Inequality in Asia and the Pacific

Asia's rapid growth in recent decades has led to a significant reduction in extreme poverty, however this has also been accompanied by rising inequality in many countries.

This book, based on recent research undertaken at the Asian Development Bank, deals with three broad questions: What have been the recent trends of inequality in Asia and the Pacific? What are the key drivers of rising inequality in the region? How should Asian countries respond to the rising inequality? It consists of two parts, preceded by an introduction chapter. Part I contains four chapters, presenting a region-wide overview and synthesis of recent trends of inequality in Asia, their key drivers (particularly, technological change, globalization, market-oriented reform, and inequality of opportunity), and policy options to address rising inequality. Part II contains 12 background papers, each providing an in-depth analysis of a particular issue related to inequality and income distribution, including gender inequality, structural transformation, role of institutions, fiscal policy and redistribution, growth strategy, middle class, and inequalities in Southeast Asia, the People's Republic of China, India, and Pakistan.

The book highlights that technological change, globalization, and market-oriented reform have been the key drivers of Asia's remarkable economic growth and poverty reduction, but they have also had significant distribution consequences. It also argues that the three drivers of growth cannot be hindered because they are the sources of productivity improvement and betterment of quality of life. This book will be of importance to those interested in policy options that could be deployed by Asian countries in confronting rising inequality.

Ravi Kanbur is T. H. Lee Professor of World Affairs, International Professor of Applied Economics and Management, and Professor of Economics at Cornell University. He holds a bachelor's degree in economics from the University of Cambridge and a doctorate in economics from the University of Oxford. Dr. Kanbur has served on the staff of the World Bank and as Director of the World Bank's World Development Report.

Changyong Rhee is the Chief Economist of the Asian Development Bank (ADB). He is the chief spokesperson for ADB on economic and development trends, and oversees the Economics and Research Department, which publishes ADB's flagship knowledge products. Dr. Rhee has over 20 years of professional experience as an economist, financial adviser, and academic. He was the Secretary General and Sherpa of the Presidential Committee for the 2010 G-20 Seoul Summit, as well as Vice Chairman of the Financial Services Commission (FSC) and Chairman of the Securities and Futures Commission of the Republic of Korea. Dr. Rhee obtained his PhD in economics from Harvard University, and his bachelor's degree in economics from Seoul National University.

Juzhong Zhuang joined ADB in 1997 and is currently Deputy Chief Economist. His recent research focuses on various development issues in Asia, including growth, poverty and inequality, structural transformation, the economics of climate change, and the Chinese economy. From 1992 to 1997, he was a research officer of the Development Economics Research Programme at the London School of Economics. He holds a PhD in economics from the University of Manchester.

Inequality in Asia and the Pacific

Trends, drivers, and policy implications

Edited by Ravi Kanbur, Changyong Rhee, and Juzhong Zhuang

Co-publication of the Asian Development Bank and Routledge

Routledge
Taylor & Francis Group
LONDON AND NEW YORK

ADB

First published 2014 by Routledge
2 Park Square, Milton Park, Abingdon, Oxon, OX14 4RN

and by Routledge
711 Third Avenue, New York, NY 100117

Routledge is an imprint of the Taylor & Francis Group

Library of Congress Cataloging-in-Publication Data
Inequality in Asia and the Pacific : trends, drivers, and policy implications/
edited by Changyong Rhee, Juzhong Zhuang and Ravi Kanbur.
pages cm
Includes bibliographical references and index.
1. Equality–Asia. 2. Equality–Pacific Area.
3. Fiscal policy–Asia. 4. Fiscal policy–Pacific Area.
5. Asia–Social conditions–21st century.
6. Pacific Area–Social conditions–21st century. I. Rhee, Changyong.
HM821.I5344 2013
323.42095–dc23 2013015920

ISBN: 978-0-415-82865-9 (hbk)
ISBN: 978-1-315-88373-1 (ebk)

Note:
In this publication, "$" refers to US dollars.

6 ADB Avenue, Mandaluyong City
1550 Metro Manila, Philippines
Tel +63 2 632 4444
Fax +63 2 636 2444
www.adb.org

For orders, please contact:
Public Information Center
Fax +63 2 636 2584
adbpub@adb.org

Typeset in Times New Roman
by Sunrise Setting Ltd, Paignton, UK

MIX
Paper from responsible sources
FSC www.fsc.org FSC® C013604

Printed and bound by CPI Group (UK) Ltd, Croydon, CR0 4YY

Contents

Figures

Tables

Boxes

Contributors

Joshua Aizenman, Professor, Economics Department, University of California, Santa Cruz, CA, United States

Talat Anwar, Economic Advisor, Program Support Unit, Canadian International Development Agency, Islamabad, Pakistan

Nancy Birdsall, President, Center for Global Development, Washington, DC, United States

J. Salcedo Cain, Graduate Research Assistant, Department of Agricultural and Applied Economics, University of Missouri, Columbia, MO, United States

Aekapol Chongvilaivan, Fellow, Regional Economic Studies Programme, Institute of Southeast Asian Studies (ISEAS), Singapore

Iris Claus, Senior Economist, Economics and Research Department, Asian Development Bank, Philippines

Jesus Felipe, Advisor, Economics and Research Department, Asian Development Bank, Philippines

Rana Hasan, Principal Economist, India Resident Mission, Asian Development Bank, India

Sean Higgins, Doctoral student, Economics Department, Tulane University, New Orleans, LA, United States

Ravi Kanbur, T. H. Lee Professor of World Affairs, International Professor of Applied Economics, Professor of Economics, Cornell University, Ithaca, NY, United States

Hyun-Hoon Lee, Professor, Department of International Trade and Business, Kangwon National University, Chuncheon, Republic of Korea

Minsoo Lee, Senior Economist, Economics and Research Department, Asian Development Bank, Philippines

Shi Li, Professor of Economics, School of Economics and Business, Beijing Normal University, People's Republic of China

Nora Lustig, Samuel Z. Stone Professor of Latin American Economics, Tulane University and Non-Resident Senior Fellow at the Center for Global Development and Inter-American Dialogue, New Orleans, LA, United States

Rhoda Magsombol, Program Analyst, Ministry of Community and Social Services, Ontario, Canada

Dalisay Maligalig, Principal Statistician, Economics and Research Department, Asian Development Bank, Philippines

Jorge Martinez-Vazquez, Regents Professor and Director (ISP), International Center for Public Policy, Andrew Young School of Policy Studies, Georgia State University, Atlanta, GA, United States

Yana van der Meulen Rodgers, Professor, Women's and Gender Studies Department, Rutgers University, New Brunswick, NJ, United States

John V. C. Nye, Frederic Bastiat Chair in Political Economy, Mercatus Center, Professor of Economics, George Mason University, Fairfax, VA, United States

Donghyun Park, Principal Economist, Economics and Research Department, Asian Development Bank, Philippines

Changyong Rhee, Chief Economist, Economics and Research Department, Asian Development Bank, Philippines

Hyun H. Son, Principal Economist, Independent Evaluation Department, Asian Development Bank, Philippines

Ajay Tandon, Senior Economist, The World Bank, Washington, DC, United States

Violeta Vulovic, International Center for Public Policy, Andrew Young School of Policy Studies, Georgia State University, Atlanta, GA, United States

Guanghua Wan, Principal Economist, Economics and Research Department, Asian Development Bank, Philippines

Juzhong Zhuang, Deputy Chief Economist, Economics and Research Department, Asian Development Bank, Philippines

Joseph E. Zveglich, Jr., Assistant Chief Economist, Economics and Research Department, Asian Development Bank, Philippines

Foreword

Widening disparities in income, wealth, and opportunities have risen to the top of policy makers' concerns in Asia. Despite the region's rapid growth, the past two decades have witnessed a rising gap between the "haves" and the "have-nots." Most people in the region – about four-fifths of them – live in countries that are becoming more unequal. Bridging this growing gap is essential to promote inclusive growth and to make growth sustainable. The social and political consequences of an Asia left to divide itself by wealth can no longer be ignored. It is time for governments in Asia to focus on policies that share the benefits of development fairly and that maintain healthy growth rates.

Policy makers need sound advice on the detailed nature of the increase in inequality and on how best to confront it. Based on conceptual and empirical analysis at the country and regional levels, the chapters in this volume show that inequitable access to new technology, education, infrastructure, and investment are fueling the divide, particularly between rural and urban areas and between coastal and inland provinces. The chapters also develop a range of policy responses based on the lessons of experience from inside and outside Asia. These policies include fiscal policy enhancements, such as increases in spending on education and health, targeted transfers for the poor, and more equitable revenue mobilization; more investment in infrastructure to reduce imbalances between developed and lagging areas; and employment-friendly measures to encourage the creation of high-quality jobs. This volume provides the analytical underpinnings of a policy discussion that must intensify in the coming years.

I would like to express my appreciation to the many staff of the Asian Development Bank and external experts who contributed to this outstanding volume on one of developing Asia's biggest development challenges.

I hope that the ideas and findings presented in this volume will enrich the policy-making discourse at global, regional, and national levels, and contribute to making the Asia and Pacific region more inclusive and free of poverty.

Bindu N. Lohani
Vice-President for Knowledge Management and Sustainable Development
Asian Development Bank

Preface

Four-fifths of Asia's population live in countries where inequality has risen over the past 20 years. This is an unprecedented phenomenon for Asia, compared with its own history and other regions of the world. In the 1960s and 1970s, East Asia was home to the much lauded "growth with equity miracle," while Latin America was the region of the world with high and rising inequality. In the past two decades, Asia has benefited from rapid economic growth, but this record has been accompanied by rising inequality. Latin America, on the other hand, has bucked its own past and the global trend, and experienced growth with falling inequality. Asian policy makers are concerned over rising inequality in Asia, and national and regional dialogue is turning to its causes and consequences.

Inequality matters for at least three reasons. First, concern about inequality of outcomes and of opportunity between individuals and between salient groups is part of the value judgments that underpin our assessment of progress. This is confirmed in a survey of the views of Asian policy makers reported in this volume. Second, even if inequality was not of direct concern, and only poverty reduction mattered, the impact of growth on poverty is mediated through inequality. Calculations in the volume show that had Asian growth been achieved without rising inequality, an additional 240 million people would have been lifted out of poverty over the past two decades. Third, inequality in its different dimensions may undermine the growth process itself through a number of channels. Thus, even if inequality was held to be normatively not important, and only growth mattered, inequality would still matter instrumentally as a determinant of growth.

This volume brings together the background papers that were prepared as inputs to the theme chapter "Confronting Rising Inequality in Asia" of the Asian Development Bank's *Asian Development Outlook 2012*. The chapters cover a range of conceptual, empirical, and policy topics. At the conceptual level, the volume distinguishes between inequality of outcomes and inequality of opportunity. At the empirical level, it presents estimates of both dimensions of inequality for Asia, and also assesses Asian trends in the context of global experience, especially that of Latin America. At the policy level, it develops a framework of drivers of inequality and identifies key policy interventions that Asian governments will have to consider in order to address rising inequality.

The first five chapters in the volume present an overview and assessment of the Asian experience, conducting a range of empirical analyses and drawing on the detail of the technical chapters that follow, as well as examining policy options. They discuss concepts of inequality and the reasons inequality matters to policy makers. They establish the basic facts of rising inequality in Asia and why this is of concern. While Asia has had fast growth and poverty reduction, the rise in inequality has blunted the impact of growth on poverty. The chapters present the results of an original survey of Asian policy makers, which captures their views on a range of issues connected with inequality. They develop a framework in which the main drivers of inequality in Asia are identified as (i) increasing skill premiums in the returns to human capital; (ii) falling labor income shares; and (iii) increasing spatial inequality, especially in its rural–urban dimension. This diagnosis then leads to the major policy conclusions in Chapter 5 of this volume that are brought together under the three headings of efficient fiscal policy measures, interventions to address lagging regions, and more employment-friendly growth.

The remaining chapters of the volume provide detailed analyses of the issues raised in the first five overview chapters. Chapters 6–10 cover a number of broad conceptual issues including (i) gender inequality; (ii) structural change and inequality; (iii) the interactions between institutions and inequality; (iv) fiscal policy and redistribution; and (v) diagnosing equity in fiscal policy. Chapters 11–17 in turn provide a range of country studies that dig deeper into the patterns and nature of inequality evolution at the country level. These include (i) growth policy and inequality in developing Asia; (ii) a study of the middle class in Latin America as a comparative benchmark; (iii) urbanization and inequality in the People's Republic of China (PRC), India, Indonesia, and the Philippines; (iv) inequality patterns in Southeast Asia; (v) income inequality and redistributive policy in the PRC; (vi) inequality in Pakistan; and (vii) accounting for inequality in India.

Taken together, the 17 chapters of this volume provide a comprehensive and in-depth assessment of trends, patterns, causes, and consequences of inequality in developing Asia. They provide specific country studies, multi-country comparative perspectives, and detailed examinations of specific issues.

The editors would like to express their deepest thanks to all the Asian Development Bank staff and external experts who contributed conceptual and empirical support to the underlying research and discussions that made this volume possible. In addition to those in the list of contributors, Arsenio Balisacan, Maria Socorro Bautista, Sekhar Bonu, Douglas H. Brooks, Jerome Destombes, Bart W. Edes, Christopher Edmonds, Yolanda Fernandez, Tatsuji Hayakawa, Shikha Jha, Kaushal Joshi, Niny Khor, Jayant Menon, Sandra Nicoll, Cyn-Young Park, Ernesto Pernia, Ganesh Rauniyar, and Paul Vandenberg provided inputs at various stages of the study, including the two workshops held in the headquarters of the Asian Development Bank in Manila in December 2011 and February 2012. We would also like to thank Arnelyn May Abdon, Anneli S. Lagman-Martin, Nedelyn C. Magtibay-Ramos, and Iva Sebastian for excellent research assistance. Thanks also go to Kae Sugawara for editorial assistance.

We hope that the volume will become a reference work to which scholars and policy makers will turn as they conduct the detailed policy analysis that must underpin the challenge of confronting rising inequality in Asia.

Finally, the views and opinions expressed in this volume are those of the authors and do not necessarily reflect those of the Asian Development Bank or its Board of Governors or the governments they represent.

Ravi Kanbur
Professor of Economics, Cornell University

Changyong Rhee
Chief Economist, Asian Development Bank

Juzhong Zhuang
Deputy Chief Economist, Asian Development Bank

Abbreviations

ADB	Asian Development Bank
ASEAN	Association of Southeast Asian Nations
CCT	conditional cash transfer
CEQ	Commitment to Equity Assessment
CHIP	Chinese Household Income Project
CIT	corporate income tax
CLMV	Cambodia, Lao People's Democratic Republic, Myanmar, and Viet Nam
CPI	consumer price index
CWB	collective wage bargaining
DHS	Demographic and Health Survey
FDI	foreign direct investment
GDP	gross domestic product
GTGS	general taxes on goods and services
HOI	Human Opportunity Index
ILO	International Labour Organization
IMF	International Monetary Fund
LAC	Latin America and the Caribbean
Lao PDR	Lao People's Democratic Republic
LFPR	labor force participation rate
MLD	mean log deviation
MUS	Manpower Utilization Survey
OECD	Organisation for Economic Co-operation and Development
OLS	ordinary least squares
PIT	personal income tax
PPP	purchasing power parity
PRC	People's Republic of China
SMEs	small and medium-sized enterprises
SSC	social security contribution
VAT	value-added tax

1 Introduction

Ravi Kanbur, Changyong Rhee, and Juzhong Zhuang

Asia's rising inequality amid rapid economic growth

The Asia and Pacific region has recorded remarkable achievements in growth and poverty reduction in recent decades. From 1990 to 2010, the average annual growth rate of the gross domestic product (GDP) for developing Asia reached 7.0% in terms of 2005 purchasing power parity (PPP) dollars, three times as high as that for the Middle East and North Africa at 2.4% and more than double that for Latin America and the Caribbean at 3.2% (Figure 1.1). Much of the growth was driven by the People's Republic of China (PRC) and India – the world's two most populous countries – with annual GDP growth of 9.9% and 6.3%, respectively. Developing Asia's outstanding growth performance has played a critical role in pulling the global economy out of recession quickly during the recent global economic crisis.

This rapid growth has significantly improved living standards and reduced extreme poverty. During 1990–2010, the region's average per capita GDP in 2005 PPP terms increased from $1,602 to $4,982. The proportion of the population living on or below the $1.25-a-day poverty line fell from 54% in 1990 to 22% in 2008, as 700 million people were lifted out of poverty. Taking the $2-a-day poverty line, the poverty rate declined from close to 80% to about 45%. Seventeen countries reduced poverty during the period by more than 15 percentage points at either poverty line.

This performance in growth and poverty reduction has, however, been accompanied by rising inequality in a large part of the region. Of the 30 countries that have comparable data, 12 – accounting for about 82% of developing Asia's population in 2010 – experienced rising inequality of per capita expenditure or income, as measured by the Gini coefficient,[1] during the period from the early 1990s to the late 2000s (Figure 1.2). Asia has historically been a region with relatively low levels of inequality, especially compared with other regions, such as Latin America. Unlike developing Asia, though, most Latin American countries have seen narrowing inequality in the past two decades – even if the average inequality in that area is still much wider than in developing Asia.

[1] A common measure of inequality, ranging from 0 indicating perfect equality to 1 (or 100) indicating perfect inequality. See Chapter 2 for technical details.

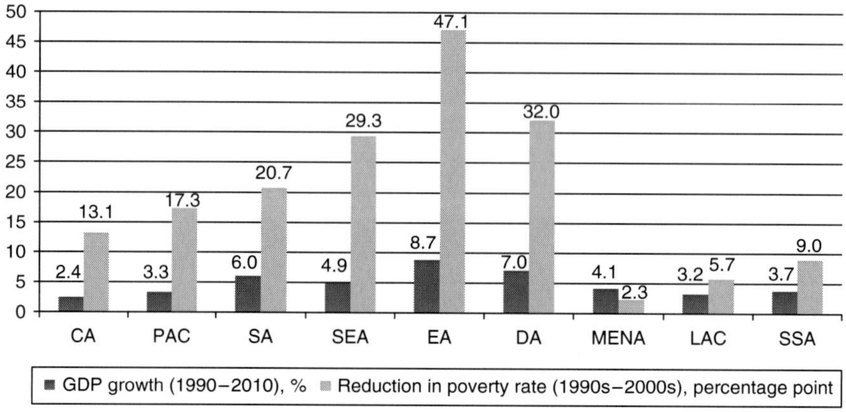

Figure 1.1 Annual GDP growth (1990–2010) and cumulative poverty reduction (1990s–2000s).

CA = Central Asia; DA = Developing Asia; EA = East Asia; GDP = gross domestic product; LAC = Latin America and the Caribbean; MENA = Middle East and North Africa; PAC = Pacific; SA = South Asia; SEA = Southeast Asia; SSA = Sub-Saharan Africa.

Notes

1 The cumulative reduction in poverty rate is estimated as the difference in the percentage of poor people between the latest year in the 2000s and the earliest year in the 1990s for which data are available, weighted by the 2010 and 1990 population, respectively.
2 For Asia and the Pacific, these include Armenia, Azerbaijan, Georgia, Kazakhstan, the Kyrgyz Republic, Tajikistan, and Turkmenistan (Central Asia); the People's Republic of China (East Asia); Fiji and Timor-Leste (Pacific); Bangladesh, Bhutan, India, Maldives, Nepal, Pakistan, and Sri Lanka (South Asia); and Cambodia, Indonesia, the Lao People's Democratic Republic, Malaysia, the Philippines, Thailand, and Viet Nam (Southeast Asia).

Sources: Authors' estimates using data from PovcalNet, http://iresearch.worldbank.org/PovcalNet/index.htm (accessed 9 March 2012) and World Development Indicators, http://data.worldbank.org/data-catalog/world-development-indicators (accessed 19 July 2012).

Inequality of outcome versus inequality of opportunity

In discussing inequality, it is useful and important to distinguish two concepts: inequality of outcome and inequality of opportunity. A principal building block of economics is the idea of human welfare – a broad sense of an individual's "well-being." Individuals will use the resources that they have available to maximize their well-being, subject to factors that may constrain their options. In the study of inequality, income or expenditure is commonly used to proxy the outcome of this process. However, focusing solely on income or expenditure can be limiting. Non-income dimensions like education and health have come to the fore in recent years, offering a multidimensional perspective on inequality and poverty. Good health, for example, confers on individuals benefits that are not fully captured by the increment it provides to incomes.

While the concept of inequality of outcome suggests the endpoint of a process, one can usefully think of how to distinguish between the resources to which one

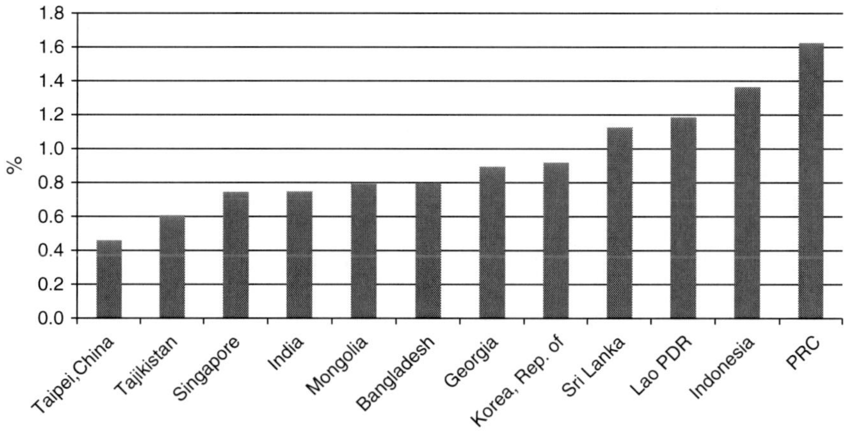

Figure 1.2 Annualized change in inequality of expenditure or income, Asian economies with rising inequality, 1990s and 2000s.

Lao PDR = Lao People's Democratic Republic; PRC = People's Republic of China.

Notes

1 The annualized growth of the Gini coefficient refers to growth between the earliest available figure in the 1990s (except in Singapore for which data are from the early 2000s) and the latest available figure in the 2000s.
2 The Gini coefficient is based on per capita income for Singapore and Taipei,China, and per capita consumption expenditures for all other economies.

Sources: PovcalNet, http://iresearch.worldbank.org/PovcalNet/index.htm (accessed 11 July 2012), supplemented by household survey data for India, and publications of official statistics offices (Republic of Korea, Singapore, and Taipei,China).

has access and the level of effort applied. Inequality of opportunity is the portion of the inequality of outcome that can be attributed to differences in "individual circumstances" (Roemer 1998). Circumstances refer to those features that are outside the control of an individual, such as gender, race, ethnicity, or place of birth. The same is true of a child's parental characteristics, such as the father's education or income. On the other hand, given an individual's circumstances, what level of efforts the individual makes in the labor market or in education – "individual effort" – will also influence their outcomes.

In the real world, a clear distinction between inequality of outcome and of opportunity is not straightforward. There could also be differences in opinion on what constitutes circumstances and what constitutes efforts in a society (Roemer 1998; Paes de Barros *et al.* 2009). Even with these difficulties, in many low-income countries, it is relatively easy to observe extreme circumstances that severely limit opportunities for a large segment of the population. These circumstances include the lack of, or unequal access to, the high-quality jobs and public services to which every citizen is meant to have equal access, irrespective of his or her circumstance – variations in this access reflect inequality of opportunity. For children, variations in access to education and health are indicators of inequality of opportunity because these are outside children's control.

The distinction between inequality of opportunity and inequality of outcome can be particularly useful in guiding public policy. Equality of opportunity is not only intrinsically important but also a critical condition for a prosperous society. Public policy must be put in place to reduce or eliminate inequality of opportunity. Governments must work hard to promote equality of opportunity and to ensure that everybody has equal opportunity to participate in the growth process and benefit from its fruits. To the extent that inequality of parents' income leads to inequality of opportunity for children, this inequality needs to be overcome by interventions to assure equal access to public services and to markets for all in society.

Apart from the conceptual differences, two pieces of empirical evidence suggest that policy makers and the general public in Asia treat the two types of inequality – of outcomes and of opportunity – differently. Results from a web-based policy makers' survey carried out by the Asian Development Bank (ADB) show about 60% of the respondents *agree* or *strongly agree* with the statement that it is more important to reduce inequality of opportunity (such as access to education, health, and employment services) than to reduce inequality of income; and 84% of the respondents *agree* or *strongly agree* with the statement that income inequality is acceptable if it is due to differences in individual efforts and an outcome of fair competition (Figure 1.3).

Another piece of empirical evidence is from the World Values Survey, which asked representative samples of people in 57 economies about their views on the importance of income redistribution versus individual efforts. On a scale of 1–10 (with 1 meaning that income should be made more equal and 10 meaning that larger income differences are needed as incentives for individual efforts), about 16% of the respondents surveyed in 10 Asian economies said 10, 39% said 7–9, and 11% said 1 (Figure 1.4). Overall, the responses are skewed toward 10, showing

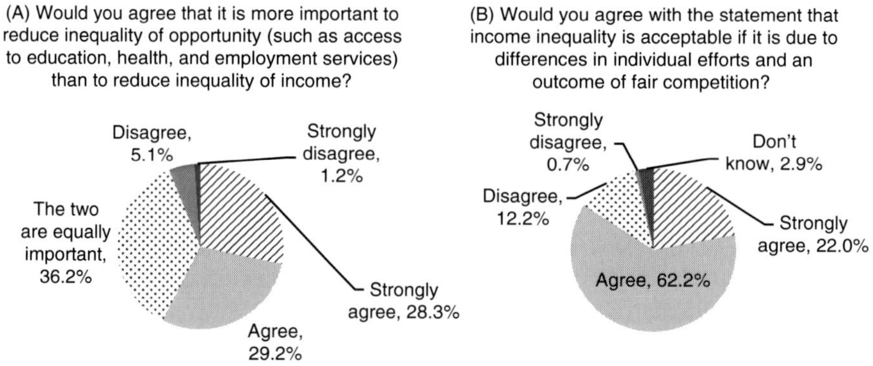

Figure 1.3 Inequality of outcomes and of opportunity – Informal Policy Makers' Survey.

Source: Web-based survey of policy makers by ADB, January–February 2012. See Box 1.2 for survey details.

that the majority recognizes the importance of individual efforts. In comparison, responses from Latin America and the Organisation for Economic Co-operation and Development (OECD) are spread more evenly over the 10 categories.

Beyond the intrinsic value of equality of opportunity – the idea of fairness, for which most humans are hardwired – does inequality make any difference for a country's development?

Why rising inequality matters

Inequality is an important dimension of development in its own right, but it also has consequences for governments' fight against poverty and efforts to sustain growth. Both poverty reduction and the foundations for future growth can be strengthened by ensuring that the benefits of development are shared broadly and equitably.

Inequality and poverty reduction

Rising inequality hampers poverty reduction. For Asian countries with comparable data, Figure 1.5 compares actual poverty headcount rates (using the $1.25-a-day poverty line) in 2008 with the poverty headcount rates simulated by keeping

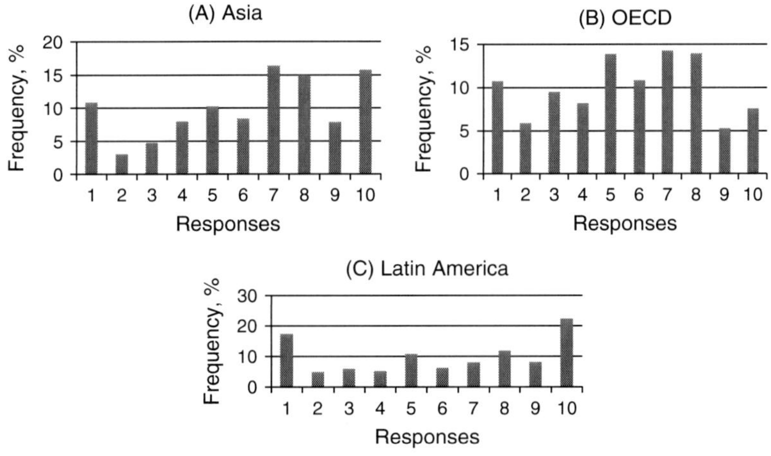

Figure 1.4 World Values Survey 2005 – more or less income inequality?

OECD = Organisation for Economic Co-operation and Development.

Notes

1 1 = incomes should be made more equal; 10 = we need larger income differences as incentives.

2 The survey results pertain to 14,359 respondents from Asia (People's Republic of China; Georgia; Hong Kong, China; India; Indonesia; Republic of Korea; Malaysia; Taipei,China; Thailand; and Viet Nam); 23,032 respondents from 19 OECD member countries; and 10,888 respondents from 8 Latin American countries.

Source: World Values Survey 2005, http://www.wvsevsdb.com/wvs/WVSData.jsp

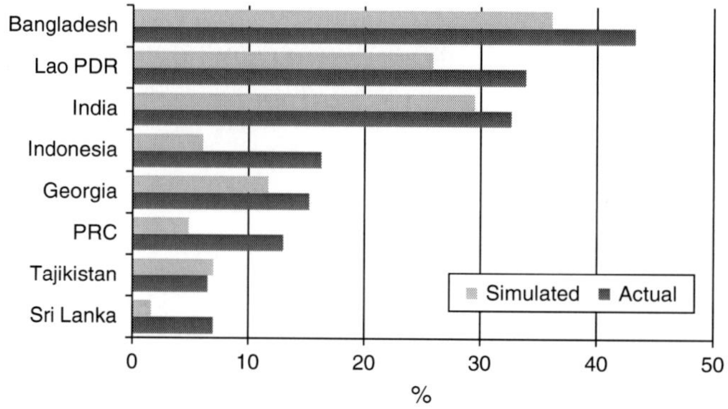

Figure 1.5 Actual and simulated poverty rates at $1.25-a-day poverty line, 1990s–2000s.

Lao PDR = Lao People's Democratic Republic; PRC = People's Republic of China.

Note: The simulated poverty rate is the poverty rate that would have been observed in the final year (with the same mean per capita expenditure) had inequality remained at its level during the initial year.

Sources: Simulations using PovcalNet, http://iresearch.worldbank.org/PovcalNet/index.htm (accessed 9 March 2012) and synthetic expenditure data derived from household surveys.

inequality unchanged from the 1990s to the 2000s. The simulations highlight the degree to which rising inequality holds back the region's poverty reduction. Note in the following results that if inequality had not increased between the early 1990s and the late 2000s:

- In India, the poverty headcount rate would have been reduced to 29.5%, instead of the actual 32.7%.
- In the PRC, extreme poverty would have declined to 4.9%, instead of the actual 13.1%.
- In Indonesia, the poverty rate would have fallen to 6.1%, instead of the actual 16.3%.

For the 12 economies with rising inequality, the cost of that widening comes to 240 million more people trapped under the $1.25-a-day poverty line – 6.5% of the region's population today. In contrast, those countries with decreasing inequality had smaller poverty rates than they would have had with stable inequality.

Inequality, institutions, and growth

Not only does inequality dampen the poverty reduction impact of growth, it can also affect growth itself, through a number of economic, social, and political mechanisms.

Inequality of wealth and income can lead to a misallocation of human capital. Those with little wealth or low income are unable to invest in human capital, or wealth- and income-enhancing activities, and will remain poor. In principle, they may be able to borrow to finance investment, but imperfect financial markets, coupled with other market failures, often heavily constrain their ability to borrow and invest. Similarly, much of the evidence shows that small enterprises have high potential rates of return to investment but are constrained from accessing capital (see, e.g., de Mel *et al.* (2008)).

Widening inequality – leaving more people at the top and bottom of the income ladder – can also mean a hollowing out of the middle class. The importance of the middle class for stability and growth has been emphasized and analyzed in recent years. Birdsall (2010), for example, has argued that "growth driven by and benefiting a middle class is more likely to be sustained – both economically, to the extent that the rent-seeking and corruption associated with highly concentrated gains to growth are avoided, and politically, to the extent that conflict and horizontal inequalities between racial and ethnic groups are easier to manage. . . ."

In fact, there is a broad consensus among analysts on the link between inequality and the quality of institutions. Along several dimensions, ranging from political stability, through institutional stability to property rights, the negative impact of inequality on institutional quality seems to be well established, although the two-way causality is also widely recognized (Zhuang *et al.* 2010; see Chapter 8 in this volume by Nye). At the same time, there is also a literature on the effect of inequality on crime and violence and, through that, on the investment climate (see, e.g., Fajnzylber *et al.* (2002); Özler and Demombynes (2002)).

Finally, greater inequality may lead to a political backlash in which pressure grows for governments to enact populist policy measures. In response to the rising demands, the political process may favor policies which, in the short term, would benefit the lower end of the income distribution, but which in the long term could hold back efficiency and growth (Alesina and Rodrik 1994). Under such conditions, the interests of the political system diverge from the interests of the economy as a whole. This is a widespread concern in developing and developed countries alike.

Empirically establishing the linkage between inequality and growth is not easy, because numerous factors are at work, and economic analysis is often subject to data and methodological limitations. Unsurprisingly, the empirical evidence is itself mixed (see, e.g., Kanbur and Lustig (2000); Barro (2008)). Recent studies by Berg and Ostry (2011a, b), however, provide convincing evidence on the inequality–growth relationship. The studies make a key distinction between growth over the short term and growth over the long term (Box 1.1). This corresponds to the different issues involved in "igniting" growth versus sustaining it over the long term. Many countries can ignite growth in the short term, but far fewer can sustain it (Hausmann *et al.* 2005). The econometric analysis by Berg and Ostry confirms that inequality is a key variable explaining long-term growth. Thus, not only does rising inequality dent the poverty impact of a given growth rate, but it can also affect the sustainability of a growth path.

Box 1.1 Inequality and sustained growth

In analyzing the determinants of growth, one needs to make an important distinction between short-term and long-term growth. The course of economic growth does not run smooth. Growth over a long period is made up of "growth spells," where growth accelerates to a higher rate, then falls again. Some of this is purely cyclical, but recent literature focuses on finding policy and structural determinants of the frequency and length of these spells.

This literature suggests that accelerating growth in the short term may be easier than sustaining it over the longer term – and at the very least the determinants of these two types of growth can be very different. The former can be achieved by a set of conventional reforms that lead to a burst of investment and output – liberalization of trade or finance, for example. Sustaining this growth, however, requires longer-term institutional underpinnings (Rodrik 2005).

Furthermore, economies are subject to shocks, even more so in an era of globalization. How policy makers respond to these shocks will determine the speed and sustainability of the rebound and the subsequent growth path. Yet, because any policy response will invariably have distributional consequences, the ability of policy makers to push through efficient responses to shocks depends on their ability to manage the distributional consequences of these responses (Rodrik 1999).

Inability to manage these shocks, and more generally, the distributional consequences of efficient reforms, will mean that growth accelerations will peter out sooner than if these shocks are managed well, and growth spells will be shorter. Long-term growth will therefore be lower.

Berg and Ostry (2011b) argued that inequality can influence the duration of growth spells through several channels:

- With credit market imperfections, inequality inhibits private investment in human capital.
- If the distribution of political power follows the distribution of income, this may lead, on the one hand, to pressure for populist policies from the bottom end and, on the other, to efforts by the elite to resist this pressure through corruption – both of which are inefficient and detrimental to growth.
- Inequality may increase the risk of political instability.

Berg *et al.* (2008) tested for the effect of inequality on growth, focusing on its impact on the duration of growth spells. The empirical results show that income distribution survives as one of the most robust and important factors associated with growth duration. A 10-percentile decrease in inequality increases the expected length of a growth spell by 50%. They concluded that inequality is a more robust predictor of growth duration than many variables widely understood to be central to growth.

Sources: A. Berg and J. D. Ostry. 2011a. Equality and Efficiency: Is There a Tradeoff between the Two or Do the Two Go Hand in Hand? *Finance and Development*. 48 (3). pp. 12–15; A. Berg and J. D. Ostry. 2011b. Inequality and

Unsustainable Growth: Two Sides of the Same Coin? *IMF Staff Discussion Note*. SDN 11/08 Washington, DC: International Monetary Fund. p. 13; A. Berg, J. D. Ostry, and J. Zettelmeyer. 2008. What Makes Growth Sustained? *IMF Working Paper* 08/59. Washington, DC: International Monetary Fund; D. Rodrik. 1999. Where Did All the Growth Go? External Shocks, Social Conflict, and Growth Collapses. *Journal of Economic Growth*. 4 (4). pp. 385–412; D. Rodrik. 2005. Growth Strategies. In P. Aghion and S. Durlauf, eds. *Handbook of Economic Growth*. 1A. North-Holland.

Inequality on the policy agenda

Governments are not blind to the problem. Indeed, in recent years, more have embraced the concept of inclusive growth to make income distribution more equitable:

- In the PRC, where the Gini coefficient of per capita consumption expenditure worsened from about 32.4 in 1990 to 43.4 in 2008,[2] the government set about building a "harmonious society" as the development goal in its Eleventh Five Year Plan (2006–2010). This goal has been reaffirmed in the Twelfth Five Year Plan (2011–2015), with greater emphasis on the quality – not just the rate – of growth, and making growth inclusive.
- In India, where the Gini coefficient deteriorated from 32.5 in 1993 to 37 in 2010, the government made an explicit commitment to inclusive growth in its Eleventh Five Year Plan (2007–2012). The central vision of the plan is "... not just faster growth but also inclusive growth, that is, a growth process which yields broad-based benefits and ensures equality of opportunity for all."
- In Indonesia, the 2010–2014 Development Plan for the country, which saw its Gini coefficient worsen from 29 in 1990 to 39 in 2011, offers a vision of a society supported by five national development agendas, among them inclusive and just development.
- In Malaysia, the 2011–2015 Development Plan is based on the "1Malaysia: People First, Performance Now" concept and adopts an inclusive development approach to ensure equitable access to economic participation among all Malaysians, particularly aiming at improving the livelihood of the poorer 40% of households.

[2] According to the government figures released in early 2013, the PRC's Gini coefficient was 49.1 in 2008. The difference between the government estimate and the figure reported in this chapter is due to the fact that the former is based on per capita disposable income, while the latter is estimated from per capita consumption expenditure. According to Chapter 2 in this volume, the difference between the two measures can be as high as 10 when the Gini coefficient is measured so that it ranges from 0 to 100.

- In the Philippines, the vision of the 2011–2016 medium-term Development Plan is to achieve inclusive growth, create employment opportunities, and reduce poverty.
- In Thailand, the 2012–2016 Development Strategy is based on the "sufficiency economy" philosophy and people-centered development, with a vision of equity, fairness, and resilience.

To gauge the extent of the rising concerns over inequality among Asian policy makers, ADB carried out a web-based survey in early 2012 (Box 1.2). Over 65% of respondents agreed that income inequality in their countries was *high* or *very high*. Almost all felt that incomes in their countries were becoming more unequal. Importantly, for a region with considerable success in lifting its citizens out of poverty, a majority of the respondents felt that widening inequality was not acceptable even with these declines in the poverty rate.

Box 1.2 How important is inequality to developing Asia's policy makers?

To better understand the views of regional policy makers, the Asian Development Bank (ADB) used an informal survey covering different aspects of the inequality problem. ADB targeted officials of ministries of finance, planning authorities, and other government agencies in the region.

The survey was administered online from 11 January to 29 February 2012. In some cases, the questionnaire was translated into local languages. From key government agencies in 25 of ADB's developing member countries, 504 respondents registered their opinions. The results confirm that policy makers consider rising inequality an increasingly serious problem (see Box 1.2, Figure 1):

- About two-thirds of the respondents indicated that the level of income inequality is *high* or *very high* and that it has increased from 10 years ago;
- 44% of the respondents indicated that the level of concern over inequality among policy makers is *high* or *very high*, and 70% indicated that the concern has increased;
- 95% of the respondents think that it is *important* or *very important* to have policies in place to prevent rises in inequality in order to maintain stability and sustain growth; and
- More than 52% *disagree* or *strongly disagree* with the statement that higher income inequality is acceptable as long as poverty is declining.

A simple analysis of thc survey results shows that respondents from countries with rising inequality have a higher level of concern over inequality and a greater sense of urgency for addressing it than those from countries with declining inequality.

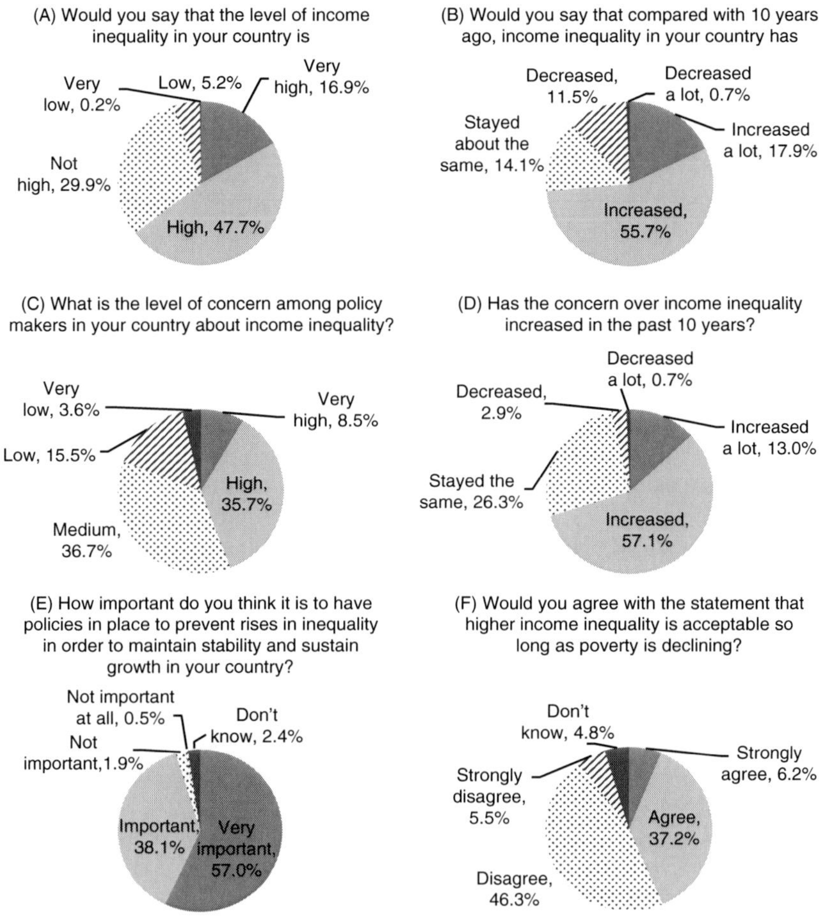

Figure 1.6 Concerns about inclusiveness of growth and rising inequality – Policy Maker Survey.

Source: Web-based survey by ADB from January to February 2012.

Summary of key findings

The rest of this volume consists of 16 papers prepared by ADB staff and their collaborators under a technical assistance project of the Economics and Research Department (ADB 2010). These papers provided background materials for the theme chapter of *Asian Development Outlook 2012: Confronting Rising Inequality in Asia* (ADB 2012). The 16 papers are grouped into two parts. The first part, comprising Chapters 2–5, provides a regional overview and synthesis of rising inequality in Asia and policy issues. The second part, comprising Chapters 6–17, contains background studies.

In Chapter 2, Zhuang, Kanbur, and Maligalig provide an update on the recent trends of inequality in Asia and the Pacific using a variety of measures. They show that 12 of the 30 Asian economies with comparable data experienced an increase in inequality in the past two decades. The increase was more pronounced when measured by the ratio of the income share of the richest 20% of households to that of the poorest 20% than by the Gini coefficient. Further, most of the economies with rising inequality saw the consumption expenditure shares of the top 1% and 5% of households increasing. These results suggest that rising inequality in developing Asia is closely associated with a rapid increase in the very top income groups – that is, the rich are getting richer much faster. The chapter also shows that income inequality in developing Asia on average is still lower than in other parts of the developing world. It argues, however, that the fact that inequality is rising in developing Asia while it is declining elsewhere is a major concern.

In Chapter 3, Zhuang, Kanbur, and Rhee ask the question what drives developing Asia's rising inequality. On the basis of a conceptual framework for thinking about income inequality, they argue that technological progress, globalization, and market-oriented reform, which have been the key drivers of Asia's rapid growth, are the basic forces behind the rising inequality in many developing countries. The chapter provides empirical evidence that these forces have changed income distribution through three channels: capital, skill, and spatial biases. The bias toward physical capital reduces labor's share of national income while increasing the income share of the owners of capital. The heightened demand for better-skilled workers raises the premium on their earnings. Spatial disparities become more acute, with locations with superior infrastructure, market access, and scale economies – such as urban centers and coastal areas – better able to benefit from changing circumstances. The chapter argues that inequality of opportunity, due largely to weaknesses in governance, market distributions, and social exclusion, magnifies the distributional consequences of these driving factors.

In Chapter 4, Son examines inequality of opportunity in basic education and infrastructure services in seven developing Asian countries: Bangladesh, Bhutan, Indonesia, Pakistan, the Philippines, Sri Lanka, and Viet Nam, using the Human Opportunity Index, a method that has been applied elsewhere. The index measures the contribution of individuals' socioeconomic and demographic circumstances to inequality of opportunity in accessing basic services. In the chapter, Son also proposes a new methodology to quantify the relative contribution of each circumstance variable to the inequality of opportunity. Results of the empirical analysis indicate that opportunities to access basic education and infrastructure services in the seven countries vary widely in terms of availability and distribution, and that inequality of opportunity is driven mainly by per capita household expenditure. These suggest that household poverty plays a crucial role in determining equitable access to basic services. The chapter concludes that more needs to be done to improve the distribution of economic benefits in these countries.

In Chapter 5, Rhee, Zhuang, Kanbur, and Felipe look at policy options to confront rising inequality in Asia and the Pacific. They argue that, while technological progress, globalization, and market-oriented reform are the basic driving forces behind rising inequality in Asia, these forces cannot be reversed because they generate productivity growth that underpins Asia's poverty reduction, economic expansion, and improvements in living standards. They propose that Asian governments should respond to rising inequality via three sets of policy measures: (i) efficient fiscal policy – increasing spending on education and health, developing better targeted social protection programs, switching from inefficient general subsidies to targeted transfers, and greater and more equitable revenue mobilization; (ii) interventions to support lagging regions – improving regional connectivity, developing new growth centers, more effective fiscal transfers, and removing barriers to migration; and (iii) more employment-friendly growth – maintaining a more balanced sectoral composition of growth, supporting the development of small and medium-sized enterprises, removing factor market distortions that favor capital over labor, and strengthening labor market institutions.

Rodgers and Zveglich, in Chapter 6, examine gender inequality in labor markets in Asia and the Pacific, with a focus on the structural drivers of women's labor force participation. Demographic survey data indicate that in Asia's lower-income countries, economic necessity is an important push factor behind women's employment. Also, being married and having young children both reduce the likelihood that a woman is employed. In a separate analysis for Taipei,China, this disincentive effect from young children on women's employment has increased over time. These results point to the importance of policies that support women's roles as caregivers while they are employed in market-based activities.

In Chapter 7, Aizenman, Lee, and Park argue that structural change has a far-reaching impact on inequality by exposing the population to challenges and opportunities. They note that trade and technological progress have been widely put forth as structural drivers of inequality. Broader structural change, such as demographic transition, can also impinge upon inequality. Structural change in developing Asia has been unprecedented in its scale and speed. The heterogeneity of the population implies that the adjustment capacity to these changes varies. They argue that the fundamental solution to mitigating the adjustment costs arising from structural change lies in empowering individuals to become more productive, adaptable, and versatile through access to education and employment. The chapter reviews the experiences of the advanced countries and argues that these provide valuable lessons for developing Asia. The chapter notes that the region has already begun the difficult and complex task of addressing inequality arising from structural change, and argues that more sustainable growth requires an inclusive growth strategy that provides equality of opportunity, especially in education, employment, and social protection.

In Chapter 8, Nye asks if good economic and political institutions affect income inequality in Asia. He notes that the literature suggests that there is a weak, albeit ambiguous, link between institutions and inequality. In general, growth-promoting economic institutions seem to be favorable to lower inequality. Democratization and other political institutions do not clearly favor higher or lower income inequality at the margin. He argues that Asia is especially noted for having weak democratization but strong growth and lower inequality. He notes that, generally, scholars have found that the link is much stronger from historical patterns of economic and social inequality to weak institutions, rather than vice versa. Given that underlying technological shifts in globalized markets favoring certain types of human capital often result in unequal incomes, institutions may not easily be used to control income inequality, especially once efficiency considerations are taken into account. Moreover, concerns about inequality often mask worries about unequal access and political favoritism, not easily captured by income changes. This suggests that policy to blunt macro shifts in inequality in Asia is a very crude instrument to address these concerns.

Claus, Martinez-Vazquez, and Vulovic in Chapter 9 assess the impact of government fiscal policies on income inequality in Asia. They discuss the role and effectiveness of redistributive fiscal policies and quantify the effects of taxation and government expenditure on income distributions. Panel estimation for 150 countries with data between 1970 and 2009 confirms international empirical findings for Asia. Tax systems tend to be progressive, but government expenditures are a more effective tool for redistributing income. Moreover, the results suggest some distinctive differential distributive effect for government expenditures on social protection. Social protection spending appears to increase income inequality in Asia, but reduces it in the rest of the world. Also adversely affecting the distribution of income in Asia is government expenditure on housing. The chapter discusses some options for improving the effectiveness of fiscal policies in Asia as well.

In Chapter 10, Lustig and Higgins argue that fiscal policy can change inequality and poverty substantially or slightly, depending on the government's resources and how they are allocated. The chapter proposes a diagnostic framework for assessing how aligned fiscal policy is with supporting a minimum living standard, accumulating human capital, and reducing inequality. The Commitment to Equity Assessment (CEQ) evaluates efforts based on whether governments (i) collect and allocate enough resources to support a minimum living standard and (ii) collect and distribute resources equitably. CEQ uses standard inequality, poverty, and tax and benefit incidence analyses. As an illustration, the chapter applies the framework to Brazil.

Chapter 11 by Lee, Lee, and Park examines the relationship between growth policies/strategy and inequality in developing Asia, with the aim of deriving policy lessons that can help the region achieve more inclusive growth. A comparison of the experiences of the PRC and India indicates that while both countries are now explicitly pursuing more inclusive growth, the PRC has so far had more success in this regard. The experiences of the Republic of Korea provide a benchmark for developing Asia since the country achieved growth with equity during its high growth period. The most important policy factor that enabled the Republic of Korea to contain inequality was large investments in public education. A rural development program also helped. Finally, while there is no one-size-fits-all set of inclusive growth policies/strategy, there are a number of recurrent themes that resonate across all countries and income levels. Access to education, in particular, seems to be an effective policy tool.

Chapter 12 by Birdsall sets out basic information on the middle class in eight Latin American countries over the past two decades. The middle class is identified as people living in households with income per capita between $10 and $50 per day, adjusted for purchasing power parity. In the countries studied (between about 1990 and 2010), the population share of the middle class increased from 17% to 30%, and its income share increased from 40% to nearly 50%. Adults in the typical middle-class household have at least some secondary education – that is true for all countries in the entire 20-year period – and all children in those households go to school, many to private school. Adults are likely to be employees in urban, formal jobs, and less likely than their richer counterparts to hold jobs in the public sector. Though rich in relative terms, they are closer in median income to the majority of households that are poorer than to the small minority that are richer. To close on an optimistic note, the profiles tell a story of an increasingly educated, middle-class region, in which a growing proportion of the population is relatively secure in the escape from poverty, while probably more reliant than the rich on the rule of law and stable and effective government. In the long term, this suggests that the middle class is likely to support market-friendly, poverty-reducing social and economic reforms.

Chapter 13 by Kanbur and Zhuang provides a quantitative analysis of how urbanization affects inequality in Asia, using a model in which inequality is determined by urban inequality, rural inequality, urban–rural income gap, and urbanization (measured by the share of urban population). Focusing on data for four countries from the early 1990s to late 2000s, the chapter finds that urbanization contributed about 300% of the increase in inequality at the national level in the Philippines, more than 50% in Indonesia, slightly less than 15% in India, but helped reduce inequality somewhat in the PRC. The change in the urban–rural income gap, on the other hand, contributed about 50% of the increase in inequality at the national level in India and one-third in the PRC, but helped reduce national inequality in Indonesia and the Philippines. The analysis also suggests that, in the coming years, urbanization alone – keeping other determinants constant – will contribute to rising inequality in India and Indonesia, but to reducing inequality in the PRC and the Philippines. The chapter also looks at how Asian governments should prioritize the four drivers of inequality on which the chapter has focused.

Chapter 14 by Chongvilaivan examines recent trends of inequality in Southeast Asia; looks at proximate, structural, and policy drivers of rising inequalities; assesses impacts and implications of recent policy developments addressing the problems of income and non-income inequalities in the region; and discusses policy lessons for putting in place inclusive growth. The chapter brings out a number of findings. First, impressive economic performance and persistent poverty reduction in many parts of the region have been coupled with increases in income inequality. Second, the estimates based on the Theil decomposition suggest that growth has been unevenly distributed along a range of dimensions and point to various proximate drivers of inequality. Third, the structural drivers, particularly trade and financial liberalization, have catalyzed inequality in Southeast Asia. Last, a closer look into redistributive policies in the region highlights the need for more policy actions.

Chapter 15 by Li, Wan, and Zhuang provides insights into the dynamics and driving forces of the PRC's income inequality using household survey data in 1995 and 2007 and reviews some of the recent income distribution policies in the PRC. They find that after increasing from about 30 in the early 1980s to over 40 in the 1990s, the PRC's Gini coefficient continued to rise in much of the 2000s, with the national coefficient standing at 47.4 in 2007. Their regression-based decomposition shows that between 1995 and 2007, the share of the total Gini coefficient explained by urban–rural residency increased from 13% to over 25%, that explained by provincial location increased from 14% to 16%, and that by household head's education attainment increased from 4% to 9%. They argue that if the spatial inequality can be considered as largely being caused by unequal access to opportunity, then more than 40% of the PRC's income inequality reflects inequality of opportunity. The policy review in the chapter covers areas of the tax system; minimum wage regulation; minimum income guarantee system; farmers' support policies; social security system; the Western Development Strategy; and poverty alleviation programs. They argue that these measures have been very effective in reducing poverty, but so far less so in reducing income inequality. They note that reducing inequality is one of the policy priorities in the government's Twelfth Five Year Plan, and argue that the challenge is to ensure effective implementation of the proposed policy actions.

In Chapter 16, Anwar evaluates the trends and main drivers of inequality in Pakistan. He notes that inequality increased in the 1970s when growth slowed down and declined in the 1980s when growth was high, suggesting a weak link between high growth and increased inequality in Pakistan. Inequality increased in the 1990s and 2000s mainly due to a rise in wage inequality in the wake of globalization and trade liberalization. The adverse effects on inequality may have been compounded by finance sector reforms. Thus, trade and financial liberalization may have been important drivers of inequality in Pakistan over the past two decades. Nevertheless, other important factors, including partial implementation of reform, seem to have compromised the benefits of reforms. Structural drivers of inequality, such as unequal access to education along with highly unequal land ownership patterns, are also important determinants of inequality in Pakistan. He argues that, to reduce inequality, the government needs to ensure that wages increase in line with the inflation rate and provide access to finance to the poor. Unequal access to human capital is an outcome of low public spending on education, health, and social protection, which needs to be increased significantly. The government needs to exit from production, remove untargeted subsidies, raise the ratio of tax to gross domestic product, and improve the governance profile to achieve inclusive growth.

In the last chapter, Cain, Hasan, Magsombol, and Tandon utilize household-level consumption expenditure data from India and regression-based decomposition techniques to examine the evolution of and accounting for inequality during 1983–2004. Various measures of inequality show that inequality levels were relatively stable during 1983–1993, but increased during 1993–2004. The increases in inequality have not precluded reductions in poverty, however. They are also more of an urban phenomenon and can be accounted for by increases in returns to education in the urban sector to a considerable extent, especially among households that rely on income from education-intensive services and/or education-intensive occupations. Some of the increases in the returns to education can be linked to economic liberalization undertaken in the 1990s.

References

Alesina, A., and D. Rodrik. 1994. Distributive Politics and Economic Growth. *Quarterly Journal of Economics*. 109 (2). pp. 465–90.

Asian Development Bank (ADB). 2010. *Technical Assistance for Establishing Global Research Alliances*. Manila.

——. 2012. *Asian Development Outlook 2012: Confronting Rising Inequality in Asia*. Manila.

Barro, R. J. 2008. Inequality and Growth Revisited. *ADB Working Paper Series on Regional Economic Integration* No. 11. Manila: ADB.

Berg, A., and J. D. Ostry. 2011a. Equality and Efficiency: Is There a Tradeoff between the Two or Do the Two Go Hand in Hand? *Finance and Development*. 48 (3). pp. 12–15.

——. 2011b. Inequality and Unsustainable Growth: Two Sides of the Same Coin? *IMF Staff Discussion Note* SDN 11/08. Washington, DC: International Monetary Fund. p. 13.

Berg, A., J. D. Ostry, and J. Zettelmeyer. 2008. What Makes Growth Sustained? *IMF Working Paper* 08/59. Washington, DC: International Monetary Fund.

Birdsall, N. 2010. The (Indispensable) Middle Class in Developing Countries. In R. Kanbur and M. Spence, eds. *Equity and Growth in a Globalizing World*. Washington, DC: The World Bank on behalf of The Commission on Growth and Development. p. 158.

de Mel, S., D. McKenzie, and C. Woodruff. 2008. Returns to Capital in Microenterprises: Evidence from a Field Experiment. *Quarterly Journal of Economics*. 123 (4). pp. 1329–72.

Fajnzylber, P., D. Lederman, and N. Loayza. 2002. Inequality and Violent Crime. *Journal of Law and Economics*. 45 (1). pp. 1–40.

Hausmann, R., L. Pritchett, and D. Rodrik. 2005. Growth Accelerations. *Journal of Economic Growth*. 10 (4). pp. 303–29.

Kanbur, R., and N. Lustig. 2000. Why is Inequality Back on the Agenda? In *Proceedings of Annual World Bank Conference in Development Economics*. pp. 285–313. Washington, DC: World Bank.

Özler, B., and G. Demombynes. 2002. Crime and Local Inequality in South Africa. *World Bank Policy Research Working Paper* No. 2925. Washington, DC: World Bank. http://www-wds.worldbank.org/external/default/WDSContentServer/WDSP/IB/2002/12/14/000094946_02120504013794/Rendered/PDF/multi0page.pdf

Paes de Barros, R., F. H. G. Ferreira, J. R. Molinas Vega, J. S. Chanduvi, M. de Carvallo, S. Franco, S. Freije-Rodríguez, and J. Gignoux. 2009. *Measuring Inequality of Opportunities in Latin America and the Caribbean. Conference Edition*. Washington, DC: World Bank.

Rodrik, D. 1999. Where Did All the Growth Go? External Shocks, Social Conflict, and Growth Collapses. *Journal of Economic Growth*. 4 (4). pp. 385–412.
——. 2005. Growth Strategies. In P. Aghion and S. Durlauf, eds. *Handbook of Economic Growth*. Volume 1A. Amsterdam, North Holland: Elsevier.
Roemer, J. 1998. *Equality of Opportunity*. Cambridge, MA: Harvard University Press.
World Bank. PovcalNet: the Online Tool for Poverty Measurement Developed by the Development Research Group of the World Bank. http://iresearch.worldbank.org/PovcalNet/index.htm
——. World Development Indicators. http://data.worldbank.org/data-catalog/world-development-indicators
Zhuang, J., E. de Dios, and A. Lagman-Martin. 2010. Governance and Institutional Quality and the Links with Growth and Inequality: How Asia Fares. In J. Zhuang, ed. *Poverty, Inequality, and Inclusive Growth: Measurement, Policy Issues, and Country Studies*. London: Anthem Press and Manila: ADB.

Part I

Regional overview and synthesis

2 Asia's income inequalities

Recent trends

Juzhong Zhuang, Ravi Kanbur, and Dalisay Maligalig

Data sources and estimation methods

This chapter takes a closer look at the levels and trends of income inequality in developing Asia during the past two decades. Estimation of income inequality draws on data from several sources. The first is the World Bank's PovcalNet, which provides Gini coefficients for more than half of the countries covered. PovcalNet also provides grouped per capita income or expenditure data (by decile), from which the quintile ratios and growth incidence by quintile can be computed. The grouped expenditure data (together with rural and urban populations) were also used to estimate the national Gini coefficients for the People's Republic of China (PRC) and Indonesia for more recent years because they are not available in PovcalNet.

The second is unit-level household survey data, which are used for estimating growth incidence curves, the top 5% and 1% income (or expenditure) shares, and for decomposition analysis. Unit-level survey data are also used to estimate Gini coefficients and quintile ratios when PovcalNet does not provide sufficient data, as is the case for most Pacific countries. Inequality measures for India are all calculated from unit-level household survey data. The third source is official statistical publications or databases for all Organisation for Economic Co-operation and Development (OECD) countries, the Republic of Korea, Singapore, and Taipei,China.

Inequality can be estimated for per capita income or per capita expenditure. The two measures usually give different results, with income inequality normally higher than expenditure inequality. As shown in Table 2.1, the income measure of the Gini was 47 in the Philippines in 2009, while the expenditure measure was 43. Viet Nam provides a starker example: the income measure was 46 in 2008 and the expenditure measure 37. For most developing Asian economies, this chapter estimates inequality measures from expenditure data, with the exception of those for Malaysia, Singapore, and Taipei,China that are based on income data. Estimates for sub-Saharan African countries are also based on expenditure data, while those for Latin American and OECD countries are based on income data. These are largely determined by data availability.

Table 2.1 Income and expenditure-based Gini coefficients in the Philippines and Viet Nam

		Gini coefficient	
	Survey year	*Income measure*	*Expenditure measure*
Philippines	2009	47.4	43.0
Viet Nam	2008	44.5	35.6

Source: Authors' estimates from unit-level household survey data.

This chapter uses several standard measures of income inequality, including the Gini coefficient, quintile ratio, Theil index, income (or expenditure) shares of the top 1% and 5% of population, and growth incidence curve.

The *Gini coefficient* is a measure of dispersion of a frequency distribution, for example, of how income or consumption expenditures are distributed across households. For an income distribution, the Gini is computed as

$$Gini = \frac{-(n+1)}{n} + \frac{2}{n^2 \mu_x} \sum_{i=1}^{n} i x_i \tag{2.1}$$

where x_i is the income (or expenditure) of an individual i, μ_x is the mean income of the population, and n is the total number of individuals in the population. The Gini will range from 0 (all individuals have the same income: perfect equality) to 1 (income is held by only one person in the population: perfect inequality). For convenience, this chapter cites the Gini multiplied by 100.

The *quintile income (or expenditure) ratio* is the ratio of the total income (or expenditure) of the top (richest) 20% of the population to that of the bottom (poorest) 20%.

The *generalized entropy index GE(0)* is one of a set of measures derived from the notion of entropy in information theory. It is also known as Theil's second measure and can be computed as

$$GE(0) = \frac{1}{n} \sum_{i=1}^{n} \ln\left(\frac{\mu_x}{x_i}\right) \tag{2.2}$$

A major attraction of this index is that total inequality can be decomposed into two components: one measuring inequality between groups and the other measuring inequality within groups.

Income (or expenditure) shares of the top 1% and 5% of the households in the distribution focus on income (or expenditure) shares of the richest households.

The *growth incidence curve* plots per capita income (or expenditure) growth at each point of an income distribution between two periods, which can provide more detailed insight into what is driving changes in the distribution over time than any summary measure of inequality.

Recent trends of income inequality in developing Asia

Gini coefficients

Of the 37 economies with available data in the 2000s (Table 2.2),[1] 14 had a Gini coefficient of or greater than 40, widely considered the threshold for "high inequality." These include one in East Asia (PRC), four in Southeast Asia (Malaysia, the Philippines, Singapore, and Thailand), one in South Asia (Sri Lanka), one in Central Asia (Georgia), and seven in the Pacific (Fiji, Kiribati, Nauru, Palau, Samoa, Solomon Islands, and Vanuatu). The Gini coefficient reached 48.2 for Singapore and 46.2 for Malaysia, but these are income-based, whereas the rest, except for that for Taipei,China, are expenditure-based. As noted earlier, for a given country, the income-based Gini could be 5–10 points higher than the expenditure-based Gini. The Gini for the rest of the economies ranged from 27.8 (Afghanistan) to 38.9 (Indonesia). The average Gini for the 37 economies is 37.7.[2]

Twelve of the 30 economies with comparable data showed an increase (worsening) in the coefficient in the past two decades. These 12 cover 82% of the region's population. On an annual basis, the increase in inequality was most pronounced in the PRC, where the Gini worsened from 32.4 in 1990 to 43.4 in 2008 (1.6% a year). Indonesia's increased from 29.2 in 1990 to 38.9 in 2011 (1.4% a year). There appears to be a positive and statistically significant relationship between the increase in the Gini (rising inequality) and gross domestic product (GDP) growth (Figure 2.1). The economies where growth has been higher tend to experience large increases in inequality; however, there are large variations in this relationship.

The trend of rising inequality is widespread in the region, yet 14 economies with comparable data (five in Central Asia) recorded an improvement in their Gini.[3] Part of the former Soviet Union, these five underwent dramatic economic and social transformation from the late 1980s onward, when the Gini surged, but the coefficient declined in more recent years as their economies became more stable. In the Kyrgyz Republic, for example, the Gini worsened from 26 in 1988 to 53.7 in 1993 and then declined to 36.2 in 2009.

Most of the other countries that saw an improving Gini coefficient (sometimes sharply) have a small economy: Bhutan, Fiji, the Maldives, Nepal, Samoa, Timor-Leste, and Tuvalu. Some of them are vulnerable to shocks. The Maldives, for instance, experienced a devastating tsunami in 2004 and Timor-Leste underwent civil strife. These are likely to have impacted on incomes of different classes and on income distribution.

To gain more insight into the pattern of inequality and its change over time, we look at the Gini coefficient of urban and rural subpopulations within a country, focusing on the PRC, India, and Indonesia, the region's three most populous

---

[1] Of these, 25 have data for both the 1990s and 2000s.

[2] This is a simple arithmetic average. If three countries with data only in the 1990s (Federated States of Micronesia, Papua New Guinea, and Turkmenistan) are included, the average is 38.3.

[3] The Gini declined in 18 economies if those with initial data only in the early 2000s are included.

Table 2.2 Trends in inequality in developing Asia

Developing member economy			*Gini coefficient*			*Top/bottom 20%*		
	Initial year	*Final year*	*1990s*	*2000s*	*Annualized growth rate (%)*	*1990s*	*2000s*	*Annualized growth rate (%)*
Central Asia								
Armenia	1998	2008	36.0	30.9	−1.53	5.8	4.5	−2.46
Azerbaijan	1995	2008	35.0	33.7	−0.28	6.1	5.3	−1.11
Georgia	1996	2008	37.1	41.3	0.90	7.1	8.9	1.88
Kazakhstan	1996	2009	35.3	29.0	−1.51	6.2	4.2	−2.98
Kyrgyz Republic	1993	2009	53.7	36.2	−2.47	22.7	6.4	−7.95
Tajikistan	1999	2009	29.0	30.8	0.61	4.5	4.8	0.61
Turkmenistan	1998	–	40.8	–	–	7.7	–	–
Uzbekistan	1998	2003	45.3	36.7	−4.21	–	–	–
East Asia								
PRC	1990	2008	32.4	43.4	1.62	5.1	9.6	3.56
Korea, Rep. of	1992	2010	24.5	28.9	0.92	–	–	–
Mongolia	1995	2007	33.2	36.5	0.79	–	–	–
Taipei,China	1990	2010	31.2	34.2	0.46	5.2	6.2	0.88
South Asia								
Afghanistan	–	2007	–	27.8	–	–	–	–
Bangladesh	1991	2010	27.6	32.1	0.80	3.9	4.7	0.94
Bhutan	2003	2007	46.8	38.1	−5.18	9.9	6.8	−9.37
India	1993	2010	32.5	37.0	0.75	4.8	5.7	1.05
Maldives	1998	2004	62.7	37.4	−8.62	46.6	6.8	−32.09
Nepal	1995	2010	35.2	32.8	−0.47	5.5	5.0	−0.66
Pakistan	1990	2007	33.2	30.0	−0.59	5.2	4.2	−1.31
Sri Lanka	1990	2006	32.5	40.3	1.34	4.8	6.9	2.26
Southeast Asia								
Cambodia	1994	2008	38.3	37.9	−0.08	5.8	6.1	0.32
Indonesia	1990	2011	29.2	38.9	1.36	4.1	6.6	2.18
Lao PDR	1992	2008	30.4	36.7	1.18	4.3	5.9	1.91

Table 2.2 Continued

Developing member economy	*Initial year*	*Final year*	*Gini coefficient*			*Top/bottom 20%*		
			1990s	*2000s*	*Annualized growth rate (%)*	*1990s*	*2000s*	*Annualized growth rate (%)*
Malaysia	1992	2009	47.7	46.2	−0.19	11.4	11.3	−0.03
Philippines	1991	2009	43.8	43.0	−0.10	8.6	8.3	−0.19
Singapore	2000	2011	44.4	48.2	0.75	10.1	12.8	2.15
Thailand	1990	2009	45.3	40.0	−0.65	8.8	7.1	−1.16
Viet Nam	1992	2008	35.7	35.6	−0.02	5.6	5.9	0.25
Pacific								
Fiji	2002	2008	46.8	42.8	−1.48	12.6	8.0	−7.50
Kiribati	–	2006	–	40.0	–	–	7.8	–
FSM	1998	–	45.0	–	–	10.3	–	–
Nauru	–	2006	–	48.0	–	–	16.2	–
Palau	–	2006	–	42.0	–	–	7.6	–
Papua New Guinea	1996	–	50.9	–	–	12.5	–	–
Samoa	2002	2008	45.0	43.0	−0.76	9.2	7.9	−2.51
Solomon Islands	–	2006	–	46.0	–	–	10.3	–
Timor-Leste	2001	2007	39.5	31.9	−3.55	7.0	4.6	−6.91
Tonga	–	2001	–	34.0	–	–	6.0	–
Tuvalu	1994	2004	45.0	37.0	−1.96	8.9	6.2	−3.57
Vanuatu	–	2006	–	46.0	–	–	10.4	–

– = not available; FSM = the Federated States of Micronesia; Lao PDR = Lao People's Democratic Republic; PRC = People's Republic of China.

Notes

1 Gini coefficients and quintile ratios are mainly from earliest available data in the 1990s (except for Bhutan, Fiji, Samoa, Singapore, and Timor-Leste, which are from the early 2000s) and latest available data, based on per capita expenditures, except for those of Malaysia, Singapore, and Taipei,China that are income-based.

2 Estimates for the PRC and Indonesia combine the separate urban and rural distributions, weighted by share of urban/rural to total population.

Sources: PovcalNet, http://iresearch.worldbank.org/PovcalNet/index.htm (accessed 11 July 2012), supplemented by household survey data (most Pacific countries and India), and publications of official statistics offices (Republic of Korea, Singapore, and Taipei,China).

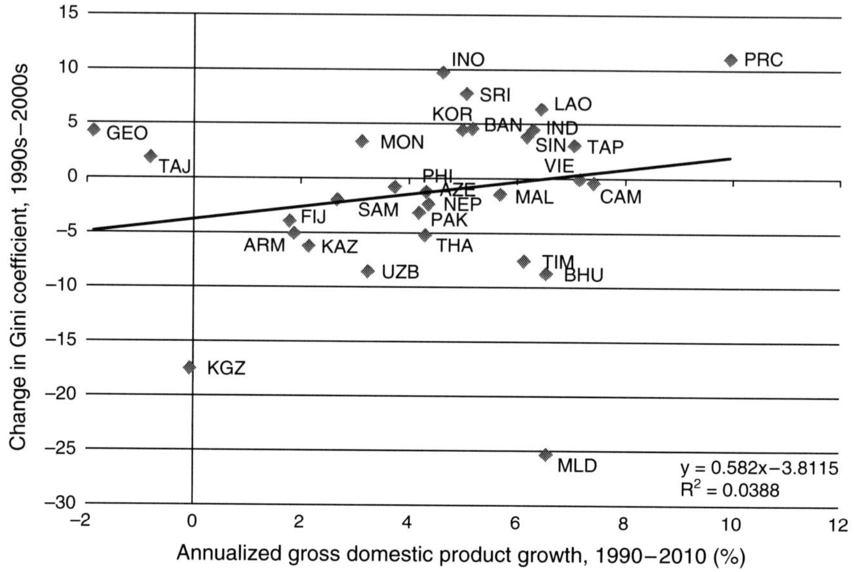

Figure 2.1 Gross domestic product growth and change in Gini coefficient.

ARM = Armenia (1998–2008); AZE = Azerbaijan (1995–2008); BAN = Bangladesh (1991–2010); BHU = Bhutan (2003–2007); CAM = Cambodia (1994–2008); FIJ = Fiji (2002–2008); GEO = Georgia (1996–2008); IND = India (1993–2010); INO = Indonesia (1990–2011); KAZ = Kazakhstan (1993–2009); KOR = Republic of Korea (1992–2010); KGZ = Kyrgyz Republic (1993–2009); LAO = Lao People's Democratic Republic (1992–2008); MAL = Malaysia (1992–2009); MLD = Maldives (1998–2004); MON = Mongolia (1995–2007); NEP = Nepal (1995–2010); PAK = Pakistan (1990–2007); PHI = Philippines (1991–2009); PRC = People's Republic of China (1990–2008); SAM = Samoa (2002–2008); SIN = Singapore (1998-2011); SRI = Sri Lanka (1990–2006); TAJ = Tajikistan (1999–2009); TAP = Taipei,China (1990–2010); THA = Thailand (1990–2009); TIM = Timor-Leste (2001–2007); UZB = Uzbekistan (1998–2003); VIE = Viet Nam (1992–2008).

Sources: PovcalNet, http://iresearch.worldbank.org/PovcalNet/index.htm (accessed 11 July 2012), World Development Indicators, http://data.worldbank.org/data-catalog/world-development-indicators (accessed 19 July 2012), International Monetary Fund, http://www.imf.org/external/pubs/ft/weo/2012/01/weodata/index.aspx (accessed April 2012).

countries. In the PRC, urban and rural inequalities increased in 1990–2008 – urban from 25.6 to 35.2 and rural from 30.6 to 39.4 (Figure 2.2). The pace for both was similar, leaving inequality greater in rural areas than in urban areas, a position unlike that in most developing countries. The rate of increase, however, appears to have been slowing since the early 2000s, for both areas.[4]

In India, the urban Gini grew from 34.4 in 1993 to 39.3 in 2010, much faster than the contemporaneous growth of the rural Gini from 28.6 to 30.0. India's rural

[4] "Appears" is used because the rural Gini had a sharp fall in 2002–2005 but a steep rise in 2005–2008. It is unclear whether this switch reflects data problems or changes in income distribution.

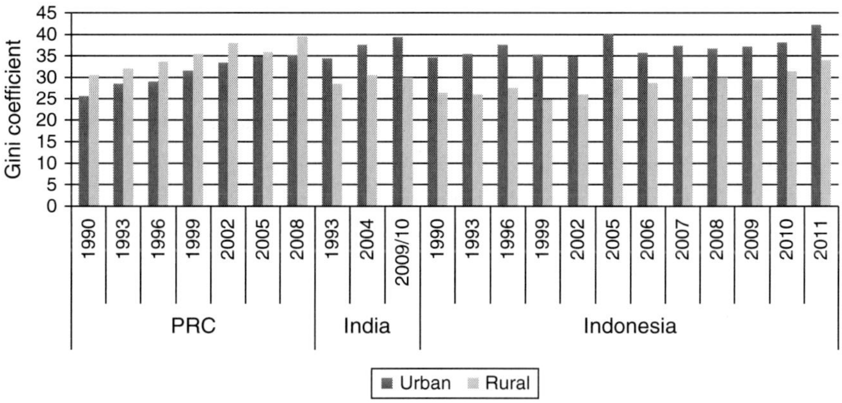

Figure 2.2 Urban and rural inequality in the People's Republic of China, India, and Indonesia.

PRC = People's Republic of China.

Sources: Authors' estimates using PovcalNet, http://iresearch.worldbank.org/PovcalNet/index.htm (accessed 9 March 2012) and household survey data (India).

inequality is lower and its urban inequality higher than in the PRC and, unlike the PRC but like most developing countries, India's urban inequality is higher than its rural inequality.

Similarly in Indonesia, urban inequality has been consistently higher than rural inequality – 42.2 and 34.0, respectively, in 2011. During 1990–2011, both urban and rural inequalities increased (but urban inequality increased faster).

Quintile ratios

The Gini coefficient presents an aggregate measure of inequality in a distribution, and it may hide detailed patterns of differences across different levels of income. Table 2.2 also presents the quintile ratios – the ratio of the per capita expenditure of the top 20% to that of the bottom 20%. In the late 2000s, 13 out of the 33 economies with available data had a quintile ratio of or above 7; that is, the average per capita expenditure of the richest 20% households was at least seven times as high as that of the poorest 20%. These include the PRC, Fiji, Georgia, Kiribati, Malaysia, Nauru, Palau, the Philippines, Samoa, Singapore, Solomon Islands, Thailand, and Vanuatu. The mean quintile ratio for the 33 economies was 7.2.[5]

Table 2.2 also shows that on an annual basis, the change in the quintile ratio is more pronounced than the change in the Gini for almost all the countries. For example, the PRC's annualized rate of increase of the Gini was 1.6%, but

[5] This is a simple arithmetic average.

3.6% for the quintile ratio (the ratio grew from 5.1 in 1990 to 9.6 in 2008). The larger increase in inequality when measured by the quintile ratio than by the Gini suggests that rising inequality may have been driven by households at the top.

Growth incidence curves

Growth incidence curves provide more detail on distributional changes by allowing one to look at income growth between two periods at various points of an income distribution. Figure 2.3 shows the annual growth of mean per capita expenditure by quintile, as well as for the entire population for the countries experiencing rising inequality in the last two decades with available data.[6]

All income groups of households (apart from Georgia's) experienced per capita expenditure growth during the periods reviewed. This suggests that economic growth has raised living standards for all people in these countries. However, per capita expenditure grew much faster for households in the top quintile than in the lower quintiles, especially than those in the bottom quintile. In the PRC, for example, mean expenditure growth for the bottom quintile in 1990–2008 was only 4%, but 7.6% for the top quintile. In India, mean growth was only 0.8% for the bottom quintile, but 1.9% for the top quintile. Even in Georgia, where income fell for all quintile groups in 1996–2008, the decline was more significant for the bottom quintile than for the top quintile and inequality widened.

Figure 2.3 also compares mean growth for each quintile with that of the population. It shows that in all the countries (except the PRC and Tajikistan), rising inequality involves a shift of income from the bottom 80% of the population to the top 20%, as indicated by lower mean expenditure growth for quintiles 1 to 4 than

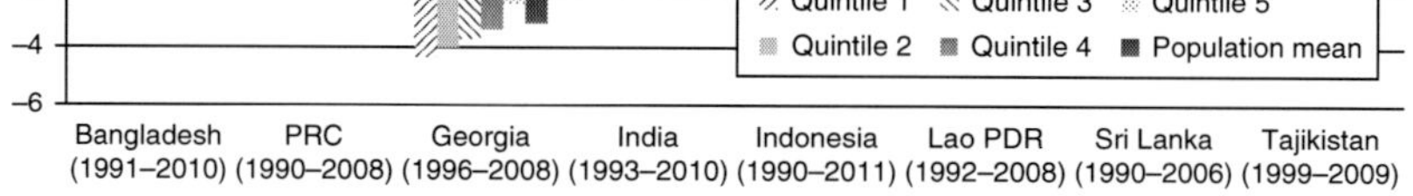

Figure 2.3 Growth incidence by quintile, countries with rising inequality.

Lao PDR = Lao People's Democratic Republic; PRC = People's Republic of China.

Note: Growth refers to annualized growth rate of per capita expenditure.

Sources: Authors' estimates using PovcalNet, http://iresearch.worldbank.org/PovcalNet/index.htm (accessed 9 March 2012) and household survey data (India).

[6] Data are not available for the Republic of Korea, Mongolia, Singapore, or Taipei,China.

that for the whole population. In the PRC and Tajikistan, with mean expenditure growth for quintiles 1 to 3 lower than and for quintile 4 close to that of the top quintile, rising inequality involves a shift of income from the bottom 60% to the top 20% of population.

Figure 2.4 shows growth incidence curves for India and Indonesia using unit-level survey data. The results largely confirm the findings from mean expenditure growth by quintile. The growth incidence curve cuts across the line of growth of population mean per capita expenditure close to the 80th percentile, suggesting that rising inequality in the two countries has been driven by income redistribution to the top 20%, at a cost to the bottom 80%. The growth incidence curve increases monotonically for Indonesia. For India, however, expenditure growth in the lowest few percentiles was higher than growth of population mean per capita expenditure.

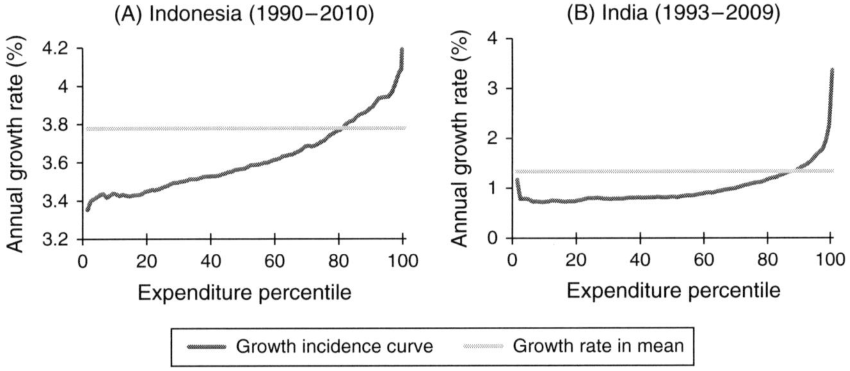

Figure 2.4 Growth incidence curves in Indonesia and India.

Source: Authors' estimates using household survey data.

Expenditure shares of the top 5% and 1%

Figure 2.5 goes further up the income distribution, focusing on the very top. In terms of levels, there are large variations in the expenditure shares of the top 5% and 1%. Except for the Pacific countries, in the late 2000s the shares of the richest households were relatively close across countries, in the range of 17–22% for the top 5% and 6–9% for the top 1%. For the Pacific countries, the shares of the top 5% and 1% were higher with a wider variation: 15–28% for the top 5% and 5–16% for the top 1%.

Consistent with the changes in the Gini and quintile ratios, most of the countries in Figure 2.5 show that the expenditure shares of the top 1% and 5% increased during the review periods. In the PRC, for example, in 1995–2008 the share of the top 5% rose from 17.0% to 20.5%, and that of the top 1% from 4.6% to 6.4%. In India, the share of the top 5% increased from 17.7% to 21.3% and that for the top 1% from 6.5% to 9.0%, respectively, in 1993–2010. These results back up the

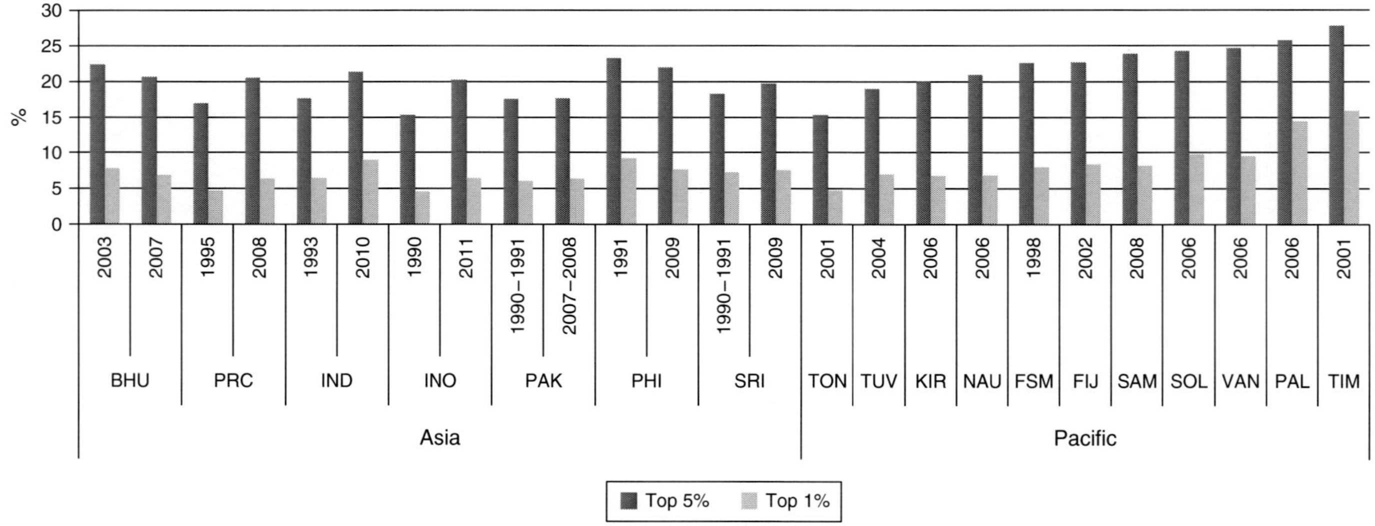

Figure 2.5 Expenditure shares of the top 5% and 1%.

BHU = Bhutan; FIJ = Fiji; FSM = Federated States of Micronesia; IND = India; INO = Indonesia; KIR = Kiribati; NAU = Nauru; PAK = Pakistan; PAL = Palau; PHI = Philippines; PRC = People's Republic of China; SAM = Samoa; SOL = Solomon Islands; SRI = Sri Lanka; TIM = Timor-Leste; TON = Tonga; TUV = Tuvalu; VAN = Vanuatu.

Source: Authors' estimates using household survey data.

earlier point that rising inequality in developing Asia is closely associated with very rapid increases in the top income groups – that is, the rich are getting richer much faster.

Within- and between-country inequality

Although the focus of this chapter is on inequality within each country, it is useful both to look at Asia-wide inequality that considers developing Asian countries as one entity and to ask how important within-country inequality is compared with between-country inequality.

The Asia-wide Gini coefficient increased from 39 in the mid-1990s to 46 in the late 2000s, or 1.4% a year. Both within-country and between-country inequality as measured by the GE(0) index widened (Figure 2.6). However, between-country inequality grew faster as its contribution to Asia-wide inequality rose from about 22.6% in the mid-1990s to 29.6% in the late 2000s, while the contribution of within-country inequality to Asia-wide inequality declined from 77.4% to 70.4% in the same period. The between-country income differences can be largely explained by much faster growth in the PRC than in the rest of the region.

Asia's inequality in a global context

Historically, incomes in Asian societies as a whole are more equally distributed compared with other parts of the developing world. With recent increases in inequality, does this still hold? This section looks at Asia's inequality in a global context. Before going into a detailed comparison of Asia's inequality in relation to other groupings, a word of caution: inequality measures are largely based on per capita incomes for OECD and Latin American countries, but based on per

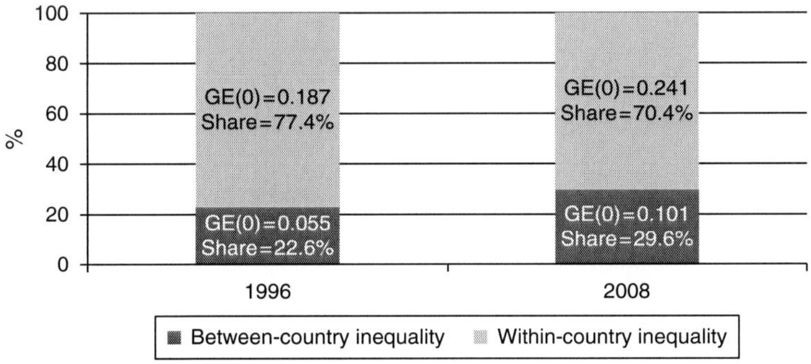

Figure 2.6 Decomposition of Asia-wide inequality.

GE(0) = generalized entropy index (see the section "Data sources and estimation methods").

Note: Asia-wide inequality pertains to 23 countries where comparative data are available for 1996 and 2008, or closest available.

Source: Authors' estimates using grouped expenditure data from PovcalNet, http://iresearch.worldbank.org/PovcalNet/index.htm (accessed 9 March 2012).

capita expenditure in most developing Asian countries (as well as sub-Saharan Africa). As noted earlier, income-based inequality measures tend to run higher than expenditure-based ones.

Despite recent increases, Gini coefficients in developing Asia are still on average lower than in other regions of the developing world (Table 2.3 and Figure 2.7). Developing Asia's range of Gini coefficients of 28–51 is tighter than that of sub-Saharan Africa at 30–66, and lower than that of Latin America and the Caribbean at 45–60. This conclusion is likely to hold even if we consider the differences between income-based and expenditure-based inequalities.

Still, developing Asia compares less favorably when one looks at *changes* in inequality. During the past decade, most sub-Saharan African countries and more than half of Latin American and Caribbean countries experienced declines in their Gini. In developing Asia, 12 of the 30 economies with comparable data, covering 82% of the region's population, experienced increases in inequality (Figure 2.8).

In the case of Latin America, recent studies have identified a number of contributing factors to the declining inequality. These include (i) falling skill premiums in labor markets, (ii) falling educational inequality, and (iii) equalizing public transfers. Policies that encouraged employment (including trade policies), policies that targeted inequality of human capital (especially education but also health), and policies that targeted transfers and used them to incentivize human capital accumulation, all contributed to the historical reversal of inequality trends in Latin America. Of particular note are the large-scale conditional cash transfer programs such as *Bolsa Família* in Brazil and *Progresa/Oportunidades* in Mexico, which have played a central role in the turnaround (Esquivel *et al.* 2010).

Table 2.3 Gini coefficients, 2000s

	Developing Asia	*Latin America and the Caribbean*	*Middle East and North Africa*	*OECD*	*Sub-Saharan Africa*
Median	37.4	52.0	36.8	30.4	42.7
Minimum	27.8	44.8	30.8	23.6	29.8
Maximum	50.9	59.2	41.4	49.4	65.8

OECD = Organisation for Economic Co-operation and Development.

Notes

1 Gini coefficients for Latin America and the Caribbean and for OECD are estimated from per capita income.

2 For developing Asia (except Malaysia, Singapore, and Taipei,China), sub-Saharan Africa and the Middle East and North Africa, coefficients are estimated from per capita consumption expenditure.

Sources: PovcalNet, http://iresearch.worldbank.org/PovcalNet/index.htm (accessed 11 July 2012), supplemented by household survey data (most Pacific countries and India) and publications of official statistics offices (Statistics Korea, http://kostat.go.kr/portal/english/index.action (accessed January 2012); Directorate-General of Budget, Accounting, and Statistics. 2012. *Statistical Yearbook*. Taipei,China; Statistics Singapore. 2012. Key Household Characteristics and Household Income Trends 2011, http://www.singstat.gov.sg/Publications/population.html#household_income_and_expenditure (accessed 13 June 2012) and OECD Stat database, http://stats.oecd.org/index.aspx (accessed February 2012)).

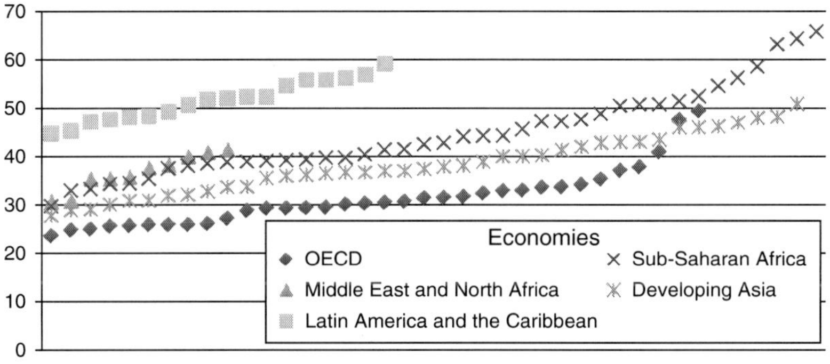

Figure 2.7 Gini coefficients, 2000s.

OECD = Organisation for Economic Co-operation and Development.

Notes

1 Markers indicate individual country observations for each region ranked by the value of their Gini coefficient.
2 Gini coefficients for Latin America and the Caribbean and for OECD are estimated from per capita income.
3 For developing Asia (except Malaysia, Singapore, and Taipei,China), sub-Saharan Africa, and the Middle East and North Africa, coefficients are estimated from per capita consumption expenditure.

Sources: PovcalNet, http://iresearch.worldbank.org/PovcalNet/index.htm (accessed 11 July 2012), supplemented by household survey data (most Pacific countries and India) and publications of official statistics offices (Statistics Korea, http://kostat.go.kr/portal/english/index.action (accessed January 2012); Directorate-General of Budget, Accounting, and Statistics. 2012. *Statistical Yearbook*. Taipei,China; Statistics Singapore. 2012. Key Household Characteristics and Household Income Trends 2011, http://www.singstat.gov.sg/Publications/population.html#household_income_and_expenditure (accessed 13 June 2012) and OECD Stat database, http://stats.oecd.org/index.aspx (accessed February 2012)).

Compared with OECD countries, however, developing Asia's inequality is much higher overall. Of the 34 OECD countries with comparative data, most countries had a Gini in the range of 25–35. Excluding Chile, Mexico, and Turkey, the United States is the most unequal country among OECD countries, and the latest Gini coefficient stood at 37.8. High taxes and transfers are key reasons for their low income inequality. Thirty-one OECD countries had a Gini coefficient before taxes and transfers greater than 40 in the late 2000s (Figure 2.9).

Yet, even in OECD countries, as in developing Asia, inequality is on the rise: 14 OECD countries saw increases in their Gini coefficient from the mid-1990s to the late 2000s (Figure 2.8).[7] A study by OECD (2011) reports that in many of its member countries household incomes increased much faster at the top income ranges from the mid-1990s to the late 2000s, similar to the experiences of many developing Asian countries. On average, income growth for households in the top decile was 1.5 times as high as that in the bottom decile from the mid-1980s to

[7] The increases were more pronounced in Denmark, Finland, and Sweden.

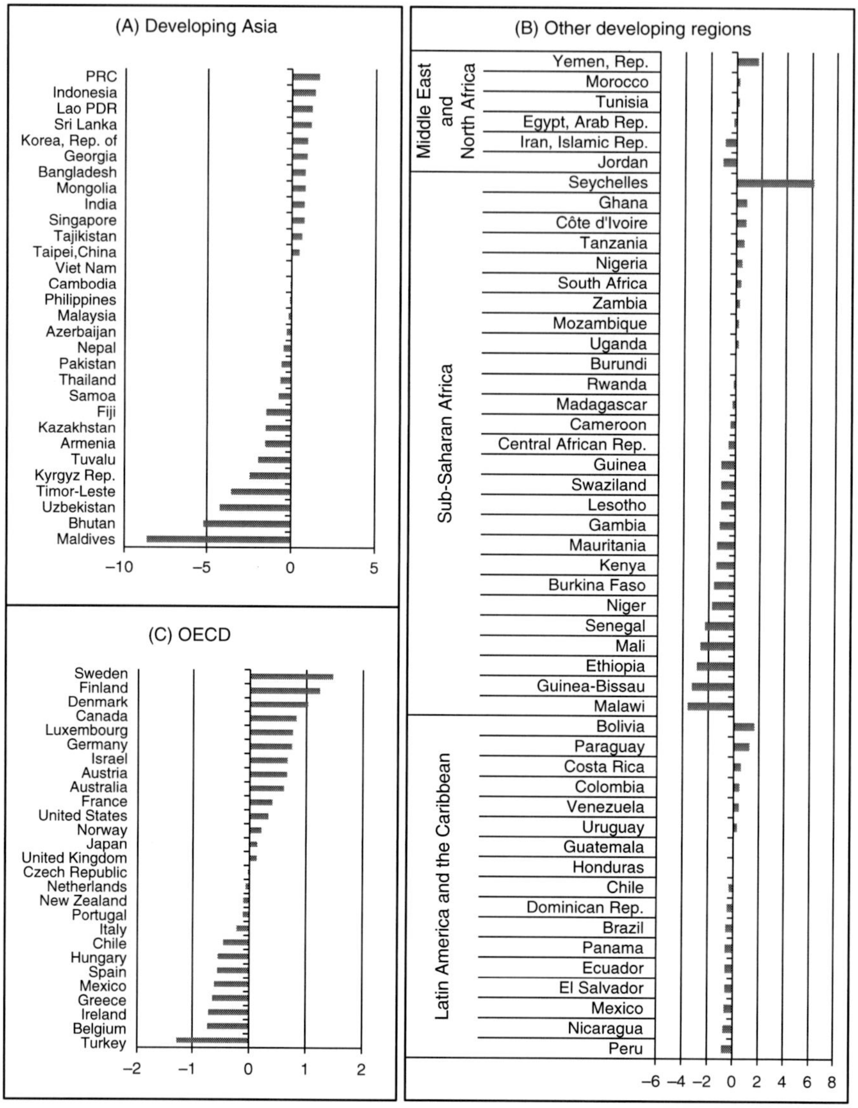

Figure 2.8 Annualized change in Gini coefficient in developing Asia and other regions, 1990s and 2000s (%).

Lao PDR = Lao People's Democratic Republic; OECD = Organisation for Economic Co-operation and Development; PRC = People's Republic of China.

Sources: Authors' estimates using PovcalNet, http://iresearch.worldbank.org/PovcalNet/index.htm (accessed 11 July 2012), supplemented by household survey data (most Pacific countries and India) and publications of official statistics offices (Statistics Korea, http://kostat.go.kr/portal/english/index.action (accessed January 2012); Directorate-General of Budget, Accounting, and Statistics. 2012. *Statistical Yearbook*. Taipei,China; Statistics Singapore. 2012. Key Household Characteristics and Household Income Trends 2011, http://www.singstat.gov.sg/Publications/population. html#household_income_and_expenditure (accessed 13 June 2012) and OECD Stat database, http://stats.oecd.org/index.aspx (accessed February 2012)).

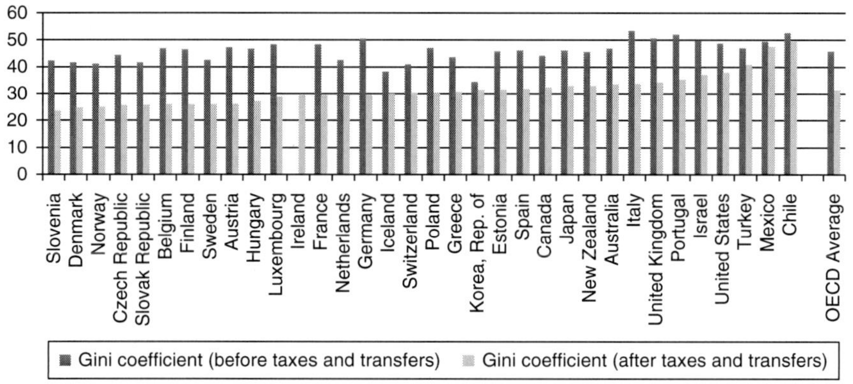

Figure 2.9 Gini coefficients in Organisation for Economic Co-operation and Development countries, late 2000s.

OECD = Organisation for Economic Co-operation and Development.

Source: OECD Stat database, http://stats.oecd.org/index.aspx (accessed February 2012).

the late 2000s for 27 OECD countries. The difference in income growth between the top and bottom deciles was particularly significant in Germany, Sweden, the United States, and the Netherlands – in the range of 3–15 times as high.

The OECD study identified various factors contributing to rising inequality including increased financial integration and technological change; increased imports from low-income countries, reducing employment prospects for less-skilled workers; changes in labor market policies that tended to reduce income and benefits for less-skilled workers; increased prevalence of part-time work; greater numbers of single-headed households; increased income shares for capital, benefiting rich households; increased incomes from self-employment, which reward the more highly skilled workers; and declining effectiveness of redistribution through taxes and transfers.

Summary

This chapter looks at recent trends of income inequality in Asia and the Pacific using a number of standard measures. Key findings are summarized as follows.

First, 12 of the 30 Asian economies with comparable data showed an increase (worsening) in the Gini coefficient in the past two decades. These 12 include the region's three most populous countries – the PRC, India, and Indonesia – and cover 82% of the region's population. The Gini coefficient worsened from 32.4 in 1990 to 43.4 in 2008 in the PRC, from 32.5 in 1993 to 37 in 2010 in India, and from 29.2 in 1990 to 38.9 in 2011 in Indonesia.

Second, on an annual basis, the change in the quintile ratio is more pronounced than the change in the Gini for almost all the countries. The larger increase in inequality when measured by the quintile ratio than by the Gini suggests that rising inequality may have been driven by households at the top.

Third, except for the Pacific countries, the expenditure shares in the late 2000s of the richest households were relatively close across developing Asian countries, in the range of 17–22% for the top 5% and 6–9% for the top 1%. For the Pacific countries, the shares of the top 5% and 1% were higher with a wider variation: 15–28% for the top 5% and 5–16% for the top 1%. Further, most countries in Asia and the Pacific with comparable data saw the expenditure shares of the top 1% and 5% increasing during the review periods. These results back up the earlier point that rising inequality in developing Asia is closely associated with rapid increases in the very top income groups – that is, the rich are getting richer much faster.

Fourth, considering Asia as a single unit, its Gini coefficient increased from 39 in the mid-1990s to 46 in the late 2000s. Breaking down the Asia-wide inequality into between-country and within-country components, the contribution of the former increased and that of the latter declined, suggesting the between-country inequality has risen faster than the within-country inequality.

Finally, on a global scale, levels of income inequality in developing Asia are still on average lower than in other regions of the developing world. The range of Gini coefficients is 28–51 for developing Asia, as opposed to 30–66 for sub-Saharan Africa and 45–60 for Latin America and the Caribbean. However, the fact that inequality is rising in developing Asia is a major concern. In many Latin American countries, income equality has been on the decline in the past two decades.

References

Directorate-General of Budget, Accounting, and Statistics. 2012. *Statistical Yearbook.* Taipei,China.

Esquivel, G., N. Lustig, and J. Scott. 2010. A Decade of Falling Inequality in Mexico: Market Forces or State Action? In L. F. López-Calva and N. Lustig, eds. *Declining Inequality in Latin America: A Decade of Progress?* Washington, DC: Brookings Institution and United Nations Development Programme.

International Monetary Fund. 2012. World Economic Outlook Database. http://www.imf.org/external/pubs/ft/weo/2012/01/weodata/index.aspx

Organisation for Economic Co-operation and Development (OECD). 2011. *Divided We Stand: Why Inequality Keeps Rising.* Paris.

Statistics Korea. 2012. Household Income and Expenditure. http://kostat.go.kr/portal/english/index.action

Statistics Singapore. 2012. Key Household Characteristics and Household Income Trends, 2011. http://www.singstat.gov.sg/Publications/population.html#household_income_and_expenditure

World Bank. PovcalNet: the Online Tool for Poverty Measurement Developed by the Development Research Group of the World Bank. http://iresearch.worldbank.org/PovcalNet/index.htm (accessed 11 July 2012).

——. World Development Indicators. http://data.worldbank.org/data-catalog/world-development-indicators (accessed 19 July 2012).

3 What drives Asia's rising inequality?

Juzhong Zhuang, Ravi Kanbur, and Changyong Rhee

A framework of thinking about income inequality

A basic framework for thinking about drivers of income inequality can start with defining income as the product of an asset and its rate of return: capital multiplied by its rate of return equals income to capital. The unskilled wage is the return to labor – the basic asset of most poor people. The return to human capital is reflected in the skill premium earned by successively higher levels of human capital, for example, as reflected in higher wages earned by more educated workers. Inequality of income is thus a function of the distribution of assets – among individuals, between groups of individuals (e.g., between men and women and between rural and urban populations), and across different provinces. Changes in income inequality can then be thought of as following a combination of changes in the distribution of assets and changes in relative returns to these assets.

In any society, the distribution of assets is determined by the ownership structure of capital and land and inequality in education and health, which together determine the human capital of an individual. Over time, this distribution is shaped by many factors, including its initial distribution, household savings behavior and investment decision, demographic changes, differences in individual efforts and entrepreneurships, political economy factors (e.g., pressures for land redistribution), the quality of governance and institutions (e.g., the presence or absence of corruption), and changes in relative returns to assets. The relative returns to assets and their changes, on the other hand, reflect demand and supply conditions in the marketplace, how efficiently the market works – for instance, the presence or absence of a monopoly or discrimination against a particular group (e.g., women) – and government income redistribution through taxation. The demand and supply conditions are further affected by market forces such as globalization and technological progress.

Within this framework, income inequality is likely to intensify if changes in the relative returns or in asset distribution are in favor of those better-off in society, such as owners of capital and land, skilled labor, and, in the context of developing countries, urban dwellers and residents in coastal regions. Increases in returns to higher levels of education, for example, will compound the inequality in human capital and escalate income inequality. Similarly, increases in returns to physical capital relative to those to labor will also add to inequality because capital incomes are less equally distributed than labor incomes. Another example is higher returns to assets and labor in urban areas relative to those in rural areas, or in coastal areas relative to interior regions – perhaps because of better infrastructure provision, better market access, or agglomeration economies in urban areas, which will add to inequality between rural and urban areas and across regions. On the other hand, policy measures such as public investment in human capital, land redistribution, and tax increases for high-income earners will reduce income inequality.

With this setting, opportunity means the opportunity to earn incomes – to have assets that can generate incomes and to have access to market rates of return to those assets. For many, this means having access to employment opportunities and to education and healthcare so as to accumulate human capital. Unequal access to employment and to basic education and healthcare especially for those for whom employment is the only source of income, means inequality of opportunity. This inequality can be across individuals with different circumstances, as characterized by levels of parental income, gender, religious background, or location of residence. Further, if these same factors are associated with differences in rates of return for the same level of human capital, due to discrimination or market distortions, then inequality of opportunity is compounded.

In this chapter, we will focus on shifts in the relative returns to assets as the primary reason for rising inequality in Asia. In particular, we will provide evidence that technological progress, globalization, and market-oriented reform – ironically the three key drivers of Asia's rapid economic growth in recent decades – can explain a large part of the movements in relative returns to assets (e.g., skilled vs. unskilled labor, capital vs. labor, and capital and labor in urban vs. in rural areas as well as those in coastal and in interior regions) and, hence, increases in inequality in many Asian countries. The next chapter will look at inequality of opportunity, focusing on access to education and health and inequality in human capital.

Key drivers of rising inequality in Asia

Technological progress, globalization, and market-oriented reform have been the key drivers of developing Asia's rapid growth in the past two decades – but they also had huge distributional consequences. Together, they have favored skilled rather than unskilled labor, capital rather than labor, and urban and coastal areas rather than rural and inland regions. These changes can explain a large part of the movements in inequality in many regional countries.

Technological change can impact the distribution of income among different factors of production. If it favors skilled labor (more educated or more experienced) over unskilled labor by increasing its relative productivity, we could expect the skill premium – the ratio of skilled to unskilled wages – to go up, which would most likely increase income inequality. Technological change could also affect the distribution of income between labor and capital. If it is biased in favor of capital, it could increase inequality because capital incomes, in general, are less equally distributed and accrue to the rich more than to the poor.

In a similar fashion, *globalization* can affect income distribution. Trade integration, for example, could change relative demand for, and hence relative wages of, skilled and unskilled workers. It could also affect income distribution between capital and labor because capital and skills often work together due to their complementarity. Financial integration could broaden access to finance by the poor – but could also increase the risk of financial crises and hurt the poor more than the rich. Globalization could magnify the distributional impact of technological progress. A large literature has emerged in recent years attempting to understand the impacts of trade integration, financial integration, and technological change on income distribution (Box 3.1), though it has yet to provide a clear-cut answer. One complication is that there are several, closely linked, confounding factors.[1]

Market-oriented reform is an important driver of growth, but it can also have significant distributional consequences. Trade policy reform is often part of the driving forces of globalization. Labor market reforms can change the bargaining position of labor in relation to capital owners, impacting wage rates and income distribution between labor and capital. Economic transition from a command to a market economy can improve efficiency and make returns to assets more closely reflective of resource scarcity, which can affect income distribution among different productive assets in a significant way.

Box 3.1 Globalization and inequality

There is general consensus among researchers and policy makers that Asia's extremely good growth performance could not have been achieved without its embrace of globalization. All countries in Asia are committed to greater integration with the global economy in the coming decades. How does greater openness of an economy influence income inequality? Economic analysis does not provide a clear answer.

The simplest trade theory predicts that for countries with abundant unskilled labor, opening the economy should raise the wages of unskilled labor and depress the wages for skilled workers and returns to capital because the country specializes in low-skill production, thereby increasing equality (Stolper and Samuelson 1941). The historical evidence on "growth with equity" from the Republic of Korea, Singapore, and Taipei,China seems to support this thesis (Wood 1999).

The recent evidence on trade, openness, and inequality, however, is mixed, especially for economies that are not readily characterized as being abundant in unskilled labor, resource-rich, or have production structures not easily captured by the simple model. The channels between market opening and inequality are complex, and the quest for clarity in results remains elusive (see Table 3.1).

[1] A cross-country study by the International Monetary Fund (2007) found that global trade integration helps reduce inequality (as measured by the Gini coefficient), global financial integration increases it, and technological progress is the most important contributor to rising inequality globally in the past two decades. The study also found that these impacts are particularly pronounced in developing Asia.

Empirically, a number of variables that affect inequality can confound the effect of trade openness on inequality, most notably financial integration, skill-biased technological change, and rising skill premiums.

Table 3.1 Empirical studies on globalization and inequality

Mechanism and net effect on inequality	*Sample or data*	*Literature*
Decrease		
Financial integration can spur growth and benefit the poor.	Meta-survey	Demirgüc-Kunt and Levine (2007)
No effect		
Trade liberalization	Survey of results for Mexico, Colombia, Brazil, and Chile (1990s)	Goldberg and Pavcnik (2007)
Inconclusive or varying		
Trade liberalization may decrease or increase wage differentials.	Survey for Latin America and East Asia (1960–1970s, 1980s–1990s)	Wood (1999)
Financial integration may increase access to finance by the poor, but gains may be captured by the elite: inequality increases at low income levels and decreases as income rises.	Meta-survey	Claessens and Perotti (2007)
Trade openness benefits the rich more than the poor in very poor countries; it benefits the poor and middle class more as income rises.	Household surveys, World Income Distribution database (1988, 1993, 1998)	Milanovic (2005)
Financial globalization increases Gini coefficient by about 0.04; trade globalization decreases Gini coefficient by about 0.05.	Global dataset (1980s–2000s)	IMF (2007)
Increase		
Foreign direct investment (FDI) increases demand for high-skilled workers.	119 countries (1993–2004) from World Development Indicators 2004	Choi (2006)

Table 3.1 Continued

Mechanism and net effect on inequality	*Sample or data*	*Literature*
FDI increases demand for skilled workers, explains 11% of wage inequality.	101 manufacturing industries in the United Kingdom (1983–1992)	Taylor and Driffield (2005)
FDI increases demand for high-skilled workers, and thus explains 50% of the increase in share of skilled labor.	Data on foreign assembly plants in Mexico (1975–1988)	Feenstra and Hanson (1997)
Trade induces skill intensification in the traded manufacturing sector, resulting in a 0.1% change in wage premium.	Micro-level data from approximately 1 million workers in Mexico (1987–1993)	Cragg and Epelbaum (1996)
The *trade* index explains 10–12% of the wage gap between workers with different schooling; the financial index explains 12–33% of the gap; and the capital account index explains 25–30%.	Household surveys from 18 Latin American countries (1977–1998)	Behrman *et al.* (2003)
Financial integration may lead to crises that hurt the poor: poverty incidence increased in 1997–1998 in Indonesia by 11–19.9%; in the Republic of Korea by 2.6–7.3%; in Malaysia by 8.2–10.4%; and in Thailand by 9.8–12.9%.	Country data for Indonesia, Republic of Korea, Malaysia, Thailand, and some Latin American countries (Asian financial crisis period)	Fallon and Lucas (2002)
Financial integration may lead to crises that hurt the poor; macroeconomic volatility increases the poverty index by about 0.35–0.40.	Macroeconomic data on various countries (World Bank Live Database) (1980s–1990s)	Agénor (2002)

Source: Authors' compilation.

Moreover, the impacts of the three drivers of growth – technological progress, globalization, and market-oriented reform – can be geographically uneven, leading to a further channel of changing income distribution: spatial inequality. This is because new economic opportunities released by these drivers are often most easily seized by locations closer to the existing trade routes (coastal areas, for example, not inland ones) and areas with better public infrastructure such as urban locations, not rural areas. This leads to shifts in income distribution among different geographic locations.

Complicating the analysis is that the impacts of the three drivers are intertwined. Although they can be disentangled conceptually, it is difficult to do so empirically. In the next three sections, therefore, instead of trying to isolate their impacts, we will look at three channels through which the three drivers affect income inequality: shifts in income distribution between skilled and unskilled labor by examining returns to human capital and the skill premium; between labor and capital by analyzing labor and capital income shares; and between different locations by estimating spatial inequality.

Yet, those individuals and groups excluded from the market because of individual circumstances beyond their control or discrimination would certainly not benefit from these opportunities – inequality of opportunity magnifies the distributional consequences of the three drivers.

Increasing skill premiums

Inequality of education is a major contributor to inequality of income. There is significant global evidence that the rates of return to progressively higher levels of education have been trending upward in recent years. In Organisation for Economic Co-operation and Development (OECD) countries, for instance, those who do not complete an upper secondary education could earn an average of 23% less than their counterparts who do. A person with a tertiary education can expect to earn over 50% more than a person with an upper secondary or postsecondary non-tertiary education (OECD 2011).

In Asia, empirical studies find that the returns to education increase with educational attainment and that the relationship has been getting steeper over time. An ADB study (2007) found that from the mid-1990s to mid-2000s, real wages grew much faster for wage earners with tertiary or higher education than for those with lower educational attainment in India and the Philippines, leading to wider wage differentials. The same study also found that education is the single most important factor among those variables included in analyzing wage inequality. In the case of India, the Gini coefficient of wages increased from 40.5 in 1993 to 47.2 in 2004. Half the increase can be explained by individual characteristics. Of this explained increase, about 50% is accounted for by education.

Many other studies have provided direct or indirect evidence of rising skill and/or education premiums in developing Asia. Son (2010) found that education increases individuals' employability in the Philippines. In 2003, the probability of being employed was 57% for individuals with a tertiary education and 34% for those with a primary education only. This difference in employability increased from 1997 to 2003. Furthermore, the difference in employability due to differences in educational attainment was more pronounced among poorer households.

A study on India, the Philippines, and Thailand found that the rate of return to college education rose relative to that of secondary education between the mid-1990s and mid-2000s (Mehta *et al.* 2011). This rise was related to the expansion of high-skill services jobs: employing only 7–11% of the labor force, they contributed 40–70% of the rate of return to college education.

A more recent study (World Bank 2012) reported that the tertiary education premium[2] stood at 90% for Cambodia (2007), 60% for the People's Republic of China (PRC; 2005), 84% for Indonesia (2007), 70% for Mongolia (2007), 70% for the Philippines (2006), 120% for Thailand (2004), and 55% for Viet Nam (2006). In Cambodia, the PRC, Mongolia, and Viet Nam, the premium has increased in recent years across sectors. The tertiary education premium increased In Indonesia in the manufacturing sector and in the Philippines in the services sector.

Household survey data help reveal patterns of income inequality due to educational attainment (in this case, of the household head) (Figure 3.1). First, education inequality almost always accounts for more than 20% of total income inequality. Second, the share of total income inequality explained by educational inequality has largely been on the increase. The share of inequality accounted for by differences in educational attainment increased in all the countries during the periods looked at, with the increase most significant in the PRC, from 8.1% in 1995 to 26.5% in 2007.

As in the rest of the world, developing Asia is facing strong upward pressure on the wage gap between skilled and unskilled labor. Is this because of skill-biased technological progress? There are empirical difficulties in isolating this factor because the wage premium depends on both demand- and supply-side factors. Unsurprisingly, analysts have come down on both sides of the explanation.[3] To the extent that skill-biased technological change happens, its impact can be transmitted through globalization. It is unlikely that policy makers can reverse this trend – nor should they want to because technological progress is delivering higher levels of productivity and growth in the economy. The answer, rather, is to address inequality in human capital itself.

---

[2] Tertiary education premium refers to the wage premium for workers with at least tertiary education compared with workers with a lower level of education.

[3] Acemoglu (2002) noted that for the late 20th century, there has been a rise in returns to education and a decrease in low-skill wages, despite an increase in the supply of college graduates, which suggests that supply has not kept up with demand for high-skilled labor. Studies have also argued for evidence of skill-biased technological change in developing economies (Goldberg and Pavcnik (2007); Robbins (1996); Sanchez-Paramo and Schady (2003); and Attanasio *et al.* (2004) for Latin America; Hsieh and Woo (2005) for Hong Kong, China; and Kijima (2006) for India). However, Card and DiNardo (2002) pointed out that wage inequality stabilized in the United States despite continuing developments in computer technology. They also argued that skill-biased technological change does not fully explain wage gaps across genders, and racial and demographic structures. The debate between competing explanations for the United States is ongoing (see Autor *et al.* (2008); Marquis *et al.* (2011)).

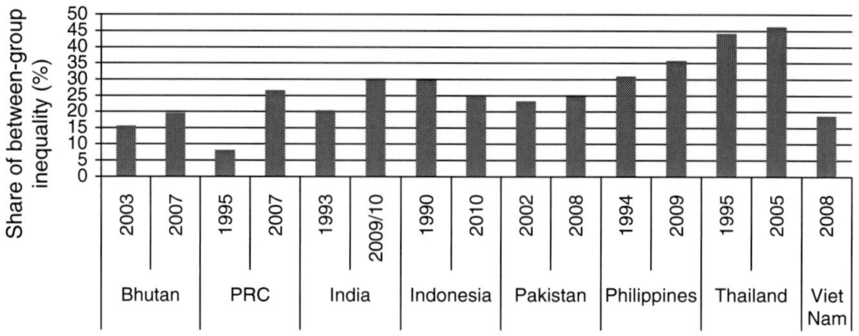

Figure 3.1 Income inequality decomposition by educational attainment of household head.

PRC = People's Republic of China.

Notes

1 Estimates are based on per capita expenditure in nominal terms, except for the PRC, which is based on income.
2 The decomposition is based on GE(0), which is a special form of the generalized entropy index.

Source: Authors' estimates using household survey data and data from the Chinese Household Income Project.

Declining share of labor income

In the past two decades, the income share of labor has been on the decline and that of capital on the rise in many OECD countries. In the United States (US), for example, the labor income share in industry declined from 65% in 1992 to 52.4% in 2009 (Figure 3.2). For the entire US economy, the labor income share fell from 68.7% to 64.2% in the same period. Similarly in Germany, the labor income share of industry peaked at 79.5% in 1993 from the rise that started in the mid-1980s, and has been declining since then. A declining labor income share means that the growth of wage rates lags behind growth of labor productivity. A number of contributing factors have been identified.

The first is that technological change, especially connected with improvements in information and communication technologies, has raised the productivity of and return to capital relative to labor. The second is the decrease in the bargaining power of labor, due to changing labor market policies and declining union membership in these countries. The third is increased globalization and trade openness, which led to migration of relatively more labor-intensive sectors from advanced economies to emerging economies – with the sectors remaining in the advanced economies relatively less labor-intensive and having a lower average share of labor income (Jacobson and Occhino 2012; Arpaia *et al.* 2009). It has also been noted that globalization and trade openness increase the elasticity of labor demand, which also weakens labor's bargaining position (Rodrik 1997; Harrison 2005).

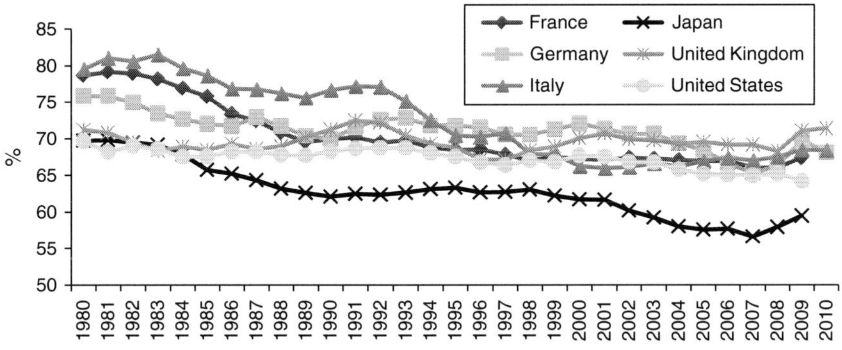

Figure 3.2 Labor income share of industry in major Organisation for Economic Co-operation and Development countries, 1980–2010.

Note: The annual labor income share is calculated as total labor costs in nominal terms divided by nominal output.

Source: Organisation for Economic Co-operation and Development. 2012. OECD Stat database, http://stats.oecd.org/index.aspx (accessed 1 March 2012).

Empirical evidence suggests that Asia is following this trend – all the economies in Figure 3.3 saw declines in labor income shares during the mid-1990s to mid-2000s.

What are the causes of these declines? Technological progress in the region appears to have been labor-saving and capital-using. This can be partly explained by a high level of capital accumulation in many Asian countries (Felipe 2009). As a result, the wage employment elasticity of growth[4] has been on the decline in many countries in recent years (Figure 3.4) – for example, in the PRC from 0.44 in 1991–2001 to 0.28 in 2001–2011 and in India from 0.53 to 0.41 for the same periods. This decline means that each percentage of employment growth now requires a higher percentage of output growth than in the past – a phenomenon sometimes referred to as "jobless growth."

A declining employment elasticity of growth implies increases in labor productivity. Annual growth of manufacturing labor productivity in 2000–2008 reached 6.7% in the PRC and 5.5% in Malaysia, and was in the range of 3–4% in Indonesia, Pakistan, the Philippines, Thailand, and Viet Nam (Asian Productivity Organization 2011).

The fact that labor productivity is increasing but labor income share is declining implies that real wage growth has lagged behind labor productivity growth, partly because of the presence of a large pool of rural surplus labor in many countries

[4] Wage employment refers to wage-earning employment, mostly in the formal sector. Wage employment elasticity is the ratio of employment growth to gross domestic product (GDP) growth between two periods. It thus measures the amount of employment growth required to generate each percentage point of GDP growth.

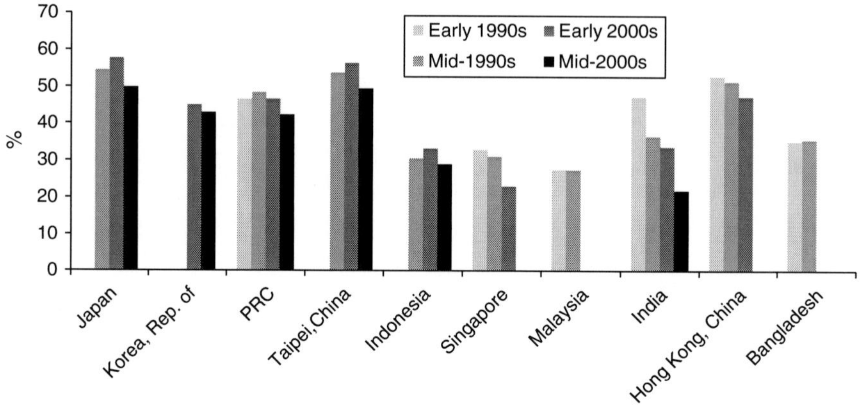

Figure 3.3 Share of labor income in industrial/manufacturing value added in selected Asian economies.

PRC = People's Republic of China.

Note: Early 1990s (1990–1992), mid-1990s (1994–1996), early 2000s (2000–2002), and mid-2000s (2004–2006) for the PRC; India; Singapore; Malaysia; India; Hong Kong, China; and Bangladesh.

Sources: Organisation for Economic Co-operation and Development. 2012. OECD Stat database, http://stats.oecd.org/index.aspx (accessed 1 March 2012) for Japan, Republic of Korea; Taipei,China; and Indonesia; J. Felipe and G. C. Sipin. 2004. Competitiveness, Income Distribution, and Growth in the Philippines: What Does the Long-Run Evidence Show? *ERD Working Paper Series* No. 53. Manila: ADB for Singapore; Malaysia; Hong Kong, China; and Bangladesh; C. Bai and Z. Qian. 2009. Factor Income Distribution: The Story behind the Statistics. Tsinghua, People's Republic of China: Tsinghua University for the PRC; and J. Felipe and U. Kumar. 2010. Technical Change in India's Organized Manufacturing Sector. *Levy Economics Institute of Bard College Working Paper* No. 626. New York, NY: Levy Economics Institute for India's organized manufacturing sector.

associated with their dual-economy structure.[5] The surplus labor pool weakens the bargaining power of labor and depresses wages in the non-agriculture sectors, contributing to declines in the labor income share when globalization and market-oriented reform lead to rapid growth.

In India, for instance, average annual growth of labor productivity was 7.4% in 1990–2007, while average annual real wage growth was only 2% (Box 3.2). In the case of the PRC, Zhuang (1996) showed that if the labor market had been fully liberalized and controls over labor transfer from rural to urban areas fully relaxed in the early 1980s, urban wage rates would have fallen and the labor income share of the urban sector would have been decreased by half.

[5] A dual economy consists of two sectors: one a low-income, rural subsistence sector with surplus population, and the other an expanding urban modern (manufacturing and services) sector. The urban economy absorbs labor from rural areas, which holds down urban wages until rural surplus labor is exhausted. See Lewis (1954).

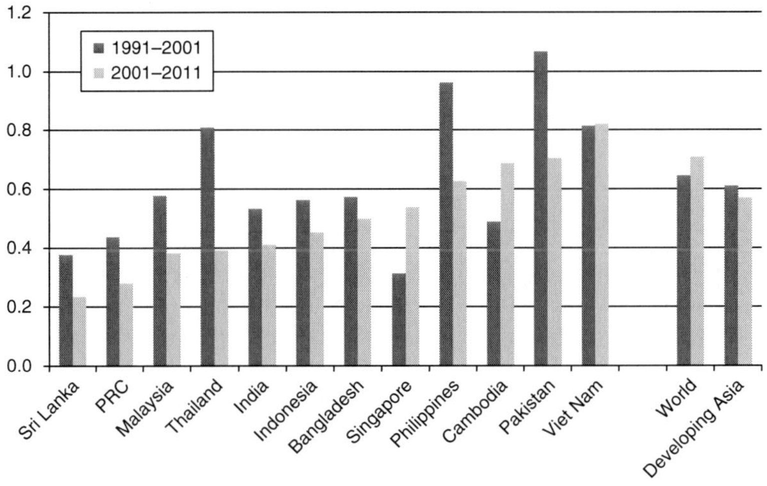

Figure 3.4 Wage employment elasticity of growth in selected Asian economies, 1991–2001 and 2001–2011.

PRC = People's Republic of China.

Note: Simple average for world and developing Asia.

Source: International Labour Organization (ILO). 2011. *Trends Econometric Models*.

Box 3.2 India's formal sector: real wage rate and labor productivity growth

Figure 3.5 shows that in 1990–2007 labor productivity in India's organized manufacturing sector grew much faster than the real wage rate. While the latter did not even double during the period, labor productivity increased three-fold, from about Rs 80,000 to about Rs 250,000. This implies that gains in productivity were not passed on to wages and, consequently, the labor share of India's organized manufacturing sector declined significantly.

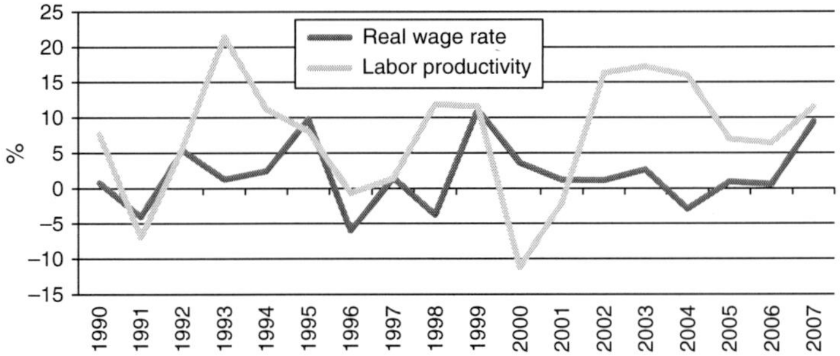

Figure 3.5 Growth of real wage rate and labor productivity in India's formal sector, 1990–2007.

Note: Growth rates are based on wage rate and labor productivity in constant 1993/1994 Indian rupees.

Source: U. Kumar and J. Felipe. 2011. A Reassessment of the Use of Unit Labor Costs as a Tool of Competitiveness and Policy Analyses in India. *Economic and Political Weekly*. 46 (40). pp. 66–70.

A lower share of income going to labor and a higher share of income going to capital tend to increase inequality because capital income is more unequally distributed (due to asset inequality) than income from basic wage labor. Figure 3.6 shows the Gini coefficients for wealth of selected Asian economies and some comparator countries – they are much higher than those for income inequality.

The declining employment elasticity in Asia is of concern because the poor and middle class rely heavily on labor for their income. Figure 3.7 shows that a higher wage employment elasticity is associated with a smaller increase in inequality. The policy implications of the close relationship between employment and inequality are significant. They suggest a search for policies that promote employment.

Spatial inequality

As the distribution of economic activity is structured geographically – high concentrations and incomes in some locations, and low on both counts in others –

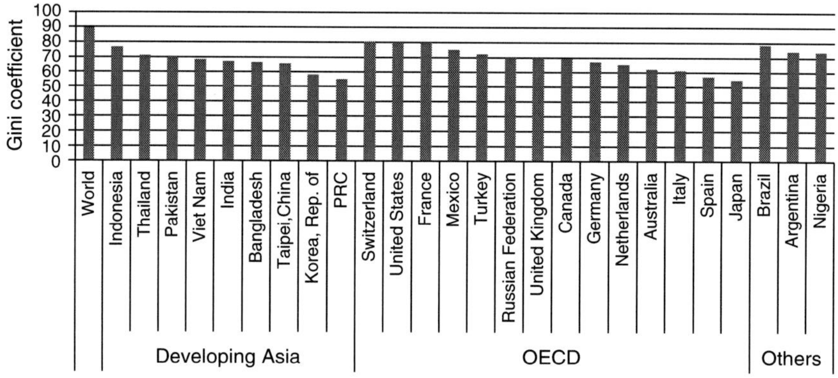

Figure 3.6 Inequality in wealth distribution in selected economies.

OECD = Organisation for Economic Co-operation and Development; PRC = People's Republic of China.

Notes

1 The Gini coefficient pertains to inequality in wealth distribution, where wealth refers to net worth or the value of physical and financial assets less liabilities.
2 The data are for around the year 2000.

Source: J. B. Davies, S. Sandstrom, A. Shorrocks, and E. N. Wolff. 2008. *The World Distribution of Household Wealth.* Discussion Paper No. 2008/03. United Nations University World Institute for Development Economics Research.

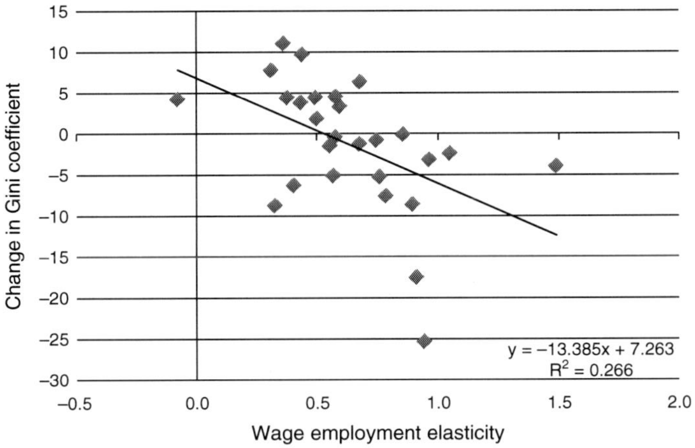

Figure 3.7 Wage employment elasticity and change in Gini coefficient in Asia and the Pacific, 1991–2011.

Sources: Authors' estimates using International Labour Organization (ILO). 2011. *Trends Econometric Models* (October 2011); and PovcalNet, http://iresearch.worldbank.org/PovcalNet/index.htm (accessed 11 July 2012), supplemented by household survey data (most Pacific countries and India), and publications of official statistics offices (Republic of Korea and Singapore).

so is the distribution of income and its evolution. Some locations have natural advantages, like fertile soil for agriculture or proximity to a coastline for trade.[6] Economic analysis has also highlighted the role of agglomeration benefits where, once concentration starts because of natural advantages or because of advantages conferred by infrastructure, there is a self-perpetuating process of increasing concentration (Krugman 2008).

Rural–urban inequality

The large rural–urban income gap is a significant contributor to inequality in several Asian countries (Figure 3.8), especially the PRC (around 45%). Its importance has even increased in some.

The possibility of rising inequality due to urbanization as part of the development process was first pointed out by Kuznets (1955). The particular mechanisms that he highlighted in his contribution (Box 3.3) start with a two-sector model with the population divided between a low mean income, low

---

[6] Several decades ago, Nobel Laureate in Economics Arthur Lewis pointed out the tendency of the development process to be inegalitarian: "Development must be inegalitarian because it does not start in every part of the economy at the same time...There may be one such enclave in an economy, or several; but at the start, development enclaves include only a small minority of the population" (Lewis 1976).

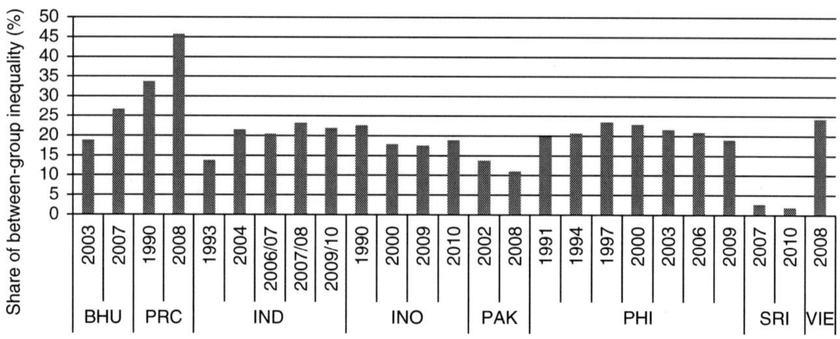

Figure 3.8 Urban–rural income inequality decomposition.

BHU = Bhutan; IND = India; INO = Indonesia; PAK = Pakistan; PHI = Philippines; PRC = People's Republic of China; SRI = Sri Lanka; VIE = Viet Nam.

Note: Estimates are based on per capita expenditure in nominal terms. Decomposition is based on GE(0), which is a special form of the generalized entropy index.

Source: Authors' estimates using household survey data.

inequality sector (rural/agriculture) and a high mean income, high inequality sector (urban/industrial). In this model, the drivers of inequality are changes in inequality within the two sectors, a widening of the gap between average incomes in the two sectors, and a shift of population from agriculture in the rural sector to industry in the urban sector – or the process of urbanization.

Box 3.3 The Kuznets theory and evidence

The basic Kuznets model is a well-defined process of distributional shift as a population moves from the agriculture (rural, traditional) to non-agriculture (urban, modern) sectors during the course of development. The process was set out by Kuznets (1955, pp. 12–15) in his classic paper:

> The basic assumptions used throughout are that the per capita income of sector B (nonagricultural) is always higher than that of sector A; that the proportion of sector A in the total population declines; and that the inequality of the income distribution within sector A may be as wide as that within sector B but not wider. With the assumptions concerning three sets of factors – intersector differences in per capita income, intrasector distributions, and sector weights – varying within the limitations just indicated, the following conclusions are suggested: . . .[E]ven if the differential in per capita income between the two sectors remains constant and the intrasector distributions are identical for the two sectors, the mere shift in the proportions of populations produces slight but significant changes in the distribution for the country as a whole. In general, as the proportion of A drifts from 0.8 downwards, the range tends first to widen and then to diminish.

This is the famous Kuznets inverted-U in the original: "the range tends to first widen and then to diminish."

Evidence on the Kuznets inverted-U is mixed. Kuznets himself presented evidence for his hypothesis from the United Kingdom, the United States, and some other developed economies in the late 19th and the first half of the 20th century. During this period, in fact, these economies were already on the downward part of the inverted-U.

The possibility of a Kuznets inverted-U for developing economies was tested two decades later by Ahluwalia (1976), who found support for it using cross-sectional data. However, subsequent rigorous econometric testing, with better techniques and better data, did not support the inverted-U in cross-country data (Anand and Kanbur 1993).

Focusing on the middle- and low middle-income countries, Cornia *et al.* (2004) found that, out of 34 developing countries for which they had several observations between the 1950s and the mid-1990s, inequality is higher in the terminal period for 15, equal for 14, and lower for 5. When data are available, a U-shape was observed in a number of cases where inequality is found to be increasing when comparing the terminal and the initial years.

Barro (2008), on the other hand, appeared to have found support for the Kuznets inverted-U in the cross-sectional data, although he recognized that many factors are important in providing a full explanation.

Thus, the scant empirical evidence validating the Kuznets hypothesis calls for a multifactor analysis, recognizing that the contributions of the various factors explaining growth and inequality may change over time. There is no single overarching driver of inequality. Rather, a detailed exploration of a number of mechanisms is needed.

Sources: K. Kanbur. 2011. Does Kuznets Still Matter? Paper written for a Festschrift in honor of Montek Ahluwalia. September; S. Anand and R. Kanbur. 1993. Inequality and Development: A Critique. *Journal of Development Economics*. 41 (1). pp. 19–43; and Chapter 7 of this volume by Aizenman, Lee, and Park.

Inequality changes within the two sectors will most likely be affected by the same factors discussed in the previous sections, in particular the widening wage premium for skills, and the regional disparity (to be discussed in the next section). To the extent that the urban labor force has a higher level of human capital than the rural labor force, this factor would also tend to widen the rural–urban gap in average incomes. Perhaps the strongest driver of that gap, however, is the cumulative force of agglomeration economies and its impact on productivity (de Groot *et al.* 2008). For whatever combination of reasons, the rural–urban income gap in Asia has been widening in the past two decades, and it has been a key driving force of rising inequality in the PRC (Figure 3.9). Thus the first two – change in inequality within the two sectors and a widening of the gap in the average income between the two sectors – are likely to put upward pressure on inequality in Asian countries.

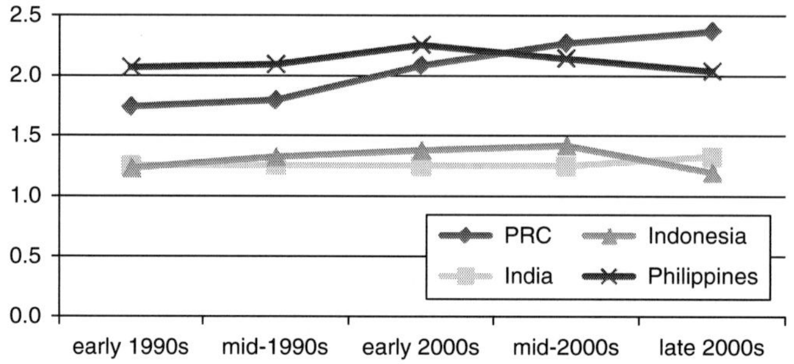

Figure 3.9 Urban–rural income gaps in selected Asian economies, early 1990s to late 2000s.

PRC = People's Republic of China.

Note: Urban–rural income gaps are measured by the ratio of urban per capita income to rural per capita income.

Source: Authors' estimates using PovcalNet, http://iresearch.worldbank.org/PovcalNet/index.htm (accessed 9 March 2012).

What about the third factor? As is well known, urbanization in Asia has been rapid. Kuznets explored this with the aid of a numerical example (Box 3.3), which showed increasing inequality to start with as urbanization begins, followed by a decrease at the later stages. Anand and Kanbur (1993) showed that if there is no difference between urban inequality and rural inequality, with the only difference between the two sectors being the higher income in the urban area, then inequality will indeed follow an inverse U shape, so that this driver will tend to raise inequality in the early stages of urbanization. If, further, urban inequality is higher than rural inequality, this effect will be reinforced. In Chapter 13 of this volume, Kanbur and Zhuang find that, during the period from the early 1990s to the late 2000s, urbanization can explain about 54% of the increase in inequality in Indonesia and 14% in India, but it helped reduce inequality in the PRC.

Regional inequality

Regional inequality has also been a key contributor to total inequality in many Asian countries, particularly in the PRC and India (Figure 3.10). Notably for the PRC, in 1990–2003, regional inequality increased more or less concurrently with overall inequality.

In the PRC, there appears to be a general consensus that increased openness contributed to sharpening income disparities between coastal and interior regions. As Lin (2005) noted, an important feature of the country's global integration is the depth of concentration of international trade along the east coast – which has far lower transport costs to the country's major markets such as Hong Kong, China; Europe; Japan; and the United States. Since 2003, the PRC's regional inequality

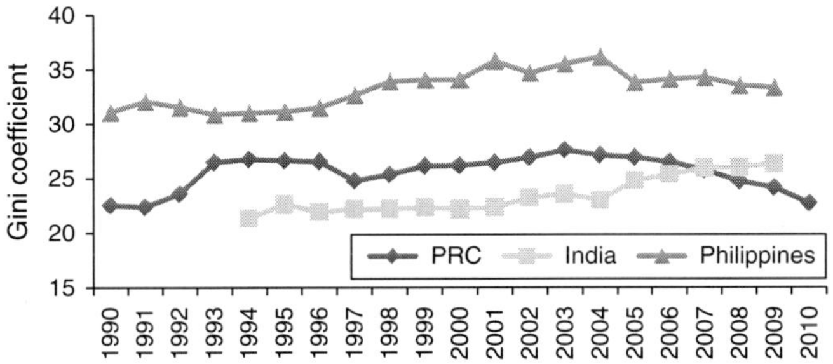

Figure 3.10 Inequalities in provincial per capita incomes in selected Asian economies, 1990–2010.

PRC = People's Republic of China.

Note: Gini coefficients are weighted by group population.

Sources: Authors' estimates using province-level data for the PRC and the Philippines from the CEIC database, http://www.ceicdata.com/search_campaign.html?ui_lang=EN&how_hear=110&spage=11318#page=page-1 (accessed 5 March 2012) and data for India from the Ministry of Statistics and Programme Implementation (accessed 5 March 2012).

has declined somewhat. This has been partly attributed to the government's Great Western Development Strategy (Fan *et al.* 2011).

In India, coastal states have also fared better than inland states, although here a set of compounding factors such as initial level of human capital and public infrastructure is also important (Kanbur *et al.* 2007). New private sector industrial investments typically take place in existing industrial and coastal districts to reduce costs, and overall investments have become more concentrated.

More generally, the interplay between market-oriented reforms and economies of agglomeration appears to have given certain regions within countries an edge when it comes to economic growth. Indeed, this interplay has been linked to increasing inequality in Southeast Asia and East Asia's middle-income economies (Gill and Kharas 2007). Figure 3.11 provides decomposition results for regional inequality in selected Asian countries. Between-region inequality can explain 20–30% of the national inequality in the late 2000s in Bhutan, the Philippines, and Viet Nam, and 10–15% in the PRC, Indonesia, India, and Sri Lanka.

Spatial inequality: the combined contribution

Combining the two components of spatial inequality and calculating the fraction of total inequality explained by rural–urban and interregional (provinces or states) divides, we see a share of more than half for the PRC (Figure 3.12).

In sum, the widening gaps between provinces and states on the one hand, and between urban and rural areas on the other, provide and will provide the geographic driver of inequality in Asia. These divides are important in themselves and also because they account for a significant proportion of observed inequality

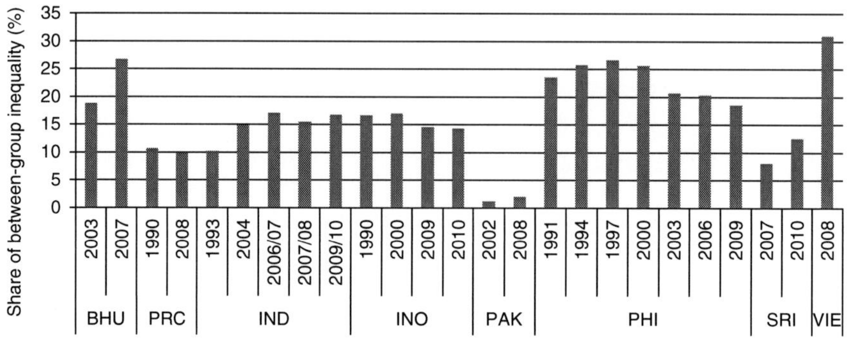

Figure 3.11 Provincial/regional income inequality decomposition.

BHU = Bhutan; IND = India; INO = Indonesia; PAK = Pakistan; PHI = Philippines; PRC = People's Republic of China; SRI = Sri Lanka; VIE = Viet Nam.

Note: Estimates are based on per capita expenditure in nominal terms. Decomposition is based on GE(0), which is a special form of the generalized entropy index.

Source: Authors' estimates using household survey data.

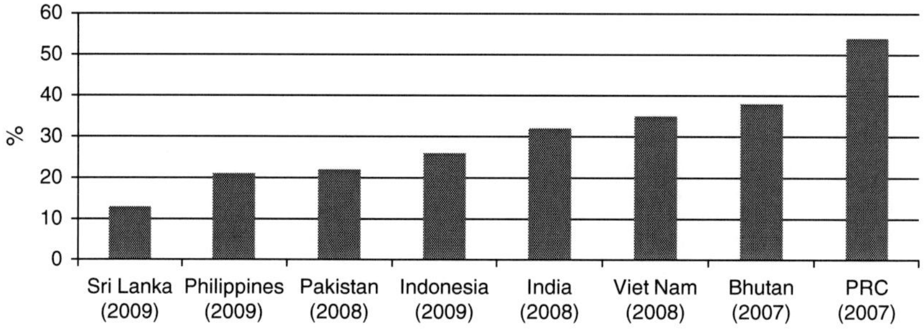

Figure 3.12 Combined contribution of spatial inequality to overall inequality in selected Asian countries.

PRC = People's Republic of China.

Notes

1 Spatial inequality covers both between-region and urban–rural inequality. The estimation involves dividing all sample households into groups classified by both region and urban/rural. For example, if a country has 20 provinces, the total groups will be 40 (20 urban and 20 rural).
2 The between-group inequality is the combined spatial inequality.

Source: Authors' estimates using household survey data.

in Asian countries. The driver of inequality in the spatial dimension is the interaction between new opportunities through trade, technology, and market-oriented reform, interacting with the structure of geography and infrastructure. The rise in spatial inequality is not a reason to reverse openness and technological progress, or stop the reform process, but rather to reorient infrastructure investment to lagging regions, and to remove barriers to migration to the fast-growing regions.

Summary

This chapter argues that technological progress, globalization, and market-oriented reform – the key drivers of Asia's rapid growth – are the basic forces behind the rising inequality in many Asian countries in the past two decades, and these forces have changed income distribution through three channels: capital, skill, and spatial bias.

The bias toward physical capital reduces labor's share of national income while increasing the income share of the owners of capital. Similarly, the heightened demand for better-skilled workers raises the premium on their earnings. Spatial disparities are also becoming more acute: locations with superior infrastructure, market access, and scale economies, such as urban centers and coastal areas, are better able to benefit from changing circumstances. Empirical evidence is consistent with these arguments. Inequality of opportunity magnifies the distributional consequences of these driving factors.

References

Acemoglu, D. 2002. Technical Change, Inequality and the Labor Market. *Journal of Economic Literature*. 40. pp. 7–72.

Agénor, P.-R. 2002. Does Globalization Hurt the Poor? *World Bank Working Paper* No. 2922. Washington, DC: World Bank.

Ahluwalia, M. 1976. Income Distribution and Development: Some Stylized Facts. *American Economic Review*. 66 (2). pp. 128–35.

Anand, S., and R. Kanbur. 1993. Inequality and Development: A Critique. *Journal of Development Economics*. 41 (1). pp. 19–43.

Arpaia, A., E. Pérez, and K. Pichelmann. 2009. Understanding Labour Income Share Dynamics in Europe. *MPR.000A Paper 15649*. Munich, Germany: University Library of Munich.

Asian Development Bank (ADB). 2007. *Asian Development Outlook 2007*. Manila.

Asian Productivity Organization (APO). 2011. *APO Productivity Databook 2011*. Tokyo: Keio University Press.

Attanasio, O., P. K. Goldberg, and N. Pavcnik. 2004. Trade Reforms and Wage Inequality in Colombia. *Journal of Development Economics*. 74 (2). pp. 331–66.

Autor, D. H., L. F. Katz, and M. S. Kearney. 2008. Trends in US Wage Inequality: Revising the Revisionists. *Review of Economics and Statistics*. 90 (2). pp. 300–23.

Bai, C., and Z. Qian. 2009. Factor Income Distribution: The Story behind the Statistics. Tsinghua, People's Republic of China: Tsinghua University.

Barro, R. J. 2008. Inequality and Growth Revisited. *ADB Working Paper Series on Regional Economic Integration* No. 11. Manila: ADB.

Behrman, J. R., N. Birdsall, and M. Székely. 2003. Economic Policy and Wage Differentials in Latin America. *Working Paper 29*. Washington, DC: Center for Global Development.

Card, D., and J. E. DiNardo. 2002. Skill-Biased Technological Change and Rising Wage Inequality: Some Problems and Puzzles. *Journal of Labor Economics*. 20 (4). pp. 733–83.

Choi, C. 2006. Does Foreign Direct Investment Affect Domestic Income Inequality? *Applied Economics Letters*. 13. pp. 811–14.

Claessens, S., and E. C. Perotti. 2007. Finance and Inequality: Channels and Evidence. *Journal of Comparative Economics*. 35 (4). pp. 748–73.

Cornia, G. A., T. Addison, and S. Kiiski. 2004. Income Distribution Changes and Their Impact in the Post-Second World War Period. In G. Cornia, ed. *Inequality, Growth and*

Poverty in an Era of Liberalization and Globalization. Oxford, UK: Oxford University Press.

Cragg, M. I., and M. Epelbaum. 1996. Why Has Wage Dispersion Grown in Mexico? Is It the Incidence of Reforms or the Growing Demand for Skills? *Journal of Development Economics*. 51 (1). pp. 99–116.

Davies, J. B., S. Sandstrom, A. Shorrocks, and E. N. Wolff. 2008. *The World Distribution of Household Wealth*. Discussion Paper No. 2008/03. Helsinki, Finland: United Nations University World Institute for Development Economics Research.

de Groot, H. L. F., J. Poot, and M. J. Smit. 2008. Agglomeration Externalities, Innovation and Regional Growth: Theoretical Perspectives and Meta-Analysis. *Working Paper in Economics 01/08*. Hamilton, New Zealand: University of Waikato.

Demirgüc-Kunt, A., and R. Levine. 2007. *Finance and Opportunity: Financial Systems and Intergenerational Persistence of Relative Incomes*. Washington, DC: World Bank.

Fallon, P. R., and R. E. B. Lucas. 2002. The Impact of Financial Crises on Labor Markets, Household Incomes, and Poverty: A Review of Evidence. *World Bank Research Observer*. 17 (1). pp. 21–45.

Fan, S., R. Kanbur, and X. Zhang. 2011. [People's Republic of] China's Regional Disparities: Experience and Policy. *Review of Development Finance*. 1 (1). pp. 47–56.

Feenstra, R. C., and G. H. Hanson. 1997. Foreign Direct Investment and Relative Wages: Evidence from Mexico's Maquiladoras. *Journal of International Economics*. 42. pp. 371–93.

Felipe, J. 2009. *Inclusive Growth, Full Employment and Structural Change: Implications and Policies for Developing Asia*. London: Anthem Press.

Felipe, J., and G. C. Sipin. 2004. Competitiveness, Income Distribution, and Growth in the Philippines: What Does the Long-Run Evidence Show? *ERD Working Paper Series* No. 53. Manila: ADB.

Felipe, J., and U. Kumar. 2010. Technical Change in India's Organized Manufacturing Sector. *Levy Economics Institute of Bard College Working Paper* No. 626. New York, NY: Levy Economics Institute.

Gill, I., and H. Kharas. 2007. *An East Asian Renaissance: Ideas for Economic Growth*. Washington, DC: World Bank.

Goldberg, P. K., and N. Pavcnik. 2007. Distributional Effects of Globalization in Developing Countries. *Journal of Economic Literature*. 45 (1). pp. 39–82.

Harrison, A. E. 2005. *Has Globalization Eroded Labor's Share? Some Cross-Country Evidence*. MPRA Paper No. 39649, posted 25 June 2012. http://citeseerx.ist.psu.edu/viewdoc/download?doi=10.1.1.198.9065&rep=rep1&type=pdf

Hsieh, C., and K. Woo. 2005. The Impact of Outsourcing to [the People's Republic of] China on [Hong Kong, China]'s Labor Market. *American Economic Review*. 95. pp. 1673–87.

International Labour Organization (ILO). 2011. *Trends Econometric Models*. October 2011.

International Monetary Fund (IMF). 2007. Globalization and Inequality. *World Economic Outlook 2007: Globalization and Inequality*. Washington, DC: IMF.

Jacobson, M., and P. Occhino. 2012. Behind the Decline in Labor's Share of Income. *Economic Trends*. 3 February. Federal Reserve Bank of Cleveland.

Kanbur, K. 2011. Does Kuznets Still Matter? Paper written for a Festschrift in honor of Montek Ahluwalia. September.

Kanbur, R., K. Gajwani, and X. Zhang. 2007. Comparing the Evolution of Spatial Inequality in [the People's Republic of] China and India: A Fifty-Year Perspective. *Annual World Bank Conference on Development Economics*. pp. 155–77.

Kijima, Y. 2006. Why Did Wage Inequality Increase? Evidence from Urban India 1983–99. *Journal of Development Economics*. 81. pp. 97–117.

Krugman, P. 2008. The Increasing Returns Revolution in Trade and Geography. http://www.nobelprize.org/nobel_prizes/economics/laureates/2008/krugman_lecture.pdf (accessed January 2012).

Kumar, U., and J. Felipe. 2011. A Reassessment of the Use of Unit Labor Costs as a Tool of Competitiveness and Policy Analyses in India. *Economic and Political Weekly*. 46 (40). pp. 66–70.

Kuznets, S. 1955. Economic Growth and Income Inequality. *American Economic Review*. 45. pp. 1–28.

Lewis, W. A. 1954. Economic Development with Unlimited Supply of Labour. *The Manchester School*. 22 (2). pp. 139–91.

——. 1976. Development and Distribution. In A. Cairncross and M. Puri, eds. *Employment, Income Distribution and Development Strategy: Problems of the Developing Countries (Essays in Honour of H. W. Singer)*. New York, NY: Holmes & Meier Publishers. pp. 26–42.

Lin, S. 2005. International Trade, Location and Wage Inequality in [the People's Republic of] China. In R. Kanbur and A. J. Venables, eds. *Spatial Inequality and Development*. Oxford, UK: Oxford University Press.

Marquis, M. H., B. Trehan, and W. Tantivong. 2011. The Wage Premium Puzzle and the Quality of Human Capital. *Working Paper 2011–06*. San Francisco, CA: Federal Reserve Bank of San Francisco.

Mehta, A., J. Felipe, P. Quising, and S. A. Camingue. 2011. Where Have All the Educated Workers Gone? Services and Wage Inequality in Three Asian Economies. *Working Paper*. Santa Barbara, CA: University of California-Santa Barbara, Global & International Studies Program.

Milanovic, B. 2005. Can We Discern the Effect of Globalization on Income Distribution? Evidence from Household Surveys. *World Bank Economic Review*. 19. pp. 21–44.

Organisation for Economic Co-operation and Development (OECD). 2011. *Divided We Stand: Why Inequality Keeps Rising*. Paris: OECD.

——. 2012. OECD Stat database. http://stats.oecd.org/index.aspx

Robbins, D. 1996. Evidence on Trade and Wages in the Developing World. *OECD Technical Paper* No. 119. Paris: OECD.

Rodrik, D. 1997. Trade, Social Insurance, and the Limits to Globalization. *NBER Working Papers 5905*. National Bureau of Economic Research.

Sanchez-Paramo, C., and N. Schady. 2003. Off and Running? Technology, Trade, and the Rising Demand for Skilled Workers in Latin America. *World Bank Policy Research Working Paper 3015*. Washington, DC: World Bank.

Son, H. H. 2010. Growth, Inequality, and the Labor Market: The Philippines. In J. Zhuang, ed. *Poverty, Inequality, and Inclusive Growth: Measurement, Policy Issues, and Country Studies*. London: Anthem Press and Manila: ADB.

Stolper, W. F., and P. A. Samuelson. 1941. Protection and Real Wages. *Review of Economic Studies*. 9. pp. 58–73.

Taylor, K., and N. Driffield. 2005. Wage Inequality and the Role of Multinationals: Evidence from UK Panel Data. *Labour Economics*. 12. pp. 223–49.

Wood, A. 1999. Openness and Wage Inequality in Developing Countries: The Latin American Challenge to East Asian Conventional Wisdom. In R. Baldwin, D. Cohen, A. Sapir, and A. Venables, eds. *Market Integration, Regionalism and the Global Economy*. Cambridge, UK: Cambridge University Press.

World Bank. 2012. *Is Higher Education Meeting Its Promises? Putting Higher Education to Work: Skills and Research for Growth in East Asia. World Bank East Asia and Pacific Regional Report.* Washington, DC.

——. PovcalNet: The On-line Tool for Poverty Measurement Developed by the Development Research Group of the World Bank. http://iresearch.worldbank.org/PovcalNet/index.htm (accessed 11 July 2012).

Zhuang, J. 1996. Estimating Distortions in the Chinese Economy: A General Equilibrium Approach. *Economica*. 63 (252). pp. 543–68.

4 Inequality of human opportunities in developing Asia

Hyun H. Son

Introduction

Inequality remains a persistent challenge in many economies today. In Asia and the Pacific, inequality has risen over the past decade despite rapid growth that has significantly lowered poverty incidence (Asian Development Bank 2007). In 16 countries in developing Asia, the Gini coefficient increased from 46.8 in 1993 to 52.4 in 2003.

While inequality is usually measured in terms of income or consumption, the concept of inequality is now being extended to cover many other standard-of-living dimensions, such as inequality of outcomes in health, education, basic infrastructure, and so on. In recent studies, Zhang and Kanbur (2005) and Tandon and Zhuang (2007) showed that disparities in health outcomes in the People's Republic of China (PRC) have worsened.

Although any society's ultimate objective is to eliminate or reduce inequality of outcomes, the 2006 World Development Report (World Bank 2006) has argued that it is not appropriate to focus on this alone when assessing the fairness of a social system. Inequality of opportunity, not of outcome, should inform the design of public policy. According to this view, public policies need not necessarily aim to eliminate or reduce all outcome inequalities but may instead focus on reducing inequalities that arise from unequal opportunity. Thus, a just society is one that provides equal opportunity to all.

Governments usually provide people with opportunities in education, health, nutrition, security, and basic infrastructure. However, not all citizens can avail of these opportunities equally. Many school-age children in developing countries, for instance, are unable to attend school due to family circumstances. Similarly, many of those children have no access to clean water, electricity, and sanitary toilets. Measurement of the inequality of opportunity in such basic services is therefore essential prior to designing policies aimed at universal provision of these basic opportunities.

The World Bank has developed the Human Opportunity Index (HOI), which measures inequality of opportunity contributed by individuals' socioeconomic and demographic circumstances. Inequality of opportunity caused by differences in circumstances is considered unjust and should be of concern to society. When a child is unable to get proper education because his or her family belongs to a low socioeconomic group, for instance, it is a gross injustice. In a study on Latin America, Paes de Barros *et al.* (2009) considered six circumstance variables: (i) urban or rural area, (ii) gender, (iii) number of siblings, (iv) parent's education, (v) per capita income, and (vi) presence of parents. The number of circumstance variables included was determined by the availability of data in 19 Latin American countries.

This chapter seeks to measure inequality of opportunity in seven Asian developing countries: Bangladesh, Bhutan, Indonesia, Pakistan, the Philippines, Sri Lanka, and Viet Nam. The HOI is measured for a set of opportunities related to education and basic infrastructure: school attendance among children aged 6–11 years for primary school and 12–17 years for secondary school, as well as access to safe water, electricity, and sanitation.

Human Opportunity Index

Let us define a variable z_i, which takes a value of 1 if the ith individual has access to an opportunity (such as education) and takes a value of 0 if the ith individual lacks access to the opportunity. It can be easily seen that $E(z_i) = \pi_i = P(z_i)$, where π_i is the probability that the ith individual has access to a given opportunity. A distinction is made between circumstance and effort variables (Roemer 1998). Circumstance variables are exogenous variables in the sense that an individual has no control over them. Effort variables, meanwhile, reflect an individual's efforts and capacity to innovate and take risk. Inequality caused by differences in effort is deemed acceptable, while inequality caused by circumstances is considered unjust and unacceptable, and should thus be reduced. The HOI measures the contribution of inequality of opportunities by the circumstance variables. Therefore, we estimate π_i by means of a logit model using a set of k circumstance variables $x_{i1}, x_{i2}, \ldots, x_{ik}$. Accordingly, we have a logit model:

$$\pi_i = \frac{e^{\sum_{j=1}^{k} \beta_j x_{ij}}}{1 + e^{\sum_{j=1}^{k} \beta_j x_{ij}}} \tag{4.1}$$

This model can be estimated using the maximum likelihood method. $\hat{\pi}_i$, the maximum likely estimate of π_i, is the probability of access to a given opportunity explained by the circumstance variables. Any measure of inequality of $\hat{\pi}_i$ will be the inequality of opportunity that is explained by the circumstance variables. Paes de Barros *et al.* (2009) use the relative mean deviation defined as

$$D = \frac{1}{2\bar{\pi}} \sum_{i=1}^{n} w_i |\hat{\pi}_i - \bar{\pi}| \tag{4.2}$$

where n is the number of sample households, w_i is the population weight attached to the ith sample household, and $\bar{\pi}$ is the proportion of the population with access to a given opportunity.[1] Note also that $\bar{\pi}$ may be called level or coverage. D measures the degree of inequality of opportunity that is explained by the individual's circumstances. As such, $(1 - D)$ may be interpreted as equity of opportunity.

The HOI is then defined as

$$\text{HOI} = \bar{\pi}(1 - D) \tag{4.3}$$

which is a composite index of two factors: (i) the level or coverage and (ii) equity of opportunity. The policy makers' objective will be to maximize HOI, which can be achieved either by enhancing total opportunity (coverage) or by increasing equity of opportunity (more equitably distributing opportunity) or by increasing both coverage and equity.

Contribution of individual circumstance variables

The relative mean deviation defined in equation (4.2) measures the total contribution of all circumstance variables to inequality of opportunity. Although it is useful to determine the total impact of all circumstance variables on inequality of opportunity, determining the impact of individual circumstance variables would be more useful to policy makers. These individual contributions will identify the circumstance variables having the most impact on inequality of opportunity. In this section, we present a method of calculating the relative contributions of individual circumstance variables to the inequality of opportunity.

A variable $y_i = \frac{\pi_i}{(1-\pi_i)}$ is the ratio of the odds of $z_i = 1$ against $z_i = 0$; thus the larger the y_i, the greater the odds for the ith person to have access to an opportunity. A special feature of the odds ratio is that, in using equation (4.1), it can be written as

$$\ln(y_i) = \sum_{j=1}^{k} \beta_j x_{ij} \tag{4.4}$$

The maximum likelihood estimate of y_i is then given by

$$\ln(\hat{y}_i) = \sum_{j=1}^{k} \hat{\beta}_j x_{ij} \tag{4.5}$$

where $\hat{\beta}_j$ is the maximum likelihood estimate of β_j derived from the logit model in equation (4.1). $\hat{y}_i$ is the ith person's odds ratio that is explained by the circumstance variables.

Since y_i is a monotonically increasing function of π_i, there is a one-to-one relationship between them. This implies that inequality of π_i will be equivalent to

[1] Note that $\bar{\pi}_i$ is the mean of π_i across all individuals.

inequality of y_i. This in turn suggests that inequality of $\hat{y}_i$ will be equivalent to inequality of π_i, which, as shown earlier, is also equal to the inequality of opportunity explained by the circumstance variables. We can thus measure inequality of opportunity explained by the circumstance variables through measuring inequality of $\hat{y}$.

We may measure inequality of opportunity by any of the inequality measures that have been proposed in the literature. As discussed, Paes de Barros *et al.* (2009) used the relative mean deviation to measure inequality of opportunity. In this study, we use a log variance measure of inequality, which has an attractive feature of decomposability.

Following Fields (2003), we took the variance of both sides of equation (4.5) to obtain

$$\sigma^2(\ln(\hat{y}_i)) = \sum_{j=1}^{k} \hat{\beta}_j \operatorname{cov}(x_{ij}, \ln(\hat{y}_i)) \tag{4.6}$$

which decomposes the inequality in opportunity (measured by the log variance) in terms of the contributions made by each of the individual circumstance variables. Dividing both sides of equation (4.6) by $\sigma^2(\ln(\hat{y}_i))$ gives the percentage contribution of individual circumstance variables as

$$100\% = \sum_{j=1}^{k} S_j \tag{4.7}$$

where

$$S_j = \frac{100\ \hat{\beta}_j \operatorname{cov}(x_{ij}, \ln(\hat{y}_i))}{\sigma^2(\ln(\hat{y}_i))} \tag{4.8}$$

is the percentage contribution of the jth circumstance variable to the total inequality of opportunity.

The decomposition presented in equation (4.7) is based on log variance as a measure of inequality. This may appear to be a restricted result, but it is in fact not. Using the famous Shorrocks theorem (1982), we can easily show that this result holds for a wide variety of inequality measures including the Gini index, Atkinson index, generalized entropy family, and coefficient of variation.

Empirical analysis

In this section, the methodologies outlined in the previous sections are applied to seven developing countries in Asia: Bangladesh, Bhutan, Indonesia, Pakistan, the Philippines, Sri Lanka, and Viet Nam. The section provides analysis of the inequality of opportunity related to basic education and infrastructure. There are five outcome variables used in our analysis, namely (i) primary school attendance among children aged 6–11 years, (ii) secondary school attendance among children aged 12–17 years, (iii) access to safe water, (iv) access to electricity, and (v) access to sanitation. Similarly, we used a set of circumstance variables required to estimate the D-Index and the HOI. These circumstance variables are (i) gender, (ii) location of household (urban or rural area), (iii) education of household head, (iv) per capita household expenditure as an indicator of household living standard, (v) age of household head, (vi) gender of household head, and (vii) household size. Circumstances, as used here, consist of personal or family socioeconomic and demographic characteristics over which an individual has no direct control. These seven circumstance variables are available from household datasets for the seven countries selected for the study.

Inequality of opportunity in basic education

The distribution of opportunity for children to access basic primary education is highly variable across countries in Asia. As indicated by the high value of the HOI in Table 4.1, the playing field is level for primary school-age children in Sri Lanka, where 99.27% of primary education services are available and equitably allocated. In contrast, only 68.09% of the basic services in Pakistan are available and are distributed inequitably among children. Countries in Southeast Asia, such as Indonesia, the Philippines, and Viet Nam, are moving toward universal access of basic primary education. For each of these countries, the estimated HOI is higher than 90%, suggesting that more than 90% of primary education services required for universal coverage are available and distributed equitably. Three countries are at the bottom of the ranking, with HOIs lower than 80: Bangladesh, Bhutan, and Pakistan (Figure 4.1).

Children in the secondary school-age group (12–17 years old) in developing Asia are more likely to have lower levels of equitably allocated education services than their younger cohorts: the HOI for primary school attendance is far lower than the corresponding figure for secondary school across the seven countries. As shown in Table 4.2 and Figure 4.2, the HOI for secondary education services ranges from a high of 84.49 for Sri Lanka to a low of 47.64 for Pakistan. These

Table 4.1 Inequality of opportunity in primary education, 6–11 years

Country	*Survey year*	*Average opportunity*	*D-Index*	*Human Opportunity Index*
Bangladesh	2000	75.59	3.53	72.92
Bhutan	2007	83.05	4.98	78.91
Indonesia	2009	94.29	0.92	93.42
Pakistan	2007–2008	74.59	8.71	68.09
Philippines	2002	93.92	1.80	92.22
Sri Lanka	2009–2010	99.39	0.12	99.27
Viet Nam	2008	96.31	1.29	95.07

Source: Author's estimates based on household surveys.

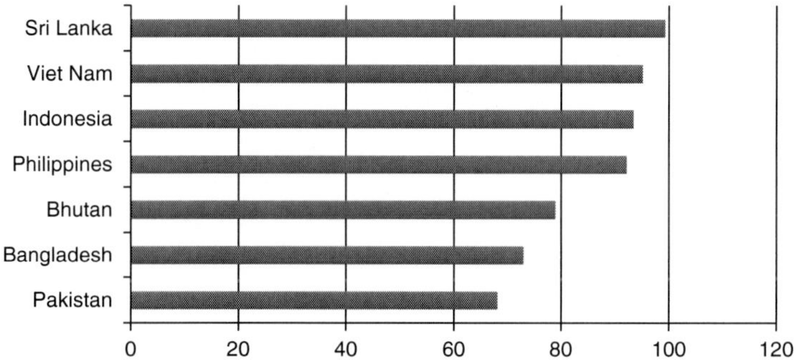

Figure 4.1 Human Opportunity Index for primary education for selected developing Asian countries.

Source: Author's estimates based on household surveys.

Table 4.2 Inequality of opportunity in secondary education, 12–17 years

Country	*Survey year*	*Average opportunity*	*D-Index*	*Human Opportunity Index*
Bangladesh	2000	58.25	8.08	53.54
Bhutan	2007	72.04	5.81	67.86
Indonesia	2009	80.58	3.74	77.57
Pakistan	2007–2008	56.15	15.15	47.64
Philippines	2002	83.09	4.03	79.74
Sri Lanka	2009–2010	86.39	2.19	84.49
Viet Nam	2008	81.97	4.43	78.33

Source: Author's estimates based on household surveys.

findings suggest that countries in the region face greater challenges in equitably ensuring that all children aged 12–17 attend school than ensuring that all children at primary school age attend school. This result would be expected because the opportunity costs of sending children to school are higher at the secondary than the primary level. This also implies that financial incentives, such as conditional cash transfer programs, could be more effective in targeting older children if the main objective is to improve school enrollment.

Inequality of opportunity in basic infrastructure

Basic infrastructure services make significant contributions to well-being. Basic services, such as safe water and sanitation (e.g., flushing toilets), have a direct impact on health status and overall well-being. Having access to services, such as electricity, helps households increase their productivity for income generation. A number of studies reveal that a household's access to basic infrastructure

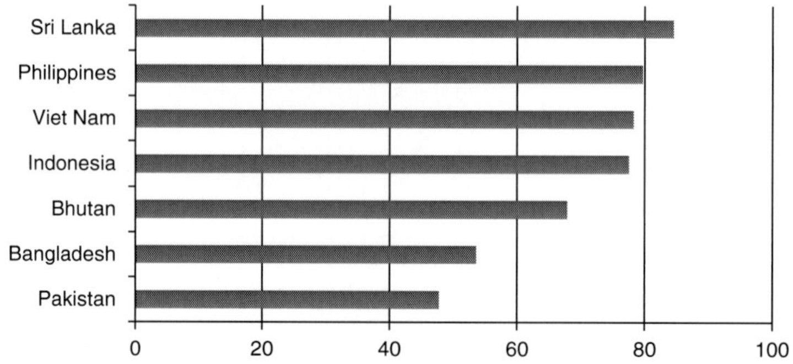

Figure 4.2 Human Opportunity Index for secondary education for selected developing Asian countries.

Source: Author's estimates based on household surveys.

services is highly and significantly correlated with a lower probability of being poor.

Compared with basic education services, our results for the HOIs suggest that Asia faces a greater challenge in providing basic infrastructure services. As presented in Tables 4.3–4.5, the HOIs for access to basic infrastructure services, such as safe water, sanitation, and electricity, show lower values for all countries and higher dispersion across countries than those for access to basic education services, highlighting the uneven rates of progress in expanding opportunities for basic infrastructure services in the region.

As seen in Table 4.3, Bhutan takes the lead in the provision of access to safe water, with its HOI of 86.91. In contrast, Bangladesh and Viet Nam have HOIs lower than 20 for this service. In sanitation, three of the seven countries examined in this study display an HOI higher than 50, while Bangladesh and Bhutan have HOIs lower than 20 (Table 4.4). In the area of electricity provision, Sri Lanka and Viet Nam lead with HOIs higher than 90, compared with Bangladesh with an HOI of about 20 (Table 4.5). These findings suggest that in Bangladesh, less than one out of five people has equal opportunity to live in households with access to safe water, electricity, and sanitation.

Contribution of circumstance variables to inequality of opportunity

This section quantifies the relative contribution of each of the seven circumstance variables to inequality of educational opportunity for both primary and secondary education, as well as inequality of opportunity to access basic infrastructure, such as safe water, electricity, and sanitation.

For primary education, the most important circumstance variable is per capita household expenditure, which influences whether a child has fair access to education opportunities. Its contribution to inequality of opportunity for primary

Table 4.3 Inequality of opportunity in access to safe water

Country	*Survey year*	*Average opportunity*	*D-Index*	*Human Opportunity Index*
Bangladesh	2000	6.66	76.34	1.58
Bhutan	2007	89.94	3.38	86.91
Indonesia	2009	26.80	21.34	21.08
Pakistan	2007–2008	34.15	24.07	25.93
Philippines	2002	61.54	12.05	54.12
Sri Lanka	2009–2010	40.54	16.34	33.92
Viet Nam	2008	26.38	42.66	15.12

Source: Author's estimates based on household surveys.

Table 4.4 Inequality of opportunity in access to sanitation

Country	*Survey year*	*Average opportunity*	*D-Index*	*Human Opportunity Index*
Bangladesh	2000	20.33	34.20	13.38
Bhutan	2007	26.47	43.51	14.95
Indonesia	2009	55.18	10.61	49.33
Pakistan	2007–2008	66.01	17.72	54.31
Philippines	2002	85.64	6.38	80.17
Sri Lanka	2009–2010	94.19	2.22	92.10
Viet Nam	2008	40.24	30.96	27.78

Source: Author's estimates based on household surveys.

Table 4.5 Inequality of opportunity in access to electricity

Country	*Survey year*	*Average opportunity*	*D-Index*	*Human Opportunity Index*
Bangladesh	2000	32.55	38.30	20.08
Bhutan	2007	70.05	13.28	60.75
Indonesia	2009	89.51	3.21	86.63
Pakistan	2007–2008	90.24	4.66	86.03
Philippines	2002	78.45	12.53	68.62
Sri Lanka	2009–2010	93.83	2.05	91.90
Viet Nam	2008	97.19	1.45	95.78

Source: Author's estimates based on household surveys.

education ranges from 60.6% in Pakistan to more than 95% in Bangladesh and the Philippines (Table 4.6). This suggests that overall standards of living for households play a major role in affecting the ability of a child to improve his or her situation over time and achieve intergenerational mobility through education.

For equal opportunity for primary education, education of household head, urban or rural location (where a child lives), and household size are also important

Table 4.6 Contribution of circumstance variables to inequality of opportunity for primary education, 6–11 years (%)

Country	*Survey year*	*Gender*	*Area of residence (urban/rural)*	*Per capita household expenditure*	*Age of household head*	*Gender of household head*	*Education level of household head*	*Household size*
Bangladesh	2000	2.8*	−2.7*	97.1*	−0.0	0.7	2.1*	−0.0
Bhutan	2007	0.2	16.1*	77.6*	−1.1	0.9*	6.8*	−0.5
Indonesia	2009	0.9*	12.4*	74.6*	4.5*	−0.0	3.4*	4.0*
Pakistan	2007–2008	5.8*	10.5*	60.6*	−0.0*	2.4*	20.5*	0.2
Philippines	2002	0.8*	1.3	95.2*	0.6*	0.2	0.3*	1.7*
Sri Lanka	2009–2010	0.4	5.1*	76.4	3.8	2.1	0.0	12.1*
Viet Nam	2008	0.1	10.5	72.8*	0.0	−0.4	6.3*	10.74*

*Indicates that the estimated coefficient was found to be statistically significant at the 5% level in the logit regression model of the probability of school attendance among the primary school-age children, 6–11 years.

Source: Author's estimates based on household surveys.

circumstance variables in Asia. In Pakistan, whether the head of household received any level of formal education accounts for more than 20% of the inequality of educational opportunity for the primary school-age children, 6–11 years. This suggests a direct association between the household head's education and his or her perception of education. A recent study by Lodhi *et al.* (2011) found that less-educated parents in Pakistan are more likely to view education as a trivial factor to future income. In turn, parents with these perceptions are significantly more likely to send their children to *madrassahs* or let them find paid work.

Similarly, the location circumstance (urban or rural residence) substantially contributes to inequality of opportunity for primary education in countries like Bhutan (16.1%) and Indonesia (12.4%). In addition, a significant proportion of children aged 6–11 years in Sri Lanka and Viet Nam are often deprived of basic opportunities to help them gain access to education due to large household size, which accounts for 12.1% and 10.7% of the inequality of opportunity, respectively. Controlling for factors such as household expenditure, parents' education, and others, households with more members tend to invest less in the education of school-age children (Dang and Rogers 2009).

Our results in Table 4.6 suggest that circumstance variables, such as age and gender of household head, have little influence on whether a primary school-age child has fair access to education opportunities.

In terms of school attendance for children aged 12–17, the inequality of educational opportunity is also driven mainly by their per capita household expenditure. Table 4.7 shows that per capita household expenditure has a higher level of contribution to inequality of opportunity for secondary education compared with the other six circumstance variables in the seven selected countries. The contribution of household expenditure to inequality of opportunity for secondary education ranges from 61% in Pakistan at the minimum to 96% in Sri Lanka at the maximum. Apart from per capita household expenditure, the gender of the child, urban or rural residence, and education of household head make a sizable contribution to the inequality of educational opportunity for secondary school-age children.

In Bangladesh, a child's gender accounts for 20.8% of the inequality of opportunity for secondary education, and in Pakistan about 10%. These findings call for strategic government policies that could redistribute the available education services toward girls to help achieve equality of opportunity in secondary education. In Bangladesh, a major hindrance to girls' attendance in secondary school is early marriage and fertility, prompting the government to introduce the highly successful Girls' Stipend Program aimed at encouraging girls to continue their schooling (Raynor and Wesson 2006). However, despite recent increases in enrollment, girls still face inequity in achieving education outcomes especially in secondary school (Hossain and Zeitlyn 2010). A similar story of gender bias can also be found in Pakistan. For children of secondary-school age, households exhibit a pro-male bias both in the decision to enroll children as well as in the amount to spend on education conditional on enrollment, while at primary-school age, the bias is only in the decision whether or not to enroll (Aslam and Kingdon 2008).

The results in Table 4.7 also show that the rural–urban divide in terms of residence affects whether the child has access to opportunities for secondary education. The contribution of this location circumstance is particularly prominent for Bhutan, where the urban or rural residence accounts for 42.4% of the total inequality of opportunity. The urban or rural residence is the most important circumstance in Bhutan's case, following per capita household expenditure (54.7%). Children living in rural areas in Bhutan have limited access to schools due to their remote and mountainous location. According to the Ministry of Education of Bhutan (2004), a continuing problem is that children tend to drop out if the schools are distant, and many teachers do not wish to be assigned in remote areas. A study conducted by the World Bank (2006) found that teachers are a critical constraint to improving quality of education in Bhutan. In particular, it is more difficult to recruit and motivate teachers to work in rural and remote areas.

Furthermore, the results also reveal that the education level of the household head has a significant influence on whether a child at secondary school age has fair access to education opportunities. More importantly, the relative contribution of parental education to inequality of opportunity among children is far higher for secondary education than for its primary counterpart: its contribution jumps to 17.2% for secondary education from 3.4% for primary education in Indonesia, and to 11% from 6.3% in Viet Nam.

As indicated by Table 4.7, other circumstances, such as age, gender of household head, and household size, seem to have a relatively negligible or statistically insignificant effect on the inequality of opportunity for secondary education.

For access to safe water, electricity, and sanitation, the inequality of opportunity is driven mainly by per capita household expenditure and, to the same extent, by where an individual lives (urban or rural residence). As can be seen from Tables 4.8–4.10, the location circumstance dominates in six (out of the seven) countries in the case of safe water, while per capita household expenditure is the most important circumstance in five countries in the cases of electricity and sanitation.

In the case of water and sanitation, their access is generally higher in urban areas than rural areas (WHO and UNICEF 2010). This can also be seen from Tables 4.8 and 4.9. In rural areas, the main challenge is the relatively higher cost of building water and sanitation infrastructure, as well as the presence of rural poverty. Given this, rural areas often lack an enabling environment that encourages public or private investment in water services, leading to low provision of such services (UNESCAP 2011; WHO and UNICEF 2006). This is a particular problem in South Asia, where there is low overall public or private investment in these types of infrastructure, particularly in Bangladesh, India, and Pakistan (WaterAid 2011). Moreover, even if investments are made in these countries, poor maintenance in rural areas still persists due to poor planning and lack of support (UN 2005). Even in Sri Lanka, which is on track to meet its Millennium Development Goal commitments on water and sanitation, rural areas are relatively underserved because the National Water Supply & Drainage Board has concentrated its efforts on providing services to densely populated areas (Asian Development Bank 2007).

Table 4.7 Contribution of circumstance variables to inequality of opportunity for secondary education, 12–17 years (%)

Country	*Survey year*	*Gender*	*Area of residence (urban/rural)*	*Per capita household expenditure*	*Age of household head*	*Gender of household head*	*Education level of household head*	*Household size*
Bangladesh	2000	20.8*	−2.6*	76.9*	−0.4	2.5*	0.5	2.5*
Bhutan	2007	3.4*	42.4*	54.7*	4.1*	1.4*	−4.5*	−1.6
Indonesia	2009	0.2*	11.6*	69.1*	0.4*	1.5*	17.2*	0.1
Pakistan	2007–2008	9.5*	5.2*	61.0*	0.2	1.2*	24.0*	−1.1*
Philippines	2002	6.4*	2.4*	90.7*	0.3*	−0.5*	0.0	0.6
Sri Lanka	2009–2010	1.3*	0.8*	96.0*	0.6	0.7	0.0	0.6
Viet Nam	2008	4.0*	6.6*	65.7*	1.2	−0.4	11.0*	12.0*

*Indicates that the estimated coefficient was found to be statistically significant at the 5% level in the logit regression model of the probability of school attendance among the secondary school-age children, 12–17 years.

Source: Author's estimates based on household surveys.

On top of financial constraints in providing water and sanitation services in rural areas, the perceptions and behavior of people in such areas relating to water use and sanitation also pose challenges. Many rural households do not see the need to invest in tap water or sanitary toilets in their households because there are free options available. This leads to low demand and further decreases the financial viability of projects addressing the provision of these services. Such behavior has been observed in Indonesia, where low consumer demand and community acceptance for water and sanitation services in rural areas are deemed important constraints to investment (AusAID 2009; Yuerlita *et al.* 2008). Similarly, lack of community participation in water and sanitation projects, and poor hygiene behaviors in rural areas contribute to low demand and are seen as constraints to improving health and sanitation outcomes in Bhutan (Collett 2010). In Viet Nam, this problem is exacerbated by the decentralized structure of delivering water and sanitation services. Households and communes in Viet Nam are expected to pay for the construction, use, and maintenance of such infrastructure. However, in rural areas, there is less appetite among households to invest in such costly infrastructure (Sijbesima *et al.* 2010).

In the Philippines, household poverty is a more important constraint to accessing water and sanitation services than is residing in a rural area. This has been reflected by our results in Tables 4.8 and 4.9 that per capita household expenditure is the main contributor to inequality of opportunity to access water and sanitation services in the Philippines. Although, in general, the rural population still has less access to safe water or sanitation services than urban dwellers, poor people in rural and urban areas suffer the most deprivation, and thus tend to bear higher burdens of diseases or economic costs. Hence, investments in water and sanitation in the country should focus on rural areas and urban slum dwellers.

As shown in Table 4.10, the inequality of opportunity for access to electricity is largely dependent on two circumstance variables: location (i.e., whether residence is in urban or rural areas) and economic status (as measured by per capita household expenditure). The first circumstance is straightforward to explain – there are high costs associated with building an electricity grid in rural areas (World Bank 2010). As such, people living in rural areas are expected to be less likely to have access to electricity than their urban counterparts. However, this is not the entire story because there are other constraints to achieving universal electrification in rural areas. In the case of Viet Nam, early attempts at rural electrification were hampered by inefficient coordination and lack of a regulatory framework (World Bank 2010). The high cost of building a rural grid and lack of central coordination also hampered electrification in Sri Lanka, but in response, the government took a decentralized approach by encouraging off-grid electrification, such as the use of solar panels (Independent Evaluation Group 2008).

A particular problem for rural electrification in Bhutan and Indonesia is their terrain, remoteness, and scattered settlements. In Bhutan, a major challenge is the ruggedness and remoteness of the mountainous terrain, compounded by the fact that the rural population is scattered in small settlements (Kumar 2011).

Table 4.8 Contribution of circumstance variables to inequality of opportunity for access to safe water (%)

Country	*Survey year*	*Area of residence (urban/rural)*	*Per capita household expenditure*	*Age of household head*	*Gender of household head*	*Education level of household head*	*Household size*
Bangladesh	2000	82.0*	17.5*	0.4*	−0.0*	0.1*	0.1
Bhutan	2007	55.6*	32.4*	0.5	−0.2*	13.8*	−2.1*
Indonesia	2009	67.7*	29.5*	0.7*	0.3*	0.5*	1.3*
Pakistan	2007–2008	70.8*	19.0*	0.0*	0.0*	10.2*	−0.1
Philippines	2002	8.5*	89.0*	2.6*	0.6*	0.5*	−1.2*
Sri Lanka	2009–2010	89.0	9.1*	0.2*	0.2*	0.0*	1.5*
Viet Nam	2008	82.8*	11.9*	2.5*	2.6*	0.1	0.1*

*Indicates that the estimated coefficient was found to be statistically significant at the 5% level in the logit regression model of the probability of having access to safe water.

Source: Author's estimates based on household surveys.

Table 4.9 Contribution of circumstance variables to inequality of opportunity for access to sanitation (%)

Country	*Survey year*	*Area of residence (urban/rural)*	*Per capita household expenditure*	*Age of household head*	*Gender of household head*	*Education level of household head*	*Household size*
Bangladesh	2000	20.4*	71.0*	1.8*	0.2*	0.0	6.6*
Bhutan	2007	43.7*	33.7*	1.7*	1.4*	21.0*	−1.6*
Indonesia	2009	79.6	17.0*	0.6*	0.1*	2.7*	0.1*
Pakistan	2007–2008	38.7*	50.6*	0.6*	0.8*	10.1*	−0.8*
Philippines	2002	2.5*	97.2*	1.1*	0.1*	0.7*	−1.5*
Sri Lanka	2009–2010	−0.3*	98.9*	2.4*	0.0	0.0*	−0.9*
Viet Nam	2008	29.0*	67.0*	0.8*	1.5*	2.3*	−0.6*

*Indicates that the estimated coefficient was found to be statistically significant at the 5% level in the logit regression model of the probability of having access to sanitation.

Source: Author's estimates based on household surveys.

Table 4.10 Contribution of circumstance variables to inequality of opportunity for access to electricity (%)

Country	*Survey year*	*Area of residence (urban/rural)*	*Per capita household expenditure*	*Age of household head*	*Gender of household head*	*Education level of household head*	*Household size*
Bangladesh	2000	35.1*	63.1*	0.2*	0.1*	0.0	1.7*
Bhutan	2007	53.3*	39.4*	–0.4*	–0.1*	9.1*	–1.3*
Indonesia	2009	86.5*	2.0*	6.0*	–0.3*	1.4*	4.5*
Pakistan	2007–2008	29.8*	58.6*	0.1*	1.3*	9.9*	0.3*
Philippines	2002	7.0*	93.6*	0.2*	0.2*	0.5*	–1.4*
Sri Lanka	2009–2010	23.8*	72.6*	1.6*	0.2*	0.0*	1.9*
Viet Nam	2008	15.3*	72.2*	2.8*	3.0*	2.7*	4.1*

*Indicates that the estimated coefficient was found to be statistically significant at the 5% level in the logit regression model of the probability of having access to electricity.

Source: Author's estimates based on household surveys.

In Indonesia, many islands are so sparsely populated that electrifying them is not financially viable (World Bank 2005). In fact, it is unlikely that the Indonesian State Electricity Company will achieve its electrification targets outside the islands of Java and Bali. Similarly, community remoteness is an important factor explaining the lack of access to electricity in Pakistan (Mirza and Kemp 2011). Thus, even rich households in rural areas can be considered living in energy poverty.

On the other hand, in Bangladesh and the Philippines, it is household-level constraints – i.e., poverty – that are a major constraint to electrifying rural areas (World Bank 2010). Poor rural households are unlikely to be able to pay for connection fees or electricity consumption, which in turn makes it less financially viable to invest in rural electrification. However, the recent success of Bangladesh shows the importance of central planning to map out subsidies and investments in rural electrification, as well as the need to provide rural households with financial assistance through cooperatives (Barnes 2007). However, in the Philippines, household poverty is a particularly binding constraint to having access to electricity because of high costs, as confirmed by studies that show that the country has among the highest electricity rates in Asia due to inefficiencies in energy production and transmission (Department of Energy 2008; Woodhouse 2005).

Conclusions

Inequality has become a major item on the development agenda in recent years. After decades of rapid economic growth around the world, economic gains were threatened by the global financial crisis of 2008 and the ongoing eurozone crisis. While economic theory has always maintained that economic growth is a necessary but not sufficient condition for improving standards of living, the recent economic crises have reinforced this view, even in developed countries. Concepts such as equity, fairness, and justice in the distribution of economic benefits are no longer in the realm of philosophers and theorists. Rather, they are now at the forefront of policy design and economic reform in both developed and developing countries.

This study is concerned with analyzing the equity of distribution of opportunity in basic education and infrastructure services. The analysis was carried out using HOI (the product of average opportunity and the equity of opportunity), which was introduced by the World Bank. The HOI shows both coverage and distribution of opportunity in an outcome variable, such as school attendance, access to safe water, access to electricity, or access to sanitation. The methodology is applied empirically using available household data from Bangladesh, Bhutan, Indonesia, Pakistan, the Philippines, Sri Lanka, and Viet Nam.

The HOI measures the total contribution of all circumstance variables to inequality of opportunity. From the perspective of policy makers, determining the impact of individual circumstance variables would be more useful because these individual contributions will help to identify circumstance variables that have the most impact on inequality of opportunity. This study presents a method of quantifying the relative contributions of individual circumstance variables to the inequality of opportunity. The new methodology introduced in this study would be helpful in analyzing binding constraints to providing equitable opportunities across countries.

Opportunities to access basic education services in the seven countries vary widely. At the primary and secondary levels, Sri Lanka is a good example in equitably providing opportunities to access education, with school attendance among children aged 6–11 years reaching nearly 100% and an HOI of more than 99. The country also has the highest attendance rate among secondary school-age children (86.38%) and an HOI of about 85. Sri Lanka's educational achievements are remarkable considering that it does not have the highest per capita gross domestic product among the seven countries – the Philippines ranked higher in 2007.

In contrast, Sri Lanka's neighbors (Bangladesh, Bhutan, and Pakistan) have yet to reach 90% attendance rates among primary school-age children, while attendance rates for secondary school-age children are still below 60% in Bangladesh and Pakistan. HOIs in these South Asian countries are also among the lowest, indicating that they need to both improve overall access to basic education services and ensure that education opportunities among children are equally distributed, even to the poorest segments of the population.

In Southeast Asian countries, access to and distribution of opportunities for basic education services have been impressive in Indonesia and Viet Nam in recent years, pointing to the effectiveness of their governments' efforts to provide basic education for all.

Likewise, there is wide variation in the availability and distribution of opportunities to access basic infrastructure services, such as safe water, electricity, and sanitation. Bhutan has the highest level of access to safe water (89.94%), Viet Nam has the highest level of electrification (97.19%), and Sri Lanka has the highest percentage of population living in homes with sanitation (94.19%). Our findings highlight the uneven rates of progress in expanding opportunities to access quality infrastructure services in the region as compared with education opportunities.

Unfortunately, for all basic infrastructure, Bangladesh shows the lowest levels of overall opportunities available and distribution across the population. Less than one-third of the population has household access to electricity, about one-fifth has sanitation facilities, and only a little more than one-twentieth have safe water. For all these facilities, only the richest 20% of the population has access rates of 50% or higher. These findings suggest that these basic infrastructure services are luxuries to most people in Bangladesh.

Clearly, a lot needs to be done to improve the distribution of economic benefits in developing countries in Asia. While Bangladesh may be a particularly urgent case, all countries considered in this analysis need to bolster their efforts to improve access to basic education and infrastructure services, especially among the poor and marginalized groups. Sri Lanka's achievements in equitably providing basic education opportunities demonstrate the importance and possible effectiveness of public policy in achieving equity of opportunity, particularly in education.

An important factor to consider in improving the delivery of basic services could be decentralization. Many countries have decentralized the delivery of services in education, water, electricity, and sanitation, mainly to improve transparency, accountability, and responsiveness in providing these services. However, decentralization could also exacerbate existing inequities across various local government units. Moreover, these local government units will have their own solvency and liquidity issues, which could affect their access to financial services. This could cause highly inequitable distribution of services across districts, with affluent areas having much better services than poorer areas. As such, national governments will have to balance the costs and benefits of decentralizing the responsibility of delivering these services. More rigorous research would be required to determine the best method to deliver public services more effectively and efficiently.

It may also be noted that household poverty – as manifested in the contribution of per capita household expenditure in the inequality of opportunity in accessing education and infrastructure services – plays an extremely significant role in determining equitable access to education and infrastructure. Household poverty defines the ability of households to pay for and access these services. This study showed a significant correlation between household resources and the demand for education and infrastructure services. Thus, policy makers may opt to explore policies that address the demand side of the provision of education and infrastructure. Targeted subsidies or loans may be used to provide incentives to households to increase their demand for education and infrastructure. For education, cash transfers have been widely used to encourage school attendance, one example being the conditional cash transfer program of the Government of the Philippines that provides stipends to poor households whose children meet the required school attendance rate, among others.

Acknowledgment

A revised version of this chapter has been published in *Asian Development Review*. 2013. 30 (2).

References

Asian Development Bank. 2007. *Sri Lanka Country Assistance Program Evaluation: Water Supply and Sanitation Sector*. Manila.

Aslam, M., and G. Kingdon. 2008. Gender and Household Education Expenditure in Pakistan. *Applied Economics*. 40 (20). pp. 2573–91.

AusAID. 2009. Independent Evaluation of Australian Aid to Water Supply and Sanitation Service Delivery in East Timor and Indonesia. *ODE Working Paper*. http://www.ode.ausaid.gov.au/publications/documents/aus-water-supply-and-sanitation-indonesia-working-paper.pdf (accessed February 2012).

Barnes, D. F., ed. 2007. *The Challenge of Rural Electrification: Strategies for Developing Countries*. Washington, DC: RFF Press.

Collett, J. 2010. Thirty-Five Years of Searching for Answers to Rural Sanitation and Hygiene in Bhutan. Paper presented at the South Asia Hygiene Practitioners' Workshop.

Dang, H., and F. H. Rogers. 2009. The Decision to Invest in Child Quality over Quantity: Has Declining Fertility Increased Household Investment in Education in Vietnam? Paper presented at the Population Association of America 2009 Meeting.
Department of Energy, Government of the Philippines. 2008. *Philippine Energy Summit Summary Report*. Manila.
Fields, G. 2003. Accounting for Income Inequality and its Change: A New Method with Application to the Distribution of Earnings in the United States. *Research in Labor Economics*. 22. pp. 1–38.
Hossain, A., and B. Zeitlyn. 2010. *Poverty and Equity: Access to Education in Bangladesh. CREATE Pathways to Access*. Research Monograph No. 51. University of Sussex, Brighton and BRAC University, Dhaka.
Independent Evaluation Group, World Bank. 2008. *The Welfare Impact of Rural Electrification: A Reassessment of the Costs and Benefits*. Washington, DC: World Bank.
Kumar, S. 2011. Is Electrification Welfare Improving: Non-Experimental Evidence from Rural Bhutan. Harvard School of Public Health Research Paper.
Lodhi, A. S., D. Tsegai, and N. Gerber. 2011. Determinants of Participation in Child's Education and Alternative Activities in Pakistan. *ZEF-Discussion Papers on Development Policy* No. 159. Bonn, Germany: University of Bonn.
Ministry of Education of Bhutan. 2004. National Report on the Development of Education. Paper presented at the 47th International Conference on Education. Geneva. 8–11 September.
Mirza, B., and R. Kemp. 2011. Why the Rural Rich Remain Energy Poor. *Journal of Sustainable Development*. 6 (1). pp. 133–55.
Paes de Barros, R., F. H. G. Ferreira, J. R. Molinas Vega, and J. S. Chanduvi. 2009. *Measuring Inequality of Opportunities in Latin America and the Caribbean*. Conference Edition. Washington, DC: World Bank.
Raynor, J., and K. Wesson. 2006. The Girls' Stipend Program in Bangladesh. *Journal of Education for International Development*. 2 (2). pp. 1–12.
Roemer, J. 1998. *Equality of Opportunity*. Cambridge, MA: Harvard University Press.
Shorrocks, A. 1982. Inequality Decomposition by Factor Components. *Econometrica*. 50 (1). pp. 193–211.
Sijbesima, C., T. X. Truong, and J. Devine. 2010. *Case Study on Sustainability of Rural Sanitation Marketing in Viet Nam*. Global Scaling Up Sanitation Project. Water and Sanitation Program: Technical Paper. Washington, DC: World Bank.
Tandon, A., and J. Zhuang. 2007. *Inclusiveness of Economic Growth in the People's Republic of China: What Do Population Health Outcomes Tell Us?* ERD Policy Brief Series No. 47. Economics and Research Department. Manila: ADB.
United Nations (UN). 2005. *Scaling-Up Rural Sanitation in South Asia*. WPS Report 34873. Water and Sanitation Programme. http://esa.un.org/iys/docs/san_lib_docs/Scaling%20Up%20Rural%20Saniltation.pdf (accessed February 2012).
United Nations Economic and Social Commission for Asia and the Pacific (UNESCAP). 2011. *Statistical Yearbook for Asia and the Pacific 2011*. Bangkok.
WaterAid. 2011. *South Asian People's Perspective on Sanitation: Synthesis Review*. London: WaterAid.
Woodhouse, E. 2005. The Philippines Electricity Market Investment Context. Paper presented at PESD Seminar. Stanford University, CA. 2–3 June.
World Bank. 2005. *Electricity for All: Options for Increasing Access in Indonesia*. Jakarta: World Bank Office.
——. 2006. *World Development Report 2006: Equity and Development*. Washington, DC.
——. 2010. *Addressing the Electricity Access Gap: Background Paper for the World Bank Group Energy Sector Strategy*. Washington, DC.
World Health Organization (WHO) and United Nations Children's Fund (UNICEF). 2006. *Meeting the MDG Drinking Water and Sanitation Target: The Urban and Rural Challenge of the Decade*. Geneva.

——. 2010. *Progress on Sanitation and Drinking Water: 2010 Update*. Geneva.

Yuerlita, R. Febriamansyah, and A. Saptomo. 2008. People's Participation in Rural Water Supply and Sanitation Project: A Case Study in Jorong Kampung Baru, Solok, West Sumatra, Indonesia. Paper presented at the 3rd WEPA International Forum on Water Environmental Governance in Asia. http://www.wepa-db.net/pdf/0810forum/paper09.pdf (accessed February 2012).

Zhang, X., and R. Kanbur. 2005. Spatial Inequality in Education and Health Care in [the People's Republic of] China. *China Economic Review*. 16 (2). pp. 199–204.

5 Confronting Asia's rising inequality

Policy options

Changyong Rhee, Juzhong Zhuang, Ravi Kanbur, and Jesus Felipe

Introduction

Developing Asia's rapid growth in recent decades has led to a significant reduction in extreme poverty, but it has also been accompanied by rising inequality in many countries. Income inequality has increased in 12 out of the 30 countries with comparable data, the 12 accounting for 82% of the total population. In many countries, income inequality coexists with non-income inequality in the form of unequal access to education, health, and basic services among different population groups classified by gender, location, and income. Asia's rising inequality contrasts with the "growth with equity" story that characterized the transformation of the newly industrialized economies in the 1960s and 1970s, and with recent trends in other parts of the developing world, in particular Latin America where income inequality has been on the decline since the 1990s. Technological change, globalization, and market-oriented reform – the main drivers of Asia's rapid economic growth – are the basic driving forces behind the rising inequality in Asia. Working together, they have significantly impacted inequality through a number of channels.

First, increasing skill premiums and returns to human capital. The emergence of vast new economic opportunities, unleashed by trade and financial integration, technological progress, and market-oriented reform, has increased returns to human capital and the skill premium, with individuals who have higher educational attainment and skill endowment being able to benefit more from the new opportunities. Our analysis shows that, in many countries, as much as 25–35% of the total income inequality can be explained by interperson differences in human capital and skill endowments.

Second, falling labor income shares. As in many countries in other parts of the world, technological progress appears to have favored capital over labor. The abundance of labor relative to capital, which depresses wage rates, is also a contributing factor to the declining labor income share in developing Asia. Since capital is less equally distributed, this has contributed to rising inequality.

Third, increasing spatial inequality. Some regions, especially urban and coastal areas, are better able to respond to the new opportunities because of their advantages in infrastructure and market access, as well as agglomeration economies from a self-perpetuating process of increasing concentration. The process of urbanization reinforces the inequality effects of agglomeration. Our analysis shows that in many Asian countries, about 30–50% of income inequality is accounted for by spatial inequality due to uneven growth.

Finally, the impact of the basic driving forces of inequality has been compounded by various forms of unequal access to opportunity – to earn income from labor and to build human capital – caused by institutional weaknesses, market distortions and failures, and social exclusion.

The basic driving forces of inequality cannot – and should not – be reversed. They generate productivity growth, which underpins Asia's poverty reduction, betterment of quality of life, and prosperity. However, high inequality could undermine social cohesion, political stability, and sustainability of growth, and a divided and highly unequal nation cannot be prosperous, as shown by international experience. Rising inequality could also lead to demands for populist measures that would be detrimental to efficiency and growth.

How should Asian governments respond to the rising inequality? Via the following sets of policy measures. While these measures cannot eliminate inequality, they will go a long way toward reducing it and, at the same time, not endanger development or hurt growth.

First, efficient fiscal policy. Measures include increasing spending on education and health, especially for the poorer; developing better targeted social protection schemes, including conditional cash transfers that target income to the poorest but also incentivize the building of human capital; and mobilizing greater revenue by broadening the tax base and improving tax administration, and switching spending from inefficient general subsidies to targeted transfers.

Second, interventions to address lagging regions. Measures include improving regional connectivity; developing new growth poles in lagging regions; strengthening fiscal transfers for greater investment in human capital and better access to public services in lagging regions; and removing barriers to migration from poor to more prosperous areas.

Third, more employment-friendly growth. Policies include facilitating structural transformation and maintaining a balanced sectoral composition of growth between manufacturing, services, and agriculture; supporting the development of small and medium-sized enterprises (SMEs); removing factor market distortions that favor capital over labor; strengthening labor market institutions; and introducing public employment schemes as a temporary bridge to address pockets of unemployment and underemployment.

Finally, these measures, designed to create more opportunities and equalize access to the opportunities, must be supported by good governance in the form of wider participation, strengthening rule of law, reducing corruption, and eliminating social exclusion.

All these constitute key elements of an inclusive growth strategy. The rest of this chapter provides more detailed examinations of these policy options.

Efficient fiscal policy

Fiscal policy is a key part of the policy responses to rising inequality in Asia. Both government spending and taxation can affect inequality. Asian governments have ample room to maneuver in using fiscal policy to address the challenge of rising inequality, depending on individual country circumstances. This could involve increasing human capital investment and social protection provision – financing the increased spending on these through greater and more equitable revenue mobilization – and switching spending on inefficient general price subsidies (as for fuel) to targeted transfers.

Fiscal spending

A large part of inequality in developing Asia is explained by differences in individual attainments in education and human capital. Returns to human capital are largely driven by the market, and it may not be efficient or even desirable for governments to try to alter them. However, it is efficient and desirable for governments to reduce inequality in the distribution of human capital in the population, by making public investments in education and health and by ensuring that all members of society have equal access to these basic services, regardless of their individual circumstances. A recent study shows that government spending on education and health helps reduce income inequality (Box 5.1). It has also been well documented that a key contributing factor to the recent decline in income inequality in many Latin American countries has been improved access to education by the poor (e.g., Esquivel *et al.* 2010).

Box 5.1 Estimating the impact of fiscal policies on income inequality

Both taxation (particularly personal income taxes) and public spending reduce inequality, but public spending has a larger impact on the distribution of income, according to a study of 150 countries with data for 1970–2009.

The results in Table 5.1 suggest that government expenditures on health and education reduce income inequality in Asia and the rest of the world. Yet, expenditure on social protection and housing appears to increase income inequality in Asia, whereas it is lower in the rest of the world.

Asia has made substantial progress toward achieving the Millennium Development Goals and targets on education and health. These achievements are consistent with the finding that education and health expenditures reduce inequality.

However, social protection policies generally remain limited in Asia, and, in countries where they exist, they tend to have a narrow coverage, extended mainly to the urban population and the formal sector. This could explain the paradoxical finding of social protection spending increasing inequality in Asia. The finding suggests that universal social protection, which covers the entire population, would help reduce inequality.

For taxation, the results provide evidence that personal income taxes reduce inequality, with a greater effect in Asia than in the rest of the world, possibly because of a larger number of people not paying income tax. Although taxes by themselves are less effective in redistributing income, taxation is crucial to raise finances for government expenditure to achieve distributional objectives.

Table 5.1. Estimated marginal impact of government spending on income inequality

	Asia	*Rest of the world*
Social protection	0.490	−0.276
Education	−0.483	−0.034
Health	−0.241	−0.330
Housing	2.162	−0.614

Note: A negative sign means that an increase in government spending reduces the Gini coefficient. The numbers show the percentage point change in income inequality (measured by the Gini coefficient) associated with a one-percentage-point increase in the government expenditure variable.

Source: Chapter 9 of this volume by Claus, Martinez-Vazquez, and Vulovic.

Increasing spending on education and health. Figures 5.1 and 5.2 show wide variations in spending on education and health as a share of gross domestic product (GDP) among developing Asian economies. In the late 2000s, in 19 out of 30 Asian economies, government spending on education as a share of GDP was less than 4%,

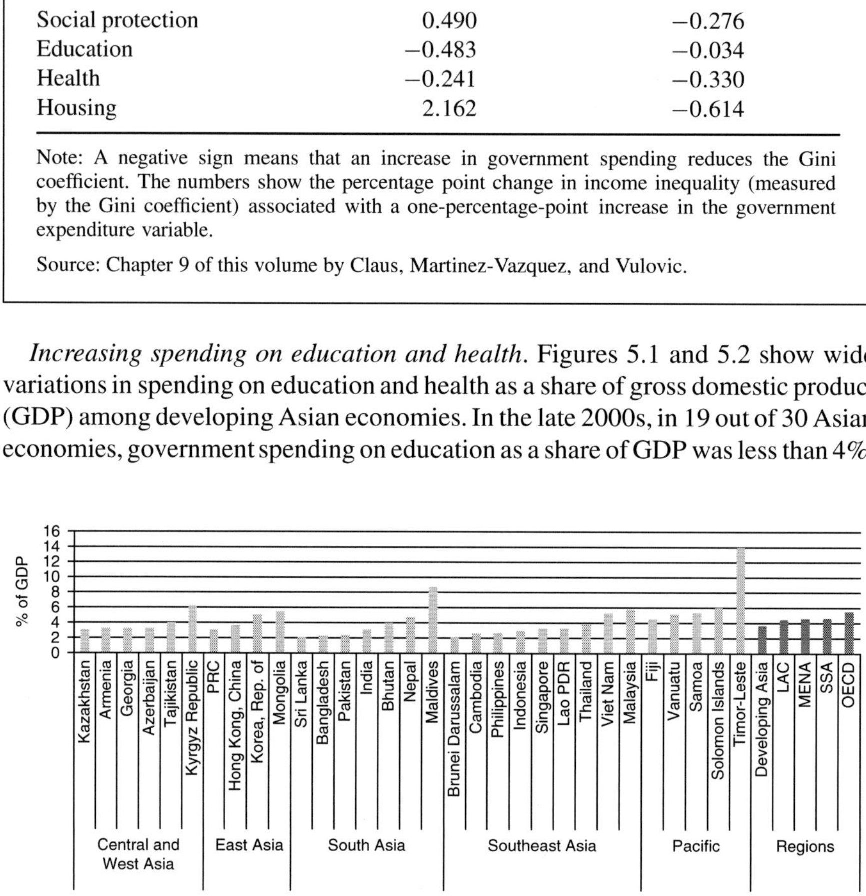

Figure 5.1 Government expenditure on education, 2000s.

GDP = gross domestic product; LAC = Latin America and the Caribbean; Lao PDR = Lao People's Democratic Republic; MENA = Middle East and North Africa; OECD = Organisation for Economic Co-operation and Development; PRC = People's Republic of China; SSA = Sub-Saharan Africa.

Note: The data are the latest available in the 2000s. Regional averages are simple averages.

Source: World Development Indicators, http://data.worldbank.org/data-catalog/world-development-indicators (accessed 20 July 2012).

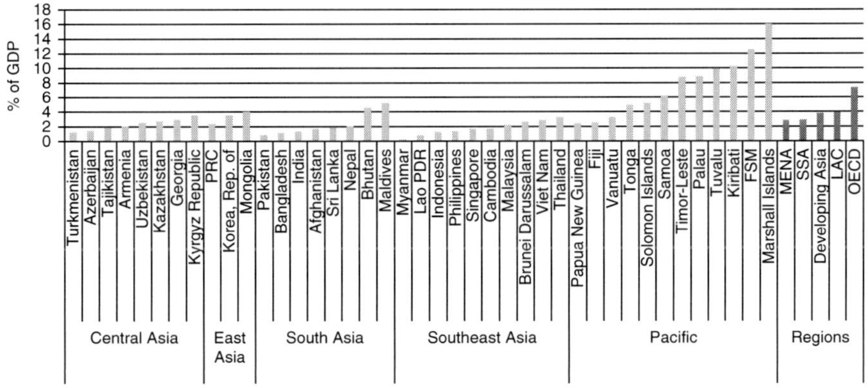

Figure 5.2 Government expenditure on health, 2009.

FSM = Federated States of Micronesia; GDP = gross domestic product; LAC = Latin America and the Caribbean; Lao PDR = Lao People's Democratic Republic; MENA = Middle East and North Africa; OECD = Organisation for Economic Co-operation and Development; PRC = People's Republic of China; SSA = Sub-Saharan Africa.

Note: Regional averages are simple averages.

Source: World Development Indicators, http://data.worldbank.org/data-catalog/world-development-indicators (accessed 20 July 2012).

including in the People's Republic of China (PRC), India, Indonesia, Pakistan, and the Philippines, compared with an Organisation for Economic Co-operation and Development (OECD) average of 5.2%. In 2009, in the majority of Asian countries, government spending on health as a share of GDP was less than 5%, with the exception of most Pacific countries, averaging 3.8% of GDP, compared with the OECD average of 7.4%. These figures suggest that there is scope for developing Asian economies to increase spending on education and health.

In practice, even if education and health services are available, poor households may not able to use them because of economic pressures (such as losing income by sending children to school). To address the demand-side constraints, the policy community has developed the instrument of conditional cash transfers (CCTs). They have been designed to have long-term benefits by providing poor households with an incentive to invest in human capital (education and health). For example, poor families receive cash transfers conditional on their children attending school.

CCTs have expanded rapidly in Latin America since the 1990s and have been found to be effective in improving education and health indicators for poor households in many countries (Schultz 2004; Schady and Araujo 2006). In Asia, CCTs have been implemented in Bangladesh, Cambodia, Pakistan, and, more recently, Indonesia and the Philippines (Box 5.2). CCT programs, which are financially sustainable and combined with complementary programs to improve the delivery of healthcare and education services, could play an important role in reducing poverty and inequality in Asia.

Box 5.2 Conditional cash transfers in the Philippines: the Pantawid Pamilyang Pilipino Program

The Pantawid Pamilyang Pilipino Program (4Ps) in the Philippines has run since January 2008. It aims to provide cash grants to extremely poor households and allows them to meet certain human development goals – health, nutrition, and education of children below 15 years – set by the government. Around 3 million households nationwide were targeted under 4Ps in 2012, out of 18.5 million households in 2009.

The targeting involves a number of steps, including selecting the poorest municipalities and cities within each selected province based on poverty incidence, and identifying poor households in the selected municipalities and cities using a proxy means testing that assesses household socioeconomic characteristics, such as ownership of assets, type of housing units, educational attainment of household head, family livelihood, and access to water and sanitation facilities.

To be eligible for 4Ps, a household must have an income equal to or below the provincial poverty threshold; have children 0–14 years old and/or a pregnant woman at the time of assessment; and agree to meet the program conditions.

The conditions have both health and education components. In particular, pregnant women must avail themselves of pre- and postnatal care, and childbirth must be attended by a health professional. Parents are required to attend "family development sessions" conducted by local governments.

Children aged 0–5 must get regular preventive health checkups and vaccines, and those aged 6–14 must receive deworming pills twice a year. Children 3–14 years old must attend classes at least 85% of the time. Schools are required to report the attendance rate of program beneficiaries to their municipal governments.

The program benefits include P500 (around $12) a month per household for health and nutrition expenses, and P300 a month per child attending school for 10 months, up to a maximum of three children per household. Transfers are generally handed to the most responsible adult in the household and are credited to the "cash card facility" of the government-owned Land Bank of the Philippines.

Source: Department of Social Welfare and Development, http://pantawid.dswd.gov.ph (accessed 28 March 2012).

Increasing social protection spending. Social protection also has an important role in reducing inequality. Social safety nets mitigate the risks of external and transitory livelihood shocks, as well as helping to meet the minimum needs of the chronically poor. Exposure to such shocks can have a profound and long-lasting impact not only on economic well-being but also on accumulation of human capital, such as education and health. Social safety nets act as a coping mechanism for poor and vulnerable people and help improve well-being by investing in human capital in the long run, which, in turn, can enhance accessibility of those with limited assets and capabilities to opportunities (Ali and Zhuang 2007).

Despite the increasing recognition of the importance of social safety nets in the region, their provision remains limited. ADB (2008) shows that very few developing Asian countries have adequate social safety nets, compared with Japan

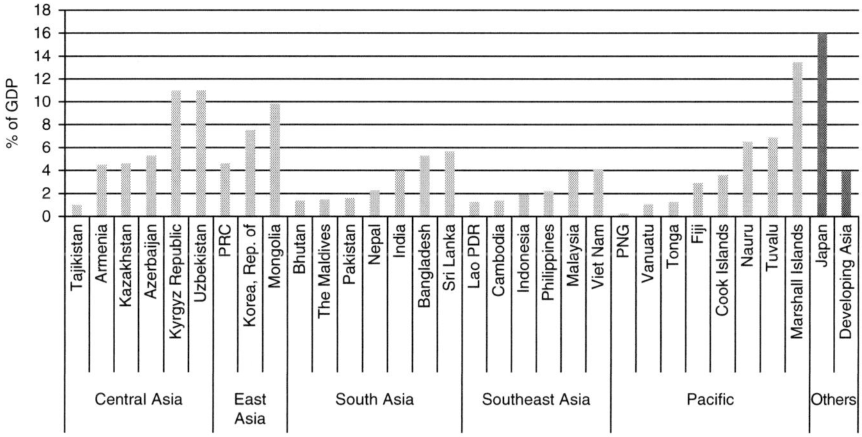

Figure 5.3 Social protection expenditure, 2008.

GDP = gross domestic product; Lao PDR = Lao People's Democratic Republic; PNG = Papua New Guinea; PRC = People's Republic of China.

Note: Social protection expenditure covers labor market programs, social insurance, social assistance, micro- and area-wide programs (including microcredit), and child protection. The figure for developing Asia is a simple average.

Source: ADB. 2008. *Social Protection Index for Committed Poverty Reduction. Volume 2: Asia.* Manila.

or the Republic of Korea. One reason is the limited resources allocated to social protection (Figure 5.3).

Countries often face many challenges in increasing the provision of social protection, including affordability, targeting, and institutional and administrative capacity. As for affordability, while this is often raised as an issue, studies have shown that the costs of basic universal social protection are not beyond the reach of most developing countries (for example, Ortiz and Yablonski (2010)). The International Labour Organization (2008) shows that virtually all countries can afford basic social security.[1] On targeting, poor beneficiaries of social protection programs on average account for only about 54.8% of the poor population in developing Asia, pointing to a clear case for improving targeting (Figure 5.4). In terms of institutional and administrative capacity, examples include better accounting, rigorous financial controls, human resource development, computerization, and greater disclosure to stakeholders.

Switching general price subsidies to targeted transfers. Increased spending on education, health, and social protection can be partly financed by reducing

[1] According to the United Nations (2007), the cost of a universal social pension scheme designed to keep the elderly out of poverty (at the $1-a-day poverty line) was estimated at 0.25% of GDP for Malaysia and about 0.50% of GDP for the Philippines and Thailand in 2005.

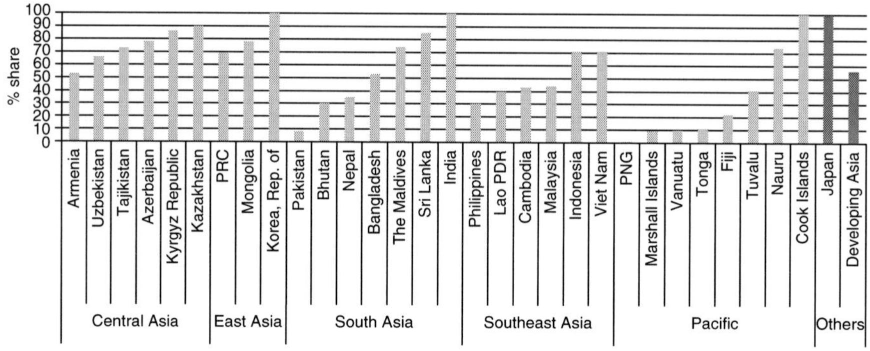

Figure 5.4 Share of the poor receiving social protection, 2008.

Lao PDR = Lao People's Democratic Republic; PNG = Papua New Guinea; PRC = People's Republic of China.

Note: The figure for developing Asia is a simple average.

Source: ADB. 2008. *Social Protection Index for Committed Poverty Reduction. Volume 2: Asia.* Manila.

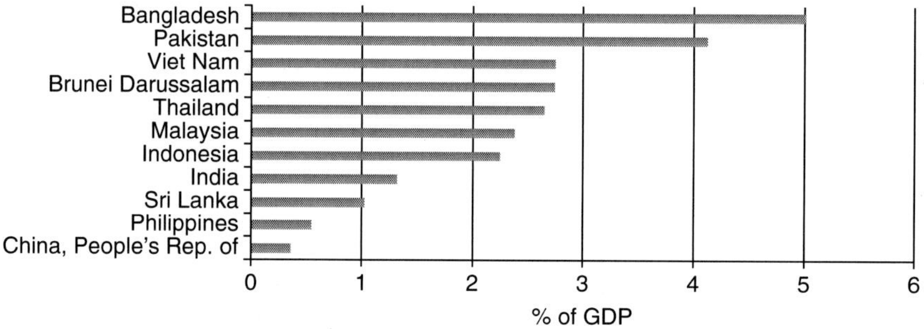

Figure 5.5 Fossil fuel consumption subsidy, 2010.

GDP = gross domestic product.

Sources: Authors' estimates using the International Energy Agency database on fossil fuel subsidies, http://www.iea.org/subsidy/index.html (accessed 23 July 2012) and World Development Indicators, http://data.worldbank.org/data-catalog/world-development-indicators (accessed 23 July 2012).

some other spending items. In most Asian countries, infrastructure investment is inadequate and should not be the target for a spending reduction through switching. However, switching government spending from general subsidies to human capital investment and social protection provision could be an effective means to reduce inequality in human capital and in income. Many countries allocate large sums to general price subsidies, which entail significant fiscal costs, but benefit the nonpoor more than the poor. A typical example is fuel subsidies (Figure 5.5). In Indonesia, for example, fuel and electricity subsidies in 2011 amounted to 3.4%

of GDP, which was larger than government spending on infrastructure that year. It is estimated that the richest 10% of households consumed 40% of the total subsidized gasoline, and the top half of households used almost 84% of it (Ginting and Aji 2012).

Encouragingly, the Indonesian Government is taking some action to tackle this issue. In March 2012, the government proposed a revised 2012 budget bill to reduce untargeted fuel subsidies and to use the saved budget resources for infrastructure investment, promotion of green growth, and transfers to poor regions and households.[2] Although what was passed by the parliament was far short of what the government originally proposed, it was still welcome.

Greater and more equitable revenue mobilization

Given the large need for more human capital investment and social protection provision in many developing Asian economies, governments will inevitably have to mobilize more revenue. The share of government revenue in GDP is low in many Asian economies. For example, in 2011, the share of central government revenue in GDP was about 12–14% in Bangladesh, Cambodia, Myanmar, Pakistan, and the Philippines, compared with the world average of close to 25% (Figure 5.6).

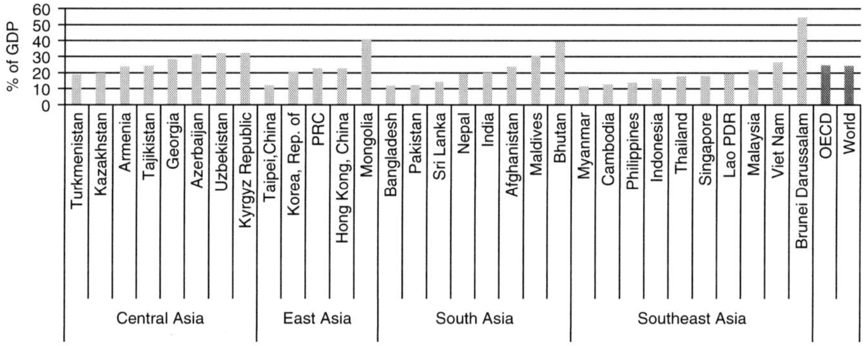

Figure 5.6 Central government revenue in selected Asian economies, 2011.

GDP = gross domestic product; Lao PDR = Lao People's Democratic Republic; OECD = Organisation for Economic Co-operation and Development; PRC = People's Republic of China.

Notes

1 Data are for 2011, except for Brunei Darussalam (2010); and OECD and World (2009). For Cambodia, the PRC, India, Kazakhstan, the Kyrgyz Republic, Mongolia, and Tajikistan, transactions are those reported by the general government.

2 OECD (2009) and world averages refer to revenues, excluding grants.

Sources: ADB. 2012. *Asian Development Outlook 2012: Confronting Rising Inequality in Asia.* Manila; World Development Indicators, http://data.worldbank.org/data-catalog/world-development-indicators (accessed 25 March 2012).

[2] The revised 2012 Budget Law gives a mandate to the government to increase fuel prices if the average Indonesian crude oil price in the previous 6-month period increases to $120.80 per barrel (15% above the budget assumption of $105).

The majority of government revenues are from taxation. In many Asian countries, more tax revenues can be mobilized by broadening tax bases and improving tax administration.

Broadening the tax base. The tax base can be broadened by reducing various exemptions, deductions, and incentives. Despite tax rates comparable to the world average (though lower than the OECD average), personal income tax collection is low in Asia (Figure 5.7). This is partly because of relatively high tax-free (minimum exempt) thresholds and a relatively high threshold of income, above which the top marginal personal income tax rate applies (Figure 5.8).

Also contributing to the lower tax collection are tax concessions. In the PRC, for example, only 11 types of personal income are liable to tax, and others not. Some of these categories are taxed at progressive rates (wages and salaries), while others are taxed at a flat rate (such as incomes of personal services, royalties, and rental and lease incomes). Tax reform is a key policy measure to improve income distribution in the PRC's Twelfth Five Year Plan (State Council of the People's Republic of China 2011).

Corporate income taxes are also low in some Asian countries partly because of tax incentives to attract investment and for activities seen as having social or economic merit. However, tax incentives can reduce the progressivity of income taxation if resources are captured by high-income interest groups lobbying for concessions. Moreover, they are often inefficient because they simply subsidize activities that firms would have undertaken anyway. Tax collection could thus also be increased by broadening the corporate tax base.

Value-added tax (VAT) receipts are low as a share of GDP in many Asian countries and are thus a potential source of additional government revenue. It is true

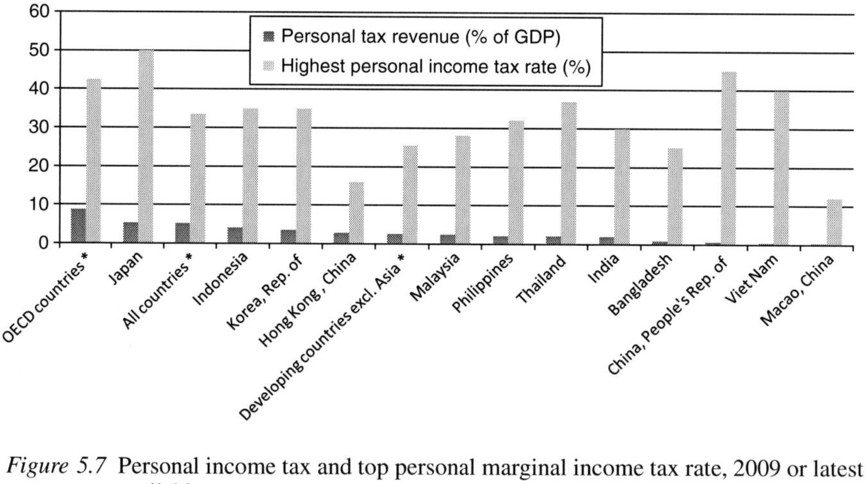

Figure 5.7 Personal income tax and top personal marginal income tax rate, 2009 or latest available year.

* simple averages; OECD = Organisation for Economic Co-operation and Development.

Source: Chapter 9 of this volume by Claus, Martinez-Vazquez, and Vulovic.

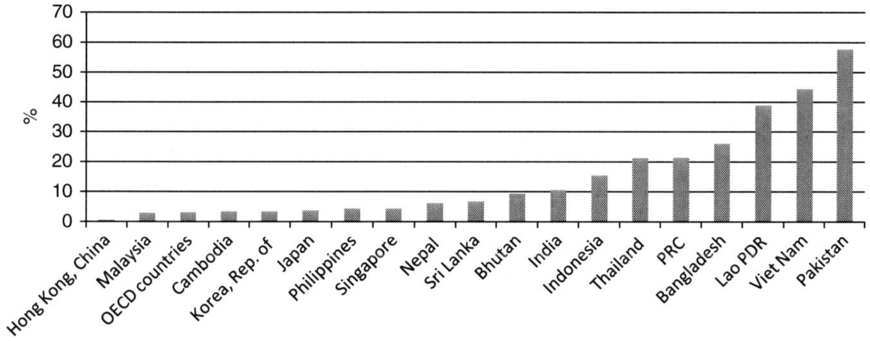

Figure 5.8 Ratio of top personal income tax threshold to gross national income per capital, late 2000s.

Lao PDR = Lao People's Democratic Republic; OECD = Organisation for Economic Co-operation and Development; PRC = People's Republic of China.

Notes: For OECD countries, data refer to 2008 or 2009 and the figure is a simple average (excluding Turkey). For Asian economies, data are for 2012. It is assumed that per capita gross national income of these economies in 2012 grows at the average rate of 2000–2010.

Source: Chapter 9 of this volume by Claus, Martinez-Vazquez, and Vulovic.

that VAT is regressive and not an effective tool for reducing income inequality, but it is less distortionary than income and sales taxes and easier to collect. VAT does not exist in, for example, Bhutan, Malaysia, the Maldives, and Myanmar. For those countries where VAT exists, its collection can be increased by broadening its base. VAT exemptions or reduced tax rates for necessities are often used to address its potential regressivity. However, these two mechanisms are costly and not well targeted at the poor. A more effective policy would be direct transfer payments to those in need. In countries where the VAT tax rate is low, it could be raised.

Improving tax administration. Government revenue can be increased by improving tax administration. In the Philippines, for example, poor tax administration has been identified as a critical constraint to increasing government revenue (ADB 2009b). Complicated tax systems with many tax rates, exemptions, deductions, and concessions increase tax administration and compliance costs as well as the opportunity for tax planning and tax avoidance. They are also often seen as unfair because higher income taxpayers generally have greater scope and resources to shift income to avoid higher tax rates. Unfair tax systems can reduce people's and businesses' willingness to pay taxes. Strengthening governance and institutions is also key to improving tax collection.

Reducing regional inequality

Spatial inequalities account for a large part of Asia's inequality. Reducing spatial inequality should therefore be a key element of the policy responses. A key

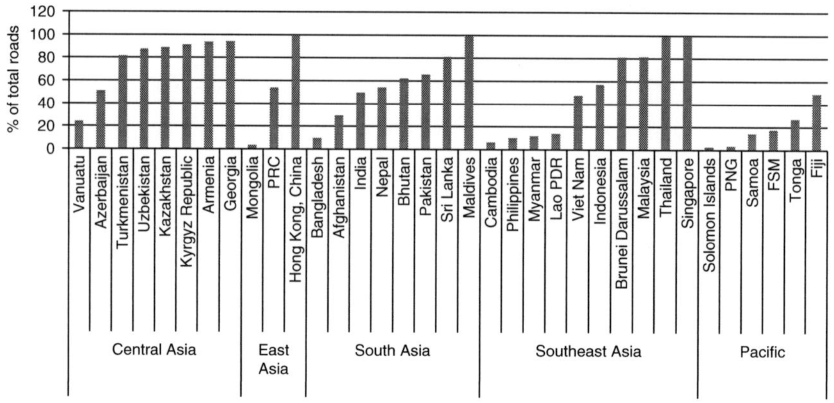

Figure 5.9 Paved roads in Asia and the Pacific, 2000s.

FSM = Federated States of Micronesia; Lao PDR = Lao People's Democratic Republic; PNG = Papua New Guinea; PRC = People's Republic of China.

Note: The figure is based on the latest available data between 2000 and 2009.

Source: World Development Indicators, http://data.worldbank.org/data-catalog/world-development-indicators (accessed 13 July 2012).

component of such inequality is that between provinces or states. Four policy options for reducing regional inequality are discussed next.

Improving regional connectivity. Poor connectivity due to lack of adequate transport and communication infrastructure is often a major constraint for interior states or provinces in engaging in global trade and attracting investment. The proportion of paved roads in total roads (Figure 5.9) was close to 100% in Thailand (as of 2000), while it was only 6.3% in Cambodia (as of 2004), 9.9% in the Philippines (as of 2003), 11.9% in Myanmar (as of 2005), 13.5% in the Lao People's Democratic Republic (Lao PDR; as of 2009), 47.6% in Viet Nam (as of 2007), and 49.5% in India (as of 2008).

Several ADB studies have found that the lack of adequate infrastructure including transport is a critical constraint to private investment in the Philippines, Indonesia, and Nepal (ADB 2009b, 2010, 2011). Improving infrastructure therefore should be one of the key policy measures to reduce regional inequality.

Developing growth poles in lagging regions. To a large extent, interregional inequality is due to coastal areas' proximity to overseas markets. This is an exogenous factor and no one can change it. However, developments in economic theory have also emphasized the importance of agglomeration economies, increasing returns, and clustering in shaping regional development (Krugman 2008). This means that countries can identify areas of potential growth poles and use policy tools and public investment to trigger growth. Countries could develop strategies for generating growth in lagging regions for equity as well as efficiency considerations. The PRC's Great Western Development Strategy presents a good example (Box 5.3).

Box 5.3 The People's Republic of China's Great Western Development Strategy

The Great Western Development Strategy was adopted in 2000 to boost the People's Republic of China's (PRC) less developed western region. It covers 11 provinces (Gansu, Guizhou, Qinghai, Shaanxi, Sichuan, Yunnan, Guangxi Zhuang Autonomous Region, Inner Mongolia Autonomous Region, Ningxia Hui Autonomous Region, Tibet Autonomous Region, and Xinjiang Uygur Autonomous Region) and one municipality (Chongqing). This region covers nearly three-quarters of the area of the country, but only one-quarter of its population and one-fifth of its total economic output (as of 2010).

The main components of the strategy include the development of infrastructure (transport, hydropower plants, energy, telecommunications, and urban development), attraction of foreign investment, increased efforts on ecological protection (e.g., reforestation), promotion of education, and retention of talent flowing to richer provinces.

During 2000–2009, total state investment in major projects in the western region reached CNY2.2 trillion (about $349 billion); fiscal transfers from the central government reached more than CNY3 trillion; the region's volume of imports and exports grew by nearly one-quarter each year on average, with its share in the national total increasing from 3.8% to 4.2%; and annual average regional gross domestic product (GDP) growth reached 11.9%, higher than the national average, with the region's share in national GDP increasing from 17.1% to 18.5%.

What has been the overall impact of the strategy on regional inequality? This is, of course, difficult to estimate because the counterfactual is difficult to specify. However, Fan *et al.* (2011) argued that regional inequality in the PRC has begun to stabilize and perhaps even turn downward since the mid-2000s, partly as a result of the strategy.

Based on primary survey data in two poor provinces – Guizhou and Gansu – Zhang *et al.* (2011) showed that real wages have risen rapidly since 2003.

Finally, Khan and Riskin (2005) argued that overall inequality has begun to level off and identified the strategy as a key factor.

Sources: S. Fan, R. Kanbur, and X. Zhang. 2011. [People's Republic of] China's Regional Disparities: Experience and Policy. *Review of Development Finance*. 1 (1). pp. 47–56; X. Zhang, J. Yang, and S. Wang. 2011. [People's Republic of] China Has Reached the Lewis Turning Point. *China Economic Review*. 22 (4). pp. 542–54; A. R. Khan and C. Riskin. 2005. [People's Republic of] China's Household Income and Its Distribution, 1995 and 2002. *The China Quarterly*. 182. pp. 356–84; and http://www. chinawest.gov.cn/web/NewsInfo.asp?NewsId=55943 (in Chinese) (accessed 20 June 2012).

Transferring fiscal resources for greater investment in human capital and better access to public services in poor regions. Fiscal transfers from richer regions to poorer regions also have an important part to play in reducing regional inequality. However, such transfers are likely to encounter political resistance from the richer regions, all the more so as even better-off regions in developing countries face a raft of pressing fiscal demands. Further, high levels of fiscal transfers may be seen as penalizing successful regions and rewarding unsuccessful ones, hence undermining incentives. Fiscal transfers should therefore be carefully designed and linked to targets and performance in improving development outcomes in recipient regions, and they should aim to build poor regions' own capacity for self-sustaining regional development, such as staving off extreme poverty, investing in human capital, and improving public services.

Reducing barriers to within-country migration. Migration from poor to prosperous areas is one of the major means for reducing regional inequality. Migration and labor mobility often come up against significant barriers. One comes from the bureaucratic and administrative obstacles to moving from one part of the country to another. For example, in the PRC, the *hukou* (registration) system constrains rural–urban migration by limiting rural migrants' access to basic public services such as education, healthcare and social protection in urban areas. Lack of necessary skills and suitable job opportunities in prosperous areas is another barrier. Absence of portability of pension benefits also discourages individuals from seeking better opportunities elsewhere. Improving connectivity, as mentioned, will facilitate the movement not only of goods but also of people.

Making growth more employment-friendly

Since the declining share of labor income is associated with rising inequality, a key issue is how to maintain and even raise this share during the growth process. This requires shifting the labor demand curve in the productive sectors of the economy as output increases. If demand outstrips supply, wages will rise, increasing the labor income share and containing inequality. Therefore, making growth more employment-friendly so as to create productive and well-paid jobs for a much wider section of the population is one of the keys to confronting rising inequality in developing Asia. Various policies stand out.

Facilitating structural transformation

Agriculture is still the largest (or at least substantial) employer in most Asian developing countries, and its dominance in providing jobs is closely associated with the high proportion of vulnerable employment, which contributes to inequality (Figure 5.10). A key challenge for most developing Asian countries is therefore to facilitate the process of structural transformation to transfer large amounts of rural agriculture surplus labor to urban manufacturing and services sectors, where most productive jobs will be generated in the future.[3] These include making the business environment more conducive to investment, improving infrastructure, reducing regulatory burdens on enterprises, promoting innovation, and upgrading industry.

[3] ADB (2007) provides a comprehensive discussion of the issues involved.

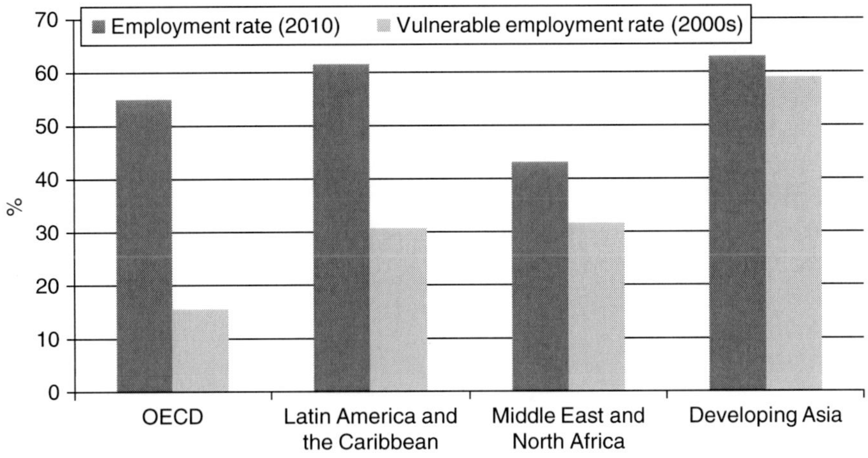

Figure 5.10 Vulnerable employment.

OECD = Organisation for Economic Co-operation and Development.

Notes

1 Vulnerable employment refers to unpaid family workers and own-account workers as a percentage of total employment.
2 The employment rate refers to the ratio of employment to the population aged 15+.
3 Weighted averages are based on the 2010 population.

Sources: World Development Indicators, http://data.worldbank.org/data-catalog/world-development-indicators (accessed 23 July 2012) and ADB estimates using NBS. 2011. *[People's Republic of] China Statistical Yearbook 2011*. Beijing.

Sectoral composition of growth has received some attention on development experiences in Asia (ADB 2007). In 2010, India's share of manufacturing in GDP was close to the average of low-income countries, but lower than the average of both lower and upper middle-income countries (Figure 5.11).[4] In the PRC, on the other hand, the share of services in GDP was much lower than the averages of low-, lower middle- and upper middle-income countries.[5]

A country's sectoral composition is determined by its comparative advantages and other factors, but development policy often plays a role. For instance, India is making greater efforts to develop manufacturing, while the PRC is aiming to increase the share of services as a source of growth and job creation. International experiences suggest that both manufacturing and services are important for

[4] Although India's share of services in GDP is high, it has been argued that jobs in the sector are mostly of low productivity and poorly paid. While the booming business outsourcing sector has generated many productive and well-paid jobs, this has only benefited a small group of the educated (ADB 2007).

[5] Some argue that the PRC's low share of services is also related to the way the data for services are collected and included in national income accounting (Pant 2007).

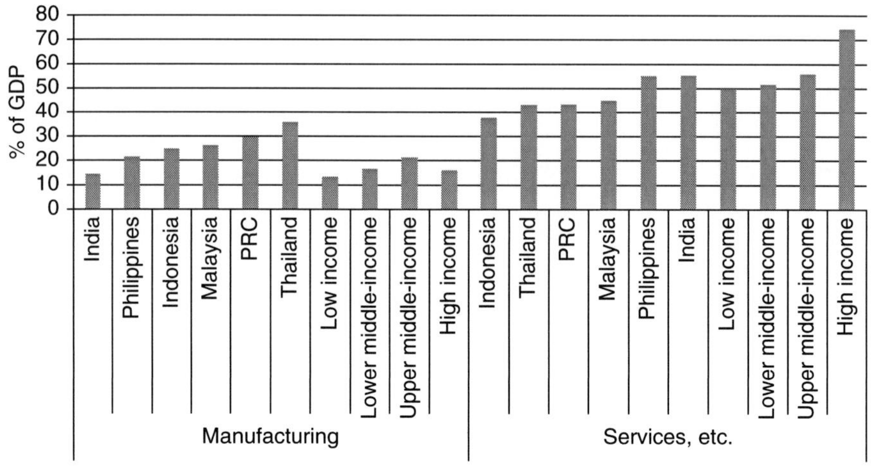

Figure 5.11 Share of manufacturing and services in gross domestic product, 2010.

GDP = gross domestic product; PRC = People's Republic of China.

Source: World Development Indicators, http://data.worldbank.org/data-catalog/world-development-indicators (accessed 23 July 2012).

growth and job creation, and the two often support each other during economic development.

Structural transformation also involves maintaining a high pace of agricultural productivity growth. This requires governments to implement agricultural policies to produce more output per hectare. Improving the access of the rural poor to irrigation, electricity, transport services, new technology and improved seeds, agricultural extension services, and financial services is vital for raising farm productivity. If ownership or access to land is highly skewed, implementing mechanisms that improve the access of the poor to land is also essential. In the PRC, rural nonagricultural village and township enterprises have played an important role in lifting income levels of the rural population and reducing rural poverty. Such enterprises could be promoted by other Asian countries.

Supporting the development of small and medium-sized enterprises

SMEs provide most jobs in developing and developed countries alike; however, they often face constraints, especially in accessing finance, human capital, and markets. Three ADB studies found that access to finance was ranked among the top constraints to business growth by SMEs in the Philippines, Indonesia, and Nepal (ADB 2009b, 2010, 2011). In the PRC, access to finance and human capital is also considered among the major constraints by SMEs, many of which are in rural areas.

Governments should support SME development by facilitating their creation, removing unnecessary and cumbersome restrictions on their development, and addressing market failures in their access to finance. Governments can also help SMEs adopt new technologies and access new markets (ADB 2009b).

On access to finance, recent international experience suggests that one of the most important ways governments can increase access to finance is to improve the institutional underpinnings of financial transactions by strengthening creditor rights, defining property rights so property can be used as collateral for credit, and enhancing credit registries and systems to screen borrowers. They can also improve the information infrastructure that underlies the workings of financial markets.

To help SMEs adopt technologies and enter new markets, governments can provide information on improved production methods, products, and markets; technical support services; and vocational training. They can also foster links between SMEs and large enterprises and encourage cluster-based development by exploiting the fact that many enterprises that make and sell related or complementary products are grouped close together, often with their suppliers and buyers.

Removing factor market distortions

One of the reasons why developing countries with relatively abundant labor prefer labor-saving and capital-intensive techniques could be distortions in factor markets: market prices of factors of production fail to reflect relative abundance, due to underdevelopment of the finance sector or financial repression, among others. In the PRC, for instance, factor market reform has lagged behind product market reform, and interest rate control has kept borrowing costs low, especially for state-owned enterprises. During 1990–2010, the PRC's real lending rate was one of the lowest among 50 middle- and high-income countries (ADB 2012b). The low cost of capital has been put forward as one of the causes of the imbalances of growth sources in the PRC (Huang 2010; World Bank 2012).

In India, the financial repression, as evidenced by persistently negative real savings deposit rates, could also be a contributing factor to the low cost of capital relative to labor in the formal sector (Reserve Bank of India 2011). It has also been suggested that some of the earlier policies of industrialization, which were intended to promote labor-intensive industries and adoption of labor-intensive techniques, had some unintended consequences of encouraging the use of capital-intensive technology (Kochhar *et al.* 2006; Felipe *et al.* forthcoming).

Reducing factor market distortions could therefore promote job creation. A key policy measure is to reduce or eliminate financial repression by further developing the finance sector. This includes decreasing and removing distortions in the cost of capital by gradually adopting market-determined interest rates; allowing greater competition and private sector participation in the finance sector; further strengthening the regulatory framework and governance of financial institutions; carefully managing the liberalization of the capital account; and making the exchange rate more flexible. For instance, India liberalized deposit interest rates in November 2011 (Reserve Bank of India 2011).

Labor market institutions

Employment generation also needs to be supported by effective labor market institutions. On the one hand, labor market institutions should help improve the employability of labor through provision of skills training and assistance with job searches (e.g., employment services) as well as provide necessary protection of workers' rights. On the other hand, they should not impose excessive costs on enterprises and hurt job creation.

There are significant disagreements on the effects of labor market interventions on job creation. Some believe that interventions such as employment protection legislation, minimum wages, and collective bargaining are important to protect the rights of workers, while others think that these interventions will raise labor costs and only protect those who have already been employed (or "insiders"), but make employers reluctant to hire new workers or find ways to bypass these (e.g., by replacing regular, formal jobs with contract labor that offers less protection, lower wages, and little social security), hence damaging job creation. Empirical evidence on these is mixed (Felipe and Hasan 2006).

In some countries, there has been an implicit or explicit move to a "flexicurity system," which involves giving employers greater flexibility in adjusting the workforce based on their needs as determined by market fluctuations, while the security of workers is "socialized" through policies and programs administered by or through the state, such as retraining or unemployment insurance (Auer 2007). This approach reduces the retrenchment burden on firms, making it more likely that they will hire and provide better security for workers. In Asia, some countries have moved in this direction, including the Republic of Korea and the PRC, while others have found it hard to restructure labor market institutions (Vandenberg 2010).

In sum, while there is room for many Asian countries to build effective labor market institutions, the exact form and approach to follow will have to be decided by each country on the basis of their specific circumstances. For countries that have transitioned from a planned economy to a market economy and where basic labor market institutions are yet to be established, there is a case for moving toward establishing or strengthening formal arrangements. For countries where labor market regulations have been seen as too restrictive and a major constraint to growth and job creation in the formal sector, there is a need to examine the specific elements that are likely to act as constraints and ensure that they are appropriately addressed.

Public employment schemes

Governments can also introduce public employment schemes to act as a buffer stock or mechanism for employment: when the private sector downsizes in recessions, workers who lose their jobs can find work in such a scheme. The government pledges to hire anyone satisfying certain criteria and willing to work on projects, such as small infrastructure (e.g., clean water and sewage projects, roads), at a basic public sector salary. Many developing countries in Asia (including Bangladesh, Cambodia, Indonesia, the Republic of Korea, and Sri Lanka) and in Latin America (including Argentina, Brazil, Chile, Peru, and Mexico) as well as developed countries (including Australia and France) have public employment programs, many of which are temporary (Felipe 2009).

Some countries have implemented such programs to counter the major problems associated with persistent unemployment. In Asia, a well-known case is India's National Rural Employment Guarantee Scheme (Box 5.4).

Box 5.4 India's National Rural Employment Guarantee Scheme

The Mahatma Gandhi National Rural Employment Guarantee Scheme was launched in 2006 in the 200 most backward districts of India (of 640 districts in all). It is a program that explicitly recognizes the "right to a job."

Under the program, every rural adult willing to be engaged in unskilled manual labor has the right to demand work from the state government for up to 100 days per household annually. The core funding for the program is provided by the central government, and state governments make additional contributions.

The program has been extended and now covers the entire country (apart from 100% urban districts). The number of households that were provided with employment increased from 21 million in 2006/2007 to 38 million in 2010/2011, which amounted to more than 1,200 million person-days of work. A notable aspect of the scheme is the large number of women who have sought work – female participation increased from 41% to 49% in this period.

The program has had several achievements: lifting rural wages; reducing distress migration; creating community assets; promoting empowerment and making politicians more responsive to the demands of the poor; reducing unemployment and underemployment; encouraging growth of agricultural production; reducing discrimination; and reducing malnutrition.

It has also drawn criticism, however, including allegations of corruption, weakening work incentives, undermining fiscal sustainability, distorting the labor market, and causing wage inflation.

Sources: K. Bonner, J. Daum, J. Duncan, E. Dinsmore, K. Fuglesten, L. Lai, J. Lee, K. Manchester, F. Tadesse, and R. Quinn. 2012. *MGNREGA Implementation: A Cross-State Comparison*. The Woodrow Wilson School's Graduate Policy Workshop, Princeton University. January; P. Jagannathan. 2011. *Ministry Wants NREGS Shut in Farming Season*; and D. Sjoblom and J. Farrington. 2008. ODI Project Briefings 7, http://www.odi.org.uk/resources/details.asp?id=440&title=indian-national-ruralemployment-guarantee-act-will-reduce-poverty-boost-economy

Toward inclusive growth in Asia

Driven by globalization, technological progress, and market-oriented reform, developing Asia has had a remarkable period of growth and poverty reduction. However, the drivers of growth are also magnifying the effects of inequalities in physical and human capital, leading to rising income inequality. These forces require Asian policy makers to redouble their efforts to generate more productive jobs, equalize opportunities in employment, education, and health, and address spatial inequality. Without such policies, which will enhance growth further, Asia may be pulled into inefficient populist policies, which will benefit neither growth nor equity.

The policy options outlined constitute key elements of a strategy for inclusive growth. Broadly, inclusive growth can be defined as "growth coupled with equality of opportunity," and it needs three policy pillars: sustained growth to create productive jobs for a wide section of the population; social inclusion to equalize access to opportunity; and social safety nets to mitigate vulnerability and risks and prevent extreme poverty (Zhuang and Ali 2010). Such a strategy would ensure that all members of society could participate in the development process productively and benefit equitably from the opportunities generated by economic growth.

It is encouraging that more and more developing Asian countries are embracing the concept of inclusive growth, with an increasing number of countries – including the PRC, India, and many Southeast Asian countries – placing inclusive growth at the heart of their development policy, as reflected in their recent medium-term development plans. Indeed, the entire development community is embracing the concept of inclusive growth. These developments will go a long way toward reducing poverty and inequality and making the world a more equitable place.

Acknowledgments

The authors would like to thank staff of the Asian Development Bank's Economics and Research Department, especially Shikha Jha and Iris Claus, for providing inputs to this chapter.

References

Ali, I., and J. Zhuang. 2007. Inclusive Growth toward a Prosperous Asia: Policy Implications. *ERD Working Paper Series* No. 97. Manila: ADB.

Asian Development Bank (ADB). 2007. *Asian Development Outlook 2007*. Manila.

——. 2008. *Social Protection Index for Committed Poverty Reduction. Volume 2: Asia*. Manila.

——. 2009a. *Key Indicators for Asia and the Pacific 2009*. Manila.

——. 2009b. *Philippines: Critical Development Constraints*. Manila.

——. 2010. *Indonesia: Critical Development Constraints*. Manila.

——. 2011. *Nepal: Critical Development Constraints*. Manila.

——. 2012a. *Asian Development Outlook 2012: Confronting Rising Inequality in Asia*. Manila.

——. 2012b. *[People's Republic of] China 2030: Growing beyond the Low-Cost Advantage: Policy Issues and Options*. Manila.

Auer, P. 2007. Security in Labour Markets: Combining Flexibility with Security for Decent Work. *Economic and Labour Market Papers* 2007/12. Geneva: Employment Analysis and Research Unit, Economic and Labour Market Analysis Department, International Labour Organization.

Bonner, K., J. Daum, J. Duncan, E. Dinsmore, K. Fuglesten, L. Lai, J. Lee, K. Manchester, F. Tadesse, and R. Quinn. 2012. *MGNREGA Implementation: A Cross-State Comparison*. The Woodrow Wilson School's Graduate Policy Workshop, Princeton University. January.

Department of Social Welfare and Development (DSWD). *Pantawid Pamilyang Pilipino Program*. Philippines. http://pantawid.dswd.gov.ph (accessed 28 March 2012).

Esquivel, G., N. Lustig, and J. Scott. 2010. A Decade of Falling Inequality in Mexico: Market Forces or State Action? In L. F. López-Calva and N. Lustig, eds. *Declining Inequality in Latin America: A Decade of Progress?* Washington, DC: Brookings Institution and United Nations Development Programme.

Fan, S., R. Kanbur, and X. Zhang. 2011. [People's Republic of] China's Regional Disparities: Experience and Policy. *Review of Development Finance*. 1 (1). pp. 47–56.

Felipe, J. 2009. *Inclusive Growth, Full Employment and Structural Change: Implications and Policies for Developing Asia*. London: Anthem Press.

Felipe, J., and R. Hasan, eds. 2006. *Labor Markets in Asia: Issues and Perspectives*. London: Palgrave Macmillan for the Asian Development Bank.

Felipe, J., U. Kumar, and A. Abdon. Forthcoming. Exports, Capabilities, and Industrial Policy in India. *Journal of Comparative Economics*.

Ginting, E., and P. Aji. 2012. Macroeconomic Management. In H. Hill, M. E. Khan, and J. Zhuang, eds. *Diagnosing the Indonesian Economy*. London: Anthem Press and Manila: ADB.

Huang, Y. 2010. [People's Republic of] China's Great Ascendancy and Structural Risks: Consequences of Asymmetric Market Liberalization. *Asian Pacific Economic Literature*. 24 (1). pp. 65–85.

International Labour Organization (ILO). 2008. Can Low-Income Countries Afford Basic Social Security? *Social Security Policy Briefings Paper* 3. Geneva: Social Security Department, ILO.

Jagannathan, P. 2011. *Ministry Wants NREGS Shut in Farming Season*. http://epaper.timesofindia.com/Default/Scripting/ArticleWin.asp?From=Archive&Source=Page&Skin=ETNEW&BaseHref=ETBG/2011/07/19&PageLabel=1&EntityId=Ar00100&ViewMode=HTML (accessed March 2012).

Khan, A. R., and C. Riskin. 2005. [People's Republic of] China's Household Income and Its Distribution, 1995 and 2002. *The China Quarterly*. 182. pp. 356–84.

Kochhar, K., U. Kumar, R. Rajan, and A. Subramanian. 2006. India's Pattern of Development: What Happened, What Follows? *Journal of Monetary Economics*. 53 (5). pp. 981–1019.

Krugman, P. 2008. The Increasing Returns Revolution in Trade and Geography. http://www.nobelprize.org/nobel_prizes/economics/laureates/2008/krugman_lecture.pdf

National Bureau of Statistics. 2011. *[People's Republic of] China Statistical Yearbook 2011*. Beijing.

Ortiz, I., and J. Yablonski. 2010. Investing in People: Social Protection for All. In S. W. Handayani. ed. *Enhancing Social Protection in Asia and the Pacific: The Proceedings of the Regional Workshop*. Manila: ADB.

Pant, B., ed. 2007. *The National Accounts of the People's Republic of China: Measurement Issues, Recent Developments, and the Way Forward*. Manila: ADB.

Reserve Bank of India (RBI). 2011. Deregulation of Savings Bank Deposit Interest Rate: A Discussion Paper. Mumbai.

Schady, N., and M. C. Araujo. 2006. Cash Transfers, Conditions, School Enrollment, and Child Work: Evidence from a Randomized Experiment in Ecuador. *World Bank Policy Research Working Paper Series 3930*. Washington, DC: World Bank.

Schultz, P. 2004. School Subsidies for the Poor: Evaluating the Mexican Progresa Program. *Journal of Development Economics*. 74 (1). pp. 199–250.

Sjoblom, D., and J. Farrington. 2008. ODI Project Briefings 7. http://www.odi.org.uk/resources/details.asp?id=440&title=indian-national-ruralemployment-guarantee-act-will-reduce-poverty-boost-economy

State Council of the People's Republic of China. 2011. *The 12th Five Year Plan of National Economy and Social Development of People's Republic of China 2011–2015*. Beijing.

United Nations (UN). 2007. *Development in an Ageing World: World Economic and Social Survey 2007*. New York, NY: Department of Economic and Social Affairs.

Vandenberg, P. 2010. Is Asia Adopting Flexicurity? *International Labour Review*. 149 (1). pp. 31–58.

World Bank. 2012. *[People's Republic of] China 2030: Building a Modern, Harmonious, and Creative High-Income Society*. Conference Edition. Washington, DC: World Bank.

——. World Development Indicators. http://data.worldbank.org/data-catalog/world-development-indicators (accessed 20 July 2012).

Zhang, X., J. Yang, and S. Wang. 2011. [People's Republic of] China Has Reached the Lewis Turning Point. *China Economic Review*. 22 (4). pp. 542–54.

Zhuang, J., and I. Ali. 2010. Poverty, Inequality, and Inclusive Growth in Asia. In J. Zhuang, ed. *Poverty, Inequality, and Inclusive Growth: Measurement, Policy Issues, and Country Studies*. London: Anthem Press and Manila: ADB.

Part II

Background studies

6 Inclusive growth and gender inequality in Asia's labor markets

Yana van der Meulen Rodgers and Joseph E. Zveglich, Jr.

Introduction

A growing body of evidence shows that gender inequalities can make the process of development less inclusive by weakening the ability of household members to care for each other or to engage in productive activities. For example, gender discrepancies in education can make the labor force less effective, undermining the economy's growth potential. At the same time, structural changes that accompany the development process – as a result of technological change, international competition, or policy liberalization – can substantially alter the constraints that women and men face when they approach new economic opportunities. The extent to which these forces lead to greater gender parity or greater divisions will influence the extent of inclusiveness of future growth.

Policy and scholarly discourse offer alternative notions of gender equality, with varying degrees of emphasis on equality of opportunity and equality of outcome. Equality of opportunity is most often associated with formal, legal equality in access to education, health services, and employment. It is also associated with equal chances for men and women to participate in decision making and to have a voice within and outside of the household. In contrast, equality of outcome commonly refers to gender parity in income, wealth, assets, market-based work, and household work. The two concepts are closely related and mutually reinforcing. Giving women greater opportunities can improve their economic outcomes, while more equal outcomes can foster more balanced gender relations that in turn help equalize opportunities.

To shed light on these ideas, this chapter examines gender inequality in developing Asia's labor markets, with an in-depth focus on the structural drivers of women's labor force participation. Women's labor force participation is viewed as both an opportunity and outcome. As an opportunity, labor force participation enables women to enhance their individual and household income and wealth, and it gives women more autonomy and greater say over household decisions. As an outcome, participation in income-earning production has intrinsic value deriving from the more favorable way it is viewed relative to uncompensated household production.

At the macro level, although globalization has been seen primarily as a positive development, women constitute the largest group who have not fully benefited.

For many developing countries in Asia, the emphasis on maintaining competitiveness in the world market has meant staking a claim to the low-wage niche, resulting in downward pressure on women's wages and segregation into jobs characterized by insecurity and poor working conditions. At the micro level, women's labor market participation has risen without any relief from domestic-based obligations. In order to facilitate more inclusive growth, these structural drivers of women's employment thus call for policy reforms that promote decent and productive employment opportunities for women, a macroeconomic environment that supports women's roles as income and care providers, and greater public investment in infrastructure and social services.

Links between economic growth and gender inequality

While the understanding of how gender inequality and the macroeconomy interact is needed to formulate supportive policies, the relationship is complex. Considerable debate has emerged regarding both the direction of causality and the distributional consequences.[1] Theoretically, rising income levels can narrow gender inequality through such channels as the demise of traditional structures that reinforce human capital differences between men and women, the rising opportunity cost of women's time outside of the labor force, the strengthening of women's economic and property rights, and the introduction of labor-saving consumer durables through technological progress.

Yet economic growth does not necessarily mean inequality will decline, especially if unpaid work burdens, biased laws, differential access to resources, and social norms continue to constrain women's ability to take advantage of new, well-paid employment opportunities (World Bank 2011). Gender differences in the drivers of labor market opportunities play a crucial role in constraining women's advancement and achievement of gender equality in the labor market. These drivers include household dynamics (especially women's relatively greater time burdens in performing unpaid household work), formal institutions (including statutory laws that favor men and inadequate public infrastructure that contributes to women's domestic work burdens), markets (particularly unequal access to credit, agricultural inputs, and investments in human capital), and informal institutions (such as employers' discriminatory attitudes toward women workers and social norms that restrict women from engaging in market-based work). These drivers are mutually reinforcing and can generate persistent obstacles toward more equitable occupational distributions and narrowing pay differentials.

In the reverse direction, gender inequality can harm economic growth through a complex set of channels, including the reduction of the human capital of women and their children, inefficient allocation of resources, suboptimal governance in business and governments, and reduced aggregate productivity. Yet some aspects of gender inequality may well induce more rapid economic growth, especially in

---

[1] The discussion of these theoretical channels draws from World Bank (2011).

the short term when women's concentration in low-paid jobs helps to keep labor costs low and improve competitiveness in world markets. Given the contradictory theoretical links, ultimately it comes down to the empirical evidence.

Growth affects gender inequality

A growing number of empirical studies have shown causal links between economic growth and gender inequality, with inequality improving or worsening depending on the gendered indicator under consideration. A considerable body of evidence indicates that economic development reduces the disadvantages faced by women, especially in educational attainment, life expectancy, and labor force participation (World Bank 2011). Economic development brings higher incomes and improved service delivery, which helps close gender gaps in educational attainment, health outcomes, and employment. For some countries, technological improvements worked to women's relative advantage as the returns to cognitive skills rose relative to the returns to manual skills.

Growth together with globalization has also provided opportunities for girls and women to embark on education and labor market tracks from which they had previously been blocked by traditional institutions. For example, low-caste girls in India have increased their enrollment in English language schools, thus preparing them for a broader range of jobs in the global economy, while traditional networks have still channeled low-caste boys into local language schools (Munshi and Rosenzweig 2006). More generally, growth can improve multiple dimensions of women's well-being. Forsythe *et al.* (2000) found that economic growth from 1970 to 1992 led to improvements in overall women's status, as measured by the United Nations Development Programme's Gender-Related Development Index. Yet economic growth may not be sufficient to improve gendered well-being in all its dimensions. In particular, Klasen and Wink (2003) argue that rising per capita income is associated with mixed evidence for improvements in women's relative status, with an increase in the absolute number of "missing women" and a growing incidence of sex-selective abortions in Asian economies contrasting with gains women experienced in education and labor-market outcomes.

Increased openness to trade and foreign direct investment (FDI) has been a key growth driver in many Asian countries, often giving women greater access to employment in export-oriented labor-intensive manufacturing. However, women may not receive net benefit from these new paid employment opportunities if their employment gains have been accompanied by precarious working conditions and an expansion of informal-sector jobs (which lack basic legal and social protections and are not subject to formal economic regulations). Pressure from international markets to keep production costs low may induce firms to offer increasingly insecure jobs that are temporary, casual, flexible, and characterized by poor working conditions.[2] For example, Bhaumik (2003) found that following India's sweeping

[2] See especially Balakrishnan (2011); Benería (2007); and Barrientos *et al.* (2004) for more support of these arguments.

trade liberalization in 1991, the share of the workforce considered to be casual grew, with larger increases for women workers compared with men in both rural and urban areas.

Across countries, the casualization of the workforce can be partly explained by the growing tendency of final-goods producers to subcontract smaller-scale, home-based operations.[3] Home-based workers are predominantly women who work for lower pay (often on a piece-rate basis), receive few (if any) fringe benefits, pay their own utility costs, and work long hours. In view of their informal status, most home-based workers remain uncovered by labor regulations that raise the cost of labor. They are predominantly new labor-market entrants, women who have lost their formal-sector jobs, and women who need to combine paid work with childcare obligations.

Further economic growth generated through openness to trade may put downward pressure on the wages of workers in the export sector and, to the extent that women workers account for a high proportion of employment, contribute to wider gender wage gaps. Supporting this argument, Berik *et al.* (2004) used data for Taipei,China and the Republic of Korea and found that increasing competition from international trade is associated with larger wage gaps between men and women. Because the analysis controlled for gender differences in productivity characteristics, the widening wage gap was interpreted as a sign of increased wage discrimination. The authors argued that rising wage gaps with international trade may be associated with wage concessions from workers in a manner that disadvantages women workers. Similar results were found for India in Menon and Rodgers (2009). In particular, after India's sweeping trade liberalization, firms appeared to favor male workers over female workers in the wage bargaining process, and the residual gender wage gap grew.[4] Yet others have argued that jobs in the export sector offer better pay compared with the alternatives for women workers (Kabeer 2004).

Technological change, a key driver of economic growth, can also affect gender inequality. Studies have shown that in middle- and higher-income economies, technological improvements have displaced women from low-paying jobs in import-competing sectors. In particular, women in middle- and higher-income economies tend to cluster in manufacturing industries that have begun to upgrade their technologies, reduce the size of their workforce, and move production to lower-wage countries. In the case of Taipei,China, technological upgrading and rising capital intensity of export-oriented manufacturing after 1980 was linked to a relative decline in employment opportunities for women (Berik 2000). Women in lower-income countries can also experience job displacement when technological change makes traditional female jobs redundant and when women face barriers to training for new jobs. For example, the adoption of new rice-husking equipment

---

3 Carr *et al.* (2000) provide further support for this argument.

4 In contrast, Black and Brainerd (2004) found declining residual gender wage gaps in industries in the United States that experienced greater competition from imports.

in India's food processing industry and new technologies in India's textiles and garment industry led to job losses for women (Jhabvala and Sinha 2002).

Gender inequality affects growth

In the reverse direction, gender inequality can also have a causal impact on economic growth. A growing body of empirical evidence indicates that gender inequality can promote some macroeconomic aggregates when considering shorter-term effects, while gender inequality serves as a drag on growth when considering longer-term effects.[5] In particular, gender inequality in wages and employment can actually stimulate export growth in the shorter term. Since the 1970s, women's jobs in highly competitive export industries (especially in garments, textiles, and electronics) have been important in generating foreign currency earnings.[6] Reliance on women workers in labor-intensive, export-oriented manufacturing has become a common pattern across Asia's high-growth economies as women's share of manufacturing employment rose during their export drives. While the concentration of women in export manufacturing has received the most attention, even in agriculture, women's seasonal or daily wage labor on farms has proven critical to keeping costs low and export demand high.

In the longer term, a number of compelling studies indicate that gender inequality in education and employment act as a drag on economic growth. Educational gender gaps, for example, are linked to higher rates of fertility and lower saving rates. Rising fertility can reduce investment in children's education and health. Moreover, educational inequality can contribute to women's unequal household bargaining power, affecting the distribution of household resources, given women's greater tendency to allocate spending to children's needs. By lowering the resources invested in children, gender inequality reduces the quality of the future labor supply and long-term productivity growth. Further, systematic differences in investments in girls' and boys' education can be inefficient due to distortions in skill levels (Boschini 2003). Investing too much in less-talented men while investing too little in competent women reduces the average skill level in the economy, with negative repercussions for total productivity. Such distortions may arise from cultural forces around gender norms that channel men and women into gendered occupations. Hence, social norms can influence gender-specific educational choices, which in turn can result in a suboptimal allocation of ability. Cross-country evidence in Boschini (2003) showed that the presence of gender stereotypes reduces skill acquisition, technological change, and economic growth.

Closely related, cross-country regressions in Busse and Nunnenkamp (2009) demonstrated that foreign firms responded positively to gender equality in education over the period 1980–2005. This statistically significant effect is limited to

---

[5] This discussion on gender inequality and economic growth is based on a comprehensive review in Berik *et al.* (2009).

[6] The feminization of foreign exchange earnings is discussed further in Samarasinghe (1998) and Seguino (2010).

middle-income, developing host countries and developed source countries, with the interpretation that gender equality and growth goals are complementary in countries that are aiming to reduce gender education gaps. Greater equality in education helps to boost FDI by expanding the pool of skilled labor, and it also enhances economic growth through spillover effects from FDI on growth. Finally, Klasen and Lamanna (2009) confirmed the substantial negative effect of gender gaps on growth previously reported in the literature. Their analysis, which covers 93 countries over the period 1960–2000, found that countries with wider gender differences in labor force participation rates grow more slowly, with simulations showing lower growth in the Middle East and Northern Africa and South Asia regions due to this effect.

Gender inequality in Asian labor markets: macro-level evidence

Aggregate labor market statistics for Asia and the Pacific indicate improvements in gender equality for some metrics, but persistent gaps in others. In particular, women's representation in the labor force has approached near equality with that of men in the lower-income and the developed member economies, but it has remained low in many middle-income countries in the region. Yet occupational segregation and gender wage gaps remain problematic across the region. On average, women are more likely than men to engage in work as unpaid helpers in family businesses, and their self-employment endeavors are often smaller in scale.

Among developing member economies, some of the highest labor force participation rates for women in 2010 are found in East Asia and the Pacific (Table 6.1). Women's labor force participation rates are particularly high in the People's Republic of China (PRC; 68%), Cambodia (79%), and the Lao People's Democratic Republic (77%). Women have low labor force participation rates – relative to women in other regions and relative to men in the same region – in South Asia. Among individual countries, women's labor force participation is especially low in Afghanistan (16%), Pakistan (22%), and India (29%). Barriers to women's presence in the workforce due to religion, conflict, and social attitudes help explain some of these very low female labor force participation rates.

A number of countries exhibit substantial changes, both negative and positive, in female labor force participation between 1990 and 2010. Stagnation and even some declines are found across the region, especially in Armenia (from 61% to 49%) and the PRC (from 72% to 68%), largely reflecting the transition from socialism to market economies in the early 1990s. Men's labor force participation rates have also fallen in this region. In the opposite direction, increases were particularly strong in Bhutan and the Maldives. Led by Australia and New Zealand, developed member economies also showed an increase in women's participation in the labor market following the implementation of more family-friendly work policies and the continuation of a policy environment conducive to women's progress in the labor market.

Data in Table 6.1 show a nonlinear relationship between women's share of the labor force and income levels. Across Asia and the Pacific, women's share of

Table 6.1 Labor force participation and women's share of the labor force, 1990 and 2010

	Adult (15+) labor force participation rate (%)				*Women's share of the adult labor force (%)*	
	1990		*2010*		*1990*	*2010*
	Women	*Men*	*Women*	*Men*		
Central and West Asia	**54.7**	**74.9**	**55.2**	**74.2**	**44.3**	**44.6**
Armenia	60.7	77.2	49.0	69.6	46.5	46.5
Azerbaijan	54.0	70.6	61.1	67.8	45.7	49.0
Georgia	55.1	74.5	55.6	73.8	46.1	47.0
Kazakhstan	62.3	78.0	66.4	76.8	47.0	49.4
Kyrgyz Republic	58.4	74.3	55.2	78.2	46.1	42.7
Tajikistan	58.2	75.7	57.3	74.8	44.5	45.2
Turkmenistan	46.4	74.8	46.4	75.7	39.7	39.3
Uzbekistan	46.1	73.2	47.6	74.4	40.0	39.8
East Asia	**70.8**	**84.1**	**66.8**	**79.6**	**44.4**	**44.5**
China, People's Rep. of	72.4	84.7	67.9	80.2	44.6	44.6
Hong Kong, China	47.2	79.3	51.0	68.3	36.5	46.0
Korea, Rep. of	47.1	73.4	49.2	71.6	39.7	41.3
Mongolia	52.3	62.5	53.9	65.0	46.6	46.4
Taipei,China	44.5	74.0	49.9	66.5	37.5	43.6
South Asia	**35.8**	**85.3**	**31.8**	**81.3**	**28.0**	**27.1**
Afghanistan	15.5	81.5	15.5	80.4	14.9	15.2
Bangladesh	61.7	88.4	56.9	84.4	39.4	39.9
Bhutan	49.6	78.2	65.5	76.0	37.1	42.5
India	34.8	85.1	29.0	80.7	27.4	25.3
Maldives	20.2	77.2	55.1	76.4	19.0	41.8
Nepal	80.0	90.5	80.3	87.7	46.9	49.2
Pakistan	13.4	84.6	22.4	83.3	12.8	20.7
Sri Lanka	36.3	78.0	34.6	76.2	31.5	32.2
Southeast Asia	**59.9**	**82.6**	**58.5**	**82.0**	**42.8**	**42.4**
Brunei Darussalam	44.0	82.2	55.7	76.8	31.4	42.1
Cambodia	77.7	84.3	79.3	86.6	52.6	49.8
Indonesia	50.2	81.1	51.0	84.2	38.6	38.2
Lao People's Democratic Republic	80.0	83.0	76.6	79.4	49.7	49.8
Malaysia	43.1	80.9	43.7	77.1	34.3	35.8
Myanmar	72.1	79.0	75.0	82.0	48.4	48.9
Philippines	48.0	82.8	49.5	79.4	36.6	38.8
Singapore	50.7	79.3	56.7	77.0	39.1	42.3
Thailand	75.8	87.3	63.8	80.2	47.4	45.7
Viet Nam	75.6	84.7	73.1	81.1	49.6	48.5
The Pacific	**60.2**	**76.2**	**62.4**	**75.2**	**43.2**	**44.7**
Cook Islands	41.3	61.9	64.2	76.1	–	–
Fiji	29.1	83.4	39.3	79.6	25.6	32.3
Kiribati	76.1	86.1	56.3	71.5	–	–
Marshall Islands	35.4	66.3	34.1	66.1	–	–

Continued

Table 6.1 Continued

	Adult (15+) labor force participation rate (%)				*Women's share of the adult labor force (%)*	
	1990		*2010*		*1990*	*2010*
	Women	*Men*	*Women*	*Men*		
Micronesia, Fed. States of	30.1	56.8	50.1	67.2	–	–
Palau	59.5	77.2	59.7	76.9	–	–
Papua New Guinea	70.9	73.9	70.6	74.1	48.0	48.3
Samoa	39.8	76.5	42.9	78.2	32.1	34.3
Solomon Islands	52.8	77.1	53.1	79.9	39.1	38.4
Timor-Leste	40.7	78.6	38.4	74.4	33.0	33.2
Tonga	35.9	75.5	53.6	75.2	31.3	42.9
Vanuatu	78.6	88.1	61.3	79.7	46.4	42.9
Developing Asia	**56.1**	**84.1**	**51.1**	**80.6**	**38.9**	**38.1**
Developed member economies	**50.4**	**77.1**	**51.1**	**72.1**	**40.8**	**42.9**
Australia	52.2	75.7	58.7	72.5	41.3	45.3
Japan	50.1	77.4	49.5	72.0	40.7	42.4
New Zealand	53.5	74.3	61.5	74.2	43.2	46.8

Notes

1 Regional averages are population-weighted averages.

2 Data for Nauru and Tuvalu are not available.

3 Data for the Cook Islands, Kiribati, Marshall Islands, the Federated States of Micronesia, and Palau are for the closest year available.

Sources: ADB. 2011. *Key Indicators for Asia and the Pacific 2011*. Manila; International Labour Organization (ILO). 2011. *Key Indicators of the Labour Market*. Seventh Edition. Geneva; and Directorate-General of Budget, Accounting and Statistics. 2012. *Statistical Yearbook*. Taipei,China.

the labor force is fairly high in the lower-income economies, drops noticeably in many middle-income countries, and then rises again in higher-income economies. For example, women's share of the labor force is relatively high, close to 50%, in Nepal, Cambodia, the Lao People's Democratic Republic, Myanmar, Viet Nam, and Papua New Guinea (lower-income economies). Women constitute closer to 30–40% of the labor force in many of the middle-income economies, and then this share rises back up to an average of 43% for the developed member economies (Australia, Japan, and New Zealand). All regions except for South Asia and Southeast Asia saw an average increase in women's representation in the labor force between 1990 and 2010.

The relationship between economic development and women's participation in the formal labor market exhibits a fairly predictable and well-documented relationship. In countries that still have relatively large agriculture sectors and an emphasis on household farm production, the female labor force participation rate is often quite high. In such economies, the distinction between paid work and home production is blurred, pushing up the number of women who are considered economically active. Women in these economies often play the primary role in collecting and managing water and firewood, and in developing and maintaining the land. When countries begin to industrialize, female labor force participation rates fall as the household farm model becomes less common and more women engage exclusively in nonmarket activities such as childcare and housework.

This drop in women's labor force participation as per capita income increases can thus be viewed as a substitution effect, in which production moves away from the household and small farms toward market-based activity, and as an income effect, in which women can afford to stay at home (Goldin 1994). In more advanced economies, the substitution effect outweighs the income effect, and female participation rates begin to rise again as growing numbers of women engage in market-based economic activity, often in combination with raising children. This trend in women's labor force participation rates as countries industrialize generates a U-shaped function that fits time-series and cross-sectional data for a number of countries at different stages of development.[7]

The pattern across countries in Asia and the Pacific in Panel A of Figure 6.1 is consistent with this U-shaped relationship between economic development and women's participation in the labor market. The figure shows a scatterplot of women's labor force participation rates across countries in Asia and the Pacific in 2010 against real per capita gross domestic product (GDP) in 2010 (adjusted by purchasing power parity [PPP] indices in constant 2005 international dollars), fitted with a quadratic function. This quadratic function readily shows the U-shaped relationship between current female labor force participation rates and real GDP per capita across Asian economies.[8] This U-shaped relationship stands in contrast to the downward-sloping relationship for men, as depicted in Panel B. Some of the main explanations given for the decrease in men's labor force participation with increasing income across countries and over time include earlier retirement for men who are still of working age, as well as younger men in the working-age population staying in school longer.

These arguments about gender differences in labor force participation rates are supported not only with data across economies, but also time-series data for individual economies. For example, evidence on labor force participation rates constructed from the Manpower Utilization Survey for Taipei,China indicates a sharp increase in women's labor force participation rates from 1978 to 2010 (Figure 6.2, Panel A), while men have exhibited a steady decline in labor force participation. The labor force participation rate for all women in Taipei,China rose from 42% in 1978 to 55% in 2010. Strong increases in participation of young women drove the aggregate upward trend. In fact, by 2006, the labor force participation rate for young women (75.4%) even surpassed the average rate for men

---

[7] This U-shaped hypothesis for the relationship between women's labor force participation rates and national income is supported with evidence in Goldin (1994) and Mammen and Paxson (2000).

[8] Afghanistan, an extreme outlier due to conflict and the Taliban's oppression of women, had to be dropped from the scatterplot analysis in order to generate the U-shaped relationship. This U-shaped relationship is robust to using current gross national income per capita in US dollars instead of PPP-adjusted GDP per capita in constant 2005 US dollars.

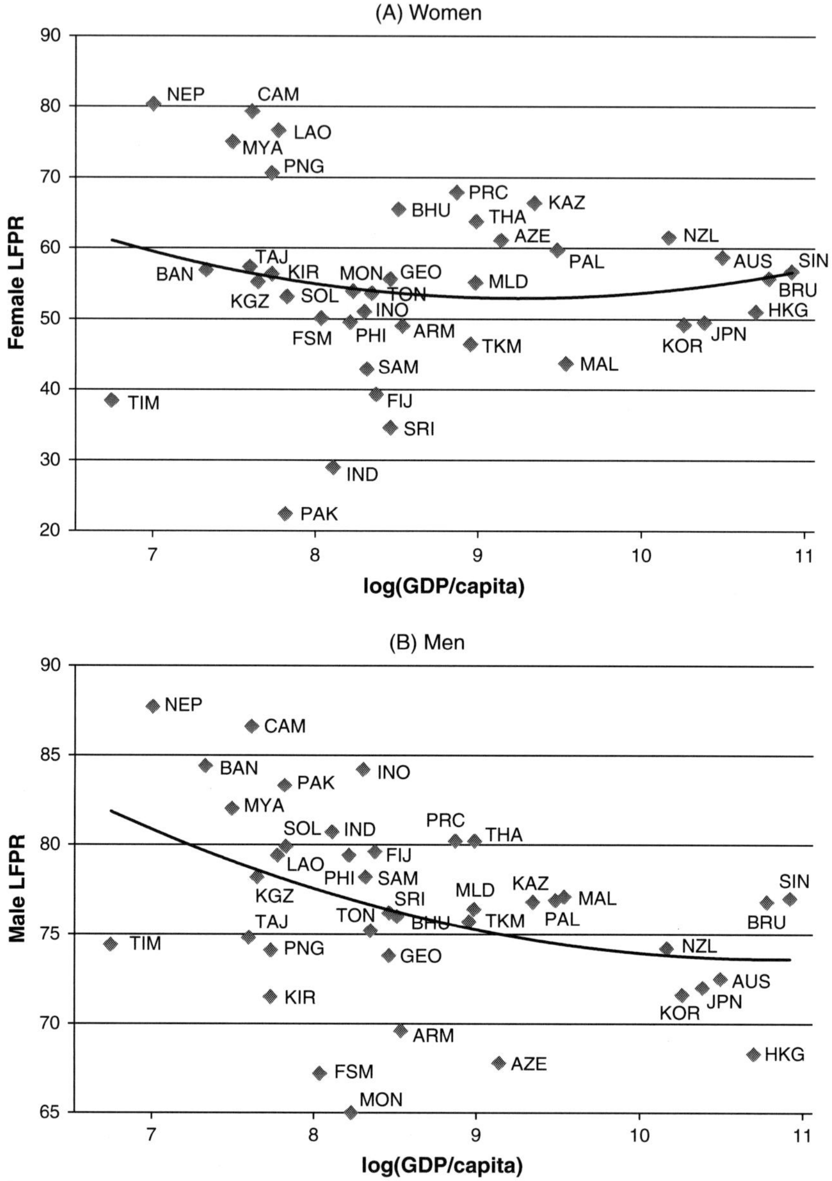

Figure 6.1 Labor force participation rates (LFPR) and per capita gross domestic product in Asia, 2010.

Figure 6.1 Continued

ARM = Armenia; AUS = Australia; AZE = Azerbaijan; BAN = Bangladesh; BHU = Bhutan; BRU = Brunei Darussalam; CAM = Cambodia; FSM = Federated States of Micronesia; GDP = gross domestic product; GEO = Georgia; HKG = Hong Kong, China; IND = India; INO = Indonesia; JPN = Japan; KAZ = Kazakhstan; KGZ = Kyrgyz Republic; KIR = Kiribati; KOR = Republic of Korea; LAO = Lao People's Democratic Republic; LFPR = labor force participation rate; MAL = Malaysia; MON = Mongolia; MYA = Myanmar; NZL = New Zealand; PAK = Pakistan; PAL = Palau; PHI = Philippines; PNG = Papua New Guinea; PRC = People's Republic of China; SAM = Samoa; SIN = Singapore; SOL = Solomon Islands; SRI = Sri Lanka; TAJ = Tajikistan; THA = Thailand; TIM = Timor-Leste; TKM = Turkmenistan; TON = Tonga.

Notes

1 All data are for 2010 or the closest year available.
2 GDP per capita in 2005 purchasing power parity dollars.

Sources: LFPR from International Labour Organization (ILO). 2011. *Key Indicators of the Labour Market*. Seventh Edition, Geneva (accessed 19 March 2012); and per capita GDP from World Development Indicators, http://data.worldbank.org/data-catalog/world-development-indicators (accessed 19 March 2012).

(73.9%). Additional increases for mid-career women further boosted the average increase for all women. In contrast, men's labor force participation remained fairly stagnant through the mid-1990s and then dropped steadily, from 79% in 1995 to 73% by 2010.

Changes in the age structure of labor force participation between 1980 and 2010 show a dramatic rise for women of all ages past the age of 22, with the largest gains occurring for women in their childbearing years (Figure 6.2, Panel B). Another noticeable change during this 30-year period is that while women in their 20s had declining labor force participation rates in 1980, this pattern reversed itself, and in 2010, women in their early to mid-20s were experiencing a surge in labor force participation. This general argument about the increase in women's labor force participation is also shown in a pseudo-cohort analysis tracking age cohorts over time as they age (Figure 6.3). In contrast, men at every age showed a drop in labor force participation between 1980 and 2010, with steeper drops at both tails of the age distribution. This conclusion also holds in the cohort analysis in Figure 6.3, which shows that the pseudo-cohorts follow roughly the same declining path. This pattern suggests that, for men at least, the pattern of the falling aggregate labor force participation rate is being driven by changes in the demographic structure.

Despite the closing gap between women and men in labor force participation rates across Asia, disparities in the labor market remain, especially in terms of earnings and the types of jobs in which women and men are employed. There is extensive evidence of persistent earnings gaps across developing and industrialized countries around the world, including in Asia and the Pacific (World Bank 2011). Gender pay gaps occur in both the public and private sectors and in the formal and informal sectors, where women disproportionately do piecework and casual work. A narrowing in the education gap between men and women in many countries has contributed to smaller gender pay gaps over time, but differentials

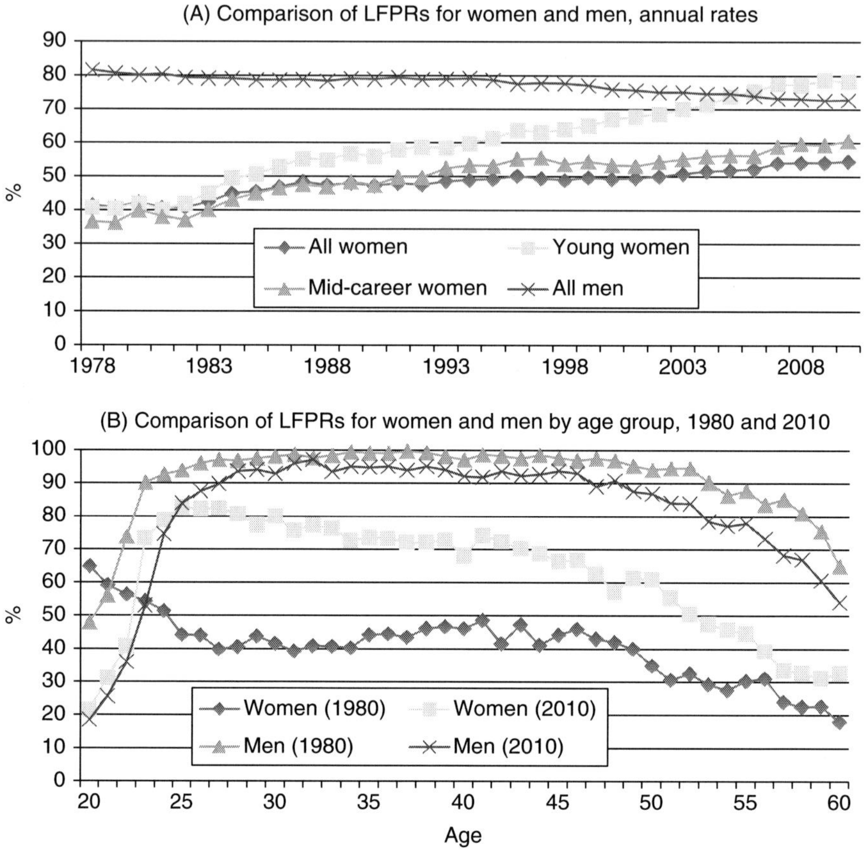

Figure 6.2 Labor force participation rates in Taipei,China, 1978–2010.

LFPR = labor force participation rate.

Source: Authors' estimates using data from Taipei,China's Manpower Utilization Surveys.

remain substantial, especially in countries such as India and the Republic of Korea, noted for long-term discrepancies.

As an example of an Asian economy that has made substantial progress in narrowing the gender earnings ratio, Taipei,China has exhibited a steady increase in women's relative earnings since the mid-1990s. As shown in Figure 6.4, the unadjusted female-to-male wage ratio remained fairly flat from 1978 to 1994, at about 64%, and then rose steadily to 78% in 2010. A similar conclusion regarding the post-1994 relative gain applies when controlling for observed productivity characteristics for women and men, including their hours worked, education, potential experience, region, occupation, and industry. In fact, once observable characteristics are factored in, the earnings differential between men and women

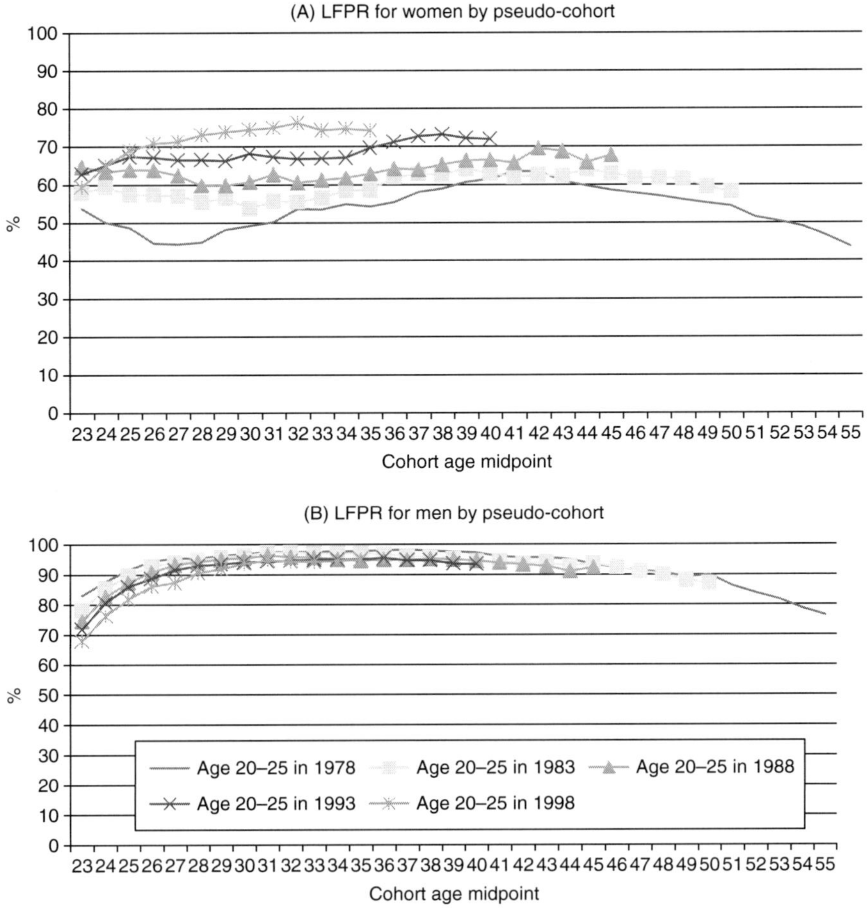

Figure 6.3 Pseudo-cohort analysis of labor force participation rates in Taipei,China, 1978–2010.

LFPR = labor force participation rate.

Source: Authors' estimates using data from Taipei,China's Manpower Utilization Surveys.

becomes quite small. However, the adjusted earnings ratios (with and without the controls for occupation and industry) showed a rather substantial decline in the earlier years as compared with the unadjusted ratio, suggesting that unobservable characteristics and potentially labor-market discrimination played an increasingly important role before the mid-1990s in preventing women from achieving earnings equality.

Moreover, in the majority of countries for which there are data, women hold a disproportionate number of unpaid jobs. As shown in Figure 6.5, which reports the number of own-account workers and contributing family workers per 100 wage

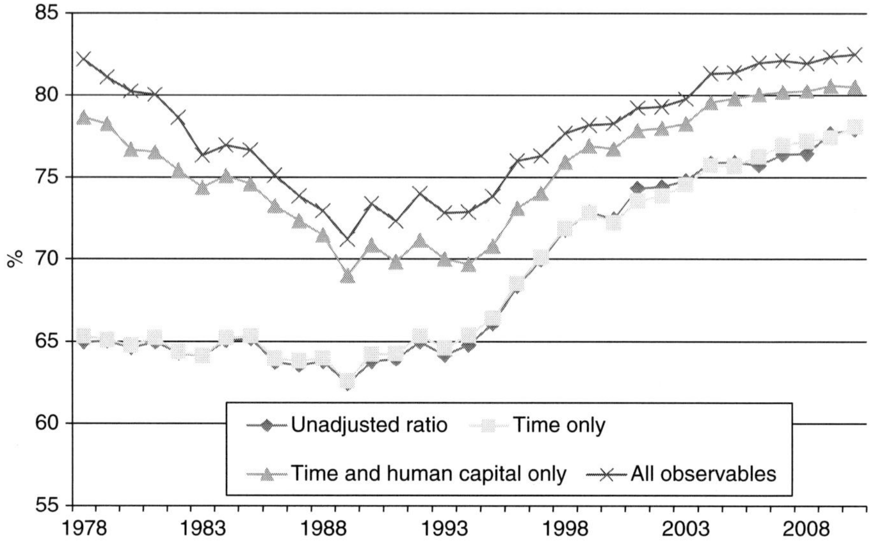

Figure 6.4 Female-to-male earnings ratio in Taipei,China, 1978–2010.

Source: Authors' estimates using data from Taipei,China's Manpower Utilization Surveys.

and salaried workers by gender, in most countries women have proportionately more jobs involving own-account work and unpaid family work compared with men. Because own-account workers and contributing family workers are mostly engaged in informal jobs without access to social protection, they are considered more vulnerable to poverty and hardship relative to wage and salaried workers. The overrepresentation of women in these vulnerable types of jobs is especially pronounced in Bhutan, Cambodia, Nepal, and Pakistan. Hence, this figure indicates that vulnerability to unstable compensation and insufficient access to decent employment are still gendered phenomena.

Drivers of women's labor force participation: micro-level evidence

Data and methodology

The analysis of micro-level drivers of women's labor force participation uses two different sources of data. The first source is repeated cross-sections of the Manpower Utilization Survey (MUS) from Taipei,China, an extremely rich household-survey database.[9] The surveys have collected information every year since 1978 on labor force status, monthly earnings, and weekly hours worked

[9] See http://eng.dgbas.gov.tw/mp.asp?mp=2

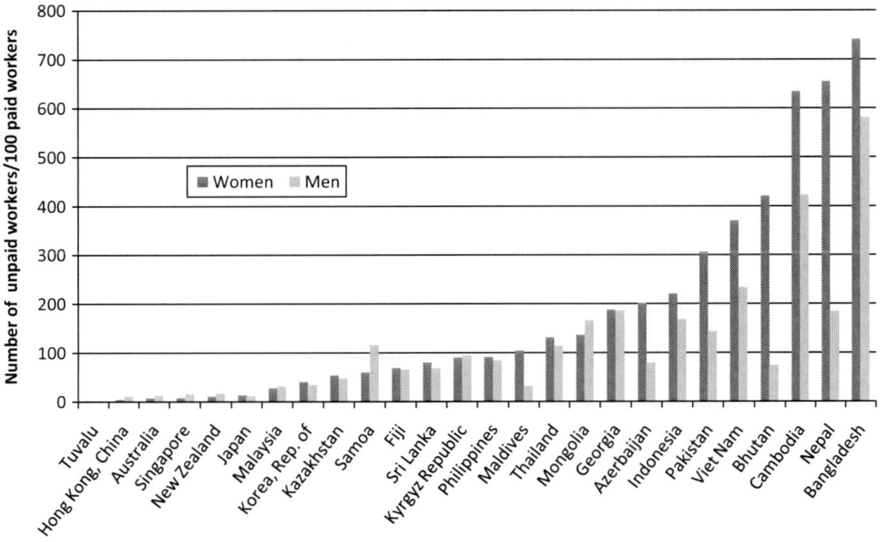

Figure 6.5 Own-account workers and unpaid family workers by gender, 2007.

Note: Data represent the number of own-account workers and contributing family workers per 100 wage and salaried workers in 2007 or the most recently available year.

Source: ADB. 2011. *Key Indicators for Asia and the Pacific 2011*. Manila.

in addition to the demographic characteristics of the respondents. Our sample consists of civilian women of working age (15–65) from 1978 to 2010. The sample contains an average 24,975 observations for each year.

Sample statistics for the MUS indicate that the average age is 36, with close to 40% of the sample working in urban areas. Almost two-thirds of the sample is married, and close to 20% of the women in the sample have preschool-aged children. About 40% of the women, almost all of whom are older, only have a primary school education, while almost 10% of the women have a college education or more. About 15% of the sample claims schoolwork as their primary activity, while another 40% claims housework as their primary activity. About 46% of the women are engaged in full-time or part-time employment.

The second source of data is the Demographic and Health Survey (DHS) data from nine Asian countries spanning the period 2005–2009. For each country, the DHS data provide a large nationally representative sample of women between the ages of 15 and 49 and the members of their households. Country selection for the case study's sample was determined by several criteria, including geographical coverage (South and Southeast Asia), the availability of a recent wave of DHS data (no earlier than 2005), and the availability of DHS Individual and Household Member Recodes. These selection criteria resulted in a nine-country sample covering 2005–2009: Bangladesh (2007), India (2005–2006), the Maldives

(2009), Nepal (2006), and Pakistan (2006–2007) in South Asia; and Cambodia (2005), Indonesia (2007), the Philippines (2008), and Timor-Leste (2009) in Southeast Asia.[10] The sample for each country consists of women respondents between the ages of 15 and 49, with sample sizes ranging from 7,131 women in the Maldives to 124,385 in India.

In accordance with the way in which the DHS coded responses to the employment question, employment status is categorized as whether or not the woman is currently employed. Note that the main potential weakness in using the DHS to examine women's labor force participation is that employment may be measured with more error compared with a labor force survey because the survey question simply asks the woman if she is currently employed. Moreover, if a woman was officially unemployed, she would be considered as not employed according to the DHS, while she would still be considered part of the labor force according to a labor force survey. Counteracting this potential weakness are various advantages that come with the DHS, including the ability to do comparable regressions across different countries as well as the extensive information on women's productivity characteristics, household composition, socioeconomic status, and household wealth that is not contained in most labor force surveys.

Sample means indicate that as many as 64–71% of all women (in Cambodia and Nepal) reported that they were currently employed. In contrast, as few as 26–32% of women (in Pakistan and Bangladesh) reported that they were currently employed, with the remaining countries falling in between these extremes. The low percentages of women currently employed in Bangladesh and Pakistan partly reflect long-standing social norms that place a heavier premium on men's capacity to generate earnings in the labor market as compared with women's capacity to generate an income. In contrast, the very high percentages of women who are currently employed in Cambodia and Nepal partly reflect the necessity of women's labor input to support the household in these low-income economies, together with less restrictive social norms, especially in Cambodia, regarding women's employment. Both countries have histories of civil war and violent conflict, which have contributed to pressure on women to support their households by becoming employed.

Other indicators related to women's employment include dummy variables for women working in agriculture and for the type of compensation (unpaid, cash only, in-kind only, or cash and in-kind). Among employed women, the region exhibits substantial variation across countries in terms of women's primary occupations. While almost 90% of women in Nepal hold agricultural jobs, just 4% of women in the Maldives work in agriculture, and in the remainder of the countries, the figure is dispersed fairly evenly across the distribution. Also among employed women, countries exhibit much variation in terms of the extent to which women work for pay. While the vast majority of women in Timor-Leste are unpaid workers (mostly in household enterprises), about three-quarters or more

[10] Access to all DHS data sets used in this case study comes from http://www.measuredhs.com/

of women workers in Bangladesh, the Maldives, Pakistan, and the Philippines work for cash only. Among the relatively lower-income economies, Cambodia and Nepal have high percentages of women who work for in-kind reimbursement. The independent variables of the analysis include various individual-level characteristics, different dimensions of socioeconomic status, and household composition. Because the DHS data do not include information on income and wages, these direct measures of household economic status cannot be included. Rather, alternative measures based on household assets, amenities, and relative wealth are employed to represent household socioeconomic status.

The MUS data and the DHS samples for the nine Asian countries are used to estimate the likelihood of a woman engaging in employment, conditional on the full set of personal and household characteristics. The empirical strategy estimates a standard labor supply equation for women in each country of the following form:

$$y_i = a + bX_i + \theta_i \tag{6.1}$$

The dependent variable y_i is a dummy that takes on the value 1 if each woman, i, is employed, and 0 otherwise. The notation X_i is the set of individual and household characteristics that influence women's decisions to be employed, and θ_i is a woman-specific idiosyncratic error term. Given the binary nature of the dependent variable, a probit model is used to estimate the labor supply function for each country, with probit coefficients converted into marginal probabilities following standard computations. Tolerance statistics are estimated to test for the presence of multicollinearity among the full set of independent variables.

Results over time using the Manpower Utilization Survey for Taipei,China

Table 6.2 reports regression results for the drivers of women's employment decisions in Taipei,China from 1978 to 2010. Results are reported for a selected number of years for the sake of brevity, but other years are consistent with those shown in the table.

In general, women with more education are more likely to be employed compared with women with just a primary school education or less, although there are some exceptions. For example, by 2010, women with college educations in technical fields were 26% more likely to be employed compared with women with primary school and below, and this likelihood is just slightly lower for women with a college education in commercial and other fields. These probabilities for college-educated women to be employed have risen substantially since the late 1970s and early 1980s, when college-educated women were no more likely and possibly even less likely than women with little education to engage in employment. A similar pattern emerges for women with a vocational school and junior college education. Women with just a middle school or high school education, however, for most of the period, have been less likely or just as likely to be employed compared with less educated women.

Table 6.2 Marginal probabilities and standard errors of women's employment determinants in Taipei,China, 1978–2010

	1978	*1983*	*1988*	*1993*	*1998*	*2003*	*2010*
Educational attainment (reference: primary school and below)							
Middle school	−0.028*	−0.028*	0.008	−0.044**	0.042**	0.019	0.031
	(0.017)	(0.016)	(0.017)	(0.018)	(0.021)	(0.021)	(0.021)
High school	−0.087***	−0.100***	−0.056**	−0.050**	−0.023	0.022	0.045*
	(0.026)	(0.023)	(0.024)	(0.024)	(0.026)	(0.026)	(0.024)
Vocational technical	0.018	−0.021	0.022	0.009	0.059	0.115***	0.147***
	(0.057)	(0.041)	(0.035)	(0.035)	(0.038)	(0.037)	(0.038)
Vocational commerce	0.037	−0.001	0.038**	0.021	0.067***	0.080***	0.103***
	(0.023)	(0.018)	(0.019)	(0.019)	(0.022)	(0.022)	(0.022)
Vocational other	−0.112	−0.068	0.034	−0.001	0.098**	0.152***	0.152***
	(0.084)	(0.062)	(0.055)	(0.049)	(0.044)	(0.040)	(0.040)
Junior college technical	−0.132	−0.027	0.043	0.016	0.118***	0.164***	0.213***
	(0.091)	(0.063)	(0.051)	(0.044)	(0.042)	(0.038)	(0.041)
Junior college commerce	0.095*	−0.082**	0.018	0.015	0.109***	0.171***	0.138***
	(0.053)	(0.037)	(0.037)	(0.034)	(0.032)	(0.029)	(0.030)
Junior college other	0.009	−0.065	−0.030	0.026	0.078	0.081*	0.058
	(0.061)	(0.049)	(0.047)	(0.050)	(0.053)	(0.048)	(0.049)
College technical	0.046	−0.185**	−0.019	0.069	0.049	0.138***	0.259***
	(0.098)	(0.073)	(0.071)	(0.068)	(0.060)	(0.042)	(0.035)
College commerce	−0.013	−0.056	0.065	0.046	0.111***	0.126***	0.226***
	(0.068)	(0.058)	(0.052)	(0.050)	(0.042)	(0.033)	(0.027)
College other	0.086***	−0.023	−0.111***	0.023	0.130***	0.114***	0.193***
	(0.051)	(0.044)	(0.041)	(0.041)	(0.040)	(0.032)	(0.028)

Table 6.2 Continued

	1978	*1983*	*1988*	*1993*	*1998*	*2003*	*2010*
Age	0.037***	0.042***	0.041***	0.041***	0.044***	0.045***	0.050***
	(0.003)	(0.003)	(0.003)	(0.003)	(0.003)	(0.003)	(0.004)
$Age^2/100$	−0.056***	−0.064***	−0.060***	−0.060***	−0.065***	−0.065***	−0.074***
	(0.004)	(0.004)	(0.004)	(0.004)	(0.004)	(0.004)	(0.004)
Regional location (reference: North)							
Central	0.129***	0.094***	0.019	0.061***	−0.018	0.009	0.033**
	(0.013)	(0.013)	(0.014)	(0.014)	(0.016)	(0.016)	(0.015)
South	0.095***	0.015	0.002	0.046***	−0.024	−0.026*	−0.037***
	(0.012)	(0.012)	(0.012)	(0.013)	(0.015)	(0.014)	(0.014)
East	0.274***	0.136***	0.150***	0.264***	0.052	0.080***	−0.016
	(0.026)	(0.028)	(0.030)	(0.027)	(0.032)	(0.031)	(0.029)
Lives in urban area	−0.070***	−0.016	−0.020*	0.049***	0.054***	0.048***	0.064***
	(0.011)	(0.011)	(0.012)	(0.012)	(0.014)	(0.013)	(0.013)
Major activity is school	−1.396***	−1.308***	−1.489***	−1.423***	−1.505***	−1.356***	−1.269***
	(0.027)	(0.024)	(0.028)	(0.026)	(0.031)	(0.027)	(0.027)
Major activity is housework	−1.044***	−1.188***	−1.261***	−1.321***	−1.460***	−1.463***	−1.452***
	(0.014)	(0.015)	(0.013)	(0.014)	(0.016)	(0.016)	(0.018)
Married	−0.019	0.115***	0.078***	0.115***	0.233***	0.246***	0.246***
	(0.017)	(0.018)	(0.018)	(0.018)	(0.019)	(0.017)	(0.015)
Has preschool child	−0.104***	−0.125***	−0.097***	−0.120***	−0.128***	−0.090***	−0.160***
	(0.014)	(0.014)	(0.015)	(0.017)	(0.020)	(0.022)	−(0.025)
Pseudo R^2	0.576	0.649	0.709	0.735	0.799	0.776	0.736
Wald χ^2	16,335***	21,515***	26,090***	26,338***	29,079***	27,714***	24,265***
Sample size	20,875	24,308	26,595	25,856	26,269	25,777	23,938

Note: Standard errors (shown in parentheses) and significance levels are calculated from the marginal probabilities of a probit regression for each year. * $p < 0.10$, ** $p < 0.05$, *** $p < 0.01$.

Source: Authors' estimates.

Other substantive predictors of women's employment decisions include their age; namely, as women become older, they are more likely to be engaged in employment. Not surprisingly, women who responded that housework and schoolwork are their primary activities are substantially less likely to engage in any kind of employment, not even part-time employment. In contrast, for most of the period, married women have shown a greater probability of engaging in employment compared with their single counterparts. This result contrasts noticeably with those in Table 6.3 for the nine lower-income Asian countries, where married women are less likely to be employed. Finally, having at least one preschool-aged child in the house serves as a major disincentive for employment. In 2010, women with a preschool-aged child at home were 16% less likely to be employed compared with women with no young children. This disincentive to join the labor force when there is a young child at home has actually increased over time.

Cross-country results using the Demographic Health Survey

Table 6.3 reports regression results for individual and household-level drivers of women's employment decisions for the nine Asian countries in the sample. As shown in the table, household wealth is strongly associated with women's employment decisions, but the direction of this effect varies across countries. In Bangladesh, India, Indonesia, Nepal, Pakistan, and Timor-Leste, women from wealthier households are substantially less likely to be employed as compared with those from the lowest wealth households. This finding supports the assertion that in these six sample countries, economic necessity is pushing women from low-wealth households to engage in market-based work, so lower socioeconomic status appears to be an important push factor behind women's employment decisions. Note also that this effect becomes stronger (more negative) for higher wealth-quintile households.

In contrast, women from wealthier households are more likely to be employed as compared with women from the poorest households in Cambodia, the Maldives, and the Philippines. At least for the Maldives and the Philippines, this result is likely due to the fact that these two economies are more developed compared with the rest of the sample, and low socioeconomic status among households does not play as strong a role in pushing women to be employed. For Cambodia, the most likely reason that the household wealth variables are not exhibiting the expected negative coefficients is that other variables related to income are capturing the income effect. In particular, women with more education, with access to safe water, and in urban areas – each an indicator of higher socioeconomic status – are substantially less likely to be employed when compared with their counterparts with less education, with no access to safe water, and in rural households.

This argument that education is capturing socioeconomic status effects also holds for most of the other lower-income Asian economies in the sample, with more education being associated with lower probabilities of employment in six of the nine economies. In particular, women with at least a secondary school education are substantially less likely to be employed when compared with women

Table 6.3 Marginal probabilities and standard errors of women's employment determinants in South Asia and Southeast Asia, 2005–2009

	BAN	*CAM*	*IND*	*INO*	*MLD*	*NEP*	*PAK*	*PHI*	*TIM*
Women's characteristics									
Age (linear)	0.004***	0.009***	0.008***	0.010***	0.006***	0.011***	0.003***	0.016***	0.013***
	(0.001)	(0.001)	(0)	(0.001)	(0.001)	(0.001)	(0.001)	(0.001)	(0.001)
Married	−0.192***	−0.055***	−0.140***	−0.102***	−0.156***	−0.018	−0.138***	−0.005	−0.044***
	(0.024)	(0.012)	(0.006)	(0.022)	(0.027)	(0.015)	(0.03)	(0.013)	(0.014)
Educational attainment (reference: no schooling)									
Primary school	−0.043***	0.038***	−0.066***	−0.100***	−0.026	0.041**	−0.043***	0.033	0
	(0.013)	(0.012)	(0.006)	(0.02)	(0.021)	(0.016)	(0.016)	(0.038)	(0.014)
Secondary or higher	−0.071***	−0.031*	−0.132***	−0.111***	0.128***	−0.037*	0.068***	0.015	−0.089***
	(0.016)	(0.016)	(0.006)	(0.022)	(0.028)	(0.021)	(0.019)	(0.038)	(0.016)
Source of information									
Reads newspaper	0.033*	−0.009	0.017***	0.013	0.099***	0.009	..	0.042***	−0.002
	(0.019)	(0.012)	(0.006)	(0.011)	(0.014)	(0.018)	..	(0.011)	(0.014)
Watches television	0.013	0.030**	0.007	−0.021	−0.003	0.034**	..	0.005	0.059***
	(0.013)	(0.012)	(0.005)	(0.018)	(0.052)	(0.017)	..	(0.021)	(0.014)
Listens to radio	0.044***	0.007	0.002	0.029***	−0.006	0.123***	..	0.022*	0.048***
	(0.014)	(0.011)	(0.004)	(0.01)	(0.022)	(0.022)	..	(0.013)	(0.013)

Table 6.3 Continued

	BAN	*CAM*	*IND*	*INO*	*MLD*	*NEP*	*PAK*	*PHI*	*TIM*
Household economic characteristics									
Household wealth index (reference: 1st quintile)									
2nd quintile	−0.021	0.001	−0.042***	−0.017	−0.009	−0.130***	−0.073***	0.015	−0.050***
	(0.017)	(0.015)	(0.007)	(0.015)	(0.019)	(0.024)	(0.016)	(0.019)	(0.016)
3rd quintile	−0.102***	0.029*	−0.104***	−0.028*	−0.031	−0.209***	−0.113***	−0.007	−0.042**
	(0.017)	(0.015)	(0.007)	(0.016)	(0.019)	(0.026)	(0.015)	(0.021)	(0.017)
4th quintile	−0.120***	0.034**	−0.206***	−0.063***	0.032	−0.275***	−0.186***	0.038*	−0.082***
	(0.02)	(0.017)	(0.007)	(0.018)	(0.026)	(0.029)	(0.014)	(0.022)	(0.018)
5th (richest) quintile	−0.216***	−0.006	−0.294***	−0.027	0.100**	−0.439***	−0.248***	0.115***	−0.050**
	(0.02)	(0.025)	(0.007)	(0.019)	(0.042)	(0.03)	(0.014)	(0.023)	(0.025)
Owns land	0.022*	0.011	0.018***	..	..	0.100***	−0.019	..	0.070***
	(0.012)	(0.013)	(0.004)	..	..	(0.015)	(0.012)	..	(0.017)
Has electricity	0.062***	0.061***	0.127***	−0.042***	0.068	0	−0.014	−0.003	−0.069***
	(0.016)	(0.019)	(0.005)	(0.015)	(0.059)	(0.015)	(0.018)	(0.019)	(0.015)
Has access to safe water	−0.02	−0.050***	0.079***	−0.053***	0.031**	0.032*	−0.045**	−0.019*	−0.057***
	(0.021)	(0.011)	(0.005)	(0.016)	(0.016)	(0.018)	(0.021)	(0.011)	(0.015)
Geographical region (reference: rural)									
Capital city	0.009	−0.027	−0.017**	−0.101***	−0.131***	0.075**	0.02	0.012	−0.063***
	(0.02)	(0.022)	(0.007)	(0.018)	(0.031)	(0.029)	(0.021)	(0.017)	(0.022)
Other urban area	0.051***	−0.049***	−0.063***	−0.059***	..	−0.055***	−0.029*	0.027**	−0.017
	(0.016)	(0.015)	(0.006)	(0.011)	..	(0.018)	(0.016)	(0.012)	(0.014)

Table 6.3 Continued

	BAN	*CAM*	*IND*	*INO*	*MLD*	*NEP*	*PAK*	*PHI*	*TIM*
Household composition									
Number of children (linear)									
< 5 yrs old	−0.047***	−0.034***	−0.037***	−0.095***	−0.029***	−0.027***	−0.014***	−0.046***	−0.018***
	(0.007)	(0.007)	(0.003)	(0.007)	(0.009)	(0.007)	(0.005)	(0.006)	(0.006)
5–12 yrs old	0.010*	0.003	0.009***	−0.006	0.002	0.008**	−0.002	0.005	−0.019***
	(0.005)	(0.004)	(0.002)	(0.005)	(0.007)	(0.004)	(0.004)	(0.005)	(0.004)
13–17 yrs old	−0.029***	−0.038***	−0.022***	−0.003	0.003	−0.016**	−0.002	−0.031***	−0.019***
	(0.007)	(0.006)	(0.003)	(0.007)	(0.008)	(0.007)	(0.005)	(0.006)	(0.006)
Has 3 or more adults	−0.064***	0.034***	−0.034***	−0.008	−0.026	0.003	−0.003	0.031***	−0.003
	(0.012)	(0.01)	(0.004)	(0.009)	(0.019)	(0.013)	(0.012)	(0.011)	(0.011)
Female-headed household	0.005	−0.023	0.024***	0.071**	−0.009	−0.014	0.01	0.073***	0.118***
	(0.021)	(0.018)	(0.009)	(0.028)	(0.021)	(0.018)	(0.024)	(0.024)	(0.031)
Pseudo R^2	0.099	0.04	0.092	0.057	0.032	0.16	0.06	0.091	0.087
Wald χ^2	882***	559***	7,367***	997***	200***	1,086***	455***	1,314***	1,131***
Sample size	10,996	16,823	124,385	32,895	7,131	10,793	9,999	13,594	13,137

BAN = Bangladesh; CAM = Cambodia; IND = India; INO = Indonesia; MLD = Maldives; NEP = Nepal; PAK = Pakistan; PHI = Philippines; TIM = Timor-Leste; yrs = years.

Notes

1 Weighted to national levels with weights provided by the Demographic and Health Survey.

2 Clustered standard errors (shown in parentheses) and significance levels are calculated from the marginal probabilities of a probit regression for each country.

3 $^{*}p < 0.10$, $^{**}p < 0.05$, $^{***}p < 0.01$.

4 Regressions include the survey month to control for seasonality.

5 The notation .. denotes that this question was not answered by respondents for that particular country; in the case of the Maldives, the variables other urban and capital city were combined.

Source: Authors' estimates.

with no schooling in Bangladesh, Cambodia, India, Indonesia, Nepal, and Timor-Leste. In contrast, women in the Maldives and Pakistan who have secondary schooling or beyond are more likely to be employed. For the Maldives, the most likely explanation again is that the country is more economically developed compared with the rest of the sample, and low socioeconomic status, as measured in this case by lack of schooling, does not play as strong a role in pushing women to be employed. For Pakistan, the result could be specific to Pakistani social norms of discouraging higher education for most women, so those women who do have more schooling are pulled into the labor market.

Estimation results also indicate that being married and having young children serve as strong drivers of women's employment decisions. In every country, married women are less likely to be employed when compared with their single counterparts, and this relationship is statistically significant and fairly large in seven of the nine economies (the exceptions being Nepal and the Philippines). Moreover, across all countries, having very young children reduces women's employment. In particular, having one additional child in the home under the age of 5 reduces the probability that a woman is currently employed by anywhere from 1% in Pakistan to 10% in Indonesia, with an average of about a 4% decline across the region. However, that effect tends to fade as children get older, and in three of the nine countries, women with children between the ages of 5 and 12 are significantly more likely to be employed. In contrast, having older children between the ages of 13 and 17 again reduces the likelihood of a woman being employed. One potential explanation is a longer-term intermittency effect, as women with older children who have stayed out of the labor market for a while experience a decline in skills. Another explanation is that these older children are contributing to household income and reducing the economic need for their mothers to engage in the labor market. Overall, these results point to the importance of policy actions that support women's roles as caregivers of young children at the same time that they are employed in market-based activities.

Conclusions and policy implications

A better understanding of drivers of women's labor force participation can contribute to more effective policy responses that will promote women's status in the labor market, which in turn can lead to long-term benefits for individuals and for society as a whole. Comprehensive and up-to-date statistical evidence on the determinants of women's employment is particularly important given the heavy weight in international policy dialogues that is placed on generating employment opportunities for women. As argued in this chapter, GDP growth has the potential to minimize the wedges and facilitate progress toward gender equality. Yet there is a strong rationale for policy reforms that alleviate the constraints that women face, especially those related to heavy time burdens devoted to unpaid work, regulations that favor men, inadequate public infrastructure, lack of credit, insufficient access to agricultural inputs, discriminatory practices in the labor market, and traditional social norms.

Results from this study support the implementation and enforcement of a number of policy interventions. Of particular importance is a transformative approach that boosts the remunerative value and security of women's jobs, improves the compatibility of women's market work with childcare, and promotes enabling policies so that women in the informal sector become less marginalized and more integrated in the labor market. Such enabling policies include providing women with greater access to credit, strengthening women's property rights, promoting skills development for women beyond gender stereotypes, improving the productivity of women farmers, and implementing gender-responsive social protection measures. The bottom line of most of these reforms and programs is that effective targeting can help tight budgets go a long way in improving societal well-being.

Boosting the value and security of women's jobs. Improving the pecuniary returns that women receive for their jobs in the form of higher wages, greater job security, and improved terms of employment will have a direct bearing on their employment decisions. Policy measures to achieve these goals are most commonly embedded in national labor standards that cover formal sector workers. In an effort to eliminate discrimination in employment and pay against women, most countries have adopted policies that promote equal treatment in the workplace. In particular, "equal pay for equal work" requires employers to provide equal pay for workers performing the same job with equal efficiency, regardless of gender. Moreover, governments have tackled occupational segregation through equal opportunity provisions that prohibit sex-based discrimination in hiring, training, promotion, and firing. Enforcing antidiscrimination measures will provide women with more rewarding career opportunities, and it will also promote essential workforce training for meeting macroeconomic growth objectives.

Measures such as safe workplace conditions, overtime pay, and paid benefits, although potentially costly to implement, promote lower turnover rates, improve well-being for workers, and contribute to extended firm-specific tenure. These measures need to be provided to a broader range of workers by removing exemptions, promoting awareness of benefit availability, and strengthening enforcement efforts. That said, a high proportion of women work in low-paid or unpaid jobs that remain uncovered by national labor standards. In addition to enforcing labor standards in paid jobs that are supposedly covered by national labor laws, a related policy goal is to create more wage-employment and productive self-employment opportunities for women through policy reforms that incentivize opportunities to switch from low-paid work in marginally productive activities to more remunerative work in productive activities.

Improving compatibility of market work with childcare. Crucial to bolstering women's progress toward equality in the formal sector, maternity leave benefits allow women to keep their position with a particular employer while they take time off to care for a newborn.[11] In terms of labor market impacts, studies

[11] Parental leave policies have similar terms, except that new fathers are also eligible to use the benefits. In most countries, however, parental leave is predominantly taken up by women.

on maternity and parental leaves have generally found that these policies have a positive impact on women's employment, although not always statistically significant. For example, Zveglich and Rodgers (2003) found that enforcement of maternity leave legislation in Taipei,China led to a 2.5-percentage-point increase in women's employment. This positive employment effect is interpreted as an indication that women value the financial benefits of paid leave and the opportunity to return to their previous employers after childbirth. Previous studies have generally found maternity benefits to have a negative wage effect, reflecting variations in such factors as mandated versus voluntary provision by firms, financing by national insurance, maternity leave duration, and the wage compensation rate. If public funding covers beneficiary payments, then wages will not decline as much, if at all. In addition to supporting women's efforts to remain and advance in the labor market, maternity benefits can contribute to the health of an infant by encouraging women in the labor force to spend more time at home following childbirth.[12]

In addition, public support of out-of-home childcare services helps to relieve the time and budgetary constraints that women experience. Public support of childcare also helps women to compete on a relatively more level playing field in the labor market, given that women's greater work burdens at home make it more difficult for them to maintain labor force attachment levels equal to those of men. Public support for early education programs also directly benefits those children who otherwise could be receiving inferior-quality care from alternative providers, as well as children who otherwise might have to accompany their mothers to work in unhealthy environments. Public support of childcare services also promotes higher levels of educational attainment among older children, especially girls, who otherwise might be pulled out of school to care for younger siblings.

Improving women's access to credit. A substantial proportion of women engage in self-employment in order to support themselves and their families. Self-employment commonly takes the form of a household enterprise, and women-operated household enterprises are often smaller in scale than those operated by men. Women's self-employment can entail an unstable income stream and less job security, and these jobs usually remain uncovered by formal labor regulations. An effective policy intervention in mitigating these risks and promoting more productive employment is the provision of small-scale loans that are mediated via rural banking reforms and microfinance initiatives. Such initiatives target individuals who have difficulty obtaining conventional loans through commercial banks, often due to a lack of collateral, and are left to rely on informal-sector money lenders and other expensive sources of credit. Providing women with increased access to credit serves as a viable means of incentivizing the shift from low-paid work in marginally productive activities to more remunerative work in productive activities. Both microfinance and rural banks have aided in reducing poverty by providing a diverse range of financial services to the poor and the

[12] For cross-country evidence, see Ferrarini and Norström (2010).

disenfranchised. Moreover, McKenzie's (2009) assessment of microenterprises and finance in developing countries concluded that additional policies designed to improve business training, provide business-development services, and facilitate shifts into more profitable sectors were most useful in enhancing the impact of credit on small business ventures.

In addition to better supporting viable household business ventures, dissemination of know-how on accounting and management practices would also serve as a useful mechanism for increasing the productivity of household businesses and for increasing their ability to generate employment. Public and nongovernment institutions can play key roles by providing subsidized loans that facilitate the purchase of new profit-enhancing technologies and by offering assistance for the marketing and sale of products created by women-run businesses. A good model is the Women Workers Employment and Entrepreneurship Development (WEED) program in the Philippines, which provides entrepreneurship training, skills development, and credit assistance to underemployed and home-based women workers, as well as women in the informal sector (Manasan 2009). Programs such as WEED can facilitate movement from low-paid work to work that is more remunerative.

Strengthening women's property rights. Improving women's control over assets, such as land, can also have powerful consequences for women's autonomy and the well-being of their families. The availability of collateral facilitates additional borrowing, which in turn gives households the capital required to finance home-based self-employment work. Such work is often the province of women in Asian developing-country households. In addition to facilitating greater access to credit, land rights can also affect households' economic decision making through increased security of land tenure. For example, Viet Nam's 1993 Land Law created a land market by giving households the power to exchange, lease, and mortgage their land use rights. Households increased their labor supply in nonfarm work as a consequence of the additional land rights, and because household borrowing did not exhibit much variation after the legal change, this outcome is attributed mainly to the additional security of land tenure rather than increased access to credit (Do and Iyer 2008).

In principle, women's land rights are positively associated with women's autonomy and empowerment, as embodied in their decision-making power, security, authority within the household, and respect from other family members. For example, women's land and home ownership are associated with a lower incidence of domestic violence in India (Panda and Agarwal 2005). Closely related, in rural Bangladesh, the value of assets that women bring into a marriage and the value of their current assets both have a positive impact on the portion of household expenditures allocated toward children's clothing and education (Quisumbing and de la Brière 2000). This effect is mediated primarily through the value of non-land assets, including livestock and durable goods. Finally, because additional income in the hands of women has been shown to have larger effects on expenditures on children when compared with male-controlled resources, women's land rights have the potential to affect child well-being. For example, Allendorf (2007) found that children in Nepal are less likely to be severely underweight if their mothers own land. This relationship is attributed primarily to the additional income and resources that women's ownership of land brings, rather than the empowering effect of land ownership.

Promoting skills development beyond gender stereotypes.[13] Gender-sensitive policies to promote skills development focus on both meeting current economic needs and building the capacity for meeting future development needs. Relevant polices focus on identifying and tackling gender norms that lead to the clustering of girls in what are considered appropriate fields. This clustering in turn constrains their employability. Such policies also include initiating mentoring programs in which women who have successfully broken the glass ceiling serve as mentors to younger women with less seniority in the labor market. Promoting skills development also includes improving the quality of education for both boys and girls. Although many Asian countries have successfully closed gender gaps in educational attainment, there are still imbalances in the quality of the education that young people are getting.

Moreover, depending on the types of activities in which women choose to engage, public support of vocational training can also be useful in preparing women for better-paying jobs. Closely related is the need for training programs, built around women's labor market intermittency due to childcare, to help promote their employability upon re-entry into the workforce. Women may also face more barriers than men when they first enter the labor market, thus providing a rationale for policies that facilitate the transition of women from school to their first job. Finally, to better reach women in the informal sector and in remote areas, specially designed training programs, such as those that are community-based or geographically mobile, can provide training opportunities to women who otherwise remain unreached by standard education and training initiatives.

Improving productivity of women farmers. Transformative policies supporting women's employment must also pay close attention to the needs of women farmers, especially given the relatively greater dependence of women in the poorest Asian economies on earning their livelihoods from agriculture. Most broadly, technological progress and investment in agriculture will help promote greater diversification and agricultural productivity. However, these and more targeted reforms need to address women's relatively limited access to assets, information, and training compared with their male counterparts.

A potential gain from more land titles and formal recognition of property rights for women is improved productivity of women farmers, with greater access to formal credit, extension services, and subsidized inputs acting as key channels. Greater access to these inputs in turn will help to lower women's cultivation costs and bring them closer to those of men, who often enjoy more state protection. Additional proposed reforms include integrated programs that enable women to group together and collectively buy land, as well as training in environmentally

[13] This policy discussion draws on recommendations in ILO and ADB (2011).

sound farming techniques. Specialized agricultural extension services that cater to small-scale farms will also help to reach more women, as will greater policy focus on nonfarm activities in rural areas conducted by small enterprises, such as cooperatives and other community-based organizations.

Implementing gender-responsive social protection measures. Asian governments have paid relatively limited attention to gendered vulnerabilities in their social protection policies (ILO and ADB 2011). Improvements in social protection that address gendered concerns include the establishment of a social floor consisting of universal healthcare access, income security for all children and the elderly, and social assistance to people living in poverty so as to save them from living in destitution. Of particular importance are social protection policies that support retired women and widows. Closely related are measures that extend the coverage of social protection to workers in the informal sector. Possible measures include promoting new micro-insurance and area-based schemes, and encouraging tax-based social benefits. Examples of such measures include India's Unorganized Sector Workers Social Security Bill 2005 and the more recent National Social Security Fund for informal sector workers. Strengthening the enforcement of occupational safety and health provisions and extending their reach into the informal sector will also go a long way toward reaching vulnerable female workers. More broadly, interventions that address gendered vulnerabilities need to be more transformative in that they promote economic and social equity and eliminate exclusion by creating more balanced power relations between women and men.

References

Allendorf, K. 2007. Do Women's Land Rights Promote Empowerment and Child Health in Nepal? *World Development.* 35 (11). pp. 1975–88.

Asian Development Bank (ADB). 2011. *Key Indicators for Asia and the Pacific 2011.* Manila.

Balakrishnan, R. ed. 2011. *The Hidden Assembly Line: Gender Dynamics of Subcontracted Work in a Global Economy.* Bloomfield, CN: Kumarian Press.

Barrientos, S., N. Kabeer, and N. Hossain. 2004. The Gender Dimensions of Globalization of Production. *ILO Working Paper* No. 17. Geneva: International Labour Organization.

Benería, L. 2007. Gender and the Social Construction of Markets. In I. van Staveren, D. Elson, C. Grown, and N. Çağatay, eds. *Feminist Economics of Trade.* London and New York: Routledge. pp. 13–32.

Berik, G. 2000. *Feminist Economics.* 6 (3). pp. 1–26.

Berik, G., Y. Rodgers, and J. Zveglich. 2004. International Trade and Gender Wage Discrimination: Evidence from East Asia. *Review of Development Economics.* 8 (2). pp. 237–54.

Berik, G., Y. Rodgers, and S. Seguino. 2009. Feminist Economics of Inequality, Development, and Growth. *Feminist Economics.* 15 (3). pp. 1–33.

Bhaumik, S. K. 2003. Casualisation of the Workforce in India, 1983–2002. *Indian Journal of Labour Economics.* 46 (4). pp. 907–26.

Black, S., and E. Brainerd. 2004. Importing Equality? The Impact of Globalization on Gender Discrimination. *Industrial and Labor Relations Review.* 57 (4). pp. 540–59.

Boschini, A. 2003. The Impact of Gender Stereotypes on Economic Growth. *Research Papers in Economics* 2003:4. Department of Economics, Stockholm University.

Busse, M., and P. Nunnenkamp. 2009. Gender Disparity in Education and the International Competition for Foreign Direct Investment. *Feminist Economics.* 15 (3). pp. 61–90.

Carr, M., M. A. Chen, and J. Tate. 2000. Globalization and Home-Based Workers. *Feminist Economics.* 6 (3). pp. 123–42.

Directorate-General of Budget, Accounting and Statistics. 2012. *Statistical Yearbook.* Taipei,China.

Do, Q.-T., and L. Iyer. 2008. Land Titling and Rural Transition in Viet Nam. *Economic Development and Cultural Change.* 56 (3). pp. 531–79.

Ferrarini, T., and T. Norström. 2010. Family Policy, Economic Development and Infant Mortality: A Longitudinal Comparative Analysis. *International Journal of Social Welfare.* 19 (S1). pp. S89–S102.

Forsythe, N., R. Korzeniewicz, and V. Durrant. 2000. Gender Inequalities and Economic Growth: A Longitudinal Evaluation. *Economic Development and Cultural Change.* 48 (3). pp. 573–617.

Goldin, C. 1994. The U-Shaped Female Labor Force Function in Economic Development and Economic History. *NBER Working Paper Series* No. 4707. Cambridge, MA: National Bureau of Economic Research.

International Labour Organization (ILO). 2011. *Key Indicators of the Labour Market.* Seventh Edition. Geneva.

International Labour Organization and Asian Development Bank (ADB). 2011. Women and Labour Markets in Asia: Rebalancing for Gender Equality. http://www.adb.org/documents/reports/women-labor-markets/women-labor-markets.pdf

Jhabvala, R., and S. Sinha. 2002. *Liberalization and the Woman Worker.* Ahmedabad, India: Self Employed Women's Association.

Kabeer, N. 2004. Globalization, Labor Standards, and Women's Rights: Dilemmas of Collective (In)action in an Interdependent World. *Feminist Economics.* 10 (1). pp. 3–35.

Klasen, S., and F. Lamanna. 2009. The Impact of Gender Inequality in Education and Employment on Economic Growth: New Evidence for a Panel of Countries. *Feminist Economics.* 15 (3). pp. 91–132.

Klasen, S., and C. Wink. 2003. "Missing Women": Revisiting the Debate. *Feminist Economics.* 9 (2–3). pp. 63–300.

McKenzie, D. 2009. Impact Assessments in Finance and Private Sector Development: What Have We Learned and What Should We Learn? *World Bank Policy Research Working Paper* No. 4944. Washington, DC: World Bank.

Mammen, K., and C. Paxson. 2000. Women's Work and Economic Development. *Journal of Economic Perspectives.* 14 (4). pp. 141–64.

Manasan, R. 2009. Reforming Social Protection Policy: Responding to the Global Financial Crisis and Beyond. *Philippine Institute for Development Studies (PIDS), Discussion Paper* No. 2009–22. Makati City, Philippines: PIDS.

Menon, N., and Y. Rodgers. 2009. International Trade and the Gender Wage Gap: New Evidence from India's Manufacturing Sector. *World Development.* 37 (5). pp. 965–81.

Munshi, K., and M. Rosenzweig. 2006. Traditional Institutions Meet the Modern World: Caste, Gender, and Schooling Choice in a Globalizing Economy. *American Economic Review.* 96 (4). pp. 1225–52.

Panda, P., and B. Agarwal. 2005. Marital Violence, Human Development and Women's Property Status in India. *World Development.* 33 (5). pp. 823–50.

Quisumbing, A., and B. de la Brière. 2000. Women's Assets and Intrahousehold Allocation in Rural Bangladesh: Testing Measures of Bargaining Power. *FCND Discussion Paper* No. 86. Washington, DC: International Food Policy Research Institute.

Samarasinghe, V. 1998. The Feminization of Foreign Currency Earnings: Women's Labor in Sri Lanka. *Journal of Developing Areas.* 32 (3). pp. 303–26.

Seguino, S. 2010. Gender, Distribution, and Balance of Payments Constrained Growth in Developing Countries. *Review of Political Economy.* 22 (3). pp. 373–404.

World Bank. 2011. *World Development Report 2012: Gender Equality and Development.* Washington, DC.

——. World Development Indicators. http://data.worldbank.org/data-catalog/world-development-indicators

Zveglich, J., and Y. Rodgers. 2003. The Impact of Protective Measures for Female Workers. *Journal of Labor Economics.* 21 (3). pp. 533–55.

7 Structural change and inequality

A conceptual overview with reference to developing Asia

Joshua Aizenman, Minsoo Lee, and Donghyun Park

Introduction

On a basic level, structural change refers to changes in the structure of the economy. The rise in the relative share of manufacturing is typically followed by a rise in the relative share of services as the manufacturing sector matures and the economy moves into a postindustrial phase. One Asia-wide structural change has been economic globalization, or growing integration into the global trade and financial systems. An indispensable core ingredient behind developing Asia's remarkable economic success has been the explosive growth of trade with the rest of the world and with other countries within the region. Equally important to the region's rapid growth has been the large inflows of foreign direct investment (FDI) and other foreign capital into the region. The region has now become a globally significant exporter of capital, and such capital outflows will benefit its growth. Another Asia-wide structural change is technological progress, which has steadily shifted the region's technological level toward the global technology frontier.

At a broader level, structural change encompasses social, political, cultural, societal, and other changes. Many countries in developing Asia, most notably the People's Republic of China (PRC) but also Mongolia, CLMV countries (Cambodia, Lao People's Democratic Republic, Myanmar, and Viet Nam), and former Soviet republics in Central Asia, are in the midst of a transition from centrally planned to market-oriented economies. While this transition clearly has far-reaching economic implications, it is much more than a narrow economic shift because it entails a drastic change in the relationship between the state and the citizens, and indeed in the mind-set and worldview of individuals. There has also been a gradual shift toward more open and pluralistic forms of government throughout the region. Family structure is also undergoing a major shift. Developing Asia is currently experiencing a seismic demographic transition, which will result in substantially older population age structures.

There is a great deal of interaction between different kinds of structural changes, both narrow and broad; therefore, it is unproductive to think of each structural change in isolation. It is, instead, conceptually more useful to think of structural change as a constellation of a wide range of economic, political, social, and other factors, which collectively alter the structure of the economy and the society at large. For example, large-scale migration of rural workers to urban areas contributes to the change in family structure from extended to nuclear families. At the same time, the same phenomenon accelerates the trend toward urbanization and the expansion of manufacturing and services sectors. What is unique about structural change in developing Asia is its sheer scale and speed due to the region's exceptionally rapid economic growth and development. In fact, far-reaching structural change has been both a cause and consequence of historically unprecedented growth rates. Structural change, which has occurred over centuries in the advanced economies, has been replicated within a few decades or even just a few years in developing Asia.

In general, structural change has a far-reaching impact on inequality. Foreign trade can exacerbate inequality by rewarding industries and firms that are able to compete in the global marketplace while punishing those that cannot. Furthermore, in the case of advanced economies, imports from low-wage developing countries compete with domestic production of labor-intensive products, thereby hurting unskilled workers who compete with low-wage workers in developing countries. This line of reasoning explains the widespread popular belief that globalization has been one of the key drivers of widening inequality in advanced economies and also helps to explain the often vehement protests against globalization in those economies. Technological progress has also been widely put forth as a structural driver of inequality. Skilled workers are better able to adopt and use new, improved technology than other unskilled workers, thereby increasing the skill premium and widening the wage gap between skilled and unskilled workers. Broader structural change, such as demographic transition, can also impinge upon inequality. In the absence of well-functioning pension systems, demographic change worsens inequality.

Because structural change in developing Asia has been unprecedented in its scale and speed, the impact of structural change on inequality in the region is potentially very large. We can expect the Schumpeterian, revolutionary technological shifts, which are constantly rocking developing Asia's industrial landscape, to even further increase the skill premium and widen the wage gap between skilled and unskilled workers. Likewise, the region's high degree of openness and heavy dependence on trade exposes it to extensive and frequent changes in its output mix. The constant change of firms and industries benefits the economy in the long term but entails serious adjustment costs in the short term. Providing adequate, yet affordable and sustainable old-age income support is challenging for the region's countries due to the lack of sound and efficient pension systems. In short, because developing Asia is a region in flux and in the midst of a wide range of extensive and far-reaching structural changes, we can expect the impact of those changes on inequality to be potentially extensive and far-reaching as well.

Conceptual overview of the relationship between inequality and structural change

Structural changes in the economy expose the population to challenges and opportunities. The heterogeneity of the population implies that the adjustment capacity to these changes varies. At the broad level, the impact of structural changes on inequality is the outcome of the complex interaction between the initial conditions of a country and five broad time-varying channels: incentives; technological change; accumulation of physical and human capital, and access to capital markets and education; social changes; and political changes. We elaborate first on these five channels, and provide some examples of the complex interaction between these channels.

(i) *Economic incentives.* Reforms impact private incentives. Starting from a highly distorted equilibrium, where private incentives are not aligned with efficient allocation and use of resources, reforms may trigger a takeoff, with large effects on poverty and inequality. The initial takeoff may be associated less with accumulation of capital and the adaptation of new technologies, and more with the more efficient use of existing resources and technologies. The performance of the PRC in the late 1970s and 1980s illustrates the gains of reforms at the level of the community, freeing entrepreneurship potential and allowing greater private ownership of the resultant surpluses.

Another class of incentives stem from international and interregional trade and the mobility of inputs, mainly capital and labor. Incumbents frequently engage in policies that may protect their quasi rents, stifling competition and future growth (Parente and Prescott 2005). These policies include "protection" against foreign competition by means of commercial policy, or protection against the emergence of domestic competitors by means of red tape, labor unions opposing immigration, and controlling new hires, among others. Higher exposure to international and interregional trade and greater input mobility curb these rent-seeking activities, thereby increasing growth. Changing the exposure to competitive market forces would also impact inequality in numerous ways.

(ii) *Technological changes.* Technological changes include the adaptation of better technologies, rising productivity via "learning by doing," and efforts leading to technological innovations at the producer and plant levels (research and development, etc.). These changes can affect relative demand for and relative productivity of different productive factors, such as unskilled labor, skilled labor, and capital and, hence, impact income distribution and inequality.

(iii) *Accumulation of capital and access to finance and education.* With proper incentives, the accumulation of physical and human capital has a large effect on future income. Unequal access to finance and to quality education has profound implications for income inequality as well.

(iv) *Social changes.* The first three factors may impact households and communities in profound ways. There are low-frequency changes, which over a span of a generation or two have huge implications for income distribution too. Examples of these are changing patterns of gender inequality and fertility, and inducing demographic transitions. A key development associated with takeoffs is the rural-to-urban migration, reducing over time the employment share in rural areas, thereby transforming agriculture from subsistence family farming into large and efficient corporate production. This transition may increase urban poverty, thus impacting income inequality.

(v) *Political changes.* Economic takeoffs and the resultant changes in social organization and the distribution of income have been associated with political changes, where the underrepresented groups (women, the poor, periphery, etc.) may gain influence. Similarly, the emerging new sectors may reduce the political clout of the declining sectors. These changes may lead to more equal access to education or health services, among others, and the formation of safety nets.

The quest for a stable association between inequality, growth, and these five factors is illusive because in the long term there is no reason to expect stability of the relevant feedback. Thus, technological changes may enhance equality if they increase the marginal product of labor; on the other hand, they may reduce equality if they hollow out the middle class, as may be the case with some of the recent trends in information technology (IT). Similarly, greater exposure to trade and FDI flows may impact the distribution of income in different directions, determined by the initial endowments of countries. The ability to adapt to the greater penetration of domestic markets by foreign competition and growing exposure to foreign technologies may determine the ultimate impact of globalization on income inequality.

To illustrate, in a country with a comparative advantage in agriculture, opening the economy to free trade would increase the price of food, possibly increasing urban poverty and reducing urban areas' real income, with opposite trends in villages producing food. The gross domestic product (GDP) would increase, but the ultimate impact of free trade on inequality would be ambiguous. Inequality would increase if most of the population is in the non-farming sector and the urban income is below that of the rural areas. The opposite would be the case if poverty is concentrated in the rural areas. Similarly, the adaptation of better technology in agriculture in the open economy would gradually induce large emigration from the rural to urban areas. This in turn may increase poverty in the urban areas, and on balance would increase the income of landowners, who may replace rural workers with capital (tractors, trucks, etc.). While GDP would increase, the net impact of these technological changes on inequality is ambiguous.

The association between inequality and the structural change encompassed in economic growth is summarized by the Kuznets curve (1955). A decade later, Kuznets (1967) outlined the link between income distribution, fertility rates, and economic growth.

Dyson and Murphy (1985) documented that the rate of fertility rises before it declines during the development process. While fertility rates fluctuate, they tend to peak just before starting a prolonged decline, leading to the conclusion that the first sign of an impending decline in fertility is a rise, which often starts many years before the pre-decline peak. These observations were interpreted by Dahan and Tsiddon (1998) in a growth model with endogenous fertility, deriving endogenously the demographic transition along with a Kuznets-type dynamic of income distribution, in a framework where economic growth is based on human capital accumulation. In line with the Kuznets hypothesis, in the first phase of development, the average rate of fertility increases and income becomes less equally distributed. In the second phase, fertility declines and income becomes more equally distributed. The economy also accumulates human capital more rapidly in this stage. The demographic transition and the U-shaped dynamics of equality are necessary for knowledge-based growth. A comprehensive analysis of this fertility–human capital–growth nexus was provided in several papers by Galor and colleagues, as summarized in Galor (2005).

Another possible take on the Kuznets curve hypothesis may link it to the characterization of economic development by Lewis (1954). A large share of workers in the poorest countries are in the rural sector, surviving at close to subsistence levels of income earned in low-efficiency farming. Frequently, the takeoff of growth is associated with the growing importance of industry and services in urban areas, offering the prospect of higher income. Yet, the transition from rural areas to urban environments may come with greater inequality associated with the growing importance of access to human and physical capital, the accumulation of which is affected by differential access of the population to the credit market and to self-financing opportunities. This suggests that the first stage of growth may increase inequality, especially when it involves gradual migration from the rural areas to the vibrant urbanized sectors, where differential access to finance and education, differential abilities, and luck is associated with greater inequality. After decades of growth, the low-income rural sector becomes a minority, and the greater scarcity of unskilled workers and possibly the adaptation of better technologies in farming would increase their wage, leading to the convergence phase where growth is associated with lower inequality. This outcome may be hastened if the political process provides the poor with greater bargaining clout, inducing greater redistribution and seeding the emergence of a safety net.

The evidence on the Kuznets hypothesis is, at best, inconclusive. A cross-section analysis of countries conducted in the 1970s suggests a parabolic relationship in line with the Kuznets hypothesis. Focusing on the low and low-middle income countries, Cornia *et al.* (2004) found that out of 34 developing countries between the 1950s and the mid-1990s, inequality is higher in the terminal period for 15 countries, equal for 14, and lower for 5. A U-shaped trend is observed in a number of cases where inequality is found to be increasing when comparing the terminal and the initial years. Similar to the Phillips curve, the scanty empirical evidence validating the Kuznets hypothesis calls for a multifactor analysis, recognizing that the contribution of the various factors explaining growth and inequality may change over time.

Lundberg and Squire (2003) focused on whether growth and inequality are simultaneously determined and whether they are subject to the same set of determining factors. This research provides answers about the impact of policy innovations on the observed association between growth and inequality. The authors show that the determinants of growth and inequality are not mutually exclusive; however, they did not find variables that uniquely identify in a robust manner the determinants of growth or of distribution. Consequently, the analysis, which examines each outcome independently, ignores the evidence that policies designed to improve one outcome will probably also influence the other. Increasing the Sachs–Warner index to promote growth would lead to greater inequity.[1] Improving income distribution through enhancing civil liberties may have harmful consequences for growth. Lundberg and Squire's results suggest that one can derive a set of policies that, in combination, may achieve almost any desired outcome in the growth-distribution space:

> Expanded education and more equitable land distribution will at least improve income distribution, and may also enhance growth. These policies could be used in combination with an increased value of the Sachs–Warner index to alleviate the distributional costs associated with "openness". Thus, growth could be improved without worsening income distribution by increasing the Sachs–Warner index (that is, increasing the proportion of time in a given period in which the country satisfies the Sachs–Warner criteria) by one standard deviation, and simultaneously improving the Gini index of land distribution by one standard deviation. This combination would nearly double the mean growth rate, and would also improve income distribution by four percent. These are of course very large policy shifts, but more modest policy changes could also yield improvements in both growth and distribution.
>
> (Lundberg and Squire 2003, p. 57)

Among the structural factors possibly impacting both growth and inequality is international trade. Yet, the channels are complex, and the quest for clear-cut results remains elusive. Attanasio *et al.* (2004) studied the impact of the drastic tariff reductions of the 1980s and 1990s in Colombia on the wage distribution. They identified three channels through which the wage distribution was affected: increasing returns to college education, changes in industry wages that hurt sectors with initially lower wages and a higher fraction of unskilled workers, and shifts of the labor force toward the informal sector that typically pays lower wages and offers no benefits. The increase in the skill premium was primarily driven by skill-biased technological changes, partially motivated by the tariff reductions and the increased foreign competition. Wage premiums decreased more in sectors that experienced larger tariff cuts. Sectors with larger tariff cuts and more trade exposure experience a greater increase in informality. The overall effect of the trade reforms on the wage distribution may have been minimal.

Recent contributions focus on the impact of trade in the presence of firms' and workers' heterogeneity, extending the insightful work of Melitz (2003). Sampson (2012) showed that the presence of positive matching between worker skill and

---

1 The Sachs–Warner index measures exchange rate and trade policies. It includes measures of exchange rate overvaluation, tariffs, and nontariff restrictions on trade.

firm productivity explains the employer size–wage premium and the exporter–wage premium. Trade has profound implications on the resultant matching and income inequality. Under trade, the selection of high-productivity firms into exporting raises the demand for skill and increases wage inequality in all countries, both on aggregate and within the export sector. This occurs when firm productivity is determined by a random draw, or when productivity is endogenous to firm-level research and development. With endogenous productivity, the higher demand for skill caused by trade liberalization results from technology upgrading by new exporters.

The structural changes in developing Asia have been driven by reforms inducing trade and the specialization of East Asia in manufacturing (and IT services in India). In these circumstances, the matching of firms and workers may provide the explanation for the growing skill premium and the growing recognition about the importance of investment in human capital.

While estimating the impact of international trade on the rise of the skill wage premium and inequality remains a work-in-progress, existing evidence is validating these forces. Castelló and Doménech (2002) computed the Gini coefficients and the distribution of education by quintiles for 108 countries over 5-year intervals from 1960 to 2000. They found that inequality in human capital negatively influences economic growth rates not only through the efficiency of resource allocation but also through a reduction in investment rates. Overall, education inequality is associated with lower investment rates and, consequently, lower income growth. Therefore, policies conducted to promote growth should not only take into account the level but also the distribution of education. Consequently, aiming at universal access to quality education ought to both reduce inequality and increase economic growth.[2] This task is complicated by the public sector support required to move toward universal access to quality education because the cost of such education is beyond the reach of a large fraction of the population. Furthermore, greater inequality implies that a wider segment of the population is unable to fund quality education, requiring deeper commitment of the public sector. While the fiscal challenges associated with funding education are daunting, the experience of countries reviewed in the next sections suggests that major strides in improving access to education have been accomplished within a generation or two in countries starting with a low tax base.

While the link between higher inequality and lower growth may be tenuous in the short term, the adverse effects of inequality on future growth may emerge. Growing income inequality seeds growing discontent, leading to future political and economic instability (Alesina and Perotti 1996). Evidence shows the negative effect of economic volatility on private investment and economic growth

[2] The focus on quality of education follows the work of Hanushek and Woessmann (2010), finding that there is strong evidence that the cognitive skills of the population – rather than mere school attainment – are powerfully related to long-term economic growth. The relationship between skills and growth proves extremely robust in empirical applications. Growth simulations reveal that the long-term rewards to educational quality are large but also require patience.

(Aizenman and Marion 1993, 1999; Ramey and Ramey 1995). Thus, access to quality education would increase growth directly, mitigate income inequality, and reduce the downside risk of growth-reducing economic instability.

Inequality–structural change nexus in the advanced economies

Insight can be gained by tracing the inequality–structural changes in advanced countries during the past 200 years. As developing Asia is converging to the development level of the advanced countries, the experience of the Organisation for Economic Co-operation and Development (OECD) countries may provide insight on the inequality–structural change associations during varying stages of growth and convergence.[3]

The history of Europe – England being among the best-documented examples – provides useful lessons. In the first phase of the Industrial Revolution, prior to the implementation of significant education reforms, physical capital accumulation propagated by technological improvements was the prime engine of economic growth. In the absence of significant human capital deepening, the concentration of capital among the capitalists widened wealth inequality. The industrialization set in motion a process whereby education reforms were propagated by the increase in the return to labor relative to capital and by the higher demand for skills. In the second phase of the Industrial Revolution, the pace of capital accumulation sharply decreased, whereas the education of the labor force increased, and skills became necessary for production. The investment ratio increased in England from 6% in 1760 to 11.7% in 1831, and remained at around 11% on average in the years 1856–1913 (Crafts 1985; Matthews *et al.* 1982). In contrast, the average years of schooling of males in the labor force was stable overall until the 1830s, and it had tripled by the beginning of the 20th century (Matthews *et al.* 1982).[4] All these changes, and the associated accumulation of assets by the workers, brought a gradual decline in inequality (Williamson 1985; Clark 2002, 2003).

Education reforms in the second phase of the Industrial Revolution were associated with a sharp increase in real wages, along with a sharp increase in the wage–rental ratio. During the period 1823–1915, wealth inequality in the United Kingdom peaked (around 1870) and declined thereafter, in close association with the sharp increase in the enrollment rates of children in public primary schools from about 20% in 1870 to about 80% in 1910 (Flora *et al.* 1983). During that period, wages almost doubled, with mild changes in land and rental

[3] See Galor (2005), Parente and Prescott (2005), and Maddison (2008) for comprehensive overviews of long-term growth patterns.

[4] Education reforms in England followed the pressure by capitalists as well as labor unions, which recognized the importance of technical skills for maintaining competitiveness against other European countries. The 1889 Technical Instruction Act allowed the new local councils to set up technical instruction committees, and the 1890 Local Taxation Act provided public funds that could be spent on technical education (Green 1990).

rates. The decline in inequality was associated with sizable changes that occurred around 1870 in the relative return to the main factors of production possessed by capitalists and workers. The changes in factor prices reflect the capital accumulation triggered by technological innovations, inducing higher demand for skilled workers as well as the increase in enrollment rates and its delayed effect on the skill level per worker. Similar patterns were observed in France and Germany (Morrisson and Snyder 2000). The decline in inequality in France appears to be associated with the significant changes in the relative returns to the main factors of production possessed by capitalists and workers in the second part of the 19th century. Levy-Leboyer and Bourguignon (1990) documented that real wages and the wage–rental ratio increased significantly as of 1860, reflecting the rise in the demand for skilled labor and the effect of the increase in enrollment rates on the skill level per worker.

The transformation of employment from agriculture to industry and services has been a key part of the growth process triggered by takeoffs, with massive rural to urban relocation of population. In the United Kingdom, the employment share of agriculture dropped from about 35% in 1800, to 5% in 1950, reaching below 3% in 2010. The results are more dramatic for the United States, where the agriculture employment share at the beginning of 1800 was well above 70%, reaching about 2% in 2010. For latecomers to industrialization, this process accelerated: the agriculture employment share dropped in Spain from about 67% in 1900 to well below 10% in 2012. This process was driven by two factors: improvements in agricultural technology combined with Engel's law released resources from agriculture (labor push from agriculture), and improvements in industrial technology attracted labor out of agriculture (labor pull). Empirical analysis of 11 OECD countries suggests that since 1800, the "pull" channel dominated until about the time of the Second World War, with the "push" channel dominating thereafter. The "pull" channel seems to matter more in countries in early stages of the structural transformation (Gollin *et al.* 2002; Alvarez-Cuadrado and Poschke 2011).

Wealth inequality in the United States, which increased gradually from colonial times until the second half of the 19th century, reversed its course at the turn of the century and maintained its declining pattern during the first half of the 20th century (Lindert and Williamson 1976). The emergence of the "new economy" in the early 20th century increased the demand for educated workers. In tandem, the creation of publicly funded mass modern secondary education from 1910 to 1940 provided general and practical education, contributed to workers' productivity, and broadened college education (Goldin 2001), facilitating social and geographic mobility. It generated a large decrease in inequality in economic outcomes. This process was magnified by the onset of demographic transitions.

The Industrial Revolution in Western Europe set in motion a complex process of demographic transition. While the growth rate of output per capita increased in the first phase of the Industrial Revolution, the Malthusian effect of income per capita on population growth was maintained for a transitional period. During that period, the sizable increase in population growth mitigated some of the potential gains in income per capita. In England, the acceleration in technological progress and the accumulation of physical capital, and to a lesser extent human capital, generated a gradual rise in real wages in the urban sector. Partly due to labor mobility and demand effects, it induced a gradual rise in real wages in the farming sector. The relaxation in the household budget constraint following the takeoffs was associated with an increase in fertility rates along with an increase in literacy rates and years of schooling. Concurrent with the decline in mortality rates, fertility rates and population growth increased in most of Western Europe until the second half of the nineteenth century (Coale and Treadway 1986). The takeoff was associated with the acceleration in industrialization and rise in urbanization, and a persistent decline in the share of agriculture production in total GDP (Mitchell 1981; Bairoch 1988). The increasing skill requirements in the process of industrialization increased the demand for education, which was boosted also by the significant increase in life expectancy. Over time, the contribution of human capital accumulation to the growth process increased (two-fold in the United States), whereas the contribution of physical capital declined significantly (Goldin and Katz 2001).

Following the growth takeoff, the population growth rate accelerated. However, after a significant lag (about a century in Western Europe, and about 70 years in Australia, Canada, and the United States), there was a dramatic drop in the population growth rate (Maddison 2001). The decline in population growth followed the dramatic decline in fertility rates – in Europe levels reached well below the population replacement level. Importantly, the decline in fertility during the demographic transition outpaced the decline in mortality rates and brought about a decline in the number of children who reached their reproductive age. While this process fits well with the secular increase in the demand for human capital, it may induce higher inequality if the demographic transition is distributed unevenly and tilted toward the higher end of the income distribution.

The process of industrialization in developed economies was magnified by the growth of international trade. The United Kingdom and Northwest Europe were net importers of primary products and net exporters of manufactured goods, whereas the exports of Asia, Oceania, Latin America, and Africa were overwhelmingly composed of primary products (Findlay and O'Rourke 2003). O'Rourke and Williamson (2005) found that trade was a significant force behind the rise in productivity in the United Kingdom. Therefore, while technological advances could have triggered the Industrial Revolution without an expansion of international trade, the growth in exports increased the pace of industrialization and the growth rate of output per capita of the United Kingdom and Western Europe.

Common threads of these experiences were that the accumulation of physical capital raised the role of human capital in the growth process, reflecting the complementarities between capital and skills. Investment in human capital, however, was suboptimal due to credit market imperfections. Limited access to and affordability of quality education, where wealth, gender, race, and ethnicity affected schooling availability, propagated unequal accumulation of human capital, inducing rising inequality at times of higher average real wages. Consequently, deeper public investment in education has been growth-enhancing, reducing income inequality. However, the low degree of complementarity between human capital and land during the Industrial Revolution implies that universal public education increased the cost of labor beyond the increase in average labor productivity in farming, probably reducing the return to land.[5]

International trade enhanced the specialization of industrial economies in the production of manufacturing and other skill-intensive goods during the second phase of the Industrial Revolution. The resultant rise in the demand for skilled labor induced a gradual investment in the quality of the population, expediting a demographic transition, in all probability stimulating follow-up technological progress and further enhancing the comparative advantage of Western Europe in the production of skill-intensive goods. In contrast, in nonindustrial economies, international trade has generated the opposite forces – greater specialization in nonindustrial goods produced by unskilled, low wage workers. The resultant low demand for human capital has provided limited incentives to invest in the quality of the population. Therefore, the gains from trade in nonindustrial economies likely delayed their demographic transition, increasing further the relative abundance of unskilled labor. Consequently, international trade affected, in complex ways, the distribution of population, skills, and technologies in the world economy.

The degree to which the education system and the social norms allow wide accessibility to human capital accumulation is a key factor accounting for the impact of structural changes on the distribution of income. Quality private education is frequently beyond the reach of the poorer segment of the population. Capital market imperfections associated with the inability to collateralize human capital imply that public funding and public education are critical for the wide accessibility to education. The history of Western Europe, Canada, and the United States suggests that, in the second phase of the Industrial Revolution, the emergence of public education and greater labor mobility facilitated growth accompanied by lower inequality.

Nevertheless, the rosy outcome of growth with lower inequality in the second phase of the Industrial Revolution is not guaranteed. Widely available quality public education requires significant tax support, redistributing income toward the poorer segments of the population. Popular support for redistributive policies may decrease with inequality (Bénabou 2000). With imperfect credit and insurance markets, some redistributive policies can improve ex ante welfare, and this implies that their political support tends to decrease with inequality. Conversely, with credit constraints, lower redistribution translates into more persistent inequality; hence the potential for multiple steady states, with mutually reinforcing high inequality and low redistribution, or vice versa. Bénabou's framework also

[5] Therefore, landowners had limited economic incentives to support growth-enhancing educational policies because their stake in the productivity of the industrial sector was insufficient. Thus, an unequal distribution of land ownership put a drag on the support and the accumulation of human capital (see Galor *et al.* (2004)).

provides an interpretation for the documented negative relationship between initial disparities of income or wealth and subsequent aggregate growth (Alesina and Rodrik 1994; Persson and Tabellini 1994). Recognizing that pretax inequality has a significantly negative effect on social transfers (de Mello and Tiongson 2006), it follows that greater inequality may hinder the support for quality public education and overall accumulation of human capital, thereby reducing growth.

The rise in inequality in the United States from 1980 may represent a new development phase, associated with technological changes propagated by the ongoing IT innovation. Autor *et al.* (2008) explain the rise in wage inequality in the United States since 1980 as the outcome of two trends. First, the rapid secular growth in the relative demand for skills, attributable to skill-biased technical change, and a sharp deceleration in the relative supply of college workers in the 1980s capture the evolution of the college/high school wage premium over four decades. Second, the recent "polarization" of skill demands in which employment has expanded in high-wage and low-wage work at the expense of middle-wage jobs may reflect the role of IT in complementing abstract (high-education) tasks and substituting for routine (middle-education) tasks. The authors conclude that computerization and international outsourcing may have raised the demand for skill among higher-educated workers, depressed skill demands for "middle-educated" workers, while leaving the lower end of the wage distribution comparatively intact. This interpretation may account for the "hollowing out" of the wage distribution observed in OECD countries.

Analytical review of the inequality–structural change nexus in developing Asia

The global trend since the 1960s has been "catch-up" and convergence across countries (Maddison 2008). Developing Asia has led this trend, with unprecedented growth of GDP per capita from 1952 to 1978 in Japan; Taipei,China; the Republic of Korea; Hong Kong, China; and Singapore at annual rates ranging from 4.8% (Singapore) to 6.7% (Japan). The next step was the tectonic shift propagated by the takeoff of the PRC in the 1980s, followed by India in the 1990s. A common feature of these takeoffs has been the high levels of investment in human and physical capital, rapid increases of international trade and inflows of FDI, and the transfer of technology. In most Asian takeoffs, the leading sector was manufacturing. The rapid growth rates following these takeoffs were reinforced by large investment in physical and human capital, financed by very high investment and saving rates in developing Asia.

The experience of developing Asia differs from that of emerging Latin America in the key role played by the export-led growth strategy, with heavy emphasis on industrialization. Frequently, this strategy was supported by direct allocation of available credit by state-owned banks in ways linked to the realized growth and export performance. Japan (from the 1950s) and the Republic of Korea (from the 1970s) are among the countries that used these credit policies for several decades, applying elaborate institutional mechanisms for selection and monitoring

(World Bank 1993). The growth was also propagated by trade liberalization efforts, increasing the Sachs–Warner index of openness and resulting in a large increase in investment, growth, and exports (Wacziarg and Welch 2008). Intriguingly, Japan and the Republic of Korea were closed to inward FDI and refrained from large hoarding of international reserves during the first decades of their economic takeoffs. The emergence of manufacturing as a leading sector provided the pull factor for rural-to-urban migration. The agriculture sector in developing Asia managed to increase its productivity in tandem with the growth takeoff. This was the outcome of land reforms, notably in the Republic of Korea and Taipei,China; improvement in agriculture extension services to speed up the diffusion of Green Revolution technologies; and investment in infrastructure (World Bank 1993). Thus, in the first stage of the takeoffs, growth benefits reduced poverty across the board. Yet, the preferential treatment of industrialization imposed an implicit tax on agriculture, resulting in lagged income growth in the rural relative to the more industrialized, mostly urban areas.

The experience of the past three decades in the PRC differs from that of Japan, the Republic of Korea, and other countries in developing Asia in the key role of inward FDI and joint ventures. These activities facilitated more rapid technological transformation. International trade remains a vital part of the PRC's growth strategy, with a growing role for complex network trade with the Republic of Korea, Japan, and other Asian countries. The strategy seems to work, allowing the PRC to climb rapidly up the ladder of product sophistication, at rates faster than those observed earlier in Japan, the Republic of Korea, and other economies in developing Asia (Schott 2008). FDI inflows to the PRC may contribute to greater inequality because the geographical distribution of the inward FDI has been skewed toward the southeastern provinces. Fleisher *et al.* (2010) pointed out that FDI had a much larger effect on total factor productivity before 1994 than after, attributing this finding to the increasing success of private and quasi-private enterprises. Regional differences in physical, human, and infrastructure capital, and regional differences in FDI flows account for the differential regional growth patterns. Human capital investment in less-developed areas is justified on efficiency grounds and on the grounds that it contributes to a reduction in regional inequality.

While the export-led growth strategy may fit small countries, short of the emergence of a "new demander of last resort," the PRC growth path has been challenged by its own success (Aizenman and Sun 2010). This is especially the case at times of diminishing growth prospects of the United States and the eurozone. Feenstra and Hong (2010) concluded that the growth in domestic demand led to three times more employment gains than did exports during 2000–2005. Therefore, the PRC could turn toward domestic demand instead of export and consumer expenditures, in particular as an engine to stimulate employment. The policies associated with such a turn would reduce the inequality between the urban and the rural areas.

This intriguing observation is in line with the growth performance of India, which managed to grow fast in a more balanced way without relying on external demand as its engine of growth. India's growth takeoff took place against the background of prior inequality in access to opportunities and income, which in turn put a drag on the speed of poverty reduction, and probably magnified the increase of inequality. The prior inequality in India, combined with the higher growth rate of the PRC, accounts for the faster poverty reduction accomplished by the PRC (Ravallion 2011).

The inequality debate in India is generally discussed in relation to the major economic reforms in the 1990s. India underwent radical external sector liberalization – average manufacturing tariffs dropped from 117% in 1990–1991 to 39% in 1999–2000. Trade liberalization and other structural reforms, along with technological change, accelerated growth and reduced poverty (Datt and Ravallion 1998). Nevertheless, geographic and sector divergence in India's growth process and heterogeneous access to opportunities dampened the poverty reduction effect of growth (Datt and Ravallion 2002, 2009). The remarkable increase in the growth rate triggered by takeoff was helped occasionally by the ability to "leapfrog," bringing advanced technologies to communities that were not exposed to the gains from older technologies. The fast adaptation of cell phones and IT networking in communities without access to reliable phone lines allowed India to become a key global provider of back office and software services, despite its infrastructure deficits.[6] As much as the service sector's growth comes from relatively skill-intensive subsectors such as IT, process outsourcing, and financial services, this growth contributed more to the well educated and households with better access to schools and colleges. The relatively small employment share of services and manufacturing in India accounts for the increased inequality in recent decades.

Kumar and Mishra (2008) provided evidence that trade liberalization in India led to decreased wage inequality between unskilled and skilled workers. Hasan and Mehta (2011) found that most of the shift in inequality could not be attributed directly to liberalization. They found that 29% of the change in wage inequality from 1993 to 2004 could be attributed to liberalization, 25 percentage points of which were linked to services reforms and 4 percentage points to trade liberalization.

Burua and Chakraborty (2010), on the other hand, found a positive relationship between trade openness and interregional inequality. India experienced a higher rate of increase in income inequality across the country during the post-reform period (1995–2000) as India's openness increased, and interregional income inequality also rose due to the concentration of manufacturing in the metropolis area.

In Malaysia, inequality, particularly between races, was given specific attention in policy making in the aftermath of the racial turbulence in the late 1960s. The

---

[6] While "leapfrogging" may allow infrastructure deficiencies to be overcome, the degree to which countries are able to leapfrog in a wide range of manufacturing remains debatable (see Hobday (1994)). However, the development patterns of the People's Republic of China suggest that climbing very fast on the quality ladder is feasible.

government put emphasis on diversifying agriculture output and export-oriented manufacturing to facilitate growth and increase employment opportunities. The government also focused on education and human resource development.

Further liberalization and deregulation in Malaysia during the period 1991–1995 facilitated the decline in poverty incidence by 9.6%, helping more than 400,000 individuals out of poverty. Income inequality during this period, however, increased by 4.3%. Ragayah (2008) pointed to the government's liberalization and privatization policies after the mid-1980s as the reason for worsening inequality since 1990. Concerns that wage increases in the early 1990s would erode export competitiveness induced policy makers to open the economy to foreign workers who kept wages down. The resultant depressed wages deteriorated the income distribution.

The Asian financial crisis of 1997–1999 induced a decline in inequality because the adverse effect of the crisis appears to have been greater in the top quintiles of the households. The impact on the bottom two quintiles was rather mild because the crisis did not lead to massive unemployment for the locals, while, shortly after the crisis, inequality resumed an upward trend. Malaysia's preferential treatment of the *Bumiputra* (indigenous people) seemed to reduce poverty and interethnic income disparity, yet intra-ethnic income inequality has widened.

In postcrisis years, Malaysia has been experiencing growth of about 5–6% with no significant improvements in the unemployment rate. In order to maintain its competitiveness in the global market, it has been moving from labor-intensive toward capital- and technology-intensive production.

Consequently, the demand for skilled and highly educated workers increased, pushing up their wages relative to those of the unskilled workers, thereby increasing inequality. This may reflect the maturing of the Malaysian economy climbing up the value chain and substituting labor-intensive operations for skill/knowledge-intensive activities. Intriguingly, these interpretations are reminiscent of the development in the United States discussed in the previous section.

Most Asian economies are characterized by their dual economic structure, where the agrarian sector is engaged in subsistence farming. Hence, the adaptation of better farming technologies has the by-product of pushing surplus labor to urban areas. Transferring more than half of the population from rural to urban communities took about 100 years in Europe, yet the faster convergence of East Asia implies that this transformation may happen within less than 50 years. The challenges associated with this transformation are enormous because it is not obvious that the push forces inducing rural labor to move to cities (better farming technologies) would match the pull forces (higher demand for labor in manufacturing and services, mostly concentrated in rapidly growing urban communities). As the pull factors may play a greater role in the first stage of economic development, the transition may impose key economic and social challenges. While restrictions on labor mobility may help in the first stages (see the PRC's experience), it may lead to segmented labor markets, with a growing underclass of discontented workers. The fast industrialization experienced in developing Asia also implies a rapid increase in the demand for skilled workers, leading to bottlenecks with widening wage gaps between skilled and unskilled workers. Distortions associated with uneven access to the capital market and education may expose Asian countries to faster increases in wealth and income inequalities, and may put a drag on the sustainability of fast growth.

The PRC's experience provides a key case study of the five forces shaping growth and inequality dynamics described at the beginning of this chapter. Changing economic incentives induced by reforms of the early 1980s prompted rapid growth in the rural economy and accounted for the majority of the PRC's success in poverty reduction since 1980 (Ravallion and Chen 2007). The rapid industrialization of the southeastern provinces, facilitated by selective incentives, FDI inflows, and the export-led growth strategy, induced rapid technological changes and accumulation of capital. The combination of these factors led to massive migration from rural areas toward the growing industrialized urban centers in southeastern PRC and the growth of urban poverty (Li 2006; Knight *et al.* 2007). The process was shaped by the initial conditions of the PRC, including the *hukou* system.[7] Its power in controlling people's lives has declined in the reform era in the wake of enormous social and economic changes and dramatic rise in rural-to-urban mobility. Despite all the reforms, the system still functions to constrain free migration and contribute to societal segregation. The gross inequality of the system has triggered a political and social process, putting in motion a slow trend toward further relaxation of the *nongzhuanfei* process (i.e., the process of converting the *hukou* status from an agricultural to a nonagricultural one). The growing demand for human capital, labor market pressures, and social fragmentation may provide the impetus for further reforms.

The fast initial growth rates of developing Asia observed during the second half of the 20th century may also imply faster demographic transitions. This reflects several factors: modern technology allowing gender screening and selective abortions, the enforcement of the "one child policy" in the PRC, and the rapid drop in infant mortality propagated by adopting modern medical standards. This is in contrast to the slower demographic transitions in Western Europe, where the control mechanism impacting the family size in the 19th century was the endogenous adjustment of women's age of marriage (Wrigley and Schofield 1981). Consequently, developing Asia has been aging faster than Western Europe throughout the demographic transition. This may account for the increase of FDI outflows from Japan in recent decades, which were needed to compensate for its shrinking and expensive labor force, and possibly increasing the wage inequality between workers and owners of capital. Similar challenges would affect the PRC,

[7] The PRC household registration system (*hukou*) divides the population into agricultural and nonagricultural sectors. It may be the most important determinant of differential privileges in state socialist PRC, determining access to good jobs, education for one's children, housing, healthcare and even the right to move to a city (Wu and Treiman 2004). Transforming one's *hukou* status from rural to urban is a central aspect of upward social mobility. Education and membership in the Communist Party are the main determinants of upward social mobility.

the Republic of Korea, and other countries projected to enter the stage of rapid increase in the old dependency ratio within less than a decade.[8]

The dilemma facing developing Asia is that while the developed countries became rich before they became old, the developing countries will become old before they become rich. The growing intergenerational tension associated with rapidly aging societies would aggravate the drag on the growth rate of developing Asia. While there are no quick and easy fixes to demographic challenges, possible policies do exist that may mitigate the downside risks:

(i) Prioritizing equal access to publicly supported quality education. This would facilitate faster growth and act to mitigate rising inequality.
(ii) Minimizing the debt overhang associated with unfunded liabilities, and improving the foreign asset position of developing Asia would help. Stockpiling foreign assets in the form of international reserves well above 15% of GDP, a common practice in most of developing Asia, may be suboptimal. A better policy stance may involve diversifying reserves into a well-run sovereign wealth fund, investing globally in equities.
(iii) Policies that would reduce the private cost of rearing children would help. Access to quality public education is important, but one should go beyond this. Dealing with the root causes of the tendency to "overeducate" children due to the "rat race" to top universities would be useful. Other steps such as reducing the burden of rearing children, typically borne by the mother, may help in mitigating the collapse of fertility in developing Asia.
(iv) Adopting policies that are friendlier to immigrants would help. This would be especially helpful in smaller countries (for the experience of Singapore and Malaysia, see Ruppert (1999)), but it would alleviate bottlenecks even in large countries. Arguably, developing Asia can apply its monopsony power to encourage a human capital profile of its immigrant and foreign labor that would fit its economic aspirations and challenges, as has been the practice of Canada and Australia.

Concluding observations and policy implications

Structural change – or changes in the structure of the economy or broader changes in noneconomic, political, social, cultural, or other spheres – has a major impact on inequality. Greater openness to foreign trade intensifies competition and thus accelerates changes in a country's industrial structure and output mix. In the short term, openness increases adjustment costs because some industries and firms will be unable to withstand foreign competition. Analogously, technological progress

---

[8] The Republic of Korea's speed of population aging has been unprecedented. The average fertility rate (birth per woman) is by now about 1.3, among the lowest in the world. By 2050, the median age of the population of the Republic of Korea is projected to be 57 years, making it one of the most elderly nations in the world. In contrast, at present, Japan has the oldest median age at 43 years, while the Republic of Korea's stands at 37 years (Klassen 2010).

will benefit higher-skilled workers, who are able to use the new and improved technology, but disadvantage lower-skilled workers. In the process, the skill premium will increase, widening the wage gap between the two groups of workers. Structural change exerts a significant effect on inequality in both advanced and developing countries. What sets developing Asia apart from the rest of the world is not the close link between structural change and inequality but the sheer speed and scale of structural change. Extensive structural change is both a cause and consequence of the exceptionally rapid economic growth that enabled the region to raise living standards and reduce poverty at a historically unprecedented rate.

Our review of developing Asia's experience confirms that the region has experienced seismic structural change during its growth and development process. Of course, each country faces different structural changes and the relative importance of a given structural change differs across countries. Furthermore, even for the same country, a given structural change can become more or less important over time. For example, the increase in inequality arising from the PRC's transition from a centrally planned economy to a market-oriented economy is becoming less important as it moves farther away from the market reforms of 1978. In the case of Malaysia, the economically disadvantaged position of the majority Malay population has traditionally been a main source of inequality. In response, the government has implemented discriminatory policies, which explicitly sought to help the majority Malays bridge the income gap with the other ethnic groups. A relatively high level of illiteracy stands in the way of India's efforts to make growth more inclusive. India differs too by its poor infrastructure, which impedes interregional connectivity and thus impedes interregional income convergence. In short, while many countries in developing Asia are buffeted by structural changes that impinge upon inequality, the relative importance of different structural changes differs across countries, and, for a single country, over time.

Given the interconnectedness between different types of structural changes, what separates countries in developing Asia matters less than what unites them, namely the collective scale of the structural change confronting them. At a broader level, structural change entails adjustment costs. Therefore, addressing the inequality resulting from structural change requires mitigating those adjustment costs.

Developing Asia has already begun the difficult and complex task of addressing inequality arising from structural change. In response to growing popular demand for more equity, governments across the region are seeking to include more of the population in the growth process and spread the fruits of growth to more of the population. While the dominant growth philosophy among the region's governments in the past was "grow first, redistribute later," there is now a growing recognition that more sustainable growth supported by broad-based political and social support requires a growth strategy that provides equality of opportunity, especially in education and employment. The newly developing more inclusive growth philosophy also envisions expanded social protection systems and social safety nets to protect the poor and the vulnerable. Although this new growth philosophy is geared toward reducing inequality and promoting equity in general, the fact that structural change is likely to be a major source of inequality in developing Asia reconfirms and validates the basic direction of the philosophy. The fundamental solution to mitigating the adjustment costs arising from structural change lies in empowering individuals to become more productive, adaptable, and versatile through access to education and employment.

Finally, the experiences of the advanced economies entail a number of valuable lessons for developing Asia. First, the impact of the adaptation of new technology on income inequality is frequently large, varying depending on initial conditions and the nature of the technology. While some technologies lead to widespread gains and higher equality, some may lead to greater inequality, generating losers and gainers, with "hollowing out" effects. Second, international trade reinforces the takeoff and growth in economies where manufacturing is the leading sector. Faster technological adaptation magnifies growth and benefits from investments in education. On the other hand, new technologies tend to generate winners and losers, and may increase inequality. Third, ensuring equal access to quality public education is extraordinarily important. This would facilitate faster growth and act to mitigate the rising inequality that characterizes the first phase of takeoffs. Fourth, the downside of growing inequality is breeding sociopolitical instability and lower economic growth. Quality public education helps, but in the second stage of the growth takeoff, a state-sponsored safety net would mitigate the downside risk of growing inequality. A safety net would also reduce the opposition to rapid changes and the adaptation of new technologies. Fifth, demographic transitions following a successful takeoff are unavoidable, imposing new challenges. While the drop in net fertility may act to increase investment in human capital, the final phase of the demographic transition may impose acute fiscal challenges. Widening the tax base and curbing unfunded liabilities help in avoiding stagnation. All of these are valuable lessons for Asia.

References

Aizenman, J., and N. Marion. 1993. Policy Uncertainty, Persistence and Growth. *Review of International Economics*. 1 (2). pp. 145–63.

——. 1999. Volatility and Investment: Interpreting Evidence from Developing Countries. *Economica*. 66. pp. 157–79.

Aizenman, J., and Y. Sun. 2010. Globalization and the Sustainability of Large Current Account Imbalances: Size Matters. *Journal of Macroeconomics*. 32 (1). pp. 35–44.

Alesina, A. F., and D. Rodrik. 1994. Distributive Politics and Economic Growth. *Quarterly Journal of Economics*. 109 (2). pp. 465–90.

Alesina, A. F., and R. Perotti. 1996. Income Distribution, Political Instability, and Investment. *European Economic Review*. 40 (6). pp. 1203–28.

Alvarez-Cuadrado, F., and M. Poschke. 2011. Structural Change out of Agriculture: Labor Push versus Labor Pull. *American Economic Journal: Macroeconomics*. 3 (3). pp. 127–58.

Attanasio, O., P. K. Goldberg, and N. Pavcnik. 2004. Trade Reforms and Wage Inequality in Colombia. *Journal of Development Economics*. 74 (2). pp. 331–66.

Autor, D. H., L. F. Katz, and M. S. Kearney. 2008. Trends in US Wage Inequality: Revising the Revisionists. *Review of Economics and Statistics*. 90 (2). pp. 300–23.

Bairoch, P. 1988. *Cities and Economic Development*. Chicago, IL: University of Chicago Press.
Bénabou, R. 2000. Unequal Societies: Income Distribution and the Social Contract. *American Economic Review*. 90 (1). pp. 96–129.
Burua, A., and P. Chakraborty. 2010. Does Openness Affect Regional Inequality? A Case for India. *Review of Development Economics*. 14 (3). pp. 447–65.
Castelló, A., and R. Doménech. 2002. Human Capital Inequality and Economic Growth: Some New Evidence. *The Economic Journal*. 112. pp. C187–C200.
Clark, G. 2002. Farmland Rental Values and Agrarian History: England and Wales, 1500–1912. *European Review of Economic History*. 6 (3). pp. 281–308.
——. 2003. The Condition of the Working-Class in England, 1200–2000: Magna Carta to Tony Blair. UC Davis. http://eh.net/content/condition-working-class-england-1200-2000-magna-carta-tony-blair (accessed 10 December 2011).
Coale, A. J., and R. Treadway. 1986. A Summary of the Changing Distribution of Overall Fertility, Marital Fertility, and the Proportion Married in the Provinces of Europe. In A. J. Coale and S. C. Watkins, eds. *The Decline of Fertility in Europe*. Princeton, NJ: Princeton University Press.
Cornia, G. A., T. Addison, and S. Kiiski. 2004. Income Distribution Changes and their Impact in the Post-Second World War Period. In G. Cornia, ed. *Inequality, Growth and Poverty in an Era of Liberalization and Globalization*. Oxford, UK: Oxford University Press.
Crafts, N. F. R. 1985. *British Economic Growth during the Industrial Revolution*. Oxford, UK: Oxford University Press.
Dahan, M., and D. Tsiddon. 1998. Demographic Transition, Income Distribution, and Economic Growth. *Journal of Economic Growth*. 3 (1). pp. 29–52.
Datt, G., and M. Ravallion. 1998. Farm Productivity and Rural Poverty in India. *Journal of Development Studies*. 34 (4). pp. 62–85.
——. 2002. Is India's Economic Growth Leaving the Poor Behind? *Journal of Economic Perspectives*. 16 (3). pp. 89–108.
——. 2009. Has India's Economic Growth Become Less Pro-Poor in the Wake of Economic Reforms? *Policy Research Working Paper* 5103. Washington, DC: World Bank.
de Mello, L., and E. R. Tiongson. 2006. Income Inequality and Redistributive Government Spending. *Public Finance Review*. 34 (3). pp. 282–305.
Dyson, T., and M. Murphy. 1985. The Onset of Fertility Transition. *Population and Development Review*. 11. pp. 399–440.
Feenstra, R. C., and C. Hong. 2010. [People's Republic of] China's Exports and Employment. In R. C. Feenstra and S.-J. Wei, eds. *[People's Republic of] China's Growing Role in World Trade*. Chicago, IL: University of Chicago Press.
Findlay, R., and K. H. O'Rourke. 2003. Commodity Market Integration, 1500–2000. In M. D. Bordo, A. M. Taylor, and J. G. Williamson, eds. *Globalization in Historical Perspective*. Cambridge, MA: National Bureau of Economic Research. pp. 13–64.
Fleisher, B., H. Li, and M. Q. Zhao. 2010. Human Capital, Economic Growth, and Regional Inequality in [the People's Republic of] China. *Journal of Development Economics*. 92 (2). pp. 215–31.
Flora, P., F. Kraus, and W. Pfenning. 1983. *State, Economy and Society in Western Europe 1815–1975*. Volume 1. Chicago, IL: St. James Press.
Galor, O. 2005. From Stagnation to Growth: Unified Growth Theory. In P. Aghion and S. N. Durlauf, eds. *Handbook of Economic Growth*. Volume 1A. Amsterdam: Elsevier.
Galor, O., O. Moav, and D. Vollrath. 2004. Land Inequality and the Origin of Divergence and Overtaking in the Growth Process: Theory and Evidence. *Brown Economics Working Paper* No. 2003-04. Providence, RI: Department of Economics, Brown University.
Goldin, C. 2001. The Human Capital Century and American Leadership: Virtues of the Past. *Journal of Economic History*. 61 (2). pp. 263–92.

Goldin, C., and L. F. Katz. 2001. On the Legacy of US Educational Leadership: Notes on Distribution and Economic Growth in the 20th Century. *American Economic Review.* 91 (2). pp. 18–23.

Gollin, D., S. Parente, and R. Rogerson. 2002. The Role of Agriculture in Development. *American Economic Review.* 92 (2). pp. 160–4.

Green, A. 1990. *Education and State Formation.* New York, NY: St. Martin's Press.

Hanushek, E. A., and L. Woessmann. 2010. Education and Economic Growth. In D. J. Brewer and P. J. McEwan, eds. *Economics of Education.* Amsterdam: Elsevier.

Hasan, R., and A. Mehta. 2011. The Effects of Trade and Services Liberalization on Wage Inequality in India. *International Review of Economics and Finance.* 23 (C). pp. 75–90.

Hobday, M. 1994. Technological Learning in Singapore: A Test Case of Leapfrogging. *Journal of Development Studies.* 30 (4). pp. 831–58.

Klassen, T. 2010. [The Republic of] Korea: Ageing Tiger. *Global Brief.* January.

Knight, J., L. Shi, and D. Quheng. 2007. Education and the Poverty Trap in Rural [People's Republic of] China. University of Oxford. Unpublished manuscript.

Kumar, U., and P. Mishra. 2008. Trade Liberalization and Wage Inequality: Evidence from India. *Review of Development Economics.* 12 (2). pp. 291–311.

Kuznets, S. 1955. Economic Growth and Income Inequality. *American Economic Review.* 45 (1). pp. 1–28.

——. 1967. Population and Economic Growth. *Population Problems. Proceedings of the American Philosophical Society* 3. pp. 170–93. Reprinted in *Population, Capital and Growth: Selected Essays.* 1973. New York: W.W. Norton & Co. pp. 1–48.

Levy-Leboyer, M., and F. Bourguignon. 1990. *The French Economy in the Nineteenth Century.* Cambridge, UK: Cambridge University Press.

Lewis, W. A. 1954. Economic Development with Unlimited Supplies of Labour. *Manchester School.* 22. pp. 139–91.

Li, S. 2006. Rising Poverty and its Causes in Urban [People's Republic of] China. In S. Li and H. Sato, eds. *Unemployment, Inequality and Poverty in Urban [People's Republic of] China.* London: Routledge.

Lindert, H. P., and J. G. Williamson. 1976. Three Centuries of American Inequality. *Research in Economic History.* 1. pp. 69–123.

Lundberg, M., and L. Squire. 2003. The Simultaneous Evolution of Growth and Inequality. *Economic Journal.* 113 (487). pp. 326–44.

Maddison, A. 2001. *The World Economy: A Millennia Perspective.* Paris: OECD.

——. 2008. Shares of the Rich and the Rest in the World Economy: Income Divergence between Nations, 1820–2030. *Asian Economic Policy Review.* 3 (1). pp. 67–82.

Matthews, C. R., F. H. Charles, and J. C. Odling-Smee. 1982. *British Economic Growth 1856–1973.* Palo Alto, CA: Stanford University Press.

Melitz, M. J. 2003. The Impact of Trade on Intra-Industry Reallocations and Aggregate Industry Productivity. *Econometrica.* 71 (6). pp. 1695–725.

Mitchell, B. R. 1981. *European Historical Statistics, 1750–1975.* Second edition. New York, NY: New York University Press.

Morrisson, C., and W. Snyder. 2000. Income Inequalities in France from the Early Eighteenth Century to 1985. *Revue Economique.* 51. pp. 119–54.

O'Rourke, K., and J. Williamson. 2005. From Malthus to Ohlin: Trade, Industrialisation and Distribution since 1500. *Journal of Economic Growth.* 10 (1). pp. 5–34.

Parente, L. S., and E. Prescott. 2005. A Unified Theory of the Evolution of International Income Levels. In P. Aghion and S. Durlauf, eds. *Handbook of Economic Growth.* Amsterdam: Elsevier.

Persson, T., and G. Tabellini. 1994. Is Inequality Harmful for Growth? *American Economic Association.* 84 (3). pp. 600–21.

Ragayah, H. M. Z. 2008. Income Inequality in Malaysia. *Asian Economic Policy Review.* 3. pp. 114–32.

Ramey, G., and V. A. Ramey. 1995. Cross-Country Evidence on the Link between Volatility and Growth. *American Economic Review.* 85 (5). pp. 1138–51.

Ravallion, M. 2011. A Comparative Perspective on Poverty Reduction in Brazil, [the People's Republic of] China, and India. *World Bank Research Observer.* 26 (1). pp. 71–104.

Ravallion, M., and S. Chen. 2007. [People's Republic of] China's (Uneven) Progress against Poverty. *Journal of Development Economics.* 82 (1). pp. 1–42.

Ruppert, E. 1999. Managing Foreign Labor in Singapore and Malaysia: Are There Lessons for GCC Countries? *World Bank Policy Research Working Paper* No. 2053. Washington, DC: World Bank.

Sampson, T. 2012. Selection into Trade and Wage Inequality. *CEP Discussion Paper* No. 1152. Centre for Economic Performance, London School of Economics.

Schott, P. K. 2008. The Relative Sophistication of Chinese Exports. *Economic Policy.* 23 (53). pp. 5–49.

Wacziarg, R., and K. H. Welch. 2008. Trade Liberalization and Growth: New Evidence. *World Bank Economic Review*. 22 (2). pp. 187–231.

Williamson, G. J. 1985. *Did British Capitalism Breed Inequality?* Boston, MA: Allen & Unwin.

World Bank. 1993. *The East Asian Miracle: Economic Growth and Public Policy*. World Bank Policy Research Report. New York, NY: Oxford University Press.

Wrigley, E. A., and R. Schofield. 1981. *The Population History of England 1541–1871: A Reconstruction*. Cambridge, MA: Harvard University Press.

Wu, X., and D. J. Treiman. 2004. The Household Registration System and Social Stratification in [the People's Republic of] China: 1955–1996. *Demography.* 41 (2). pp. 363–84.

8 Institutions and economic inequality in Asia

Disentangling policy and political structure

John V. C. Nye

Introduction

The growing literature linking economic growth and development to differential institutions has also spurred interest in the links between institutional arrangements and economic inequality. Unfortunately, distributional considerations do not fall out so easily from either the pure theories of economic growth or the theories regarding the institutional determinants of growth. Scholars now have good reason to believe that good institutions, such as sound property rights, market-promoting regulations, strong contract enforcement, and stable legal rules, support high growth. But there is no guarantee that high economic growth will lead to a more even distribution of income. There is both theoretical work and empirical evidence following the initial observations of Simon Kuznets (1955) that in the early stages of growth, inequality may rise while further growth tends to lead to more even distributions of income in advanced economies (see Barro (2000) and Glaeser (2005) for recent surveys on this issue). However, there is also evidence that initial conditions of high inequality may result in distorted political and social institutions, which hinder both economic development as well as a more even distribution of material resources. In this chapter, I treat institutions generally in the sense of political and economic "rules of the game" in the formulation of Douglass North (1990), but, in keeping with the more complex determinants of inequality, also consider the role of initial conditions that might otherwise overlap with policy or social conditions.

A recent survey of inequality and institutions (Savoia *et al.* 2010) focused on the ways in which pre-existing historical inequalities created conditions that led to poor institutions. Of course, given the persistence of political and economic institutions, these institutions can themselves subsequently affect the degree of economic and political equality that develops. Thus, any study of institutions – more specifically of the institutions of governance – and their effects on inequality is faced with disentangling the two-sided relationships between institutions and inequality. Inequality is an effect of many types of governance relations, but initial conditions of inequality may feed into the political conditions that result in particular types of governance relations.

The need to disentangle the links between economic inequality and institutions runs afoul of two major problems. The first is that it is not quite clear which one is causal. There is work that suggests that different types of political institution – notably regime choice (authoritarian versus democratic) – have some independent influence on observed economic inequality. However, there is a larger body of work that says existing political and social institutions are an outcome of long-standing economic inequalities. Second, it is necessary to try to unpack the meaning of institutions. Sometimes, this is used as a catchall, and, at other times, it can be used to mean either regime type or, just as commonly, some measure of state competence or capacity. The latter also gets entangled in the problem of corruption versus state capacity.

In addition, there is insufficient attention to the distinction between structural political institutions (whether regime type or legal origins) and policy choice. In some cases, a particular policy (e.g., protective tariffs on restrictive labor rules) might promote inequality in both democratic and authoritarian regimes but are not separately identified in many cases. Thus, while democracies can sometimes promote greater equality of income, it is not always clear whether the differences (or lack thereof) between democracies and autocracies are due to regime type or the inability to provide and administer public goods or promote open competition. Further, it is even more difficult to disentangle which policies, designed to lessen inequality, meet a standard cost–benefit calculation, or in many cases even do anything to limit inequality effectively.

Finally, measures of inequality are fraught with greater than usual problems. While most of the literature focuses exclusively on measures of monetary income or wealth, societies marked by high political and social inequality are likely to produce estimates of wealth inequality that underestimate true inequality precisely because social influence is more important than raw wealth. Conversely, societies making progress in removing certain inequalities (for example, by choosing to tax hitherto exempt perquisites for chief executive officers and managers of major corporations) might actually see measured inequality rise as companies substitute larger salaries or stock options in lieu of the previously tax-free benefits. Though nominally resulting in greater measured inequality, such compensation might actually reflect a more open economic environment in which competition is more open and people are provided with greater opportunities to become upwardly mobile.

Thus, any discussion of governance and inequality must begin by clarifying the conceptual and theoretical issues involved and by outlining the different causal possibilities before considering what the empirical literature suggests are the operationally relevant relationships.

Table 8.1 summarizes much of the literature that details the various ways in which both political and economic institutions can influence or affect economic inequality. While Table 8.2 summarizes work showing reverse causation, a cursory glance at the table suggests that institutions only ambiguously affect inequality, and not in a consistent fashion. Conversely, virtually all of the literature indicates that greater initial inequality has potentially strong effects (almost always negative) on the quality of various political and economic institutions.

Table 8.1 Claims linking better institutions to greater or lesser inequality

Direction of effect	*Causal institutions*	*Literature*
Negative to bimodal	Property rights	Amendola *et al.* (2011); Bowles (2004); Bourguignon *et al.* (2007). The exceptions are primarily a poor country effect where increasing property rights can increase income inequality. Richer or faster-growing countries see better property rights equaling lower inequality.
Negative	Labor market institutions	Checchi and García-Peñalosa (2008). Again there is something of a country split where strong labor rules are helpful for countries already blessed with other good institutions. In other cases, weak property rights or state institutions mean that labor protections equal higher unemployment and other welfare diminishing outcomes of employment assistance or union protection.
Negative	Political institutions (e.g., index combining low corruption, quality of bureaucracy, law and order, and protection of property rights)	Barro (2000); Bourguignon and Morrisson (1998); Li *et al.* (1998).
Ambiguous	Democratization or political freedom	Chong and Calderón (2000); Bourguignon and Verdier (2000); Acemoglu and Robinson (2000). Political freedom or loose measures of democratization first produce an increase in income inequality but in a second stage cause an improvement in equality.
Positive	Migration restrictions	Liu (2005) points to the *hukou* system in the People's Republic of China limiting migration as widening the rural–urban divide.

Note: Positive means stronger (or more of stated) institutions are associated with more inequality; negative is the opposite.

Source: Author's compilation.

Table 8.2 Claims linking initial inequality to subsequent institutional quality

Direction of effect	*Institutions affected*	*Literature*
Negative	General institutions	Engerman and Sokoloff (2002) is perhaps the core paper that links historical inequality to unproductive and restrictive economic and political institutions.
Negative	Property rights	Keefer and Knack (2002) show that income and land inequality, and ethnic tensions reduce security of property and contract rights.
Negative	Property rights	Sonin (2003) argues that the ability to maintain private protection systems makes the rich opponents of private property rights.
Negative	Property rights	Glaeser *et al.* (2003). Higher inequality worsens property rights and regulatory institutions.
Negative	Institutional stability	Thorbecke and Charumilind (2002). Inequality exacerbates distributive conflict and hence stability.
Negative	Institutional quality	Cervellati *et al.* (2008); Gradstein (2007). The rich do not need public protection and benefit relatively more from existing system.
Negative	Democracy	Boix (2003); Robinson (2006). Initial inequality leads to greater fear that democracy will lead to prospective redistribution.
Negative	Political stability (Democracy)	Bollen and Jackman (1985); Figueroa (1996); Muller (1995). Successful democracies with high inequality lead to resentful poor, greater turmoil and less stability.
Negative	Political stability (Democracy)	Acemoglu and Robinson (2001). The elite can retake power by mounting a coup which avoids costs of redistribution.

Note: Positive means greater inequality is associated with better institutions; negative is the opposite.

Source: Author's compilation.

In the subsequent sections, I will discuss some of the highlights of the core causal links between institutions and/or related policy and economic inequality.

Democracy and inequality

The major political structure that concerns scholars of political economics is democracy – or its lack – and its influence on both growth and inequality.

Of course, it is well known by now that there is no convincing causal link between democracy per se and economic growth. Although there is an association between the nations that have attained the highest standards of living and political democracy, there is no strong evidence that democracy in and of itself leads to higher economic growth (see Przeworski and Limongi (1993)). Democracy can lead to lower growth in many cases as some redistributive policies may lead to worse economic performance. However, higher income and economic growth may also lead societies to push for greater democracy and political freedom, thus confounding causation.

In the same way, we also need to be careful when considering the ways in which democracy may or may not promote greater economic equality. Democratic institutions might be more likely to promote greater economic equality. Conversely, more economically equal societies might be more likely to become democracies or to preserve democratic institutions. There might be indirect effects of these two causations. Successful societies that encourage economic growth might see economic inequality rise at first (see the extensive literature on the Kuznets curve) and then decline as the nations reach high levels of income. Conversely, democracies that promote growth might see countervailing political forces that lobby for greater redistribution as inequality widens, sometimes to the point of diminishing long-term growth prospects. Non-democracies may be controlled by elites who have access to both political power and greater wealth. They, in turn, may choose to use or distort institutions to further preserve their privileges so that inequality is maintained or made worse, even as the economy grows.

One strand of the literature emphasizes the ways in which democracy may promote greater equality or prolong autocracy or exacerbate economic inequality. One of the direct ways in which this might occur is by increasing accountability and limiting rent-seeking likely to generate income inequality. The key document in this literature is probably North and Weingast's 1989 paper on the importance of credible commitment to property rights and checks on executive power as key to Britain's rise as a modern power in the 18th century. The Glorious Revolution in seventeenth-century England resulted in a more constrained Crown, sharing power with Parliament. Paradoxically, a less powerful king led to a stronger central government that saw a newly influential 18th-century Britain use its influence to successfully conduct an expansive foreign policy and permanently raise government spending as a share of gross domestic product (see Brewer (1989); Nye (2007); Pincus (2009)). The modern political economy literature utilizing standard models and econometric analyses for this is surveyed in Acemoglu *et al.* (2005).

However, as Savoia *et al.* (2010) cautioned in their survey of inequality and institutions, democracies are not always so hospitable to property rights. Accountability and checks and balances may limit some forms of rent-seeking, but democracy, and its attendant susceptibility to unbridled populism, can undermine existing property rights, and hence the credibility of future property rights. This goes back to the earliest surveys of Przeworski and Limongi (1993) or Bardhan (1999) who underlined the tendency of a new majority to take advantage of democracy to promote redistribution that effectively undermines existing property arrangements. This is the theme of work on how democracy – through the promotion of more open and more widespread elections – enables populist redistribution.

Since workers may have stronger unions or otherwise interfere in the institutions of wage determination, costs may be systematically higher and labor supply less efficient than in more market-driven conditions (Savoia *et al.* 2010, p. 147). Poor labor market institutions may mitigate some of the beneficial effects of wage redistribution through lowering growth or distorting inequality in other ways. And of course, there is no guarantee that highly contested elections in less developed economies with otherwise poor social and political institutions will be able to either control inequality or deliver public goods.

Ultimately, we do not understand how a competitive democratic process necessarily mitigates or exacerbates the pre-existing social and economic inequalities that exist. It is quite likely that the effects of democracy work differently in poor nations with complementarily weak institutions.

Theoretical work by Acemoglu and Robinson (2006) has sought to formalize the intuition that initial distributions of power are more significant than political forms in limiting economic inequality. Dominant elites may not only work to preserve antimarket or anticompetitive institutions, they could also serve to offset democratic pressures to redress social inequalities. But it seems to be increasingly the view that the ways in which democracy affects inequality are heavily determined by pre-existing inequalities. Where elites have much to lose from redistribution, they may serve as interest groups resisting both reform and direct redistribution, with Robinson (2006) arguing that this is critical for preindustrial nations whose landed elite are especially vulnerable to taxation.

However, much of this literature either begs or evades the question of whether it is the initial inequality in resources that is relevant or the nature of social and political inequalities that constrain competition. For example, Mokyr and Nye (2007) noted that in 18th-century Britain, high landowner concentration did not prevent reforms that eventually eroded both the power and the income shares of the landed elite. This is because the commercial and city elites behind Parliament taxed the rural elites lightly, while promoting liberal and pro-market reforms that eventually helped to undermine the dominance of the landed aristocracy as industrialization and improved market integration destroyed the autarkic agricultural arrangements that helped to sustain aristocratic power. Ultimately, the desirability of the larger and more advanced industrial market allowed the system to "trade" social inequality for greater national income. In much the same way, there has been no systematic investigation in Asia of the ways in which entrenched rural elites in India or the Philippines derive their control of the economy primarily from the unequal initial distribution of assets or from their benefiting from economic and political rules that favor them. It is never entirely clear why direct redistribution, without structural or economic reforms, might reliably improve long-term inequality if it merely exacerbated the underlying social conflicts.

The interaction between democratic institutions and inequality is especially pronounced for Asia. As Savoia *et al.* (2010) noted, Asian countries do well on most measures of institutional quality (e.g., regulatory quality, government effectiveness, property rights protection) but score poorly on measures of democracy relative to most other nations. This highlights the importance of asking how the conflict over resources and the rules for their distribution matter in terms of determining which institutions "constrain" or worsen inequality. Indeed, the highly endogenous nature of institutions should also give us pause when considering which political interventions might serve to ameliorate economic and social inequalities.

Labor/wage rules and inequality

An important consideration for the potential channel between democracy and inequality is the degree to which democracies promote policies that are seen to be favorable to labor or to unions (including protective labor regulations like minimum wages, tenure regulations, or varieties of collective bargaining). However, wage rules may shift the distribution of resources to labor from capital and lower inequality, or they may raise labor costs to the point where higher unemployment hurts growth, income equality, and possibly development.

The difficulties of teasing out the links between labor policy and inequality can be seen in the empirical exercise by Checchi and García-Peñalosa (2008). They attempt to link labor market institutions, such as employer protection legislation, collective bargaining, or provision of unemployment benefits, to wage dispersion and therefore to income distribution. However, as they note, the theoretical impact of stronger pro-labor institutions on income inequality is ambiguous.

For example, the direct effects of higher unemployment benefits reduce inequality directly through aid to the lower end of the income strata and through lower wage dispersion. However, the potential for a higher unemployment rate due to the effects of implicitly raising the cost of labor has a negative effect on hiring. Finally, the macroeconomic effects of promoting a higher wage share (relative to capital) are ambiguous for income distribution (Checchi and García-Peñalosa 2008, p. 610). Thus, there are no clear grounds for supposing that changing labor institutions or regulatory policy should *a priori* promote greater or lesser inequality.

Checchi and García-Peñalosa (2008) considered inequality trends in different European countries and found conditional correlations between some groups of countries – particularly those with otherwise strong institutions – and the capacity of labor regulation and unemployment benefits to improve inequality. However, the lack of a clear theoretical link between these groupings and the clear negative effect of these labor institutions on inequality in other countries casts doubt on a purely empirical macroeconomic exercise to suggest policy that is clearly welfare improving. As a commenter on their paper noted, the proposed "optimal regulations" that the authors propose could not be uniformly applied to the European nations they studied, with two-thirds of the sample suffering either an increase in inequality or unemployment or both (Zweimuller in Checchi and García-Peñalosa (2008, p. 639)).

This exercise is actually useful for considering the problems in trying to draw policy implications from our empirical studies of institutions and inequality. Particularly when dealing with fundamental political changes like democracy versus autocracy or centralized versus decentralized political systems, it is hard to believe that any exogenous shift in institutions would not change so many underlying social conditions that the very characteristics that might have driven the correlations will be undone.

Asian inequality

Whatever the relationship that emerges in international comparisons, it is clear that democratic institutions are of minor importance for Asian inequality. Consider the comprehensive comparison of institutions, democracy, and inequality measures contained in Table 8.3.

Income and land equality in Asia are substantially above those of Africa and Latin America, despite having average democracy scores well below those of all the regions except Africa. What is noteworthy is how Asia performs on various economic and institutional measures. It scores high (relative to non-Organisation for Economic Co-operation and Development [OECD] countries) on property rights, regulatory quality, government effectiveness, political stability, and executive constraints. This suggests that Asian nations have somehow solved many of the problems in attaining greater material equality, despite not having the kinds of political competition that may be beneficial to promoting redistribution or open access.

Very often (as in the cases of the Republic of Korea and Taipei,China), early industrialization was also accompanied by successful land reform and opening up of their economic system to more modern production, more focused on manufacturing and industry. In the case of the Republic of Korea, land reform was facilitated by redistributing lands formerly controlled by the Japanese. In both cases, it is not clear whether the land reform's success helped propel further development or whether the success of land reform was also symptomatic of other favorable conditions that made economic reforms generally more feasible. As with many studies concerning political control and economic reform and ties to inequality, it is not clear how to disentangle the various endogeneity issues, whereby inequality breeds poor institutions or poor institutions further inequality. What is clear is that strong attention to growth-promoting institutions has led these nations to acquire a greater stake in growth-sustaining institutions, which themselves support a degree of openness that hinders extreme inequalities of income. However, these systems do not necessarily impede the accumulation of large fortunes, and it remains to be seen whether further growth is compatible with lessened inequality or whether marginal steps to lessen inequality may interfere with growth and development.

A case for the success of land reform as a condition of development emerges from a comparative study of the Republic of Korea, the Philippines, and Taipei,China (You 2011) where the argument is made that the external pressures

Table 8.3 Institutions, democracy, and inequality measures during the 1990s

Variables	*Number of countries*	*Mean*	*Standard deviation*
Property rights in 2000			
Africa	30	4.49	1.36
Asia	13	5.58	1.65
Latin America	23	4.70	1.11
OECD	24	8.60	1.06
Transition economies	13	5.82	0.83
Regulatory quality in 1998			
Africa	35	−0.33	0.66
Asia	13	0.33	0.50
Latin America	24	0.31	0.67
OECD	24	0.86	0.25
Transition economies	26	−0.22	0.81
Government effectiveness in 1998			
Africa	33	−0.46	0.58
Asia	12	0.23	0.87
Latin America	23	−0.26	0.60
OECD	24	1.36	0.46
Transition economies	26	−0.26	0.66
Political stability in 1998			
Africa	32	−0.66	0.86
Asia	12	0.06	0.93
Latin America	23	−0.25	0.56
OECD	24	1.11	0.43
Transition economies	26	0.07	0.73
Executive constraints in 1998			
Africa	36	2.86	2.00
Asia	13	5.08	1.85
Latin America	22	6.04	1.04
OECD	22	6.91	0.29
Transition economies	26	5.00	2.13
Democracy (Vanhanen's index) in 1998			
Africa	36	6.52	6.90
Asia	12	16.57	8.79
Latin America	24	18.32	8.57
OECD	24	33.78	6.56
Transition economies	26	20.26	11.36
Income inequality (Gini index) in 1994			
Africa	19	48.47	4.92
Asia	11	41.51	5.00
Latin America	17	47.58	3.33
OECD	20	36.26	3.97
Transition economies	17	41.24	8.99

Table 8.3 Continued

Variables	*Number of countries*	*Mean*	*Standard deviation*
Land inequality (family farms,%) in 1998			
Africa	36	52.86	11.31
Asia	12	66.92	16.30
Latin America	24	28.13	9.83
OECD	24	74.92	18.56
Transition economies	25	25.84	25.42

OECD = Organisation for Economic Co-operation and Development.

Note: Authors' elaboration based on the most representative observations during the 1990s.

Source: Adapted from A. Savoia, J. Easaw, and A. McKay. 2010. Inequality, Redistribution and Rent-Seeking. *World Development.* 38 (2). pp. 142–54.

on the Republic of Korea and Taipei,China to reform produced low inequality and support for meritocracy and a professional bureaucracy, while the Philippines' failures resulted in higher corruption and elite capture. The problem with this argument is that the author does not do much to disentangle the particulars of land reform or the ways in which implementation may or may not hinder industrialization. For example, the Philippine case not only exhibits the obvious problems of persistent corruption and elite capture, but also the form of the reforms seems designed to preserve low-level productivity, encourage continued state intervention, and otherwise interfere with the structural transformation from the countryside to the city that might be seen as a precondition for a successful growth transition (see Fabella (2009) on Philippine land reform or Nye (2011) on structural transformation and barriers to migration). Indeed, it is telling that You (2011) believes that the Republic of Korea and Taipei,China have succeeded because of outside pressures (the United States and the communist threat), while the Philippines failed due to capture of the land reform process (using an argument about reforms and vested interests common in the literature since the work of Olson (1984)). However, if these pressures were strong enough, it is also possible that the impetus given to structural and economic reforms was just as important in promoting growth, and that it was these changes that promoted improvements rather than the land reform per se. After all, the importance of economic institutional indicators across the region, regardless of land reform, seems to be a more general variable for explaining the success of both economic catch-up and lessened Asian inequality.

The other Asian evidence in favor of an initial inequality measure conditioning subsequent performance comes from cross-sectional work on India by Banerjee and Iyer (2005), who argued that areas with inherited unequal land distribution had more polarized politics. Democracy led to peasants promoting redistribution, while their own assets were at risk from powerful elites. The result was lessened investment. In this case, however, it is not clear whether exogenous shifts in inequality would necessarily promote improvement if it worsened conflict, and of course we do not know if wholesale, investment-favorable economic reforms would be viable under such political conditions.

In contrast, we can easily identify some major economic regulations as direct contributors to inequality in Asia. Since it is well known that structural reform (the transformation from rural agriculture to urban industry) has been the core determinant of successful development, any interference with this dynamic will hamper adjustment and potentially worsen inequality. In the People's Republic of China, the *hukou* system of internal passport control prevents most members of the rural population from moving to urban areas, thus serving as a major contributor to the existing rural–urban divide, which is the primary driver of inequality in the country today (Liu 2005).

The special case of land reform and inequality

As briefly mentioned earlier, many Asian nations have benefited from successful land reform programs and have also managed to combine relatively high growth with low inequality and rapid poverty reduction. The literature on the Asian experience, in particular, goes back to Birdsall *et al.* (1995). In that paper, the authors' in focus was on showing that in many cases, there was not necessarily a contradiction between policies that promoted growth and reduced inequality. In that regard, the ability of many Asian economies, especially the Far Eastern tigers (e.g., Republic of Korea and Taipei,China), to ignite rapid growth while engaging in rapid and effective land reform has been especially encouraging. However, it is not entirely clear to what extent the land reform and asset redistribution served as a causal factor in promoting further improvements in equality or growth-enhancing policy changes. Moreover, it is not even clear if the confluence of lowered inequality and rapid growth (seeming to go against the standard Kuznets observation that early industrialization and growth is usually accompanied by some worsening in income inequality) was itself affected by specific poverty reduction programs or asset redistribution (also see Birdsall and Londono (1997) for further discussion of asset inequality and poverty reduction).

The most likely mechanism for this claim is a political–economic one. Successful redistribution of land created a more equal polity that would more readily support growth enhancing reforms. Thc lack of overly dominant elites meant that no veto groups stood in the way of liberalization. A perception of widespread gains to the poor and the middle class allowed for the creation of more technocratic and professional bureaucracies, which in turn enhanced institutional quality and promoted further reform.

Of course, the lack of a dominant elite would itself be sufficient grounds for arguing against the relative importance of initial asset inequality because unequal distribution in a sufficiently competitive political environment does not necessarily translate into a very distorted political situation. If these nations began with dominant ruling elites, their "dominance," or lack thereof, does not give us an answer as to why successful and sustainable land reform was possible in some cases, while laggards like India or the Philippines could neither dislodge their pre-existing elites nor make a success of their own land reform programs. Once again, the tricky problem is disentangling mere material or income inequality from social and political inequality that is readily translated into material imbalance.

Birdsall *et al.* (1995) were on stronger grounds in showing how human capital investment, especially in education for the masses, can be both growth-promoting and equality-enhancing. Enhanced human capability equalizes labor in ways that are not easily seen in merely monetary terms. As is well known, a trained college graduate with no money is still richer in expected value terms than many a worker with less than secondary education who has already worked and accumulated assets but has lesser potential for long-term income growth. However, the large gains that have been made in extending elementary and secondary education to the poor do not by any means suggest that expanding education at higher and higher levels will provide us with nearly the same rate of return in the future. Indeed, the existing literature on educational improvements strongly suggests that the largest returns are to early childhood and prenatal interventions, and that later assistance has weaker outcomes and usually does little to improve things like test scores or long-term skills formation.

The urban–rural gap

Although there are many parallels between growing inequality in the developed and developing areas of the world, an important distinction is that the overriding differences in gross income inequality in most of Asia – and indeed in most developing nations – are mostly derived from the degree to which workers have moved out of the low-paid rural/agricultural sector and into the higher paying urban/industrial sector (see OECD (2011)). Countries that have made this transition quickly and smoothly are more likely to have seen income inequality decrease or plateau. In contrast, countries that are still in the process of transformation may have very wide income disparities, especially if any structural, regulatory, or other disparity restricts some groups' abilities to make the shift. Unsurprisingly, rural workers left out will suffer lower wages and also lower future prospects for growth and income, which is often the greater source of longer-term regional inequality (Liu 2005).

More recent work suggests that growth in India (Kotwal *et al.* 2011) has not followed quite the same pattern as growth in the People's Republic of China or the rest of East Asia. India is unusual in having seen very slow declines in the share of labor in agriculture, with virtually no decline in the absolute numbers living in poor, rural conditions given the reality of high population birthrates. The lack of an expanding export sector has also meant low foreign investment and little transformation. Growth in services has mostly come in the areas of software or information technology, banking, and communications. It is almost as if India is truly a dual economy with a small, highly educated urban elite being best placed to take care of the partial liberalization India has undergone by tying themselves to the global economy in ways that dramatically improve their income prospects.

Although the OECD study (2011) suggested that reforms like conditional cash transfers might alleviate some of the poverty and suffering of the poorest, there is no doubt that failure to resolve the inherent disparities in access to global markets will be the main impediment to both growth and structural transformation, hence slowing both long-term poverty reduction and observed income reduction in inequality.

Unexamined assumptions

Most authors acknowledge the difference between mere income inequality and inequalities of social or political control that are not measurable in purely material terms, but which help to promote inequality or stifle efforts to improve the lot of the masses or to open up the economic and political system to greater competition and participation. However, no one has managed to fully engage the difficulties this entails for measurement.

The fact that many Asian countries have simultaneously succeeded in having high growth, lowered poverty, and lowered inequality does not mean that these all will necessarily coincide, or that equality-enhancing measures might be undertaken in a way that hinders development. Even worse, a system that was to open up political access or reduce social inequalities might lead to increases in measured income inequalities that are spurious.

Consider simple things like the price of high-end urban land or control of corporations. In the former case, a highly restricted market that favored certain elite groups would tend to depress the nominal selling prices of the most desirable lands, even as bureaucracy or complicated legal procedures might serve as effective barriers to other groups' access. Thus, a reform that successfully opened up access to those assets would see their market value rise as more groups bid for them. In the short to medium term, this might lead to higher measured inequality as the assets of elites who held on to their lands rose in book value while in no way reflecting the effective decline in "real" value. Similarly, corporate heads able to give themselves untaxed perks or manipulate rules so as to limit takeovers and competition would need lower salaries than chief executive officers in countries with more competitive business cultures. Thus, a shift to a more egalitarian and market-oriented system would actually see the salaries of genuinely successful and productive executives rise because they would now need to be compensated more visibly in cash in lieu of the lost perks and lesser competition enjoyed by the older class of privileged elites. Any analysis of inequality that only focused on money-denominated wealth would not pick up the loss of social and positional goods that precipitated this change. Indeed, it is quite likely that more socially unequal societies would have many goods – especially status or positional goods – allocated through nonmarket mechanisms that might lead wealth measures to underestimate actual inequality (as in socialist or communist regimes). Conversely, permitting nominal inequality to rise could sometimes serve as a trade-off that promotes growth-enhancing policy and serves as partial compensation in a more open and less restricted political and economic system (see Nye (2002) for a discussion of the problem of positional goods). But of course, no existing measures of inequality even begin to touch on these issues.

Finally, even if we hold a given distribution of income constant, in periods of rising income, the "real" (or utility-adjusted) income inequality of the population would perforce fall because of diminishing marginal utility of income. More important, since technology is likely to benefit overwhelmingly the poorest (considering innovations in food, medicine, transportation, and housing have the greatest impact on those with next to nothing), effective inequality could be declining, even as measured inequalities rise (consider how the relative gaps in infant mortality or life expectancy have rapidly converged in many parts of the world, often to a greater extent than measured incomes). This, too, is not captured by income statistics.

Conclusion and future challenges

Ultimately, we cannot really do much to get around the dual causality of institutions and inequality. Chong and Gradstein (2007) have produced the most recent attempt to both model this dual causality and use macro vector autoregression techniques to decompose the relative importance of each direction. They conclude that the arrow from inequality to institutions dominates the opposite effect. As they note, "institutional reform may be an instrument to reduce inequality; political factors, however, may prevent its implementation" (Chong and Gradstein 2007, p. 464). In the Asian case, however, the strong changes in both economic policy and institutions, despite high initial inequality, are probably the best examples of exogenous and well-enforced economic reforms helpfully accompanying more direct growth-enhancing reforms. However, the continued problem of eliminating endogeneity and of distinguishing between easily measured and harder to measure sources of social and political inequality will make it hard to focus on institutional reforms that would unambiguously and safely promote desirable and growth-compatible improvements in inequality.

The more important problem is how to think about existing inequality in Asia and the challenges faced by the different Asian nations. The literature suggests that there are two issues involved. The first is a worldwide shift in the demand for many types of labor, driven by changes in technology and the rise of a new global economy. This has tended to promote outsized gains for the mobile, flexible, and highly educated elites who have been well positioned to take advantage of the new world economy of the past 30 years and for urban workers who have been plugged into international trade, especially in the quarter-century preceding the financial crisis. The second factor, largely confined to the developing world, is how to think about the structural split or rural–urban divide, which is a primary cause of observed inequality in developing and newly developed nations. To the extent that something can be done to efficiently accelerate this shift and to remove disparities in opportunity for rural and low-income workers to enter the global economy, policy will be successful in enhancing growth, reducing poverty, and eventually dampening observed income inequality.

Certain compensatory programs have been suggested as important policy features to alleviate inequality. These include improved education, with basic literacy and universal secondary education having the greatest long-term benefits. Other policies involving direct redistribution, such as poverty assistance or social assistance like retirement pension schemes, unemployment insurance, and targeted infrastructure spending, presuppose effective tax systems and fiscal spending mechanisms. However, it is also the case that countries most likely to have poor economic institutions and high inequality are least likely to be very good at establishing such systems or implementing them in an effective, neutral fashion. Corruption, of course, is commonplace in these environments and, as the large literature on the subject demonstrates, dealing with it independently of institutional reform opens up another laundry list of complications and problems.

It is also likely that as the size of the middle class rises, discontent with perceived inequality is less about the formal distribution of income (to the extent that this shows up in Gini coefficients and the like) than about positional or social differences perceived to be unfair. Income effects may increase demand for democratization or class representation in highly authoritarian cultures. Concerns about corruption or unfair advantages accruing to those tied to the government also start to matter more as incomes rise or when a crisis stalls expected growth. Issues of governance that were previously shunted aside may also achieve more prominence. Any discussion of the needed policy reforms to deal with rising or unchanged inequality in Asia must make efforts to confront the nonobvious, nonmaterial sources of inequality. In some cases, reforms that might open the workplace or industry might seemingly raise income inequality as typically measured. To the extent that this only reflects the monetization/formalization of benefits that have, up until now, been taken in the form of untaxed perks or of protection from competition, it might be possible to have a situation where perceived inequalities may have diminished, even as measured monetary inequality seems to rise. Conversely, lower measured inequality may hide socially protected differences that would be more disturbing to the populace, precisely because it is so hard to overcome these inequalities.

Aid agencies promoting reform have to be especially careful of making crude policy suggestions based on large-scale measured inequality aggregates that could damage growth prospects, limit poverty reduction, and might do little to assuage discontented citizens' perceptions of inequality, merely for the sake of improving a given set of aggregate index measurements. Given the current state of the literature, it is not at all clear that we are able to evaluate small-scale interventions and their effects on overall inequality measures in ways that solve the equity-efficiency problem effectively. Greater attention should be given to opening up economic possibilities for larger segments of the population and increasing opportunities by eroding political privileges that favor certain groups, protect them from competition, or otherwise exclude many groups in society.

References

Acemoglu, D., and J. A. Robinson. 2000. Why Did the West Extend the Franchise? Democracy, Inequality and Growth in Historical Perspective. *Quarterly Journal of Economics.* 115 (4). pp. 1167–99.

——. 2001. A Theory of Political Transition. *American Economic Review.* 91 (4). pp. 938–63.

——. 2006. De Facto Political Power and Institutional Persistence. *American Economic Association Papers and Proceedings.* 96 (2). pp. 325–30.

Acemoglu, D., S. Johnson, and J. A. Robinson. 2005. Institutions as the Fundamental Cause of Long-Run Growth. In P. Aghion and S. Durlauf, eds. *Handbook of Economic Growth.* North Holland: Elsevier.

Amendola, A., J. Easaw, and A. Savoia. 2011. Inequality in Developing Economies: The Role of Institutional Development. *Public Choice.* Published online on 3 August.

Banerjee, A., and L. Iyer. 2005. History, Institutions, and Economic Performance: The Legacy of Colonial Land Tenure Systems in India. *American Economic Review.* 95 (4). pp. 1190–213.

Bardhan, P. 1999. Democracy and Development: A Complex Relationship. In I. Shapiro and C. Hacker, eds. *Democracy's Value.* Cambridge, UK: Cambridge University Press.

Barro, R. J. 2000. Inequality and Growth in a Panel of Countries. *Journal of Economic Growth.* 5 (1). pp. 5–32.

Birdsall, N., and J. L. Londono. 1997. Asset Inequality Matters: An Assessment of the World Bank's Approach to Poverty Reduction. *American Economic Review.* 87 (2). pp. 32–7.

Birdsall, N., D. Ross, and R. Sabot. 1995. Inequality and Growth Reconsidered: Lessons from East Asia. *World Bank Economic Review.* 9 (3). pp. 477–508.

Boix, C. 2003. *Democracy and Redistribution.* Cambridge, UK: Cambridge University Press.

Bollen, K. A., and R. W. Jackman. 1985. Political Democracy and the Size Distribution of Income. *American Sociological Review.* 50 (4). pp. 438–57.

Bourguignon, F., and C. Morrisson. 1998. Inequality and Development: The Role of Dualism. *Journal of Development Economics.* 57 (2). pp. 233–57.

Bourguignon, F., and T. Verdier. 2000. Oligarchy, Democracy, Inequality and Growth. *Journal of Development Economics.* 62 (2). pp. 285–313.

Bourguignon, F., F. Ferreira, and M. Walton. 2007. Efficiency, Equity and Inequality Traps: A Research Agenda. *Journal of Economic Inequality.* 5. pp. 235–56.

Bowles, S. 2004. Institutional Poverty Traps. In S. Bowles, S. N. Durlauf, and K. Hoff, eds. *Poverty Traps.* Princeton, NJ: Princeton University Press. pp. 116–38.

Brewer, J. 1989. *The Sinews of Power: War, Money and the English State, 1688–1783.* London: Unwin Hyman.

Cervellati, M., P. Fortunato, and U. Sunde. 2008. Hobbes to Rousseau: Inequality, Institutions and Development. *The Economic Journal.* 118 (531). pp. 1354–84.

Checchi, D., and C. García-Peñalosa. 2008. Labour Market Institutions and Income Inequality. *Economic Policy.* 56. pp. 601–49.

Chong, A., and C. Calderón. 2000. Institutional Quality and Income Distribution. *Economic Development and Cultural Change.* 48 (4). pp. 761–86.

Chong, A., and M. Gradstein. 2007. Inequality and Institutions. *Review of Economics and Statistics.* 89 (3). pp. 454–65.

Engerman, S. L., and K. L. Sokoloff. 2002. Factor Endowments, Inequality and Paths of Development among New World Economies. *NBER Working Paper* No. 9259. Cambridge, MA: National Bureau of Economic Research.

Fabella, R. 2009. CARP without Coase: Redistributing Poverty in the Philippines. *University of the Philippines School of Economics Working Paper.* Manila, Philippines: University of the Philippines.

Figueroa, A. 1996. The Distributive Issue in Latin America. *International Social Science Journal.* 48 (2). pp. 231–44.
Glaeser, E. L. 2005. Inequality. *NBER Working Paper Series* No. 11511. Cambridge, MA: National Bureau of Economic Research.
Glaeser, E. L., J. Scheinkman, and A. Shleifer. 2003. The Injustice of Inequality. *Journal of Monetary Economics.* 50 (1). pp. 199–222.
Gradstein, M. 2007. Inequality, Democracy, and the Protection of Property Rights. *The Economic Journal.* 117 (516). pp. 252–69.
Keefer, P., and S. Knack. 2002. Polarization, Politics and Property Rights: Links between Inequality and Growth. *Public Choice.* 111 (1–2). pp. 127–54.
Kotwal, A., B. Ramaswami, and W. Wadwha. 2011. Economic Liberalization and Indian Economic Growth: What's the Evidence? *Journal of Economic Literature.* 49 (4). pp. 1152–99.
Kuznets, S. 1955. Economic Growth and Income Inequality. *American Economic Review.* 45 (1). pp. 1–28.
Li, H., L. Squire, and H.-F. Zou. 1998. Explaining International and Intertemporal Variations in Income Inequality. *The Economic Journal.* 108 (446). pp. 26–43.
Liu, Z. 2005. Institution and Inequality: The Hukou System in [the People's Republic of] China. *Journal of Comparative Economics.* 33 (1). pp. 133–57.
Mokyr, J., and J. V. Nye. 2007. Distributional Coalitions, the Industrial Revolution, and the Origins of Economic Growth in Britain. *Southern Economic Journal.* 74 (1). pp. 50–70.
Muller, E. N. 1995. Democracy, Economic Development, and Income Inequality. *American Sociological Review.* 60 (6). pp. 966–82.
North, D. 1990. *Institutions, Institutional Change, and Economic Performance.* Cambridge, UK: Cambridge University Press.
North, D., and B. R. Weingast. 1989. Constitutions and Commitment: The Evolution of Institutions Governing Public Choice in Seventeenth-Century England. *Journal of Economic History.* 49 (4). pp. 803–32.
Nye, J. V. 2002. Economic Growth. Part II. Irreducible Inequality. 1 April. Retrieved from Library of Economics and Liberty at http://www.econlib.org/library/Columns/Nyepositional.html (accessed November 2011).
——. 2007. *War, Wine, and Taxes: The Political Economy of Anglo-French Trade, 1689–1900.* Princeton, NJ: Princeton University Press.
——. 2011. Taking Institutions Seriously: Rethinking the Political Economy of Development in the Philippines. *Asian Development Review.* 28 (1). pp. 1–21.
Olson, M. 1984. *The Rise and Decline of Nations: Economic Growth, Stagflation, and Social Rigidities.* New Haven and London: Yale University Press.
Organisation for Economic Co-operation and Development (OECD). 2011. *Divided We Stand: Why Inequality Keeps Rising.* Paris: OECD.
Pincus, S. 2009. *1688: The First Modern Revolution.* New Haven, CT: Yale University Press.
Przeworski, A., and F. Limongi. 1993. Political Regimes and Economic Growth. *Journal of Economic Perspectives.* 7 (3). pp. 51–69.
Robinson, J. A. 2006. Economic Development and Democracy. *Annual Review of Political Science.* 9. pp. 503–27.
Savoia, A., J. Easaw, and A. McKay. 2010. Inequality, Redistribution and Rent-Seeking. *World Development.* 38 (2). pp. 142–54.
Sonin, K. 2003. Why the Rich May Favor Poor Protection of Property Rights. *Journal of Comparative Economics.* 31 (4). pp. 715–31.
Thorbecke, E., and C. Charumilind. 2002. Economic Inequality and Its Socioeconomic Impact. *World Development.* 30 (9). pp. 1477–95.
You, J.-S. 2011. *Democracy, Inequality, and Corruption.* APSA 2011 Annual Meeting Paper. http://ssrn.com/abstract=1903420

9 Government fiscal policies and redistribution in Asian countries

Iris Claus, Jorge Martinez-Vazquez, and Violeta Vulovic

Introduction

Asia's rapid economic growth in recent decades has resulted in a substantial reduction in poverty and a dramatic improvement in welfare and the standard of living for a large proportion of the population. Although poverty reduction remains the main challenge for the region, widening income inequality is emerging as a concern. In recent years, income disparity has risen in several developing Asian economies. At the same time, unequal access to basic social services, such as education and health, is seen as a significant problem that may be exacerbating growing income inequality.

A variety of public policies have been used to improve the distribution of income and reduce inequality. These can be grouped into (i) policies and strategies to make growth patterns more inclusive; (ii) public spending (e.g., on education, health, and social services) to enhance human capacity and enable everyone in society to participate in higher living standards; (iii) taxation and direct income transfers that redistribute income from higher to lower income groups; and (iv) governance and institutional reforms to level the playing field and enable everyone in society to participate in and benefit from development on an equitable basis (such as labor market policy, social protection and safety nets, land distribution, anticorruption, and antisocial exclusion).

Review of the literature on the effectiveness of redistributive fiscal policies

A fair distribution of income as one of the most important goals of government policy has meant that a great deal of effort of research in economics has gone into conceptualizing and measuring how the revenue and expenditure sides of government budgets affect the distribution of income among households and individuals and how effective they are in actually helping the poor. Formally, the study of these effects is known as tax and expenditure incidence. This section reviews the conceptual bases of the different approaches that have been used in the literature.[1]

---

[1] Some parts of this section draw on Martinez-Vazquez (2008) and Cuesta and Martinez-Vazquez (2011).

It discusses some of the key measurement issues and main techniques used, and summarizes the empirical findings in previous studies.

Tax incidence analysis

Tax incidence – the analysis of who ultimately bears the burden of government taxes in the economy – is covered in a vast literature in economics.[2] Despite this vast literature, establishing firm final evidence on the distributional impact of different taxes remains a difficult task because the varying results depend on economic conditions and the sometimes complex feedback effects that operate through the entire economy. Because of this complexity, there has always been a grain of skepticism about the empirical findings in the tax incidence literature (Bird and de Wulf 1973). However, our knowledge and understanding have improved greatly due to the analytical improvements of key economic issues in incidence analysis; greater data availability, in particular household income and expenditure surveys in many countries; and more powerful computational techniques, such as microsimulation models and computable general equilibrium models.

There are several key concepts in tax incidence analysis. First is the distinction between "statutory" (or legal) incidence and "economic" incidence, or those taxpayers who are by law required to pay the tax versus those taxpayers who ultimately bear the tax burden. The latter is what really counts. The "shifting" of taxes happens because the agents statutorily responsible to pay the taxes can alter their economic behavior and transfer or shift the burden of taxes to other agents via changes in prices charged to consumers, wages paid to workers, or the return paid on investments. The degree of shifting depends on the elasticities of demand, supply, and substitution in the use of inputs of production among the economic agents interacting in the activity or market being taxed. Economic agents with lower elasticities – that is, lower ability (or willingness) to react – are more likely to ultimately bear the burden of taxes. Because adapting or reacting to taxes takes time, the economic incidence of taxes will tend to be different in the short and the long term. For example, capital owners may bear the burden of increased profit taxes in the short term, but this burden can be shifted to workers in the longer term as decreased investment leads to lower productivity and wages and higher unemployment.

Second, it is important to realize that taxes impose total burdens that go beyond the amounts actually collected by governments. This difference receives the name "excess burdens" of taxes, also known as deadweight losses. The excess burdens arise because taxes lead to less efficient uses of economic resources and lower output and income in the economy as taxes distort the choices by economic agents. For example, income taxes affect labor–leisure choices and savings and investment decisions.

---

[2] For classic reviews of tax incidence, see for example Newbery and Stern (1987), Shah and Whalley (1991), and Musgrave and Musgrave (1989).

Third, a significant difficulty in measuring the impact of taxes is to figure out what is the appropriate "counterfactual," i.e., the situation before the taxes were implemented that should be used as the benchmark in the measurement of the impact. Different choices of the counterfactual situation can be made, but there is always a difficulty in approximating the distribution of income that would have taken place in the absence of taxes.

To have a complete view of tax incidence, we need to take into account the impact of tax expenditures, negative income taxes, and in-kind transfers. Tax expenditures are special tax law provisions pursuing a variety of policy objectives and taking the form of exemptions, rebates, special deductions, tax credits, or even special lower tax rates. They can make a tax system more progressive (i.e., increase income equality) or more regressive (i.e., lower income equality), depending on a variety of public choice issues such as lobbying power. Moreover, an important consideration is that tax expenditures cannot help the poor unless they pay taxes. And many of the poor do not pay taxes. This point highlights some of the limitations of redistributional policies from the tax side of the budget.

An important amount of redistribution can be implemented via negative taxes. These cash transfers are targeted to the poor and are by nature highly progressive.[3] However, there are some caveats in their application. To minimize fraud, a sophisticated tax administration is required. In addition, stigma among the recipients can lead to low and uneven take-up of benefits, which may affect the assumed progressivity of this type of transfer.

For in-kind transfers, their incidence typically depends on the degree of participation by income groups. In-kind transfer programs, such as food stamps, tend to be quite progressive. But not all in-kind transfer programs are progressive. For example, voucher programs for higher education tend to benefit higher income groups more than lower income groups because their uptake of higher education typically is proportionally higher, and so in general, voucher programs are regressive.

Determining the impact of taxes on income distribution

Three approaches have been used to estimate the distributional impact of taxes. The first, and most widely used, is microsimulation analysis using individual household data and conventional assumptions of tax incidence. The second is based on computable general equilibrium models for the entire economy and just a few representative individuals, and the third is based on econometric estimation models with more aggregate data.

Microsimulation models of tax incidence. These models allocate tax burdens to different income groups, ordered from rich to poor by deciles or quintiles of the population, on the basis of a series of assumptions about who bears the final burden of taxes. For each tax, a portion of the revenues collected is imputed as tax

[3] For a discussion of negative income taxes see, for example, Milanovic (1995).

burden to each income group in a way that exhausts the total revenues collected. For example, the revenues from excise taxes on tobacco products are allocated to different income groups in proportion to their relative share in the consumption of tobacco products. To arrive at an estimate of the incidence for the entire tax system, the incidence for each tax is calculated separately for each income group. These results are added up across all taxes for each income group to arrive at the total burden for each income group. Typically, the total burden is expressed as an average total tax rate, i.e., the proportion of income paid in taxes by each income group. The information on total income, sources of income, and expenditure patterns is generally obtained from data in household or consumer income and expenditure surveys. Taxes collected are obtained from the tax administration authorities.

A critical step in the process is to make explicit assumptions about the shifting and final incidence of taxes based on theoretical and empirical analyses.[4] Typically, there has been wide agreement on the assumptions used for the different taxes, and, where there is no consensus, the usual approach is to conduct sensitivity analysis to check how the results differ under alternative assumptions.

The microsimulation approach to tax incidence presents advantages and disadvantages. On the plus side, the methodology is relatively simple and easy to implement, the underlying assumptions are transparent, and the implications of alternative assumptions can be easily compared. The analysis can also include large samples of taxpayers. On the minus side, good information on income distribution is not always available, and general equilibrium second-round feedback effects are typically ignored. More importantly, the shifting assumptions that play a critical role in the results have been criticized for "stipulating" the incidence of various taxes (Devarajan *et al.* 1980).

General equilibrium models of tax incidence. This approach to tax incidence was pioneered by Harberger (1962). It analyzes the incidence of taxes within the context of a general equilibrium model of the economy, without making explicit assumptions about the final shifting of taxes. Instead, tax incidence is determined by the initial structure of the economy with the final outcome measured by observing the differences in the vector of equilibrium prices before and after the tax change. One of the greatest insights from this approach is that the final incidence of taxes depends on the values of several critical parameters in the economy, including the capital–labor ratios in different sectors and the elasticity of substitution in production among the different factors. Later on, Harberger's model was operationalized by the development of computable general equilibrium models. These are relatively complex models, which attempt to capture in more detail the general equilibrium responses to taxes in the economy. The models are numerically solved using data from the national income accounts, household expenditure surveys, and taxpayer data.[5] General equilibrium models capture all the parameters that should

4 See Shah and Whalley (1991) and Browning (1978).

5 Some of the original models include those in Fullerton *et al.* (1978, 1979) and Ballard *et al.* (1985).

play a role in final tax incidence among different income groups: different demand patterns, different endowments in resources, and variations in capital–labor ratios in different economic sectors.

The general equilibrium approach also has its advantages and disadvantages. On the positive side, it employs an explicit structural model of the economy from first bases with utility/demand functions and production/supply functions. It offers transparency in how incidence results are linked to assumptions on fundamental parameters, such as the elasticity of substitution in production, and the incidence results include measures of excess burdens. Moreover, general equilibrium models take into account indirect or second-round feedback effects of taxation or government expenditure changes. On the negative side, general equilibrium models are operationally intensive and the number of taxpayers represented needs to be small. And even though the approach does not stipulate incidence results, it does stipulate a long list of critical parameters, including elasticities of substitution in production and demand and supply (Fullerton and Rogers 1991).

Regression-based estimates of the impact of taxes on income distribution. A limited number of recent studies have used multivariate econometric analysis to investigate the impact of the tax structure on the distribution of income across countries, typically measured via Gini coefficients. For example, Weller (2007) uses cross-country data from 1981–2002 and finds positive effects of progressive taxation on income distribution. Gwartney and Lawson (2006) use panel data on changes in marginal tax rates from 1980–2002 to examine their impact on the distribution of income and find that countries with the most significantly high tax brackets rate reductions have experienced the largest increases in inequality over the sample period. Duncan and Sabirianova Peter (2008) derive a complete measure of income tax progressivity and find that inequality in the distribution of income is significantly affected by their measure of progressivity. Similarly, Martinez-Vazquez *et al.* (2011b) find that higher reliance on direct over indirect taxes improves the income distribution over time for a large number of countries.

A disadvantage of the multivariate econometric approach to tax incidence is that the impact of the different elements of the structure of taxes on income distribution cannot be examined in any detail, at least not to the extent allowed by the general equilibrium approach and especially microsimulation models. On the plus side, the econometric approach allows analysis of the impact of large variations in the level and structure of taxes across countries – variations that are unlikely to be observed within the context of a single economy. Moreover, it has fewer data requirements than the microsimulation and general equilibrium approaches and uses information typically available for most countries including developing economies. In all, the econometric approach should be considered a complement rather than a substitute for the other two approaches.

Expenditure incidence analysis

From the perspective of income redistribution policies, it is important to understand the incidence of public spending programs. However, the key difficulty in measuring the impact of public expenditure on individuals and households is that with some rare exceptions, we are not able to measure output from government expenditures. How public expenditures impact different groups depends, among other things, on the composition of public expenditures, what programs are being implemented, and how much funding is going to each, such as basic education versus university-level education, or primary healthcare versus tertiary hospitals. The impact of public expenditure on the distribution of income depends also on the efficiency of government spending, the cost effectiveness of funds in delivering services, and the matching of needs of people.

The basic problem in expenditure incidence is how to measure the benefits accruing to individuals from public goods and services. In the case of private goods and services, even though marginal private benefits are not directly observable, we can infer them from market prices. In the case of public goods and services, many are provided without direct charges, and even when there is a fee or service charge, this price cannot be interpreted in general as the marginal benefit for individuals, because the supply of most public goods and services is subsidized or rationed, and it does not respond directly to demand.[6]

Determining the impact of government expenditures on income distribution

Three general approaches have been used in the estimation of expenditure incidence. The first is the benefit incidence approach, which measures by how much the income of households would have to be raised if they had to pay for subsidized public goods and services at full cost. The second is the behavioral approach, which derives estimates of households' and individuals' willingness to pay for those goods and services. The third approach uses econometric techniques with aggregate data to analyze their differential impact on income distribution generally measured by Gini coefficients.

The benefit incidence approach. This approach, which is also known as the classic or the nonbehavioral approach, was pioneered by twin World Bank studies by Selowsky (1979) for Colombia and Meerman (1979) for Malaysia. The essence of the approach is to use information on the cost of publicly provided goods and services together with information on their uses by different income groups to arrive at estimates of the distribution of benefits. Individual beneficiaries are typically grouped by income level, but they can also be grouped by geographical area, ethnic group, urban and rural location, gender, and so on. Information on individual or household use of the public goods and services is typically obtained from surveys, and it is fundamental to know how effectively public expenditure programs target the poor. Because of the required information on unit costs in the provision of public goods and services and the rate of use of those services by different individuals in practice, benefit incidence has been estimated for three main

[6] See van de Walle (1998) and Demery (2000) for two excellent and complete reviews of the issues.

categories of public goods and services: education, healthcare, and some types of infrastructure.

The benefit incidence approach has several strengths, but also weaknesses. On the positive side, it provides simplicity and transparency of estimation procedures and allows study of which public expenditure programs are most effective in reaching and improving the status of the poor. On the negative side, the cost measures may not be a good enough approximation of true benefits or marginal valuations of the public good or service provided, and it cannot incorporate changes in the behavior of individuals in response to changes in public expenditure. For example, we may find that poor households may not send their children to school, but benefit incidence does not suggest why or provide a course of policy action. Moreover, the scope is limited to public expenditure programs for which private beneficiaries can be identified. The approach can also ignore important interaction effects with the private sector. For example, if the private education sector is able to attract a higher number of richer students, benefit incidence of education becomes more progressive. If the quality of education depends, among other things, on peer pressure, the lower number of children of better-educated and wealthier families in public schools may reduce the quality of public education for the poor.

The behavioral approach: marginal willingness to pay. In essence, this approach uses individual preferences to derive marginal willingness to pay as the measure of individual benefits from public expenditures. It was pioneered by Gertler and van der Gaag (1990), Gertler and Glewwe (1990), and Younger (1999). The methodology consists of using econometric methods to exploit variation in behaviors in the use of public goods and services, prices, incomes and other household characteristics across individuals, and time to estimate demand functions for public goods and services. These demand functions generate price elasticities and willingness to pay, generally varying by income group. With that information, one can estimate the incidence of public spending programs, in particular whether they have a pro-poor incidence and whether the poor may have a more elastic response to any changes in costs associated with the use of the public good or service. Discerning the behavioral impact of public expenditure programs opens up possibilities for the better design of public policies, and in particular for better targeting expenditures to the poor.

The behavioral approach also has several strengths and weaknesses. On the positive side, it is more theoretically sound with clear foundations in microeconomics, and allows the estimation of incidence for public expenditures for which specific users cannot be identified. Furthermore, it incorporates individual behavioral responses, and therefore provides concrete guidance for policy reform. On the negative side, this approach is more data-intensive and methodologically more complex.

Regression-based estimates of the impact of government expenditures on income distribution. Using cross-country or panel data, this approach investigates the impact of government expenditures on the distribution of income, typically measured via Gini coefficients. Regression-based estimates, going as far back as Tanzi (1974), have shown that what, in many instances, would seemingly be perceived as redistributive government spending may do nothing to improve income inequality and may actually worsen it. For example, de Mello and Tiongson (2006), in a cross-country analysis (the sample running in 27–56 countries depending on availability of data) of the impact of government spending on income distribution, found the overall effects of expenditures to be unequalizing. In fact, those countries where redistribution is most needed due to high inequality are also less likely to have effective redistributive policies in place. In a country case study for Brazil, Clements (1997) similarly found that government social expenditures contributed to exacerbated income inequality. On the other hand, Jao (2000) found that in the case of Taipei,China, public expenditures on social assistance and social insurance contributed positively to reducing income inequality. In a more recent study using panel data for a large number of countries, Martinez-Vazquez *et al.* (2011a) found that aggregate public expenditures on social welfare, education, healthcare, and housing had a significant effect on reducing income inequality.

The multivariate regression approach to the analysis of public expenditure incidence also has some clear advantages and disadvantages, and therefore should be considered a complement rather than a substitute for the benefit incidence and behavioral approaches. It can analyze the impact on income distribution of large variations in levels of expenditures and their composition across countries, variations that are often not observed within the context of country case studies. Multivariate analysis also allows the examination of the evolution over time of the impact of different government expenditures on income distribution within countries and is less data-intensive. On the other hand, the analysis of income distribution at the aggregate country level does not allow the introduction in the analysis of specific details of policies and institutions that can make a significant difference to the effectiveness and overall impact of public expenditure policies. For example, two countries can have similar expenditures on primary education and healthcare, but one of these countries may put greater effort into targeting the access to these services by poor rural or urban families. This type of information is typically not available for a large number of countries and therefore is likely to be ignored in multivariate regression studies. If the information is available, there may be the possibility of using dummy variables to account for those effects. Also, to the extent that institutions and policy approaches do not change over time, their impact can be controlled by using fixed effect panel estimation approaches.

As a manner of conclusion

Although different tools and data have been used in the incidence literature, some general results and findings about the effectiveness of redistributive fiscal policies seem to hold across the different methodological approaches.

Most tax systems tend to show a mildly progressive incidence impact. However, around the world, taxes have not been a very effective means of redistributing income. One reason for this is the potentially large excess burdens or economic losses associated with highly progressive taxation. The international experience shows that the expenditure side of the budget (including transfers) can have a more significant impact on income distribution. Direct cash transfers and in-kind transfers can be quite progressive, unless there are serious targeting problems. Moreover, expenditure programs in the social sectors (education and healthcare) are more progressive the more is spent in relative and absolute terms on those goods and services, which are frequently used by the poor (basic education and primary healthcare). However, the effective targeting of lower income groups in expenditure programs is hard to design and to implement. Whether these general findings and conclusions about the effectiveness of redistributive fiscal policies also hold for Asian countries is investigated next.

Empirical estimates of the impact of fiscal policies on income inequality in Asia

This section presents estimates of the impact of fiscal policies on income inequality in Asia. They are derived from multivariate regression analysis and quantify the effects of taxation and government expenditures on income distributions measured by Gini coefficients.

Methodology and data

Using data from 150 developed, developing, and transition economies between 1970 and 2009, Claus *et al.* (2012) estimate the impact of fiscal policies on income distributions measured by Gini coefficients. Of the 150 economies, 22 are from Asia.[7] To identify Asia-specific tax and government expenditure effects, dummy variables are used. Different regressions are estimated to assess the effects of taxes and government expenditures individually and jointly using fixed effect panel estimation methodology proposed by Blundell and Bond (1998).

All regressions include lagged inequality to capture the persistence of income inequality over time, various tax and government expenditure variables, and a set of observable control variables that are commonly used in the literature to explain income inequality. Based on data availability, the following control variables are included: population growth, youth dependency, old-age dependency, a globalization index, gross domestic product (GDP) per capita, long-term unemployment, perception of corruption, schooling, and size of government. The estimations also include dummy variables to account for differences in the computation of Gini coefficients across countries.[8]

[7] Economies in Asia included are Bangladesh; Bhutan; Cambodia; the People's Republic of China; Hong Kong, China; India; Indonesia; Japan; the Republic of Korea; the Lao People's Democratic Republic; Macao, China; Malaysia; the Maldives; Mongolia; Myanmar; Nepal; Pakistan; the Philippines; Singapore; Sri Lanka; Thailand; and Viet Nam.

[8] Gini coefficients are computed from income/consumption distribution data. They can be based on gross or net income (i.e., income before or after the deduction of taxes and social contributions) or expenditure.

The following tax variables are considered: personal income tax (PIT), corporate income tax (CIT), social security contributions (SSC) and payroll taxes, general taxes on goods and services (GTGS), excises, and customs duties – all measured as a percentage of GDP. Income taxes are generally thought to reduce income inequality. However, when evaluating the impact of PIT on income inequality, it is important to take into account the progressivity of income tax scales, i.e., how fast the average tax rate rises with income. As a result, PIT revenue is interacted with a PIT progressivity measure (progressivity) constructed by Sabirianova Peter *et al.* (2010).

When assessing the impact of CIT revenue, it is important to take into account that the progressivity of corporate income taxes may be affected by countries' openness. In his seminal paper on incidence of CIT, Harberger (1962) shows that in a closed economy with two perfectly competitive sectors and fully mobile factors of production, imposing a tax on capital in one sector would cause capital to move from the taxed to the untaxed sector, further causing a reallocation of labor between the two sectors and changes in factor and output prices. Using elasticities typical for the United States economy, Harberger finds that, in these circumstances, capital bears approximately the full burden of the CIT. In his two more recent papers, Harberger (1995 and 2006) revisits the incidence of corporate income taxes in an open economy where capital can flow freely across international borders. In this setting, he finds that the burden of CIT more than fully shifts to labor. To account for these effects, the CIT variable is interacted with a globalization index.

Social security contributions and payroll taxes are commonly shared between employees and employers. However, employers tend to almost entirely shift the burden to employees in the form of lower wages. Social security contributions and payroll taxes are expected to increase income inequality if there is a cap on income for contribution. The lower the cap, the more regressive the taxes.

The evidence for the impact on income inequality of taxes on goods and services, including value-added taxes and excises, is mixed. Studies that analyze current income generally find that they are regressive, but this regressivity is reduced substantially and may even become neutral when analyzed over a longer time frame. The sign on the coefficient for general taxes on goods and services and excises could therefore be negative or not significantly different from zero. For lack of better information, customs duties are expected to have the same direction of effect on income inequality as general taxes on goods and services.

On the government spending side, four types of expenditure are considered: on social protection, education, health, and housing – all expressed as a percentage of GDP. Ideally, subcomponents of these expenditure categories would have been included, e.g., basic education versus university-level education, or primary healthcare versus tertiary hospitals, because they are likely to affect income groups differently. However, internationally comparable disaggregated data on government spending are not available. Bearing this in mind, higher government spending on social protection, education, health, and housing is expected to reduce income inequality.

The empirical analysis consists of three sets of estimation. The first set focuses only on the effects of taxation and PIT progressivity on income inequality. Similarly, the second set of estimates investigates only the effects of government spending on income distributions, while the third set includes both taxation and government expenditure to evaluate their joint effect on income inequality in Asia and other countries. A detailed description of the data, methodology, and results is contained in Claus *et al.* (2012).

Taxation and income inequality

Table 9.1 reports the estimated marginal impact of alternative tax instruments on income inequality. It shows that PIT has the expected negative impact on income inequality and that the effect is significantly higher in Asia than in the rest of the world. A one-percentage-point increase in PIT in Asia reduces income inequality by around 0.573 percentage points compared with 0.041 percentage points in the rest of the world. The finding of a greater redistributive effect of personal income taxation may be due to a larger number of people not paying income tax in Asia because their income is below a tax-free threshold. A larger share of informal employment may also be a contributing factor.

The overall impact of progressive income tax scales is modest and somewhat smaller in Asia than in the rest of the world. A one-percentage-point increase in PIT interacted with the progressivity measure reduces income inequality by around 0.002 percentage points in Asia compared with 0.005 in the rest of the world.

Including CIT in the estimation suggests that corporate income taxation reduces income disparity in the rest of the world, but that it is regressive in Asia.[9] A one-percentage-point increase in CIT raises income inequality by around 0.598 percentage points. This regressivity of CIT in Asia may be due to larger tax concessions and subsidies for firms. However, interacting CIT with globalization reverses the sign. CIT interacted with globalization lowers inequality, which is the

Table 9.1 Estimated marginal impact of taxation on income inequality (percentage points)

	Asia	*Rest of the world*
Personal income tax	−0.573	−0.041
Personal income tax × progressivity	−0.002	−0.005
Corporate income tax	0.598	−0.338
Corporate income tax × globalization	−0.017	0.005
Social security and payroll taxes	1.324	0.165
General taxes on goods and services	0.666	0.768
Excises	0.609	−0.059
Customs duties	0.174	0.651

Source: I. Claus, J. Martinez-Vazquez, and V. Vulovic. 2012. Government Fiscal Policies and Redistribution in Asian Countries. *ADB Economics Working Paper Series* No. 310. Manila: ADB.

[9] The correlation coefficient between the Gini coefficient and CIT in Asia is about 0.06.

opposite from what is expected and what is observed in the rest of the world. The finding may be due to higher effective tax rates for foreign firms in Asia compared with domestic firms and in the rest of the world.

Theory on the incidence of SSC and payroll taxes suggests that imposing these types of tax results in lower wages and higher unemployment. While these taxes are commonly levied equally between employers and employees, they are typically shifted to employees in the form of lower wages and are expected to result in increased income inequality when capped at higher incomes. The results in Table 9.1 provide support to this hypothesis, especially in Asia where the estimated effect of SSC and payroll taxes on income inequality is substantially larger than in the rest of the world (1.324 compared with 0.165).

Empirical evidence regarding the effect of GTGS on income inequality is mixed. The results for Asia and for the rest of the world support the hypothesis that they are regressive. The results suggest that a one-percentage-point increase in GTGS in Asia increases income inequality by around 0.666 percentage points compared with 0.768 in the rest of the world. Somewhat less regressive GTGS could be due to lower tax compliance in Asia. Moreover, Asia may have a greater number of small businesses not charging value-added tax (VAT), for example, because their sales are below VAT registration thresholds. Excises and customs duties are also found to be regressive in Asia. The results in Table 9.1 show an estimated effect of 0.609 percentage points for excises and 0.174 percentage points for customs duties.

Government spending and income inequality

Table 9.2 reports the estimated marginal impact of the different types of government spending on income inequality. Including only social protection expenditure in the estimation reduces the sample size by 35%, partly reflecting that many countries do not have social safety nets. The estimates suggest that a one-percentage-point increase in social protection expenditure raises income inequality in Asia by 0.49 percentage points. In the rest of the world, social protection spending has the expected negative sign, i.e., it reduces income inequality.

Social protection expenditures consist of two components: (i) services and transfers provided to individuals and households and (ii) expenditures on services

Table 9.2 Estimated marginal impact of government spending on income inequality (percentage points)

	Asia	*Rest of the world*
Social protection	0.490	−0.276
Education	−0.486	−0.034
Health	−0.241	−0.330
Housing	2.162	−0.614

Sources: I. Claus, J. Martinez-Vazquez, and V. Vulovic. 2012. Government Fiscal Policies and Redistribution in Asian Countries. *ADB Economics Working Paper Series* No. 310. Manila: ADB.

provided on a collective basis (IMF 2001). Collective social protection services include formulation and administration of government policy, formulation and enforcement of legislation and standards for providing social protection, and applied research and experimental development into social protection services. Asian countries provide relatively few services and transfers, and the second component is likely to dominate. The unexpected positive effect of social protection on income inequality suggests that government policies and legislative enforcement, i.e., the second component of social protection expenditure, may benefit higher-income households and individuals more than those with a lower income. To test this hypothesis, information on the structure of social protection expenditures would be needed; however, this is not available. Moreover, the unexpected positive effect of social protection may be due to a narrow benefit coverage and a lack of targeting to the poor for the few services and transfers that Asian countries provide.

For education, the results suggest that government expenditures in Asia have a larger negative effect on income inequality than education spending in other countries. In the case of expenditures on health, this type of expenditure has a somewhat lower negative effect on income inequality in Asia than in the rest of the world. On the other hand, the estimates suggest that a one-percentage-point increase in housing expenditure raises income inequality in Asia by 2.162 percentage points, vis-à-vis the rest of the world where housing spending has the expected negative sign, i.e., it tends to reduce income inequality.

Joint effect of taxation and government spending on income inequality

Results from joint estimations, i.e., including all tax variables, all government expenditure variables, and both all taxation and all government expenditure variables, confirm the previous findings. Social protection expenditure in Asia appears to increase inequality, while in the rest of the world it has a negative effect on income distribution. Moreover, housing policies seem to benefit people with a higher income in Asia to a larger extent than people with a lower income compared with the rest of the world, although housing policies in the rest of the world are now also regressive, whereas they reduced inequality when included on their own.

In the case of education, when all four government expenditure policies are taken into account, spending on education reduces income inequality in Asia somewhat less than in the rest of the world, whereas previously it had a slightly larger impact. The opposite holds true for health expenditure. Health spending lowers income inequality in Asia somewhat more than in the rest of the world in the joint estimation compared with the regression that includes health expenditure only.

For taxation, the results from the joint estimation provide further support to the finding that tax policies may not have a large impact on the distribution of income, and this seems to be the case in both Asia and the rest of the world. The results from including all the tax variables (but not the expenditure variables) show that the tax variables are jointly statistically significant but not individually, except for the progressivity measure interacted with personal income tax in the rest of the world. Moreover, the signs on the tax variables reverse in several instances. Based on these results, we conclude that taxes may, at best, have a small redistributive impact, in both Asia and the rest of the world.

Improving the effectiveness of fiscal policies in Asia

The review of the literature and the empirical results for Asia and the rest of the world suggest that more effective redistributional policies can be implemented with spending programs on social welfare and the social sectors, such as health and education policies, than with taxes. However, taxation is crucial to raise finances for government expenditure to achieve distributional objectives. This section discusses the effectiveness of tax systems and tax administration in collecting tax revenue in Asia. Our focus is on corporate and personal income taxation and general taxes on goods and services, because payroll and social security taxes are less important in Asian countries and tax revenues from foreign trade taxes, including customs duties, are declining with rising trade liberalization. The section also briefly discusses government spending policies on education, health, and social protection to throw more light on the empirical findings presented in the previous section. Housing is excluded from the discussion because of lack of readily available data and information.

Tax systems

Taxes create economic costs because they distort economic behavior. A theoretically optimal tax that minimizes the behavioral impact of taxation is one that taxes activities according to their varying responses to the tax (Diamond and Mirrlees 1971). In practice, however, such an approach is not feasible because it is constrained by principles of fairness and simplicity, and because of the difficulties of reliably measuring the tax sensitivity of particular activities. Practically speaking, an efficient tax system is one that reduces the disincentive effects of taxation to work, save, and invest by using broad bases and low, fairly uniform rates. A broad-base, low-rate system also lowers administration and compliance costs, leaving more resources for productive activities, and is often seen as fairer than a narrow-base system because of horizontal equity considerations (i.e., taxpayers who have the same income should pay the same amount in taxes) and vertical equity (i.e., people with different incomes should pay different amounts of tax) (Tanzi 2011).

Composition of taxes

Corporate income taxation is an important part of economies' tax systems. Figure 9.1 plots CIT revenue as a percentage of GDP and (statutory) CIT rates in Asia compared with three country averages: all countries, Organisation for Economic Co-operation and Development (OECD) countries, and developing

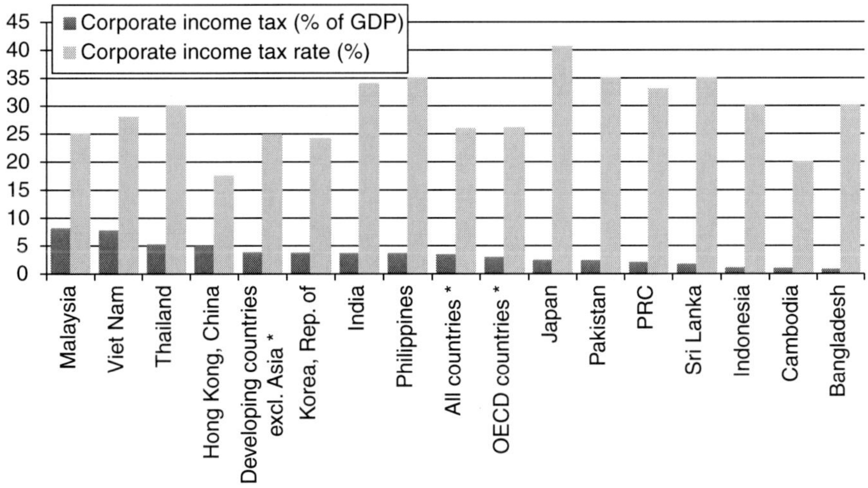

Figure 9.1 Corporate income tax and corporate income tax rate, 2009 or latest available year.

GDP = gross domestic product; OECD = Organisation for Economic Co-operation and Development; PRC = People's Republic of China.

Note: Sorted from highest to lowest tax revenue as a percentage of GDP.

*Unweighted average.

Sources: International Monetary Fund, KPMG, OECD, and United Nations Economic Commission for Latin America and the Caribbean, as used in I. Claus, J. Martinez-Vazquez, and V. Vulovic. 2012. Government Fiscal Policies and Redistribution in Asian Countries. *ADB Economics Working Paper Series* No. 310. Manila: ADB.

economies excluding those in Asia. It shows that Malaysia at 8.1% and Viet Nam at 7.7% have the highest level of CIT, while Indonesia, Cambodia, and Bangladesh have the lowest, at 1.0%, 0.9%, and 0.7%, respectively. Corporate tax collection is low in Indonesia and Bangladesh despite relatively high tax rates, partly because of various tax incentives and concessions that governments often provide for attracting investment and for activities seen as having social or economic merit.

Besides reducing tax revenue collections, there are other potential costs to tax incentive schemes. Tax incentives often become politicized, with resources being captured by interest groups. If lobbying power were concentrated among high-income groups, tax incentives and concessions would be expected to reduce the progressivity of corporate income taxation. Another difficulty with tax incentives schemes is that they are often poorly targeted and, to a large extent, just subsidize activities that firms would have undertaken regardless of the policies.

Personal income taxation is another important part of economies' tax collection. Figure 9.2 plots PIT revenue as a percentage of GDP and the top personal (statutory) marginal income tax rate. It shows that PIT collection is low in Asia

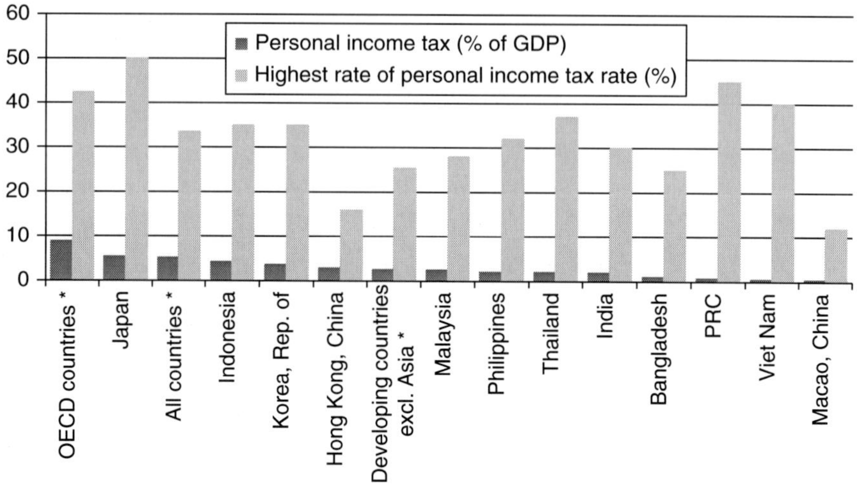

Figure 9.2 Personal income tax and top personal marginal income tax rate, 2009 or latest available year.

GDP = gross domestic product; OECD = Organisation for Economic Co-operation and Development; PRC = People's Republic of China.

Note: Sorted from highest to lowest tax revenue as a percent of GDP.

*Unweighted average.

Sources: International Monetary Fund, KPMG, OECD, and United Nations Economic Commission for Latin America and the Caribbean, as used in I. Claus, J. Martinez-Vazquez, and V. Vulovic. 2012. Government Fiscal Policies and Redistribution in Asian Countries. *ADB Economics Working Paper Series* No. 310. Manila: ADB.

compared with the rest of the world, OECD countries, and developing economies excluding those in Asia. On average, Asian economies collect about 2.2% of PIT as a percentage of GDP compared with an all-country average of 5.2%, and 8.8% and 2.7%, respectively, in OECD and developing countries excluding those in Asia. Partly contributing to this relatively low tax take are higher tax-free (minimum exempt) thresholds and a higher threshold of income above which the top marginal PIT rate applies.

Figure 9.3 plots the ratio of the tax-free threshold/individual allowance or deduction to gross national income per capita. It shows that Nepal at 3.8 and Pakistan at 3.95 have the highest ratios. Only Cambodia, the Republic of Korea, and Japan have ratios below the average of OECD countries. The higher the tax-free threshold, the larger the number of people exempt from income taxation tends to be and the higher the statutory tax rates that are needed to finance government expenditure.

Figure 9.4 plots the ratio of the top PIT threshold to per capita gross national income. Hong Kong, China has the lowest ratio at 0.45, while the Lao People's

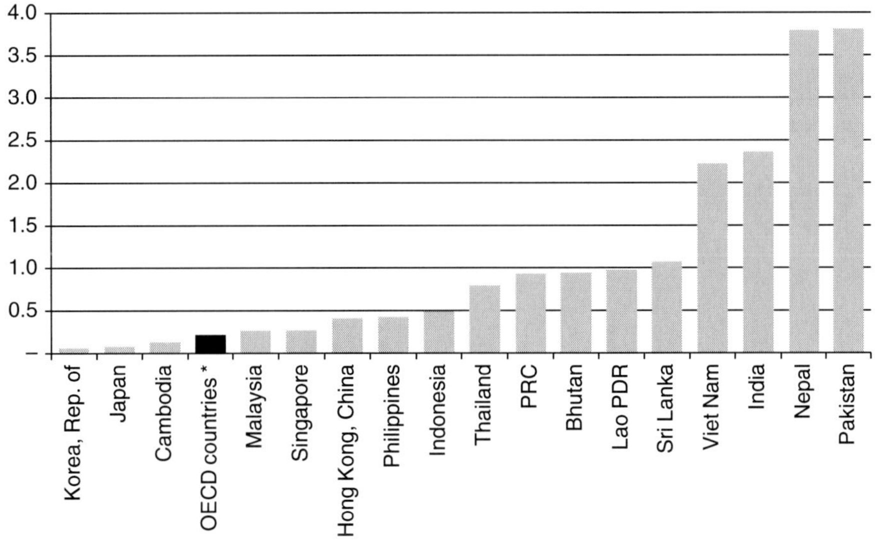

Figure 9.3 Ratio of tax-free threshold/individual allowance or deduction to gross national income per capita, 2012.

Lao PDR = Lao People's Democratic Republic; OECD = Organisation for Economic Co-operation and Development; PRC = People's Republic of China.

Note: Gross national income per capita for Asian economies is assumed to grow at the 2000–2010 rates.

*Unweighted average, data are for 2009 or 2008, no data are available for Turkey.

Sources: International Bureau of Fiscal Documentation and Asian Development Bank, as used in I. Claus, J. Martinez-Vazquez, and V. Vulovic. 2012. Government Fiscal Policies and Redistribution in Asian Countries. *ADB Economics Working Paper Series* No. 310. Manila: ADB; authors' calculations.

Democratic Republic, Viet Nam, and Pakistan have the highest thresholds with ratios of 38.8, 44.4, and 56.7, respectively.

Also contributing to the relatively low PIT take in some Asian countries are narrow PIT bases, which exempt certain types of income or tax them at lower rates. In the People's Republic of China (PRC), for example, only certain listed types of income (11 categories) are liable to tax. Some of these categories are taxed at progressive rates, while others are taxed at a flat rate. For labor income, wages and salaries are taxed at a progressive rate with a top marginal rate of 45%, but the remuneration of personal services is taxed at a flat rate of 20% after a deduction of 20% of the payment as deemed expense. Interest is also generally taxed at a flat rate (20%), while royalties and rental and lease income are taxed at 20% and 10%, respectively, with a 20% deduction being allowed. Moreover, certain types of income (e.g., monetary awards, interest on government bonds and on savings in a deposit account with banks in the PRC) and certain benefits

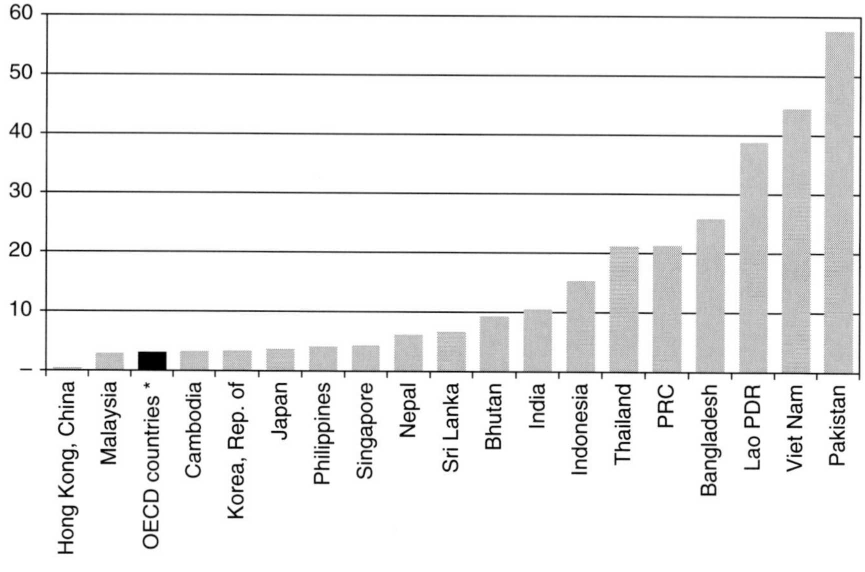

Figure 9.4 Ratio of top personal income tax threshold to gross national income per capita, 2012.

Lao PDR = Lao People's Democratic Republic; OECD = Organisation for Economic Co-operation and Development; PRC = People's Republic of China.

Note: Gross national income per capita for Asian economies is assumed to grow at the 2000–2010 rates.

*Unweighted average, data are for 2009 or 2008, no data are available for Turkey.

Sources: Asian Development Bank, International Bureau of Fiscal Documentation, and OECD, as used in I. Claus, J. Martinez-Vazquez, and V. Vulovic. 2012. Government Fiscal Policies and Redistribution in Asian Countries. *ADB Economics Working Paper Series* No. 310. Manila: ADB; authors' calculations.

in-kind (e.g., provision of or reimbursement for reasonable expenses on accommodation, travel expenses, and allowances for children's education) are exempt from personal income taxation altogether.

A further important contributor to countries' tax collection is GTGS, which include value-added (goods and services) taxes, general sales taxes, and turnover taxes. They are plotted in Figure 9.5 as a percentage of GDP together with countries' indirect tax rate, which generally coincides with the general VAT rate. The figure shows that GTGS, similar to PIT, are low in Asia, averaging 3.3% of GDP compared with an all-country average of 6.4%, and 6.9% and 6.6% in developing countries excluding those in Asia and OECD economies, respectively. This lower tax take partly results from lower indirect tax rates. Among Asian countries, Japan and Singapore, both at 5%, and Thailand, at 7%, have some of the lowest indirect tax rates in the world.

At 2.2% of GDP, the Philippines has the lowest collection of GTGS (consisting of VAT) despite its 12% indirect tax rate. The low VAT revenues are largely due to

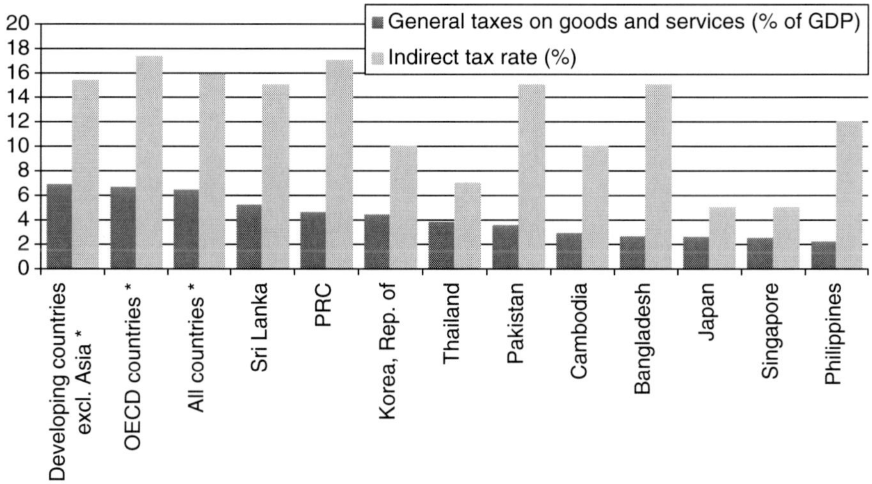

Figure 9.5 General taxes on goods and services and indirect tax rate, 2009 or latest available year.

GDP = gross domestic product; OECD = Organisation for Economic Co-operation and Development; PRC = People's Republic of China.

Note: Sorted from highest to lowest tax revenue as a percentage of GDP.

*Unweighted average.

Sources: International Monetary Fund, KPMG, OECD, and United Nations Economic Commission for Latin America and the Caribbean, as used in I. Claus, J. Martinez-Vazquez, and V. Vulovic. 2012. Government Fiscal Policies and Redistribution in Asian Countries. *ADB Economics Working Paper Series* No. 310. Manila: ADB.

a low efficiency of the VAT system. An efficiency ratio, plotted in Figure 9.6, can be calculated as VAT revenues to GDP divided by the standard statutory VAT rate (expressed as a percentage). A low efficiency ratio is taken as evidence of erosion by exemptions, reduced rates within the tax law, and/or low taxpayer compliance (Ebrill *et al.* 2001). Bangladesh has the second least efficient VAT system in Asia.

Singapore also has a relatively low efficiency given the breadth of its VAT base, resulting from an extremely high registration threshold of annual taxable turnover above S$1 million or about $620,000 (Figure 9.7).

Although the number of countries with a VAT system has been rising rapidly (Martinez-Vazquez and Bird 2011), several Asian economies have not adopted a VAT. They include Bhutan; Hong Kong, China; Macao, China; Malaysia; and Myanmar. India also does not have a VAT in the traditional sense. A central sales tax is levied on the movement of goods between states, and a central VAT is levied on all goods that are produced or manufactured in India.

Less reliance on value-added taxes in Asian countries is likely to increase the economic costs of taxation because VAT is one of the least distortionary taxes (Auerbach 2008; Banks and Diamond 2010). The economic costs of value-added

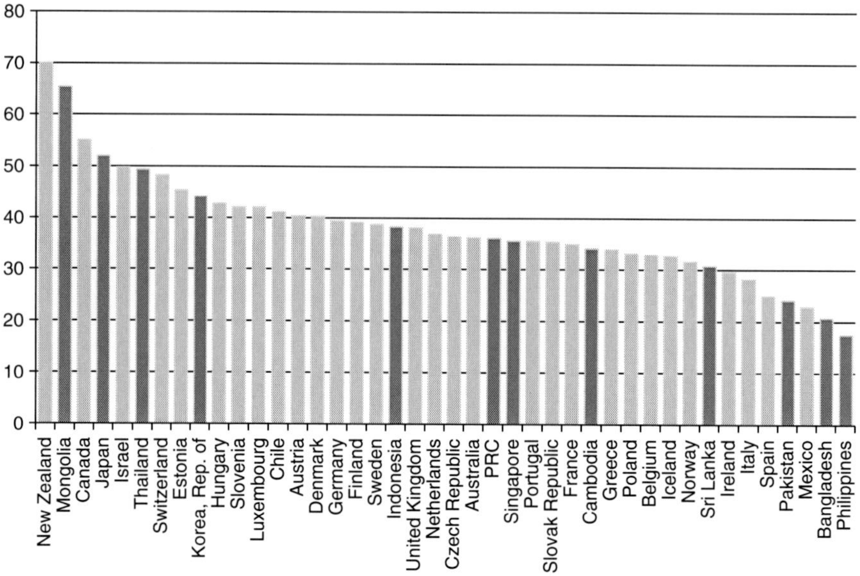

Figure 9.6 Value-added tax efficiency ratio, 2009 or latest available year.

PRC = People's Republic of China.

Sources: International Monetary Fund, Organisation for Economic Co-operation and Development, KPMG, PricewaterhouseCoopers, and Department of Statistics Singapore, as used in I. Claus, J. Martinez-Vazquez, and V. Vulovic. 2012. Government Fiscal Policies and Redistribution in Asian Countries. *ADB Economics Working Paper Series* No. 310. Manila: ADB; authors' calculations.

taxes are lower because, typically, VAT is charged at a uniform, relatively low rate to a (more or less) comprehensive and broad base. This lowers the economic costs of taxation, which tend to increase with higher tax rates and narrower tax bases. Moreover, VAT, in theory, does not distort business or export decisions. This is because the tax paid on production inputs and exports is deductible. Also, VAT is less distortionary than other taxes because it does not affect savings and investment decisions, i.e., it does not distort between current and future consumption.

Tax administration and compliance costs

Limited information is available on tax administration costs in Asian countries. Figure 9.8 plots tax administration expenditure as a percentage of GDP for six Asian countries (India, Indonesia, Japan, the Republic of Korea, Malaysia, and Singapore) and the OECD economies. It shows that administration costs in Asia are relatively low, at least in the countries for which data are available. This is

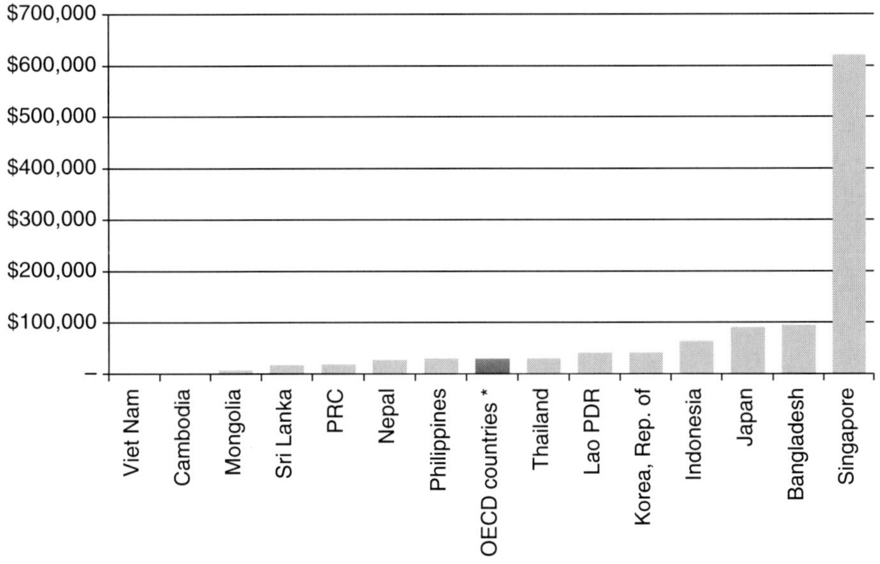

Figure 9.7 Value-added tax registration threshold, 2012.

Lao PDR = Lao People's Democratic Republic; OECD = Organisation for Economic Co-operation for Development; PRC = People's Republic of China.

Note: Average exchange rates for 2000–2010 are used.

*Unweighted average, data are for 2011.

Sources: International Bureau of Fiscal Documentation, Asian Development Bank, and OECD, as used in I. Claus, J. Martinez-Vazquez, and V. Vulovic. 2012. Government Fiscal Policies and Redistribution in Asian Countries. *ADB Economics Working Paper Series* No. 310. Manila: ADB; authors' calculations.

partly because of less revenue collection. Also contributing to low tax administration expenditure in Indonesia, India, the Republic of Korea, and Singapore is efficient tax administration. This can be seen in Figure 9.9, which compares the administrative costs of collecting 100 units of revenue. Indonesia has the 7th lowest costs, India the 10th lowest, while Singapore and the Republic of Korea rank 13th and 14th, respectively.

The ease with which taxpayers are able to comply with the tax system varies across countries and economies. Figure 9.10 plots the total time to comply with taxes in hours per year. Compliance costs in Asia are lowest in the Maldives (largely because in 2009 the Maldives did not levy taxes on goods and services or income taxes other than on the net profit of banks based on their annual financial statements); Hong Kong, China; and Singapore. They are highest in the PRC, Pakistan, and Viet Nam, partly because of complicated tax systems in these countries.

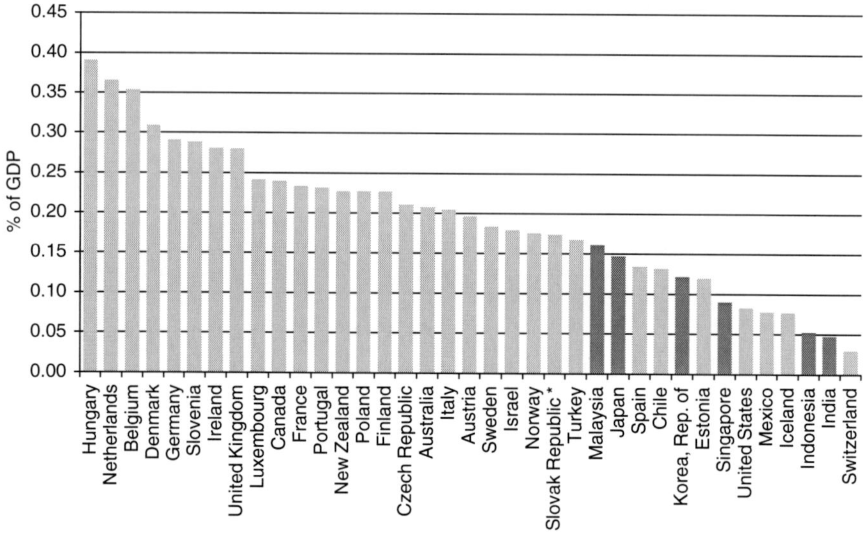

Figure 9.8 Tax administration expenditure, 2009.

GDP = gross domestic product.

*Data are for 2007.

Sources: Organisation for Economic Co-operation and Development, as used in I. Claus, J. Martinez-Vazquez, and V. Vulovic. 2012. Government Fiscal Policies and Redistribution in Asian Countries. *ADB Economics Working Paper Series* No. 310. Manila: ADB.

Complicated tax systems increase tax administration and compliance costs as well as the opportunity for tax planning and tax avoidance. Moreover, narrow-base, high-rate tax systems are often seen as unfair because higher-income taxpayers generally have greater scope and resources to shift income to avoid higher tax rates. Unfair tax systems can reduce people's and businesses' willingness to pay taxes and hence the government's ability to raise finances to fund government expenditure.

Government expenditure policies

Turning to government expenditures, Asia has made considerable progress in improving education and health outcomes and also toward achieving the Millennium Development Goals (MDGs) and targets. The MDGs were adopted by world leaders in September 2000 to reduce extreme poverty, with a deadline of achieving a series of targets by 2015. The second MDG focuses on education (achieving universal primary education) and Goals 4 to 6 center on health (reducing child mortality; improving maternal health; and combating HIV/AIDS, malaria, and other diseases). Progress in Asian countries has been substantial, particularly in education.

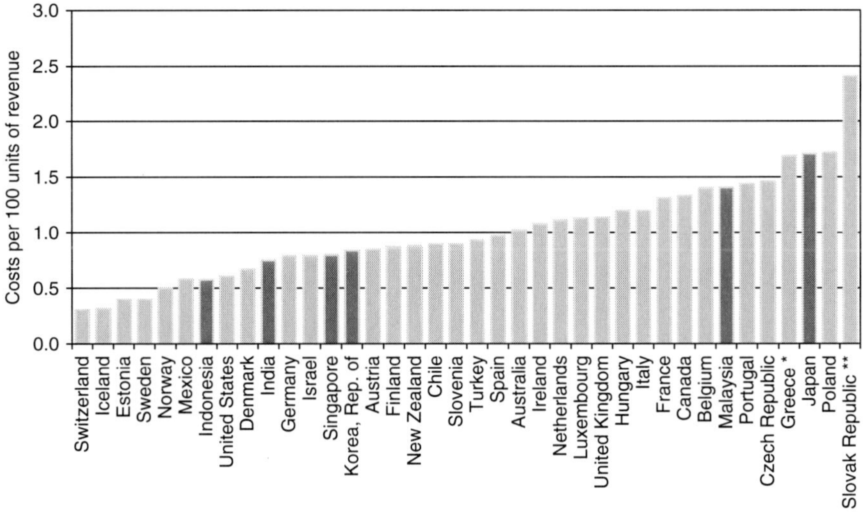

Figure 9.9 Tax administration costs to net revenue collections, 2009.

*Data are for 2004.

**Data are for 2007.

Sources: Organisation for Economic Co-operation and Development, as used in I. Claus, J. Martinez-Vazquez, and V. Vulovic. 2012. Government Fiscal Policies and Redistribution in Asian Countries. *ADB Economics Working Paper Series* No. 310. Manila: ADB.

Primary school enrollment and the number of students who start grade 1 and reach the last grade of primary education have been rising, and several countries have achieved or are expected to reach the set goals by 2015. Moreover, literacy rates in Asia are high. Most Asian countries have rates that are above the world average, and those economies with rates below (Bangladesh, Cambodia, India, the Lao People's Democratic Republic, Nepal, and Pakistan) have made considerable progress to raise them. These achievements are likely to be a contributing factor in the finding that education expenditure is reducing income inequality in Asia as government spending on primary education has been found to be progressive.

Progress has also been made toward improving health conditions. Maternal death rates have fallen sharply in Asia with better attendance at birth of trained health professionals and improved antenatal care. Infant and child mortality rates are also falling, although only a few countries so far have reached the MDG target. The progress that has been made is likely to have benefited poor families in particular because infant and child mortality is closely related to household wealth. Infants in poor households are often less than half as likely to survive their first year of life than those in higher-wealth households (ADB 2011). Death and incidence rates of tuberculosis have also been declining. But HIV/AIDS remains

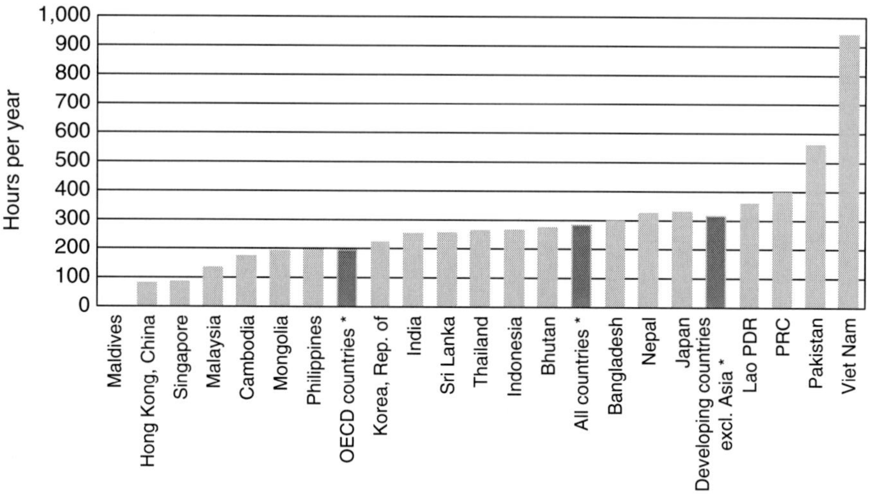

Figure 9.10 Total time to comply with taxes, 2012.

Lao PDR = Lao People's Democratic Republic; OECD = Organisation for Economic Co-operation and Development; PRC = People's Republic of China.

*Unweighted average.

Source: World Bank, as used in I. Claus, J. Martinez-Vazquez, and V. Vulovic. 2012. Government Fiscal Policies and Redistribution in Asian Countries. *ADB Economics Working Paper Series* No. 310. Manila: ADB.

a problem, with the percentage of the population with comprehensive, correct knowledge about the illness and the percentage of the population with advanced HIV infection who have access to antiretroviral drugs being relatively low and only rising slowly in some countries from a low base.

For social protection, overall coverage remains relatively low in Asia and generally only available to formal sector workers in the civil service or large enterprises. Moreover, the availability of social protection programs does not necessarily imply that they are well designed, have wide coverage, or are financially sustainable (Asher 2010). Few economies have income support systems for the unemployed (e.g., the PRC; Hong Kong, China; Japan; the Republic of Korea; Mongolia; Thailand; and Viet Nam), with coverage rates in terms of the proportion of unemployed who receive benefits being less than 10% on average (ILO 2010). Effective coverage of work-related accidents and diseases is also low with only a proportion of accidents being reported and compensated. In the informal sector, unemployment coverage is virtually nonexistent, working conditions and safety are typically poor, and work-related diseases are widespread.

With regard to income security in old age, although some Asian countries have made efforts to extend coverage beyond the formal sector, the proportion of the working-age population covered by contributory programs remains low at around 20% (ILO 2010), and few countries have social pensions to provide safety net retirement income for people who were not members of a formal scheme. Moreover, pension systems in Asian countries, outside the OECD, are often quite generous due to early retirement ages and relatively high pension levels (OECD 2012). According to OECD estimates, replacement rates, which measure the value of a person's pension as the percentage of their earnings when working, are well above OECD levels for men in Asia, especially in the PRC, Pakistan, and Viet Nam. The high replacement rates are partly due to nearly all defined-benefit schemes being based on final salaries rather than average earnings. Such schemes tend to be particularly regressive because the higher paid typically have salaries that rise more rapidly with age, while the earnings of lower paid workers generally remain flat or rise less fast. Furthermore, the OECD estimates that the expected amount of time that people spend in retirement, which can be calculated by combining information on national pension ages and life expectancy, is relatively high in Asia. Pension eligibility ages are particularly low for both men and women in Malaysia and Sri Lanka and for women in the PRC and Thailand.

This discussion offers some potential explanation for the finding that education and health expenditures in Asia have reduced income inequality, while social security spending has mainly benefited those with a higher income. Basic education and health services seem to be fairly universally available, whereas social protection spending has been restricted to those already likely to be better off, i.e., people employed in the formal sector. This suggests that labor market reform that moves workers from informal to formal employment may offer the greatest scope for reducing income inequality in Asia. Higher formal employment should also raise personal income tax collection, which could further assist governments in achieving redistributive objectives.

Conclusions and policy lessons

This chapter assessed the impact of government fiscal policies on income inequality in Asia. It discussed the role and effectiveness of redistributive fiscal policies and provided estimates of the effects of taxation and government expenditure on income distributions in Asia and other countries.

Government expenditures on health and education have reduced income inequality in both Asia and the rest of the world, but public spending on social protection shows some distinctive differential distributive effects. Social protection expenditure in Asia appears to increase income inequality, whereas it reduces it in the rest of the world. Also adversely affecting the distribution of income in Asian countries is government expenditure on housing.

For taxation, policies in Asia have a less distinctive differential distributive impact. Empirical estimates provide some evidence that personal income taxes are more progressive in Asia than in the rest of the world, possibly because of a larger number of people not paying income tax. Corporate income taxes, on the other hand, may be less progressive. This could be due to larger tax incentives, exemptions, and concessions for Asian firms.

Although taxes by themselves are less effective in redistributing income, taxation is crucial to raising finances for government expenditure to achieve distributional objectives through spending programs on social welfare and the social sectors, such as health and education policies. The discussion in this chapter suggested that taxes could be raised more efficiently in some Asian countries. Practically speaking, an efficient tax system is one that reduces the disincentive effects of taxation to work, save, and invest by using broad bases and low, fairly uniform rates. A broad-base, low-rate system also reduces administration and compliance costs and is often seen as fairer than a narrow-base system because of horizontal equity considerations (taxpayers who have the same income should pay the same amount in taxes) and vertical equity concerns (people with different incomes should pay different amounts of tax).

The tax systems in several Asian countries are characterized by relatively high tax rates and narrow bases. Moreover, there seems to be greater reliance on corporate income taxation, which tends to be more distortionary (because of internationally mobile capital) than personal income taxation and VAT. Tax reform in Asia could focus on lowering income tax rates while broadening the tax base, i.e., abolishing tax incentives, exemptions, and concessions. This would reduce the economic, compliance, and administrative costs of taxation and likely lead to increases in tax revenue. Increases in tax revenue, in turn, would allow greater government expenditure to achieve distributional objectives. Further gains could be achieved in some countries by shifting the tax burden from income taxation to VAT and broadening the VAT base. Currently, VAT exemptions and/or reduced tax rates for necessities are often used to address the potential regressivity of VAT. However, they are costly and not well targeted to the poor. A more effective policy would be direct cash transfer payments to those in need.

With respect to government spending policies, Asia has made substantial progress toward achieving the MDGs and targets on education and health. However, social protection policies generally remain limited in Asia, and in countries where they exist they tend to have a narrow benefit coverage and lack targeting to the poor. For instance, unemployment benefits are typically restricted to those in formal employment and do not include the large proportion of those working in the informal sector. Pensions are another example. In Asian countries, outside the OECD, pension systems are often quite generous due to early retirement ages and relatively high pension levels, but they are typically only available to a privileged minority.

References

Asher, M. 2010. The Global Economic Crisis: An Opportunity for Strengthening Asia's Social Protection Systems? *ADBI Working Paper* 198. Tokyo: Asian Development Bank Institute.

Asian Development Bank (ADB). 2011. *Key Indicators for Asia and the Pacific 2011.* Manila.

Auerbach, A. J. 2008. Tax Reform in the Twenty-first Century. In J. W. Diamond and George R. Zodrow, eds. *Fundamental Tax Reform: Issues, Choices and Implications*. Cambridge, MA: MIT Press.

Ballard, C., D. Fullerton, J. Shoven, and J. Whalley. 1985. *A General Equilibrium Model for Tax Policy Evaluation*. Chicago, IL: University of Chicago Press.

Banks, J. W., and P. A. Diamond. 2010. The Base for Direct Taxation. In Institute for Fiscal Studies, ed. *Dimensions of Tax Design*. New York, NY: Oxford University Press.

Bird, R. M., and L. H. de Wulf. 1973. Taxation and Income Distribution in Latin America: A Critical Review of Empirical Studies. *International Monetary Fund Staff Papers*. 20. pp. 639–82.

Blundell, R., and S. Bond. 1998. Initial Conditions and Moment Restrictions in Dynamic Panel Data Models. *Journal of Econometrics*. 87 (1). pp. 115–43.

Browning, E. K. 1978. The Burden of Taxation. *Journal of Political Economy*. 86 (4). pp. 649–71.

Claus, I., J. Martinez-Vazquez, and V. Vulovic. 2012. Government Fiscal Policies and Redistribution in Asian Countries. *ADB Economics Working Paper Series* No. 310. Manila: Asian Development Bank.

Clements, B. J. 1997. Income Distribution and Social Expenditure in Brazil. *International Monetary Fund Working Papers* 97/120. Washington, DC: International Monetary Fund.

Cuesta, J., and J. Martinez-Vazquez. 2011. Analyzing the Distributive Effects of Fiscal Policies: How to Prepare (Analytically) for the Next Crisis. In O. Canuto and B. Moreno-Dobson, eds. *When Fiscal Policy Is the Solution to a Global Crisis*. Washington, DC: World Bank.

de Mello, L., and E. R. Tiongson. 2006. Income Inequality and Redistributive Government Spending. *Public Finance Review*. 34 (3). pp. 282–305.

Demery, L. 2000. *Benefit Incidence: A Practitioner's Guide*. Washington, DC: World Bank.

Devarajan, S., D. Fullerton, and R. A. Musgrave. 1980. Estimating the Distribution of Tax Burdens: A Comparison of Different Approaches. *Journal of Public Economics*. 13 (2). pp. 155–82.

Diamond, P. A., and J. A. Mirrlees. 1971. Optimal Taxation and Public Production II: Tax Rules. *American Economic Review*. 61 (3). pp. 261–78.

Duncan, D., and K. Sabirianova Peter. 2008. Tax Progressivity and Income Inequality. *Andrew Young School of Policy Studies Research Paper Series* 08-26. Atlanta, GA: Georgia State University.

Ebrill, L. P., M. Keen, J.-P. Bodin, and V. P. Summers. 2001. *The Modern VAT*. Washington, DC: International Monetary Fund.

Fullerton, D., and D. L. Rogers. 1991. Lifetime versus Annual Perspectives on Tax Incidence. *National Tax Journal*. 44 (3). pp. 277–88.

Fullerton, D., J. B. Shoven, and J. Whalley. 1978. A General Equilibrium Analysis of US Taxation Policy. *1978 Compendium of Tax Research*. Washington, DC: US Government Printing Office.

Fullerton, D., A. T. King, J. B. Shoven, and J. Whalley. 1979. Corporate and Personal Tax Integration in the US: Some Preliminary Findings from a General Equilibrium Analysis. In R. H. Haveman and K. Hollenbeck, eds. *Microeconomic Simulation*. Madison, WI: Institute for Research on Poverty.

Gertler, P., and P. Glewwe. 1990. The Willingness to Pay for Education in Developing Countries: Evidence from Rural Peru. *Journal of Public Economics*. 42 (3). pp. 251–75.

Gertler, P., and J. van der Gaag. 1990. *Willingness to Pay for Medical Care*. Washington, DC: World Bank.

Gwartney, J. D., and R. A. Lawson. 2006. The Impact of Tax Policy on Economic Growth, Income Distribution, and Allocation of Taxes. *Social Philosophy and Policy.* 23 (2). pp. 28–52.

Harberger, A. C. 1962. The Incidence of the Corporate Income Tax. *Journal of Political Economy.* 70 (3). pp. 215–40.

—. 1995. *The ABCs of Corporation Tax Incidence: Insights into the Open Economy Case, Tax Policy and Economic Growth.* Washington, DC: American Council for Capital Formation.

—. 2006. Corporate Tax Incidence: Reflections on What Is Known, Unknown and Unknowable. In J. W. Diamond and G. R. Zodrow, eds. *Fundamental Tax Reform: Issues, Choices, and Implications.* Cambridge, MA: MIT Press.

International Labour Organization (ILO). 2010. *World Social Security Report 2010/11.* Geneva.

International Monetary Fund (IMF). 2001. *Government Finance Statistics Manual 2001.* Washington, DC.

Jao, C.-C. 2000. *Journal of the Asia Pacific Economy.* 5 (1). pp. 73–90.

Martinez-Vazquez, J. 2008. The Impact of Budgets on the Poor: Tax and Expenditure Benefit Incidence Analysis. In B. Moreno-Dobson and Q. Wodon, eds. *Public Finance for Poverty Reduction: Concepts and Case Studies from Africa and Latin America.* Washington, DC: World Bank.

Martinez-Vazquez, J., and R. M. Bird. 2011. Value Added Tax: Onward and Upward. In E. Albi and J. Martinez-Vazquez, eds. *The Elgar Guide to Tax Systems.* Cheltenham (UK) and Northampton, MA (US): Edward Elgar Publishing.

Martinez-Vazquez, J., B. Moreno-Dodson, and V. Vulovic. 2011a. The Impact of Tax and Expenditure Policies on Income Distribution: Evidence from a Large Panel of Countries. Paper prepared for the 4th International Tax Dialogue Global Conference on Tax and Inequality, New Delhi, India, 7–9 December.

Martinez-Vazquez, J., V. Vulovic, and Y. Liu. 2011b. Direct versus Indirect Taxation: Trends, Theory and Economic Significance. In E. Albi and J. Martinez-Vazquez, eds. *The Elgar Guide to Tax Systems.* Cheltenham (UK) and Northampton, MA (US): Edward Elgar Publishing.

Meerman, J. 1979. *Public Expenditure in Malaysia: Who Benefits and Why.* New York, NY: Oxford University Press.

Milanovic, B. 1995. Impact of Cash and In-Kind Transfers in Eastern Europe and Russia. In D. van de Walle and K. Nead, eds. *Public Spending and the Poor – Theory and Evidence.* Baltimore, MD: The Johns Hopkins University Press.

Musgrave, R. A., and P. B. Musgrave. 1989. *Public Finance in Theory and Practice.* Columbus, OH: McGraw-Hill.

Newbery, D. M. G., and N. Stern. 1987. *The Theory of Taxation for Developing Countries.* Oxford, UK: Oxford University Press.

Organisation for Economic Co-operation and Development (OECD). 2012. *Pensions at a Glance Asia/Pacific 2011.* Paris.

Sabirianova Peter, K., S. Buttrick, and D. Duncan. 2010. Global Reform of Personal Income Taxation, 1981–2005: Evidence from 189 Countries. *National Tax Journal.* 63 (3). pp. 447–78.

Selowsky, M. 1979. *Who Benefits from Government Expenditures?* Washington, DC: Oxford University Press for the World Bank.

Shah, A., and J. Whalley. 1991. Tax Incidence Analysis of Developing Countries: An Alternative View. *World Bank Economic Review.* 5 (3). pp. 535–52.

Tanzi, V. 1974. Redistributing Income through the Budget in Latin America. *Banca Nazionale del Lavoro Quarterly Review.* March. pp. 3–25.

——. 2011. Tax Systems in the OECD: Recent Evolution, Competition and Convergence. In E. Albi and J. Martinez-Vazquez, eds. *The Elgar Guide to Tax Systems*. Cheltenham (UK) and Northampton, MA (US): Edward Elgar Publishing.

van de Walle, D. 1998. Assessing the Welfare Impacts of Public Spending. *World Development.* 26 (3). pp. 365–79.

Weller, C. E. 2007. The Benefits of Progressive Taxation in Economic Development. *Review of Radical Political Economics.* 39 (3). pp. 368–76.

Younger, S. D. 1999. The Relative Progressivity of Social Services in Ecuador. *Public Finance Review.* 27 (3). pp. 310–52.

10 Commitment to equity

A diagnostic framework to assess governments' fiscal policy

Nora Lustig and Sean Higgins

Introduction: what is the Commitment to Equity Assessment?

Based on the economics of the welfare state,[1] the Commitment to Equity Assessment (CEQ) is a diagnostic framework used to measure and evaluate how aligned government expenditures and taxes are with supporting a minimum living standard and reducing inequality in ways that are broadly consistent with macroeconomic stability, microeconomic efficiency, and growth.[2] CEQ evaluates government efforts in individual countries in terms of the following criteria. Do governments collect and allocate enough resources to support a minimum living standard and human capital accumulation for all? Is the collection and distribution of fiscal resources consistent with eradicating extreme income and human capital poverty gaps? Do governments collect and distribute resources equitably? Do they ensure that spending is fiscally sustainable and that programs are compatible with incentives? Do they collect and publish relevant information, and are programs subject to independent evaluations? For each criterion, there are quantitative and qualitative indicators derived from poverty and inequality analysis, tax and benefit incidence analysis, and best practices in macroeconomic management, program and policy design and evaluation, and accountability indicators.[3]

CEQ's main purpose is to inform governments of how their fiscal policy affects their equity goals, recommend practical measures, and enhance accountability and transparency through better data collection and evaluation systems. In the case of heavily indebted poor countries (HIPCs), and very poor countries more broadly, CEQ can be used to inform donors on the orders of magnitude of resource shortfalls to achieve certain goals (for example, reducing poverty by half and realizing

[1] See, for example, Musgrave (1957) and Barr (2004).

[2] The first two sections of this chapter are based on Lustig and Higgins (2012).

[3] For the limitations of standard incidence analysis see, for example, Bergh (2005). Other important references related to incidence analysis include Adema and Ladaique (2005); Atkinson (1983); Bourguignon and Pereira da Silva (2003); Barr (2004); Barros *et al.* (2009); Birdsall *et al.* (2008); Breceda *et al.* (2008); Dilnot *et al.* (1990); Ferreira and Robalino (2010); Fiszbein *et al.* (2009); Goñi *et al.* (2008); Grosh *et al.* (2008); Kakwani (1977); Lambert (2002); Lora (2006); Lustig (2000); Morra-Imas and Rist (2009); O'Donnell *et al.* (2008); Shah (2003); Suits (1977); van de Walle and Nead (1995); and World Bank (2000/2001, 2006, 2009, 2011).

universal coverage of primary education) as well as on the actual use and ability of foreign aid to help achieve these goals. Of course, CEQ can be used for other purposes, for example, participatory budgeting processes and nongovernment social observatories.

While there has been substantial progress in the methods and approaches to evaluate individual policies and programs, there is currently no comprehensive instrument to evaluate social policy as a system. CEQ has been created to fill that void. It is one of the first frameworks to comprehensively assess social policy – or, rather, public policy with social equity objectives – and to make the assessment comparable across countries.

Before proceeding, some caveats are in order. One of the advantages of using our proposed diagnostic framework is that it provides a systematic and logical order of how to prepare a diagnostic assessment of governments' antipoverty and redistributive policies through fiscal interventions. A second is that it homogenizes concepts, definitions, and methods that in the literature are often not clear. In its present form, the core of the diagnostic framework is based on standard incidence analysis. As such, it does not include a formal assessment of the fiscal sustainability of the policies or take into account second-round (or, more ambitiously, general equilibrium) behavioral and inter-temporal effects. However, these aspects are included in the framework and the discussion to contextualize the findings in specific countries.

A diagnostic framework

Following Barr (2004), we assume that the first main objective of a welfare state is *supporting a minimum living standard*. This, in turn, entails three goals: (i) *poverty reduction*: ensuring that everyone has a minimum level of consumption; (ii) *insurance*: preventing individuals from falling (or falling further) below the minimum level of consumption due to adverse shocks, both idiosyncratic (unemployment, illness, disability, bad harvests, etc.) and systemic (economic crises, natural disasters, spikes in food prices, etc.); and (iii) *income smoothing*: ensuring that a minimum level of consumption is achieved throughout an individual's life cycle (maternity/paternity leave and retirement, in particular). Welfare states are also concerned with equity (Barr 2004). In particular, welfare states want to equalize opportunities. Thus, the second main objective of the welfare state is *supporting a minimum level of human capital accumulation* – that is, ensuring that everyone has a minimum level of access to education and healthcare – especially for the income poor.[4] Finally, welfare states are also concerned with egregious inequalities; in particular, those arising from market failures, exploitative and predatory behavior, or perverse social norms.

---

[4] These dimensions are consistent with perceptions by the poor about poverty and the analytics of the multidimensionality of poverty. See, for example, Narayan *et al.* (2000), World Bank (2000/2001), Alkire and Santos (2010), and Alkire and Foster (2011). One could add other dimensions such as building access for the poor to basic infrastructure and/or housing.

Governments can work toward supporting a minimum living standard and reducing inequality through four main channels: taxes and transfers (fiscal policy);[5] non-budgetary/regulatory interventions;[6] redistribution of assets; and interventions that change the distribution of voice and power among different groups in society[7] and/or alter cultural norms.[8] Actions in these areas will affect poverty through two main channels: growth and distribution, either by the effect on market (primary) incomes and/or income after net transfers. CEQ confines its assessment to government efforts in fiscal policy (also called fiscal or budgetary interventions). It uses standard incidence analysis and does not include behavioral responses or general equilibrium effects.

The welfare state improves not only equity but also efficiency. For example, transfers can help the credit-constrained poor to invest in human capital and thereby result in lower poverty *and* higher growth.[9] Directly producing or regulating certain social services can correct market failures in markets where information asymmetries are large (e.g., healthcare).[10] However, as economic theory also predicts, state interventions through taxes and transfers can have important efficiency costs. In these instances, there will be a trade-off between efficiency and equity. Fiscal interventions should be such that distortions are kept to a minimum; in particular, the financing and construction of benefits should not result in large negative incentives to labor supply, investment in human capital, savings, fertility, informality, or private transfers. Thus, CEQ also attempts to assess whether fiscal interventions are designed and implemented in ways that minimize distortions.

In addition to causing microeconomic distortions, poorly designed or badly implemented fiscal interventions can cause unsustainable macroeconomic imbalances. These imbalances can lead to economic downturns or crises that, in turn, result in large increases in poverty.[11] That is why tax and transfer policies should avoid cost explosions and unfunded spending commitments. In addition, governments should collect sufficient revenues from sustainable sources (e.g., not rely on occasional windfalls from commodity booms).[12] CEQ assesses the extent to which

[5] "Taxes" here refer to all government revenues (including "profits" from public sector enterprises) and "transfers" refer to current expenditures and include consumer subsidies. Depending on the country, they may include some producer subsidies, especially in agriculture. More precise definitions are discussed later.

[6] For example, price controls, minimum wage policies, land reform, import or export restrictions, labor market regulations, antitrust legislation, and competitiveness policies.

[7] These include changes in fostering and supporting the mobilization of certain groups (landless peasants, informal workers, unions, women, ethnic minorities, etc.).

[8] Examples are campaigns to reduce fertility rates or to denounce domestic violence.

[9] On the effect of credit constraints on poverty, inequality, and growth see Aghion *et al.* (1997), Aghion and Howitt (1992), and Mookherjee and Ray (2003, 2006).

[10] See Barr (2004).

[11] See, for example, Lustig (2000) and Ravallion (2008).

[12] See Birdsall *et al.* (2008).

the combination of tax and transfer policy is consistent with the overarching goal of macroeconomic stability.

Finally, the success of fiscal interventions in reducing poverty and inequality requires having the ability to measure progress and evaluate mechanisms to determine the effectiveness of fiscal interventions. CEQ assesses the extent to which governments are accountable, that is, whether needed information is produced and shared, whether there are mechanisms to independently validate this information, and, finally, whether there are mechanisms to independently evaluate the design and implementation of taxes and transfers.

Policy instruments

In order to assess and quantify the impact of policies and programs, we must identify which redistributive instruments[13] will be included in the diagnostic tool and organize them in some fashion. There are four main types of redistributive instruments available to governments through fiscal policy: (i) taxes on income, consumption, and assets; (ii) cash transfers; (iii) subsidies to consumption goods, inputs, and credit (including tax expenditures); and (iv) in-kind transfers through the fully or partially subsidized provision of goods and services, particularly in the area of education and health.[14]

Specifically, CEQ will attempt to be as comprehensive as possible in assessing government efforts on both the revenue and spending sides. The menu of policies and programs is vast: direct taxes; indirect taxes (e.g., sales tax and value-added tax); monetary transfers; consumption subsidies (e.g., housing, food, fuel, and value-added tax exemptions) and inputs (e.g., fertilizers, improved seeds, and credit); in-kind transfers, such as spending on education including pre-primary, primary, lower secondary, (upper) secondary, and tertiary; day care services; early childhood programs; youth programs; scholarships; student credit programs (subsidy component); fee waivers; pensions (subsidized component); healthcare for the insured and uninsured population (subsidized component); housing subsidies; school feeding programs; targeted food subsidies; and rural roads, electricity, water, and sanitation in poor regions and neighborhoods. Some of the transfers will take the form of investments (e.g., rural roads, electricity grids, drainage, schools, health facilities, etc.), but the vast majority are recurrent expenditures (e.g., teachers' and doctors' salaries, educational and medical inputs, etc.). CEQ will quantify and assess the impact of the most significant policies and programs[15] on the income poverty and human capital poverty gaps, and on inequality.

---

[13] "Redistributive" here refers to state actions and policies that can potentially result in a more equal distribution of income.

[14] Transfers in the form of food will be included under direct or cash transfers and not under in-kind transfers.

[15] Examples of policies are tax systems, public education systems, public health systems, pension systems, price subsidies, price support systems, and subsidies to specific sectors (e.g., agriculture) to mention the most important. Examples of programs are conditional or unconditional cash transfer programs; workfare or employment (or employment guarantee) programs; programs to protect poor

The design of the Commitment to Equity Assessment

CEQ consists of a diagnostic framework that helps identify the main causes and constraints (successful fiscal interventions) that prevent a country from achieving (enable a country to achieve) a universal minimum standard of living and lower inequality in ways that are consistent with macroeconomic and microeconomic efficiency. A diagnostic framework follows a logical sequence to identify or discard factors that may be either obstacles or crucial to achieving a particular objective or essential to understanding a specific phenomenon. Diagnostic exercises usually rely on a combination of predictions from theory, rigorous empirical evidence, practical knowledge, and what we call "common sense." The diagnostic approach has been widely used to identify the binding constraints for economic growth.[16] CEQ is one of the first attempts to apply it to a social equity goal. In broad terms, one would like to know whether a government (i) has enough resources and allocates them well enough to meet social equity policy objectives; (ii) has appropriate policies and programs, and collects and distributes resources equitably; (iii) ensures spending is fiscally responsible and that programs minimize distortions and negative incentives; and (iv) collects and publishes relevant information, as well as subjects itself to independent evaluations. For simplicity, these criteria are called resources, equity, quality, and accountability with the following definitions:

- *Resources*: Assess whether government revenues and redistributive spending are *potentially* sufficient with what would be required for supporting a minimum standard of living.
- *Equity*: Assess whether the *actual* level and allocation of redistributive spending, as well as the range, design, and implementation of programs and policies, are consistent with supporting a minimum standard of living.
- *Quality*: Assess whether the design and implementation of programs and policies[17] to support a minimum standard of living are broadly consistent with macroeconomic and microeconomic efficiency, and whether the programs and

households from the financial impact of illness, disability, or death; programs to provide noncontributory health insurance; programs to prevent people from falling into poverty during old age; programs or policies specifically addressed to building human capital and assets of the poor; early childhood development programs for poor children; programs for pregnant and lactating poor women; programs for poor youth at risk; programs to increase school attendance of the poor (e.g., scholarships, school feeding programs, conditional cash transfers); programs to improve nutrition and health of the poor (e.g., food coupons, subsidized basic foodstuffs, nutritional supplements, etc.); programs to improve access of the poor to housing; programs to improve access of the poor to energy (e.g., differential prices); programs to improve access of the poor to credit and private insurance; programs to empower the poor; programs to reduce social exclusion and discrimination; programs to support ethnic minorities; programs to empower women; and programs to achieve other socially desirable objectives.

16 Hausmann *et al.* (2006); Rodrik (2007); and Hausmann *et al.* (2008).

17 Throughout this section, "programs" refer to programs designed to support a minimum standard of living and "policies" refer to policies designed to support a minimum standard of living.

policies implemented have high social returns and are also cost-effective, of high quality, and incentive-compatible.

- *Accountability*: Assess the degree of accountability and transparency with respect to programs and policies designed to support a minimum standard of living.

In sum, CEQ is among the first frameworks to comprehensively assess social policy and to make the assessment comparable across countries. It is based on extensive research and expert opinion that give it high content validity.[18] In particular, the diagnostic framework and indicators for CEQ are selected according to existing analysis of what is constituted as essential to achieving significant reductions in poverty and inequality through fiscal policy.

Diagnostic framework

To understand the diagnostic framework, it is best to visualize it as a diagnostic tree as in Figure 10.1. Let us consider the first objective of the welfare state: supporting a minimum living standard for all. If that objective were met, the disposable income poverty gap with an agreed upon poverty line would equal zero. If it is zero, two situations may arise: the market income (income before net transfers) poverty gap is very low to begin with – that is, the country is an equity success story – or the state made substantial efforts to reduce the poverty gap through fiscal policy. Of course, if a country is already successful before fiscal interventions, their direct impact becomes relevant only to the extent they make things worse. Understanding the causes for this kind of success is very important, but CEQ would not be the appropriate instrument. Instead, if the country's success is determined by direct fiscal policy, CEQ will help unveil which specific interventions account for success and why. Likewise, if the government is not successful in supporting a minimum living standard after taxes and transfers, CEQ will help identify the causes of failure and policy actions to improve the government's performance.

Suppose that, as in most developing countries, the disposable income poverty gap is not zero. There are a number of reasons for such a case. In searching for the causes, we follow a logical sequence that will help us to identify the contributing factors and binding constraints. The first reason the poverty gap is not zero might be that the government either collects too little revenue and/or spends too little for redistributive purposes. We can check that by comparing total revenues and total redistributive spending (defined below) with the poverty gap *before* net transfers (i.e., the poverty gap estimated with market income). If it turns out that either or both are the cause, the next step is to check whether this is so because the country is too poor, the government's capacity to tax is too low, or public spending is mainly on other items (e.g., military expenditures or debt servicing).

[18] For more on content validity, see Morra-Imas and Rist (2009, p. 294) and Adcock and Collier (2001).

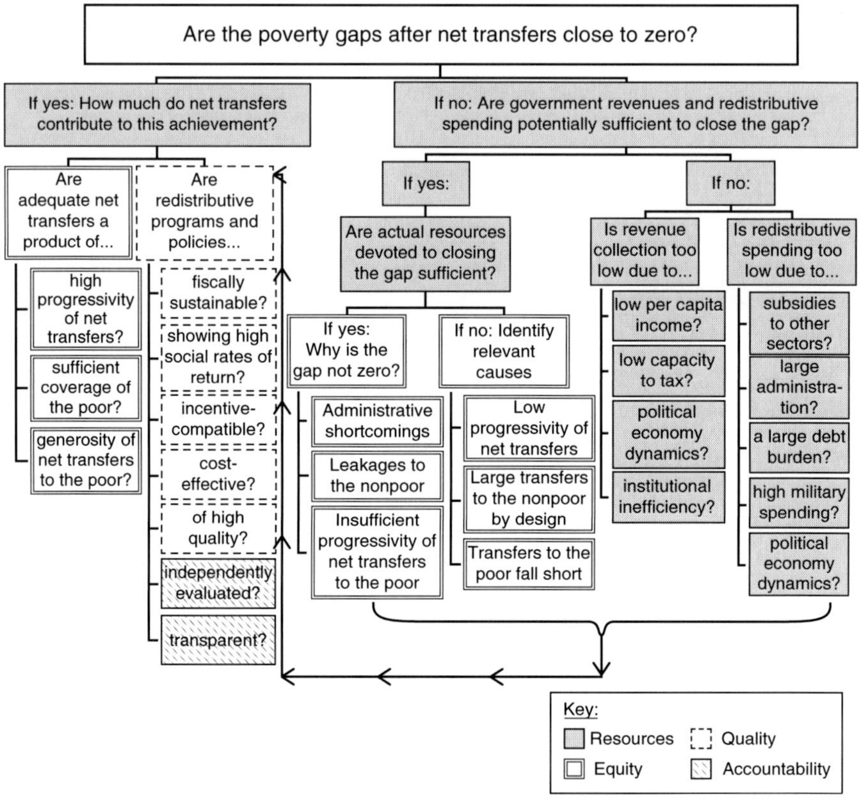

Figure 10.1 Commitment to Equity Assessment (CEQ): diagnostic tree.

Source: N. Lustig. 2012. Commitment to Equity: diagnostic Questionnaire. *CEQ Working Paper* No. 3, September. New Orleans, LA: Tulane University.

In middle-income countries, insufficient total fiscal resources or redistributive expenditures are not likely to be a cause of the disposable income poverty gap not being equal to zero. Even if enough resources are spent on redistributive programs and policies, redistributive spending allocated *to the poor* might not be enough to close the poverty gap. There are at least four – not mutually exclusive – causes of this. First, redistributive spending is regressive or not progressive enough. Second, regardless of how much is allocated to the nonpoor – and even if what is allocated to the poor is potentially sufficient – the poverty gap may not be zero because the safety net system does not cover the universe of the poor.[19] Third, the per poor

[19] Transfers could bring a portion of the poor way above the poverty line, for example, yet leave out some of the poor by design.

person transfer might be lower than required. Fourth, transfers among the poor might not be sufficiently progressive.[20]

In turn, the reasons mentioned above may be the result of several factors. First, the safety net system may benefit the nonpoor or leave out some poor households intentionally. For example, "universal" social security systems often do not include agricultural workers and housekeepers. Cash transfers to the poor can exclude households without children, individuals who are below the age of 65, or undocumented migrants. Second, the design of programs may have unintended effects. For example, the participation costs may be too high for the poorest of the poor, or the eligibility cutoff and amount transferred might not be adjusted for differences in prices across regions within a country. Third, in practice, the programs may leave out eligible individuals and include non-eligible individuals due to corruption, clientelistic politics, or honest mistakes.

In the literature, the share of the poor who do not receive benefits of safety net programs are called errors of exclusion and the share of the nonpoor who are beneficiaries are called errors of inclusion. However, we consider that it is useful to classify the "errors" of exclusion and inclusion into two groups: intentional and unintended errors of exclusion and inclusion. For simplicity, we shall refer to the *intentional* exclusion of the poor and inclusion of the nonpoor as exclusion and leakage *by design*. The unintended errors will be called *errors of exclusion* and *errors of inclusion*. The latter could be caused by unintended failures in design or implementation of programs, such as higher-than-anticipated participation costs, deficient information systems, clientelistic politics or corruption, underestimation of geographic isolation, higher-than-expected administrative costs, unanticipated leakages, lack of accrediting documentation among potential beneficiaries, or self-exclusion.

Definitions and data requirements

In this section, we describe the main concepts used by CEQ. A detailed technical description of variables and concepts can be found in Lustig and Higgins (2012).

Income concepts: market, net market, disposable, post-fiscal, and final income

As usual, any incidence study must start by defining the basic income concepts. In our study, we use five: market, net market, disposable, post-fiscal, and final income. One area in which there is no agreement is how pensions from the contributory system should be considered. Some authors treat them as part of market income and others place them under government transfers. Since this is an unresolved issue, we defined in our study a benchmark case in which contributory pensions are part of market income. We also conducted a sensitivity analysis where

[20] Of course, another reason may be that direct taxes are not sufficiently progressive.

pensions are classified under government transfers. Fortunately, we found that including pensions as part of government transfers changes results quantitatively, but the order of magnitude is small; qualitative results are not affected. The results presented here are for the benchmark case. Results for the case when pensions are placed under government transfers can be seen in Lustig *et al.* (2012).

Market income is defined as

$$I^m = W + IC + AC + IROH + PT + SSP$$

where I^m = market income;[21] W = gross (pre-tax) wages and salaries in the formal and informal sectors (also known as earned income); IC = income from capital (dividends, interest, profits, rents, etc.) in the formal and informal sectors (excludes capital gains and gifts); AC = auto-consumption (also known as self-production); $IROH$ = imputed rent for owner occupied housing (also known as income from owner occupied housing); PT = private transfers (remittances and other private transfers such as alimony); SSP = retirement pensions from the contributory social security system.

Net market income is defined as

$$I^n = I^m - DT - SSC$$

where I^n = net market income; DT = direct taxes on all income sources (included in market income) that are subject to taxation; SSC = all contributions to social security except the portion going toward pensions.[22]

Disposable income is defined as

$$I^d = I^n + GT$$

where I^d = disposable income; GT = direct government transfers (mainly cash but can include transfers in kind such as food).

Post-fiscal income is defined as

$$I^{pf} = I^d + IndS - IndT$$

where I^{pf} = post-fiscal income; $IndS$ = indirect subsidies (e.g., lower electricity rates for small-scale consumers); $IndT$ = indirect taxes (e.g., value-added tax, sales tax, etc.).

Final income is defined as

$$I^f = I^{pf} + InkindT - CoPaym$$

---

21 Market income is sometimes called primary income.

22 We are treating contributory pensions as part of market income, and the portion of the contributions to social security going toward pensions is treated as "savings."

where I^f = final income; *InkindT* = government transfers in the form of free or subsidized services in education and health; *CoPaym* = co-payments, user fees, etc., for government services in education and health.[23]

Because some countries do not have data on indirect subsidies and taxes, we also defined

$$Final\ income^* = I^{f^*} = I^d + InkindT - CoPaym$$

The definitions are summarized in Figure 10.2.

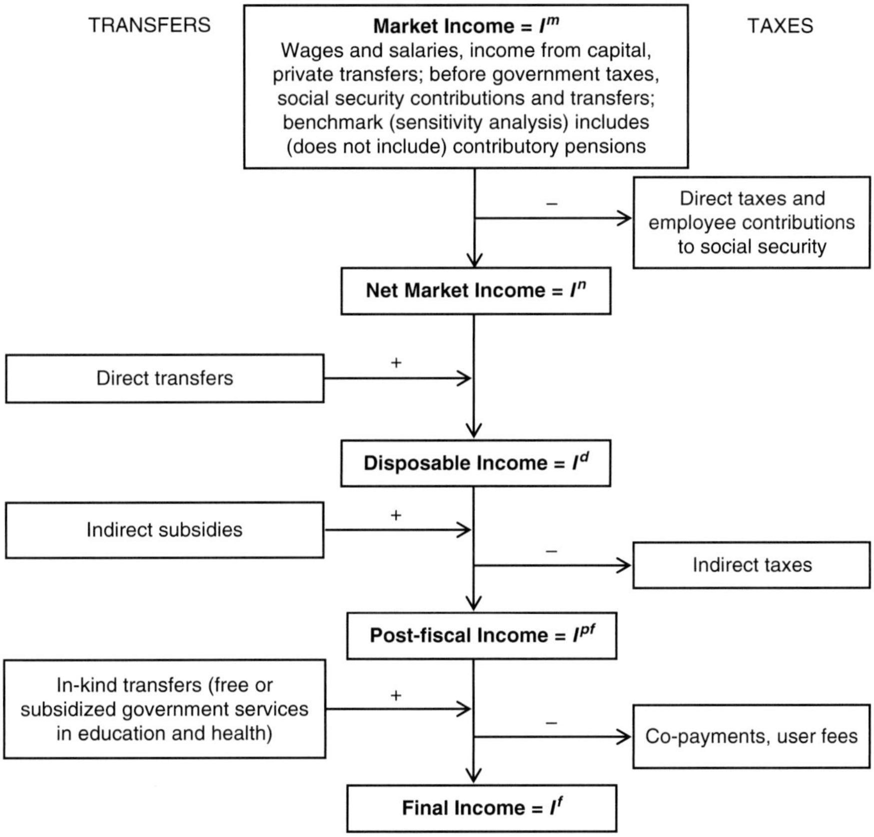

Figure 10.2 Definitions of income concepts: a stylized presentation.

Source: N. Lustig and S. Higgins. 2012. Commitment to Equity Assessment (CEQ): Estimating the Incidence of Social Spending, Subsidies and Taxes Handbook. *Tulane Economics Working Paper Series* No. 1219. Tulane University.

[23] One may also include participation costs, such as transportation costs or foregone incomes because of use of time in obtaining benefits. In our study, they were not included.

Data on household market and disposable income can be obtained from standard household surveys (although sometimes there is no information on nonmonetary income sources such as auto-consumption). Disposable income is obtained as a combination of available and imputed information depending on how data on income and taxes is collected in the surveys.[24] Indirect subsidies and indirect taxes to calculate post-fiscal income are usually imputed based on consumption data from household surveys (income–expenditure surveys). In-kind transfers are usually imputed based on the reported use of public services by individual households and the direct average cost of supplying the service based on public expenditure accounts.

Because there is no convention regarding where to place contributory pensions, we suggest conducting a sensitivity analysis placing contributory pensions under government transfers instead of market income.

Total government revenue

Total government revenue includes the total budgetary income of the federal government: tax and nontax revenue plus income generated by direct budgetary controlled entities or public enterprises. In countries where revenue collected at the provincial or state level is important, the total will include the revenues obtained by governments at the subnational level.

Social and redistributive spending

To assess government efforts on the spending side, we use *social spending* from public sector accounts and the concept of *redistributive spending*. Social spending as commonly defined in official government budgetary classifications and the concept of redistributive spending can be different. Social spending as reported in public sector accounts will typically include spending on education, health, social assistance, and social security payments (only included in countries with a pay-as-you-go pension system).[25] It may also include other forms of social expenditures,

---

[24] This varies by country. In some countries, household surveys report only income after direct taxes and social security contributions; in other countries, they report it before taxes. The problem is compounded because wage income is often after taxes, but the situation of self-employment income is left unclear.

[25] For the purposes of CEQ, two versions of social security payments are used in the analysis, which leads to two versions of social spending and redistributive spending. The first version is total social security payments, equal to the total amount of pensions paid out by the government (from the contributory system). The second version is the subsidized portion of social security or the "social security deficit," equal to the total pensions paid out by the government (from the contributory system) minus employer and employee contributions to the contributory system. Note that noncontributory pensions (sometimes called "minimum pensions") are included as part of social assistance rather than social security.

such as spending on water and sewerage, etc.[26] Redistributive spending includes spending on education, health, social assistance, and social security (only included in countries with a pay-as-you-go pension system) *plus* spending on indirect consumer subsidies (e.g., food, electricity, and gasoline subsidies), some producer subsidies (e.g., agricultural producer subsidies), and "social" tax expenditures (exemption of value-added tax for certain foodstuffs). The information on redistributive spending has to be teased out from public sector accounts at the federal level (and subnational level in the countries where the study includes subnational spending in the analysis). In some countries, there is no information on other forms of redistributive spending; in such cases, one should confine the analysis to social spending.

Progressivity and regressivity of taxes and transfers

Since one criterion of the assessment of government fiscal interventions is based on the extent of their progressivity, this is a good place to review the definitions used in the literature of what constitutes a progressive tax and progressive transfer system. The most frequently used method to measure the progressivity (or regressivity) of government taxes and transfers is incidence analysis. In essence, incidence analysis consists of comparing the amount of transfers (taxes) received (paid) by population quantiles. Progressivity is measured in absolute terms, comparing transfers or taxes per capita among quantiles, or it is measured in relative terms, comparing transfers or taxes as a share of each quantile's income. Here we define as progressive (regressive) any tax or transfer that reduces (increases) market income inequality to obtain the following:

(i) A tax (transfer) will be regressive if the tax (transfer) in relation to the individual's market income is larger (smaller), the poorer an individual is.
(ii) A tax (transfer) will be progressive if the tax (transfer) in relation to the individual's market income is smaller (larger), the poorer an individual is.
(iii) A transfer will be progressive in absolute terms if the transfer in per capita terms is larger, the poorer an individual is.[27]
(iv) A tax (transfer) will be neutral if the tax (transfer) in relation to an individual's market income is the same for everyone.

The four cases are illustrated in Figure 10.3.[28]

---

[26] For comparability across countries, we also define "CEQ Social Spending" as exactly equal to the sum of education, health, social assistance, and (in countries with a pay-as-you-go pension system) social security spending.

[27] Although, in theory, taxes could be regressive in absolute terms, this never really happens in practice.

[28] See Lambert (2002) for a formal discussion. If a transfer is progressive (regressive) in absolute (relative) terms, it follows by definition that it must be progressive (regressive) in relative (absolute) terms, but the converse is not true. If a tax is progressive (regressive) in relative (absolute) terms, it follows by definition that it must be progressive (regressive) in absolute (relative) terms, but the converse is not true.

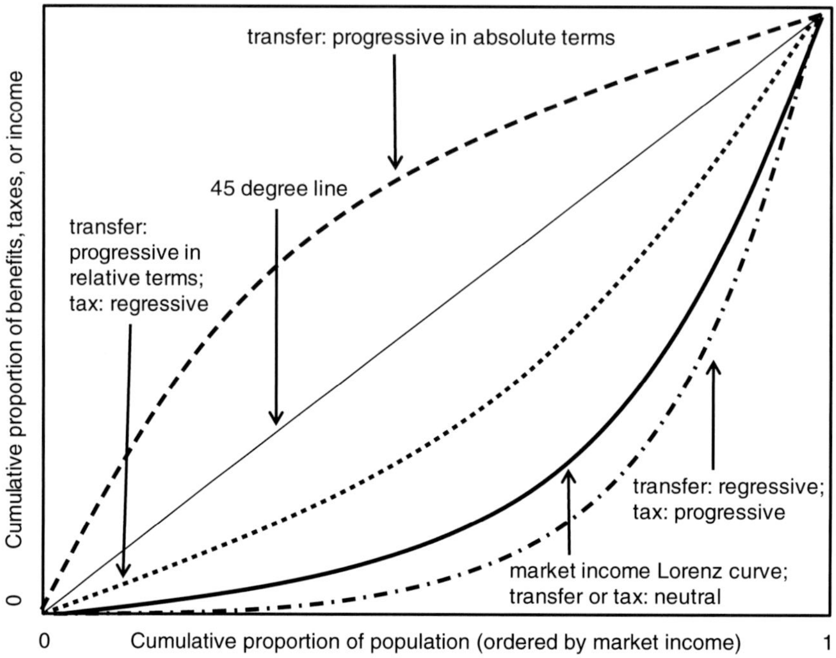

Figure 10.3 Concentration curves for progressive and regressive transfers and taxes.

Source: N. Lustig and S. Higgins. 2012. Commitment to Equity Assessment (CEQ): Estimating the Incidence of Social Spending, Subsidies and Taxes Handbook. *Tulane Economics Working Paper Series* No. 1219. Tulane University.

An assessment of fiscal policies and redistribution in Brazil

This section illustrates the use of the diagnostic questionnaire to assess fiscal policies and redistribution in Brazil.[29] For the sake of conciseness, this section uses a streamlined version of the diagnostic questionnaire (see Box 10.1). The calculations were done using the national household survey called Pesquisa de Orçamentos Familiares (POF) for 2008–2009.

Box 10.1 Applying the diagnostic questionnaire to Brazil

Initial question: Are the income and human capital poverty gaps after net transfers (poverty gaps, henceforth) zero?

Poverty gaps are not zero. The following are the after-transfers poverty gaps (in millions of reais per year):

[29] The application to Brazil of the diagnostic questionnaire presented here is based on the analysis by Pereira and Higgins (2012) and Higgins and Pereira (forthcoming).

Gap	\$2.50 PPP	\$4.00 PPP
Income poverty gap	10,674	41,075
Human capital gap	23,315	43,396
Overall poverty gap	33,989	84,471

PPP = purchasing power parity.

Having established that the extreme and total poverty gaps are not zero, we now proceed to analyze whether this is the result of (i) insufficient overall resources, (ii) how they are allocated between the poor and the nonpoor, (iii) the share of poor individuals not covered by existing anti-poor programs, and/or (iv) the per beneficiary size of transfers.

Resources: Assess whether government revenues and redistributive spending are *potentially* sufficient with what would be required for supporting a minimum standard of living.

R1. *Revenue collection*

R1.1 Does the government collect sufficient combined resources to close the (i) income poverty gap before net transfers (market income poverty gap), (ii) human capital gap before net transfers, and (iii) overall (market income and human capital) poverty gap before net transfers?

The overall poverty gap before transfers, using a poverty line of \$4.00 per day adjusted for purchasing power parity (PPP), is 12% of total revenues (including contributions to social security and other sources of public revenue, but excluding revenue from public enterprises) and 29% of tax revenues (excluding contributions to social security).

The overall poverty gap using a poverty line of \$2.50 PPP per day is 6% of total revenues (including contributions to social security and other sources of public revenue, but excluding revenue from public enterprises) and 14% of tax revenues (excluding contributions to social security).

R2. *Redistributive spending*

R2.1 Does the government allocate sufficient budgetary resources for redistributive spending purposes to potentially close the poverty gaps?

Yes. Brazil allocated 552,621 million reais to redistributive spending (excluding non-subsidized spending on contributory pensions) or 17.4% of gross domestic product (GDP). The overall poverty gap before transfers at \$4.00 PPP (\$2.50 PPP) is 31% (15%) of total redistributive spending, meaning that the government allocates sufficient budgetary resources for redistributive spending purposes to potentially close the poverty gap.

R2.2 Is total government spending and government spending for redistributive purposes (as a percentage of GDP) consistent with the country's GDP per capita?[30]

Primary government spending (total government spending minus debt servicing) was 1,318,169 million reais, or 41.4% of GDP, which exceeds the international benchmark. Since we do not have benchmarks for primary government spending, we use social spending as a proxy. Social spending (including all social security spending so that it is comparable to the international data) was

[30] The answer to this question depends on benchmarks available upon request.

803,668 million reais in 2009 or 25.2% of GDP. This exceeds the international benchmark. Thus, total government spending and spending for redistributive purposes (proxied by social spending) are consistent with the country's GDP per capita.

R2.3 Why does the government not allocate sufficient budgetary resources for redistributive spending purposes? Is it due to subsidies to other sectors, overblown administration, a large debt burden, high military spending, political economy dynamics, or others (specify)?

Not applicable; the government does allocate sufficient budgetary resources for redistributive spending purposes. Nevertheless, the government faces high interest rates on its debt, which could be an obstacle in the future.

Equity: Assess whether the *actual* level and allocation of redistributive spending as well as the range, design, and implementation of programs and policies are consistent with supporting a minimum standard of living.

E1. *Allocation of spending to the poor*

E1.1 Is targeted antipoverty spending sufficient to close the poverty gaps before net transfers?

Targeted antipoverty spending is sufficient to close the before-transfers income poverty gap at $2.50 PPP per day assuming perfect targeting, but likely to be insufficient if we account for the fact that targeting is not perfect. Furthermore, targeted antipoverty spending is *insufficient* to close the before-transfers income poverty gap at $4.00 PPP per day. Note that targeted antipoverty spending only includes direct transfers, so we do not compare it with the human capital or overall poverty gaps. The before-transfers income poverty gap using the $2.50 PPP per day poverty line is 58% of targeted antipoverty spending, while for $4.00 PPP the before-transfers income poverty gap is nearly double (172%) the income poverty gap. Thus, even with perfect targeting, Brazil would need to allocate double what it is currently spending on targeted antipoverty direct transfers to close the income poverty gap at $4.00 PPP.

E2. *Progressivity of net transfers*

E2.1 Are net transfers to the nonpoor "too large"? How equalizing is the distribution of net transfers? If the distribution of net transfers is not sufficiently equalizing, is it due to "universalistic" welfare systems (by design everybody has a right to a benefit and hence benefits going to the poor are too small), state-capture by ruling elites, distribution rules or patterns among federal and subnational governments, or others (specify)?

Direct transfers to the nonpoor are too large. A sum of 73.5% of the total benefits of direct transfers reach the nonpoor, while only 26.5% reach the market-income poor (those living on less than $4.00 PPP per day before government intervention). Furthermore, only 16.8% of total direct transfers reach the market-income extreme poor (those living on less than $2.50 PPP per day before government intervention). These percentages can be compared with the market-income poverty headcount index: 26.7% at $4.00 PPP and 15.4% at $2.50 PPP. Thus, the poor receive slightly less in direct transfers than the nonpoor in relation to their proportion of the population, while the extreme poor receive slightly more in direct transfers than the not extremely poor in relation to their proportion of the population. To eliminate poverty, the poor should instead be receiving a disproportionately large share of direct transfers.

The amount of direct transfers reaching the poor (extreme poor) is approximately 33,437 (20,991) million reais based on the size of budget of all direct transfer programs in public accounts and the percentages above, which are estimated from the household survey microdata (i.e., the amounts reaching the poor when income reported in the survey is scaled by item). The amount of direct transfers reaching the poor is approximately 23,555 (14,943) million reais if it is instead estimated based on the amount of benefits received by the poor, according to the microdata (i.e., when income in the survey is not scaled).[31] These numbers are lower than the before-transfers income poverty gap at $4.00 PPP of 56,843 million reais (at $2.50 PPP of 19,178 million reais), meaning that "what remains" for the poor after direct transfers to the nonpoor is insufficient to close the income poverty gap.[32] As a consequence, direct transfers to the nonpoor are too large.

The distribution of net direct transfers reduces the Gini by 5.5% (percent reduction between the market income Gini and the disposable income Gini). The distribution of net (direct and in-kind) transfers reduces the Gini by 19.1% (percent reduction between the market income Gini and the final income Gini). A few programs are particularly equalizing: Bolsa Família, Brazil's signature conditional cash transfer program, has a concentration coefficient of −0.58 and by itself contributes to a 1.4% decrease in the net market income Gini. Brazil's noncontributory pension system, Benefício de Prestação Continuada (BPC), is also particularly progressive, with a concentration coefficient of −0.48. BPC alone causes a 1.0% reduction in the market income Gini. Other direct transfer programs are not sufficiently progressive: unemployment benefits, special circumstances pensions, scholarships, and basic food baskets are only relatively progressive. In this study, contributory pensions were considered as market income rather than a government transfer. However, if contributory pensions are considered a government transfer, as in some studies, they have a concentration coefficient (with respect to market income excluding contributory pensions) of 0.06.[33]

[31] Deaton (2005) argues that the methodologies of computing income in national accounts should not be used to scale up income when estimating poverty because data from national accounts are upward biased and designed to generate macroeconomic aggregates rather than poverty statistics, in addition to using different definitions and having different coverage than household surveys.

[32] The exception to this statement occurs when comparing the scaled-up transfers going to the extreme poor (20,991 million reais) with the before-transfers income poverty gap at $2.50 PPP (19,178 million reais). In this case, the two numbers are almost equal; nevertheless, because targeting of "what remains" cannot be perfect, even in this case we can conclude that direct transfers to the nonpoor are too large.

[33] Lustig and Higgins (2012) and Higgins and Pereira (forthcoming) explain why the concentration coefficient of contributory pensions should be calculated with respect to market income *not including contributory pensions*. See also Immervoll *et al.* (2009).

With regard to in-kind transfers, public spending on health and education are progressive in absolute terms, with concentration coefficients of −0.12 and −0.16, respectively. However, education spending is less so for the higher levels. While preschool education spending, primary education spending, and secondary education spending are absolutely progressive, with concentration coefficients of −0.33, −0.31, and −0.21, respectively, tertiary education spending is large and only slightly progressive in relative terms, with a concentration coefficient of 0.43. This may be a result of the universal education system. While all Brazilians are theoretically eligible to receive benefits from public universities, the poor face barriers in accessing tertiary education because they tend to receive lower-quality primary and secondary education and perform worse on entrance exams.

E2.2 Are benefits going to the nonpoor by design (i.e., intentional), or are there errors of inclusion (i.e., leakages to unintended beneficiaries)? If there are errors of inclusion, are they due to shortcomings in the diagnostic, design, dissemination, and/or implementation of existing policies and programs; clientelistic politics or corruption; shortcomings in targeting mechanisms; or others (specify)?

For Bolsa Família, 29.5% of benefits go to the nonpoor. Higgins (2012) finds that some benefits go to the rural nonpoor by design when the poverty line being considered is based on the real cost of food and housing and allowed to vary by region to account for spatial price differences within Brazil. These rural nonpoor have household per capita income that exceeds the cost of a basket of basic food and nonfood needs in their area, but they are included by design because the program's eligibility cutoff is based on nominal income. Another example of inclusion by design is based on the recent revision of the program's exit strategy; previously, if a family's income surpassed the eligibility criteria, the family exited the program immediately. However, the exit strategy changed in 2010 to a minimum two-year period in the program to address the high income volatility faced by the poor (and possibly the alleged labor disincentives of the program) (Britto and Soares 2011). Thus, a family that escapes poverty while enrolled in the program will remain a beneficiary for the remainder of the two-year period, and thus some nonpoor (but near-poor) are included by design.

There are also errors of inclusion of Bolsa Família, in part due to shortcomings in the program's targeting mechanism. Brazil uses a partially verified means test based on self-reported income to determine eligibility instead of the proxy means test employed by many other countries with conditional cash transfer programs. Households have an incentive to underreport their incomes to the municipal workers responsible for determining program eligibility. Although incomes are being increasingly cross-checked with formal sector employment accounts and social program accounts, households not registered in these systems can be included in the program by error when they underreport their income. If we take into account the program eligibility rules rather than the poverty line to measure leakages, more than 1.2 million households (about 10% of recipients) receiving Bolsa Família in 2009 had an income above the threshold, according to an auditing of the Tribunal de Contas da União (according to Medeiros *et al.* (2007), 21% of transfers went to recipients with incomes above the threshold in 2004, based on the Pesquisa Nacional por Amostra de Domicílios [PNAD] household survey).[34]

In addition, since Bolsa Família beneficiaries are selected by local governments who have minimum quotas of recipients, clientelistic politics can play a role in the allocation of resources.

It is worth noting that very few middle-class or rich individuals receive leakages from the program, if the lower bound of the middle class is defined as not being vulnerable to falling into poverty and set at $10.00 PPP per day (the line calculated econometrically by López-Calva and Ortiz-Juarez (2011) and used by Kharas (2010) and Ferreira *et al.* (2013)). In this case, only 3.8% of all the program benefits go to those who are middle class or rich.

BPC, the noncontributory pension system, has more leakages than Bolsa Família. The nonpoor are not included by design; the eligibility requirement is to be elderly or incapacitated and have an income less than one-fourth of the monthly minimum salary in Brazil, which equaled 116.25 reais per month in September 2009 – less than the $2.50 PPP per day extreme poverty line. Thus, the 43.1% of benefits going to the nonpoor (those with household per capita income greater than $4.00 PPP per day) are entirely due to leakages. The cause of these errors of inclusion is unclear. As in the case of Bolsa Família, shortcomings in the targeting mechanism could be a factor.

Other direct transfer programs include the nonpoor by design: scholarships are not all need-based, and those that are may include a significant portion of the nonpoor under their threshold; unemployment benefits are targeted based on unemployment rather than poverty; and special circumstance pensions are intended to dampen the impact of idiosyncratic shocks, but only some are means-tested, and most are reserved for formal-sector employees.

E3. *Coverage of the poor*

E3.1 Is coverage of the poor universal? If program/policy coverage is not close to 100%, what is the cause? Is this due to gaps in the safety net system? Do programs and policies intentionally leave out some of the poor? Who are they?

Coverage of the poor is not universal. Of the poor, 84.7% (93.3% of the extreme poor) are covered by at least one direct transfer. Bolsa Família accounts for the majority of this with coverage for 85.3% of poor households (75.8% of extremely poor households).[35]

For the poorest of the poor (those with household per capita income of less than 70 reais per month in September 2009, or approximately $1.35 PPP per day), there are theoretically no gaps in the safety net system because any such

[34] We use a secondary source to measure leakages based on program eligibility rules because income in the POF microdata is temporally deflated because the survey is carried out over the course of one year. It would be incorrect to compare temporally deflated (real) income to the (nominal) eligibility requirement.

[35] These numbers reflect the application of a methodology (Souza *et al.* 2011) to correct for the fact that some recipient households do not report receiving Bolsa Família. See Higgins and Pereira (forthcoming) for more details.

household is eligible for the unconditional portion of Bolsa Família, regardless of whether the household has children. However, for poor families with income above this threshold who have no children (making them ineligible for Bolsa Família) and no elderly family members (making them ineligible for BPC), there are virtually no social programs aimed at helping them to escape poverty – especially if they are not in the formal sector – considering that the two largest social programs are special circumstance pensions and unemployment benefits. It is worth noting that only 17.8% of the total poor receive a direct transfer other than Bolsa Família or BPC. Furthermore, given the low coverage of the poor of all programs other than Bolsa Família and BPC, the low eligibility cutoffs of Bolsa Família (140 reais per month in September 2009, or approximately $2.70 PPP per day) and BPC (one-quarter of one monthly minimum salary, or 116.25 reais in September 2009 or approximately $2.25 PPP per day) imply that many families with household per capita income less than $4.00 PPP per day, who are thus poor by regional standards (CEDLAS and World Bank 2011), are not eligible for any transfer. While Brazil does not have official poverty lines, the Brazilian Government's Institute of Applied Economic Research (IPEA) produces poverty lines based on the cost of a basic needs basket in different regions, and their lines range from 134 to 250 reais per month ($2.57–$4.80 PPP per day). Even if we define poverty by IPEA's standards, rather than the $4.00 PPP per day line, a number of poor Brazilians are excluded from Bolsa Família and BPC based on their income.

Even for those who are eligible to be covered by the safety net system, it is still a problem for people living in remote rural areas to be reached. According to the federal government, almost 1 million potential beneficiaries of Bolsa Família are not included. One of the objectives of the new social program Brasil Sem Miséria is to identify these households and enroll them in the program. Another problem can arise from the decentralized nature of Bolsa Família. Since beneficiaries are selected by the local government, local governments may use the distribution of resources to gain political power. Several cases have been reported in Brazil of the distribution of social program benefits being determined by dominant political parties attempting to "buy votes" rather than on true criteria.

E4. *Size of net transfers going to the poor*

E4.1 Do net transfers per beneficiary to the poor fall short of what is needed to close the poverty gaps? Does the design of programs and policies intentionally keep net transfers below sufficient levels? If yes, why? Is this due to budget constraints or a fiscal austerity program, or to minimize negative incentive effects or ensure long-term fiscal sustainability, etc.?

Direct transfers to the poor per beneficiary equal 464 reais (511 reais) per year for those living on less than $4.00 PPP ($2.50 PPP) per day. In PPP-adjusted dollars per day, direct transfers per beneficiary to the poor (extreme poor) equal $0.74 PPP ($0.82 PPP) per day. To assess whether benefits to those poor who receive at least one direct transfer still fall short of what is needed to close the income poverty gap, we compare these numbers with the average poverty gap[36] of 1,119 (656) reais per year, or \$1.79 PPP (\$1.05 PPP) per day. Average benefits per poor beneficiary are less than the average poverty gap; direct transfers per beneficiary hence fall short of what is needed to close the poverty gap. This means that even if 100% of the poor were covered, direct transfers per beneficiary would fall short of what is needed to close the poverty gaps and poverty would not be eradicated.

There are a number of reasons why direct transfers are kept below sufficient levels to eradicate income poverty. The only program that covers a large proportion of the poor, Bolsa Família, has a small transfer size. This is potentially to minimize negative incentive effects on labor. Although Bolsa Família has a nonexistent or negligible negative incentive effect on labor currently (Foguel and Barros 2010; Tavares 2010; and Teixeira 2010), a larger transfer size could potentially lead to disincentives to work or a higher incentive to underreport income when applying for the benefit. An argument in favor of limiting the number of children for which a parent can receive benefits, which in turn keeps the per capita transfer low for larger poor families, has been that Bolsa Família could increase fertility by providing an incentive to have more children. However, Rocha (2009) finds that the program has no impact on fertility, while Signorini and Queiroz (2011) find that the program caused beneficiaries to *decrease* fertility.

The low transfer size cannot be ascribed to budget constraints or long-term fiscal sustainability, because the budget size of Bolsa Família is only 0.39% of GDP. The government's priority seems to be to expand program coverage rather than to increase transfer size. Although President Dilma Rousseff increased the minimum transfer from 22 reais to 32 reais (in March 2011), the transfer remains small in real terms, especially for poor households in metropolitan Brasília, São Paulo, Rio de Janeiro, and Belém, who face a significantly higher cost of living than those in rural and other urban areas (Higgins 2012). Bills on the table in Brazil's Senate and Chamber of Deputies propose further increases to the transfer size but have a low probability of being passed (Britto and Soares 2011), implying that political economy dynamics may be keeping the transfer size low. One bill currently under consideration proposes to raise the minimum benefit to half of the monthly minimum wage; increasing each beneficiary household's monthly transfer to half of the monthly minimum wage would increase the size of the Bolsa Família program by a factor of 10.

E4.2 Do net transfers to the poor fall short due to errors in design, planning, and/or implementation? If yes, why?

Yes.

For Bolsa Família and BPC, errors in implementation cause errors of inclusion that divert resources that could otherwise be going to poor households, via either expanded coverage or increased transfer size. The new

[36] Here, the average poverty gap refers to the sum of all poor individuals' shortfall below the poverty line (*not* normalized by the poverty line), divided by the number of poor. We choose this indicator because it tells us the average transfer per poor person that would eradicate poverty if all poor individuals received the transfer.

program announced in 2011, Brasil Sem Miséria, seems to be a step in the right direction because it seeks to both expand the coverage of Bolsa Família and provide additional resources to the poor in urban areas (mainly focused on the insertion of Bolsa Família recipients into the labor market) and rural areas (mainly focused on providing technical assistance and improved technology to poor farmers).

For education, more resources should be devoted to early childhood development spending, pre-primary education spending, and primary education spending, which are (highly) absolutely progressive. These resources could be diverted from tertiary education spending, which has a concentration coefficient barely lower than the Gini coefficient, meaning it is only very slightly equalizing. Currently, there is a large discrepancy between the amount spent on public education for younger students and university students: the government spends 2,276 reais per student per year for "initial education" (early childhood development and pre-primary), while it spends 15,582 reais per student per year for public universities. Such a large discrepancy is not seen in most of the other countries analyzed by the CEQ project and is an area where Brazil could improve the design, planning, and implementation of redistributive spending.

E4.3 Do net transfers fall short because the tax, fees, co-payments burden, or other factors (such as transportation or labor opportunity costs) on the poor are too high?

Indirect taxes are very high, especially on items important for poor families (food and domestic fuel). Food expenditures are one-fifth to one-quarter of the budget of the poorest fifth of Brazilians, and taxes on items in the basic food basket are highly regressive, making up 3.3% of the total expenditure of the poorest decile. When all food items (not just those in the basic basket) are considered, the poorest decile spends 4.8% of its expenditures on indirect food taxes (Siqueira *et al.* 2010).

In addition, participation costs may be high for the poor, leading them to self-exclude from certain social programs. Again, using the example of Bolsa Família, because it is the social program with the highest coverage rate among the poor, families face transportation and opportunity costs that comply with the health and education conditions. The participation costs related to enrolling in the program and receiving benefits are minimized due to the program's decentralized nature (beneficiaries can enroll online or at a municipal office) and the magnetic ATM-style cards used to automatically pay benefits (which reduce time waiting in line to receive the benefit and promote financial inclusion, especially among poor women) (Soares and Silva 2010).

Conclusion

CEQ provides a systematic and logical order of how to prepare a diagnostic assessment of governments' antipoverty and redistributive policies through fiscal interventions. After completing the assessment, one is able to answer the following questions for the country being studied: do governments collect and allocate enough resources to support a minimum living standard and human capital accumulation for all? Is the collection and distribution of fiscal resources consistent with eradicating extreme income and human capital poverty gaps? Do governments collect and distribute resources equitably?

In addition, CEQ homogenizes concepts, definitions, and methods that in the literature are often not clear. This ensures that studies undertaken by different researchers for different countries use the same methodology, which in turn maximizes the comparability of results across countries. As a result, the analysis for a particular country can be placed in comparative perspective with results from other countries, without needing to wonder if different results are due to methodological differences or policy differences. As part of the analysis, any country-specific methodological assumptions (e.g., necessitated by data limitations or unique programs) are described in detail, so that differences in results, which might be due to methodological differences, are not mistakenly attributed to policy differences. To date, CEQ has been applied to 12 countries.

In this chapter, we apply the framework to Brazil as an illustration. There are several important and policy-relevant findings. Revenue collection and redistributive spending are sufficient to close the poverty gaps and are consistent with Brazil's GDP per capita when compared with international benchmarks. However, poverty is not eradicated. We use the diagnostic framework to determine the reasons. First, transfers to the nonpoor are too large: the share of direct transfers received by the poor is approximately equal to their population share. For direct transfers to reduce poverty and inequality, the poor should receive more than their population share in direct transfers. Benefits go to the nonpoor both by design and due to errors of inclusion. Second, coverage of the poor is not universal: 15% of the poor are not covered by at least one direct transfer program. In fact, some families that are moderately poor by Latin American and national standards are not eligible for any targeted antipoverty program (even if the family has children or elderly) due to the programs' low eligibility cutoffs. Third, the average transfer per poor beneficiary is less than the average poverty gap. This implies that there are many poor families receiving direct transfers but remaining in poverty due to the low transfer size. Furthermore, it implies that if all poor were covered, poverty would still not be eradicated.

In sum, CEQ entails a rigorous and data-intensive analysis, the results of which serve as an important policy tool to inform governments of how their fiscal policy affects their equity and poverty reduction goals. The diagnostic framework enables governments to learn why their redistributive spending is unsuccessful at eradicating poverty and recommends practical policy measures.

Acknowledgments

This chapter is based on a paper prepared for the Asian Development Bank (ADB). An earlier draft was presented at the Forum on Equalizing Opportunities for Inclusive Growth, 7–8 December 2011 at ADB headquarters in Manila, Philippines. The authors are very grateful to Maria Socorro Bautista for her very useful comments on an earlier draft, and to Samantha Greenspun and Emily Travis for their excellent research assistance. The application of the framework to Brazil is based on joint research with Claudiney Pereira. The chapter is part of the Commitment to Equity project. Developed under the leadership of Nora Lustig, the project is a joint initiative of the Center for Inter-American Policy and Research (CIPR) and Department of Economics at Tulane University and the Inter-American Dialogue. The Commitment to Equity project has received generous support from the Canadian International Development Agency (CIDA), the Development Bank of Latin America (CAF), the General Electric Foundation, the Inter-American Development Bank (IADB), the International Fund for Agricultural Development (IFAD), the Norwegian Ministry of Foreign Affairs, the United Nations Development Programme's Regional Bureau for Latin America and the Caribbean (UNDP/RBLAC), and the World Bank. See http://commitmenttoequity.org.

References

Adcock, R., and D. Collier. 2001. Measurement Validity: A Shared Standard for Qualitative and Quantitative Research. *American Political Science Review.* 95 (3). pp. 529–46.

Adema, W., and M. Ladaique. 2005. Net Social Expenditure, 2005 Edition: More Comprehensive Measures of Social Support. *OECD Social, Employment and Migration Working Papers* 29. Paris: OECD.

Aghion, P., C. Harris, and J. Vickers. 1997. Paper and Proceedings of the Eleventh Annual Congress of the European Economic Association. *European Economic Review.* 41 (3–5). pp. 771–82.

Aghion, P., and P. Howitt. 1992. A Model of Growth through Creative Destruction. *Econometrica.* 60 (2). pp. 323–51.

Alkire, S., and M. E. Santos. 2010. Acute Multidimensional Poverty: A New Index for Developing Countries. *OPHI Working Paper* No. 38. Oxford University.

Alkire, S., and J. Foster. 2011. Counting and Multidimensional Poverty Measurement. *Journal of Public Economics.* 95 (7–8). pp. 476–87.

Atkinson, A. B. 1983. *Social Justice and Public Policy.* Cambridge, MA: MIT Press.

Barr, N. 2004. *Economics of the Welfare State.* Fourth edition. New York, NY: Oxford University Press.

Barros, R. P., F. Ferreira, J. M. Vegas, and J. S. Chanduvi. 2009. *Measuring Inequality of Opportunities in Latin America and the Caribbean.* Washington, DC: World Bank. http://siteresources.worldbank.org/BRAZILEXTN/Resources/322340-1222953505624/BookHOI.pdf

Bergh, A. 2005. On the Counterfactual Problem of Welfare State Research: How Can We Measure Redistribution? *European Sociological Review.* 21 (4). pp. 345–57.

Birdsall, N., A. de la Torre, and R. Menezes. 2008. *Fair Growth: Economic Policies for Latin America's Poor and Middle-Income Majority.* Washington, DC: Brookings Institution Press.

Bourguignon, F., and L. A. Pereira da Silva, eds. 2003. *The Impact of Economic Poverty and Income Distribution.* Washington, DC: World Bank.

Breceda, K., J. Rigolini, and J. Saavedra. 2008. Latin America and the Social Contract: Patterns of Social Spending and Taxation. *Policy Research Working Paper* 4604. World Bank Latin American and Caribbean Region Poverty Department Poverty Reduction and Economic Management Division. Washington, DC: World Bank.

Britto, T., and F. V. Soares. 2011. *Conditional Cash Transfers and the Basic Income Grant in Brazil: Will They Ever Merge?* One Pager 124. February. International Policy Centre for Inclusive Growth, United Nations Development Programme.

Centro de Estudios Distributivos, Laborales y Sociales (CEDLAS) and World Bank. 2011. *A Guide to the SEDLAC Socio-Economic Database for Latin America and the Caribbean.*

Deaton, A. 2005. Measuring Poverty in a Growing World (or Measuring Growth in a Poor World). *Review of Economics and Statistics.* 87 (1). pp. 1–19.

Dilnot, A., J. Kay, and M. Keen. 1990. Allocating Taxes to Households: A Methodology. *Oxford Working Papers.* 42 (1). pp. 210–30.

Ferreira, F., and D. Robalino. 2010. Social Protection in Latin America: Achievements and Limitations. *Policy Research Working Paper* 5305. Latin America and Caribbean Region Office of the Chief Economist, and Human Development Network Social Protection and Labor Unit. Washington, DC: World Bank.

Ferreira, F., J. Messina, J. Rigolini, L.-F. López-Calva, M. A. Lugo, and R. Vakis. 2013. *Economic Mobility and the Rise of the Latin American Middle Class.* Washington, DC: World Bank.

Fiszbein, A., N. Schady, F. Ferreira, M. Grosh, N. Kelleher, P. Olinto, and E. Skoufias. 2009. *Conditional Cash Transfers: Reducing Present and Future Poverty.* Washington, DC: World Bank.

Foguel, M. N., and R. P. Barros. 2010. The Effects of Conditional Cash Transfer Programmes on Adult Labour Supply: An Empirical Analysis Using a Time-Series-Cross-Section Sample of Brazilian Municipalities. *Estudos Economicos.* 40 (2). pp. 259–93. Available at http://www.scielo.br/

Goñi, E., J. H. López, and L. Servén. 2008. Fiscal Redistribution and Income Inequality in Latin America. *Policy Research Working Paper* 4487. World Bank Development Research Group Macroeconomics and Growth Team. Washington, DC: World Bank.

Grosh, M., C. del Ninno, E. Tesliuc, and A. Ouerghi. 2008. *For Protection and Promotion: The Design and Implementation of Effective Safety Nets.* Washington, DC: World Bank.

Hausmann, R., D. Rodrik, and A. Velasco. 2006. Getting the Diagnosis Right: A New Approach to Economic Reform. *Finance and Development.* 43 (1). pp. 12–15.

Hausmann, R., B. Klinger, and R. Wagner. 2008. Doing Growth Diagnostics in Practice: A "Mindbook." *CID Working Paper* 77. Center for International Development at Harvard University.

Higgins, S. 2012. The Impact of Bolsa Família on Poverty: Does Brazil's Conditional Cash Transfer Program Have a Rural Bias? *Journal of Politics & Society.* 23 (1). pp. 88–125.

Higgins, S., and C. Pereira. Forthcoming. The Effects of Brazil's Taxation and Social Spending on the Distribution of Household Income. *Public Finance Review.*

Immervoll, H., H. Levy, J. R. Nogueira, C. O'Donoghue, and R. Bezerra de Siqueira. 2009. The Impact of Brazil's Tax-Benefit System on Inequality and Poverty. In S. Klasen and F. Nowak-Lehmann, eds. *Poverty, Inequality, and Policy in Latin America.* Cambridge, MA: MIT Press. pp. 271–302.

Kakwani, N. C. 1977. Measurement of Tax Progressivity: An International Comparison. *The Economic Journal.* 87 (345). pp. 71–80.

Kharas, H. 2010. The Emerging Middle Class in Developing Countries. *OECD Development Centre Working Paper* 285. Paris, France: OECD Development Centre.

Lambert, P. 2002. *The Distribution and Redistribution of Income.* Third edition. Manchester, UK: Manchester University Press.

López-Calva, L.-F., and E. Ortiz-Juarez. 2011. A Vulnerability Approach to the Definition of the Middle Class. *Policy Research Working Paper* 5902. Washington, DC: World Bank.

Lora, E., ed. 2006. *The State of State Reforms in Latin America.* Washington, DC: World Bank.

Lustig, N. 2000. Crises and the Poor: Socially Responsible Macroeconomics. *Economía: Journal of the Latin American and Caribbean Economic Association.* 1 (Fall). pp. 1–45. Washington, DC: Brookings Institution Press.

——. 2012. Commitment to Equity: Diagnostic Questionnaire. *CEQ Working Paper* No. 3, September. New Orleans, LA: Tulane University.
Lustig, N., and S. Higgins. 2012. Commitment to Equity Assessment (CEQ): Estimating the Incidence of Social Spending, Subsidies and Taxes Handbook. *Tulane Economics Working Paper Series* No. 1219. New Orleans, LA: Tulane University.
Lustig, N., G. Gray-Molina, S. Higgins, M. Jaramillo, W. Jimenez, V. Paz, C. Pereira, C. Pessino, J. Scott, and E. Yañez. 2012. The Impact of Taxes and Social Spending on Inequality and Poverty in Argentina, Bolivia, Brazil, Mexico and Peru: A Synthesis of Results. *Tulane Economics Working Paper Series* No. 1216. New Orleans, LA: Tulane University.
Medeiros, M., T. Britto, and F. Soares. 2007. Transferência de Renda no Brasil. *Novos Estuodos – CEBRAP*. 79. pp. 5–21.
Mookherjee, D., and D. Ray. 2003. Persistent Inequality. *Review of Economic Studies*. 70 (2). pp. 369–93.
——. 2006. Occupational Diversity and Endogenous Inequality. *Working Paper*. Institute for Economic Development. Boston, MA: Boston University.
Morra-Imas, L. G., and R. C. Rist. 2009. *The Road to Results: Designing and Conducting Effective Development Evaluations*. Washington, DC: World Bank.
Musgrave, R. A. 1957. A Multiple Theory of Budget Determination. *Finanzarchiv*. 17 (3). pp. 333–43.
Narayan, D., R. Chambers, M. K. Shah, and P. Petesch. 2000. *Crying Out for Change: Voices of the Poor*. Oxford, UK: Oxford University Press.
O'Donnell, O., E. van Doorslaer, A. Wagstaff, and M. Lindelow. 2008. Analyzing Health Equity Using Household Survey Data: A Guide to Techniques and Their Implementation. *WBI Learning Resources Series*. Washington, DC: World Bank.
Pereira, C., and S. Higgins. 2012. *Fiscal Policy, Urban-Rural Inequality and Rural Poverty in Brazil*. Report prepared for the International Fund for Agricultural Development. Rome, Italy: International Fund for Agricultural Development.
Ravallion, M. 2008. Bailing out the World's Poorest. *Policy Research Working Paper* 4763. World Bank Development Research Group. Washington, DC: World Bank.
Rocha, R. 2009. Programas Condicionais de Transferência de Renda e Fecundidade: Evidências do Bolsa Família. Rio de Janeiro: PUC-Rio. http://www2.dbd.puc-rio.br/pergamum/tesesabertas/0510700_09_cap_03.pdf
Rodrik, D. 2007. *One Economics, Many Recipes: Globalization, Institutions, and Economic Growth*. Princeton, NJ: Princeton University Press.
Shah, A. ed. 2003. *Handbook on Public Sector Performance Reviews*. Washington, DC: World Bank.
Signorini, B., and B. Queiroz. 2011. The Impact of Bolsa Família on Beneficiaries' Fertility. *Texto para Discussão* 439. Belo Horizonte: UFMG/Cedeplar.
Siqueira, R., J. Nogueira, and E. Souza. 2010. Aliquotas Efetivas e a Distribuição da Carga Tributária Indireta entre as Famílias no Brasil. XV Prêmio Tesouro Nacional. Brazil: Tesouro Nacional.
Soares, F. V., and E. Silva. 2010. Conditional Cash Transfer Programmes and Gender Vulnerabilities: Case Studies of Brazil, Chile and Colombia. *Working Paper* No. 69. Brazil: International Policy Centre for Inclusive Growth, Overseas Development Institute.
Souza, P., R. Osorio, and S. Soares. 2011. Uma Metodologia para Simular o Programa Bolsa Família. *Texto para Discussão* 1654. Brasilia: IPEA.
Suits, D. B. 1977. Measure of Tax Progressivity. *American Economic Review* 67 (4). pp. 747–52.
Tavares, P. A. 2010. Efeito do Programa *Bolsa Família* Sobre a Oferta de Trabalho das Mães. *Economia e Sociedade*. 19 (3). pp. 613–35. http://www.scielo.br/pdf/ecos/v19n3/08.pdf
Teixeira, C. G. 2010. A Heterogeneity Analysis of the Bolsa Família Programme Effect on Men and Women's Work Supply. *International Policy Centre for Inclusive Growth Working Paper* 61. Brazil: International Policy Centre for Inclusive Growth.

van de Walle, D., and K. Nead, eds. 1995. *Public Spending and the Poor: Theory and Evidence.* Baltimore and London: Published for the World Bank by the Johns Hopkins University Press.

World Bank. 2000/2001. *World Development Report 2000/2001: Attacking Poverty.* Washington, DC and New York: Published for the World Bank by Oxford University Press.

——. 2006. Country Policy and Institutional Assessments. Washington, DC: Operations Policy and Country Services, World Bank.

——. 2009. *The World Bank's Country Policy and Institutional Assessment: An Evaluation.* Independent Evaluation Group. Washington, DC: World Bank.

——. 2011. CPIA Public Sector Management and Institutions Cluster Average. http://data.worldbank.org/indicator/IQ.CPA.PUBS.XQ (accessed October 2011).

11 Growth policy/strategy and inequality in developing Asia

Hyun-Hoon Lee, Minsoo Lee, and Donghyun Park

Introduction

Growth policy refers to the various government policies that influence the economic growth of a country. Some of those policies are explicitly geared toward promoting growth while others impinge upon growth even though they serve other objectives. For example, many governments in developing countries try to foster domestic savings and thus promote investment and the accumulation of physical capital as an explicit means of stimulating growth. Indeed, high savings and investment rates induced by supportive government policies were one of the key ingredients of the East Asian Miracle. On the other hand, heavy investment in public education aims to impart literacy, numeracy, and other basic knowledge to as much of the population as possible. Educating the youth is in and of itself a key policy objective in all countries. At the same time, a better educated population and hence labor force contributes to a higher stock of human capital and hence higher growth. Growth strategy refers to a country's constellation of policies that directly and indirectly affect economic growth. In fact, many developing countries have 5- or 10-year national economic plans that specify a target growth rate and a collection of policies – i.e., growth strategy – to achieve the target.

While the central objective of a growth strategy is to foster economic growth, a growth strategy inevitably has significant ramifications for inequality. Virtually all growth policies have an impact on inequality, but some specific examples include promotion of export-oriented manufacturing, promotion of manufacturing over services, adoption of labor-intensive versus capital-intensive production technologies, the relative role of small and medium-sized enterprises versus big companies, the relative role of skilled versus unskilled workers, and regional development priorities. For example, in many developing countries, the government pursued policies that favored the urban sector at the expense of the rural sector, by artificially keeping down the prices of staple foods. Such policies exacerbated inequality between urban and rural areas. In the case of developing Asia, the top priority of policy makers up to now has been to maximize economic growth. Growth strategy has focused almost entirely on its central objective – i.e., growth – with limited consideration for inequality.

More recently, however, there is a growing recognition among developing Asia's policy makers that sustainable growth requires including the largest possible segment of the population in the economic growth process. Sustainable growth also requires spreading the fruits of growth to as much of the population as possible. Thus was born the concept of inclusive growth, which has direct and far-reaching implications for growth strategy. Up to now, developing Asia's growth strategies implicitly assumed that the fruits of growth would eventually trickle down to the poor, and in fact, the region's exceptionally rapid growth reduced poverty on a massive scale. However, there is now a growing popular unhappiness at what is perceived to be a persistently wide income gap between the rich and the rest. Policy makers are aware of the increasingly vocal popular demand for more equality. For example, policy makers in the People's Republic of China (PRC) recently set forth the agenda for a "harmonious society" to address the growing popular demand for a more inclusive growth process.

Spreading the fruits of growth to the broadest swathe of the population requires at least some redistribution from the rich to the poor. In fact, many developing Asian countries have already begun to strengthen their social protection systems, and to expand and improve social safety nets for the poor and the vulnerable. However, in light of its still-low income levels, the region needs to maintain high growth rates in order to continue to reduce poverty at a meaningful scale and speed. Therefore, the more fundamental challenge for the region is to sustain growth while, at the same time, tackling inequality. Put differently, the region must continue to vigorously expand the size of the pie, even while it seeks to divide up the pie more equitably. Therefore, devising and implementing a growth strategy that delivers both growth and equity holds the key to ensuring politically and socially sustainable growth in the post-crisis period. The two cornerstones of such a growth strategy are equal access to education and equal access to employment, which jointly constitute the core of equality of opportunity.

Inclusive growth policy/strategy: a comparison of the People's Republic of China and India

With a population of 1.3 billion in the PRC and 1.2 billion in India as of 2010, both are mammoth countries not only in Asia but also in the world, accounting for 19.6% and 17.1% respectively of the world's population of 6.8 billion. Indeed, they are the two largest countries in the world in terms of population size. For the past two decades, these two giants have undertaken fairly extensive market-oriented economic reforms and have been growing very rapidly with an annual growth rate of around 10%. Interestingly, both countries have recently embraced "inclusive growth" as an important feature of their development plans.

The two countries are, however, not uniform in terms of cultural background, political system, and other factors. For instance, the PRC maintains the so-called socialist market economic system under the leadership of one political party, while India is characterized in its constitution as a "sovereign socialist secular democratic republic." These countries are also different in terms of income level as shown in Figure 11.1. Gross domestic product (GDP) per capita (purchasing

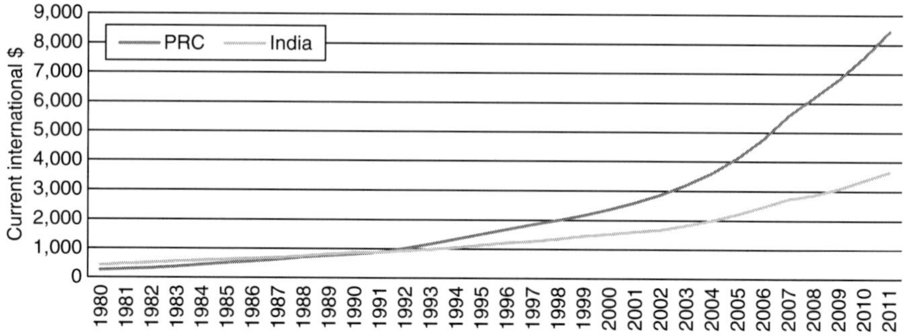

Figure 11.1 Gross domestic product per capita in the People's Republic of China and India, 1980–2011.

PRC = People's Republic of China.

Note: Gross domestic product per capita is in purchasing power parity terms.

Source: World Development Indicators, http://data.worldbank.org/data-catalog/world-development-indicators (accessed 27 August 2012).

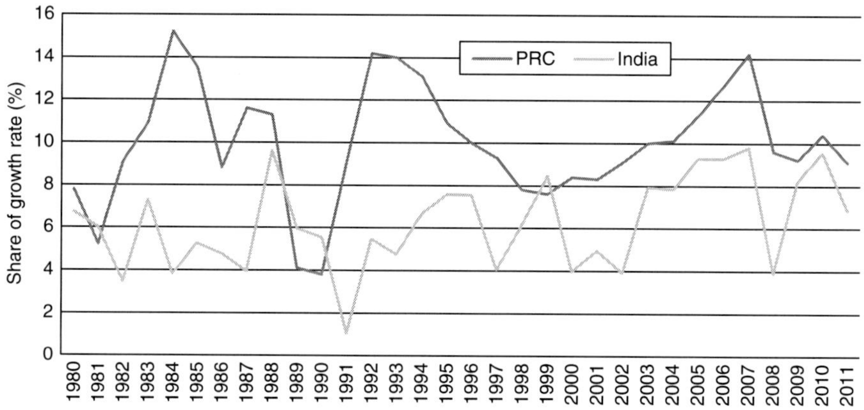

Figure 11.2 Gross domestic product growth rate in the People's Republic of China and India, 1980–2011

PRC = People's Republic of China.

Source: World Development Indicators, http://data.worldbank.org/data-catalog/world-development-indicators (accessed 27 August 2012).

power parity [PPP] international dollars) of the PRC was lower than that of India in the 1980s, but in the early 1990s, the PRC surpassed India. In 2011, the PRC's GDP per capita was $8,442, while that of India was $3,650. This is, of course, because economic growth in the PRC was a lot faster than in India during the period, as seen in Figure 11.2.

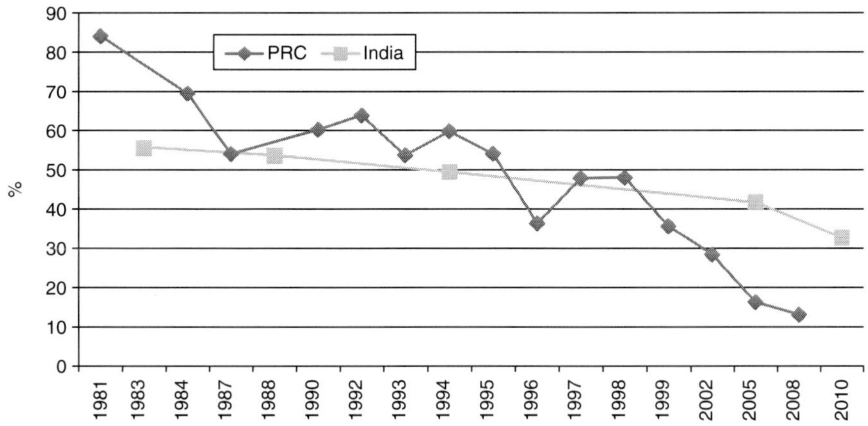

Figure 11.3 Population living below $1.25 a day in the People's Republic of China and India, 1981–2010.

PRC = People's Republic of China.

Note: $1.25 a day in 2005 purchasing power parity dollars.

Source: World Development Indicators, http://data.worldbank.org/data-catalog/world-development-indicators (accessed 3 April 2013).

As shown in Figure 11.3, both the PRC and India have made progress against poverty since the early 1980s, albeit at different rates. The PRC in particular has been successful in reducing the percentage of people living under the global poverty line of $1.25 per day – 16.3% in 2005 compared with 41.6% in India. However, income inequality in both countries, as measured by the Gini coefficient, has been increasing during the period of economic reforms (in the PRC since the early 1980s and in India since the early 1990s), but at different rates again: the rise in inequality has been far greater for the PRC than for India. The Gini coefficient for India rose from 30.8 in 1993 to 33.4 in 2005, while that for the PRC rose from 35.5 to 41.5 during the same period (Figure 11.4).

The next section first provides a general overview of the policies and strategies related to inclusive growth of the two countries. Because these policies and strategies are very broadranging from fiscal and monetary policies to industry-specific policies, we will first compare the development plans of the two countries. We will then evaluate the policies and strategies of inclusive growth in terms of providing equal education and employment opportunities for disadvantaged groups, such as women, who account for about half of the population but have been given unequal treatment in education and employment.

People's Republic of China

In the past 30 years, the PRC has enjoyed one of the fastest economic growth rates in the world and has lifted about 500 million–600 million people out of poverty.

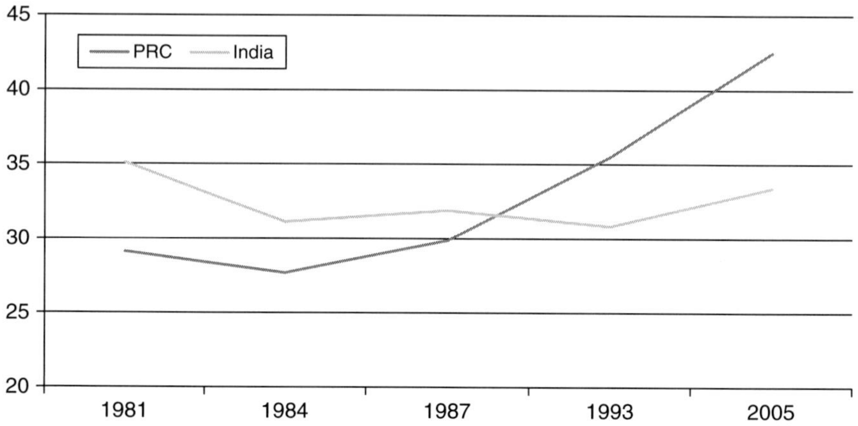

Figure 11.4 Gini coefficients in the People's Republic of China and India.

PRC = People's Republic of China.

Source: PovcalNet, http://iresearch.worldbank.org/PovcalNet/index.htm (accessed 27 August 2012).

There are, however, still many Chinese who are suffering from poverty. There were over 170 million people in the PRC (13.06% of the total population as seen in Figure 11.3) living under the global poverty line in 2008. Furthermore, inequality in the PRC has risen sharply in the past 30 years. In particular, the gap has risen rapidly between urban and rural incomes. The rising gap between the PRC's urban and rural residents has contributed to a range of problems, including social unrest in some rural areas (APCO Worldwide 2010).

With mounting inequalities and disparate interests that need accommodating, the PRC Government has recently taken up plans to address the growing gap between rich and poor and to upgrade social welfare. Specifically, under the leadership of President Hu Jintao and Premier Wen Jiabao, the government made the creation of a "harmonious society" the top priority in its Eleventh Five Year Plan for National Economic and Social Development for the period 2006–2010. During the plan period, however, the income disparity continued to grow.

The concept of a "harmonious society" has also been incorporated in the PRC's Twelfth Five Year Plan which covers the period 2011–2015. In October 2010, the Central Committee of the Communist Party approved the guiding principles of the plan and it was approved by the National People's Congress in March 2011. According to President Hu Jintao, an important feature of the new development plan is the concept of "inclusive growth," acknowledging that the country's rapid growth during the past 30 years has lifted millions of its people out of poverty, but resulted in the issue of increasing income and wealth disparity. The new development plan also emphasizes "higher quality growth," acknowledging the question of sustainability as the PRC grapples with challenges such as pollution, intensive energy use, and resource depletion.

Important goals of the Twelfth Plan are to (i) develop the PRC's western regions, (ii) protect the environment and improve energy efficiency, and (iii) continue transitioning to an economy driven by domestic consumption instead of exports and improve the lives of its citizens. Some new plans related to inclusive growth are the (i) housing target: develop 36 million units of affordable housing; (ii) wellbeing target: increase average life expectancy by one year; and (iii) education target: increase the high school enrollment ratio from 82.5% to 87% (KPMG China 2011).

The government plans to provide improved social safety nets for the PRC's rural population, such as basic healthcare coverage and improved rural land distribution. It also plans to raise the minimum wage and hence increase income and improve the livelihoods of the poor. It is expected that minimum wages will increase by more than 13% per year and this in turn is expected to boost consumption and economic growth (KPMG China 2011).

Thus, the PRC Government is now attempting to change its policy direction from the country's previous emphasis on short-term growth to prioritizing policies and strategies to ensure long-term prosperity for the entire nation.

However, some outside skeptics argue that it is not clear that the country's political system, reform of which is widely considered as lagging behind that of the economic system, is up to the task (*The Economist* 2010a). Also, income disparities between rural and urban residents are partly because of the *hukou* (household registration) system, which limits internal migration to cities. People with a city *hukou* can live and work there freely. Those with a rural *hukou* can go to a city only as guest workers. About 150 million rural Chinese live in cities without a city *hukou*. They often have no or less access to public schools, clinics, and housing. The government has promised to reform the *hukou* system, but it is the city authorities that will implement the reform and may face many constraints including financing (*The Economist* 2011a).

The PRC Government has also been trying to provide better quality education for their young generation for a greater number of years. For example, the National Outline for Medium- and Long-term Education Reform and Development (2010–2020) was drafted in 2009 to build the foundation for a learning society by modernizing the current educational system. The main goal for a modernized education system in the PRC is to be able to provide globally competitive workforce. Some important aspects of the plan are to (i) consolidate and enhance the level of 9-year compulsory education, (ii) provide migrant children's education managed by the city governments and operated by full-time public schools ensuring equal access to compulsory education, (iii) establish a modern vocational education system that can adapt to economic changes and restructuring demands, (iv) accelerate the development of internationally renowned colleges and universities with a number of universities at or near the world-class level, (v) accelerate the development of continuing education and establish a learning society, (vi) improve the level of education for minorities and in ethnic areas, and (vii) improve the overall quality of education for disabled students (Quosdorf 2010).

Special efforts have also been made to provide equal education opportunities to the female population. For example, the government has enacted and implemented outlines for the development of women, and included women's development in the overall plans of economic and social development. The Outline for the Development of Chinese Women was a national program of action to carry out the Platform for Action adopted in 1995 and push forward gender equality in a comprehensive way for the period 1995–2000. In 2001, the PRC promulgated a new version of its Outline for the Development of Chinese Women (2001–2010). The new document outlined 34 major goals and 100 policies and measures in six fields: women and the economy, women's participation in decision making and administration, women and education, women and health, women and the law, and women and the environment. In 2011, the updated government policy was again promulgated in the National Program on the Development of Chinese Women (2011–2020), which covers the seven fields of health, education, economy, political participation, social security, environment, and law, with 57 main objectives and 88 strategies and measures. In the field of education, it aims to promote equal opportunities for men and women in the education process, raising women's education levels, and controlling and reducing the rate of illiteracy among young and middle-aged women.

India

India is the second-largest country by population in the world, after the PRC, and has also enjoyed very fast economic growth. India has recently switched to a development strategy of making growth more inclusive and this orientation with the theme "towards faster and more inclusive growth" was visibly manifested in the theme of the Eleventh Five Year Plan (2007–2012) (Planning Commission of India 2006).

The plan set the annual GDP growth target at 9.0%, and it aimed "first, to generate the income and employment opportunities that were needed for improving living standards for the bulk of the population; and second, to generate the resources needed for financing social sector programmes, aimed at reducing poverty and enabling inclusiveness" (Planning Commission of India 2011, 1). The Indian economy achieved an average GDP growth of around 8% over the plan period 2007–2012. This was lower than the 9.0% originally targeted, largely because of the global financial and economic crisis in 2008–2009.

Reducing poverty was a key element in India's inclusive growth strategy. As seen in Figure 11.3, the proportion of the population living under the global poverty line had been decreasing, but as of 2010, there were over 400 million Indians (32.67% of the total Indian population) under the global poverty line. The Eleventh Plan had set an ambitious target of achieving a decline in the poverty ratio of 2 percentage points per year. Preliminary estimates suggest that the percentage of the population in poverty declined by about 1 percentage point per year, during the 5-year period from 2004/2005 to 2009/2010 (Planning Commission of India 2011).

The Eleventh Plan articulated the need for expanding educational facilities and improving quality of education as key instruments for achieving faster and inclusive growth. The Right to Education Act, which makes education a fundamental right for all children in the 6–14 age group, became operational in 2009.

The Planning Commission of India claims that according to the 66th round of the National Sample Survey on employment, the total number of young working-age people (ages 15–24) who continued in educational institutions doubled from about 30 million in 2004/2005 to over 60 million during 2009/2010. The survey also shows that in the 5–14 age group, 89.3% of children were in school during 2009/2010, up from 82.4% during 2004/2005. Further, this increase was higher for girls, rising from 79.6% during 2004/2005 to 87.7% during 2009/2010. In the 15–19 age group, 59.5% of young people were in the educational system during 2009/2010 as compared with 46.2% during 2004/2005.

The survey on employment also shows that the vast majority of new jobs created between 2004/2005 and 2009/2010 were in construction. As an increasing number of children finish primary education, expansion of capacity in secondary and higher secondary schools is also in great need. Therefore, the Central Government of India introduced a program of creating new central universities and other institutions of higher learning in the Eleventh Plan.

India's Government is currently implementing its Twelfth Five Year Plan, which covers the period 2012–2017, and the Planning Commission's focus is once again on instilling "inclusive growth." An important aspect of generating "inclusive growth" is shifting the target of government aid to rural areas (2point6billion.com 2011). The 2011 Census of India estimated that over 800 million people live in rural India. Therefore, there is a great need for the expansion of employment and income opportunities in farm activities. It has been reported that, according to Prime Minister Manmohan Singh, the key components of the inclusive growth strategy include a sharp increase in investment in rural areas, rural infrastructure, and agriculture; a spurt in credit for farmers; increase in rural employment through a unique social safety net; and a sharp increase in public spending on education and healthcare. Thus, the Indian Government believes that expansion of nonfarm employment and income opportunities in rural areas also has enormous potential and it has therefore put in place various development programs to support the rural transformation process by improving rural infrastructure.

In this sense, India's Twelfth Five Year Plan is similar to the PRC's Twelfth Five Year Plan, which seeks to improve the livelihood of rural Chinese by increasing urbanization and industrial efforts in central and western PRC. By contrast, however, while the PRC Government seems to be continuing with nationwide industrialization efforts, the Indian Government may be attempting to promote a policy of reverse migration by making rural living more attractive with some access to modern amenities (2point6billion.com 2011).

The plan is also expected to encourage the development of India's education, health, and social welfare, and to create employment by developing India's manufacturing sector. For India to genuinely embrace inclusive growth, it also needs to rebut the discrimination and denial of opportunity that the caste system has created. "As millions have moved to urban areas in search of work, they have left the rigid social groupings of their villages for the relative anonymity of cities, and swapped hereditary trades for jobs in which family background is largely immaterial" (*The Economist* 2010b). However, even after India's constitution banned caste discrimination in 2004, it is still evident in the bleak living conditions of *dalits* (formerly "untouchables"), who remain India's poorest and least educated people (*The Economist* 2010b).

An evaluation

There is as yet no agreed definition of inclusive growth. Ali and Zhuang (2007) define it as "growth coupled with equality of opportunity." That is, inclusive growth focuses on creating economic opportunity and making opportunity accessible to all. In other words, "growth is inclusive when it allows all members of society to participate in, contribute to, and benefit from growth on an equal basis, regardless of individual circumstances" (Zhuang and Ali 2010, p. 9).

Ali and Zhuang (2007) argued that social inclusion is essential to equalizing opportunity, and the first area of social inclusion relates, especially among the poor and women, to lack of access to basic education, healthcare, and social protection, while the second area relates to lack of access to productive employment and assets such as credit and land. They maintained that enhancing social inclusion requires public interventions in two areas: (i) investing in education, health, and other services to expand human capacity, especially of the disadvantaged; and (ii) eliminating various market and institutional failures and social exclusion to level the playing field. To do so, the government needs to address all the market, institutional, and policy failures, and to ensure that people would not be excluded from participating in and benefiting from growth because of individual circumstances.

In the first area, provision of high-quality basic education seems most important in expanding human capacity, while in the second area, elimination of barriers to access productive employment is most crucial. Felipe (2010) argued that if developing countries are serious about making growth inclusive, they must place full employment at the top of the policy agenda. Cuaresma and Raggl (2011) also noted that employment lies at the heart of the concept of inclusive growth.

Therefore, this subsection will evaluate policies and strategies related to inclusive growth in the PRC and India in terms of providing equal education and employment opportunities for the disadvantaged groups, including women.

India has a younger population in comparison with not only advanced countries but also the PRC and other developing countries. In 2011, about 30% of the total population in India was aged below 15, while *only* 19% of the total population in the PRC was below 15, as seen in Figure 11.5. The labor force in India is expected to increase by 32% over the next 20 years (Planning Commission of India 2011). This "demographic dividend" can add to growth potential and it can be realized only when the extent and quality of education and skills development

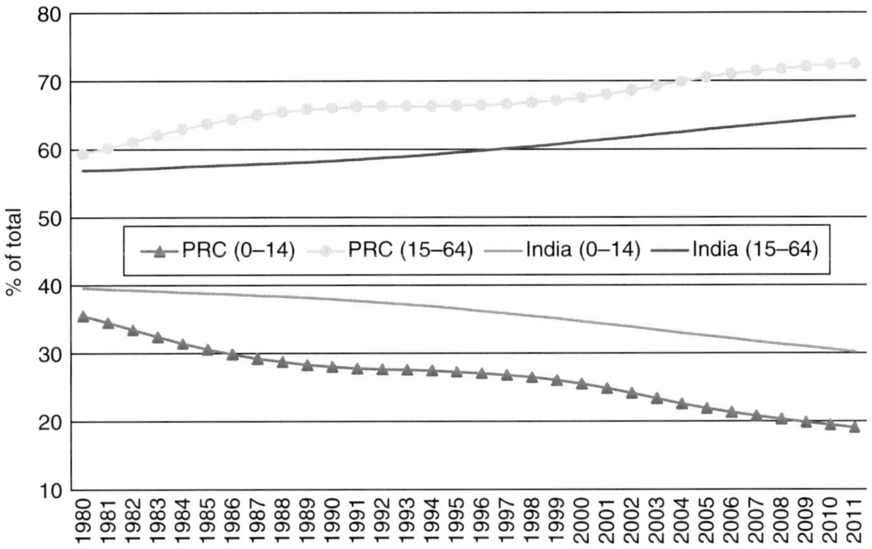

Figure 11.5 Population aged 0–14 and 15–65 in the People's Republic of China and India, 1980–2011.

PRC = People's Republic of China.

Source: World Development Indicators, http://data.worldbank.org/data-catalog/world-development-indicators (accessed 27 August 2012).

among new entrants to the workforce is enhanced and when the economy provides high-quality employment opportunities.

As seen in Figure 11.6, both the PRC and India have been providing increased years of schooling for their people, but the rate of increase is far greater in the PRC than in India. Because of this, while the average number of years of schooling had been similar in both countries in 1960, there was a big gap between the two countries in 2010, with 8.2 years for the PRC and 5.1 years for India.

However, the average number of years of total schooling in the Republic of Korea, which is drawn here as a benchmark, has expanded more rapidly than these two countries. Indeed, such an outstanding emphasis on education has been regarded as one of the key ingredients of the remarkable growth performance of the Republic of Korea (Harvie and Lee 2003).

There have been many reports that gender inequality in education leads to lower growth. Using cross-country and panel regressions, Klasen (2002) found that gender inequality in education adversely affects long-term economic growth. His results suggest that gender inequality in education directly affects economic growth by lowering the average level of human capital, and, in addition, growth is indirectly affected through the impact of gender inequality on investment and population growth. On the other hand, Chaudhry and Rahman (2009) showed

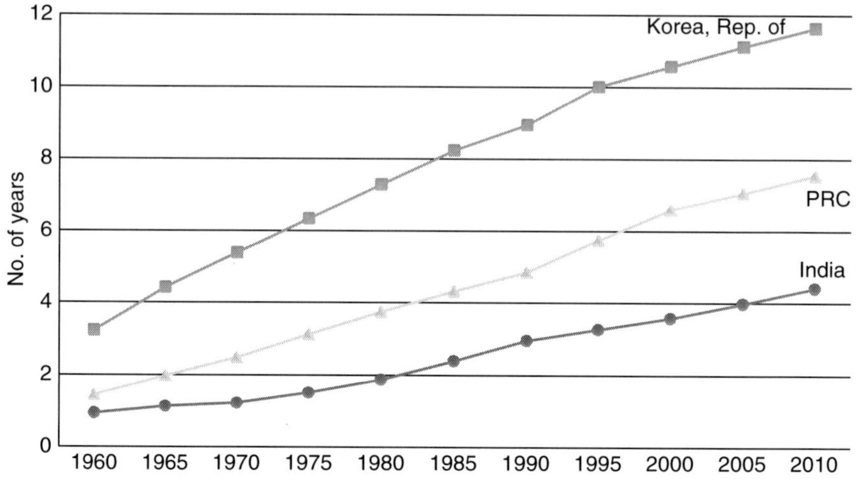

Figure 11.6 Average years of total schooling in the People's Republic of China, India, and the Republic of Korea, 1960–2010.

PRC = People's Republic of China.

Source: R. Barro and J. W. Lee. Educational Attainment Dataset, http://www.barrolee.com (accessed 27 August 2012).

that gender inequality in education has an adverse impact on rural poverty in Pakistan.

Figure 11.7 shows that the female-to-male ratio in enrollment rates for both primary school and secondary school in the PRC and India increased very rapidly during the period between 1981 and 2010. In 2008, the female-to-male ratio in the enrollment rate for primary school had reached 100% in both the PRC and India; in the case of secondary school, the ratio also reached 100% in the PRC, but it was only 88% in India.

Figure 11.8 reports the average number of years of schooling for the female population as of 2010. As can be seen, the female population has fewer years of schooling compared with the total population in both countries. However, such a gap appears bigger in India than in the PRC. When these two countries are compared with the Republic of Korea, women in both countries stay in school for fewer years than in the Republic of Korea.

Many reports acknowledge that gender equality, not only for education but also for employment and political empowerment, among others, is an important means of fostering economic growth and poverty reduction (e.g., Morisson *et al.* 2007; World Bank 2008). Klasen and Lamanna (2008) updated the results of previous studies on impacts of education gaps on growth and extended the analysis to employment gaps using panel data. They found that gender gaps in education and employment significantly reduced economic growth.

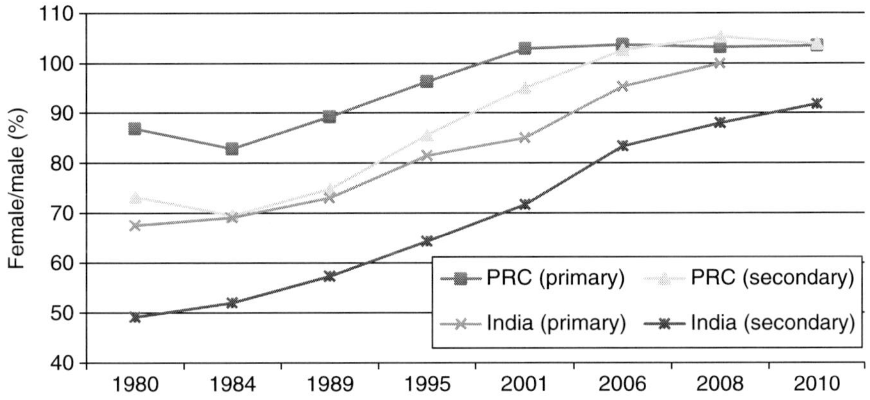

Figure 11.7 Primary and secondary school female-to-male enrollment ratios in the People's Republic of China and India, 1980–2010.

PRC = People's Republic of China.

Source: World Development Indicators, http://data.worldbank.org/data-catalog/world-development-indicators (accessed 11 December 2011).

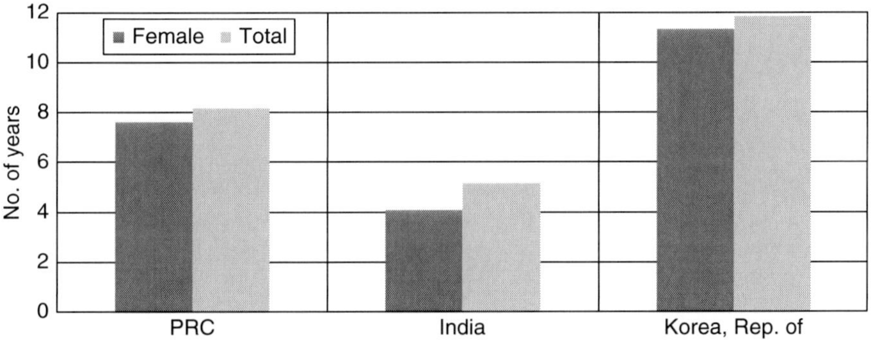

Figure 11.8 Average years of total schooling for females and total population in the People's Republic of China, India, and the Republic of Korea, 2010.

PRC = People's Republic of China.

Source: R. Barro and J. W. Lee. Educational Attainment Dataset, http://www.barrolee.com (accessed 27 August 2012).

The PRC and India have made progress in reducing gender inequality over the past few decades, but women still remain a disadvantaged group in many countries, according to the United Nations Development Programme's Gender Inequality Index (http://hdr.undp.org/en/statistics/gii/) (Figure 11.9). In particular, India is shown as the country with the greatest gender inequality among the three countries, including the Republic of Korea.

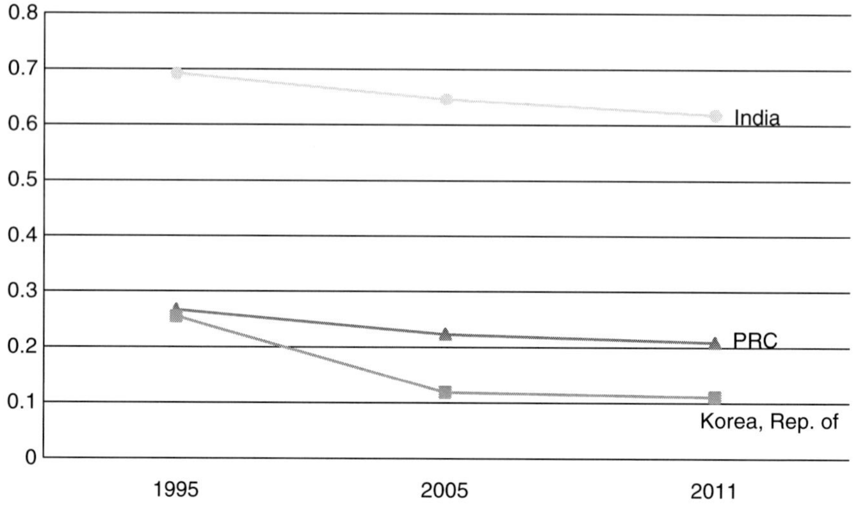

Figure 11.9 Gender inequality index in the People's Republic of China, India, and the Republic of Korea.

PRC = People's Republic of China.

Note: The greater the number, the greater the gender inequality.

Source: United Nations Development Programme, http://hdr.undp.org/en/statistics/gii/ (accessed 11 December 2011).

As noted above, elimination of barriers to access to productive employment and provision of equal opportunities for employment is also very crucial to make growth inclusive. Indeed, employment is the major means to eradicate poverty and to reduce income inequality.

Employment – and the lack thereof – has been considered as one of the biggest problems for inclusive growth and development in India because the population has been increasing at a very rapid rate since independence. The quality of employment is also very important for inclusive growth, but in India it is still very low due to low levels of education as discussed earlier. It is also noted that the labor force participation rate of women is only about 32% in 2009, as compared with 67% in the PRC (Figure 11.10). Thus, compared with the PRC, opportunities of employment are lower, especially for women.

In-depth analysis of inequality–growth nexus in the case of the Republic of Korea

It is well known that during the period from the 1960s to the 1980s, the Republic of Korea enjoyed sustained high economic growth with relatively equal income distribution. As such, it may be considered a benchmark and model for the rest of

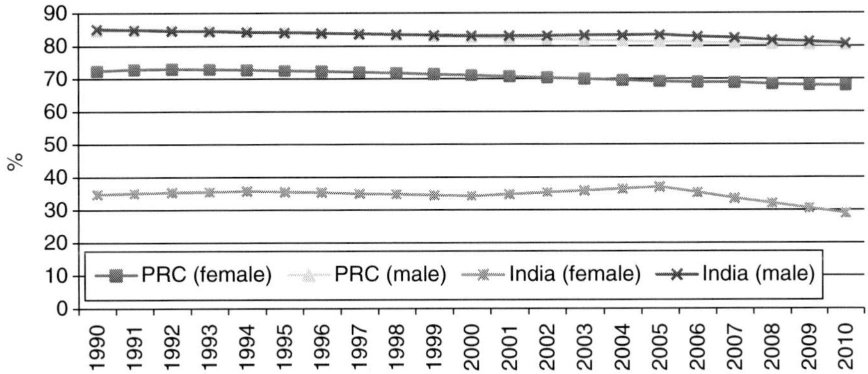

Figure 11.10 Labor force participation rate by gender in the People's Republic of China and India, 1990–2010.

PRC = People's Republic of China.

Source: World Development Indicators, http://data.worldbank.org/data-catalog/world-development-indicators (accessed 11 December 2011).

developing Asia. This section aims to provide an in-depth review of the Republic of Korea's inclusive growth policies/strategies.

Trend of economic and social development in the Republic of Korea

Since 1960, the Republic of Korea has been transformed from one of the poorest countries in the world to a leading industrial nation. Such a remarkable performance was indeed an economic miracle as such a fast economic growth was unprecedented (Harvie and Lee 2003).

Table 11.1 summarizes the trend of some key indicators regarding the Republic of Korea's economic growth and social development. As shown in the table, the Republic of Korea enjoyed a rapid economic growth rate from 1960 onward, even though the momentum has slowed since the Asian crisis of 1997/1998. By 2010, the country's GDP per capita surpassed $20,000, firmly placing it in the echelons of high-income countries. It is also among the world's 15 largest economies. Both inflation and unemployment have remained generally low. By any measure, the Republic of Korea's performance has been spectacularly successful.

The Republic of Korea's economic miracle is all the more remarkable because it combined rapid growth with equity. The World Bank (2004) and the Organisation for Economic Co-operation and Development (OECD 2011) praised the Republic of Korea as one of the exceptional success stories in achieving "growth with equity," and thus contradicting Kuznets' inverted-U hypothesis. The country's official Gini coefficient (Gini 2 in Table 11.1) shows that there was no

Table 11.1 Overall economic performance of the Republic of Korea, 1960–2011

	GDP per capita (current $)	*Annual GDP growth (%)*	*Annual inflation[a] (%)*	*Gini 1[b]*	*Gini 2[c]*	*Gini 3[d]*
1960	155					
1961	92	4.9				
1962	104	2.5				
1963	142	9.5				
1964	121	7.6				
1965	106	5.2		33.7	34.4	
1966	130	12.7	11.3	32.9		
1967	157	6.1	10.9	36.4		
1968	195	11.7	10.8	34.6		
1969	239	14.1	12.4	34.6		
1970	279	8.3	16.0	31.3	33.2	
1971	302	8.2	13.5	30.7		
1972	323	4.5	11.7	31.2		
1973	403	12.0	3.2	36.8		
1974	556	7.2	24.3	38.2		
1975	608	5.9	25.3	37.7		
1976	824	10.6	15.3	39.0	39.1	
1977	1,042	10.0	10.1	37.8		
1978	1,383	9.3	14.5	37.0		
1979	1,747	6.8	18.3	37.5		
1980	1,674	−1.5	28.7	35.7		
1981	1,846	6.2	21.4	34.7		
1982	1,938	7.3	7.2	37.7	35.7	
1983	2,118	10.8	3.4	37.4		
1984	2,307	8.1	2.3	38.0		
1985	2,368	6.8	2.5	38.0		
1986	2,703	10.6	2.8	37.7	33.7	
1987	3,368	11.1	3.0	37.8		
1988	4,466	10.6	7.1	38.4		
1989	5,438	6.7	5.7	41.3		
1990	6,153	9.2	8.6	40.2	33.2	25.6
1991	7,123	9.4	9.3	40.1		25.0
1992	7,555	5.9	6.2	38.8		24.5
1993	8,220	6.1	4.8	38.0	31.0	25.0
1994	9,525	8.5	6.3	38.5		24.8
1995	11,468	9.2	4.5			25.1
1996	12,249	7.0	4.9			25.7
1997	11,235	4.7	4.4			25.7
1998	7,463	−6.9	7.5			28.5
1999	9,554	9.5	0.8			28.8
2000	11,347	8.5	2.3			26.6
2001	10,655	4.0	4.1			27.7
2002	12,094	7.2	2.8			27.9
2003	13,451	2.8	3.5			27.0
2004	15,029	4.6	3.6			27.7
2005	17,551	4.0	2.8			28.1
2006	19,676	5.2	2.2			28.5

Table 11.1 Continued

	GDP per capita (current $)	*Annual GDP growth (%)*	*Annual inflation[a] (%)*	*Gini 1[b]*	*Gini 2[c]*	*Gini 3[d]*
2007	21,590	5.1	2.5			29.2
2008	19,028	2.3	4.7			29.4
2009	16,959	0.3	2.8			29.5
2010	20,540	6.3	3.0			28.9
2011	22,424	3.6	4.0			

GDP = gross domestic product.

Notes

1 [a]Consumer price index; [b]time series data from Ahn (1997) until 1981 and from Ahn (1995) from 1982 onward; [c]the figures for 1965, 1970, 1976, 1982, and 1990 are from Choo and Kim (1978) and Choo and Yoon (1984); those for 1980, 1985, 1988, and 1993 are from the Social Statistics Survey; [d]Korean Statistical Information Service.

2 Gini coefficients are income-based and originally defined as a ratio ranging from 0 to 1.

3 The values expressed in this table have been adjusted to range from 0 to 100.

Sources: World Development Indicators, http://data.worldbank.org/data-catalog/world-development-indicators (accessed 30 August 2012) for GDP per capita and GDP growth rates; Korean Statistical Information Service for inflation rates; K. Ahn. 1992. Review of [the Republic of] Korea's Social Development. In D. Cha, K. S. Kim, and D. H. Perkins, eds. *The Korean Economy 1945–95: Performance and Vision for the 21st Century*. Seoul: Korea Development Institute Press; K. Ahn. 1995. Economic Development and Income Distribution in [the Republic of] Korea. *Journal of Economic Development*. 1 (1). pp. 53–76. Korea Development Economics Association (in Korean); K. Ahn. 1997. Trends in and Determinants of Income Distribution in [the Republic of] Korea. *Journal of Economic Development*. 22 (2). pp. 27–56; H. Choo and D. Kim. 1978. *Probable Size Distribution of Income in [the Republic of] Korea: Over Time and by Sector*. Seoul: Korea Development Institute (in Korean); H. Choo and J. Yoon. 1984. *Size Distribution of Income in [the Republic of] Korea, 1982: Its Estimation and Sources of Change*. Seoul: Korea Development Institute (in Korean); Social Statistics Survey; and Korean Statistical Information Service for Gini coefficients.

significant change in the size of income inequality during the period 1965–1993.[1] In fact, income distribution improved between the mid-1960s and the early 1970s, although it worsened in the mid-1970s, before steadily improving in the 1980s. Still, the Gini coefficient calculated by Ahn (1997) (Gini 1 in Table 11.1 and Figure 11.11) showed that the Republic of Korea's income distribution deteriorated in the mid-1970s and again in the late 1980s.[2] Thus, it is generally accepted that the Republic of Korea's income distribution improved or at least did not consistently deteriorate up until the early 1990s (Kang 2001).

However, the Republic of Korea's income inequality has worsened since 1998 when post-crisis structural reforms were implemented. Thus, the country is becoming more unequal than it used to be and discontent is rising about inequality (*The Economist* 2011b).

1 There are no reliable data to infer overall income distribution in the Republic of Korea until 1964.

2 Ahn (1997) argued that income distribution in the Republic of Korea deteriorated in the late 1980s, largely due to the high rise of real estate prices, which also caused a prevalent sense of relative deprivation. Indeed, as Leipziger *et al.* (1992) noted, income distribution data may yield a biased view of the equity situation as they fail to capture accurately the gains from land and real estate holdings.

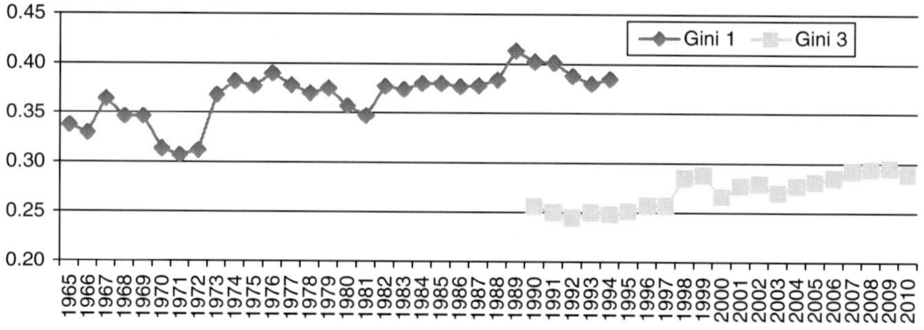

Figure 11.11 Gini coefficients in the Republic of Korea, 1965–2010.

Note: Gini coefficients are income-based.

Sources: For Gini 1 from 1965 to 1981: K. Ahn. 1992. Review of [the Republic of] Korea's Social Development. In D. Cha, K. S. Kim, and D. H. Perkins, eds. *The Korean Economy 1945–95: Performance and Vision for the 21st Century*. Seoul: Korea Development Institute Press; for Gini 1 from 1982 to 1994: K. Ahn. 1995. Economic Development and Income Distribution in [the Republic of] Korea. *Journal of Economic Development*. 1 (1). pp. 53–76. Korea Development Economics Association (in Korean) and K. Ahn. 1997. Trends in and Determinants of Income Distribution in [the Republic of] Korea. *Journal of Economic Development*. 22 (2). pp. 27–56; and Korean Statistical Information Service for Gini 3.

Regional disparities and polarization have also been a major concern for the Republic of Korea because the Seoul area has attracted a disproportionate share of investment and enjoys greater economic dynamism than the rest of the country.

Overview of the economic and social development policies

The Republic of Korea has undergone seven political regime changes since 1961. Each regime placed different emphasis on economic growth and social welfare, in response to various political and economic circumstances. In terms of the degree of political freedom, the seven political regimes can be categorized into three different periods. Each of the three different periods is also different from others in terms of welfare policies, which are summarized in Table 11.2.

The fundamental economic philosophies of the authoritarian regimes of Park Chung-hee (1961–1979) and Chun Doo-hwan (1980–1988) can be characterized as "Growth first, distribution later." The basis for the Republic of Korea's economic miracle, based largely on export-oriented industrialization, was primarily laid during this period. The welfare system during this time period is often referred to as the developmental welfare state or the minimalist welfare state. However, despite the limited welfare system, the extent of the income inequality of the low-income households was tolerable due to rapid economic growth. Indeed, income equity in terms of the Gini coefficient was kept at a reasonable rate during the period of rapid economic development until the mid-1990s, as shown in Table 11.1. This is partly due to the fact that the size of the pie multiplied and the income level of middle- and low-income households also increased.

Table 11.2 Development of welfare policies in the Republic of Korea

Period	*Regimes*	*Economic policies*	*Welfare policies*
Authoritarian dictatorship	Park Chung-hee (1961–1979) Chun Doo-hwan (1980–1987)	Industrialization (government-dominant growth strategy)	Growth first, distribution later (developmental welfare state or minimalist welfare state)
Democratization	Roh Tae-woo (1988–1992) Kim Young-sam (1993–1997)		Transition period
Democratic government	Kim Dae-jung (1998–2002) Roh Moo-hyun (2003–2007) Lee Myung-bak (2008–present)	Globalization and post-industrialization (balance between growth and redistribution)	Productive welfare Participatory welfare Active welfare

Source: Authors' compilation.

In fact, the Republic of Korea was viewed as one of the most equitable developing countries during this time period. This is remarkable because welfare policy was not widely used to reduce inequality during this period. The World Bank (2004) and Choi and Kwon (1997) described how, because of the land reform conducted in the late 1940s and total destruction of industrial facilities during the Korean War (1950–1953), the Republic of Korea was equalized in terms of income and assets. Also, an outward-oriented development strategy, which focused primarily on labor-intensive manufacturing industries, boosted employment and wages and helped spread the benefits of growth throughout the population (Leipziger *et al.* 1992). The expansion and improvement of primary and secondary education contributed greatly to a more equitable income distribution, even though the primary goal of the education policy was to promote economic growth (Choi and Kwon 1997; Kang 2001). Indeed, as Lee (1997) showed, the Republic of Korea accumulated a stock of educated workers at an unprecedented rate. The country's high level of education contributed not only to its rapid economic growth but also to equitable income distribution, because with basic education available to virtually all segments of population, most Koreans were able to take part in the industrialization process.

One noteworthy government program during this period of limited welfare, which helped address urban–rural inequality, was Saemaul Undong (new village movement). This was a community-based integrated rural development program implemented during the 1970s (Park 2009). As discussed, the government's development policy focused on industrial development with export orientation, but this resulted in the widening gap between cities and rural areas. In order to close the gap, the government initiated Saemaul Undong, hoping to develop rural community conditions to match those of the cities. The major objectives of Saemaul Undong were (i) income generation, (ii) living environment and basic rural infrastructure improvement, and (iii) capacity building and attitudinal change (Park 2009). The Saemaul movement brought about some success in rural development and helped the rural community generate not only farm-based income but also nonfarm income sources, thus contributing to a more equitable income distribution between urban and rural areas.

The next phase was democratization and social development – from 1988 to 1997. As the economy in the Republic of Korea reached middle-income country levels, workers and the poor began to demand democracy and a greater portion of the pie. During the period of transition from authoritarianism to democracy, workers' strikes erupted across the country. The major goal of labor strikes was wage increase and free union activity. For example, there were 3,749 strikes with almost 1.26 million participants in the second half of 1987 (Shin 2008). Democratization proceeded with the successful struggle for democracy.

The Roh Tae-woo Government (1988–1992) at last yielded to the social pressure and enacted a minimum wage law and implemented a national pension program for private sector workers. The Kim Young-sam Government (1993–1997) introduced an unemployment social insurance scheme and expanded the national pension program to farmers and fisherfolk. Even though many welfare policies and schemes were introduced, the degree of social welfare in the Republic of Korea was still not as good as those observed in the advanced countries. Still, it should be recognized as the period of transition that forced the government to have concerns about distribution and poverty issues.

The final phase – 1998 to present – centered on democratic governments and the quest for a better balance between growth and redistribution. After a long period of rapid economic growth, the Republic of Korea ran into a sudden financial crisis in late 1997. This financial crisis was a turning point for the country to rapidly expand its welfare system. Massive corporate restructuring was carried out for many companies to retain their competitiveness, and this led to an unprecedented high rate of unemployment in the process. The government needed to handle a sharply increasing unemployment rate and poverty rate.

While the Kim Dae-jung administration implemented a neoliberal economic reform package following the International Monetary Fund bailout program, the government also paid much attention to inclusive and equitable measures to handle its side effects. The Kim Dae-jung administration brought out a new model of welfare system called "productive welfare" and dealt with the increased demand for social welfare during and after the crisis. According to the World Bank (2004), "productive welfare" was an ideology that sought to secure minimum living standards for all low-income households by providing human resource development programs to support self-reliance among the poor and by expanding the coverage of social insurance to all people.

The Presidential Committee on Social Inclusion adopted six specific strategies on productive welfare: (i) National Basic Livelihood Security Act and four major social insurance programs – employment insurance, national pension system, national health insurance system, and industrial injury insurance system; (ii) job security through job creation and human capital development; (iii) self-reliance programs; (iv) community-based public–private cooperation; (v) realization of industrial democracy; and (vi) expansion of the welfare budget. Significant changes were made to the decision-making process of labor market policies. More specifically, a tripartite committee comprising representatives of government, business, and labor was set up to form social consensus on reforms of labor market policies.

The Roh Moo-hyun administration shared with the Kim Dae-jung administration many of the political principles but proposed a different welfare scheme called "participatory welfare initiative." While productive welfare focused more on reducing absolute poverty and unemployment in the wake of the financial crisis of 1997, the participatory welfare initiative was concerned more with relative poverty and social polarization.

The issue of social polarization has caught much attention, partly as a result of the liberalization reform in the wake of the financial crisis of 1997/1998. Polarization was reflected in the widening income gap between regular and irregular workers, between workers in large companies and small and medium-sized enterprises, and between income classes (Chan 2006).

The participatory welfare initiative aimed to (i) develop a fully fledged national healthcare system; (ii) promote national welfare with focus on guaranteeing minimum livelihood, childcare, and support for senior citizens and the handicapped; and (iii) create a prosperous and stable society. It also aimed to (iv) foster a society of balanced development between economic growth and distribution, different regions, different classes, and between labor and management; and (v) promote sustainable development and gender equality.

Compared with the Kim Dae-jung and Roh Moo-hyun administrations, the Lee Myung-bak administration is rather conservative and claims to support business-friendly policies and tax reduction. Therefore, the welfare system of the Lee Myung-bak administration pursues market-based policies. The administration has brought out many notions such as "shared growth," "fair society," and "symbiosis society" to define its welfare policies, but they can be summarized into one: "active welfare."

The Lee Myung-bak administration advocated "active welfare," which aimed for "welfare through work." Active welfare is a market-friendly welfare system that tries to transfer welfare beneficiaries or pre-beneficiaries to the labor market. Kim (2011) described the characteristics of active welfare as a liberalistic welfare system that raises social productivity rather than a consumption-centered or passive welfare system. For example, the Sunshine Loan Program and the Smile Microcredit Program increase self-reliance among the poor by providing loans, not cash. *Bogeumjari* housing supports people in buying their own house through long-term savings, not just providing public rental houses. Thus, the objectives of the "active welfare state" are similar to those of "inclusive growth," which seeks both equity promotion and economic growth.

An evaluation

This section discusses some important economic and social policies and strategies of the Republic of Korea, focusing on education and employment.

Education policies

Equal opportunity. Various policies have been established and implemented to support education for all children. Usually the concept of "inclusive education" has been understood as policies ensuring educational access at regular schools for students with disabilities (Kim 2007). In particular, for low-income families, the government has been implementing a Master Plan to Assist Regions that Require Priority Investment in Educational Welfare. Priority regions with many low-income families are to receive concentrated educational welfare support. Under this plan, the government supports the students in the most needy areas with orientation and psychotherapy programs, meal provision, health education, after-school voucher programs, and edu-care for infants and children under the age of 6, in an integrated manner.

For college students, a new income-contingent student loan program, the Study-Now-Pay-Later program, was introduced in January 2010. The loans are available to students from households in the lowest to the seventh income deciles. The loans can cover annual tuition fees plus 2 million won in living expenses per year. The interest rate has been set low compared with other regular loans. Students make no payments during the study period and are required to pay back interest and principal in installments spread over a maximum of 25 years after their annual earnings reach 16 million won.

As shown in Figure 11.6, the average number of years of schooling in the Republic of Korea is far greater than that in the PRC and in India. Besides, as can be seen in Figure 11.8, the average number of years of schooling for women is also greater than that for men in both the PRC and India, even though it is slightly lower than that for men in the Republic of Korea. Indeed, the Republic of Korea's rapid economic growth was accompanied by extensive investment in human resources. Public and private expenditure on education regularly exceeded 10% of GDP, the highest among all developing countries, and this investment in education also led to a high degree of income equality (Harvie and Lee 2003).

Vocational education and training and lifelong education. Vocational education and training takes place at the senior high school and tertiary levels. It also encompasses a range of measures aiming to provide vocational training to the adult population, including training for employees, the unemployed, and those outside the labor market. However, vocational high schools have been regarded as inferior to the regular high schools, which aim to prepare students for college entrance. Even students in vocational high schools often desire to go to college after graduation instead of finding a job.

During the Lee Myung-bak administration, the government has been attempting to fight such tendencies. Using job training schools in Germany as a benchmark, 21 vocational Meister high schools opened in 2010. Meister high schools specialize in vocational education in fields such as shipbuilding, mechanical engineering, semiconductors, and medical equipment. Students pay no tuition fees, and they are given the chance to get a job after graduation. The government plans to increase the number of such schools to 50.

Vocational training is mostly administered under the Ministry of Labor throughout vocational training centers. Overall, the government has made flexible options for citizens to become lifelong learners. Currently, there are nine cyber universities to make education accessible in the country, and there are open-class, part-time registration, major-advanced, and special courses in order to make traditional universities more accommodating for working adults. Nonetheless, education policy has been primarily focused on education for children, and the rate of adult participation in education is among the lowest among the OECD member countries.

Labor market policies

Labor market dualism. A major problem in the labor market of the Republic of Korea is the high degree of dualism. According to the official data released by the Ministry of Labor, the share of non-regular workers[3] exceeds one-third of employees (Figure 11.12). The largest category of non-regular employment is temporary workers, despite long-standing restrictions on fixed-term contracts.

The country's share of temporary workers was the second highest in the OECD in 2007 (Jones and Tsutsumi 2009). The high proportion of temporary workers is a drag on growth as it increases worker turnover and hence reduces firm-provided training, which plays a very important role in the Republic of Korea. It also raises equity issues as non-regular workers face precarious jobs, wage discrimination, and less social protection.

The government has announced a number of countermeasures for non-regular workers. For instance, it has enacted a law to protect non-regular workers from "undue discrimination" and to avoid their "excessive use." It has also expanded active labor market policies for non-regular workers to improve their employability by providing vocational training for them. Furthermore, since July 2007, workers with fixed-term contracts in all firms regardless of size are considered to be regular employees after 2 years of work. The government has also taken steps to increase their social safety net coverage.

However, the OECD (2007) cautioned that prohibiting discrimination against non-regular workers may subject firms to costly and time-consuming litigation that would discourage the employment of non-regular workers and lead to higher

---

[3] The Economic and Social Development Commission defines non-regular workers as contingent workers who have fixed-term contracts or who expect their work arrangement to have a limited duration for involuntary reasons; part-time workers who work "fewer hours" than full-time workers; and atypical workers, including temporary agency workers (dispatched workers), individual contract workers (who work independently from the firm), home-based workers, on-call workers, and other new forms of employment.

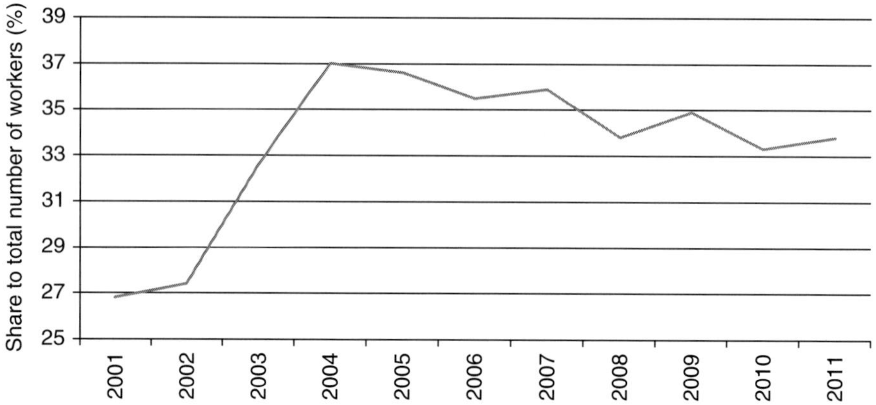

Figure 11.12 Non-regular workers in the Republic of Korea, 2001–2011.

Source: Korean Statistical Information Service, http://kosis.kr/eng/ (accessed 11 December 2011).

unemployment. To reduce the incentives to hire non-regular workers, it has been recommended that employment protection for regular workers be relaxed and the social insurance coverage of non-regular workers be broadened in order to reduce labor market dualism and its negative effect on growth and equity.

Youth employment. As shown in Figures 11.13 and 11.14, the low employment rate and high unemployment rate of youths in the Republic of Korea are other important issues related to inclusive growth strategies. Indeed, the employment rate for young men is the lowest in the OECD. This is explained to some extent by high enrollment in tertiary education and 2-year military service obligation for men. However, the higher unemployment rate for youths is not easily explainable. A possible explanation is that there is a mismatch between the kind of jobs that the job seekers are looking for and the kind of workers that the firms are looking for. For example, youths with a tertiary degree might be looking for high-wage jobs, although there are only a few such jobs available.

Public spending on active labor market policies for the youth has increased for direct job creation, training, employment subsidies, and job experience programs. However, the fragmented policy approach, increased administrative costs, and complicated monitoring and evaluation have made it difficult for youths to find the proper program (OECD 2007). In 2008, the government introduced a more comprehensive and coordinated package of measures, known as the Youth Employment Service, which sought to improve labor market opportunities for youths. In 2011, it became the youth component of the Employment Service Package Program, a broader employment support program targeting people with low incomes, youths who are less educated, and long-term job seekers.

Female employment. As can be seen in Figure 11.15, women's employment in the labor market in the Republic of Korea is remarkably lower than that for men. Indeed, the employment rate and participation rate of women in the labor force are

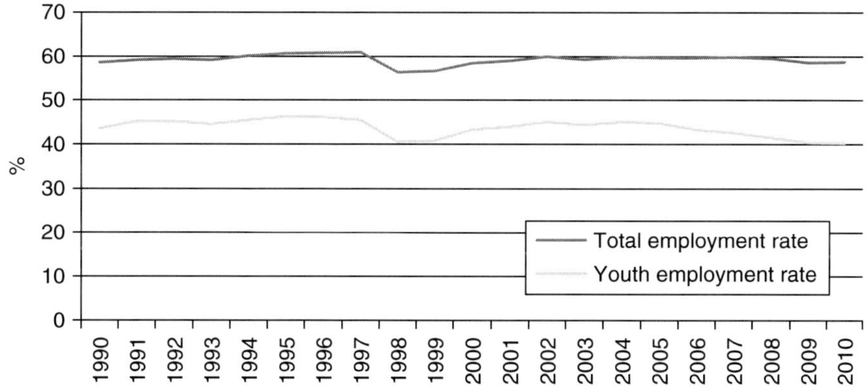

Figure 11.13 Total vs. youth employment rate in the Republic of Korea, 1990–2010.

Note: Youths are defined as the age group of 15–29.

Source: Korean Statistical Information Service, http://kosis.kr/eng/ (accessed 11 December 2011).

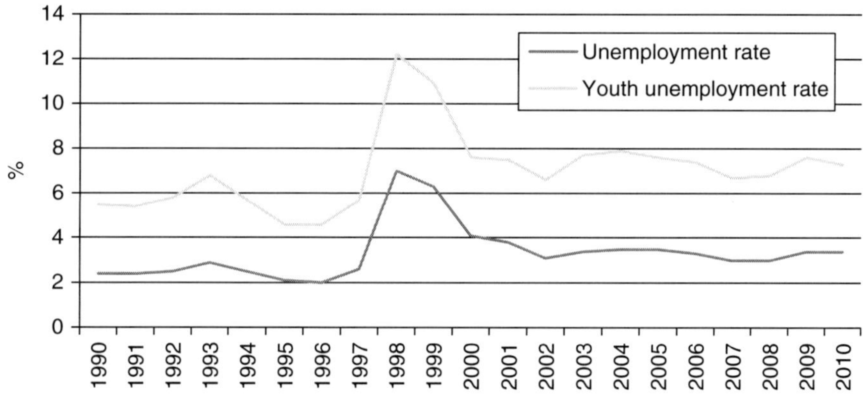

Figure 11.14 Total vs. youth unemployment rate in the Republic of Korea, 1990–2010.

Note: Youths are defined as the age group of 15–29.

Source: Korean Statistical Information Service, http://kosis.kr/eng/ (accessed 11 December 2011).

among the lowest in OECD member countries. This is largely because a significant proportion of women withdraw from the labor force at the time of marriage or childbirth. It has been said that boosting female employment is key to mitigating the impact of rapid population aging, and the government has attempted various measures: alleviating the burden of bearing and caring for children, creating more family-friendly workplaces, lengthening parental leave, and increasing the availability of childcare.

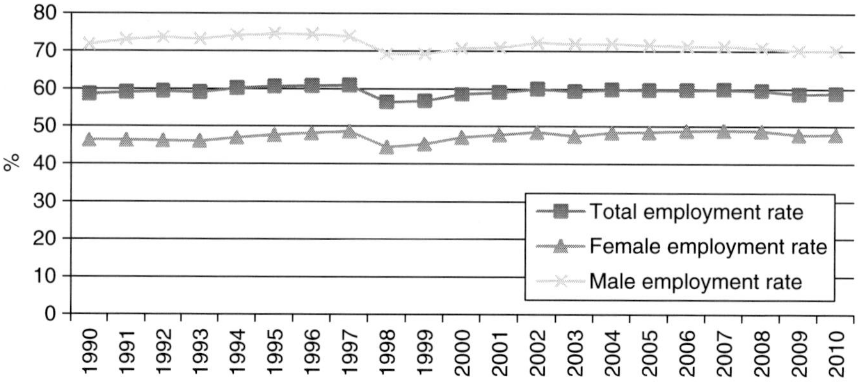

Figure 11.15 Female vs. male employment rate in the Republic of Korea, 1990–2010.

Source: Korean Statistical Information Service, http://kosis.kr/eng/ (accessed 11 December 2011).

However, there is no sign yet of women's employment and participation rates increasing, so there is a strong need for the government to step up its efforts to boost female labor force participation.

Concluding observations and policy implications

As developing Asia turns from a low-income region into a largely middle-income region, there is growing popular demand for political and social participation. Related to this, there is also an increasingly vocal demand for more inclusive growth, which includes as much of the population as possible in the growth process and spreads the fruits of growth to the entire population. In the past, growth strategies, which were geared almost exclusively toward growth with little regard for equity, helped deliver rapid growth and poverty reduction. However, in light of the rising demand for more equality and inclusion, growth strategies will have to be adjusted if the region is to continue to enjoy the economic success it enjoyed prior to the global financial crisis. There is a growing recognition among the region's policy makers of the need to respond to the popular pressure for more inclusive growth. While there is some scope for redistributive policies, in light of the region's still low income levels and development gaps, a more fundamental solution lies in modifying the pattern of the growth process in a more inclusive direction.

Indeed, in the absence of substantial modifications to the growth strategy, it may be politically and socially difficult to sustain rapid growth. The reason is that political and social discontent due to widening inequality may undermine the bedrock of sociopolitical stability, which facilitated the region's growth for the past few decades. An annual GDP growth rate of 8% rather than 10%, but which is more inclusive, is likely to be more politically and socially sustainable. In the context of a more inclusive growth strategy, two sets of policies are especially important: those delivering equal access to education and those delivering equal access to employment. Expanded access to education and employment not only helps to level the playing field among the rich and the poor, but also helps to raise a country's overall productive capacity and hence potential growth. A growth strategy that equalizes opportunity may also have an economy-wide incentive effect by rewarding those who seek to improve themselves and their lives. The region can thus continue to grow rapidly on a more stable sociopolitical foundation.

The PRC, India, and the Republic of Korea have recently placed greater emphasis on inclusion in their respective development plans. An important consequence of the new focus on inclusive growth is heightened awareness about inclusiveness among the general public. This trend is not inconsistent with the pursuit of high rates of GDP growth. Indeed, all three countries continue to seek rapid growth. While the higher priority on inclusive growth is a welcome trend, a comprehensive assessment of policies and strategies related to inclusive growth is inherently difficult. This is not only because inclusiveness is a multidimensional concept and achieving inclusiveness in different dimensions requires multiple interventions, but also because such policies usually require a long time period to bear fruit. Therefore, we focused our evaluation of the inclusive growth-related policies and strategies of the PRC, India, and the Republic of Korea on two specific areas: providing equal education and employment opportunities for the disadvantaged groups, including women.

The following are some of the key lessons that emerge from the review of the experiences of the three countries:

First, there is no single, one-size-fits-all set of policies and strategies of inclusive growth that would work for all developing countries. This is because different countries are at different levels in terms of income and development and are subject to different cultural backgrounds and socioeconomic systems. For instance, India needs to target not only the removal of income inequalities, but also social inequalities stemming from gender, social class, and geographical location, such as urban versus rural or different states. On the other hand, a much more immediate priority in the PRC is the income inequalities stemming from the widening urban–rural gap.

Second, even within one country, there is no single set of policies and strategies of inclusive growth that would work throughout different levels of development. This is evident from our in-depth review of the experiences of the Republic of Korea, which moved from a low-income to a high-income country within a generation. For instance, during the earlier period of economic development, the priority needs to be the removal of poverty rather than income inequality. Indeed, in the earlier period of development, some kind of unbalanced growth strategy might be conducive for growth, especially in a small country not endowed with natural resources or a large domestic market, as was the case of the Republic of Korea in the 1960s and 1970s.

Third, even though there is no single set of inclusive growth-related policies and strategies that would work for all countries or for all levels of economic development, there are some important policy issues that are common to all countries at all times. That is, there are some common recurrent themes in the pursuit of inclusive growth. Above all, there is the need to provide high-quality education to all segments of society, including the disadvantaged. In particular, gender equality in education directly affects economic growth by enhancing the average level of human capital. In this regard, ensuring gender equality not only in education but also in employment is particularly crucial for making growth more inclusive because one of the biggest consequences of gender inequality in access to economic opportunity is the inefficient allocation and/or underutilization of resources, subsequently hindering economic growth. Another common challenge is to provide productive employment opportunities for all groups.

Fourth, there is a compelling need to develop an index of inclusive growth with which we can evaluate cross-country and/or time-series performance of inclusive growth. The current absence of such a measurement tool is hardly surprising in light of the current lack of consensus on the meaning and definition of inclusive growth. Nevertheless, the development of such an index will allow us to measure how different countries compare with respect to the inclusiveness and hence sustainability of growth, along with whether a country's growth process is becoming more or less inclusive and hence sustainable over time. Such an index would enable us to compare the quality of growth across countries and over time.

Acknowledgments

This chapter is based on a paper presented at the Forum on Equalizing Opportunities for Inclusive Growth at the Asian Development Bank on 7–8 December 2011. We are grateful to Donna Yoo, Hyung-suk Byun, and Suejin Lee for their excellent research assistance.

References[4]

2point6billion.com. 2011. India's 12th Five Year Plan to Focus on "Inclusive Growth." 25 April. http://kostat.go.kr/portal/english/surveyOutlines/3/1/index.static (accessed August 2011).

Ahn, K. 1992. Review of Korea's Social Development. In D. Cha, K. S. Kim, and D. H. Perkins, eds. *The Korean Economy 1945–95: Performance and Vision for the 21st Century*. Seoul: Korea Development Institute Press.

——. 1995. Economic Development and Income Distribution in Korea. *Journal of Economic Development*. 1 (1). pp. 53–76. Korea Development Economics Association (in Korean).

—— . 1997. Trends in and Determinants of Income Distribution in Korea. *Journal of Economic Development*. 22 (2). pp. 27–56.

Ali, I., and J. Zhuang. 2007. Inclusive Growth toward a Prosperous Asia: Policy Implications. *ERD Working Paper Series* No. 97. Manila: Asian Development Bank.

APCO Worldwide. 2010. China's 12th Five Year Plan: How It Actually Works and What's in Store for the Next Five Years. http://apcoworldwide.com/content/PDFs/Chinas_12th_Five-Year_Plan.pdf (accessed August 2011).

[4] The Asian Development Bank recognizes China by the name People's Republic of China, and Korea by the name Republic of Korea.

Barro, R., and J. W. Lee. Educational Attainment Dataset. http://www.barrolee.com (accessed September 2011).

Chan, R. K. H. 2006. Participatory Welfare in Korea: Meaning and Issues. *Working Paper Series* No. 174. Hong Kong, China: Center for Asian Pacific Studies.

Chaudhry, I. S., and S. Rahman. 2009. The Impact of Gender Inequality in Education on Rural Poverty in Pakistan: An Empirical Analysis. *European Journal of Economics, Finance and Administrative Science.* 15. pp. 174–88.

Choi, K., and S. Kwon. 1997. Social Welfare and Distribution Policies. In D. Cha, K. S. Kim, and D. H. Perkins, eds. *The Korean Economy 1945–1995: Performance and Vision for the 21st Century*. Seoul: Korea Development Institute.

Choo, H., and D. Kim. 1978. *Probable Size Distribution of Income in [the Republic of] Korea: Over Time and by Sector*. Seoul: Korea Development Institute (in Korean).

Choo, H., and J. Yoon. 1984. *Size Distribution of Income in [the Republic of] Korea, 1982: Its Estimation and Sources of Change*. Seoul: Korea Development Institute (in Korean).

Cuaresma, J. C., and A. Raggl. 2011. Inclusive Growth and Employment: Conceptual and Methodological Challenges. World Bank's Inclusive Growth Diagnostic Analysis Conference. Nairobi, Kenya. 28–29 September.

The Economist. 2010a. The Elusive Fruits of Inclusive Growth. 13 May.

——. 2010b. The Indian Census and Caste: Caste in Doubt. 13 May.

——. 2011a. Inequality: The Rich and the Rest. 20 January.

——. 2011b. Korea's Economy: What Do You Do When You Reach the Top? 12 November.

Felipe, J. 2010. Inclusive Growth through Full Employment: The Role of Investment and Industrial Policy. In J. Zhuang, ed. *Poverty, Inequality, and Inclusive Growth in Asia: Measurement, Policy Issues, and Country Studies*. London: Anthem Press and Manila: ADB. pp. 161–98.

Harvie, C., and H.-H. Lee. 2003. *Korea's Economic Miracle – Fading or Reviving?* London, UK: Palgrave Macmillan.

Jones, R. S., and M. Tsutsumi. 2009. Sustaining Growth in Korea by Reforming the Labour Market and Improving the Education System. *OECD Economics Department Working Paper* No. 672. Paris: OECD.

Kang, S. 2001. Globalization and Income Inequality in Korea: An Overview. Paper presented at the Technical Meeting on FDI, Human Capital, and Education in Developing Countries. Paris, France. 13–14 December. Paris: OECD Development Centre.

Kim, K.-O. 2007. Inclusive Education in the Republic of Korea. Country Paper for the Regional Preparatory Workshop on Inclusive Education. Hangzhou, People's Republic of China. 3–5 November. UNESCO International Bureau of Education.

Kim, Y.-S. 2011. *Size and Reality of Non-Regular Workers*. Seoul: Korea Labour & Society Institute (in Korean).

Klasen, S. 2002. Low Schooling for Girls, Slower Growth for All? Cross-Country Evidence on the Effect of Gender Inequality in Education on Economic Development. *World Bank Economic Review* 16(3):121–54.

Klasen, S., and F. Lamanna. 2008. The Impact of Gender Inequality in Education and Employment on Economic Growth in Developing Countries: Updates and Extensions. *IAI Discussion Paper* No. 175. Göttingen, Germany: Ibero America Institute for Economic Research.

KPMG China. 2011. *China's 12th Five Year Plan*. March. http://kpmg.com/cn/en/IssuesAndInsights / ArticlesPublications / Documents / China-12th-Five-Year-Plan-Overview-201104.pdf (accessed August 2011).

Korean Statistical Information Service. http://kosis.kr/eng/

Lee, J.-W. 1997. Economic Growth and Human Development in the Republic of Korea. *Human Development Occasional Papers* HDOCPA-1997-02. United Nations

Development Programme. http://hdr.undp.org/en/reports/global/hdr1997/papers/jong-wha_lee.pdf
Leipziger, D. M., D. Dollar, A. F. Shorrocks, and S. Y. Song. 1992. *The Distribution of Income and Wealth in Korea*. Washington, DC: EDI Development Studies, Economic Development Institute of the World Bank.
Morisson, A. R., D. Raju, and N. Sinha. 2007. Gender Equality, Poverty and Economic Growth. *Policy Research Working Paper* No. 4349. Washington, DC: World Bank.
Organisation for Economic Co-operation and Development (OECD). 2007. *Economic Survey of Korea*. Paris.
—-. 2011. *A Framework for Growth and Social Cohesion in Korea*. Paris.
Park, Y. 2009. Analysis of Saemaul Undong: A Korean Rural Development Programme in the 1970s. *Asia-Pacific Development Journal*. 16 (2). pp. 113–40.
Planning Commission of India. 2006. *Towards Faster and More Inclusive Growth: An Approach to the 11th Five Year Plan*. Delhi, India.
—– . 2011. *Faster, Sustainable and More Inclusive Growth: An Approach to the 12th Five Year Plan*. Delhi, India.
Quosdorf, F. 2010. China Defines Road Map for Becoming a Learning Society by 2020. *The China Education Blog*. http://www.chinaeducationblog.com/chinese-education-policy/2010-06-14/china-defines-road-map-for-becoming-a-learning-society-by-2020/
Shin, K.-Y. 2008. The Development of Welfare Regime in Korea. Paper presented at the International Symposium on Globalization and the Future of East Asian Welfare Capitalism. National Chung-Cheng University, Chia-Yi, Taipei,China. 29–30 May.
Social Statistics Survey, Republic of Korea. Various years.
United Nations Development Programme. Gender Inequality Index. http://hdr.undp.org/en/statistics/gii/
World Bank. 2004. Republic of Korea: Four Decades of Equitable Growth. *Working Paper* No. 30781. Washington, DC.
—–. 2008. *Gender Equality as Smart Economics: A World Bank Group Action Plan*. Washington, DC.
—–. PovcalNet: The On-line Tool for Poverty Measurement Developed by the Development Research Group of the World Bank. http://iresearch.worldbank.org/PovcalNet/index.htm
—–. World Development Indicators. http://data.worldbank.org/data-catalog/world-development-indicators
Zhuang, J., and I. Ali. 2010. Poverty, Inequality, and Inclusive Growth in Asia. In J. Zhuang, ed. *Poverty, Inequality, and Inclusive Growth in Asia: Measurement, Policy Issues, and Country Studies*. London: Anthem Press and Manila: ADB. pp. 161–98.

12 A note on the middle class in Latin America

Nancy Birdsall

Introduction

In this chapter, I set out basic information on the middle class for eight countries in the Latin America and Caribbean (LAC) region, over the past two decades. The middle class is identified as people living in households with income per capita between $10 and $50 per day, in purchasing power parity dollars. This income-based identification, summarized below, is explained and justified in the World Bank report on mobility and the middle class (Ferreira *et al.* 2013). It is conceptually and empirically grounded in the analysis of household surveys and is meant to apply region-wide.

The first part of this chapter provides a brief review of the literature on the middle class and explains the motivation of this chapter; that is, to provide new information on the characteristics at the household and individual level of the growing middle class in Latin America and the Caribbean. The profiles presented are an input to the analysis of social mobility in the region. The profiles can also provide a basis for the analysis of whether and how economic policy has affected growth of the middle class independent of economic growth itself, and what the political consequences of this growth have been in different countries.

At some point, when the middle class is large or powerful enough, the nation in which it lives is likely to take on and sustain characteristics associated with a "middle-class" society. The second part of this chapter summarizes information on the size and economic command of the LAC middle class as identified above and suggests simple measures for representing a middle-class society.

The third part describes the characteristics of the middle class including in terms of education, household size, and participation in the labor force. It also discusses differences across countries and over time. The resulting profiles suggest that middle-class households in LAC are not particularly different from what might be expected given that their household income is greater than that of poorer and less than that of richer households. Over time and across countries, household income per capita is a reasonably good summary indicator of "status" broadly conceived.[1]

---

[1] The same can be said of values, for which household income per capita is a good summary indicator. See López-Calva *et al.* (2012).

This chapter concentrates on description. I try to be careful about implying causation from correlation, and about inviting conclusions about middle-class exceptionalism or particularism in values or behavior when, at most, supposition is warranted. However, in a short conclusion, I speculate about two major policy questions that the summary measures of middle-class "societies" in the second part and the profile information in the third part raise: What, if any, economic programs and policies have contributed to LAC's larger and more economically salient middle class in the past two decades? And what, if any, consequences of a larger middle class are emerging in LAC? Improved governance? Less or more redistribution? Is the middle class a political force, and is it aligning itself with the interests of those less rich or more rich? Given the likelihood that the middle class will continue to grow, what are the economic prospects and political directions that the LAC countries in our sample are likely to take?

Why another note on the middle class

Only in the past decade have economists working on development issues begun studying the emergence of a new, income-based class of the not poor but not rich in developing countries.[2] Interest has grown, largely because with rapid economic growth in the People's Republic of China, the number of poor by international standards (income of $2 or less per capita per day, and $1.25 or less per capita per day for extreme poverty) has declined.

Economists tend to identify the middle class using income. However, there is no consensus about whether relative or absolute income matters, or within what ranges of relative or absolute income the middle class lies. One approach simply categorizes anyone who is not poor as middle class. Banerjee and Duflo (2008) describe households in a set of countries with income between $2 and $10, calling them middle class. Ravallion (2010) assesses the increase in the number of people in the middle class over the past several decades, defining the developing country middle class as those people with income per capita between $2 and $13.

Yet, earlier studies of household-level data in low-income countries suggest that a large share of households that are "not poor" as defined by some income threshold still face a high risk of falling (back) below such a threshold. Pritchett *et al.* (2000) analyze the variability of household expenditures in two panel data sets from Indonesia and conclude that 30–50% of households have a chance of 50% or more of falling into poverty. By most conventional definitions of the middle class,[3] they are too vulnerable and insecure in a material sense to qualify.

Other economists have defined the "middle stratum" or sometimes (misleadingly) the middle "class" in developing countries in strictly relative terms, namely as those in the middle of their own countries' income distributions, e.g., within specific ranges of median income per capita (Birdsall *et al.* 2000) or in the middle

[2] Sumner (2012) provides a comprehensive review of the literature.

[3] See López-Calva and Ortiz-Juarez (2011) for a useful review of the sociological literature.

three quintiles (Easterly 2001). Still others have used average country per capita income proxies as a way to represent a group that is in the middle of the global income distribution (Milanovic 2010; Cardenas *et al.* 2011).

A few studies have been concerned with identifying the middle class in developing countries in terms of its potential as an economic, social, and political force. This approach reflects the view that the middle class in the currently advanced economies has been key to economic growth as consumers and entrepreneurial producers, and has constituted the bulwark of democracy and stable and accountable government. Birdsall (2010) refers to the "indispensable" middle class, suggesting that a larger and more economically salient middle class is likely to be a force for more sensible economic policy, stronger and more responsive political institutions, and thus more sustained growth.[4] The concept as defined by sociologists emphasizes white-collar occupation, relatively good education, and the ability to plan. Most recent studies by economists have concentrated on descriptions of the size, characteristics and, to some extent, the welfare of developing country households that they predefine as middle class using one or another income-based definition.[5] Beyond description, analysis of the determinants or causes of the increase in the size and income command of the middle class, or of its consequences for growth and governance, is still relatively rare.[6]

This chapter also concentrates on description. However, the income thresholds that identify the LAC middle class are empirically based proxies for an economic conception of the "middle class" – independent of whether the resulting households fall in the middle of the income distribution. This makes it all the more important to provide a detailed background on the characteristics of these households, as well as compare them with poorer and richer households, by country and within the region. The resulting comparative "profiles" provide a basis for analysis of social mobility, including into and out of the middle class. They also constitute a basis for further work on the determinants of middle-class growth (in population and economic power) in Latin America; and the longer-term consequences of a larger and more economically and politically salient middle class for growth, governance, and democracy in the region.

---

[4] Birdsall and Sumner (2011) define a "catalytic" class that is less secure and poorer than the middle class. The catalytic class likely depends, more than the secure middle, on good government that ensures competition and adherence to the rule of law, and that minimizes unfair business practices and insider privileges.

[5] In the past several years, the Asian Development Bank (2010) and African Development Bank (Ncube *et al.* 2011) have published reports that include a discussion of the middle class in their member countries. The income increases have also been of obvious interest to the global consumer goods industry (see, e.g., a Goldman Sachs report by Lawson and Gilman (2009)).

[6] Easterly (2001) assesses the effect of the income share of the three middle quintiles of the income distribution on growth. He finds that a higher income share of the middle stratum and a lower level of ethnic fractionalization are good for economic growth. Birdsall *et al.* (2011) discuss the effects of various political regimes on the income share of the top quintiles. They find that in social democratic regimes compared with populist regimes, a higher share of income at the top of the distribution increases the incidence of social spending on lower-income groups.

For those purposes, the middle "class" is identified using an absolute income range, so that the characteristics of its members should be reasonably stable across countries and over time.

The $10 minimum threshold is grounded in two findings. First, López-Calva and Ortiz-Juarez (2011) show that at a household income per capita of at least $10, households in Chile, Mexico, and Peru are relatively invulnerable to falling into poverty. Based on data from three panel surveys, they show that households around this income only had a 10% probability of falling below their national poverty lines.

Second, in the analysis of surveys in which respondents in seven countries of the region were asked to report their class, it was at or around $10 a day that respondents identified themselves as middle class rather than poorer.[7] On the one hand, self-identification as middle class at about $10 could be a coincidence; on the other hand, it suggests that respondents in the region, when asked to put themselves into one or another class, view middle-class status – whether explicitly or intuitively – in some part as having to do with reasonably good income security. It may also mean that reasonably good income security is closely associated with other characteristics that respondents perceived as middle class.

The $50 threshold is less defensible, though not completely arbitrary. In the same set of surveys, a small proportion of respondents identified themselves as "rich" (on average 0.8% across all countries surveyed). Oddly, their estimated incomes ranged from the top to the bottom quintile, suggesting some coding problems or reporting issues. Respondents who identified themselves as "upper middle class" had estimated incomes somewhat better distributed around $20, with a long tail stretching beyond $60. The groups that identify themselves as "lower middle" and "middle" have estimated incomes peaking just below $10, but in contrast to those that self-identify as "lower," they have a long tail stretching to or beyond $50. The actual number of people sampled at $40–$50 is of course relatively small, but $50 as an upper threshold seems reasonable given these distributions.

Across all eight countries, the percentage of the population living in households that are classified as rich at $50 ranges from below 1% (in the Dominican Republic, Mexico, and Peru), to 3% in Brazil, and to almost 5% in Chile. For a family of four, a household income per capita of $50 a day would be about $73,000 (perhaps a middle bank manager's income in Sao Paulo). Since top incomes of a small percentage of households in LAC exceed that amount by several multiples, it is likely there is considerable underreporting of income by the rich (Székely and Hilgert 2000). This underreporting, however, is probably concentrated among households that are well above the $50-a-day line. Its effects will hence occur within the category of rich, reducing the average reported income of the group while leaving unaffected, for example, their average education compared with the middle class.

---

7 Ferreira *et al.* (2013) discusses the methodology of matching class and income using data from ECOSOCIAL and SEDLAC surveys.

In the discussion, I will sometimes refer to the characteristics of these "richer" households, but I am not assuming that they form a representative sample, given their small sampled numbers.

What constitutes a middle-class society?

At what size, income share, or other characteristic of the "middle class" in a country or region does that country or region become a middle-class society in which the virtues or vices of the middle class – in terms of values, aspirations, political views, savings, consumption, and work habits – dominate in their society?

Table 12.1 lists the population and income shares of the middle class for various years, in ascending order of national per capita income. Norway and the United States are included for comparison.

By 2009, almost one-third of the LAC population was in the middle class – between just under 20% in Honduras and over 40% in Chile, compared with our rough estimates of about 60% and 90% for the United States and Norway (using thresholds of $40–$100 a day), respectively. The middle class in LAC had grown substantially since the early 1990s. In five of the seven countries for which we have at least two survey years, it had nearly doubled in size.

Across countries and over time, middle-class population shares are statistically associated with higher mean income per capita and lower inequality measured by the Gini coefficient (Table 12.2, column 1). Declines in inequality are now well documented in most LAC countries, particularly since about 2000 (López-Calva and Lustig 2010). Whether those declines are the cause or consequence of growing middle-class population shares is not clear from the association alone. The association with increases in average income in most countries suggests that the population share of the middle class has increased from the bottom. Increases in median income (not shown) reflect the fact that overall growth is sufficiently shared with households below $10 per capita to ensure many were lifted above that threshold.

For comparison with countries outside of LAC, Table 12.3 lists population shares of the middle class in other parts of the developing world. In 2008/2009, the estimated share for urban People's Republic of China was only about 13%, compared with 18% for Thailand and 36% for Turkey. The implication is that many countries in Latin America are at least as "middle class" as East Asian countries such as Thailand, and more middle class than most developing countries in Africa and South Asia.

The 2008/2009 figures in Table 12.3 suggest that a large share of the increase in middle-class population size in Honduras, Brazil, and Chile has occurred since 2005. The very small increase in the middle-class population size in Mexico suggests that the country benefited less than most of its South American neighbors from the boom years 2005–2009 because of its dependence on exports to the United States, which declined as economic growth in the United States faltered after 2006. The data also suggest the sensitivity of middle-class population share to growth.

Table 12.1 Mean household income per capita, income share, and population share of the middle class

Country	*Year*	*Total population*		*Middle class*					
		Mean household income		*Mean household income*		*Income share*		*Population share*	
		$ per capita (1)	*% change (2)*	*$ per capita (3)*	*% change (4)*	*% of total (5)*	*% change (6)*	*% of total (7)*	*% change (8)*
Honduras	1992	4.38		18.05		32.78		5.94	
	1999	5.61	+28.2	17.91	−0.8	38.41	+5.6	9.55	+3.6
	2009	7.03	+25.3	18.01	+0.6	49.28	+10.9	16.57	+7.0
Dominican	2000	11.79		18.90		51.81		26.83	
Republic	2008	9.49	−19.4	18.34	−3.0	40.40	−11.4	20.40	−6.4
Peru	1999	7.71		19.28		34.85		13.25	
	2009	9.87	+28.0	18.29	−5.1	45.91	+11.1	28.13	+14.9
Mexico	1992	11.63		19.39		43.86		22.42	
	1998	9.54	−17.9	18.55	−4.3	41.88	−2.0	17.90	−4.5
	2008	12.62	+32.3	19.08	+2.8	49.95	+8.1	28.25	+10.3
Colombia	2006	13.66		19.87	+0.0	47.03		25.76	
Costa Rica	1992	7.79		17.12		40.58		18.15	
	1999	10.87	+39.6	18.99	+10.9	52.26	+11.7	27.93	+9.8
	2009	15.67	+44.1	20.57	+8.3	53.57	+1.3	37.20	+9.3
Brazil	1992	6.95		18.43		44.24		14.73	
	1999	11.19	+60.9	19.93	+8.2	44.91	+0.7	21.95	+7.2
	2009	14.07	+25.7	19.38	−2.8	48.65	+3.7	31.55	+9.6

Table 12.1 Continued

Country	*Year*	*Total population*		*Middle class*					
		Mean household income		*Mean household income*		*Income share*		*Population share*	
		$ per capita (1)	*% change (2)*	*$ per capita (3)*	*% change (4)*	*% of total (5)*	*% change (6)*	*% of total (7)*	*% change (8)*
Chile	1992	12.04		19.28		40.26		23.67	
	1998	15.90	+32.0	20.24	+5.0	44.47	+4.2	31.93	+8.3
	2009	19.07	+20.0	19.90	−1.7	53.64	+9.2	42.32	+10.4
Norway	1991					41.60		23.50	
	2000					83.90	+42.3	67.60	+44.1
	2004					92.40	+8.5	81.80	+14.2
United States	1991					60.50		34.10	
	2000					86.20	+25.7	68.30	+34.2
	2004					91.70	+5.5	76.60	+8.3

Notes: All dollar figures are purchasing power parity (PPP) dollars, based on the 2005 International Comparison Program. The "middle class" is defined as all households with a daily household income of $10–$50 per capita, below which is considered "poor" and above which is considered "rich." For Norway and the United States, we define the middle class as all households with a daily income of $40–$100 per capita.

Source: Socio-Economic Database for Latin America and the Caribbean (CEDLAS and the World Bank), http://sedlac.econo.unlp.edu.ar/eng/ (accessed 18 July 2012).

Table 12.2 Middle-class society regressions

Independent variable	*Dependent variable*					
	Population share of the middle class		*Income share of the middle class*		*Overlap of middle class and three middle quintiles*	
	(1)	*(2)*	*(3)*	*(4)*	*(5)*	*(6)*
Gini coefficient	−1.121	0.201	−0.127	0.176	0.843	3.498
	(2.22)*	(0.63)	(0.47)	(0.73)	(0.44)	(2.44)*
Mean income	1.243		0.283		2.377	
	(14.61)**		(6.25)**		(3.97)**	
Median income		1.294		0.298		2.469
		(23.59)**		(7.19)**		(5.52)**
Constant	4.595	−0.028	3.647	2.578	−6.993	−16.305
	(2.30)*	(0.02)	(3.43)**	(2.66)*	(0.96)	(2.81)*
R^2	0.95	0.98	0.77	0.81	0.70	0.82
N	15	15	15	15	11	11

Note: Linear regression model. $^*p < 0.05$, $^{**}p < 0.01$. *t*-statistics in parentheses. All variables are log-transformed.

Source: Socio-Economic Database for Latin America and the Caribbean (CEDLAS and the World Bank), http://sedlac.econo.unlp.edu.ar/eng/ (accessed 18 July 2012).

Along with population shares of the middle class, Table 12.1 also shows income shares of the middle class for each country and year. The middle class in most LAC countries "resides" in the top three deciles of the income distribution. It follows that its income shares (between 40% and 54% in 2008/2009) are much higher than its population shares.

Income shares have increased in most countries of the region, though by much less than population shares. They are, like population shares, closely associated with higher country mean and median income, but in contrast to population shares, not with lower inequality (Table 12.2, columns 3 and 4). At the same time, with income growth over time, income shares relative to population shares have fallen (Table 12.1, column 5 compared with column 7).

The change in income shares in Brazil between 1992 and 2009 indicates a healthy decline (from about 3:1 to about 1.5:1) in the ratio of income to population share – healthy in the sense that it occurs because rising incomes push more people into the middle class from below than out of the middle class to above. In Brazil, median income within the middle class rose over the two decades, making the overall picture benign. In this period, Brazil benefited from rapid growth and, since about 2001, from a decline in inequality (López-Calva and Lustig 2010).

That economic growth in the developing world has been good for the poor, by reducing their absolute numbers, is a well-accepted dogma in the development literature. Ravallion (2010) shows that economic growth in the developing world

Table 12.3 Population shares of the middle class in selected countries and years

Country	*Survey type*	*Population share (%)*		*Mean income*
		2005/06	*2008/09*	*2008/09*
India – urban	(C)	0.99	1.54	2.40
Indonesia – urban	(C)	2.29	1.81	2.68
People's Republic of China – urban	(C)	7.80	13.43	6.50
Honduras	(I)	10.78	17.37	6.67
Thailand	(C)	16.66	17.74	7.06
South Africa	(C)	15.87	17.96	8.45
Turkey	(C)	25.16	35.36	10.05
Mexico	(I)	26.92	27.98	10.15
Brazil	(I)	24.20	31.55	11.95
Russian Federation	(C)	34.31	51.97	14.71
Chile	(C)	38.59	42.35	16.24

Notes

1 Countries sorted in ascending order of mean income. Mean income refers to average daily per capita income or consumption expenditure from the corresponding survey, in 2005 purchasing power parity dollars.
2 Survey type refers to the welfare measure used: (I) income or (C) consumption.
3 No adjustment is made to account for different welfare measures.
4 Divergence from Table 12.1 is due to differences in underlying data and estimation methodology.
5 For better comparability, this table uses consistent data from PovcalNet for all countries.

Source: PovcalNet, http://iresearch.worldbank.org/PovcalNet/index.htm (accessed March 2012).

has pushed a large number of people above the $2 poverty line because of the high concentration of households around that line. In LAC, growth combined with falling inequality has apparently been good for building middle-class societies. The number of people in the middle class in the region as a whole (extrapolating roughly from growth in the countries for which we have data) has grown from about 70 million in 1992 (about 15% of the LAC population then) to about 170 million in 2009 (almost 30% of the larger 2009 population).

Are countries in LAC becoming more middle-class societies in the political realm? Are they more likely to collaborate implicitly or explicitly in demanding rights, rents, or a more market-driven or a more welfare-oriented political regime? When does a country's political system or regime primarily reflect middle-class demands? The answer has to do not only with a sufficient share of households reaching some minimum absolute income; for political salience, it also has to do with the group's implicit – if not explicit – sense of identity as a group with shared political interests that are different from the interests of the "richer" and the "poorer."

One measure of middle-class identity is the Gini coefficient of the LAC middle class itself, that is, a Gini in which the middle class in each country and year is treated as the entire population. The resulting Gini coefficients are shown in column 1 of Table 12.4. The low Gini coefficients imply a reasonably good sense

Table 12.4 Measures of middle-class society

Country	*Year*	*Middle-class summary indicators*			*Ratios*	
		Gini coefficient	*Population share*	*Income share*	*Middle-class income share/ middle-class Gini coefficient*	*Middle class/three middle quintiles overlap*
			% of total	*% of total*		*% of total population*
		(1)	*(2)*	*(3)*	*(4)*	*(5)*
Honduras	1992	21	5.94	32.78	1.56	0
	1999	21	9.55	38.41	1.83	0
	2009	24	16.57	49.28	2.05	1.80
Dominican	2000	24	26.83	51.81	2.16	14.20
Republic	2008	22	20.40	40.40	1.84	0.70
Peru	1999	23	13.25	34.85	1.52	0
	2009	23	28.13	45.91	2.00	6.40
Mexico	1992	23	22.42	43.86	1.91	7.10
	1998	23	17.90	41.88	1.82	2.90
	2008	25	28.25	49.95	2.00	16.10
Colombia	2006	25	25.76	47.03	1.88	15.60
Costa Rica	1992	23	18.15	40.58	1.76	0
	1999	24	27.93	52.26	2.18	8.70
	2009	25	37.20	53.57	2.14	18.70
Brazil	1992	23	14.73	44.24	1.92	0
	1999	24	21.95	44.91	1.87	7.70
	2009	25	31.55	48.65	1.95	18.70
Chile	1992	24	23.67	40.26	1.68	6.70
	1998	24	31.93	44.47	1.85	12.80
	2009	25	42.32	53.64	2.15	23.20
Norway	1991		23.50	41.60		15.90
	2000		67.60	83.90		35.10
	2004		81.80	92.40		43.20
United States	1991		34.10	60.50		17.00
	2000		68.30	86.20		36.80
	2004		76.60	91.70		41.50

Note: In the United States and Norway, we define the middle class as all households with daily per capita income of more than $30 purchasing power parity, up to the 95th percentile of the income distribution.

Source: Socio-Economic Database for Latin America and the Caribbean (CEDLAS and the World Bank), http://sedlac.econo.unlp.edu.ar/eng/ (accessed 18 July 2012).

of identity (for example, as consumers) and in terms of likely labor productivity levels within the predefined middle class.

The middle class might be viewed as more politically salient the larger its shares of population and income, and the smaller its Gini. Those shares are shown in columns 2, 3, and 4 of Table 12.4. In column 4, the differences between countries are driven primarily by differences in their income shares. Still, the ratios provide a shorthand, if crude, portrait of a region that is becoming more middle class over time. In 2009, Chile and Costa Rica were the "most" middle class: Chile is the richest and Costa Rica has relatively low national income inequality.[8]

Finally, column 5 of Table 12.4 shows the proportion of population that is both in our LAC middle class and in the "middle" of each country's income distribution, that is, in the middle three quintiles. In 2008/2009, the overlap is tiny in Honduras because households with a daily per capita income of $10 are barely at the top of the fourth quintile; almost no households in the three middle quintiles of the income distribution are in the middle class. In contrast, in richer Chile, about two-thirds of all middle-class households are in the fourth quintile of the overall distribution.

By this measure, the most middle-class societies in the region are Chile (23% of households in both categories), Brazil, and Costa Rica (almost 19% of households in both categories). But even in those three countries, the overlap is small compared with Norway and the United States, where it is around 40% in 2004. Table 12.2 (columns 5 and 6) shows a simple regression of the size of the overlap between our middle class and the three middle quintiles. Across years and countries, higher mean income per capita is associated with a larger overlap of the two groups. Similarly, higher median income per capita is associated with a larger overlap. Its inclusion also makes the Gini coefficient positive (i.e., greater inequality increases the overlap while controlling for median income).

Some characteristics of the Latin American and Caribbean middle class

Is a sense of shared identity among members of the LAC middle class warranted in terms of economic and political, as opposed to ethnic, racial, or religious interests? Profiles of the middle class across countries and over time help address at least the following three questions.

First, how different are middle-class households from other income groups in terms of education, employment, household assets, etc.? Is there anything special about the middle class beyond their place in the income distribution (middle-class "particularism")?

Second, to what extent is there commonality across countries in the characteristics of middle-class households? Does a middle-class household in Honduras look the same as a middle-class household in Chile? If so, does it suggest that the

---

[8] In 2009, the national Gini index of Costa Rica was 50.7, just a little higher than the Dominican Republic and Peru at about 49, and lower than Brazil, Chile, Colombia, and Honduras at over 52.

region is economically integrated, with a single price for, say, labor at a specific skill level?

Third, have the characteristics of the middle class in LAC changed over time, or is the region more middle class simply because more households have entered the category of less vulnerable to poverty, though not rich by any regional standard?

I shall now describe the LAC middle class using the latest available household survey data for our eight countries, and then discuss changes in the profiles of our middle-class households over the past two decades. In doing so, I will compare middle-class households ($10–$50 daily per capita income) with three other groups: the poor (under $4 daily per capita income), the vulnerable ($4–$10 daily per capita income), and those richer than $50 per capita per day.

The Latin American and Caribbean middle class, 2009

Income. Table 12.5 shows mean and median daily household income per capita of the middle class for each country and year.

At the medians, middle-class households are about three times richer than the combined group of poor and vulnerable households (Table 12.5 and Figure 12.1). Median incomes of the middle class are far above overall median incomes (and even above overall mean incomes). This is consistent with the fact that middle-class households are heavily concentrated in the top two or three deciles of the income distribution in most countries, on average at far higher incomes than their poorer counterparts. Recall that in part by definition, our LAC middle class is relatively invulnerable to falling into poverty at about $4 a day. The great majority of households in LAC are in fact still vulnerable to that risk.

At the same time, middle-class households in all countries are four to five times poorer at the medians than richer households. The LAC middle class is closer in income to its poorer than to its richer counterparts. This is consistent with the top-heavy concentration of income in most countries of the region. Indeed, median incomes of the rich are very high – particularly assuming the relatively greater underreporting of income in richer households.

Size, age, and other demographic characteristics. Table 12.6 shows key demographic characteristics of middle-class households pooled across all eight countries, weighted by population. LAC middle-class households are small and middle-aged. They have about three people (more in poorer Honduras, less in richer Brazil and Chile) and, except for Honduras, a mean of less than one child per household. In Brazil, they have an average of just 2.7 people and 0.5 children. The average age of all middle-class adults is 39 (younger in Honduras, older in Chile and Brazil), approaching the age 40 when workers typically reach their maximum productivity (Skirbekk 2003).

These demographic characteristics of households are closely and monotonically associated with income per capita (with average size and number of children in part a function of the per capita construct), both across countries and within

Table 12.5 Daily household income per capita by income group

Country	*Year*	*Total population*		*Poor <$4*		*Vulnerable $4–$10*		*Middle class $10–$50*		*Rich >$50*	
		Mean	*Median*	*Mean*	*Median*	*Mean*	*Median*	*Mean*	*Median*	*Mean*	*Median*
Honduras	1992	4.38	2.36	1.64	1.57	6.21	5.91	18.05	14.95	78.41	68.69
	1999	5.61	3.14	1.83	1.76	6.26	5.89	17.91	14.55	73.72	69.56
	2009	7.03	3.95	1.68	1.58	6.46	6.19	18.01	15.28	86.29	64.54
Dominican	2000	11.79	6.79	2.44	2.55	6.53	6.34	18.90	15.81	98.88	71.49
Republic	2008	9.49	5.87	2.44	2.57	6.46	6.22	18.34	15.50	95.76	67.79
Peru	1999	7.71	4.10	2.08	2.06	6.32	6.06	19.28	16.15	82.51	74.75
	2009	9.87	6.44	2.37	2.40	6.58	6.41	18.29	15.33	84.83	66.18
Mexico	1992	11.63	6.28	2.35	2.45	6.42	6.10	19.39	16.27	101.52	75.92
	1998	9.54	5.37	2.22	2.27	6.41	6.16	18.55	15.78	100.41	71.47
	2008	12.62	7.40	2.38	2.53	6.67	6.50	19.08	16.03	104.57	71.59
Colombia	2006	13.66	6.67	1.96	2.06	6.57	6.31	19.87	16.77	106.26	75.25
Costa Rica	1992	7.79	5.38	2.21	2.38	6.42	6.13	17.12	14.28	80.53	72.22
	1999	10.87	6.97	2.29	2.45	6.56	6.40	18.99	15.82	74.96	66.84
	2009	15.67	9.07	2.45	2.75	6.80	6.65	20.57	17.34	89.33	68.51
Brazil	1992	6.95	4.15	1.96	1.95	6.27	5.91	18.43	15.46	74.50	63.70
	1999	11.19	5.40	2.05	2.14	6.35	5.98	19.93	16.60	93.66	73.78
	2009	14.07	8.48	2.12	2.31	6.82	6.74	19.38	16.23	95.05	72.92
Chile	1992	12.04	6.47	2.59	2.68	6.50	6.28	19.28	15.91	100.62	76.31
	1998	15.90	8.28	2.60	2.74	6.65	6.48	20.24	16.83	101.60	74.65
	2009	19.07	10.46	2.62	2.89	6.93	6.90	19.90	16.59	111.32	78.57

Note: All figures are in purchasing power parity dollars, based on the 2005 International Comparison Program.

Source: Socio-Economic Database for Latin America and the Caribbean (CEDLAS and the World Bank), http://sedlac.econo.unlp.edu.ar/eng/ (accessed 18 July 2012).

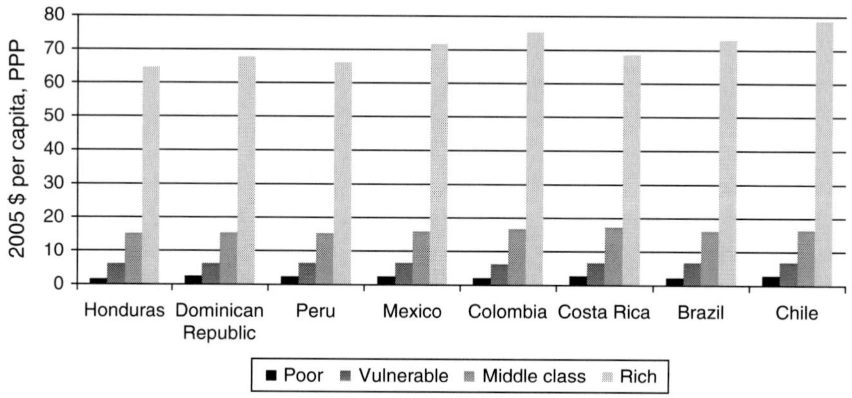

Figure 12.1 Median daily household income per capita by income group, 2008/2009.

PPP = purchasing power parity.

Note: The data for Colombia are for 2006.

Source: Socio-Economic Database for Latin America and the Caribbean (CEDLAS and the World Bank), http://sedlac.econo.unlp.edu.ar/eng/ (accessed 18 July 2012).

countries over time. Over time, household size and number of children decreased as overall incomes have risen.

Household size and fertility have been converging across income groups as overall fertility has fallen across the region. In Brazil, the mean number of children of middle-class households was 0.8 in 1992 and had fallen to 0.5 in 2009. By 2009, differences by income group were relatively small compared with the differences in 1992.

Still, the relatively small differences in average size and number of children accumulate across households in the different income categories: in 2009, 44.6% of Brazilian children under 18 years lived in poor households and another 36.8% lived in vulnerable households. In total, 81.4% of children are growing up in households that are not middle class or richer. Just 17.5% of children lived in middle-class households and a mere 1.2% in the richest households.

Schooling. I use the term schooling rather than education in this section. In developing countries, there is a strong relationship between the quantity and the quality of schooling that people receive. Those who benefit from better schooling as children tend to go farther in school (Behrman and Birdsall 1983). As a result, differences in education across classes are almost certainly understated by differences in schooling, and more so the poorer a country was when an adult was a child.[9]

[9] Filmer *et al.* (2006) and Pritchett (forthcoming) provide ample evidence of the low quality of schooling in developing countries compared with Organisation for Economic Co-operation and Development countries.

Table 12.6 Demographic characteristics of the middle class, pooled sample

		Year		
		1992	*2000*	*2009*
Middle-class population share (% of total population)		15.7	21.3	28.2
Daily household income ($ per capita (PPP))	Mean	18.9	19.5	19.3
	Standard deviation	8.8	9.3	9.1
	Median	15.7	16.4	16.2
Education (adults 18–65 years)	Mean	9.6	10.1	10.4
	Standard deviation	4.5	4.4	4.3
	Median	11	11	11
Household size	Mean	3.3	3.2	2.9
	Standard deviation	1.6	1.5	1.4
	Median	3	3	3
Children per household	Mean	0.9	0.8	0.6
	Standard deviation	1.1	1.0	0.9
	Median	1	0	0
Age	Mean	30.8	32.7	36.3
	Standard deviation	19.6	19.8	20.5
	Median	28	31	35
Age of children 0–17	Mean	8.7	9.1	9.4
	Standard deviation	5.2	5.2	5.2
	Median	9	9	10
Age of children 18–65	Mean	36.6	37.6	39.0
	Standard deviation	12.9	12.9	13.4
	Median	34	37	39

PPP = purchasing power parity.

Source: Socio-Economic Database for Latin America and the Caribbean (CEDLAS and the World Bank), http://sedlac.econo.unlp.edu.ar/eng/ (accessed 18 July 2012).

Table 12.7 shows the mean and median of years of schooling of adults (ages 25–65) and Figure 12.2 plots the median values in 2009. The median schooling of adults in middle-class households is between 10 and 12 years in most countries. In virtually every country, the average adult in a middle-class household has attended at least some secondary school. That is especially true for those at the younger end of the age range (Table 12.8). The median of years of schooling is much higher for richer households. With the exception of Honduras, the rich are far more likely to have attended or even completed university.

Three points are noteworthy about Table 12.7. First, mean and median years of schooling of middle-class adults vary little across countries and over time; there is constancy in the crude relationship between income ($10–$50) and schooling of adults throughout the region, suggesting relatively deep integration of the real cost of labor across the region and time. The lack of change over time is in part a function of the growth in the size of the middle class from below; the average

Table 12.7 Mean and median years of education by income group, adults aged 25–65

Country	*Year*	*Total population*			*Poor (<$4)*			*Vulnerable ($4–$10)*			*Middle class ($10–$50)*			*Rich (>$50)*		
		Mean	*SD*	*Median*	*Mean*	*SD*	*Median*	*Mean*	*SD*	*Median*	*Mean*	*SD*	*Median*	*Mean*	*SD*	*Median*
Honduras	1992	4.9	4.5	4	3.5	3.3	3	6.6	4.5	6	10.9	5.3	12	13.5	4.5	14
	1999	5.1	4.5	5	3.5	3.2	3	6.2	4.3	6	9.9	5.2	12	12.9	4.3	12
	2009	5.9	4.5	6	3.8	3.2	3	6.2	4.0	6	9.6	4.9	11	13.7	4.8	16
Dominican	2000	7.4	5.1	7	5.0	4.1	4	6.8	4.5	7	9.7	5.2	10	13.9	4.5	16
Republic	2008	8.2	5.2	8	6.1	4.4	6	7.9	4.9	8	11.0	5.1	12	14.4	4.6	16
Peru	1999	7.9	5.2	9	5.3	4.5	5	9.3	4.7	11	11.9	4.3	12	14.8	2.2	16
	2009	9.0	5.0	11	5.9	4.3	5	9.0	4.6	11	11.9	4.3	12	14.6	3.0	16
Mexico	1992	6.4	4.9	6	3.5	3.2	3	5.8	4.1	6	9.7	5.0	9	13.2	5.1	15
	1998	7.2	4.9	6	4.6	3.7	4	7.2	4.2	6	10.9	4.8	12	14.6	3.8	17
	2008	8.4	4.8	9	5.7	3.8	6	7.6	4.1	8	10.8	4.7	11	14.6	4.0	16
Colombia	2006	7.9	4.9	7	5.4	3.9	5	7.1	4.1	6	10.3	4.6	11	14.7	3.9	16
Costa Rica	1992	7.0	4.2	6	5.3	3.2	6	6.7	3.7	6	9.8	4.6	11	13.5	4.1	15
	1999	7.4	4.3	6	5.2	3.2	6	6.6	3.5	6	9.7	4.4	10	13.6	4.2	15
	2009	8.7	4.4	8	5.8	3.1	6	7.0	3.4	6	10.4	4.3	11	14.7	3.1	16
Brazil	1992	5.2	4.4	4	3.3	3.3	3	5.5	4.0	4	9.1	4.6	11	12.6	3.9	14
	1999	6.1	4.6	5	3.7	3.3	3	5.6	3.8	5	9.0	4.4	10	13.4	3.6	15
	2009	7.7	4.8	8	5.2	4.1	4	6.7	4.4	7	9.6	4.4	11	13.5	2.8	15
Chile	1992	8.5	4.2	8	7.3	3.8	8	8.3	4.1	8	10.1	4.2	11	11.9	3.5	12
	1998	9.8	4.3	10	7.4	3.6	8	8.9	3.9	9	11.6	4.0	12	15.2	3.0	16
	2009	11.0	3.8	12	8.9	3.4	9	9.7	3.3	10	11.8	3.7	12	15.5	3.0	17

SD = standard deviation.

Source: Socio-Economic Database for Latin America and the Caribbean (CEDLAS and the World Bank), http://sedlac.econo.unlp.edu.ar/eng/ (accessed 18 July 2012).

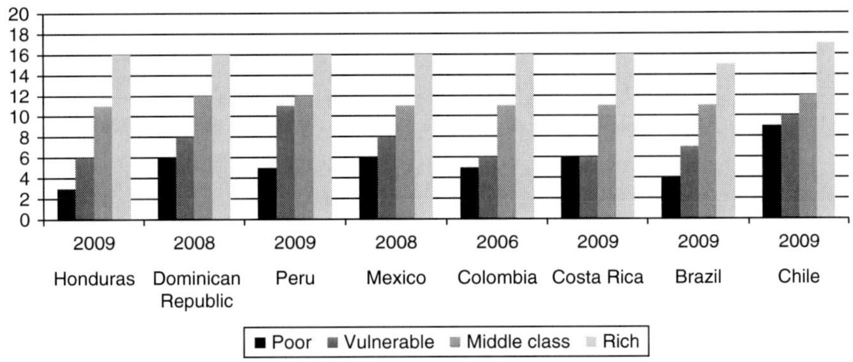

Figure 12.2 Median years of schooling by income group, adults aged 25–65.

Source: Socio-Economic Database for Latin America and the Caribbean (CEDLAS and the World Bank), http://sedlac.econo.unlp.edu.ar/eng/ (accessed 18 July 2012).

Table 12.8 Median years of schooling in Brazil by age and income group, 2009

Age group	*Poor* <*$4*	*Vulnerable* *$4–$10*	*Middle class* *$10–$50*	*Rich* >*$50*
15–19	7	8	10	10
20–24	8	11	11	13
25–29	7	11	11	15
30–34	5	8	11	15
35–39	4	8	11	15
40–44	4	8	11	15
45–49	4	5	11	15
50–54	3	4	8	15
55–59	2	4	8	15
60–65	2	3	4	15

Source: Socio-Economic Database for Latin America and the Caribbean (CEDLAS and the World Bank), http://sedlac.econo.unlp.edu.ar/eng/ (accessed 18 July 2012).

schooling of the resulting middle class has not changed much, though in absolute terms average schooling of the entire populations has been increasing steadily.

Second, except in Chile, median schooling of the middle class is 50–100% higher than that of the poorer groups. Recall that "poorer" in those countries includes 70% or more of the total population. The difference between average schooling of the LAC middle class and the absolute poor ($2 a day or less per capita income) would be far greater.

Compared with Norway and the United States, mean schooling of the LAC middle class is much lower. For example, about 88% of adults (25 years and older) in the United States have at least received high school education (United

States Census Bureau 2011), compared with 22% of adults in our sample of LAC countries.

Third, there is considerable lack of precision in the calculation of schooling means by income group (Figure 12.2). Standard deviations are high – except for the richer group. To be rich in Latin America is to be highly schooled, and vice versa.

Table 12.8 shows median years of schooling for Brazilian adults by age and income group in 2009. Higher medians at younger ages reflect the universal gains in access to schooling. Convergence by income group is also associated with these gains. Not surprisingly, the years of schooling among the rich do not decline with age as much as for other income groups. Most of those who are old and rich were apparently raised in rich households when they were younger.

What about current school attendance? Virtually all children aged 6–12 in middle-class households are in school, as are at least three-quarters of 13–19 year-olds (Table 12.9). Substantial numbers of middle-class children aged 6–12 attend private schools: 63% in the Dominican Republic, 57% in Peru, and 45% in Brazil (Table 12.10). The percentages are lower in the countries with larger and more politically salient middle classes: 27% in Mexico, 25% in Costa Rica, and 8% in Chile.[10]

In all countries, the great majority of children of secondary school age from richer households attend private schools. This is true even in Costa Rica (62%), which is probably the country with the longest history and the best reputation for good-quality public schooling. The differences in private school attendance at the secondary level between middle-class and richer households are notable, reflecting in part the high cost of private secondary schooling and the very large differences in income between middle-class and poor households (Table 12.5). At the same time, the difference is also notable between middle-class households and their poorer counterparts. Private school attendance at both the primary and secondary levels is a major marker of differences across all classes.

Residence.[11] The region is highly urbanized. With the exception of Costa Rica, Honduras, and Peru, all countries have urbanization rates of more than 60% in all income groups.[12] The rates are much higher in all countries for the middle class.

Looking at migration within countries, it is clear that the more income a household commands today, the more likely it is that its members have moved at some point. As is true for other indicators, higher income is probably both a consequence of having moved as well as a consequence of higher initial income (which is correlated with current higher income, and can be a cause or a facilitating factor for having moved).

[10] The low figure in Chile presumably excludes publicly subsidized private schools.

[11] Birdsall (2012) provides more details and descriptive tables on the residence of middle-class households.

[12] Comparisons across countries are not actually possible because the definition of "urban" varies across countries.

Table 12.9 Percentage of students enrolled in any school, 2008/2009

Country	*Between 6 and 12 years old*				*Between 13 and 18 years old*			
	Poor *<$4*	*Vulnerable* *$4–$10*	*Middle class* *$10–$50*	*Rich* *>$50*	*Poor* *<$4*	*Vulnerable* *$4–$10*	*Middle class* *$10–$50*	*Rich* *>$50*
Honduras	92.4	96.7	95.2	94.9	48.4	64.4	77.8	84.5
Dominican Republic	93.7	97.7	98.4	100.0	86.6	85.3	91.3	96.1
Peru	98.2	98.9	99.4	100.0	76.1	78.1	81.0	97.5
Mexico	96.7	98.7	99.3	94.3	63.6	67.9	80.5	91.8
Colombia	90.5	94.6	96.3	93.8	70.5	72.0	81.6	87.8
Costa Rica	97.8	99.3	99.7	100.0	74.4	79.9	86.1	90.7
Brazil	97.2	98.4	99.2	99.7	83.0	82.8	86.8	95.3
Chile	98.1	99.1	99.6	99.9	85.9	86.5	90.0	91.3

Note: Data for Colombia are from 2006.

Source: Socio-Economic Database for Latin America and the Caribbean (CEDLAS and the World Bank), http://sedlac.econo.unlp.edu.ar/eng/ (accessed 18 July 2012).

Table 12.10 Percentage of students in school enrolled in private school by age group, 2008/2009

Country	*Between 6 and 12 years old*				*Between 13 and 18 years old*			
	Poor *<$4*	*Vulnerable* *$4–$10*	*Middle class* *$10–$50*	*Rich* *>$50*	*Poor* *<$4*	*Vulnerable* *$4–$10*	*Middle class* *$10–$50*	*Rich* *>$50*
Honduras	2.2	10.3	34.8	62.9	7.5	19.3	42.5	70.0
Dominican Republic	14.0	29.8	63.4	89.9	15.3	27.0	62.9	83.2
Peru	2.6	20.0	56.5	91.8	3.4	14.9	50.4	91.7
Mexico	0.7	4.1	26.9	79.3	4.5	6.9	24.7	70.9
Colombia	6.7	13.8	41.9	83.3	8.4	14.6	40.5	84.7
Costa Rica	1.2	2.1	25.2	67.2	2.9	4.0	26.8	62.1
Brazil	4.8	13.3	45.1	90.6	2.7	8.0	35.3	85.3
Chile	0.6	0.9	8.1	68.8	1.6	1.7	10.8	64.1

Note: Data for Colombia are from 2006.

Source: Socio-Economic Database for Latin America and the Caribbean (CEDLAS and The World Bank), http://sedlac.econo.unlp.edu.ar/eng/ (accessed 18 July 2012).

There is, in short, nothing surprising or particular about the middle class in terms of current or past residence, once their income is taken into account. Perhaps this distinguishes the LAC region from less urbanized South Asia and People's Republic of China, where the middle class is probably even more heavily concentrated in urban areas.

Employment. Table 12.11 provides a breakdown of workers by employment sector in 2009. The categories aggregate across 17 sectors: primary activities include

Table 12.11 Employment sectors of workers aged 25–65 by income group and ISIC classification, 2008/2009

	Primary activities	*Health, education, public services*	*Manufacturing*	*Construction*	*Other*	*Primary activities*	*Health, education, public services*	*Manufacturing*	*Construction*	*Other*
	poor (<$4)					*vulnerable ($4–$10)*				
Honduras	57.3	5.3	11.2	4.8	21.4	17.1	10.6	18.0	8.8	45.5
Dominican Republic	23.8	15.1	11.0	5.8	44.3	11.9	14.9	14.5	8.2	50.4
Peru	73.8	7.0	2.5	13.0	3.7	30.7	22.3	6.0	28.9	12.1
Mexico	34.6	4.4	14.4	8.8	37.7	9.5	9.7	18.5	10.6	51.7
Colombia	33.1	8.5	9.4	5.9	43.2	18.6	11.2	14.1	6.5	49.6
Costa Rica	23.0	7.6	9.6	8.0	52.0	15.5	10.1	13.6	8.1	52.8
Brazil	35.6	7.2	9.4	9.5	38.3	16.1	12.0	14.6	9.5	47.9
Chile	22.6	9.1	10.8	13.2	44.4	17.8	11.7	11.8	11.8	46.9
	Middle class ($10–$50)					*Rich (>$50)*				
Honduras	7.2	19.8	13.4	6.6	53.1	10.4	24.8	8.3	2.9	53.6
Dominican Republic	5.9	21.6	12.6	6.5	53.4	1.5	17.3	25.6	4.8	50.7
Peru	15.3	33.9	6.7	27.1	17.0	13.6	27.0	10.7	16.1	32.7
Mexico	4.2	22.9	14.6	6.5	51.8	6.7	26.9	11.2	4.7	50.6
Colombia	7.5	21.0	15.6	3.9	52.1	5.6	29.4	11.8	3.2	50.0
Costa Rica	5.8	20.7	11.8	5.7	56.0	2.7	29.5	7.1	2.8	58.0
Brazil	8.1	20.0	15.4	6.2	50.3	4.0	29.2	10.0	2.5	54.4
Chile	11.1	19.8	10.3	7.3	51.5	7.2	28.2	6.2	7.1	51.3

ISIC = International Standard of Industrial Classification of All Economic Activities.

Note: Data for Colombia are from 2006. Employment sectors are categorized and rearranged using ISIC Rev 3 top-level classifications: Primary activities are A (Agriculture, hunting, and forestry), B (Fishing), and C (Mining and quarrying). Public services are L (Public administration), M (Education), N (Health and social work), and O (Other community, social, and personal service activities).

Source: Socio-Economic Database for Latin America and the Caribbean (CEDLAS and the World Bank), http://sedlac.econo.unlp.edu.ar/eng/ (accessed 18 July 2012).

agriculture, mining, and fishing. "Other" comprises mostly private activities such as real estate, and hotels and restaurants.

Within each category, there are, of course, higher- and lower-skilled jobs that command more or less pay. It is therefore not surprising that some workers in poor households work in the public sector and some in rich households work in primary activities. At the same time, some broad patterns emerge: middle-class workers are less likely to work in primary sectors and more likely to work in health, education, and public services (in both the public and the private sector) than their poorer counterparts. This is even more the case for their richer counterparts. In this regard, middle-class workers in LAC look far more like a typical "rich" than a typical "poor" worker. This is consistent with our data on schooling, where differences are greater between the poor and middle groups than between the middle and richer groups. It is also in line with the fact that the middle class in LAC is not in the "middle" of the income distribution, but concentrated in the top two or three deciles. This is particularly the case in the three poorest countries of our sample.

It is not the sector of employment but the status of employment that differentiates the middle class. Consistent with existing literature that finds most workers in the middle class earn a regular wage or salary as opposed to being entrepreneurs (Banerjee and Duflo 2008), our sample shows that between 52% (the Dominican Republic) and 76% (Honduras) of middle-class workers are "employees" (Table 12.12). In Brazil, Chile, Costa Rica, and Honduras, the percentage of workers who are "employees" is even higher in the middle class than in the group of rich households.

To what extent are middle-class workers "employers"? Not surprisingly, middle-class workers are more likely to be employers than their poorer counterparts and less likely than their richer counterparts. There is, however, a significant gap between middle-class workers and rich workers, who are much more likely to be employers. In Brazil in 2009, rich workers were three times more likely to be employers than middle-class workers. In Chile and Honduras in 2009, rich workers were more than five times more likely to be employers than middle-class workers.

Table 12.13 shows the percentage of workers reporting employment in either small private firms (five employees of less), large private firms (more than five employees), or in the public sector. Casual observation might suggest that middle-class workers are concentrated in public sector jobs, including in state-owned enterprises. That is only true to some extent. On the one hand, between 16% (Chile) and 37% (Honduras) of the middle class work in the public sector and on the other hand, the rich are similarly or even more concentrated in the public sector in most countries. The exceptions are Peru and Mexico, suggesting some sort of middle-class exceptionalism (though the differences are small and may not be statistically meaningful). Not surprisingly, the poor and vulnerable mostly work in small firms while the rich are mostly employed in large firms.

Finally, there are significant differences in the percentage of people in the labor force who are enrolled in the social insurance system of their country. Slightly

Table 12.12 Employment status of workers aged 25–65 by income group, 2008/2009

	Employer	*Employee*	*Self-employed*	*Working without salary*	*Unemployed*	*Employer*	*Employee*	*Self-employed*	*Working without salary*	*Unemployed*
	Poor (<$4)					*Vulnerable ($4–$10)*				
Honduras	11.4	33.9	34.8	17.2	2.8	10.5	49.6	27.6	8.5	3.9
Dominican Republic	2.1	41.4	47.8	2.0	6.7	3.4	50.4	41.7	1.4	3.1
Peru	3.3	20.8	44.3	28.5	3.2	4.7	44.3	35.3	10.9	4.9
Mexico	4.2	50.0	25.8	11.8	8.0	3.2	71.6	15.7	4.7	4.5
Colombia	3.0	21.0	49.9	8.3	17.7	3.2	38.9	41.1	4.8	11.9
Costa Rica	5.2	47.0	24.0	2.2	21.7	4.5	66.2	18.8	1.8	8.7
Brazil	0.9	44.6	20.7	16.6	17.2	1.7	64.2	18.3	7.4	8.4
Chile	1.4	50.0	13.9	0.7	34.1	0.7	72.2	13.7	0.4	13.0
	Middle class ($10–$50)					*Rich (>$50)*				
Honduras	5.8	76.4	11.8	3.2	2.5	29.5	51.9	14.9	2.6	1.2
Dominican Republic	7.8	52.1	35.5	1.8	2.9	19.6	64.5	12.4	3.6	–
Peru	7.9	56.0	26.5	6.1	3.6	21.4	61.4	12.1	2.4	2.7
Mexico	13.0	57.2	20.4	6.3	3.0	20.6	64.7	8.8	4.0	2.0
Colombia	5.7	54.4	30.0	2.6	7.2	12.0	62.6	20.6	0.8	4.1
Costa Rica	7.6	73.5	14.4	1.1	3.4	18.4	70.9	9.0	0.6	1.1
Brazil	6.3	66.6	18.5	4.7	3.9	20.5	59.1	16.6	2.0	1.9
Chile	2.8	69.8	21.4	0.4	5.5	15.3	57.7	22.5	0.2	4.3

Note: Data for Colombia are from 2006.

Source: Socio-Economic Database for Latin America and the Caribbean (CEDLAS and the World Bank), http://sedlac.econo.unlp.edu.ar/eng/ (accessed 18 July 2012).

Table 12.13 Percentage of workers aged 25–65 in private and public sector by income group, 2008/2009

	Private firms		*Public firms*	*Private firms*		*Public firms*
	Small	*Large*		*Small*	*Large*	
	Poor (<=$4)			*Vulnerable ($4–$10)*		
Honduras	68.8	26.4	4.9	29.4	54.7	15.9
Dominican Republic	68.6	19.6	11.8	59.5	28.2	12.3
Peru	81.9	15.5	2.7	66.6	23.0	10.4
Mexico	75.7	20.9	3.5	54.6	36.1	9.4
Colombia	84.2	14.4	1.4	68.0	28.8	3.2
Costa Rica	66.0	27.9	6.1	50.6	40.0	9.4
Brazil	75.4	19.2	5.4	56.5	33.6	9.9
Chile	51.9	38.8	9.3	39.0	50.7	10.3
	Middle class ($10–$50)			*Rich (>=$50)*		
Honduras	11.6	54.3	34.2	2.2	50.1	47.7
Dominican Republic	46.8	36.8	16.4	36.4	51.5	12.1
Peru	49.7	31.9	18.4	29.2	54.8	16.0
Mexico	37.3	38.7	24.0	27.5	51.4	21.1
Colombia	45.5	41.3	13.2	28.4	49.5	22.1
Costa Rica	35.4	39.7	24.9	20.6	43.3	36.1
Brazil	43.7	37.7	18.6	34.8	35.4	29.8
Chile	36.6	47.7	15.7	29.9	49.5	20.6

Note: Data for Colombia are from 2006. SEDLAC classifies workers into three groups according to whether they work in small firms, large firms, or the public sector. Small firms are defined as those with fewer than five workers, and large firms are those with five or more workers. The public sector includes jobs in state-owned firms, public schools, hospitals and other services, and public administration.

Source: Socio-Economic Database for Latin America and the Caribbean (CEDLAS and the World Bank), http://sedlac.econo.unlp.edu.ar/eng/ (accessed 18 July 2012).

more than 80% of middle-class workers are covered in Costa Rica, Brazil, and Chile. Coverage rates are much lower in the Dominican Republic, Peru, and especially in Mexico. These differences cannot be fully explained by different mean or median incomes of middle-class households, but likely reflect differences in coverage itself. On average, middle-class households are much better covered than poor households, but less well covered than rich households.

Female labor force participation. Reported female labor force participation is relatively high across all countries and has risen in most countries over the past two decades. This is consistent with rising levels of education and urbanization, as well as with declining fertility. For the most part, women are more likely to be in the labor force the higher the income per capita of their household. Women's contributions also drive household income per capita and, in some cases, may move their household into one of the higher income categories. In middle-class households, between 60% and 70% of women are in the labor force. In most countries, labor force participation is even higher in rich households, especially in Costa Rica and Chile (the most middle-class "societies"). In a bit of exceptionalism, female labor force participation was highest in middle-class households in Peru in 2009, as well as in Mexico in all years of our sample (when income overall was not rising). This could reflect greater pressure for female workers to supplement incomes in households that might otherwise fall out of our middle class.

Household assets.[13] The $10 income threshold for entering the middle class was partly derived based on ownership of eight household assets.[14] As a result, the middle class will, by construction, own more of those assets than the poorer groups, and probably less than the richer group.

More than 50% of the poorer households own cell phones, as do three-quarters or more of middle-class households. In Peru, for which we have two survey years with information on cell phone ownership, the proportion of middle-class households owning a cell phone rose from 14% to 80% in one decade. Home ownership is similarly widespread across all countries in our sample, even among poor households.

Among middle-class households, more than 50% own a computer in Costa Rica, Brazil, and Chile. More than 50% own a car in Costa Rica and Mexico,[15] and more than 70% own a washing machine in Mexico, the Dominican Republic, and Chile. Cross-country differences probably reflect different consumer needs and ease of access to consumer credit, rather than differences in the intrinsic characteristics of middle-class households.

Summary profile: the Latin American and Caribbean middle class in 2009. In 2009, the typical middle-class household in the LAC region was in the top quintile of the household income distribution in most countries and had a median per capita income between $15 and $17 per day (between $22,000 and $24,800 per year for a family of four). Middle-class households were "rich" relative to the great majority of the population. The median per capita income of the total population was between $4 and $10 per day.

Adults in middle-class households had at least some secondary education and worked in urban, organized sectors of the economy. Virtually all children of middle-class households aged 6–12 and about three-quarters of children aged 13–18 were in school, and large percentages attended private school.

The great majority of middle-class workers were employees with a regular salary. Relatively few are employers of other workers. Female labor force participation is high in all income groups, but particularly so in middle-class (and rich) households, in which 66% of women work.

---

[13] For a more detailed analysis, see Birdsall (2012).

[14] The assets included were fixed phone line, cell phone, cable TV, washing machine, car, motorcycle, Internet, computer, and education.

[15] Dadush and Ali (2012) suggest that ownership of a car is a good proxy for middle-class status in developing countries. In our data, using our income thresholds, 18% of poor households and 24% of vulnerable households owned a car in Costa Rica (2009), while 9% of poor households and 22% of vulnerable households owned a car in Mexico (2008).

In most countries, 20% of working middle-class adults were employed in education, health, or other public services – more than their poorer but less than their richer counterparts. About 15% worked in the public sector itself, a relatively high percentage compared with workers in poorer households. Still, the middle class generally does not rely particularly heavily on the public sector, at least not in terms of employment. Across the region, a much higher percentage of rich workers was employed in the public sector.

In all countries for which we have data, very large shares of the middle-class population owned a house and a cell phone. The same is true for sizable shares of poorer households. Middle-class households were much more likely than poorer households to own a washing machine, a car, and a computer.

Middle-class households in Latin America and the Caribbean: a few exceptions to exceptionalism

With only a few exceptions, the characteristics of middle-class households compare with their poorer and richer counterparts along the lines you would expect. The two most notable exceptions are in the area of employment.

First, the richer a household, the more likely it is on average that its workers enjoy the benefits of being "employees" with a regular salary or wage. In Brazil, Chile, Costa Rica, and Honduras, however, a worker in a middle-class household is more, rather than less, likely to be an employee than a worker in a rich household. Brazil, Chile, and Costa Rica rank high among the eight countries on measures of middle-class "society."

Second, women in middle-class households are more likely to participate in the labor force. This appears to reflect greater demand for higher income (the income effect) rather than a greater wage that women in higher-income households command (the price effect) because the exceptional pattern prevails in lower-income countries and prevailed in Mexico during the 1990s, following the financial crisis there.

The Latin American and Caribbean middle class: more like the poorer or more like the richer?

Middle-class households are, in general, more different from the small group of rich households than from the households in the vulnerable group. Their income is much closer to the poorer groups than to the richer group. They are much less likely to be employers than the rich. They have some secondary education, which distinguishes them from adults in poorer households in most countries. Except for Chile and Peru, adults in poorer households have too few years of schooling to have entered secondary school. The gap between their incomplete secondary schooling and the schooling of adults in rich households, who in most countries would have completed some post-secondary schooling or even received university-level training, is far greater. This difference matters: until the last decade, the wage return to university training has far exceeded the wage return to secondary school in Latin America. Most adults in the middle class did not attend university, but most adults among the rich did.

The middle class is far more likely to take advantage of the possibility of private schooling for their children than poorer households. Even so, the gap between private school enrollment of children in middle-class households and children in rich households is significant.

Is there commonality across Latin America and the Caribbean countries in the middle-class profile?

Yes, middle-class households share their profiles across countries. Median income per capita of the middle class varies by just about $2 across countries (Table 12.5). Median years of schooling is 11 or 12 years in all countries, and secondary school enrollment rates of children in middle-class households are universally high.

Differences across countries in private school enrollment of middle-class children do range widely; they appear to be a function of country differences in the quality of public schools. Enrollment in private schools at the primary level is lowest in Chile and Costa Rica.

Is the middle class different today than two decades ago?

With one exception, the answer to that question is no. Using our identification tied to real income thresholds, it should not be surprising that for the most part, a middle-class household in low-income Honduras in 1992 looks strikingly similar to a middle-class household in higher-income Chile in 2009 (Table 12.5). The latter household is just about 11% richer at the median. Over this period, median income per capita increased by 2.2% in Honduras and by 4.3% in Chile. With a median of 12 years, Chilean middle-class adults in 2009 received no more schooling than Honduran middle-class adults in 1992. In Honduras, the median years of schooling actually fell from 12 to 11 years between 1992 and 2009, presumably as the middle class grew because people entered from below (Table 12.7).

The increase in median income of the middle class suggests a slight shift to the right in the within-group distribution. Among the rich, mean income rose in most countries while median income fell. That implies a much stronger shift to the right and the likely appearance of more "super-rich" households in the right tail of the income distribution. The exception to the constancy of characteristics over time is that middle-class households were smaller and had fewer children in 2009 than in the 1990s. The size of middle-class households has fallen from 3.3 to 2.9 people, while the mean number of children has fallen from 0.94 to 0.59 (Table 12.6).

In our pooled sample of middle-class households, years of schooling rose by almost one year or almost 10%. Private school enrollment rose by 25% and the average age of adults by almost 10%. Mean household size fell by 0.4 members (the median remained constant at 3), and the mean number of children fell by more than 30%.

These trends, however, mostly reflect major demographic shifts that were shared across all income groups, rather than anything peculiar or particular about the middle class.

The important change at the country and regional level was not in the characteristics of the middle class, but the significant increase in the population size and the economic command of the middle class in every country. Most notably, the smaller increase in the middle-class income share compared with its population share reflects the growth of the group from the bottom.

Concluding reflections

This chapter is modest in intentions. The objective is to exploit household data to describe the middle class in LAC as well as changes in its size and characteristics over the past two decades. Analyzing the causes of the increase in the size and economic command of the middle class, including the link to social mobility and its causes across countries and over time, and assessing the likely consequences of that increase, would be a more ambitious exercise.

If the story is one of a virtuous circle (and that in itself is a hypothesis) in which a growing middle class supports economic policies and practices that ensure a growing middle class,[16] it is hard to discern causes and consequences.

Still, what this chapter demonstrates is a cause for optimism about the economic and democratic prospects in Latin America and the Caribbean. First, it is encouraging that whatever is captured in self-responses about being "middle class" seems to accord reasonably well with the objective criterion of relative invulnerability to falling into poverty.

Second, it is encouraging that across time and countries, people in households with per capita income between \$10 and \$50 share such key characteristics as education and work status. This suggests that it is reasonable to have a construct called the Latin American middle class – with potential spillovers across countries in policy norms. A secure middle class is likely to both object to corruption in government as well as be more effective in fighting it. Perhaps the exposure of high-level corruption in Brazil will reinforce intolerance for such corruption in Peru and Bolivia.

Third, that the middle class is not exceptional in its characteristics after controlling for their income[17] is another cause for optimism. It suggests, as Kenny (2011) recently argued, that the poor are no different from you and me. Most of the world's poor are poor not because they are deficient in ambition or enterprise, but because they lack the assets that provide a middle-class income. A larger middle class suggests some positive trends at the societal level; more people have one or several of those assets that are sufficient to insure reasonable economic security.

---

[16] As well as the strengthening of inclusive political and economic institutions, rules, and norms (Acemoglu and Robinson 2012).

[17] Or, as other studies show, in the values they hold or in their views about such economic policies as taxes and the role of the market (López-Calva *et al.* 2012).

Moreover, the fact that the middle class is not exceptional after controlling for current income vindicates this measure as a reasonably sensible proxy for education, permanent income, occupation, or whatever other characteristics analysts might prefer to identify the middle class – at least in the case of Latin America. An income level that is sufficient to be part of the middle class does not guarantee happiness, but it does go along with characteristics and capabilities that are associated with well-being and, in the wider sense, agency and human freedom (Sen 1999).

Fourth, the finding that the middle class is not exceptional in behavior or values does not imply that societies are not somehow different when the middle class represents a larger share of population and income. The measures of middle-class "society" discussed earlier indicate that Chile, Brazil, and Costa Rica are the most middle-class countries in our sample of eight LAC countries. This can largely, but not entirely, be explained by their higher average income.

The countries' income distributions also matter, at least in a statistical sense (Table 12.2). Costa Rica has a lower average income than Brazil, but a larger middle-class population share with a larger command of total income.

It does not follow ineluctably that lower income inequality implies a larger middle class because the middle class in the LAC region is not in the middle of the overall distribution, but is heavily concentrated in the top three deciles. Relatively speaking, the middle class is in fact "rich" in these countries. Will Latin America's "rich" middle class align itself politically with their richer counterparts or the much larger poor and vulnerable populations? There is indirect evidence that this well-off middle class is open to redistribution. Birdsall *et al.* (2011) find that in countries with center-left as opposed to populist governments, changes in social policies have benefited the bottom four quintiles more than the top quintiles in which the middle class is concentrated (see Figures 8 and 9 in Birdsall *et al.* (2011) as well as Lustig (2011)). Brazil and Chile had such center-left governments throughout most of the 2000s.

There is a fifth possible reason for optimism. Perhaps a growing middle class, with its growing political influence, supports political regimes that promise a combination of sound macroeconomic policy with a heavy emphasis on social programs that reach the majority of the population. A growing middle class perhaps even supports such policies if their own group does not directly benefit through public expenditures. This would suggest that the middle class in Latin America sees its future aligned with governments that deliver a combination of property rights protection, stability, and greater overall access to public goods. The middle class would then be a consequence of good economic policy and, in a virtuous circle, a supporter of such policy.

It is often surmised that a politically powerful middle class will discourage policies that help the poor. There is no obvious evidence that this has been the case in Latin America over the past decade. Though the LAC middle class is rich in relative terms, the profiles earlier show that in absolute income and other characteristics, it is closer to the large group of poor and vulnerable households than to the rich. This is true with respect to income itself and with respect to education once the high returns to university education – the norm only among the rich – are taken into account.

Latin America and the Caribbean is becoming a middle-class region. The middle class has grown: from about 17% to about 30% of the population, and from about 40% to about 50% of the income share. Is that only or mostly because of growth in a period of global economic expansion? Will the middle class continue to grow as overall growth rates slow? Will it grow more in countries with one set of economic policies than another? And what have been and will be the consequences? The analysis in this chapter does not address these questions of cause and consequence. But it does provide a basis for optimism. Optimism that at least in some countries of the region, the middle class is large enough to make those countries middle-class "societies," and that more middle-class societies are at least consistent with and might reinforce the inclusive politics that sustain broadly shared growth.

Acknowledgments

I am grateful to Owen McCarthy for patience in compiling the data, and for good replication of the contribution of Gonzalo Llorente, an incredible research assistant at the World Bank who lost his life in late 2011. Christian J. Meyer provided tremendous help in updating the data and in final revisions of the chapter. For thoughtful comments on an early draft, I am grateful to Hyun H. Son of the Asian Development Bank and to the LAC team at the World Bank, especially Jamele Rigolini and Francisco Ferreira whose ideas on identifying and describing the middle class are reflected here. A longer version of this chapter, published as Center for Global Development Working Paper 303, provided background for their 2012 report on mobility and the middle class in Latin America and the Caribbean (Ferreira *et al.* 2013); and background in suggesting the kind of data and analysis that could be useful for a report on inclusive growth and the middle class in Asia of the Asian Development Bank.

References

Acemoglu, D., and J. Robinson. 2012. *Why Nations Fail: The Origins of Power, Prosperity, and Poverty*. New York, NY: Crown Business.

Asian Development Bank. 2010. *Key Indicators for Asia and the Pacific 2010: The Rise of Asia's Middle Class*. Manila.

Banerjee, A., and E. Duflo. 2008. What Is Middle Class about the Middle Class around the World? *Journal of Economic Perspectives*. 22 (2). pp. 3–28.

Behrman, J. R., and N. Birdsall. 1983. The Quality of Schooling: Quantity Alone Is Misleading. *American Economic Review*. 73 (5). pp. 928–46.

Birdsall, N. 2010. The (Indispensable) Middle Class: Or, Why It's the Rich and the Rest, Not the Poor and the Rest. *Working Paper* 207. Washington, DC: Center for Global Development.

——. 2012. A Note on the Middle Class in Latin America. *Working Paper* 303. Washington, DC: Center for Global Development.

Birdsall, N., C. Graham, and S. Pettinato. 2000. Stuck in the Tunnel: Is Globalization Muddling the Middle? *Working Paper* 14. Washington, DC: Brookings Institution.

Birdsall, N., N. Lustig, and D. McLeod. 2011. Declining Inequality in Latin America: Some Economics, Some Politics. *Working Paper* 251. Washington, DC: Center for Global Development.

Birdsall, N., and A. Sumner. 2011. Who are Africa's Middle Class? And Will They Help to Reduce Poverty? *The Guardian* Poverty Matters Blog. http://www.guardian.co.uk/global-development/poverty-matters/2011/may/06/africans-middle-class-poverty-reduction (accessed 19 July 2013).

Cardenas, M., H. Kharas, and C. Henao. 2011. *Latin America's Global Middle Class. Research Paper*. Washington, DC: Brookings Institution.

CEDLAS (Universidad Nacional de La Plata) and the World Bank. Socio-Economic Database for Latin America and the Caribbean (SEDLAC). http://sedlac.econo.unlp.edu.ar/eng/

Dadush, U., and S. Ali. 2012. *In Search of the Global Middle Class: A New Index*. The Carnegie Papers. International Economics. July. Washington, DC: Carnegie Endowment for International Peace.

Easterly, W. 2001. The Middle Class Consensus and Economic Development. *Journal of Economic Growth*. 6 (4). pp. 317–35.

Ferreira, F. H. G., J. Messina, J. Rigolini, L.-F. López-Calva, M. A. Lugo, and R. Vakis, 2013. *Economic Mobility and the Rise of the Middle Class*. Washington, DC: World Bank.

Filmer, D., A. Hasan, and L. Pritchett. 2006. A Millennium Learning Goal: Measuring Real Progress in Education. *Working Paper* 97. Washington, DC: Center for Global Development.

Kenny, C. 2011. The Myth of the Middle Class. Foreign Policy. Website Article. http://www.foreignpolicy.com/articles/2011/09/19/the_myth_of_the_middle_class (accessed 20 June 2012).

Lawson, S., and D. B. Gilman. 2009. *The Power of the Purse: Gender Equality and Middle-Class Spending*. Goldman Sachs Global Markets Institute Report. 5 August. Goldman Sachs Global Investment Research.

López-Calva, L. F., and N. Lustig, eds. 2010. *Declining Inequality in Latin America: A Decade of Progress?* Washington, DC: The Brookings Institution Press.

López-Calva, L. F., and E. Ortiz-Juarez. 2011. A Vulnerability Approach to the Definition of the Middle Class. *Policy Research Working Paper* 5902. Washington, DC: The World Bank.

López-Calva, L. F., J. Rigolini, and F. Torche. 2012. Is There Such a Thing as Middle Class Values? *Working Paper* 286. Washington, DC: Center for Global Development.

Lustig, N. (coordinator). 2011. Fiscal Policy, "Fiscal Mobility," the Poor, the Vulnerable and the Middle Class in Latin America. Draft: Commitment to Equity Initiative. Tulane University and Inter-American Dialogue.

Milanovic, B. 2010. *The Haves and the Have-Notes: A Brief and Idiosyncratic History of Global Inequality*. New York, NY: Basic Books.

Ncube, M., C. L. Lufumpa, and S. Kayizzi-Mugerwa. 2011. *The Middle of the Pyramid: Dynamics of the Middle Class in Africa*. Market Brief. 20 April. Abidjan: Chief Economist Complex, African Development Bank.

Pritchett, L. Forthcoming. *The Rebirth of Education: Schooling Ain't Learning*. Washington, DC: Center for Global Development.

Pritchett, L., A. Suryahadi, and S. Sumarto. 2000. Quantifying Vulnerability to Poverty – A Proposed Measure, Applied to Indonesia. *Policy Research Working Paper* 2437. Washington, DC: The World Bank.

Ravallion, M. 2010. The Developing World's Bulging (But Vulnerable) Middle Class. *World Development*. 38 (4). pp. 445–54.

Sen, A. 1999. *Development as Freedom*. New York, NY: Random House.

Skirbekk, V. 2003. Age and Individual Productivity: A Literature Survey. *MPIDR Working Paper* 2003-028. Rostock: Max-Planck Institute for Demographic Research.

Sumner, A. 2012. The Buoyant Billions: How "Middle Class" Are the New Middle Classes? (And Why Does It Matter?). *CGD Working Paper* 309. Washington, DC: Center for Global Development.

Székely, M., and M. Hilgert. 2000. What Drives Differences in Inequality across Countries? *Latin America Research Network Working Paper* 439. Washington, DC: Inter-American Development Bank.

United States Census Bureau. 2011. Current Population Survey. Table 1. 2011 Annual Social and Economic Supplement. http://www.census.gov/hhes/socdemo/education/data/cps/2012/tables.html (accessed 18 July 2013).

World Bank. PovcalNet: The On-line Tool for Poverty Measurement Developed by the Development Research Group of the World Bank. http://iresearch.worldbank.org/PovcalNet/index.htm

13 Urbanization and inequality in Asia

Ravi Kanbur and Juzhong Zhuang

Introduction

This chapter is motivated by three stylized facts for Asia over the past two decades. First, inequality has risen significantly relative to historical trends. As highlighted by the Asian Development Bank (ADB 2012a), more than 80% of Asia's population now lives in countries where inequality has risen in the past 20 years. Second, rural–urban income gaps in Asia are significant, reflecting the dominance of, but also a changing, dual economic structure in a large part of the region. For example, the rural–urban divide accounts for close to 20% of the economy-wide inequality in Indonesia and the Philippines, 25% in Bhutan, India, and Viet Nam, and 45% in the People's Republic of China (PRC), and this divide has increased sizably in some countries. Third, urbanization has proceeded apace. Asia's share of urban population has increased from 40% to 46.2% in the past two decades (ADB 2012b). In the PRC, the share of its urban population increased from 27% in 1990 to 52% in 2012 (World Bank 2012).

The evolution of inequality at the economy-wide or national level is a complex phenomenon, impacted by history, culture, technology, demography, and policy. It is not our intention in this chapter to provide a comprehensive explanation of inequality trends in Asia. Instead, the purpose of this chapter is narrower and more focused. Given the three stylized facts and using data for four Asian countries – the PRC, India, Indonesia, and the Philippines – we look at how the changing dual economic structure in Asia and particularly urbanization have impacted the evolution of national inequality in the past and how the former might impact the latter in the future.

Urbanization features strongly in the classic analysis of inequality and development by Kuznets. In his seminal paper, Kuznets (1955) identified a number of forces that together may lead to the well-known inverted U-shaped Kuznets curve – as a country develops, inequality increases initially and declines after a certain average income level is attained. These forces include the concentration of savings among rich households, which tend to increase inequality as a country moves to higher income levels, and political pressures for income redistribution, demographic changes, the emergence of new industries, rising importance of services sector incomes (that rely more on individual excellence), and urbanization, all of which, according to Kuznets (1955), tend to help reduce inequality as a country becomes more and more developed. The Kuznets hypothesis has been tested empirically by many, although results have not been uniformly supportive (Anand and Kanbur 1993a, b; Fields 2001; Kanbur 2012).

To illustrate how urbanization affects inequality at the national level, Kuznets (1955) used numerical examples and showed that, holding within-rural and within-urban income distributions and the urban–rural income ratio constant, the mere population shift from the lower-income and lower-inequality rural sector to the higher-income and higher-inequality urban sector could lead to an inverted-U curve – inequality first increases, reaches a turning point, and then declines. The bulk of the analysis in his paper follows this framework. In reality, however, it is not realistic to assume that rural and urban inequalities and the urban–rural income ratio would stay constant when urbanization takes place because many other forces, highlighted earlier, are at work to shape income distribution. Nevertheless, it is useful to see how urbanization alone has influenced the dynamics of income distribution in the four countries and what it implies for their inequality in the coming years as urbanization proceeds.

The chapter has three specific objectives. Using Theil's second measure of income inequality, a change in national inequality over a certain period of time can be decomposed into changes in inequality within the rural sector, in inequality within the urban sector, in the gap in mean incomes between the two sectors, and in the population share of the urban sector – a measure of urbanization. The first objective of this chapter is to estimate how much of the observed changes in inequality in the four Asian countries over the past two decades can be attributed to changes in the above four components or drivers.

The second objective is to provide a more in-depth analysis of the relationship between urbanization and national inequality. We follow Kuznets' numerical examples and look at how urbanization alone has affected national inequality of the four countries, how the former may affect the latter in the coming years, and, in particular, whether these countries have passed the turning point, as numerically illustrated in Kuznets' classic paper.

The third objective is to estimate the impact of a marginal change in each of the four components on national inequality. This information is useful because it gives guidance to policy makers on where to focus interventions to mitigate the rise in national inequality in the future. This is particularly important given that Asian policy makers have identified rising inequality as one of the major policy challenges of the coming decades and urbanization as a key policy instrument to meet the challenge (Hu 2012).

Inequality index, data, and basic trends

Inequality index

Let income be denoted by y and let the two sectors – urban and rural – in the economy have income distributions with densities $f_1(y)$ and $f_2(y)$, respectively. The population share of sector 1 (urban) is x; the share of sector 2 (rural) is thus

$1 - x$. With this specification, the economy-wide or national income distribution is simply

$$f(y) = xf_1(y) + (1 - x)f_2(y) \tag{13.1}$$

National income distribution is thus a function of f_1, f_2, and x. A change in national inequality is the result of changes in urban income distribution f_1, rural income distribution f_2, and/or a shift of population from rural to urban, measured by a change in x.

This chapter focuses on the case where inequality is given by Theil's second measure, that is, the *GE(0)* measure from the generalized entropy family. Let the mean of f_1, urban mean income, be m_1 and the mean of f_2, rural mean income, be m_2, with $k = m_1/m_2$ as the ratio of the two means. National inequality is denoted by L, with L_1 and L_2 being urban and rural inequality, respectively.

Using Theil's second measure, it can be shown that national inequality L can be decomposed into a within-group component and a between-group component, i.e.,

$$L = L(x, k, L_1, L_2) = L_W + L_B$$

or

$$L = xL_1 + (1 - x)L_2 + \log[xk + (1 - x)] - [x\log(k)]. \tag{13.2}$$

In equation (13.2), L_W is the within-group component of national inequality, which is simply a population-weighted sum of urban and rural inequalities. L_B is the between-group component of national inequality – the inequality that would be present if everybody in the urban sector had the mean income of that sector, m_1, and everybody in the rural sector had the mean income of that sector, m_2. This between-group component of national inequality depends only on the ratio of urban and rural mean incomes, k, and the share of urban population, x. As shown by equation (13.2), L is an additively decomposable inequality measure.

Equation (13.2) contains the entire analytical structure that we will need for our empirical analysis. Using the equations, we will be able to trace national inequality as a function of the share of urban population x, urban–rural income ratio k, urban inequality L_1, and rural inequality L_2. Before moving to specific applications, however, we turn now to a brief account of the data and of the four countries that form the focus of this chapter.

Data

The four Asian countries included in this chapter are the PRC, India, Indonesia, and the Philippines. This chapter uses data from two sources. For India, Indonesia, and the Philippines, unit-level household survey data are used, while for the PRC, data are sourced from the World Bank's PovcalNet because the unit-level

Table 13.1 Key variables, early 1990s and late 2000s

Country	*Early 1990s*				*Late 2000s*			
	x	k	L_1	L_2	x	k	L_1	L_2
PRC	0.27	1.74	0.108	0.161	0.43	2.37	0.208	0.259
India	0.23	1.74	0.219	0.149	0.26	2.02	0.239	0.161
Indonesia	0.35	1.78	0.193	0.118	0.57	1.77	0.228	0.122
Philippines	0.39	2.07	0.338	0.211	0.55	2.04	0.300	0.233

k = urban–rural income ratio; L_1 = urban inequality; L_2 = rural inequality; PRC = People's Republic of China; x = share of urban population.

Note: Early 1990s data = 1990 for the PRC and Indonesia, 1991 for the Philippines, and 1993 for India; late 2000s data = 2008 for the PRC and India, 2010 for Indonesia, and 2009 for the Philippines.

Sources: Unit-level household survey data and PovcalNet, http://iresearch.worldbank.org/PovcalNet/index.htm (accessed 14 May 2012).

household survey data are not available. It is important to note that, for the four countries, estimated means and inequalities in this chapter are all based on per capita household consumption expenditure. As is known, for a given country, inequality estimated from per capita household consumption expenditure is normally lower than that estimated from per capita household income (ADB 2012a).

Table 13.1 gives the values of the four key variables, x, k, L_1, and L_2, for the early 1990s and late 2000s. For India, Indonesia, and the Philippines, in both instances, k was greater than 1, meaning urban mean income was higher than rural mean income, and urban inequality L_1 was higher than rural inequality L_2, consistent with the assumptions of Kuznets' numerical examples in his 1955 paper. However, in the case of the PRC, while urban mean income was higher than rural mean income, urban inequality was lower than rural inequality – not consistent with one of Kuznets' assumptions. For all the four countries, the share of urban population increased between the early 1990s and late 2000s, and the increase was very significant for the PRC, Indonesia, and the Philippines. In comparison, the pace of urbanization was much slower in India, where the share of urban population increased only by 3 percentage points in about 15 years.

In the PRC and India, the pace of growth was faster for urban mean income than for rural mean income, leading to a significant widening in the urban–rural income gap between the early 1990s and late 2000s: the ratio of urban mean income to rural mean income, k, increased from 1.74 to 2.37 in the PRC and from 1.74 to 2.02 in India. In Indonesia and the Philippines, however, k remained more or less unchanged in the past two decades, at about 1.78 in Indonesia and 2.07 in the Philippines.

In the PRC, India, and Indonesia, both urban and rural inequalities increased in the past two decades, and the increases were particularly pronounced in the PRC. For these countries, urban inequality grew faster than rural inequality, especially for the PRC. Since the PRC's urban inequality was lower than rural inequality in

Table 13.2 National inequality of per capita consumption expenditure

Country	*Gini coefficient*		*Theil index [GE(0)]*	
	Early 1990s	*Late 2000s*	*Early 1990s*	*Late 2000s*
PRC	32.4	43.4	0.179	0.329
India	32.5	37.0	0.194	0.233
Indonesia	29.2	38.9	0.183	0.221
Philippines	43.8	43.0	0.326	0.330

PRC = People's Republic of China.

Sources: Authors' estimates using unit-level household survey data and PovcalNet, http://iresearch.worldbank.org/PovcalNet/index.htm (accessed 14 May 2012).

the early 1990s, a larger increase in urban inequality implies its difference from rural inequality has declined relatively. For India and Indonesia, however, this suggests a widening in the difference between urban and rural inequalities. In the case of the Philippines, while rural inequality grew, urban inequality actually declined.

Table 13.2 shows the values of national inequality, measured in both the second measure of the Theil index [*GE(0)*] and the Gini coefficient. The PRC's Gini coefficient increased from 32.4 in 1990 to 43.4 in 2008;[1] India's Gini coefficient worsened from 32.5 in 1993 to 37.0 in 2010, and Indonesia's Gini rose from 29.2 in 1990 to 38.9 in 2011. On the other hand, inequality changed little in the Philippines, with the Gini falling from 43.8 to 43.0, but the Theil index [(*GE(0)*] increasing from 0.326 to 0.330 during 1991–2009.

A recent study by ADB (2012a) highlighted three fundamental drivers of rising inequality in Asia: technological change, globalization, and market-oriented reform. It is noted that these forces have opened enormous new opportunities for Asian economies to prosper, but have not benefited all Asian people equally. More specifically, these forces have affected income distributions through three channels: rising skill premiums, falling labor's share of total income, and increasing spatial inequality. Moreover, their impacts have been further compounded by unequal access to opportunity due to weaknesses in governance and social exclusion (ADB 2012a).

Accounting for changes in national inequality

As shown in the previous section, national inequality L in Asia has changed significantly over the past two decades, and so have its constituent components x, k,

[1] Some studies have reported much higher Gini coefficients for the PRC (see, e.g., *The Economist*, 15 December 2012). One of the major reasons for the difference is that in this chapter, the Gini coefficient is estimated from per capita household consumption expenditure, while those in other studies, which are found to be much higher, are estimated from per capita household income. According to ADB (2012a), the difference between the two measures can be as high as 10 when the Gini coefficient is measured such that it ranges from 0 to 100.

Table 13.3 Estimated coefficients

Country	*Year*	A_x	A_k	A_{L1}	A_{L2}
PRC	Base-year	0.009	0.070	0.274	0.726
	End-year	−0.053	0.089	0.431	0.569
India	Base-year	0.150	0.064	0.227	0.773
	End-year	0.182	0.077	0.260	0.741
Indonesia	Base-year	0.113	0.078	0.345	0.655
	End-year	0.069	0.074	0.574	0.426
Philippines	Base-year	0.151	0.087	0.394	0.606
	End-year	0.016	0.080	0.549	0.451

A_k = coefficient of urban–rural income ratio; A_{L1} = coefficient of urban inequality; A_{L2} = coefficient of rural inequality; A_x = coefficient of share of urban population; PRC = People's Republic of China.

Source: Authors' estimates.

L_1, and L_2. How have changes in these components contributed to the changes in national inequality? This section will develop a sense of the quantitative contribution of each of these forces to the actual changes in national inequality between the early 1990s and late 2000s for the four countries under study.

Using equation (13.2), we can write the change in national inequality as

$$dL = A_x dx + A_k dk + A_{L1} dL_1 + A_{L2} dL_2 \tag{13.3}$$

where

$$A_x = (L_1 - L_2) + [(k-1)/(x(k-1)+1)] - \log(k) \tag{13.4a}$$

$$A_k = x/(1 - x + xk) - x/k \tag{13.4b}$$

$$A_{L1} = x \tag{13.4c}$$

$$A_{L2} = (1 - x) \tag{13.4d}$$

The four coefficients, A_x, A_k, A_{L1},and A_{L2}, can all be calculated from the actual data. Notably, their numerical values will be different depending on whether the base-year or end-year data are used, as shown in Table 13.3.

In the following accounting exercise, we use the average of the two numerical values for each coefficient: one estimated from the base-year data and the other from the end-year data.[2] Multiplying the change in each of the four variables (x, k, L_1, and L_2) between the early 1990s and late 2000s by its respective coefficient

[2] Although the numerical values of the coefficients estimated from the early 1990s data differ from those estimated from the late 2000s data, the difference does not alter the conclusions of this section. The results estimated from base-year data and end-year data, separately, are available from the authors upon request.

Table 13.4 Accounting for changes in national inequality, early 1990s and late 2000s

Country	*Change in national inequality [GE(0)] between the 1990s and 2000s*	*Contribution (% share)*				*Residual*
		x	k	L_1	L_2	
PRC	0.149 (100)	−0.003 (−2.3)	0.05 (33.4)	0.035 (23.5)	0.064 (42.6)	0.004 (2.9)
India	0.039 (100)	0.005 (13.7)	0.02 (50.0)	0.005 (12.6)	0.009 (23.3)	0.00 (0.4)
Indonesia	0.039 (100)	0.021 (54.0)	−0.001 (−1.7)	0.016 (42.3)	0.003 (6.6)	0.00 (−1.1)
Philippines	0.004 (100)	0.013 (308.1)	−0.002 (−54.9)	−0.018 (−419.8)	0.012 (247.3)	−0.00 (−7.6)

k = urban–rural income ratio; L_1 = urban inequality; L_2 = rural inequality; PRC = People's Republic of China; x = share of urban population.

Note: Figures in parentheses are percentage shares.

Source: Authors' estimates.

gives an estimate of the contribution of that variable to the change in national inequality for each country. The contributions will not add up to the actual change because of nonlinearity and interaction effects and there will be a residual term. Table 13.4 reports absolute and percentage contributions to the change in national inequality by each of the four variables, as well as the residual term for the four countries.

Table 13.4 shows that, for all the four countries, changes in the four components between the early 1990s and late 2000s can explain almost all of the observed change in the national inequality. However, the relative importance of each of the four components differs from country to country:

(i) In India, half of the total observed change in national inequality was accounted for by the widening urban–rural income gap, about 23% by rising rural inequality, and about 13% each by an increase in the urban population share and urban inequality.

(ii) In the PRC, 43% of the total observed increase in the national inequality can be explained by rising rural inequality, 33% by widening in the urban–rural income gap, and 24% by rising urban inequality, while the impact of urbanization as measured by rising urban population share is negligible – in fact, it helps reduce inequality, with the resulting reduction amounting to about 2% of the total observed increase in national inequality.

(iii) In Indonesia, the most important driver of the observed increase in national inequality was urbanization explaining 54% and rising urban inequality explaining 42%, while rising rural inequality explained 6% and the impact of the urban–rural income gap was negligible.

(iv) In the Philippines, there was a small increase in national inequality. Falling urban inequality and a narrowing in the urban–rural income gap helped reduce national inequality, with the resulting reduction amounting to 420% and 54% of the observed increase in national inequality, respectively. On the other hand, urbanization and rising rural inequality increased national inequality, with the resulting increase amounting to 308% and 247% of the observed increase in national inequality, respectively.

These results suggest that rising inequalities in the four countries have different driving forces. Urbanization played a major role in driving up national inequality in Indonesia and the Philippines, mainly because of a large increase in the share of the urban population during the past two decades, higher urban inequality relative to rural inequality, and the fact that the two countries have not passed the turning point, as illustrated in Kuznets' numerical examples (see further discussion in the next section). Urbanization has also contributed to rising inequality in India, but it is not a major driver because the increase in the share of India's urban population in the past two decades has been rather modest. For the PRC, urbanization has actually helped reduce national inequality despite the large increase in the share of urban population. This is partly due to its lower urban inequality relative to rural inequality.

The widening urban–rural income gap was a major contributor to rising national inequality in both India and the PRC. It was the most important for India and second most important for the PRC. For Indonesia and the Philippines, the urban–rural income gap actually narrowed slightly, and hence helped reduce national inequality.

Neither the increase in urban inequality nor that in rural inequality was the most important contributor to rising national inequality among the four countries, with the exception of the PRC, where the increase in rural inequality was the most important contributor to rising national inequality in the past two decades. This finding is in contrast to what has been widely believed: the widening urban–rural income gap and rising urban inequality are the two most important drivers of rising inequality in the PRC in the past two decades (Lin *et al.* 2008).

Urbanization and the turning point

As noted in the introduction, Kuznets (1955) put the process of urbanization at the heart of his analysis of inequality change and he used a particular model to describe how inequality changes with the process of urbanization and to derive an inverted-U relationship between the two. The argument was made with the aid of numerical examples:

> The basic assumptions used throughout are that the per capita income of sector B (nonagricultural) is always higher than that of sector A; that the proportion of sector A in the total number[3] declines; and that the inequality of

[3] This refers to population.

> the income distribution within sector A may be as wide as that within sector B but not wider. With the assumptions concerning three sets of factors – intersector differences in per capita income, intrasector distributions, and sector weights – varying within the limitations just indicated, the following conclusions are suggested: ... [I]f the differential in per capita income between the two sectors remains constant and the intrasector distributions are identical for the two sectors, the mere shift in the proportions of numbers produces slight but significant changes in the distribution for the country as a whole. In general, as the proportion of A drifts from 0.8 downwards, the range tends first to widen and then to diminish.
>
> (Kuznets 1955, pp. 12–13)

It is important to note that urbanization is only one of the forces that underlie the well-known Kuznets curve, and other important forces identified by Kuznets include the concentration of savings among rich households; political pressures for income redistribution through, for example, tax policy; demographic changes; the emergence of new industries; and rising importance of services sector incomes that rely more on individual excellences rather than accumulated wealth.[4] Nevertheless, given that the mere population shift from the rural to urban sector may lead to an inverted-U curve after holding urban and rural inequalities and the urban–rural income gap constant, it is interesting to apply this model to the four sample countries to examine how urbanization may affect these countries' inequalities in the coming years and, in particular, to look at where the turning points as illustrated in Kuznets' numerical examples are.

The basic question posed by Kuznets through his simple numerical model was: what happens to national inequality as urbanization proceeds and the share of urban population goes from 0% to 100%? This can be answered by using the *GE(0)* measure of inequality. Differentiating equation (13.2) with respect to the share of urban population x gives

$$dL/dx = (L_1 - L_2) + [(k-1)/(x(k-1)+1)] - \log(k) \tag{13.5}$$

We assume that $k > 1$, so that sector 1 is the sector with the higher mean income. With this specification we come close to the natural specification, with sector 1 being the urban sector and x increasing with development. The mathematical expression for the turning point x^* can be obtained by setting $dL/dx = 0$, and is given by

$$x^* = 1/[\log(k) - (L_1 - L_2)] - 1/(k-1) \tag{13.6}$$

[4] Following on from Kuznets (1955), the complex nature of national inequality evolution and the key role for policy have been emphasized in the subsequent literature. See, for example, Piketty (2006) and Kanbur (2012).

Table 13.5 Predicted turning points

Country	*Share of urban population (%)*		*Predicted turning point using base-year data (%)*	*Predicted turning point using end-year data (%)*
	Base-year	*End-year*		
PRC	27	43	29.7	36.4
India	23	26	71.4	62.0
Indonesia	35	57	71.1	84.9
Philippines	39	55	73.0	58.7

PRC = People's Republic of China.

Source: Authors' estimates.

As shown in Anand and Kanbur (1993a), the turning point will be between 0 and 1 when

$$L_1 - L_2 < 1/k - 1 + \log(k) \tag{13.7}$$

Substituting the values of k, L_1, and L_2 in equation (13.6) would give us the predicted turning point following Kuznets' simulation. We used both base-year and end-year data to estimate turning points, as reported in Table 13.5. Understandably, turning points differ depending on which year's data are used. Some interesting observations emerge.

For India, Indonesia, and the Philippines, both base-year and end-year urban population shares are smaller than the predicted turning points, whether using base-year or end-year data. This suggests that national inequalities of these countries have not reached their turning points. For India and Indonesia, given that end-year urban population shares are still much smaller than the predicted turning points using the end-year data, the two countries still have many years to go before national inequality peaks even if urban and rural inequalities and the urban–rural income gap stay constant. For the Philippines, however, the end-year urban population share is very close to the predicted turning point using end-year data.

The picture for the PRC is different. The PRC's predicted turning point using base-year data lies between base-year and end-year urban population shares, suggesting that national inequality would have peaked if urban and rural inequalities and the urban–rural income gap stayed constant between the base-year and end-years. Moreover, the PRC's end-year urban population share is greater than the predicted turning point using end-year data, suggesting that its national equality has passed the turning point if urban and rural inequalities and the urban–rural income gap remain constant.

In reality, however, the assumptions of urban and rural inequalities and the urban–rural income gap staying constant are unlikely to hold as Asia's recent experiences have shown. Therefore, reducing national inequality requires efforts

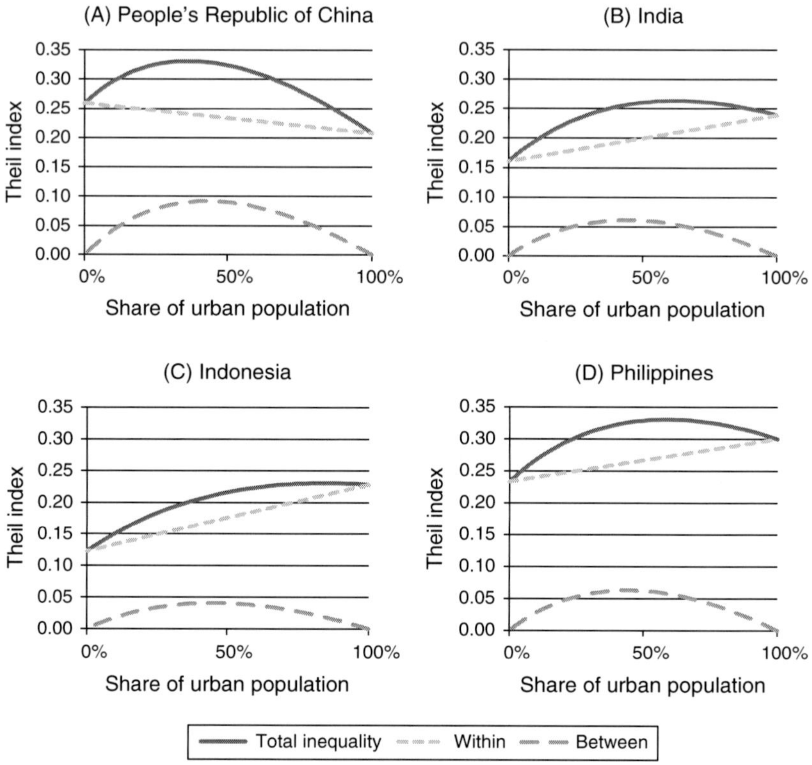

Figure 13.1 Urbanization and inequality.

Source: Authors' estimates.

on all fronts (ADB 2012a). Nevertheless, from the viewpoint of policy making, it is useful to know that shifting population from the rural to urban sectors, holding all other factors constant, will in the coming years increase national inequality for India and Indonesia, have limited impact on national inequality for the Philippines, and help reduce national inequality for the PRC.

In Panels A–D of Figure 13.1, we show graphically how inequality changes as urbanization proceeds. For this exercise, we use equation (13.2) and set other variables (k, L_1, and L_2) in the equation to their end-year values. We show national inequality as well as its two components: within-group inequality and between-group inequality.

For India, Indonesia, and the Philippines, the within-group component of inequality increases monotonically as urbanization proceeds. This is because, for these countries, urban inequality is higher than rural inequality, and so the shifting population from rural to urban sectors will always increase the within-group inequality. On the other hand, between-group inequality increases with urbanization when the level of urbanization is low and decreases with urbanization when the level of urbanization is high, with the turning point occurring at the urbanization rate of around 45% for all three countries. The turning point for national inequality, the sum of the two components, occurs at a higher rate of urbanization: 62% for India, 85% for Indonesia, and 59% for the Philippines. Given that India's actual share of urban population in the late 2000s was about 26% and Indonesia's was 57%, the two countries have many years to go to reach their turning points. The Philippines' actual share of urban population was 55% in the late 2000s, which is close to its predicted turning point.

In the case of the PRC, within-group inequality declines monotonically with urbanization because urban inequality is lower than rural inequality and shifting population from the rural to urban sectors will always reduce within-group inequality. Like the other three countries, the PRC's between-group inequality also increases with urbanization when the level of urbanization is low and decreases with urbanization when the level is high, with the turning point occurring at around 43%. The turning point for national inequality occurs at around 36%, much earlier than the other three countries. With the actual level of urbanization at 52% in 2012, the PRC has already passed this turning point.

Turning points discussed earlier are a function of k, L_1, and L_2, as shown by equation (13.5), and hence should only be interpreted from the viewpoint of how urbanization affects national inequality, holding constant other factors. Since k, L_1,and L_2 can all change independently of urbanization, the turning point is not unique for each country. It can shift, either forward or backward, depending on how urban inequality, rural inequality, and/or the urban–rural income gap change and interact with each other.[5] Therefore, a country's national inequality may still increase in the future, even if it has passed the turning point currently. In the case of the PRC, for example, if urban inequality continues to rise and becomes higher than rural inequality, shifting population from the rural to urban sectors may start to increase within-group inequality, and whether national inequality increases or decreases with urbanization will depend on the relative magnitude of the increase in within-group inequality and decrease in between-group inequality.

Prioritizing drivers of inequality

The four variables (x, k, L_1, and L_2) are the drivers of national inequality in the framework followed in this chapter. Policy makers may be able to influence these drivers through various instruments. For example, support for small farmers can moderate rural inequality, while progressive income taxation could moderate urban inequality. General support for rural development can help to reduce the urban–rural income ratio, while policies that restrict or hamper migration could reduce the share of the urban population to a lower level than it otherwise would have been.

---

[5] In the case of the PRC, Zhang *et al.* (2011) suggested that, at least in terms of wage earnings, the trend of a rising urban–rural gap may have turned. They call this the "Lewis turning point" after Lewis (1954).

Which policies should be the priority targets of policy makers in order to moderate increases in inequality? The answer depends partly on the relative power of the four drivers of national inequality. To answer this question, we estimate the elasticity of national inequality with respect to each of the four drivers – the percentage change in national inequality corresponding to each percentage change in the value of a relevant driver. A higher elasticity implies greater power.

Using equation (13.2), the elasticity of L with respect to each of the four variables can be obtained from

$$dL/L = E_x(dx/x) + E_k(dk/k) + E_{L1}(dL_1/L_1) + E_{L2}(dL_2/L_2) \quad (13.8)$$

E_x, E_k, E_{L1}, and E_{L2} are elasticities of L with respect to x, k, L_1, and L_2, respectively, and are given by

$$E_x = (x/L)A_x \quad (13.9a)$$

$$E_k = (k/L)A_k \quad (13.9b)$$

$$E_{L1} = (L_1/L)A_{L1} \quad (13.9c)$$

$$E_{L2} = (L_2/L)A_{L2} \quad (13.9d)$$

where A_x, A_k, A_{L1}, and A_{L2} are given in equations (13.4a)–(13.4d).

Table 13.6 shows that the value of the inequality elasticity varies across the four drivers and countries. For India, reducing the urban–rural income gap potentially has the largest marginal impact on national inequality, followed by reducing rural and urban inequalities, while urbanization increases national inequality. In the case of the PRC, reducing the urban–rural income gap has the largest marginal impact on national inequality, followed by reducing rural inequality, urban inequality, and urbanization. In Indonesia, reducing urban inequality and the urban–rural income gap have the same and largest marginal impact, followed by rural inequality, while urbanization increases national inequality. Finally, in the case of the Philippines, reducing urban inequality and the urban–rural income gap have similar and the largest impact on national inequality, followed by reducing rural inequality, while urbanization increases national inequality, although the impact is small.

Table 13.6 Inequality elasticities

Country	E_x	E_k	E_{L1}	E_{L2}
PRC	−0.069	0.641	0.272	0.449
India	0.202	0.664	0.265	0.510
Indonesia	0.178	0.590	0.591	0.235
Philippines	0.027	0.496	0.499	0.319

E_k = elasticity with respect to urban–rural income ratio; E_{L1} = elasticity with respect to urban inequality; E_{L2} = elasticity with respect to rural inequality; E_x = elasticity with respect to share of urban population; PRC = People's Republic of China.

Source: Authors' estimates.

An important caveat for this analysis is that, while inequality elasticity indicates the percentage change in national inequality corresponding to each percentage change in a concerned driver, policy effort needed to bring about each percentage change may differ a lot among different drivers. This should also be taken into consideration in prioritizing policy actions.

Summary and conclusions

Let us return to the three questions posed in this chapter, in light of the basic stylized facts of inequality and urbanization in Asia.

First, how much of the observed increase in inequality in Asia can be attributed to the changing dual economic structure and urbanization? The answer is highly country-specific. Urbanization contributed about 300% of the increase in inequality at the national level in the Philippines, more than 50% in Indonesia, slightly less than 15% in India, but helped reduce inequality somewhat in the PRC. The change in the urban–rural income gap, on the other hand, contributed about 50% of the increase in inequality at the national level in India and about 33% in the PRC, but helped reduce national inequality in Indonesia and the Philippines. In the PRC, the most important contributor to rising national inequality was an increase in rural inequality, accounting for 43%, in contrast to what has widely been believed. This emphasizes the importance of a widening urban–rural income gap and rising urban inequality.

Second, how might urbanization affect inequality in the future? The answer is again country-specific. The PRC has already passed its "turning point," that is, holding urban and rural inequalities and urban–rural income ratio constant, urbanization will help reduce inequality at the national level; and the Philippines has not passed but is close to such a turning point. On the other hand, India and Indonesia are still far away from their turning points, suggesting urbanization will cause national inequality to rise in these two countries. It must be noted, however, that the turning point is a function of urban and rural inequalities and the urban–rural income ratio. Since these components depend on many other factors that may not remain constant, and, in fact, they could be related to urbanization itself, the turning point is not unique for each country. Nevertheless, it remains true that urbanization is a major driving force of inequality in Asia.

Third, how should Asian governments prioritize the four drivers of inequality on which this chapter has focused as the targets? It appears that reducing the urban–rural income ratio will have the largest marginal impact on national inequality for all the four countries. In Indonesia and the Philippines, reducing urban inequality will have a similar marginal impact as reducing the urban–rural income gap. In the PRC and India, the second important driver is reducing rural inequality. The caveat is that prioritizing policy actions also needs to take into account any associated costs (both economic and social).

It is hoped that the framework developed in this chapter and calculations presented have provided more insights into the dynamics of rising inequality in Asia and can help policy makers prioritize policy actions for confronting it.

Acknowledgments

This chapter was first published in *Asian Development Review*, 30 (1), 2013. The authors would like to thank two anonymous referees for useful comments and Anneli S. Lagman-Martin for excellent research assistance.

References[6]

Anand, S., and R. Kanbur. 1993a. The Kuznets Process and the Inequality–Development Relationship. *Journal of Development Economics*. 40 (1). pp. 25–52.

——. 1993b. Inequality and Development: A Critique. *Journal of Development Economics*. 41 (1). p. 19–43.

Asian Development Bank. 2012a. *Asian Development Outlook 2012*. Manila.

——. 2012b. *Key Indicators for Asia and the Pacific 2012*. Manila.

The Economist. 2012. Inequality in China: To Each, Not According to His Needs. 15 December. http://www.economist.com/news/finance-and-economics/21568423-new-survey-illuminates-extent-chinese-income-inequality-each-not

Fields, G. 2001. *Distribution and Development, A New Look at the Developing World*. New York, NY: Russell Sage Foundation, and Cambridge, MA and London: MIT Press.

Hu, J. 2012. Political Report at the 18th National Congress of the Communist Party of China. Beijing, People's Republic of China. November.

Kanbur, R. 2012. Does Kuznets Still Matter? In S. Kochhar, ed. *Policy-Making for Indian Planning: Essays on Contemporary Issues in Honour of Montek S. Ahluwalia*. New Delhi: Academic Foundation Press. pp. 115–28.

Kuznets, S. 1955. Economic Growth and Income Inequality. *American Economic Review*. 45. pp. 1–28.

Lewis, W. A. 1954. Economic Development with Unlimited Supply of Labour. *The Manchester School*. 22 (2). pp. 139–91.

Lin, T., J. Zhuang, D. Yarcia, and F. Lin. 2008. Income Inequality in the People's Republic of China and Its Decomposition: 1990–2004. *Asian Development Review*. 25 (1&2). pp. 119–36.

Piketty, T. 2006. The Kuznets' Curve, Yesterday and Tomorrow. In A. Banerjee, R. Bénabou, and D. Mookherjee, eds. *Understanding Poverty*. Oxford, UK: Oxford University Press.

World Bank. PovcalNet: The On-line Tool for Poverty Measurement Developed by the Development Research Group of the World Bank. http://iresearch.worldbank.org/PovcalNet/index.htm

——. World Development Indicators. http://data.worldbank.org/data-catalog/world-development-indicators (accessed April 2012).

Zhang, X., J. Yang, and S. Wang. 2011. China Has Reached the Lewis Turning Point. *China Economic Review*. 22 (4). pp. 542–54.

[6] The Asian Development Bank recognizes China by the name People's Republic of China.

14 Inequality in Southeast Asia

Aekapol Chongvilaivan

Introduction

Although the economies in Southeast Asia have exhibited exceptional performance, it has become apparent that economic development in the region is uneven, and the emerging disparities pose critical challenges to inclusive and sustainable growth. There are a number of mechanisms through which rising inequality negatively affects growth of an economy. First, inequality may induce distortive redistributive policies and interventions (Alesina and Rodrik 1994). Second, inequality constitutes a root cause of sociopolitical instability and violence (Keefer and Knack 2002). Third, concentration of wealth and economic resources in small groups implies inadequate market size and aggregate demands (Murphy *et al.* 1989). Last, inequality entails a waste of human resources because the poor are often constrained in investing in education and health (Bénabou 1997).

While the subjects of inclusive growth and inequalities have already been central to public and policy debates, limitations of consistent, up-to-date household data have plagued thorough understanding and analyses of the issues in the context of Southeast Asia. The objective of this study is to examine (i) recent trends of inequality in Southeast Asia; (ii) proximate, structural, and policy drivers of inequalities; (iii) impacts and implications of recent policy developments addressing the problems of income and non-income inequalities; and (iv) policy lessons toward reducing inequalities and putting in place inclusive growth in the region.

This chapter brings out the following main findings: first and foremost, impressive economic performance and large poverty reduction in many parts of the region have been coupled with increases in or persistently high income inequality. While this pattern characterizes overall development in Southeast Asia, the level of inequality and pace of its change differ from country to country. Second, the decomposition analysis shows that growth has been unevenly distributed along a range of dimensions, pointing to various proximate drivers of inequality. Third, the structural drivers, particularly trade and financial liberalization, have had impacts on inequality in Southeast Asia. The chapter also looks at policy drivers of inequality, in particular government spending on social programs and governance and institutional quality.

Table 14.1 Current levels of income inequality in Southeast Asia

Country	*Year*	*Gini coefficient*	*Quintile ratio*	*Mean log deviation*
Cambodia	2008	37.9	6.1	0.2
Indonesia[a]	2011	42.2	7.8	0.3
Lao PDR	2008	36.7	5.9	0.2
Malaysia	2009	46.2	11.3	0.4
Philippines	2009	43.0	8.3	0.3
Thailand	2009	40.0	7.1	. . .
Viet Nam	2008	37.6	5.9	0.2

Lao PDR = Lao People's Democratic Republic; . . . = no data available.

Note: Gini coefficients are originally defined as a ratio ranging from 0 to 1. The values expressed in this table have been adjusted to range from 0 to 100.

[a]Data cover urban areas only.

Source: PovcalNet, http://iresearch.worldbank.org/PovcalNet/index.htm (accessed 31 January 2012).

Recent trends of inequality in Southeast Asia

Current status

Table 14.1 reports three conventional measures of income inequality, including the Gini coefficient, quintile ratio, and mean log deviation (MLD).[1] Malaysia's income distribution is the most uneven with all of the three measures taking the highest value: 46.2 for the Gini coefficient, 11.3 for the quintile ratio, and 0.37 for MLD. Indonesia, the Philippines, and Thailand have somewhat lower income inequality, with the Gini coefficient ranging from 40 to 43, the quintile ratio from 7 to 8.3, and MLD approximately at around 0.3. The relatively low-income countries, namely, Cambodia, the Lao People's Democratic Republic (Lao PDR), and Viet Nam, have lower levels of inequality, with the Gini coefficient at about 37, the quintile ratio at 6, and MLD at 0.21–0.24.

Pattern of change

The accelerated poverty reduction accompanied by rising income inequality is particularly discernible in Indonesia and the Lao PDR (Figure 14.1). This pattern also prevails in Cambodia, the Philippines, and, to a lesser extent, Viet Nam. In Malaysia and Thailand, large reductions in poverty have been coupled with a slight

[1] The Gini coefficient captures dispersion of income distribution and ranges from 0 to 1. The 0 value represents perfect equality when all individuals have the same level of income, while the value of 1 implies perfect inequality when only one person takes up all income. In this chapter, the values have been adjusted to range from 0 to 100. The quintile ratio is the ratio of total income of the richest 20% to that of the poorest 20%. Therefore, a higher value means more uneven income distribution. MLD is the mean of the log of the population mean income divided by individual income. A higher value of MLD implies greater income inequality.

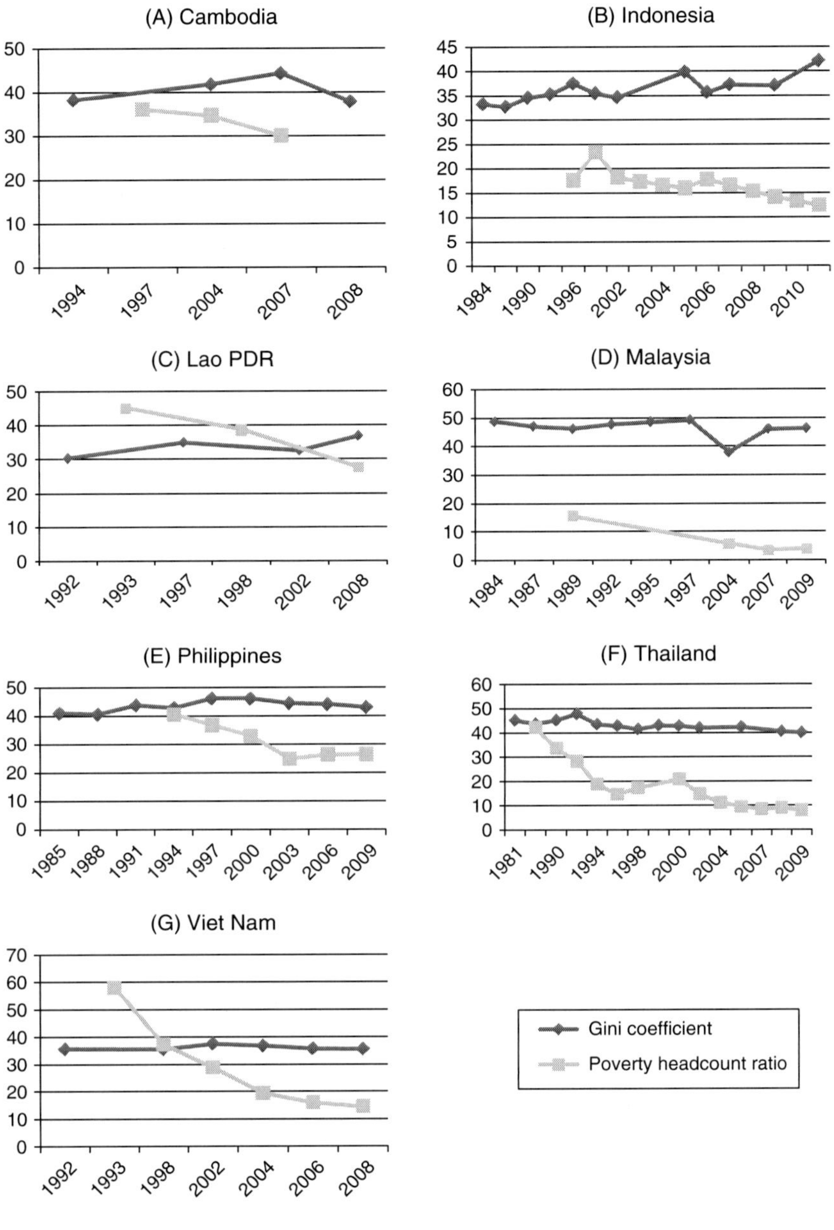

Figure 14.1 Gini coefficients and poverty headcount ratios in Southeast Asia.

Lao PDR = Lao People's Democratic Republic.

Sources: PovcalNet, http://iresearch.worldbank.org/PovcalNet/index.htm (accessed 31 January 2012) and World Development Indicators, http://data.worldbank.org/data-catalog/world-development-indicators (accessed 31 January 2012).

drop in income inequality since the 1980s, notwithstanding some spikes in the aftermath of the Asian financial crisis in Thailand and in the run-up to the global financial crisis in 2008/2009 in Malaysia. This pattern of change implies that the rising inequality in the region is driven primarily by the extent to which incomes of the rich surge at a faster pace than those of the poor. This also highlights that in the context of Southeast Asia, gains from swift economic development have not been shared widely.

Pace and direction of change

The pace and direction of change in income inequality can also be observed in Figure 14.1. In Cambodia, the Gini coefficient increased during 1994–2007, but declined somewhat after 2007. In Indonesia, income inequality rose from the late 1980s onward; however, it declined sizably in the aftermath of the Asian financial crisis, even though it soon bounced back and rose after 2002, reaching the unprecedented high level of 42.2 in 2011. In the Lao PDR, even though the Asian financial crisis resulted in a modest decrease in inequality during 1997–2002, the Gini coefficient increased from 30.43 to 34.9 during 1992–1997 and from 32.6 to 36.7 during 2002–2008. In Malaysia, the Gini coefficient increased during the late 1980s, followed by a drop during 1997–2004 and an increase in the run-up to the global financial crisis in 2009. In the Philippines, inequality increased during 1985–1997, but has since been on the decline, especially after the Asian financial crisis, although only slightly. Income inequality in Thailand declined in the 1990s, but increased slightly after the Asian financial crisis. Since then, it has also been on the decline. In Viet Nam, inequality stayed relatively stable during 1992–2008. The Gini coefficient picked up slightly during 1992–2004, followed by a modest decline in 2004–2008.

Dimensions of inequality

Generalized entropy measure of inequality

The discussions in this section essentially employ the Theil (1967) index decomposition by individual or household attributes. Based on ADB (2012), the Theil estimates are measured by per capita household expenditure in nominal terms, using various national household surveys. It should be highlighted that expenditure-based inequality estimates may be quantitatively different from income-based estimates, with the former lower than the latter. However, the use of expenditure-based inequality estimates can be justified by the fact that individuals and households derive utility from expenditures, rather than incomes (Akita *et al.* 1999). Theil's second entropy measure of inequality, $GE(0)$, can be written as

$$GE(0) = \sum_{j=1}^{n} p_j \ln(p_j / y_j) \tag{14.1}$$

where y_j is the income share of group j in total income and p_j is the population share of group j in the total population.[2] As articulated in Anand (1983), one appealing feature of the Theil indices is that the income inequality measure can be additively decomposed into within-group and between-group inequality components (denoted with the subscripts W and B, respectively). Suppose that all individuals in the population are grouped into m groups. $GE(0)$ can be partitioned into the two components as follows:

$$GE(0) = \sum_{j=1}^{m} p_j GE(0)_j + \sum_{j=1}^{m} p_j \ln(p_j/y_j) = GE(0)_w + GE(0)_B \qquad (14.2)$$

This decomposition allows us to quantify the contributions of the proximate drivers to income inequality.

Proximate drivers of inequality

Urban–rural inequality. It is usually believed that, in the development process of a developing country, the income gap between urban and rural households may widen as growth initially tends to center on developed realms such as cities and coastal areas. Figure 14.2 shows that, in Indonesia, the income gap – measured by the ratio of per capita consumption expenditure in urban areas to that in rural areas – rose from 1.23 in the 1990s to 1.42 in the mid-2000s and fell to 1.20 in the late 2000s. Similarly, the urban–rural divide in the Philippines rose from 2.07 in the 1990s and reached a peak of 2.26 in the early 2000s, but the trend seems to have since reversed. Several factors account for the urban-biased economic development, such as the different pace of human capital accumulation in the urban and rural areas, market-driven urbanization and industrialization, and agglomeration of economies (de Groot *et al.* 2008).

The urban–rural income gap contributes approximately 20% to overall inequality in three Southeast Asian countries (Figure 14.3). In Indonesia, the share of the between-group component slightly dropped from 22.5% in 1990 to 18.8% in 2010, even though a rising trend was observed in recent years. In the Philippines, the contribution of urban–rural inequality declined from a peak of 23.4% in 1997 to 18.9% in 2009. The urban–rural differential appears to be the most significant in Viet Nam where the share of the between-group component stood at 24.2% in 2008.

Interprovincial inequality. Interprovincial inequality is most pronounced in Viet Nam where disparity across provinces accounted for more than 30% of the overall inequality in 2008 (Figure 14.4). The contribution of interprovincial disparity ranged between 18.5% and 26.6% in the Philippines during 1991–2009.

[2] Some caveats apply. First, Theil measures of inequality based on information theory are rather normative and thus in contrast to other alternative concepts like the Lorenz curve. Additionally, the levels of inequality under Theil's measurement are influenced by a member with higher income.

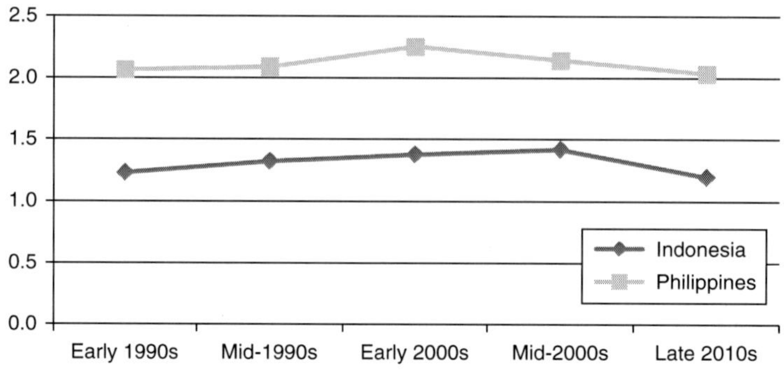

Figure 14.2 Urban–rural income gaps in selected Southeast Asian countries.

Source: ADB estimates using PovcalNet, http://iresearch.worldbank.org/PovcalNet/index.htm (accessed 31 January 2012).

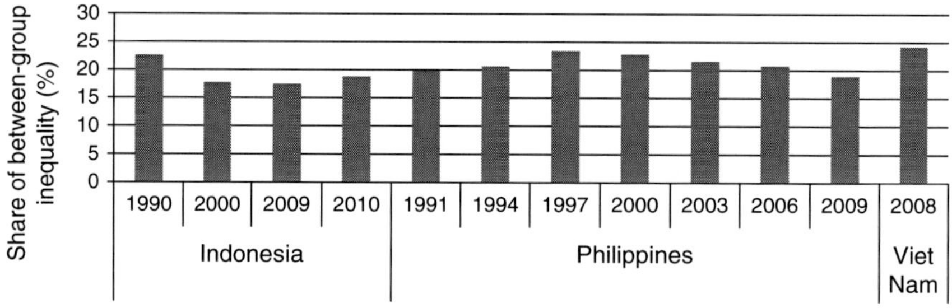

Figure 14.3 Inequality decomposition by urban–rural location.

Note: Estimates are based on per capita expenditure in nominal terms.

Source: ADB. 2012. *Asian Development Outlook 2012: Confronting Rising Inequality in Asia*. Manila.

Interestingly, interprovincial inequality in the Philippines exhibited a persistent decline from the peak of 26.6% in 1997 to 18.5% in 2009. Interprovincial inequality is relatively modest in Indonesia where the share also declined consistently from 16.6% in 1990 to 14.2% in 2010.

Between-country inequality. Another aspect of inequality in Southeast Asia is the between-country inequality (Figure 14.5) – the developmental divide between relatively advanced countries, such as Brunei Darussalam, Indonesia, Malaysia, the Philippines, Singapore, and Thailand, on the one hand, and new member states of the Association of Southeast Asian Nations (ASEAN), such as Cambodia, the Lao PDR, Myanmar, and Viet Nam (CLMV), on the other. It has been widely argued that bridging the intra-ASEAN income gap holds a key to seamless regional economic integration in that equitable development within an economic grouping serves as a prerequisite for successful regional economic integration (Viner 1950; Park 2000).

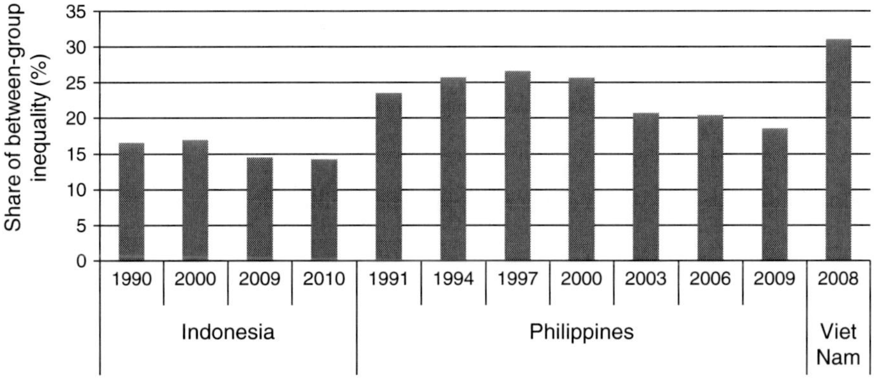

Figure 14.4 Inequality decomposition by province.

Note: Estimates are based on per capita expenditure in nominal terms.

Source: ADB. 2012. *Asian Development Outlook 2012: Confronting Rising Inequality in Asia*. Manila.

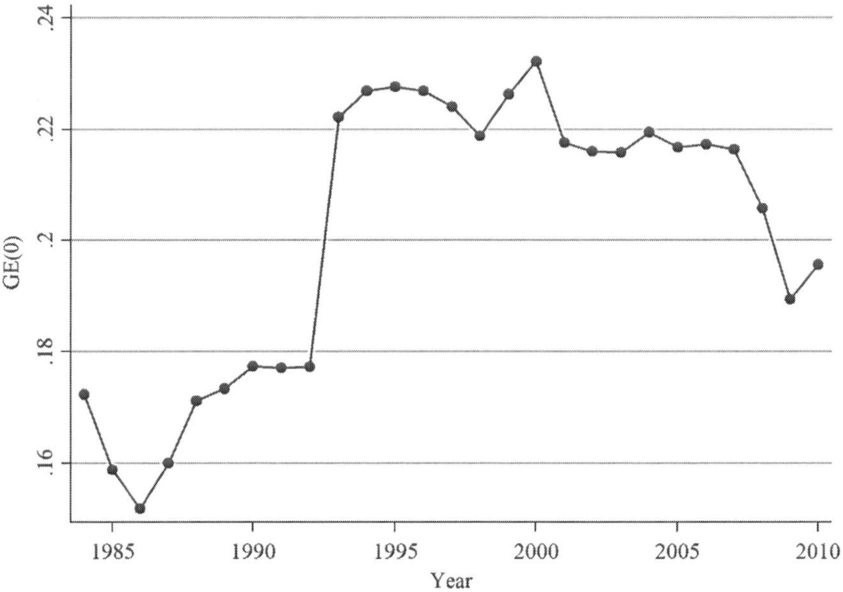

Figure 14.5 Between-country inequality in Southeast Asia.

Note: The samples include nine Southeast Asian countries excluding Myanmar. Cambodia is excluded from 1984 to 1992.

Source: Author's estimate based on World Development Indicators, http://data.worldbank.org/data-catalog/world-development-indicators (accessed 31 January 2012).

The emerging income discrepancies during 1986–2000 were driven largely by the fact that the major Southeast Asian nations, especially Malaysia, Singapore, and Thailand, had experienced staggering economic growth and rapid economic development, while most others, including Cambodia, the Lao PDR, Myanmar, and Viet Nam, had weaker physical and institutional infrastructure, concentrated on labor-intensive, low value-added production, and hence experienced lower growth. However, intra-Southeast Asia income convergence appeared in the aftermath of the Asian financial crisis. From 2001 to 2008, Indonesia, Malaysia, the Philippines, and Thailand experienced slower growth after a sharp downturn in 1997/1998, while Cambodia and Viet Nam transitioned toward a market economy and achieved rapid industrialization, poverty reduction, and economic development.

Inequality by household attributes. Figure 14.6 shows that the contribution of differences in educational attainment (of household head) to inequality is very significant, especially in Thailand where the share of the between-group component amounted to more than 46% in 2005. In the Philippines, it increased substantially from about 22% in 1985 to almost 36% in 2009. Although the contribution of educational differences was smaller in Indonesia, the share of the between-group component also showed a large dump, from 18% in 2000 to nearly 25% in 2010. In the case of Viet Nam, in 2008, differences in educational attainment explained about 18% of the overall inequality. The increasing importance of education in explaining income inequality suggests rising skill premiums, which may be related to globalization and technological change, and unequal access to education, which exacerbates inequality (ADB 2012).

On the other hand, the contribution of male–female income disparity to overall inequality is not significant (Figure 14.7). The between-group component took up merely 2–3.5% of total inequality in the Philippines during 1985–2009 and in Viet Nam in 2008, and the share was virtually negligible in Indonesia

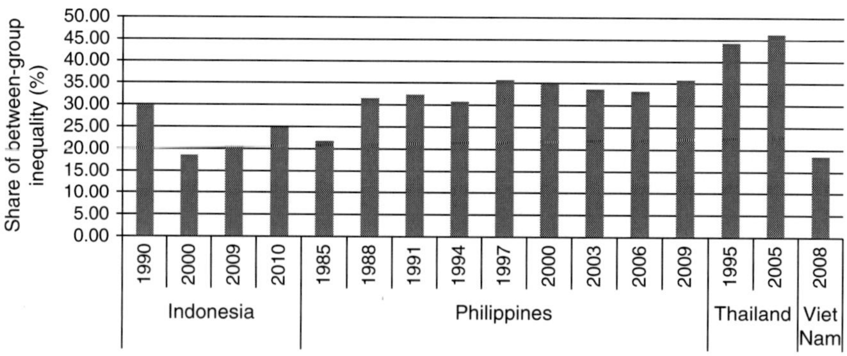

Figure 14.6 Inequality decomposition by educational attainment of household head.

Note: Estimates are based on per capita expenditure in nominal terms.

Source: ADB. 2012. *Asian Development Outlook 2012: Confronting Rising Inequality in Asia.* Manila.

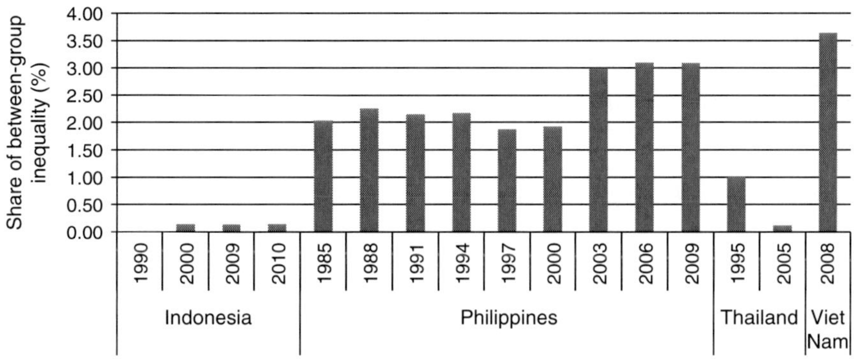

Figure 14.7 Inequality decomposition by gender of household head.

Note: Estimates are based on per capita expenditure in nominal terms.

Source: ADB. 2012. *Asian Development Outlook 2012: Confronting Rising Inequality in Asia*. Manila.

throughout the period 1990–2010. This may be partly due to the fact that the inequality is measured using household data, not income data of individual earners.

Functional distribution of income. Another important driver of income inequality is the change in functional distribution of income, defined as the labor share of income in total value added (Galbraith 2011). The existing studies on this subject have been devoted to how a shift in the functional distribution of income is related to evolving distribution of personal incomes. Giovannoni (2010), for instance, provided evidence that the wage share in member countries of the Organisation for Economic Co-operation and Development (OECD) has been consistently declining since the early 1980s, and this decline has been accompanied by rising income inequality in many OECD countries. The decline in the labor income share has been attributed to a number of factors, such as technological change and the declining bargaining power of trade unions (ADB 2012).

The falling labor income share of the industry sector is observed rather evidently in Indonesia and Singapore. Singapore experienced the most rapid decline in the labor income share, from 32.7% in the early 1990s to 22.9% in the early 2000s (Figure 14.8). In Indonesia, labor income accounted for 33.1% of total industrial value added during the early 2000s, but the share plunged to 28.8% in the mid-2000s. The labor income share in Malaysia was relatively stable at approximately 27% during the 1990s. In Southeast Asia, the falling labor income share can be explained by the fact that the manufacturing sectors, particularly electronics and automobiles, are capital- and technology-intensive; and increasing demand for capital relative to labor led to less labor employment and, consequently, a decline in the labor income share.

Inequality in opportunity versus inequality in income. At least two dimensions of non-income inequality are particularly pertinent to Southeast Asia: gender gaps and education inequality. In 2010, the Philippines ranked ninth in the world in

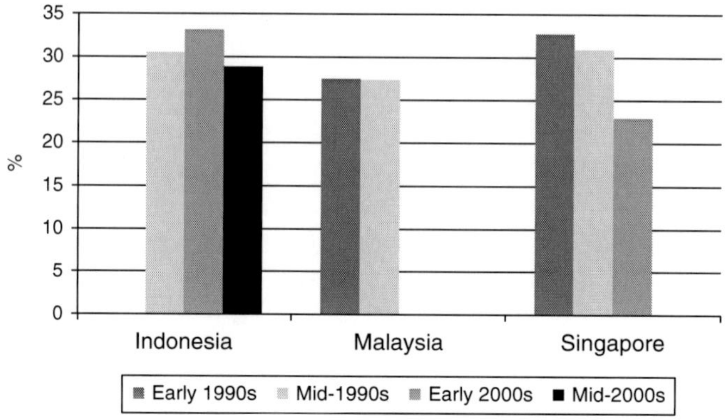

Figure 14.8 Share of labor income in industrial/manufacturing value added in selected Southeast Asian countries.

Note: Early 1990s (1990–1992), mid-1990s (1994–1996), early 2000s (2000–2002), and mid-2000s (2004–2006).

Source: ADB. 2012. *Asian Development Outlook 2012: Confronting Rising Inequality in Asia*. Manila.

terms of overall gender equality, but in other countries, there is still much room for improvement (Figure 14.9). Singapore, for instance, ranked 56th, Thailand 57th, Viet Nam 72nd, Indonesia 87th, Cambodia 97th, and Malaysia 98th, respectively. A breakdown of the Gender Gap Index into four subindicators – economic participation and opportunity, educational attainment, health and survival, and political empowerment – further reveals that the Southeast Asian countries performed better in education and health, but relatively poorly in other areas, especially in political empowerment among women. Therefore, enhancing political awareness and participation among women is imperative to reducing the gender gap in the region.

Like inequality in income, inequality in education can also be measured by the Gini coefficient, which captures unevenness of educational attainment among the population. Although access to education has been rather uneven, especially in Cambodia, Indonesia, and Viet Nam where the Gini coefficient was more than 30, the education inequality declined persistently in all countries in the past two decades, suggesting that access to education is becoming more equitable in the region (Figure 14.10). The decline in the Gini coefficient was quite significant in Cambodia and Indonesia, where the inequality in education was very high in the 1990s.

Structural and policy drivers of inequality in Southeast Asia

Structural drivers

The issue of structural drivers of inequality in Southeast Asia pivots around the consequences of globalization that advocate trade and financial

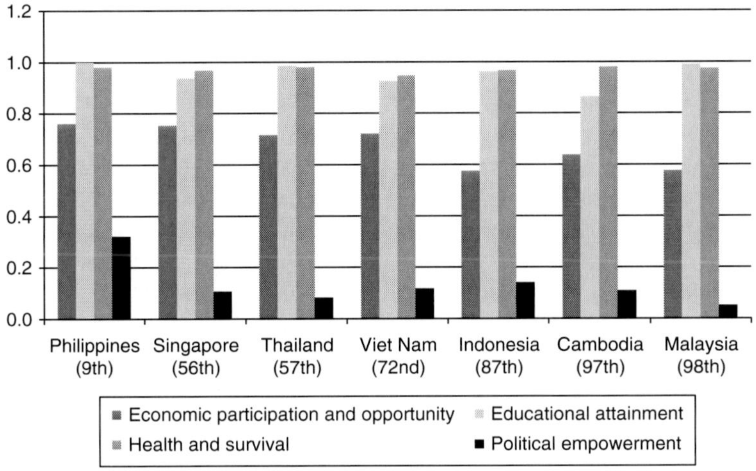

Figure 14.9 Subindicators of the gender gap in Southeast Asia, 2010.

Source: World Economic Forum. 2010. *The Global Gender Gap Report 2010*. Geneva.

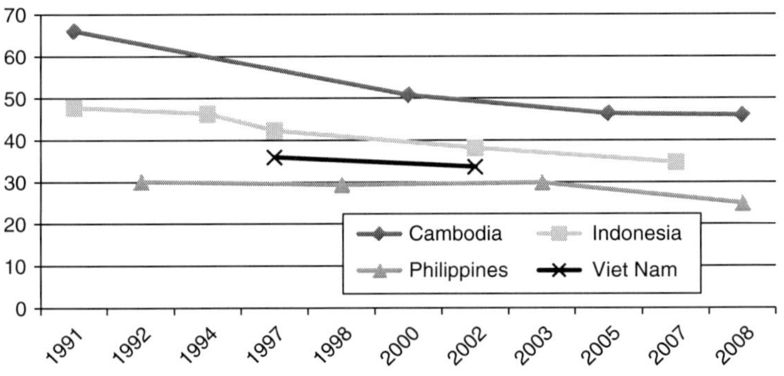

Figure 14.10 Gini coefficient of average years of schooling.

Source: EdStats, http://web.worldbank.org/WBSITE/EXTERNAL/TOPICS/EXTEDUCATION/EXTDATASTATISTICS/EXTEDSTATS/0,,menuPK:3232818~pagePK:64168427~piPK:64168435~theSitePK:3232764,00.html (accessed 31 January 2012).

liberalization.[3] The causal relationship between globalization and inequality in developing countries is complex, and different initial conditions and policy reforms mean that unskilled labor or the poor may fall out from the race toward liberalization. In the standard Stolper–Samuelson theorem, liberalization brings about reallocation of resources from capital-intensive production toward

[3] See Goldberg and Pavcnik (2005) for a survey of literature on the distributional effects of trade and financial liberalization in developing economies.

the labor-intensive sectors. It is therefore expected to deliver an upward shift in relative demand for labor, thereby mitigating within-country inequality. In reality, however, a path toward globalization is typically followed by domestic policy changes that may increase inequality, such as tax exemptions to promote foreign investment. As noted by Milanovic (2005), most studies on developing countries find that the effects of trade liberalization on inequality are statistically insignificant.

As with trade liberalization, the effects of financial sector development that facilitate cross-border movement of capital remain controversial (Agénor 2002; Fallon and Lucas 2002). On the one hand, the domestic financial deregulation helps improve resource allocation and perk up returns on financial assets by channeling capital to the most efficient uses. The rises in income accrued by the holders of financial assets could potentially be redistributed to support equitable economic development. Financial sector development, on the other hand, can exacerbate income inequality in developing countries in various ways (Taylor 2000). For instance, the appreciation of domestic currencies as a result of capital inflows may divert resources away from low skill-intensive sectors and trigger a fall in demand for unskilled workers. Moreover, undue development toward a free capital market puts the countries at risk of falling into a financial crisis in which the poor are the most affected. Finally, it has been widely received that the problems of incomplete information, herd behavior, weak supervision, excessive speculation, and inadequate institutional infrastructure often plague the liberalized international financial system.

To empirically investigate the structural drivers of inequality in Southeast Asian countries, this section develops a simple econometric model that relates the Gini coefficient to measures of trade and financial liberalization, in addition to other control variables. As in the International Monetary Fund's (IMF) *World Economic Outlook* (2007), the econometric specification can be loosely written as

$$\ln(Gini_{it}) = \alpha_0 + \alpha_1 \ln(TRADE_{it}) + \alpha_2 \ln(FINANCE_{it}) + \mathbf{x}'_{it}\boldsymbol{\beta} + u_{it} \quad (14.3)$$

where the subscripts i and t represent a country $i = 1, \ldots, N$ and a time period $t = 1, \ldots, T$, respectively, and $\mathbf{x}_{it}$ is a vector of control variables. Trade liberalization, $TRADE_{it}$, is measured by the ratio of trade (the sum of exports and imports) to gross domestic product (GDP). As discussed later, this measure can be further disaggregated into the ratio of exports to GDP and the ratio of imports to GDP to see how exports and imports may affect inequality differently. Two proxies of financial liberalization, $FINANCE_{it}$ are used: one is the ratio of foreign assets to GDP, and the other is the ratio of inward foreign direct investment (FDI) stocks to GDP. In addition to these key variables, the econometric specifications also control for four country-specific characteristics in the vector $\mathbf{x}_{it}$. The first is labor productivity measured by the ratio of value added to total employment. The other three control variables are employment shares of agriculture, industry, and service sectors, respectively. The empirical model of equation (14.3) is estimated by standard ordinary least squares (OLS), with heteroskedasticity-robust estimators. It should also be highlighted that all dependent and independent variables enter the model in terms of natural logarithm to yield more amenable OLS estimates.

Now that the objective is to examine the effects of structural drivers on inequality, the data set involves seven Southeast Asian countries: Cambodia, Indonesia, the Lao PDR, Malaysia, the Philippines, Thailand, and Viet Nam. Table 14.2 summarizes key statistics of the data set.

Table 14.3 presents the estimation results. Model 1 is the regression of the Gini coefficient on the ratio of trade to GDP, in addition to other control variables. Model 2 puts emphasis on the variables of financial liberalization by regressing the Gini coefficient on the ratio of foreign assets to GDP and the ratio of inward FDI to GDP, together with other control variables. Model 3 puts together the variables of trade and financial liberalization. Models 4 and 5 change the specification by breaking down the variable of trade liberalization into the ratio of exports to GDP and the ratio of imports to GDP to account for the possibility that exports and imports may affect inequality differently.

The main findings can be summarized as follows. First, although the coefficient of the ratio of trade to GDP appears to be statistically insignificant, the partition of the trade openness index yields a rather strong result that an expansion of exports as a result of trade liberalization helps reduce inequality in Southeast Asia, while an influx of imports puts upward pressure on inequality. As shown in Table 14.3, the coefficient of the ratio of exports to GDP is negative and statistically significant at the 1% level in both Models 4 and 5. In contrast, the coefficient of the ratio of imports to GDP turns out to be positive and statistically significant at the 1% level. The fact that the impacts of exports and imports on inequality work in opposite

Table 14.2 Summary statistics

Variable	*Number of observations*	*Mean*	*Standard deviation*	*Minimum*	*Maximum*
Gini coefficient	57	40.71	4.82	30.43	49.15
Ratio of trade to GDP	55	1.09	0.46	0.46	2.29
Ratio of exports to GDP	55	0.55	0.24	0.23	1.21
Ratio of imports to GDP	55	0.54	0.23	0.20	1.08
Ratio of foreign assets to GDP	50	0.19	0.12	0.01	0.51
Ratio of inward FDI to GDP	50	3.07	2.42	0.07	10.52
Labor productivity	52	9,504	5,294	2,567	24,059
Agriculture employment share (%)	46	43.77	14.41	13.50	72.20
Industry employment share (%)	46	18.75	5.79	8.30	33.70
Service employment share (%)	46	37.45	9.99	19.20	59.50

FDI = foreign direct investment; GDP = gross domestic product.

Note: Labor productivity is proxied by the ratio of value added to total employment.

Source: Author's estimate based on PovcalNet, http://iresearch.worldbank.org/PovcalNet/index.htm and World Development Indicators, http://data.worldbank.org/data-catalog/world-development-indicators (accessed 31 January 2012).

Table 14.3 Determinants of the Gini coefficient in Southeast Asia

Dependent variable: natural logarithm of the Gini coefficients					
Variable	*Model 1*	*Model 2*	*Model 3*	*Model 4*	*Model 5*
Trade liberalization					
Ratio of trade to GDP	0.007 (0.060)	–	0.041 (0.097)	–	–
Ratio of exports to GDP	–	–	–	−0.48*** (0.103)	−0.554*** (0.096)
Ratio of imports to GDP	–	–	–	0.449*** (0.097)	0.501*** (0.096)
Financial liberalization					
Ratio of foreign assets to GDP	–	−0.048** (0.018)	−0.055** (0.026)	–	−0.006 (0.023)
Ratio of inward FDI to GDP	–	0.037** (0.014)	0.032* (0.017)	–	0.023* (0.013)
Control variable					
Labor productivity	0.072 (0.047)	0.116*** (0.040)	0.118*** (0.042)	0.121*** (0.042)	0.161*** (0.042)
Agriculture employment share	−0.068 (0.118)	−0.077 (0.093)	−0.045 (0.132)	0.058 (0.097)	0.086 (0.105)
Industry employment share	0.021 (0.109)	−0.037 (0.085)	−0.042 (0.090)	0.056 (0.081)	0.056 (0.069)
Service employment share	−0.059 (0.142)	−0.021 (0.120)	0.012 (0.170)	0.188** (0.091)	0.209** (0.096)
Constant	3.470*** (0.959)	3.010*** (−0.792)	2.75** (1.110)	1.56* (0.899)	0.985 (0.942)
Number of observations	46	39	39	46	39
R^2	0.251	0.4	0.402	0.577	0.679
F-statistics	2.95**	7.74***	5.69***	9.68***	13.36***

FDI = foreign direct investment; GDP = gross domestic product.

Notes:

1 $^{*}p < 0.10$; $^{**}p < 0.05$; and $^{***}p < 0.01$.
2 Heteroskedasticity-robust standard errors are in parentheses.
3 All explanatory variables are in natural logarithm.
4 All specifications are estimated by ordinary least squares.
5 Selected Southeast Asian countries include Cambodia, Indonesia, the Lao People's Democratic Republic, Malaysia, the Philippines, Thailand, and Viet Nam.

Sources: Author's estimate based on PovcalNet, http://iresearch.worldbank.org/PovcalNet/index.htm and World Development Indicators, http://data.worldbank.org/data-catalog/world-development-indicators (accessed 31 January 2012).

directions may explain why the overall impact of trade liberalization captured by the ratio of trade to GDP is insignificant.

Second, financial liberalization that boosts the cross-border capital flows appears to help bring down inequality. The coefficient of the ratio of foreign assets to GDP is negative in all estimations, although it is statistically insignificant in Model 5. This may suggest that greater financial liberalization provides greater access to financial resources and opportunities for the poor.

Third, consistent with IMF (2007), an increase in inward FDI increases inequality in Southeast Asia. As shown in Table 14.3, the coefficient of the ratio of inward FDI to GDP is positive and statistically significant in all the specifications. In the context of Southeast Asia, most foreign investment is directed toward skill-intensive industries, such as automobiles and electronics, thereby shifting labor demand away from unskilled workers toward skilled ones. The widening gap between skilled and unskilled wages as a consequence of inward FDI is translated into income inequality.

Fourth, labor productivity growth may also be a source of inequality in Southeast Asia. The coefficient of labor productivity is positive and statistically significant in all the specifications (except Model 1), suggesting that the countries with higher labor productivity in terms of value added per worker tend to be characterized by a more uneven income distribution. This can be explained by the fact that higher labor productivity is associated with high-tech capital accumulation and technology advancement, which in turn bolster the premium for skilled workers and returns to capital. Since unskilled workers take up a larger share of the population in Southeast Asia, higher labor productivity leads to more uneven income disparities.

Last, the expansion of the industry and service sectors, together with the downsizing of the agriculture sector, also has implications for rising inequality in developing Southeast Asia. As shown in Table 14.3, the coefficient of the service employment share is positive and statistically significant at the 5% level in Models 4 and 5, even though the employment shares of agriculture and industry sectors do not produce statistically significant estimates. This posits that the burgeoning service sector in Southeast Asia may contribute to income inequality. One explanation perhaps rests with labor market rigidity whereby labor is hindered to move away from low-return activities in the agriculture sector to high-return service activities (Topalova 2007). The stickiness of inter-sectoral labor reallocation is attributed to, for instance, skill mismatch between service and agricultural activities and various labor market frictions that hamper low-wage workers in the agriculture sector being quickly and freely reallocated to the service sector. The widening wage differentials between the service and agriculture sectors ultimately fuel income inequality.

It should also be underlined that the empirical exercise in this section is subject to several caveats. Limitations of the Gini coefficient data impose constraints on the sample size and consistency of the data set. Limited data availability confines the control variables only to labor productivity and employment shares across sectors and may cause estimation biases arising from the omitted variables. Additionally, the limited scope of this section leaves a number of econometric issues unaddressed, including endogeneity biases as well as country- and time-specific effects. Therefore, the empirical results discussed in this section should be deemed as tentative.

Policy drivers

Redistributive policy

Redistributive policy has become a central element of public policy debates lately. There are three channels through which redistribution can be typically undertaken: taxation, social transfers, and social expenditure (Prasad 2008).

While taxation in most Southeast Asian countries has been progressive (Jomo 2001), liberalization and global competition have forced a shift in tax structures in favor of high-income groups, such as through tax exemptions on capital gains, a rise in value-added taxes, and a decline in marginal income tax rates. The declines in tax burdens as a result of these taxation changes are more pronounced for the high-income groups than the low-income ones, thus increasing income inequality. Notwithstanding this trend of taxation, some Southeast Asian countries embarked on taxation as the redistributive measure to shift tax burdens away from the low-income to high-income individuals or groups.

Social transfers, such as social assistance benefits and social insurance programs, also have redistributive effects on income. As in developed countries, Southeast Asian countries have embraced the social transfers that promote equitable access to healthcare, education, and employment opportunities, thereby narrowing income inequalities. The countries are greatly varied in terms of the programs provided (Table 14.4). Thailand seems to have the most comprehensive

Table 14.4 Coverage of social security programs in the Association of Southeast Asian Nations, 2010

		Sickness and maternity				
Country	*Old age, disability, and survivors*	*Cash benefits for both*	*Cash benefits plus medical care*	*Work injury*	*Unemployment benefits*	*Family allowances*
Brunei Darussalam	x	n	c	x	n	n
Myanmar	n	x	x	x	n	n
Indonesia	x	n	c	x	n	n
Lao PDR	x	x	x	x	n	n
Malaysia	x	n	c	x	n	n
Philippines	x	x	x	x	n	n
Singapore	x	x	x	x	n	n
Thailand	x	x	x	x	x	x
Viet Nam	x	x	x	x	x	n

Lao PDR = Lao People's Democratic Republic.

Notes: x denotes that coverage is provided; n denotes that coverage is not provided; and c denotes that only medical care is provided.

Source: United States Social Security Administration, http://www.ssa.gov/policy/docs/progdesc/ssptw/2010-2011/asia/index.html (accessed 31 January 2012).

social assistance benefits and insurance programs that cover all categories. Viet Nam provides social benefits for old age, disability and survivors, sickness and maternity, work injury, and unemployment, but not family allowances. The Lao PDR, the Philippines, and Singapore do not pursue social protection programs for unemployment and family allowances. In Brunei Darussalam, Indonesia, and Myanmar, the benefits of social protection programs appear inadequate; in particular, the benefits in terms of healthcare and work welfare are absent. It should also be highlighted that a benefit under a social transfer program does not necessarily guarantee that the coverage suffices and that potential beneficiaries are appropriately identified (Asher 2010). The United Nations Economic and Social Commission for Asia and the Pacific (2001), for instance, posited that Thailand's unemployment mitigation program provided merely 3,000 baht per person per month, and this amount was not sufficient to have significant impact on individuals or households; neither was identification of beneficiaries of the healthcare and education programs properly carried out.

Sustainability of the social protection programs also poses serious challenges to redistributive policy in Southeast Asia. The contribution rates (by employees and employers) for social protection programs are rather low in some Southeast Asian countries, at 4% for Myanmar, 9.5% for the Lao PDR, 10.2% for Thailand, and 12.9% for the Philippines (Table 14.5). The low contributions imply that the social protection programs depend largely on government funding and are thus susceptible to availability of fiscal space. For instance, in the aftermath of the Asian financial crisis in 1997/1998 and the global financial crisis in 2008/2009, there was a sharp cutback in government spending on social transfer programs in Thailand and the Philippines.

Lastly, public spending on education, health, and other social services is also an important channel of redistribution. Recent data reveal that in many Southeast

Table 14.5 Contribution rates for all social security programs in the Association of Southeast Asian Nations, 2010

Country	*Employee (%)*	*Employer (%)*	*Total (%)*
Brunei Darussalam	8.50	8.50	17.00
Myanmar	1.50	2.50	4.00
Indonesia	2.00	7.24	9.24
Lao PDR	4.50	5.00	9.50
Malaysia	11.50	13.75	25.25
Philippines	4.58	8.32	12.90
Singapore	20.00	15.00	35.00
Thailand	5.00	5.20	10.20
Viet Nam	8.50	20.50	29.00

Lao PDR = Lao People's Democratic Republic.

Source: United States Social Security Administration, http://www.ssa.gov/policy/docs/progdesc/ssptw/2010-2011/asia/index.html (accessed 31 January 2012).

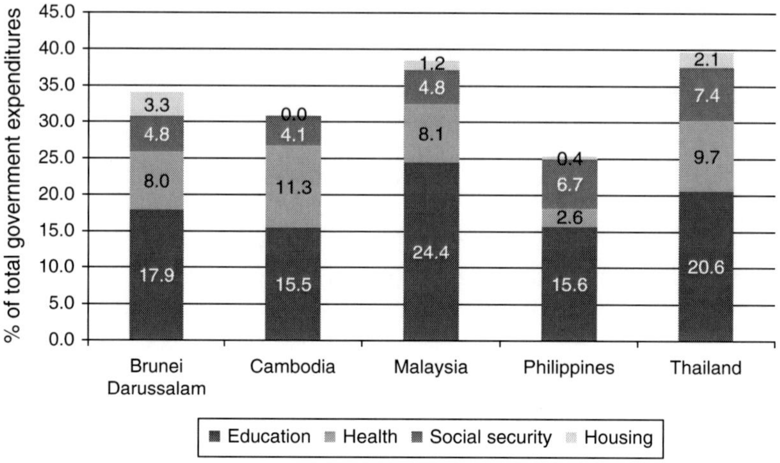

Figure 14.11 Annual social expenditures in selected Association of Southeast Asian Nations countries, 2010.

Source: ADB. 2011. *Key Indicators for Asia and the Pacific 2011*. Manila.

Asian countries, more than half of the government social expenditures are devoted to education, whereas spending on other areas such as healthcare, social security, and housing is low (Figure 14.11). For instance, in 2010, spending on social security accounted for only 4–5% of total government expenditures in Brunei Darussalam, Cambodia, and Malaysia. Similarly, government spending on public housing was also limited in Cambodia and the Philippines.

Governance and institutional reform

Corruption is often considered as being associated with prevailing, if not widening, income inequality (Johnston 1989). Corruption serves as the impetus for the rich and elites to extract resources from the poor through means such as rent-seeking actions, tax evasion, and changes in policies that are in favor of higher-income individuals (Gupta *et al.* 2002; Gyimah-Brempong 2002). In addition, the decline in and misuse of government resources hinder the social safety nets and protection programs that are imperative to bridging the income gap and ensuring equal access to facilities and opportunities.

More generally, it has been argued that improvement of institutional quality should result in more equitable income distribution for a number of reasons (Huther and Shah 2000). The egalitarian distribution of political rights (e.g., voice and accountability), in addition to political stability and regulatory enforcement, is indispensable for public policy and reform that are in favor of the majority of society. Further, a frail judicial system tends to allow the elites to extract economic rents away from the poor (Kayizzi-Mugerwa 2001). However, the empirical evidence on this relationship seems to be mixed (Zhuang *et al.* 2010). Bollen and

Table 14.6 Aggregate governance/institutional indicators in Southeast Asia, 2011

Country	*Voice and accountability*	*Political stability*	*Government effectiveness*	*Regulatory quality*	*Rule of law*	*Control of corruption*
Brunei Darussalam	−0.63	1.12	0.88	1.17	0.88	0.84
Cambodia	−0.91	−0.44	−0.75	−0.45	−1.03	−1.10
Indonesia	−0.08	−0.82	−0.24	−0.33	−0.65	−0.68
Lao PDR	−1.60	0.01	−0.91	−0.96	−0.92	−1.06
Malaysia	−0.44	0.16	1.00	0.66	0.52	0.00
Myanmar	−1.86	−1.16	−1.64	−2.13	−1.42	−1.69
Philippines	−0.01	−1.39	0.00	−0.26	−0.51	−0.78
Singapore	−0.19	1.21	2.16	1.83	1.69	2.12
Thailand	−0.45	−1.02	0.10	0.24	−0.24	−0.37
Viet Nam	−1.48	0.17	−0.28	−0.61	−0.48	−0.63

Lao PDR = Lao People's Democratic Republic.

Note: Scores range from −2.5 to 2.5, with higher values corresponding to better outcomes.

Source: Worldwide Governance Indicators, http://info.worldbank.org/governance/wgi/index.asp (accessed 31 January 2012).

Jackman (1985), for instance, found that equally distributed political rights under democracy have little to do with a more equal income distribution. In contrast, Chong and Gradstein (2007) showed that the linkage between institutions and income inequality is mutually reinforcing; good institutional quality is essential for reducing income gaps, and inequality, in turn, undermines institutions.

Table 14.6 reports the Worldwide Governance Indicators produced by the World Bank, focusing on Southeast Asia in 2011; namely, voice and accountability, political stability, government effectiveness, regulatory quality, rule of law, and control of corruption. The indicators range from −2.5 to 2.5, with higher values corresponding to better governance standards. Measured by the simple arithmetic mean of the six indicators, Singapore has the highest score, followed by Brunei Darussalam, Malaysia, Thailand, Indonesia, the Philippines, Viet Nam, Cambodia, the Lao PDR, and Myanmar.

The last column of Table 14.6 reports the current state of control of corruption in Southeast Asia. Corruption measures the extent to which "public power is exercised for private gain, including both petty and grand forms of corruption, as well as 'capture' of the state by elites and private interests" (Kaufmann *et al.* 2007). Singapore has the lowest degree of corruption, followed by Brunei Darussalam, Malaysia, Thailand, Viet Nam, Indonesia, the Philippines, the Lao PDR, Cambodia, and, lastly, Myanmar.

Recent policy developments

In response to rising or persistently high inequality, Southeast Asian governments have been taking policy actions in recent years. More and more countries are putting the promotion of inclusive growth at the heart of their development policy. This is largely reflected in their medium-term development strategies.

Cambodia

The Rectangular Strategy for Growth, Employment, Equity and Efficiency under the National Strategic Development Plan 2006–2010 has been reaffirmed in the most recent plan for 2009–2013 (Royal Government of Cambodia 2010) in response to the global economic crisis. While not explicitly anchored in the inclusive growth concept, Phase II of the Rectangular Strategy has elements to promote inclusiveness and poverty reduction. At the core of the strategy is good governance, especially in delivery and management of public goods and services. The four strategic areas are enhancement of the agriculture sector, rehabilitation and construction of physical infrastructure, private sector development and employment generation, and capacity building and human resources development. In addition, Cambodia intends to continue to deepen implementation of the Public Management Reform, which involves improving inclusiveness and integration in the budget. The plan targets an annual economic growth of 7% and a reduction in poverty by 1 percentage point per year.

Indonesia

Under its 2010–2014 development plan (Ministry of National Development and Planning, Government of Indonesia 2010), the vision for Indonesia is for a prosperous, democratic, and just society. This vision is supported by five national development agendas: economic development and increased welfare, enhancement of good governance, strengthening of the pillars of democracy, law enforcement and eradication of corruption, and inclusive and just development. National priorities for the plan period include reform of the bureaucracy and administration, education, health, poverty reduction, food security, infrastructure, and development of regions that are left behind, remote, or recovering from conflict. An annual growth rate of 6.5% is deemed necessary to achieve inclusive development if it is accompanied by more effective policies and programs to reduce poverty,[4] an enhanced role for women in increasing family welfare, and improved rural infrastructure.

---

[4] These include family-based social assistance programs that help low-income communities to meet their basic needs and give greater attention to the disabled and elderly (especially those from poor families, neglected children, and marginalized communities). In addition, the country's community-driven development program, Program Nasional Pemberdayaan Masyarakat (PNPM) Mandiri, aims to assist in empowering people toward actively participating in the efforts to bring themselves out of poverty. Programs for the empowerment of small and micro enterprises also assist informal workers to gain equal access to business opportunities.

Lao People's Democratic Republic

In reviewing the achievements under the previous development plan, the Lao PDR Ministry of Planning and Investment (2011) noted that "including all sectors in an economy can promote faster and more inclusive economic growth, and bring about change." The current development plan for 2011–2015 does not explicitly base the development strategy on the concept of inclusive growth. Nevertheless, the plan outlines various strategies and measures that support an inclusive growth strategy. The economy is projected to grow at more than 8% per year, and per capita GDP is expected to reach $1,500 in current prices by 2015. The plan calls for reducing the poverty rate to less than 19% and the percentage of poor households to less than 10% by 2015. It also aims to reduce unemployment to less than 2%.

Malaysia

Malaysia's development philosophy of growth with distribution led to decades of outstanding economic performance, resulting in significant poverty reduction, more balanced economic participation, and wider coverage of essential social services. To address the needs of low-income or disadvantaged citizens, Malaysia's plan for 2011–2015 (Economic Planning Unit 2010) calls for an inclusive development approach in line with the "1Malaysia: People First, Performance Now" concept.

The approach is anchored in two objectives. The first is to enable equitable opportunities for all Malaysians. It involves improving capacity, enhancing access to employment opportunities, and adopting a more targeted approach in encouraging innovation-driven entrepreneurship. The second objective is to provide a social safety net for disadvantaged groups. During the plan period, key strategies to provide equitable opportunity and promote greater socioeconomic inclusiveness include elevating the livelihoods of the bottom 40% of households, enhancing *Bumiputera*[5] economic participation, ensuring access by all to basic physical infrastructure, and enabling a progressive and more inclusive society in line with the 1Malaysia concept.

To improve the livelihoods of the bottom 40% of households, support will be provided through education and entrepreneurship, strengthened access to basic amenities, and implementation of tailored programs for target groups with specific needs. The government has set targets to reduce poverty incidence from 3.8% in 2009 to 2% in 2015, increase the mean income of the bottom 40% of households from RM1,440 in 2009 to RM2,300 in 2015, and reduce the Gini coefficient from 44.1 in 2009 to 42.0 in 2015. The plan details many other programs to support inclusiveness.

---

[5] *Bumiputera* is a Malay term referring to the indigenous people of the Malay archipelago.

Philippines

The Philippines has committed to the pursuit of inclusive growth in its 2011–2016 development plan (National Economic and Development Authority 2011), recognizing that sustained growth creates jobs, includes the majority in the economic and social mainstream, and reduces mass poverty. To achieve inclusive growth, the plan's key strategies include massive infrastructure development, higher governance standards, human development and human capital formation, employment generation, and access to financing. These thrusts will be complemented by a macroeconomic regime of low inflation and a sustainable fiscal balance, along with ecological integrity and mitigation of the effects of climate change. The plan also emphasizes equitable access to basic social services, as well as stronger safety nets and social protection against shocks.

Government-backed programs include the *Kapit-bisig Laban sa Kahirapan (Comprehensive and Integrated Delivery of Social Services)*, which provides funding and in-kind support from national and local governments to implement small projects by *barangays*[6] who follow their own plans, priorities, and processes. The *Pantawid Pamilyang Pilipino Program* provides conditional cash transfers targeted to the needs of vulnerable groups, particularly children, women, and the elderly and disabled. The plan targets an annual economic growth of 7–8% for at least 6 years and net employment generation of 1 million jobs per year. The plan calls for reducing the poverty rate from 33.1% in 1991 to 16.6% by 2015.

Thailand

The guiding principles of "people-centered development" and the "philosophy of sufficiency economy," which were in previous Five Year Plans for Thailand, are also included in the Eleventh National Economic and Social Development Plan 2012–2016 (National Economic and Social Development Board 2011). The plan envisions a happy society with equity, fairness, and resilience. The key development strategies are to create a just society, develop a lifelong learning society, strengthen the agriculture sector and food and energy security, restructure the economy toward quality growth and sustainability, achieve regional connectivity, and manage natural resources and the environment toward sustainability. Among other things, these strategies are aimed at better utilizing the country's economic and social capital. The plan also aims to improve the quality of human resources through better access to resources and through a fair distribution of development benefits. The Government of Thailand has set a goal of including all people, especially those in the informal sector, under the national welfare system by 2016.

Viet Nam

The country's goal for 2011–2015 is to develop the economy in a fast and sustainable manner and to restructure the economy to improve competitiveness

---

[6] A *barangay* is the smallest administrative unit of local government in the Philippines.

(Ministry of Planning and Investment, Government of Viet Nam 2011). While the development plan for 2011–2015 does not explicitly emphasize inclusive growth, it aims to ensure social welfare and enhance people's material and spiritual life and to make Viet Nam an industrialized country by 2020. GDP is expected to grow by at least 6.5–7% annually. Over the plan period, 8 million jobs are expected to be created and poverty to be reduced by 2 percentage points per year on average nationwide and by 4 percentage points in poor areas.

Policy lessons

This chapter draws at least four policy lessons and sheds light on the avenues of public policy and necessary reforms that would allow the poor to participate in and benefit from growth on an equitable basis.

Lesson 1: Enhancing and equalizing access to education

Equitable access to education holds a key to bridging income gaps. Although several human development indicators of the region have improved significantly in recent years, most countries lag behind developed countries in terms of secondary and tertiary education. This is despite the fact that education spending takes up a significant portion of public spending on the social sector. One possible explanation is that public spending on education puts more emphasis on providing access to basic education, while spending on secondary and tertiary education has been insufficient. Globalization and technological progress mean that primary education is not sufficient to equip jobseekers, especially from low-income families, with adequate skills needed for relatively high-paying jobs. Therefore, abating income inequality in the region requires reform of educational policy and allocating public resources not just to primary education, but also to secondary and tertiary education.

Lesson 2: Incorporating inclusion and equity into growth strategies

Southeast Asia is at a critical juncture when inclusion and equity need to be incorporated into every step of economic development. Inclusive growth, however, is easier said than done. Although recent developments show encouraging signs in terms of investment in human capital and public infrastructure and increasing public spending on social protection programs, the region needs to make far more progress in providing everyone with equal opportunity to participate in and benefit from the development process. Unequal access to opportunity is partly due to weaknesses in institutions that favor those with economic and political influences. Redistribution and social transfers are sometimes captured for the benefits of a few elite groups. Therefore, inclusive growth that promotes equitable access to opportunity for all cannot be achieved without a strong commitment to inclusion and equity at the policy-making level.

Lesson 3: Mitigating corruption and improving institutional quality

Corruption and poor institutional quality have been considered a cause of the vicious cycle between economic development and growing inequality. The examination of the current state in the region underlines that most developing Southeast Asian countries, especially Cambodia, Indonesia, the Lao PDR, Myanmar, the Philippines, and Viet Nam, are behind countries at the same level of development in terms of good governance and institutional quality. Given the importance of improving governance and institutional quality in alleviating inequality, it is critical that governments address political – in addition to social and economic – inclusion and participation, and strengthen accountability and transparency of political and regulatory procedures.

Lesson 4: Strengthening social protection

There are at least three areas where policy attention is needed in the region. The first is to develop or strengthen labor market institutions related to employment protection, unemployment benefits and insurance against work-related risks such as illness, disability, and accidents. In most countries, these programs have limited coverage, and exclude most vulnerable groups, such as unskilled workers and the poor. The second is to strengthen health-related social protection programs, such as subsidized health services, family allowances, and child development schemes. Government provisions and subsidies for these services help reduce household expenditure on healthcare especially among poor families; health protection programs, on the other hand, help to boost labor productivity and build human capabilities. The third area is to develop and improve public housing schemes and make them a crucial part of social safety nets. In rural areas, ownership of arable land matters for lifting the income levels of poor households. Likewise, in urban areas, public housing is critical for improved living standards of the poor because savings from lower housing costs can be set aside for more consumption in terms of food, healthcare and education.

References

Agénor, P.-R. 2002. Does Globalization Hurt the Poor? *World Bank Working Paper* No. 2922. Washington, DC: World Bank.

Akita, T., R. A. Lukman, and Y. Yamada. 1999. Inequality in the Distribution of Household Expenditures in Indonesia: A Theil Decomposition Analysis. *The Developing Economies*. 37 (2). pp. 197–221.

Alesina, A., and D. Rodrik. 1994. Distributive Politics and Economic Growth. *Quarterly Journal of Economics*. 109 (2). pp. 465–90.

Anand, S. 1983. *Inequality and Poverty in Malaysia: Measurement and Decomposition*. London: Oxford University Press.

Asher, M. G. 2010. Social Security Reform in Southeast Asia. In S. W. Handayani, ed. *Enhancing Social Protection in Asia and the Pacific: The Proceeding of the Regional Workshops*. Manila: Asian Development Bank.

Asian Development Bank (ADB). 2011. *Key Indicators for Asia and the Pacific 2011*. Manila.

——. 2012. *Asian Development Outlook 2012: Confronting Rising Inequality in Asia.* Manila.

Bénabou, R. 1997. Inequality and Growth. *NBER Working Paper* No. 5658. Cambridge, MA: National Bureau of Economic Research.

Bollen, K. A., and R. W. Jackman. 1985. Political Democracy and the Size Distribution of Income. *American Sociological Review.* 50 (4). pp. 438–57.

Chong, A., and M. Gradstein. 2007. Institutions and Inequality. *Review of Economics and Statistics.* 89 (3). pp. 454–65.

de Groot, H. L. F., J. Poot, and M. J. Smit. 2008. Agglomeration Externalities, Innovation and Regional Growth: Theoretical Perspectives and Meta-Analysis. *Working Paper in Economics* 01/08. Hamilton, New Zealand: University of Waikato.

Economic Planning Unit, Government of Malaysia. 2010. *Tenth Malaysia Plan 2011–2015.* Kuala Lumpur.

Fallon, P. R., and R. E. B. Lucas. 2002. The Impact of Financial Crises on Labor Markets, Household Incomes, and Poverty: A Review of Evidence. *World Bank Research Observer.* 17 (1). pp. 21–45.

Galbraith, J. K. 2011. Inequality and Economic and Political Change: A Comparative Perspective. *Cambridge Journal of Regions, Economy and Society.* 4 (1). pp. 13–27.

Giovannoni, O. 2010. Functional Distribution of Income, Inequality, and the Incidence of Poverty: Stylized Fact and the Role of Macroeconomic Policy. *UTIP Working Paper* No. 58. University of Texas Inequality Project.

Goldberg, P. K., and N. Pavcnik. 2005. Distributional Effects of Globalization in Developing Countries. *Journal of Economic Literature.* 45. pp. 39–82.

Gupta, S., H. Davoodi, and R. Alonso-Terme. 2002. Does Corruption Affect Income Inequality and Poverty? *Economics of Governance.* 3 (1). pp. 23–45.

Gyimah-Brempong, K. 2002. Corruption, Economic Growth, and Income Inequality in Africa. *Economics of Governance.* 3 (3). pp. 183–209.

Huther, J., and A. Shah. 2000. Anti-Corruption Policies and Programs: A Framework for Evaluation. *Policy Research Working Paper* No. 2501. Washington, DC: World Bank.

International Monetary Fund (IMF). 2007. Globalization and Inequality. In *World Economic Outlook 2007.* Washington, DC.

Johnston, M. 1989. Corruption, Inequality, and Change. In P. M. Ward, ed. *Corruption, Development and Inequality.* New York and London: Routledge.

Jomo, K. S. 2001. Globalisation, Liberalisation, Poverty and Income Inequality in Southeast Asia. *Working Paper* No. 185. Paris, France: OECD Development Centre.

Kaufmann, D., A. Kraay, and M. Mastruzzi. 2007. Governance Matters VI: Aggregate and Individual Governance Indicators. *Policy Research Working Paper* No. WPS 4280. Washington, DC: World Bank.

Kayizzi-Mugerwa, S. 2001. Globalisation, Growth and Income Inequality: The African Experience. *Working Paper* No. 186. Paris, France: OECD Development Centre.

Keefer, P., and S. Knack. 2002. Polarization, Politics, and Property Rights: Link between Inequality and Growth. *Public Choice.* 111 (1–2). pp. 127–54.

Milanovic, B. 2005. Can We Discern the Effects of Globalization on Income Distribution? Evidence from Household Surveys. *World Bank Economic Review.* 19. pp. 21–44.

Ministry of National Development and Planning, Government of Indonesia. 2010. *Regulation of the President of the Republic of Indonesia Number 5 of 2010 Regarding the National Medium-Term Development Plan (RPJMN) 2010–2014.* Jakarta.

Ministry of Planning and Investment, Government of the Lao People's Democratic Republic. 2011. *The Seventh Five-Year National Socio-Economic Development Plan (2011–2015).* Vientiane.

Ministry of Planning and Investment, Government of Viet Nam. 2011. Draft Five-Year Socio-Economic Development Plan 2011–2015. Extract of SEDP 2011–2015, unofficial translation. Ha Noi.

Murphy, K. M., A. Shleifer, and R. W. Vishny. 1989. Industrialization and the Big Push. *Journal of Political Economy.* 97 (5). pp. 1003–26.
National Economic and Development Authority, Government of the Philippines. 2011. *Philippine Development Plan 2011–2016.* Pasig City.
National Economic and Social Development Board, Government of Thailand. 2011. *Summary of the Eleventh National Economic and Social Development Plan (2011–2016).* http://thailandtoday.org/economy/elibrary/article/582
Park, D. 2000. Intra-Southeast Asian Income Convergence. *ASEAN Economic Bulletin.* 17 (3). pp. 285–92.
Prasad, N. 2008. Policies for Redistribution: The Use of Taxes and Social Transfers. *Discussion Paper* No. 194. Geneva, Switzerland: International Institute for Labour Studies.
Royal Government of Cambodia. 2010. *National Strategic Development Plan Update 2009–2013.* Phnom Penh.
Taylor, L. 2000. External Liberalisation, Economic Performance and Distribution in Latin America and Elsewhere. *UNU/WIDER Working Paper* No. 215. Helsinki, Finland: United Nations University World Institute for Development Economics Research.
Theil, H. 1967. *Economics and Information Theory.* Amsterdam: North Holland.
Topalova, P. 2007. Trade Liberalization, Poverty, and Inequality: Evidence from Indian Districts. In A. Harrison, ed. *Globalization and Poverty.* Chicago, IL: University of Chicago Press.
United Nations Economic and Social Commission for Asia and the Pacific. 2001. Strengthening Policies and Programmes on Social Safety Nets: Issues, Recommendations and Selected Studies. *Social Policy Paper* No. 8.
United States Social Security Administration. 2010. Social Security Programs Throughout the World: Asia and the Pacific. http://www.ssa.gov/policy/docs/progdesc/ssptw/2010-2011/asia/index.html
Viner, J. 1950. *The Custom Union Issue.* London: Stevens and Sons.
World Bank. Education Statistics (EdStats). http://web.worldbank.org/WBSITE/EXTERNAL/TOPICS/EXTEDUCATION/EXTDATASTATISTICS/EXTEDSTATS/0,,menuPK:3232818~pagePK:64168427~piPK:64168435~theSitePK:3232764,00.html
——. PovcalNet: The On-line Tool for Poverty Measurement Developed by the Development Research Group of the World Bank. http://iresearch.worldbank.org/PovcalNet/index.htm
——. World Development Indicators. http://data.worldbank.org/data-catalog/world-development-indicators
——. Worldwide Governance Indicators. http://info.worldbank.org/governance/wgi/index.asp
World Economic Forum. 2010. *The Global Gender Gap Report 2010.* Geneva.
Zhuang, J., E. de Dios, and A. Lagman-Martin. 2010. Governance and Institutional Quality and the Links with Growth and Inequality: How Asia Fares. In J. Zhuang, ed. *Poverty, Inequality, and Inclusive Growth: Measurement, Policy Issues, and Country Studies.* London: Anthem Press and Manila: ADB.

15 Income inequality and redistributive policy in the People's Republic of China

Shi Li, Guanghua Wan, and Juzhong Zhuang

Introduction

The rapidly rising income inequality that has accompanied the People's Republic of China's (PRC) phenomenal economic growth in the past three decades has been a key topic in policy discussions and academic research in and outside the PRC in recent years. According to the latest government releases, the Gini coefficient of per capita household disposable income hit a peak of 49.1 in 2008 and dropped somewhat to 47.4 in 2012 (NBS 2013). These figures represent a significant jump from its level of about 30 in the early 1980s (Ravallion and Chen 2007).[1]

Many studies have looked at the dynamics of the PRC's income inequality and its driving forces. However, such efforts have often been hampered by the lack of publicly available unit-level household survey data covering the entire country. One notable attempt to address this issue is by Lin *et al.* (2010) that used data extrapolated from publicly available grouped household income data of 23 provinces covering 85% of the country's population. The study found that the PRC's Gini coefficient increased from 34.5 in 1990 to 45.7 in 2005, driven by widening urban–rural income gaps and rising urban inequality. Another attempt is the Chinese Household Income Project (CHIP) of Beijing Normal University that carried out household surveys in selected years during 1995–2007 in more than 10 provinces. Results from these surveys show that the PRC's income inequality increased from 45 in 1995 to 48 in 2007 (Li *et al.* 2013).

This chapter has two objectives. The first is to provide more insights into the dynamics and driving forces of the PRC's income inequality using CHIP data in 1995 and 2007. We estimate national, urban, and rural inequalities; decompose the national inequality into between- and within-group inequalities; and look at how different household characteristics have contributed to inequality using regression-based decomposition. The second objective is to review some of the recent government policies in the PRC that aim to address the issue of rising income inequality, including tax reform, labor market policy, pro-farmer policies, social protection, regional development strategy, and fiscal transfers.

[1] The Gini coefficients presented in this chapter range from 0 to 100.

Table 15.1 Sample size of Chinese Household Income Project surveys, 1995 and 2007

	Location	*Provinces*	*Households*	*Individuals*
1995	Urban	12	6,931	21,698
	Rural	19	7,998	34,739
2007	Urban	16	10,000	29,249
	Rural	16	13,000	51,847

Source: S. Li, C. Luo, Z. Wei, and X. Yue. 2008. Appendix: The 1995 and 2002 Household Surveys: Sampling Methods and Data Description. In B. Gustafsson, S. Li, and T. Sicular, eds. *Inequality and Public Policy in [the People's Republic of] China*. New York: Cambridge University Press, pp. 337–53.

Data and methodology

Chinese Household Income Project surveys and household data

The CHIP survey in 1995 covered 6,931 urban households and 21,698 urban individuals from 12 provinces as well as 7,998 rural households and 34,739 rural individuals from 19 provinces. In 2007, it covered 10,000 urban households, 29,249 urban individuals, 13,000 rural households, and 51,847 rural individuals from 16 provinces (Table 15.1). The provinces included in both years are representative in terms of geographic coverage, including megacities and the East, Central, and West regions, and are detailed in Li *et al.* (2008) and Li *et al.* (2012). Notably, all 12 provinces in the 1995 urban survey were covered in the 2007 urban survey, and all 16 provinces in the 2007 rural household survey were covered in the 1995 survey. The household samples in the CHIP surveys were drawn from a large sample of the National Bureau of Statistics (NBS) surveys, which cover both rural and urban areas and all the provinces in mainland PRC.[2] The sampling methodology of the NBS surveys is described in Li *et al.* (2008).

The income definition adopted in this chapter is borrowed from that used by NBS so that our income inequality estimates are comparable with those published by NBS. Household incomes defined by NBS in urban areas are slightly different from those in rural areas. The urban household incomes are called "disposable cash incomes," including wages and salaries, net business incomes, property incomes, and net transfers (transfers minus taxes and fees), thus excluding income-in-kind and imputed rent of private-owned housing. The rural household incomes are called "net incomes," including both cash incomes and the monetary value of self-consumed agricultural products after subtracting production costs. It should be noted that rural household net incomes exclude private transfer payments from relatives and friends, which are part of disposable incomes of urban households. Like urban household disposable incomes, rural household net incomes do not include imputed rent of private-owned housing.

[2] The sample size of the NBS surveys was 35,520 in urban and 67,340 in rural areas in 1995, and 59,305 in urban and 68,190 in rural areas in 2007. See NBS (2003, 2008).

Methodology

This chapter uses two common measures of income inequality: Gini coefficient and Theil index. The to of the Gini coefficient, which ranges from zero indicating perfect equality and 1 (or 100 as followed in this chapter) indicating perfect inequality, is due to its wide application (see Chapter 2 for its definition). The use of the Theil index is due to its decomposability, which allows total income inequality to be decomposed into a between-group component and a within-group component. The Theil index, T, can be calculated as[3]

$$T = \frac{1}{N}\sum_{i=1}^{n}\frac{Y_i}{m}\ln\left(\frac{Y_i}{m}\right) \qquad (15.1)$$

where N is the total number of individuals in the population, Y_i is the income of individual i, and m is the mean income of the population. The Theil index can be expressed as the sum of between-group inequality (T_B) and within-group inequality (T_W):

$$T = T_B + T_W = \left[\sum_{j=1}^{j}\frac{Y_j}{Y}\ln\left(\frac{m_j}{m}\right)\right] + \left[\sum_{j=1}^{j}\left(\frac{Y_j}{Y}\right)T_j\right] \qquad (15.2)$$

where j is the number of population groups (which equals 2 in this chapter, namely, urban and rural), Y_j is the total income of the jth group, m_j is the mean income of the jth group, Y is the total income of the population, and T_j is the Theil index of the jth group, given by

$$T_j = \frac{1}{n_j}\sum_{i=1}^{n_j}\frac{Y_{ij}}{m_j}\ln\left(\frac{Y_{ij}}{m_j}\right) \qquad (15.3)$$

where n_j is the total number of individuals in the jth group, Y_{ij} is the income of individual i in the jth group.

This chapter also looks at contributions of household characteristics to income inequality using a regression-based decomposition approach. This involves employing the Shapley value decomposition proposed by Shorrocks (1999), with a combination of the methods proposed by Wan (2004) to decompose income inequality. Suppose that a general income-generation function is given by

$$Y_i = f(X_{i1}, X_{i2}, \ldots, X_{iK}) \qquad (15.4)$$

where Y_i, $i = 1, 2, \ldots, N$, is the per capita income of household i; X_{ik}, $k = 1, 2, \ldots, K$, is an independent variable corresponding to a particular household

[3] Also denoted as GE(1) in the literature.

characteristic of household i; and N and K are the total number of sample households and total number of independent variables, respectively.

Equation (15.3) can be estimated by applying simple regression analysis to the sample data. The estimate for equation (15.3) can be used to predict Y_i for each sample household, and an inequality measure (such as the Gini coefficient) can be estimated from these predicted values, which we denote as $I(Y)$. Replacing X_k in equation (15.3) by its sample mean would eliminate any difference in X_k among households. Y_i can be recomputed from equation (15.3) after this replacement. The resulting per capita income Y_{ik} differs from one household to another because other independent variables in equation (15.3) are set at their actual values. However, inequality in Y_{ik}, denoted as $I(Y_k)$, is due to differences in all the independent variables excluding X_k, which is set at the sample mean for all the sample households. The contribution of X_k to total inequality can then be computed as

$$C_k = I(Y) - I(Y_k), \quad \text{for } k = 1, \ldots, K \tag{15.5}$$

where C_k is the contribution of X_k to total inequality. These contributions can be termed the "first-round effect," which is obtained when only one independent variable X_k is replaced by its sample mean. One can obtain a second-round C_k by replacing two independent variables, X_k and X_j, with their sample means in computing Y_{jk}. The second-round contribution can be computed as

$$C_k = I(Y_j) - I(Y_{jk}), \quad \text{for } k, j = 1, \ldots, K (k \pi j) \tag{15.6}$$

By the same token, the third-round contribution can be obtained as

$$C_k = I(Y_{ij}) - I(Y_{ijk}) \quad \text{for } k, j, i = 1, \ldots, K (k \pi j \pi i) \tag{15.7}$$

This process continues until all X_k are replaced by their sample means. In each round, there will be multiple C_k, which are averaged first and then averaged across all rounds. The final average value of C_k represents the contribution of X_k to total inequality. Wan (2004) provides more technical details.

Dimensions of the People's Republic of China's income inequality

Total, urban, and rural income inequalities

Table 15.2 shows that the Gini coefficient of per capita household income of the entire sample increased from 45.2 in 1995 to 47.4 in 2007. The increase was more pronounced for urban households (with the Gini coefficient rising from 31.4 to 33.6) than for rural households (with the Gini coefficient rising from 36.4 to 37.9) during the same period. These results also confirm findings of previous studies that in the PRC, rural inequality is higher than urban inequality, unlike most

Table 15.2 Income inequality estimates, 1995 and 2007

	1995	*2007*
All households		
Gini coefficient	45.2	47.4
Theil index	0.377	0.385
Urban households		
Gini coefficient	31.4	33.6
Theil index	0.173	0.195
Rural households		
Gini coefficient	36.4	37.9
Theil index	0.237	0.249

Source: Authors' estimates based on 1995 and 2007 data from the Chinese Household Income Project, China Institute of Income Distribution, Beijing Normal University.

Table 15.3 Comparison with overall Gini coefficients reported in other studies

	1990	*1995*	*2000*	*2005*	*2007*	*2008*	*2010*	*2012*
This study	–	45.2	–	–	47.4	–	–	–
Ravallion and Chen (2007)	34.9	41.5	43.8	–	–	–	–	–
Lin *et al.* (2010)	34.5	39.7	41.1	45.7	–	–	–	–
National Bureau of Statistics (2013)	–	–	–	48.5	48.4	49.1	48.1	47.4

– = data not available.

Source: Authors' compilation.

developing countries where urban inequality is usually higher than rural inequality (ADB 2012; Chapter 13 of this volume). The Theil indices also show similar trends.

Table 15.3 compares our estimates of the overall Gini coefficients of per capita disposable household income with those reported in other selected studies, as well as the figures newly released by NBS (2013). Our estimate for 2007 is very close to that released by NBS. However, our estimate for 1995 is much higher than those reported in Ravallion and Chen (2007) and Lin *et al.* (2010).

To provide more insights into income inequalities, we computed the income share of each household decile group and the ratio of the mean income of each decile group to that of the lowest decile, separately for urban and rural households (Tables 15.4 and 15.5). In the case of urban households, in 1995 the income share of the lowest decile was only 3.2%, while that of the highest decile reached 27.8%. In 2007, the income share of the lowest decile declined to 2.8% and that of the highest decile also declined to 25.7%. In 1995, the ratio of the mean income of the highest decile to that of the lowest decile was 8.7:1. In 2007, this ratio increased to 9.1:1.

In the case of rural households, in 1995 the income share of the lowest decile was only 2.7%, while that of the highest decile reached 28.4%. In 2007, the income

Table 15.4 Urban income distribution by decile

	1995			*2007*		
	Share of total income (%)	*Cumulative share of total income (%)*	*Ratio of each decile to the lowest decile*	*Share of total income (%)*	*Cumulative share of total income (%)*	*Ratio of each decile to the lowest decile*
1 (Lowest)	3.2	3.2	1.0	2.8	2.8	1.0
2	4.8	8.0	1.5	4.4	7.2	1.6
3	5.7	13.7	1.8	5.6	12.8	2.0
4	6.6	20.3	2.1	6.6	19.4	2.3
5	7.5	27.9	2.4	7.7	27.1	2.7
6	8.6	36.4	2.7	8.9	36.0	3.1
7	9.7	46.2	3.0	10.4	46.4	3.6
8	11.4	57.6	3.6	12.4	58.8	4.4
9	14.6	72.2	4.6	15.5	74.3	5.4
10 (Highest)	27.8	100.0	8.7	25.7	100.0	9.1

Source: Authors' estimates based on 1995 and 2007 data from the Chinese Household Income Project, China Institute of Income Distribution, Beijing Normal University.

Table 15.5 Rural income distribution by decile

	1995			*2007*		
	Share of total income (%)	*Cumulative share of total income (%)*	*Ratio of each decile to the lowest decile*	*Share of total income (%)*	*Cumulative share of total income (%)*	*Ratio of each decile to the lowest decile*
1 (Lowest)	2.7	2.7	1.0	2.0	2.0	1.0
2	4.2	6.9	1.6	3.9	5.9	2.0
3	5.3	12.2	2.0	5.1	11.0	2.5
4	6.2	18.5	2.3	6.2	17.2	3.1
5	7.3	25.7	2.7	7.3	24.5	3.7
6	8.5	34.2	3.2	8.6	33.2	4.3
7	10.0	44.2	3.7	10.3	43.4	5.1
8	12.0	56.2	4.5	12.4	55.8	6.2
9	15.4	71.6	5.7	15.9	71.7	7.9
10 (Highest)	28.4	100.0	10.6	28.3	100.0	14.1

Source: Authors' estimates based on 1995 and 2007 data from the Chinese Household Income Project, China Institute of Income Distribution, Beijing Normal University.

share of the lowest decile further declined to 2% and that of the highest decile also declined but slightly, to 28.3%. During the same period, the mean income ratio of the highest to the lowest decile increased from 10.6:1 to 14.1:1, by about a third.

Table 15.6 Inequality decomposition by rural–urban division (% of total income inequality)

	Theil index	
	Within-group	*Between-group*
1995	60.3	39.7
2007	55.5	44.5

Source: Authors' estimates based on 1995 and 2007 data from the Chinese Household Income Project, China Institute of Income Distribution, Beijing Normal University.

Between- and within-group inequalities

The income gap between rural and urban areas has changed dramatically in the PRC since the beginning of economic reform. During 1995–2007, the gap increased significantly – the ratio of urban to rural household per capita income increased from 2.7:1 to 3.3:1. Table 15.6 shows that in 1995, the urban–rural income gap contributed 39.7% to total income inequality, and the rest – the sum of within-urban and within-rural inequalities – contributed 60.3%. In 2007, the share of total inequality contributed by the urban–rural income gap increased to 44.5%, while that contributed by the sum of within-urban and within-rural inequalities decreased to 55.5%. These results suggest that the rising urban–rural income gap has been a key driver of the rising income inequality in the PRC in recent years.

Determinants of inequality: regression-based decomposition

This section looks at how various household characteristics affect per capita income and hence income inequality, following the procedure described earlier. The independent variables used in the estimation include gender, age, educational attainment, marital status, retirement status, and occupation – all related to the household head; proportion of employed household members; household size; age composition of household members; and household residence location (rural or urban residence, province).[4] Table 15.7 reports the results.

In 1995, the explanatory variables combined can explain 60% of the total Gini coefficient, with the remaining 40% unexplained and denoted as residuals. Provincial location was the most important contributor of total income inequality, explaining about 14.3% of the Gini coefficient. This is followed by urban–rural residence, explaining about 13.0%; household head's occupation, 12.6%;

[4] The coefficients of most explanatory variables of the estimated income equations are statistically significant and the explanatory variables combined can explain a large part of the variations in the dependent variable, as suggested by the R-squared at 0.62 for the income equation in 1995 and at 0.68 in 2007. The detailed estimation results are available from the authors upon request.

Table 15.7 Regression-based decomposition

		1995		*2007*	
	Variable	*Gini*	*%*	*Gini*	*%*
A	Gender of household head	−0.1	−0.2	0.7	1.5
B	Age of household head	0.1	0.3	0.1	0.2
C	Educational attainment of household head	1.9	4.4	3.8	8.6
D	Marital status of household head	0.1	0.2	0.1	0.1
E	Retirement status of household head	1.2	2.7	1.2	2.6
F	Occupation of household head	5.5	12.6	1.9	4.3
G	Proportion of employed members	0.7	1.6	0.9	2.1
H	Household size	2.9	6.6	3.0	6.8
I	Age composition of household	2.2	5.1	1.7	3.9
J	Urban–rural residence	5.6	13.0	11.2	25.3
K	Province of household residence	6.2	14.3	7.0	15.7
L	Residual	17.2	39.6	12.8	28.9
Total		42.5	100.0	48.2	100.0

Source: Authors' estimates based on 1995 and 2007 data from the Chinese Household Income Project, China Institute of Income Distribution, Beijing Normal University.

household size, 6.6%; household's age composition, 5.1%; and household head's educational attainment, 4.4%.

In 2007, the explanatory variables combined accounted for about 71% of the total Gini coefficient of 48.2, increasing from 1995. Among the explanatory variables, urban–rural residence became the most important contributor, explaining 25.3% of the total Gini coefficient. This is followed by provincial location, explaining 15.7%; household head's educational attainment, 8.6%; household size, 6.8%; household head's occupation, 4.3%; and household's age composition, 3.9%.

Comparing 1995 with 2007, we can draw the following conclusions. First, the urban–rural divide made the greatest contribution to rising national income inequality, and it is now the most important determinant of inequality in the PRC. Second, cross-provincial income disparity remains a major contributor, but its relative importance has somewhat declined in recent years. It is now the second most important determinant. Third, the role of educational attainment has increased significantly in explaining household per capita income, and it is now the third most important determinant of income inequality.

The results from the regression-based decomposition analysis also allow us to examine to what extent income inequality is due to inequality of opportunity. It has been argued that income inequality due to differences in individual circumstances, such as location of residence (urban vs. rural areas and different provinces), parental education, ethnic origin, gender, and occupation (different sectors), could largely reflect inequality of opportunity because these circumstances are often out of the control of individuals (Roemer 1996; Ali and Zhuang 2007). As shown in Table 15.7, four such variables (urban–rural residence, provincial residence, occupation, and gender) together can explain a large part of the total Gini coefficient in both 1995 and 2007. Moreover, their contribution increased – from 39.6% in 1995 to 46.8% in 2007.

Recent government policies addressing income inequality

Concerns over the income distribution in the PRC have been increasing in recent years. In the Twelfth Five Year Plan, the government reiterated its commitment to "speeding up the formation of a reasonable pattern of income distribution . . ., and reversing the widening income gap as soon as possible" (State Council of the PRC 2011a). The government has set the goal to eliminate absolute poverty and narrow the income gap within the next 5 years, and this has attracted wide attention in and outside the PRC. In this section, we review recent developments in government policies for improving income distribution in some detail.

Personal income tax reform

The PRC did not have a personal income tax until the early 1980s. In 1986, the State Council issued the Provisional Regulations of PRC Personal Income Tax, which marked the start of official implementation of a personal income tax in the PRC. However, the tax was only applied to urban areas and levied on individual incomes rather than household incomes. There are 11 types of taxable personal incomes, with wages and salaries being taxed at progressive rates ranging from 5% to 45% and others, such as interest and rental incomes, royalties, remuneration of personal services, and capital gains from owning properties (recently introduced), being taxed at flat rates.

For the tax on wages and salaries, the minimum threshold (when the tax starts applying) was initially set at 800 yuan per month, which was very high compared with the average monthly urban wage in 1986 at 110 yuan (see NBS (1987)). As a result, only a very small proportion of income earners reached the threshold. As urban household incomes grew rapidly in the past two decades, more and more income earners became liable to income tax. In response to concerns over rising inequality, the government raised the minimum threshold from 800 yuan per month to 1,600 yuan per month in 2005, to 2,000 yuan per month in 2007, and to 3,500 yuan per month in 2011.

Overall, the personal income tax has not played an important role in redistributing income in the PRC due to a number of reasons. First, the tax is levied on individual sources of personal incomes separately, rather than on a consolidated basis, reducing its progressiveness. Second, wage and salary thresholds of different tax brackets are relatively high compared with the level of mean income, leading to a narrow tax base. For instance, the threshold for the top marginal tax rate is currently about 25 times as high as the PRC's gross domestic product (GDP) per capita, while this ratio is normally in the range of 4–5 on average in Organisation for Economic Co-operation and Development (OECD) countries. With the new minimum threshold adopted in 2011, it is estimated that there are now only

Table 15.8 Personal income tax burden on urban residents by decile, 2008

Income group	*Per capita income (yuan)*	*Per capita tax (yuan)*	*Tax rate (%)*
1 (Lowest)	5,427	0.2	0.004
2	8,424	1.8	0.022
3	10,666	5.8	0.054
4	12,712	8.7	0.069
5	14,831	18.2	0.123
6	17,266	29.5	0.171
7	20,277	60.7	0.299
8	24,258	117.1	0.483
9	30,535	251.9	0.825
10 (Highest)	51,467	1,059.2	2.058

Source: Authors' estimates based on 2008 urban household survey data of China National Bureau of Statistics.

less than 10% of urban income earners paying the tax.[5] Third, some high-income groups have ways to avoid paying the tax due to weaknesses in tax collection and administration.

Table 15.8 estimates the personal income tax burden of urban households by income decile using data from the 2008 urban household survey of NBS that covered 12,700 urban households. The annual per capita income ranged from 5,427 yuan for the lowest decile to 51,467 yuan for the highest decile and the corresponding per capita personal tax paid ranged from 0.2 yuan to 1,059.2 yuan. From these figures, the effective personal income tax rate is estimated to range from 0.004% for the lowest decile to 2.058% for the highest decile, with the average effective tax rate at less than 1%. These results show that while personal income tax is progressive, the progressiveness is rather limited, and, further, the overall effective tax rate is very low. Li *et al.* (2012) calculated pre-tax Gini coefficients and post-tax Gini coefficients for the period 1994–2009 using urban household data. The results, reported in Table 15.9, support the conclusion that the distributive effect of personal income tax is very limited in the PRC.

Agricultural tax reform

During the PRC's planned economy period, while urban households did not pay income tax, there existed agricultural tax, special agricultural product tax, slaughter tax, and deed tax in rural areas. In addition, farmers had to pay a variety of fees imposed by local governments, which in some localities led to an even higher burden on rural households than that of taxes. In the 1990s, the tax burden of Chinese farmers reached a very high level, causing public resentments and complaints. In

[5] It was estimated that the number of personal income taxpayers would be reduced from 84 million to 24 million when the threshold was raised from 2,000 yuan per month to 3,500 yuan per month in 2011. At the same time, urban employed people reached 360 million (see NBS (2012)).

Table 15.9 Redistribution effect of personal income tax for urban households

Year	*Pre-tax Gini coefficients*	*Post-tax Gini coefficients*
1997	30.1	29.6
1998	30.1	29.5
1999	29.7	29.2
2000	32.3	31.7
2001	32.4	31.6
2002	32.5	31.8
2003	34.4	33.6
2004	34.5	33.5
2005	35.2	34.2
2006	34.7	33.7
2007	34.5	33.2
2008	36.3	35.1
2009	34.7	33.5

Source: S. Li, G. Ma, and J. Xu. 2012. The Income Redistribution Effect of [the People's Republic of] China's Personal Income Tax: What the Micro Data Say? Discussion paper. China Institute of Income Distribution, Beijing Normal University.

Table 15.10 Average tax (fee) rate for different rural income groups

Income group	*1988*	*1995*	*2002*	*2007*
Lowest 10%	7.5	13.9	6.2	0.3
Lowest 20%	6.5	12.0	5.4	0.3
Highest 20%	4.1	3.4	1.7	0.3
Highest 10%	3.8	3.0	1.5	0.4
Average	5.0	5.3	2.8	0.3

Source: Authors' estimates based on 1988, 1995, 2002, and 2007 data from the Chinese Household Income Project, China Institute of Income Distribution, Beijing Normal University.

response, the central government repeatedly issued orders and circulars to curb excessive imposition of taxes and fees on farmers by local governments. Despite such efforts, the problem remained. A study of three counties dominated by the agriculture sector by the Development Research Center of the State Council found that the average effective tax rate facing rural households in these counties was 12% in 1997 and reached as high as 28% in one county (Chen 2003).

In 2006, to address widening rural–urban income gaps, the government abolished the agricultural tax nationwide, and also imposed strict control over local governments in collecting the fees from farmers. The 2007 household survey data showed that the rural households' tax burden had become negligible. As shown in Table 15.10, the average effective tax rate for rural households was 5% in 1988, reached 5.3% in 1995, but fell to 2.8% in 2002, and further declined to 0.3% in 2007. Table 15.10 also shows that the agricultural tax was regressive, with the rate for richer households lower than that for poorer households. This is confirmed in Table 15.11, which shows that the Gini coefficient of rural income inequality after tax was higher than that before tax in 1988, 1995, and 2002.

Table 15.11 Pre-tax and post-tax rural income inequality, 1988–2007

	1988	*1995*	*2002*	*2007*
Income Gini coefficient before tax (and fees)	30.89	36.66	36.06	37.94
Income Gini coefficient after tax (and fees)	31.29	37.66	36.16	37.94
Change in Gini coefficient (post-tax to pre-tax)	0.40	1.00	0.10	0.00

Sources: Figures for 1988, 1995, and 2002 are from H. Sato, S. Li, and X. Yue. 2006. The Redistributive Impact of Taxation in Rural [People's Republic of] China, 1995–2002: An Empirical Study Using the 1995–2002 CASS CHIP Surveys. *Discussion Papers* 2006–10. Graduate School of Economics, Hitotsubashi University; figures for 2007 are authors' estimates based on 2007 Chinese Household Income Project data, China Institute of Income Distribution, Beijing Normal University.

Labor market policies

The PRC has recently implemented two types of labor market policies: minimum wage regulation and collective wage bargaining mechanisms. The minimum wage regulation was introduced in urban areas in the late 1990s, and it has attracted greater attention and been implemented more strictly in recent years compared with collective wage bargaining. In 2004, the central government introduced a formal minimum wage regulation, which requires provincial governments to implement the regulation and set minimum wage standards for their respective urban cities. In practice, a provincial government sets a series of minimum wage standards for cities to choose from. That means there are significant differences in minimum wage levels among cities, even within a province. For example, the minimum wage was 1,120 yuan per month in Shanghai in 2011, while it was only 600 yuan per month in Kaifeng City in Henan Province.

Two issues have been raised over how effective the minimum wage regulation has been in reducing wage inequality in the PRC. One is deficient and ineffective enforcement of the regulation, especially in the informal sector (Ngok 2008). Another issue is the relatively low level of minimum wages. As shown in Figure 15.1, the average minimum wage as a percentage of the urban average wage has been declining since the 1990s. In particular, since 2005, the average minimum wage level has been below 30% of the average wage. Therefore, even with increasingly strict enforcement in recent years, the role of the minimum wage regulation in reducing wage inequality is believed to be limited.

Some cities and urban enterprises, with a push from the government, have recently experimented in the collective wage bargaining (CWB) mechanism. The number of workers covered by the mechanism has been increasing in recent years (Lee 2009). However, it is not clear if the new mechanism is effective in reducing wage inequality because there is little empirical research on this issue. There are two issues associated with the effectiveness of CWB in reducing wage inequality in the PRC context. The first is the weaker role of trade unions in enterprises in negotiating with employers. In state-owned enterprises, trade unions in general are less independent from governments and employers because the leaders of trade unions are, in general, appointed by governments or employers. The second is the

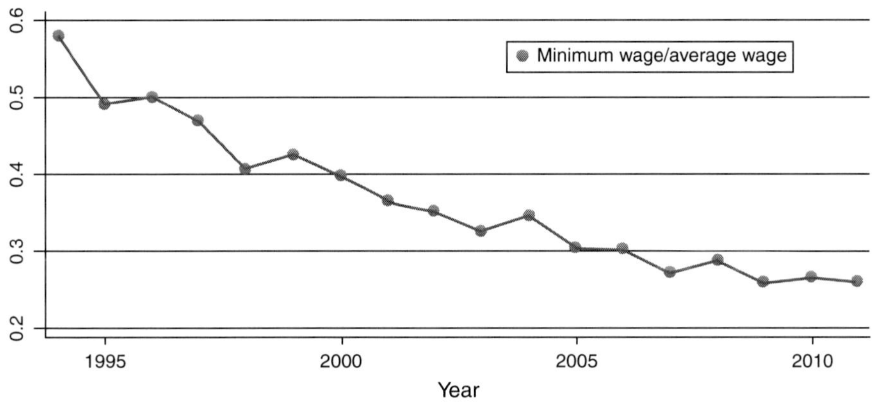

Figure 15.1 Minimum wage as a ratio of the average urban wage.

Source: S. Li and L. Ye. 2012. *Minimum Wage Policy in [the People's Republic of] China*. Discussion paper. China Institute of Income Distribution, Beijing Normal University

difficulty of applying CWB to the informal sector and small private firms, which employ mainly casual workers and unskilled labor.

The Dibao system

Dibao, or the minimum income guarantee system, was first experimented with in Shanghai in 1993. Since the State Council promulgated the Regulations on the Minimum Income Guarantee for Urban Residents in 1999, the number of beneficiaries covered by the system has grown rapidly (Table 15.12). At the end of June 2002, the Ministry of Civil Affairs announced that the PRC had achieved the goal of "guaranteeing all those who should be guaranteed" in urban areas. According to the 2010 Social Services Development Statistical Report (Ministry of Civil Affairs 2011), a total of 11.45 million urban households (23.1 million individuals) were receiving subsistence allowances at the end of 2010. The total government expenditure on urban subsistence allowances amounted to 52.47 billion yuan, 70% of which was from the central government budget. The beneficiaries included the unemployed, elderly without pensions, and children without parental support. These three groups accounted for more than 70% of all the allowance recipients. The level of the subsistence allowance has recently been raised. For instance, in 2010, the average urban subsistence allowance was 251.2 yuan per person, up 10.3% from 2009.

Empirical studies find that while the *Dibao* program does not have a significant impact on reducing income inequality, it has been effective in alleviating poverty (Li and Yang 2009). If the local minimum income is taken as the poverty line, using the CHIP 2007 urban household survey data, we can work out poverty incidence, the poverty gap, and the weighted poverty gap before and after the

Table 15.12 Urban and rural population supported by the *Dibao* system, 2000–2011 (million)

	2000	*2001*	*2002*	*2003*	*2004*	*2005*	*2006*	*2007*	*2008*	*2009*	*2010*	*2011*
Urban	4.0	11.7	20.6	22.5	22.1	22.3	22.4	22.7	23.3	23.5	23.1	22.8
Rural	3.0	3.0	4.1	3.7	4.9	8.3	15.9	35.7	43.1	47.6	52.1	53.1

Sources: Ministry of Civil Affairs. 2008. *Statistical Report of [the People's Republic of] China's Social Development in 2008*. Beijing; and NBS. 2012. *[People's Republic of] China Statistical Yearbook 2012*. Beijing: China Statistical Press.

subsistence allowance. The results show that urban poverty incidence declined by 42% on the whole as a result of the *Dibao* system. More importantly, the impact on the poverty gap and the weighted poverty gap was even stronger, reaching 57% and 63%, respectively (Li and Yang 2009). This means that the subsistence allowance has not only lifted a considerable number of people out of poverty, but also raised the income of the remaining poor households.

Compared with the urban *Dibao* program, the rural one was established a few years later and was not promoted in all rural areas until 2007. Even in 2004, the rural *Dibao* program was implemented only in a few provinces and supported fewer than 5 million people. After 2004, more provinces implemented the program, covering a growing number of people. For example, only 0.46% of rural residents received the subsistence allowance in 2004 and the percentage increased to nearly 8% in 2011. The guarantee level has also been rising over time.

Similar to the *Dibao* in urban areas, the *Dibao* in rural areas has had limited impact on narrowing income inequality but has been effective in reducing rural poverty. NBS survey data show that in 2008, among the officially designated poor counties, 3,835 rural households and 16,636 people received support from the *Dibao* program. The coverage was 7.28%, above the national average. As shown in Table 15.13, for the recipient group, using the poverty line of 1,196 yuan per person per year (the new official poverty line introduced in 2008), the *Dibao* system reduced poverty incidence by 21%, the poverty gap by 32.6%, and the weighted poverty gap by 37.5%. This means that the rural minimum income guarantee system lifted more than 20% of the recipients out of poverty.

Pro-farmer policies

Since the beginning of the new century, the PRC Government implemented a series of pro-farmer policies as part of its balanced development strategy and measures to reduce urban–rural income gaps. Pro-farmer policies can be divided into two categories. The first is subsidies aimed at directly increasing farmers' income, supporting grain production, accessing improved varieties of seeds, and purchasing farm machinery. The second is improved public services and social protection, including the establishment of a new cooperative medical system, "two exemptions and one subsidy (free textbooks, exemption from tuition fees, and

Table 15.13 Rural poverty before and after the *Dibao* system, 2008

Poverty line: 1,196 yuan per person per year	*Poverty incidence*	*Poverty gap*	*Weighted poverty gap*
Recipients			
Before *Dibao*	0.2392	0.0723	0.0357
After *Dibao*	0.1886	0.0487	0.0223
Pro-poor effect (%)	21.1500	32.6400	37.5400
All rural residents			
Before *Dibao*	0.1503	0.0462	0.0402
After *Dibao*	0.1466	0.0445	0.0392
Pro-poor effect (%)	2.4600	3.6800	2.4900

Source: Q. Deng and S. Li. 2010. *Assessment of the Rural Social Security Progress and Its Poverty Reduction Effect: Based on the Case of the Minimum Living Security System.* A background report prepared for the Evaluation Report of the Effect of "[People's Republic of] China's Rural Poverty Alleviation and Development Outline (2001–2010)." Beijing, PRC (translated from Chinese).

Table 15.14 Central government spending on rural subsidies (billion yuan)

	2004	*2005*	*2006*	*2007*	*2008*
Central government funds supporting agricultural development	167.1	297.5	339.7	431.8	595.5
Grain subsidies	11.6	13.2	14.2	15.1	15.1
Improved seed varieties subsidy	2.8	3.9	4.2	6.7	12.1
Agricultural machinery purchase subsidy	0.07	0.3	0.6	1.2	4.0
General subsidies for agricultural production supplies	–	–	12.0	27.6	63.8
Rural minimum living allowance	1.7	2.5	4.2	10.4	22.2

Source: X. Li, K. Zhang, and L. Tang. 2010. *Assessment of General Preferential Agricultural Policy and Its Poverty Reduction Effect.* Background report prepared for the Evaluation Report of the Effect of "[People's Republic of] China's Rural Poverty Alleviation and Development Outline (2001–2010)." Beijing, PRC (translated from Chinese).

subsidized accommodation)" policy for compulsory education, and rural minimum income guarantee. These pro-farmer policies have played an important role in increasing farmers' incomes and reducing the income gaps between urban and rural areas. They have also helped reduce income inequality within rural areas and alleviated rural poverty.

To implement the pro-farmer policies, the central government has increased its fiscal allocation for rural development. Table 15.14 shows that, from 2004 to 2008, the central government expenditure on supporting agriculture development increased from 167.1 billion yuan to 595.5 billion yuan, with an annual growth rate of 61%. Grain subsidies increased by 30%, seed subsidies by 140%, and the increase in subsidies for agricultural production machinery purchase and for agricultural production supplies were even higher during the four years.

Social security

During the planned economy period, the PRC's social security programs only covered urban formal sector employees, with the rural population largely not covered. One of the government's recent reform priorities is to establish a social security system that covers the entire population. The social security system has been extended to cover the urban informal sector and migrant workers, in particular in pension and medical care. In 2003, the government started to implement the New Rural Cooperative Medicare (NRCM) in rural areas, funded by the central government and local governments (80%) and the participants (20%). Official reports estimate that the rate of participation in NRCM reached more than 97% of rural people by the end of 2011, with more than 1.3 billion rural patients receiving support from the program (Ministry of Health 2012). The New Rural Pension Scheme (NRPS) was implemented first as an experiment in 20% of counties in 2009. The scheme has been quickly expanded to other counties. The government planned to have the scheme expanded to all counties in 5 years. It is reported that there were more than 326 million rural adults participating in the scheme by the end of 2011 (NBS 2012).

Due to the expansion of the social security system in recent years, employees in urban informal sectors – especially migrant workers from rural areas – and rural residents have been gradually covered. This should have some positive impacts on income distribution. However, because of the differences in the scope and level of coverage among these groups, it is not clear to what extent the social security system has narrowed the income gap between urban and rural areas, within urban areas and within rural areas, and income inequality nationwide (Zhuang *et al.* 2012). For instance, Li and Luo (2010) found that the market value of the social security and public services received by urban residents was 17 times that of rural residents in 2002. Taking this into account would increase the urban–rural per capita income ratio from 3.1 times to 4.4 times. For the social security system to play a major role in narrowing income inequality and achieving greater social equity, it is critically important for the PRC to move toward a system with equal access and coverage by all population groups.

Regional development strategy and fiscal transfer policies

During much of the reform period, economic growth was higher in the coastal region than in the western region, and this has led to widening regional disparity in household income and consumption, government revenue and expenditure, and public services delivery. In response, the government in 2000 adopted the Western Development Strategy. Its main components include the improvement of infrastructure, preferential policies for foreign investment, more efforts on ecological protection (such as reforestation), and promotion of education and public

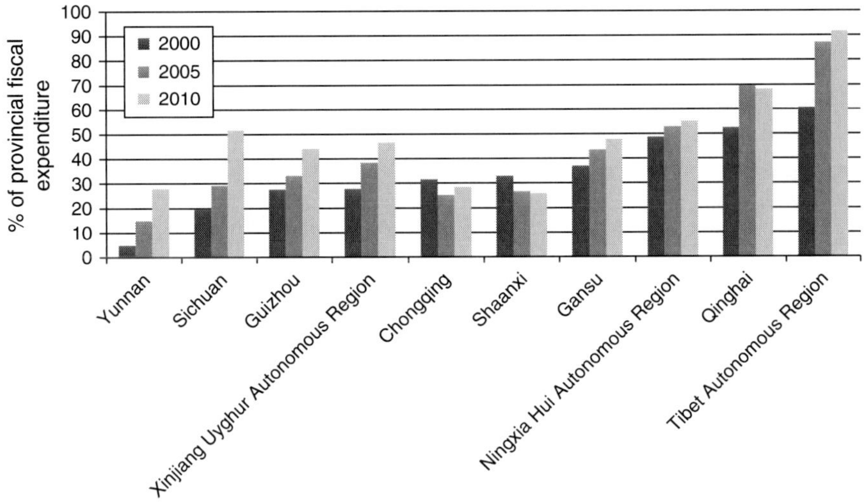

Figure 15.2 Fiscal transfers from the central government to western provinces.

Source: H. Zhang, Forthcoming. Report on Fiscal Transfer and Fiscal Expenditure Equalization in [the People's Republic of] China. In S. Li., L. Deshen, and C. Luo, eds. *Research Report on Income Distribution in [the People's Republic of] China.*

services in the western region. As part of implementing this strategy, the central government spent 2.2 trillion yuan on infrastructure projects from 2000 to 2010 (State Council of the PRC 2011b). To support local economic and social development in the western provinces, the central government also increased fiscal transfers to the region. As indicated in Figure 15.2, the fiscal transfers received from the central government by the western provinces increased significantly during 2000–2010. The poorest provinces, such as Qinghai and Tibet Autonomous Region, have particularly benefited from the fiscal transfers. For example, the fiscal transfers received as a percentage of the total fiscal expenditure increased from 52.4% to 68.2% in Qinghai and from 60.5% to 91.5% in Tibet Autonomous Region during 2000–2010.

As a result, the income gap between coastal and western PRC has decreased since the mid-2000s. It has been reported that, during 2000–2009, the western region's growth rate was higher than the national average. The share of the western region in national GDP increased from 17.1% to 18.5% during the same time (State Council of the PRC 2011b). The Western Development Strategy also contributed to narrowing household income gaps between coastal and western regions. Rural household income per capita in the western provinces as a percentage of that in the eastern provinces increased from 50.4% in 2005 to 54.3% in 2010. For urban households, the ratio increased from 65.7% to 67.9% during the same period (NBS 2006, 2011).

Poverty alleviation policies

The PRC started to implement antipoverty policies in the mid-1980s, focusing on rural areas where poverty is concentrated. One unique feature of the poverty alleviation strategy in the PRC, called "Poverty Alleviation and Development" (*fupin kaifa*), is to reduce rural poverty by promoting the local economy of the most underdeveloped areas where the poor are concentrated. In the mid-1990s, the government officially designated 592 counties as poor counties on which poverty alleviation policies would be targeted. These counties are mostly located in central and western PRC, accounting for over 60% of the total poor in rural PRC.

To speed up rural poverty alleviation, the government introduced the 8–7 National Plan for Poverty Reduction in 1994, highlighting the determination to get 80 million rural people out of poverty in 7 years. In 2001, the State Council issued the *Outline of the Poverty Alleviation and Development Policies in Rural [People's Republic of] China 2001–2010*, which contains new measures for poverty alleviation, such as a comprehensive development program for 148,000 poorest villages (*Zhengcun tuijin*) that will receive funds to improve infrastructure and implement social welfare programs until the end of 2009 (CDRF 2007).

During 1986–2005, the central government spent 322.8 billion yuan on poverty alleviation programs, consisting of 167.1 billion yuan used to subsidize the loans to poor counties and households, 83.4 billion yuan for work-for-food projects, and 72.3 billion yuan as development funds (CDRF 2007). In 2011, the central government increased the poverty alleviation fund by 21.3% and, for 2012, it committed to an increase of over 20% (China Daily 2011).

As household incomes continue to grow, the government has also raised the official poverty line in recent years. The first poverty line (called the old or absolute poverty line) was introduced in 1985 and applied only to the rural areas. It was set at 200 yuan per person per year and adjusted by the rural consumer price index (CPI) for subsequent years. In 2000, the government introduced a low-income line at 865 yuan per person per year, adjusted by CPI for subsequent years. In 2007, this low-income line was adjusted to 1,067 yuan per person per year. In 2008, the absolute poverty line and the low-income line were merged, and 1,067 yuan became the new official poverty line, which was adjusted to 1,196 yuan in 2009 and 1,274 yuan in 2010. In 2011, the government raised the official poverty line for the rural population further to 2,300 yuan per person per year (in 2010 constant prices).

As a result of both the poverty alleviation policies and high economic growth, the PRC's rural poverty rate has declined considerably (Figure 15.3). At the old poverty line, the number of rural poor declined from 152 million in 1981 to 15 million in 2007, with the decline more pronounced during the first two decades of economic reform. At the new poverty line introduced in 2007, the number of rural poor declined from 94 million in 2000 to 36 million in 2009. At the latest 2,300 yuan poverty line, the number of rural poor stood at 128 million in 2011.

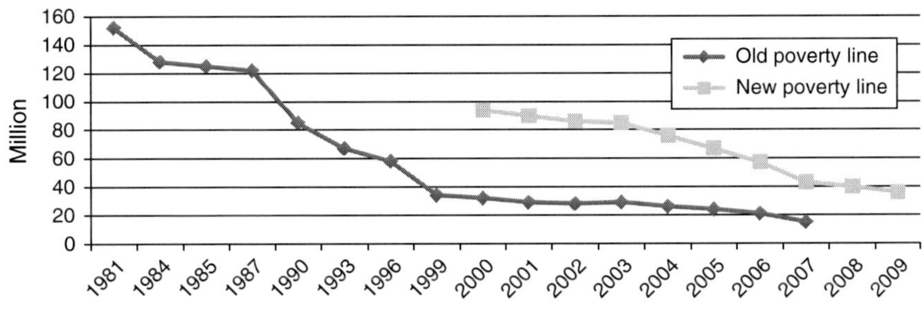

Figure 15.3 Changes in rural poor population in the People's Republic of China, 1981–2009.

Note: The old poverty line was introduced in 1985 at 200 yuan per person per year and adjusted by the rural consumer price index (CPI) for subsequent years. The new poverty line was introduced in 2008 at 1,067 per person per year and adjusted by CPI for subsequent years.

Source: NBS. 2010. *[People's Republic of] China Rural Poverty Monitoring Report 2010*. Beijing: China Statistical Press.

Conclusions and policy implications

In this chapter, we looked at the dynamics and driving forces of the PRC's income inequality using CHIP data in 1995 and 2007, and reviewed recent government policies to address the issue of rising income inequality, including tax reform, labor market policy, pro-farmer policies, social protection, regional development strategy, and fiscal transfers. The key findings can be summarized as follows.

First, after increasing from about 30 in the early 1980s to over 40 in the 1990s, the PRC's Gini coefficient continued to rise during much of the 2000s. Based on CHIP data, this chapter finds that the national, urban, and rural Gini coefficients stood at 47.4, 33.6, and 37.9, respectively, in 2007. These figures are in line with the latest income inequality estimates released by the country's national statistical bureau, which put the national Gini coefficient at 48.4 in 2007, 49.1 in 2008, and 47.4 in 2012. More detailed analysis using CHIP data shows that the income share of the richest decile of the urban population in 2007 was 26%, while that of the poorest decile was less than 3%; for the rural population, the richest decile's income share was 28% and the poorest decile's income share was 2%.

Second, conventional decomposition analysis shows that the urban–rural income gap accounted for 40% of total income inequality in the PRC, and this contribution increased to about 45% in 2007. Regression-based decomposition provides more insights into the causes of rising inequality. Between 1995 and 2007, the share of the total Gini coefficient explained by urban/rural residency increased from 13% to over 25%, by provincial location from 14% to 16%, and by household head's educational attainment from 4% to 9%. If the spatial inequality can be considered as largely being caused by unequal access to opportunity, then more than 40% of the PRC's income inequality reflects inequality of opportunity.

Third, to reduce poverty and address rising income inequality, the government has introduced many policy measures since the 1980s, including reforming the personal income tax system; abolishing agriculture tax; introducing minimum wage regulation and collective wage bargaining mechanisms; introducing the minimum income guarantee (*Dibao*) system; implementing farmer support policies; developing and strengthening the social security system; implementing the Western Development Strategy to reduce regional disparity; and introducing various poverty alleviation programs, including raising the official poverty line from time to time. These measures have been very effective in reducing poverty, but not so in reducing income inequality.

Fourth, moving forward, while the PRC should continue to implement various programs to reduce and eliminate poverty – given the fact that 128 million Chinese still live in poverty as measured by the latest updated poverty line – more efforts are also needed to confront the challenge of rising and high income inequality. Policy priorities in this regard may include, among others, (i) increasing the role of personal income tax in income distribution; (ii) increasing the targeting of transfer and social relief programs and expanding the coverage of social protection to the entire population; (iii) increasing government spending on public services (education, healthcare and so on), ensuring equal access to these services, and eliminating discrimination, particularly against rural migrant workers; (iv) continuing to implement farmer support policies and improving their effectiveness; (v) improving labor market institutions to provide adequate protection of workers' rights, especially those of vulnerable groups such as women, the disabled, and ethnic minorities, without hindering job creation; (vi) improving governance, promoting rule of law and social justice, and intensifying anticorruption efforts; and, more broadly, (vii) creating more urban jobs to absorb surplus labor in the agriculture sector.

It is encouraging that many of these policy priorities are in the government's Twelfth Five Year Plan and were reconfirmed at the recent 18th National Congress of the PRC Communist Party. They have been further detailed in the Circular for Deepening Income Distribution Reform, recently issued by the National Development and Reform Commission, Ministry of Finance, and Ministry of Human Resources and Social Security and approved by the State Council in February 2013. The circular recommends a number of new redistribution policies, such as promoting equal employment opportunities, providing training for unskilled workers, encouraging labor mobility, implementing universal social security, promoting faster income growth of low- to middle-income households, raising the minimum wage level substantially, controlling faster wage growth in monopoly sectors, increasing fiscal transfers to remote and backward areas, introducing property taxes, and so on. The challenge is to make them a reality before inequality divides society and stunts growth.

References[6]

Ali, I., and J. Zhuang. 2007. Inclusive Growth toward a Prosperous Asia: Policy Implications. *ERD Working Paper* No. 97. Manila, Philippines: Economics and Research Department, ADB.

Asian Development Bank (ADB). 2012. Confronting Rising Inequality in Asia. Theme chapter of *Asian Development Outlook 2012*. Manila, Philippines: ADB.

Chen, X. 2003. *Research on China's County and Township Finance and Income Growth of Farmers*. Shanxi, PRC: Shanxi Economic Press.

China Daily. 2011. Public Disclosure of Poverty Relief Funds Management Soon. 7 December. http://english.peopledaily.com.cn/90882/7668592.html (accessed 24 July 2013).

China Development Research Foundation (CDRF). 2007. *China Development Report 2007: The Elimination of Poverty through Development*. Beijing: Fazhan Press.

Deng, Q., and S. Li. 2010. *Assessment of the Rural Social Security Progress and Its Poverty Reduction Effect: Based on the Case of the Minimum Living Security System*. A background report prepared for the Evaluation Report of the Effect of "China's Rural Poverty Alleviation and Development Outline (2001–2010)." Beijing, PRC.

Lee, C.-H. 2009. Industrial Relations and Collective Bargaining in China. *Working Paper* No. 7. Industrial and Employment Relations Department, International Labour Organization (ILO). Geneva: ILO.

Li, S., and S. Yang. 2009. Effect of China's Urban Minimum Living Security System on Income Distribution and Poverty. *China Population Science*. 5. pp. 19–27.

Li, S., and C. Luo. 2010. Re-Estimating the Income Gap between Urban and Rural Households in China. In M. Whyte, ed. *One Country, Two Societies: Rural–Urban Inequality in Contemporary China*. Cambridge, MA: Harvard University Press.

Li, S., and L. Ye. 2012. *Minimum Wage Policy in China*. Discussion paper. China Institute of Income Distribution, Beijing Normal University.

Li, S., C. Luo, Z. Wei, and X. Yue. 2008. Appendix: The 1995 and 2002 Household Surveys: Sampling Methods and Data Description. In B. Gustafsson, S. Li, and T. Sicular, eds. *Inequality and Public Policy in China*. New York: Cambridge University Press. pp. 337–53.

Li, S., G. Ma, and J. Xu. 2012. *The Income Redistribution Effect of China's Personal Income Tax: What the Micro Data Say*? Discussion paper. China Institute of Income Distribution, Beijing Normal University.

Li, S., H. Sato, and T. Sicular, eds. 2013. *Inequality in China: Public Policy and the Pursuit of a Harmonious Society*. Cambridge, UK: Cambridge University Press.

Li, X., K. Zhang, and L. Tang. 2010. *Assessment of General Preferential Agricultural Policy and Its Poverty Reduction Effect*. Background report prepared for the Evaluation Report of the Effect of "China's Rural Poverty Alleviation and Development Outline (2001–2010)."

Lin, T., J. Zhuang, D. Yarcia, and F. Lin. 2010. Decomposing Income Inequality: People's Republic of China, 1990–2005. In J. Zhuang, ed. *Poverty, Inequality, and Inclusive Growth in Asia: Measurement, Policy Issues, and Country Studies*. London: Anthem Press and Manila: ADB.

Ministry of Civil Affairs. 2008. *Statistical Report of China's Social Development in 2008*. Beijing.

—. 2011. *2010 Social Services Development Statistics Report* (in Chinese). http://www.mca.gov.cn/article/zwgk/mzyw/201106/20110600161364.shtml

Ministry of Health. 2012. *China Health Statistical Bulletin 2011* (in Chinese). http://61.49.18.65/mohwsbwstjxxzx/s7967/201204/54532.shtml

[6] The Asian Development Bank recognizes China by the name People's Republic of China.

National Bureau of Statistics (NBS). 1987. *China Statistical Yearbook 1987*. Beijing: China Statistical Press.
——. 2003. *China Statistical Abstract 2003*. Beijing: China Statistical Press.
——. 2006. *China Statistical Yearbook 2006*. Beijing: China Statistical Press.
——. 2008. *China Statistical Abstract 2008*. Beijing: China Statistical Press.
——. 2010. *China Rural Poverty Monitoring Report 2010*. Beijing: China Statistical Press.
——. 2011. *China Statistical Yearbook 2011*. Beijing: China Statistical Press.
——. 2012. *China Statistical Yearbook 2012*. Beijing: China Statistical Press.
——. 2013. *China Statistical Yearbook 2013*. Beijing: China Statistical Press.
Ngok, K. 2008. The Changes of Chinese Labor Policy and Labor Legislation in the Context of Market Transition. *International Labor and Working Class History*. 73 (1). pp. 45–64.
Ravallion, M., and S. Chen. 2007. China's (Uneven) Progress against Poverty. *Journal of Development Economics*. 82. pp. 1–42.
Roemer, J. E. 1996. *Theories of Redistributive Justice*. Cambridge, MA: Harvard University Press.
Sato, H., S. Li, and X. Yue. 2006. The Redistributive Impact of Taxation in Rural China, 1995–2002: An Empirical Study Using the 1995–2002 CASS CHIP Surveys. *Discussion Papers* 2006–10. Graduate School of Economics, Hitotsubashi University.
Shorrocks, A. F. 1999. Decomposition Procedures for Distributional Analysis: A Unified Framework Based on the Shapley Value. Unpublished manuscript. Department of Economics, University of Essex.
State Council of the People's Republic of China. 2011a. The Twelfth Five Year Plan for National Economic and Social Development of the People's Republic of China (2011–2015) (in Chinese). http://news.sina.com.cn/c/2011-03-17/055622129864.shtml
State Council of the People's Republic of China, Western Development Bureau. 2011b. Retrospect on Achievement of Western Development in the Last Ten Years. http://www.chinawest.gov.cn/web/NewsInfo.asp?NewsId=57916
Wan, G. 2004. Accounting for Income Inequality in Rural China: A Regression-Based Approach. *Journal of Comparative Economics*. 32 (2). pp. 348–63.
Zhang, H. Forthcoming. Report on Fiscal Transfer and Fiscal Expenditure Equalization in China. In S. Li., L. Deshen, and C. Luo, eds. *Research Report on Income Distribution in [the People's Republic of] China*.
Zhuang, J., P. Vandenberg, and Y. Huang. 2012. *Growing beyond the Low-Cost Advantage: How the People's Republic of China Can Avoid the Middle-Income Trap*. Manila: ADB.

16 Drivers of inequality in Pakistan

Talat Anwar

Introduction

The recent debate on income inequality and economic liberalization in Pakistan began in the late 1990s. There has been widespread concern that liberalization and excessive reliance on market forces are increasing inequality at the national and provincial levels and in urban and rural areas. There have also been apprehensions that growing income inequality is exacerbating unequal access to basic social services such as education and health. Many studies have examined the trends of inequality in Pakistan, employing different methods, living standard indicators (household income or consumption), and data sources. Inevitably, they have generated divergent results.

This chapter has three objectives. The first is to look at the recent evolution of income as well as non-income inequality in Pakistan, paying particular attention to consistency in making comparisons over time. The second is to examine key driving forces of changing inequality in Pakistan. The third is to take stock of the policy actions that the government is taking to address the issue of inequality, draw policy lessons, and provide recommendations for future policy actions in pursuing an inclusive growth strategy.

Recent trends of income and non-income inequality

Inequality of per capita household income since the 1960s

While there are many studies on inequality in Pakistan, most of these are limited to estimating inequality using household survey data in two periods.[1] These studies employed different methods, used different data sources, and hence reported divergent and sometimes contradictory results, leading to an unambiguous conclusion about trends in inequality in Pakistan.

Anwar (2005) estimated Pakistan's income inequality during the early 1960s to early 2000s, using published household survey data and following a consistent method. As shown in Figure 16.1, the country's Gini coefficient of per capita household income declined at the end of the decade after remaining high in the

---

[1] Studies include early work by Haq (1964), Bergan (1967), Azfar (1973), Khandkar (1973), Naseem (1973), Mahmood (1984), de Kruijk and Leeuwen (1985), and more recent contributions by the Pakistan Bureau of Statistics (2001) and World Bank (2003).

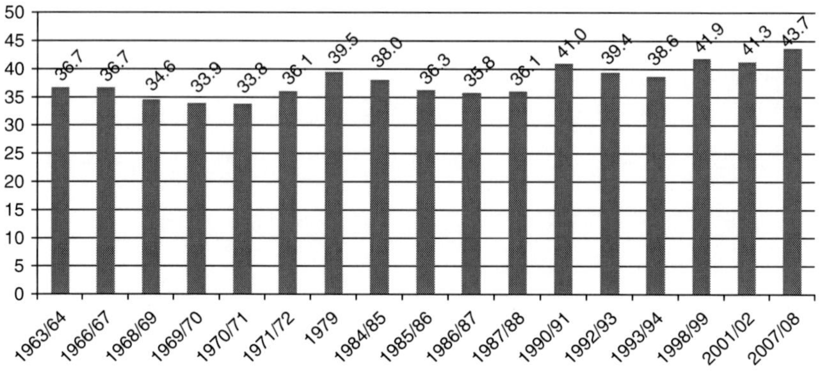

Figure 16.1 Gini coefficients in Pakistan.

Note: Gini coefficients are based on household per capita income.

Sources: Based on results from 1963/1964 to 2001/2002 in T. Anwar, 2005. Long-Term Changes in Income Distribution in Pakistan: Evidence Based on Consistent Series of Estimates. *Discussion Paper* No. 3 CRPRID. August. Islamabad; and author's estimates using data from Pakistan Bureau of Statistics. 2001. *Poverty in the 1990s*. Islamabad: Statistics Division; and Pakistan Bureau of Statistics. 2008. *Pakistan Social and Living Standard Measurement Survey (PSLM) 2007/08*. Islamabad.

mid-1960s due to relatively high economic growth. The 1970s were characterized as a slow growth period, but income inequality was on the rise. Income inequality declined in the 1980s when growth was high, at an average 6.5% per year, and increased in the 1990s despite economic growth slowing down to 4.6% per year. These results suggest a weak link between growth and inequality in Pakistan.

Anwar (2005) also found that the income shares of the poorest 20% and middle 60% of the population declined between 1987/1988 and 2001/2002, whereas that of the richest 20% grew significantly, in both urban and rural areas of Pakistan. This period coincided with the implementation of the structural adjustment and liberalization program supported by the International Monetary Fund and the World Bank. The government undertook a number of economic reforms to reduce internal and external imbalances, but these reforms failed to reduce inequality. Income inequality increased rapidly between 2001/2002 and 2007/2008, with the income distribution in 2007/2008 being the most unequal during the past six decades. This period was characterized by rapid economic growth, driven by consumption in the wake of high capital inflows in the form of foreign investment and aid as well as workers' remittances after the 9/11 event in the United States (Anwar 2004).

Recent trends in consumption inequality

The Government of Pakistan's Economic Survey (for various years) and the Planning Commission (2006) provided more detailed estimates of inequality in the

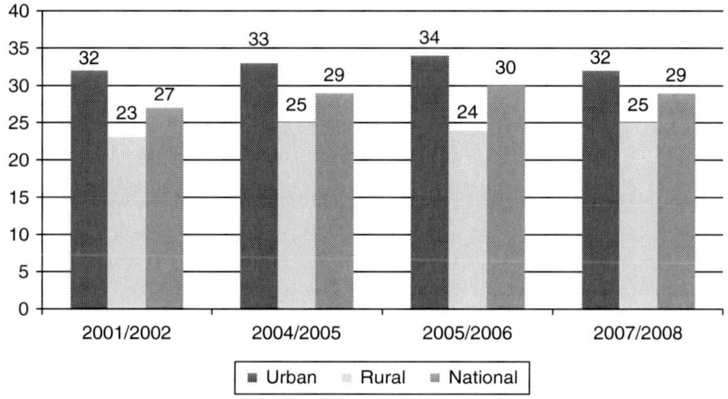

Figure 16.2 Urban, rural, and national Gini coefficients in Pakistan.

Sources: Government of Pakistan. 2006. *Economic Survey 2006*. Islamabad: Ministry of Finance; Government of Pakistan. 2008. *Economic Survey 2008*. Islamabad: Ministry of Finance; and Pakistan Bureau of Statistics. 2001. *Poverty in the 1990s*. Islamabad: Statistics Division.

2000s, based on per adult-equivalent household consumption expenditure data.[2] Figure 16.2 shows that the Gini coefficient increased between 2001/2002 and 2004/2005 and continued to widen between 2004/2005 and 2005/2006, but narrowed marginally in 2007/2008. Other studies have shown that between 2001 and 2005, the consumption share of the lowest 70% declined and that of the richest 20% increased.[3] Correspondingly, the ratio of per adult-equivalent household consumption expenditure of the highest decile to that of the lowest decile worsened from 5.5 in 2001 to 6.2 in 2005, indicating an increased income gap between rich and poor over the period.

Between 2001/2002 and 2004/2005, while the Gini coefficient increased in both rural and urban areas, the increase was more pronounced for rural than urban areas. Inequality declined in rural areas, while it continued to increase in urban areas from 2004/2005 to 2005/2006. From 2005/2006 to 2007/2008, inequality increased in rural areas but decreased in urban areas, resulting in a decline in overall inequality in Pakistan. The decline in urban inequality may have been due to the growth effect. Notably, slower growth started in 2007/2008, which seemed to have affected the incomes of the richest in urban areas. While the overall Gini coefficient declined marginally in 2007/2008 – the most recent year for which data are available – its level remained higher than that at the beginning of the decade.

---

[2] Per adult-equivalent household consumption expenditure adjusts for differences in the age structure of household members across households. Consumption-based inequality estimates are normally lower than income-based inequality estimates (see Chapter 2).

[3] See Anwar (2009, 2010) and Planning Commission (2006).

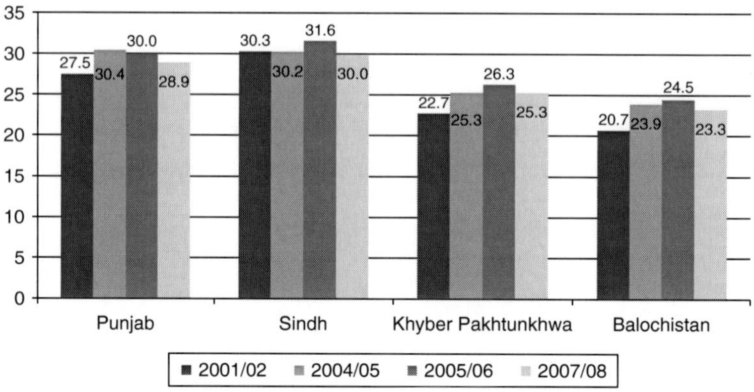

Figure 16.3 Gini coefficients in Pakistan by province.

Sources: Government of Pakistan. 2006. *Economic Survey 2006*. Islamabad: Ministry of Finance; Government of Pakistan. 2008. *Economic Survey 2008*. Islamabad: Ministry of Finance; Pakistan Bureau of Statistics. 2001. *Poverty in the 1990s*. Islamabad: Statistics Division; and computed from Pakistan Bureau of Statistics. 2008. *Pakistan Social and Living Standard Measurement Survey (PSLM) 2007/08*. Islamabad.

Figure 16.3 shows that all four provinces in Pakistan – Punjab, Sindh, Khyber Pakhtunkhwa, and Balochistan – shared the nationwide trend of changing inequality in the 2000s. During 2001/2002 to 2005/2006, inequality increased, and, from 2005/2006 to 2007/2008, it declined in all provinces. With the exception of Sindh, inequality was higher in 2007/2008 than at the beginning of the decade.

Non-income inequality

Inequality has many dimensions. However, analysis is often limited to monetary measures of income or consumption. Income or consumption inequality is actually an outcome of inequalities in the socioeconomic structure of a society; that is, it is linked to inequality in opportunities, such as educational opportunity or access to health. Non-income inequality plays a critical role in shaping income inequality.

Inequality in literacy. Household survey data show that inequality in literacy rates across consumption deciles is high in Pakistan. In 2001, the literacy rate for individuals aged 10 years and above was 24% for the poorest decile, compared with 72% for the richest decile.[4] There is also large disparity in the literacy rate between rural and urban areas. For instance, the adult literacy rate of the poorest decile in rural areas was only 19%, as opposed to 53% in urban areas.

Gender inequality in education. Recent progress in education has been disappointing in Pakistan as the net primary enrollment rate – already one of the lowest in Asia – declined, although marginal, to 56% in 2010/2011 from 57% in

[4] For a detailed analysis, see Anwar (2009).

2008/2009.[5] There appears to be a large gender disparity in basic education in Pakistan. The net primary enrollment rate for females was 50% compared with 60% for males. The net primary enrollment rate for females in rural areas was 48% compared with 57% for males. Gender disparities in educational opportunity also exist at middle and matric (i.e., secondary) levels. The net enrollment rate at the middle level was 32% for females compared with 38% for males, with the gender gap in rural areas greater – 24% for females and 34% for males. However, the gender gap is smaller at the matric level, with the net enrollment rate at 21% for females compared with 24% for males.

Inequality in access to healthcare. Large disparity across consumption deciles also exists in access to health facilities in Pakistan. In 2001, the proportion of fully immunized children aged 12–23 months was 31% among the poorest 10% compared to 78% among the richest 10%.[6] There were large rural–urban differences in this area as well. The disparity related to utilization of maternal health facilities appears to have improved. Evidence shows that the percentage of pregnant women receiving prenatal consultation increased from 35% in 2001 to 49% in 2005. The increase in prenatal consultation was mainly due to the rise in consultation received at home from traditional birth attendants, female health workers and health visitors, and doctors. Similarly, postnatal consultations within 6 weeks after delivery increased significantly from 9% in 2001 to 22% in 2005. The improvement was attributed to the rise in consultations with female health visitors, doctors, and government hospitals.

Inequality comparison with other Asian countries

Figure 16.4 compares Pakistan's consumption expenditure-based Gini coefficient with those of other countries in South Asia in the late 2000s. Pakistan's Gini coefficient at 30 was lower than Bangladesh's 32, India's 37, and Sri Lanka's 40. It is worth noting, however, that Pakistan's Gini coefficient is estimated using per adult-equivalent consumption expenditure, while for other countries it is estimated using per capita consumption expenditure. Furthermore, Pakistan's Gini coefficient has been adjusted for urban–rural cost of living differences, while this may not be the case for other countries. Adjusting for the cost of living differences between urban and rural areas could reduce the Gini's magnitude. Hence, although Pakistan's Gini coefficient is lower than those of the three other South Asian countries as shown in Figure 16.4, caution is needed in making cross-country comparisons.

Absolute poverty trends

With inequality on the rise in Pakistan, it would be interesting to know whether trends in poverty move in the same direction. In Pakistan, as in many other

[5] For a detailed analysis, see Pakistan Bureau of Statistics (2008, 2011).

[6] See Anwar (2009).

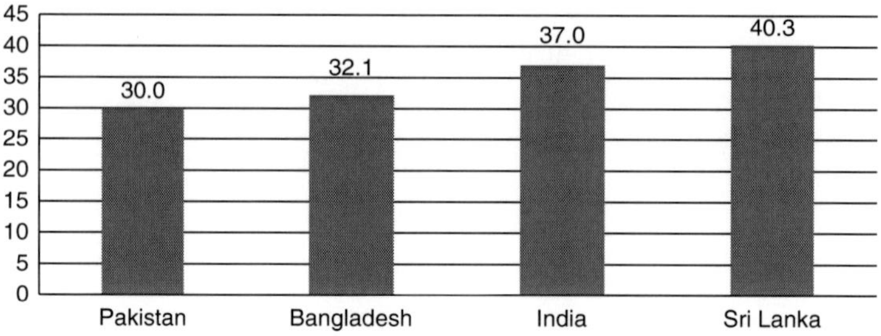

Figure 16.4 Gini coefficients in Pakistan and selected countries in South Asia.

Sources: Government of Pakistan. 2008. *Economic Survey 2008*. Islamabad: Ministry of Finance; and ADB. 2012. *Asian Development Outlook 2012: Confronting Rising Inequality in Asia*. Manila.

developing countries, poverty is defined as lack of ability to meet 2,350 calories per adult per day as the minimum food intake needed to perform the physical activities of daily life. Figure 16.5 shows that the rate of absolute poverty increased from the early 1990s to the early 2000s, and the increase coincided with rising inequality in the 1990s (Figure 16.1). The increase in poverty was mainly attributed to the slowdown in economic growth, from an annual average of 6% in the 1980s to 4% in the 1990s. However, poverty declined following rapid growth since the early 2000s, and this decline has been accompanied by a rise in inequality.

Although there is consensus on a declining trend in poverty in the wake of high growth, the level of poverty remains controversial in Pakistan. As shown in Figure 16.5, poverty as measured by the Planning Commission declined substantially, from 34.5% in 2001/2002 to 23.9% in 2004/2005 and further to 17.2% in 2007/2008. However, poverty estimates of 23.9% in 2004/2005 using official methods have been questioned by the World Bank (2006) and Anwar (2006). These studies suggested a decline in poverty to 29.2% and 29.3%, respectively, rather than 23.9% as estimated by the Planning Commission.[7]

The controversies deepened further when the World Bank (2010) adopted latest poverty estimates for 2007/2008, which the Planning Commission did not endorse, arguing that a rapid reduction in poverty to 17.2% in 2007/2008 seemed implausible in the wake of high inflation during the year of the high food price crisis. Using the same official methodology, a committee constituted by the Planning Commission estimated that poverty declined further to 12.4% in 2010/2011. However, a technical group constituted by the Planning Commission did not validate the result because it is not consistent with high inflation and declining economic growth during that period. The government still uses old poverty estimates of

[7] For a detailed discussion, see ADB (2008).

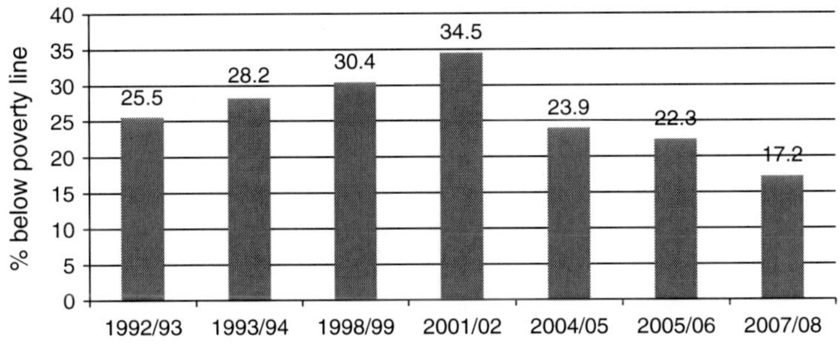

Figure 16.5 Poverty headcount in Pakistan, 1990s and 2000s.

Sources: Pakistan Bureau of Statistics. 2001. *Poverty in the 1990s*. Islamabad: Statistics Division; Government of Pakistan. 2006 and 2008. *Economic Survey 2006* and *Economic Survey 2008*. Islamabad: Ministry of Finance; T. Anwar. 2010. Role of Growth and Inequality in Explaining Changes in Poverty in Pakistan. *Pakistan Development Review*. 49 (1). pp. 1–17; World Bank. 2010. *Country Partnership Strategy, FY 2010–13*. Report No. 53553-PK.

22.3% in 2005/2006 in official documents of 2012 for planning and evaluation purposes.

Decomposition of inequality

The previous section shows that overall inequality increased in Pakistan but does not explain what contributed to the increase. Changes in economic conditions could bring many structural shifts, such as urban–rural income gaps, regional disparity, earnings differences between skilled workers and those with lower skill endowments, and wage gaps between males and females – and all these could in turn shape inequality. For instance, if market-oriented economic reforms initiated in the 1990s have had differential impacts across regions, due to factors such as advantages in physical infrastructure or human capital endowments of some locations over others, regional inequality could increase. This section decomposes Pakistan's inequality by location, individuals' educational attainment, and gender to assess the importance of these factors in shaping overall inequality.

Decomposition by location: within and between rural and urban areas

The rising rural–urban income gap can be a significant contributor to inequality in a country. In his two-sector model, Kuznets (1955) identified the possibility of rising inequality due to urbanization. In this model, the drivers of inequality are changes in inequality within each of the two sectors (rural and urban), a widening of the gap between average incomes in the two sectors, and a shift of population from agriculture in the rural sector to industry in the urban sector.

The decomposition of inequality by the urban–rural dimension in Pakistan indicates that the contribution of between rural–urban inequality was modest at

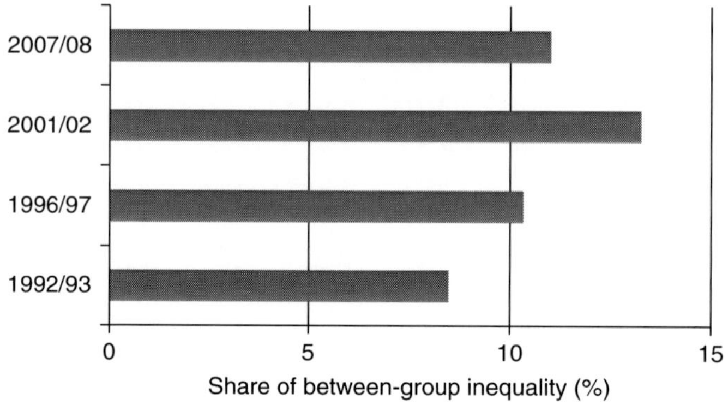

Figure 16.6 Urban–rural inequality decomposition in Pakistan.

Source: Based on results of M. Idrees. 2006. Analysis of Income and Consumption Inequality in Pakistan. PhD thesis submitted at Quad-i-Azam University, Islamabad; and ADB. 2012. *Asian Development Outlook 2012: Confronting Rising Inequality in Asia*. Manila.

around 8% in 1992/1993 (Figure 16.6).[8] This was very low compared with the 92% combined contribution of within-rural and within-urban inequalities.[9] The low contribution of between rural–urban inequality can largely be explained by a relatively small difference in household mean income between rural and urban areas of Pakistan. However, the importance of rural–urban inequality increased over time, with its contribution rising from less than 9% in 1992/1993 to 13% in 2001/2002, before declining to 11% in 2007/2008. This increase can be explained by relatively faster growth in urban than in rural areas during most of the period. It suggests that the increasing urban–rural gap has been one of the drivers of rising inequality in Pakistan. Nevertheless, the contribution of between rural–urban inequality to overall inequality in Pakistan at 11% in 2007/2008 is lower than in other Asian countries such as the People's Republic of China (PRC) at 45%, India at 22%, and Indonesia at 23%.

Decomposition by location: within and between provinces

Regional inequality has also been a key contributor to national inequality in many Asian countries, in particular in the PRC and India where between-province and between-state inequalities were 12% and 17%, respectively (ADB 2012). In Pakistan, Punjab is the largest province with the other three being much smaller. Figure 16.7 shows that between-province inequality only accounted for a share

[8] The decomposition for the period 1992/1993 to 2001/2002 is based on Theil's second measure, as reported in Idrees (2006), whereas the figure for 2007/2008 is from ADB (2012).

[9] The combined contribution of within-rural and within-urban inequalities remained dominant throughout the period.

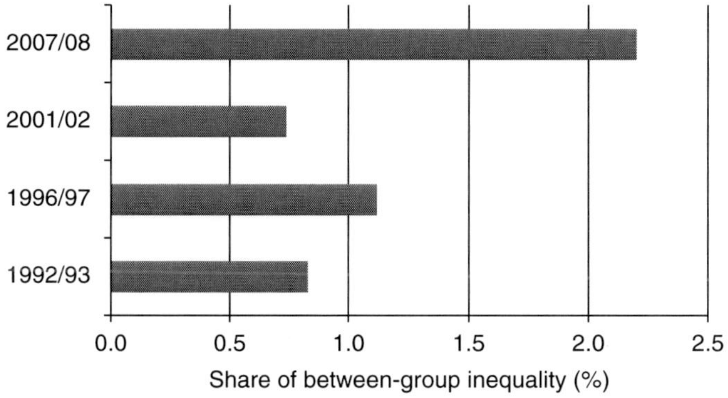

Figure 16.7 Provincial inequality decomposition in Pakistan.

Sources: For 1992/1993 to 2001/2002, M. Idrees. 2006. Analysis of Income and Consumption Inequality in Pakistan. PhD thesis submitted at Quad-i-Azam University, Islamabad; and for 2007/2008: ADB. 2012. *Asian Development Outlook 2012: Confronting Rising Inequality in Asia*. Manila.

of around 1% of total inequality during 1992/1993 to 2001/2002 and 2.2% in 2007/2008. Thus, inequality in Pakistan cannot be explained in terms of inequality across provinces; it is within-province inequality rather than inter-provincial inequality that is responsible for income inequality in Pakistan. Nevertheless, rising regional inequality has also contributed to rising overall inequality.

Decomposition of labor

Earnings of employed persons account for more than two-thirds of aggregate household incomes in Pakistan. Inequality estimates based on earnings suggest that the level of inequality is much higher. The Gini coefficient based on labor earnings of households in Pakistan increased from 46 in 1992/1993 to 47 in 2001/2002, suggesting that a sizable earnings inequality existed before economic liberalization (Idrees 2006). Earnings of an individual depend on various factors including age, gender, education, and employment status. It is thus important to analyze the contribution of these factors to the overall earnings inequality.

Decomposition of earnings inequality by gender

Gender has been found to be an important determinant of individual earnings. The decomposition of earnings inequality by gender shows that the contribution of inequality *within* the female group increased from 22.9% in 1992/1993 to 23.9% in 2001/2002, whereas the contribution of inequality *within* the male group declined from 75.4% to 74.0% during the same period.[10] On the other hand,

[10] See Idrees (2006) for decomposition of earnings inequality by gender and education.

the contribution of inequality *between* male and female groups remained low but increased from 1.6% to 2.0%.

It is noteworthy that the proportion of employed females has been quite low in Pakistan, although it increased to 17.5% in 2001/2002 from 9.4% in 1992/1993. The income share of female earners at 6.4% was even lower than their employment share, implying that average earnings of females were considerably lower than the average earnings of males. However, earnings inequality among females is much higher than inequality among males. This is because employed females are mostly from either the elite or poor classes of society. Females with higher education apply for white-collar jobs while those from the poor classes end up with low-paid informal jobs.

Decomposition of earnings inequality by education

Education is also a key determinant of individual earnings. Decomposition of earnings inequality by individual educational attainment suggests that within-group inequality accounted for 95% of the overall earnings inequality and between-group inequality accounted for only 5% in 2001/2002 (Idrees 2006). Of the total within-group inequality, earnings inequality among illiterate individuals accounted for 37.8%, 34% among those with primary education, 11% among those with secondary education, and 6% among those with tertiary education. The low contribution of within-group inequality with higher education was mainly due to the low share of individuals with such a level of education. On the other hand, an ADB study (2012) using household survey data found that the share of total income inequality that can be explained by differences in educational attainment of heads of households increased from 23% in 2002 to 25% in 2008.

Structural and policy drivers of inequality

While globalization is critical to economic development, it could increase inequality because it tends to affect income and employment of different segments of population differently. Technological change and market-oriented economic reform have been the key drivers of economic growth in Pakistan during the past two decades, but they have also had an important bearing on income inequality. In this context, it is important to identify the transmission channels of the effects of these factors on inequality.

Globalization and trade liberalization

Globalization has three main features.[11] First, it involves the integration of trade through removal of trade barriers. Second, it increases mobility of capital through removal of barriers on investment. Third, it involves technological change and

---

[11] For a good discussion of these, see Anwar (2002).

diffusion as an outcome of these two features. Globalization and trade integration could affect income distribution by increasing relative demand for skilled workers, thereby affecting the relative wages of skilled and unskilled workers. Similarly, *technological change* can also affect income distribution by increasing the relative demand for skilled labor (more educated and experienced) by increasing its productivity, resulting in increased skill premiums that can increase income inequality. Technological change could be biased in favor of capital and thus will increase inequality as capital income is less equally distributed than labor income. Likewise, *market-oriented reform* can have significant distributional consequences. If labor market reform reduces the bargaining position of labor, it could adversely impact wages and income distribution.

Pakistan liberalized its trade regime in the late 1980s in order to integrate its market with the world economy. The government undertook a major shift in trade policy from inward-looking import substitution to outward-looking export promotion. As a result, most non-tariff barriers on imports were replaced with tariffs, and maximum tariff rates were reduced from 225% in 1988 to 70% in 1994/1995, 35% in 1998/1999, and finally 25% in 2007/2008 (Anwar 2002).

Globalization and trade liberalization can affect growth and income distribution through a variety of channels. The impacts of these drivers are interconnected and difficult to disentangle empirically. In East Asian countries, trade liberalization contributed to a decline in wage inequality in the 1990s (Wood 1999). On the other hand, liberalization had a substantial effect on wage inequality in Latin America (Beyer *et al.* 1999). Technological change and structural transformation was skill-biased and thus resulted in increased wages for skilled labor.

In Pakistan, Salman and Javed (2011) showed that trade liberalization as measured through import penetration in different industries increased wage inequality for different skill levels in the 1990s and early 2000s. These results concerning increasing wage inequality matched those of Galiani and Sanguinetti (2003) whose findings suggested that an increase in import penetration ratio leads to higher wage premiums of skilled workers relative to other low-skilled labor. Salman and Javed's (2011) results also indicated a similar increase in the premium for skilled labor along with a decrease in wages for unskilled labor, significantly and further widening the wage gap in Pakistan.[12] The results showed that a 10% increase in import penetration increases the wage premiums for skilled workers by 2.1 percentage points but reduces the wage premiums for unskilled workers by 2.0 percentage points, indicating that trade openness appears to have increased wage inequality in Pakistan. Because wages contribute a major portion of aggregate household incomes, an increase in wage inequality is likely to have resulted in higher income inequality in Pakistan during the past two decades. Globalization and trade liberalization, therefore, turned out to be an important driver of inequality in Pakistan over the past two decades.

12 Anwar (1996) found that wage increases announced by the government were lower than the inflation rate. This led to a decline in real wages and prompted poverty to rise in the late 1980s.

Financial liberalization

Financial liberalization refers to the deregulation of domestic financial markets and it can facilitate finance sector development and contribute to long-term growth. A more developed and freer finance sector can increase the availability of credit, allowing the poor not only to invest in their human capital but also establish small businesses. Therefore, by widening financial opportunities for the poor, finance sector development can reduce income inequality. On the other hand, rich households may be better able to seize the opportunities created by finance sector development, while the poor may fail to do so due to their lack of collateral and connections, among other factors. In other words, financial liberalization could increase inequality (Banerjee and Newman 1993; Galor and Zeira 1993). Furthermore, financial liberalization could induce excessive risk-taking and increase macroeconomic volatility and instability to which the poor are more vulnerable.

Pakistan has undertaken a series of reforms to liberalize its finance sector since the early 1990s. To remove structural weaknesses, the government introduced government debt auctions and open market operations, imposed cash reserve requirements to control monetary expansion, reduced the statutory liquidity ratio, phased out directed credit and concessional interest rate, and allowed the private sector to open banking companies (State Bank of Pakistan 2002). These measures have increased financial depth as measured by the ratio of broad money to gross domestic product (GDP), improved efficiency of credit allocation as the share of concessionary and mandatory credit in the total private sector credit declined from 58.7% during 1980–1985 to 35.7% in the 2000s, and made the investment environment more conducive with inflows of foreign investment to Pakistan increasing from about $200 million in 1991 to about $7 billion in 2007.

The impact of finance sector reforms on income distribution in Pakistan has been a matter of debate. As the government undertook simultaneously a number of reforms to liberalize trade, investment, and the finance sector, it is difficult to isolate the effects of finance sector reforms on income inequality from others. However, some empirical evidence suggests that finance sector reforms do not seem to reduce income inequality but rather tend to aggravate it. The Gini coefficient based on per capita consumption expenditure for households headed by finance sector employees was at 39 in 2001/2002, followed by that for households headed by employees in the mining sector at 35, manufacturing sector at 33, community services sector at 30, and wholesale and retail trade sector at 29 (Anwar 2007).

Land ownership

Distribution of land ownership could be one of the important structural drivers of inequality, especially for an agrarian economy such as Pakistan where land plays a key role in livelihood. The landless population appears to be very large in Pakistan. According to the 1990 Agriculture Census, 61.4% of rural households were landless (Government of Punjab 2003). Anwar *et al.* (2004) estimated that 67% of rural households owned no land in Pakistan in 2001/2002. The same study also found that 18% of households in 2001/2002 owned less than 5 acres of land and 9.7%

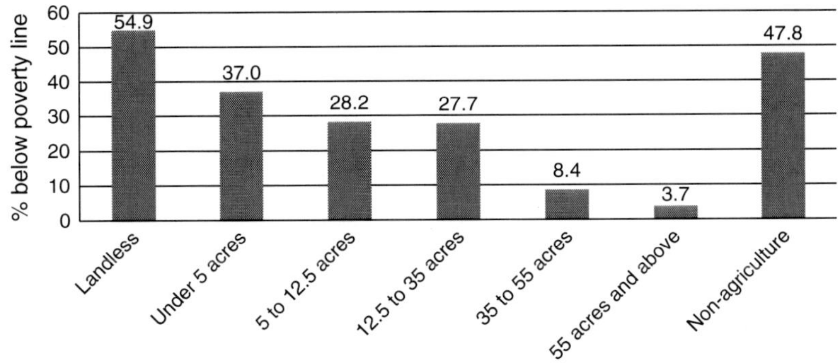

Figure 16.8 Poverty headcount in Pakistan by landholding using official poverty line, 2001/2002.

Source: T. Anwar, S. K. Qureshi, and H. Ali. 2004. Landlessness and Rural Poverty in Pakistan. *Pakistan Development Review.* 43 (19). pp. 855–74.

owned 5–12.5 acres per household. These land sizes only provide a subsistence level of living. On the other hand, 1.0% of households owned more than 35 acres of land per household, indicating a highly skewed land ownership pattern in Pakistan. This is also captured by the Gini coefficient of landholdings, which was very high at 61.5% in 2001/2002. Poverty seems to be strongly correlated with the size of landholdings in Pakistan. The poverty headcount rate was found to be the highest in rural areas among landless at 54.9%, followed by non-agriculture households at 47.8% (see Figure 16.8). Poverty incidence declines with increases in the size of landholdings. Thus, highly unequal land distribution is one of the major causes of poverty that drives and reinforces existing income inequality in rural Pakistan.

Growth, growth pattern, and growth policy

Pakistan's economy grew 5% per year on average during the past six decades, although growth slowed in the 1970s and 1990s. The lower growth rates in the 1970s were mainly due to the nationalization of major industries, banking, and insurance companies, as well as educational institutions, leading to an erosion of private investor confidence. The decline in poverty was accompanied by a rise in inequality during the 1970s. Growth declined in the 1990s in the wake of globalization and economic liberalization, leading to an unstable macroeconomic environment and increased poverty and inequality levels.

In 2001, the government built its growth paradigm on attracting capital inflows through foreign investment, privatizing public sector entities, and increasing domestic demand through credit expansion to accelerate the growth of the economy, in particular in industry and services. As a result, the country witnessed high GDP growth of around 6–9% per year. The fast pace of expansion enabled

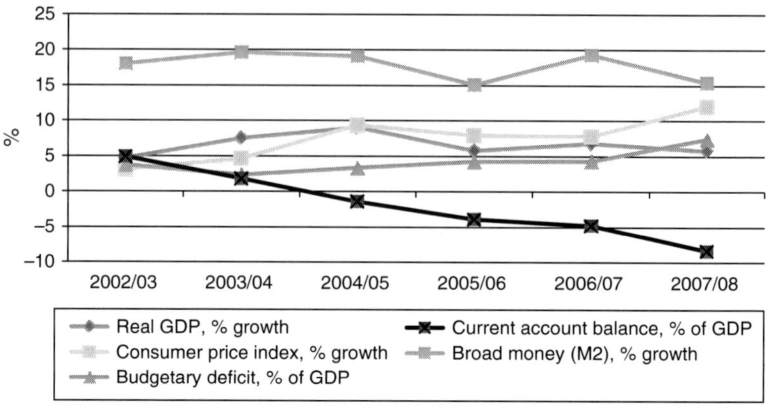

Figure 16.9 Changes in macroeconomic indicators in Pakistan, 2002/2003 to 2007/2008.

GDP = gross domestic product.

Sources: Government of Pakistan. 2006 and 2008. *Economic Survey 2006* and *Economic Survey 2008*. Islamabad: Ministry of Finance.

the country to position itself as one of the fastest growing economies in Asia (Figure 16.9). The growth paradigm benefited from high capital inflows in the form of foreign investment, foreign aid, and increased workers' remittances after 9/11 (Anwar 2004).

The central bank did not sterilize these capital inflows, which led to an expansionary monetary policy. Consequently, monetary assets increased rapidly by 19.6% in 2003/2004 and 19.3% in 2004/2005, significantly impacting domestic demand. As a result, imports grew more rapidly than exports, turning the current account balance into deficit in later years. The lax monetary policy led to an expansion in private sector credit, including personal consumption loans, which led to a surge in aggregate demand and thus higher economic growth and inflation in subsequent years. While high growth seems to have reduced poverty, it resulted in higher inequality during this period. It appears that the adverse effects of the 1990s were mitigated in the post-9/11 developments, mainly due to increased capital inflow that positively impacted economic growth and the poverty level but induced adverse effects on the level of inequality in the 2000s (Figures 16.1 and 16.5). With the rapid growth in the 2000s mainly driven by manufacturing and services sectors, where skilled labor is used that generally receives relatively higher wages, inequality increased (Anwar 2007).

Governance

The quality of governance can also affect inequality. Weak governance compromises the delivery of public services and adversely affects those who need them

Table 16.1 Percentile rank of governance indicators for Pakistan

Governance indicator	*1996*	*1998*	*2000*	*2004*	*2006*	*2007*	*2008*	*2009*	*2010*	*2011*
Voice and accountability	29.3	31.3	11.1	14.9	22.6	20.2	22.6	23.2	26.5	26.3
Political stability and absence of violence	12.5	13.5	14.4	6.7	2.4	1.0	1.0	0.9	0.5	0.5
Government effectiveness	30.7	36.1	31.2	39.5	42.0	40.3	28.6	23.9	26.3	22.3
Regulatory quality	30.9	27.9	21.1	18.1	36.3	32.0	32.0	33.0	31.1	29.9
Rule of law	28.7	24.9	20.6	20.6	23.4	19.6	19.2	20.9	25.6	20.7
Control of corruption	8.8	15.6	22.4	12.7	23.4	24.3	21.8	12.4	12.0	15.6

Source: Worldwide Governance Indicators, http://info.worldbank.org/governance/wgi/index.asp

most, particularly low- and middle-income households. Corruption can affect inequality by perpetuating the existing distribution of assets. The influence of powerful interest groups could bias policies, programs, and spending away from the low-income segments of the population. Governance has many dimensions. The World Bank regularly publishes worldwide governance indicators that capture six dimensions (voice and accountability, political instability and violence, government effectiveness, regulatory quality, rule of law, and control of corruption) for more than 200 countries including Pakistan.

Table 16.1 reports the World Bank's governance indicators for Pakistan, expressed in percentile ranks.[13] Pakistan's government effectiveness, regulatory quality, and control of corruption improved between 1996 and 2007, but all governance indicators worsened between 2007 and 2011, with the exception of voice and accountability, and rule of law. The worsening was most pronounced in government effectiveness, followed by control of corruption; however, data constraints preclude empirically establishing a link between governance and inequality.

Recent policy developments in reducing inequality

While the government has been making efforts to restore growth in recent years, it has also introduced several policy measures to address regional and provincial disparity, and thereby reduce poverty and inequality.

[13] For a particular country, a percentile rank in a particular governance indicator shows the percentage of countries worldwide that are rated below this country in this indicator. A higher value indicates a better governance rating.

Agricultural pricing policy

Pakistan is an agricultural country, and agriculture is the mainstay of the economy. It provides food to the people and raw materials to industry, and is a base for earning foreign exchange. Wheat is the most important staple crop of the country. Low wheat prices resulted in lower production in 2008 and compelled the government to import wheat to meet domestic needs. To provide better incentives to the agriculture sector and increase farmers' incomes, the government increased the minimum guaranteed wheat price between 2008 and 2011 by 68%. This increase led to a bumper harvest in 2008/2009 and has had a positive effect on income distribution (Government of Pakistan 2012).

National Finance Commission award

Pakistan is a federation comprising four provinces. Most of the fiscal revenues are collected by the federal government and then distributed vertically between federal and provincial governments and horizontally among the provinces in accordance with the Constitution under the National Finance Commission (NFC). Under the 7th NFC award in 2009, the federation has moved away from the unsatisfactory sole criterion of population to multiple criteria that include poverty/backwardness, revenue collection and generation, and inverse population density. The population weight has been reduced to 82%, while poverty, revenue generation, and inverse population density have been assigned weights of 10.3%, 5%, and 2.7%, respectively, for horizontal distribution of resources among provinces. Consequently, the provinces' share from the divisible pool increased from 46% to about 60%. In addition, the government made deliberate efforts to ensure balanced regional development with special focus on backward areas. Thus, additional specific resources were provided to these regions to bring them up to par with the other parts of the country. These reforms are likely to have a positive impact on making regional development more balanced, and hence improve income distribution between regions and provinces.

New growth strategy

The Planning Commission of Pakistan approved a new growth strategy in 2011, which is based on sustained reform that builds efficient and knowledgeable governance structures and markets in desirable, attractive, and well-connected locations. The strategy maintained that growth drivers, such as entrepreneurship and innovation, could be greatly encouraged by reforming and strengthening institutions such as the civil service, the legal and judicial framework, and the taxation system. The strategy also suggests measures such as a reform of the restrictive zoning laws that have impeded the growth of domestic commerce and hampered the role of cities as generators of economic growth.

The combined impact of the new growth framework would improve the investment climate, reduce the cost of doing business, and increase the profitability of enterprises, encouraging them to expand and improve productivity.

The strategy also proposes programs to support the youth, who suffer disproportionately from unemployment, by providing them with quality basic and college education as well as market-led skills development, and by instituting national youth service policy reforms. While Pakistan has a relatively large proportion (32%) of uneducated youths, mostly with no vocational and life skills, the proposed provision of quality education at the basic and college levels, and market-led skills development will not only increase their employability but also have a positive impact on income distribution among households.

The new growth strategy also recognizes that the current distortive policies are detrimental to the budgetary process. Public sector enterprises have been hemorrhaging about PRs300 billion annually during 2008/2009 to 2010/2011, pushing the fiscal deficit to unsustainable levels. In addition, the power sector took the largest chunk of more than 50% of total subsidies of PRs213 billion in 2009/2010. There is a need for the government to exit from production through privatization of government-owned productive units because these subsidies are untargeted and put pressure on the government to keep on resorting to borrowing, which in turn results in higher inflationary tendencies and affects poverty and inequality adversely. Thus, removing these untargeted subsidies will not only save scarce resources for the protection of the poor but also reduce inequality among households.

Redistributive policy: taxation

Taxation is an important tool for redistribution. Different types of taxes have different effects on income distribution. Personal income taxes and property taxes are progressive. In addition to partly fulfilling government expenditure requirements, these taxes are also aimed at reducing inequality of income among individuals. Corporate taxes could be regressive or progressive depending upon the size of the companies, while indirect taxes are regressive and considered to have negative effects on income distribution. Since indirect taxes in Pakistan have a larger share in total tax revenue, the overall tax system of the country can be considered regressive, which tends to have an adverse impact on inequality.

The taxation structure of Pakistan has experienced significant changes during the past decade. The share of direct taxes has increased significantly from 31% to 39%, while the share of indirect taxes declined from 69% to 61% during this period. The decline is mainly attributable to the fact that the share of trade-related taxes and excise duty has fallen significantly in the wake of economic liberalization since the late 1990s. Although the share of indirect taxes declined, its share is still high in total tax revenue, suggesting that the tax system is still regressive.

Pakistan's fiscal situation weakened in 2008 owing to a number of domestic and external factors, including oil and food price shocks in the international market. As a result, both fiscal and current account deficits reached an unsustainable level (8% of GDP) leading to an International Monetary Fund Standby Arrangement of

$7 billion between 2008 and 2010. The federal budget for 2012/2013 appears to be an election-year budget because it contains no tax reforms. There is a need to improve tax collection by broadening the tax net to improve the tax-to-GDP ratio, which, at 9.2%, is one of the lowest in the region. The tax system can be improved by imposing progressive taxes, such as agriculture income, property, and value-added taxes, which have great potential for revenue generation. While the current government has no intention to introduce tax reforms, it is anticipated that a new government after the election in 2013 will introduce tax reforms to reduce the fiscal deficit to a sustainable level.

Public spending on human capital

Investment in education and health can reduce inequality of opportunity for low-income segments of the population and thus reduce income inequality. While taxes and social transfers have an immediate effect on income distribution, public expenditure for social services tends to have a longer-term impact. Public programs in basic education and healthcare and public investment in infrastructure such as water and sanitation address the fundamental causes of inequality by creating opportunities and enhancing human capabilities.

While economic growth is essential for poverty reduction, it alone may not be sufficient because of inequality in opportunities. Enhanced human capabilities enable the deprived segments of the population to participate in the process of growth and come out of the poverty trap. In this context, it is important to examine the recent public spending on human capital in Pakistan. The budgetary poverty-related expenditure as defined by the government rose from PRs343 billion in 2006/2007 to PRs1.111 trillion in 2009/2010 (Table 16.2). The pro-poor expenditures increased from 4.9% of GDP in 2006/2007 to 7.6% of GDP in 2009/2010.

Pakistan's public spending on education was low at 1.8% of GDP in 2007, compared with 4.1% in India, 3.1% in Sri Lanka, and 2.5% in Bangladesh. This low public spending on education has fluctuated in the range of 1.5–1.7% of GDP in recent years to accommodate security- and subsidies-related spending in the event of fiscal austerity to reduce the budget deficit. As a result, the share of the education and health sectors in total poverty-related budgetary expenditure declined from 62% to 38%. On the other hand, the share of expenditure on subsidies and administrative expenses on law and order, which do not qualify under the criteria of pro-poor spending, recorded a substantial rise during this period. It is noteworthy that the rise in expenditure on subsidies was mainly due to untargeted subsidies that are not pro-poor, while the expenditure on law and order has increased mainly due to the war on terror.

The decline in spending on health and education will not only affect human capabilities adversely but also reinforce the existing unequal access to opportunities and result in a higher level of income inequality in the future. Thus, there is a critical need to increase the health and education allocation, which is one of the lowest in Asian countries if compared as a share of GDP.

Table 16.2 Budgetary poverty-related expenditure by sector (% share)

	2006/2007	*2007/2008*	*2008/2009*	*2009/2010*
Roads, highways, and bridges	17.5	14.8	10.2	8.9
Water supply and sanitation	4.8	3.5	2.3	2.3
Education	47.3	31.9	24.6	23.4
Health	15.5	10.7	8.6	8.5
Population planning	2.0	2.3	0.5	0.6
Social security and welfare	1.3	3.3	3.0	4.9
Natural calamities	1.5	1.3	1.0	1.1
Agriculture	21.8	14.6	9.1	9.4
Land reclamation	0.7	0.5	0.3	0.2
Rural development	6.5	4.1	1.7	1.8
Subsidies	1.6	9.6	22.6	21.1
Food support program	1.0	0.8	1.3	0.0
People's Works Programme-I	0.0	0.2	0.3	0.8
People's Works Programme-II	0.7	0.5	2.9	2.9
Low-cost housing	0.1	0.1	0.1	0.2
Justice administration	1.5	1.4	0.9	1.0
Law and order	0.6	0.4	10.7	12.9
Total (PRs million)	342,680	572,620	977,228	1,110,762
Total (% of GDP)	4.9	5.6	7.5	7.6

GDP = gross domestic product.

Source: Government of Pakistan. 2011. *Economic Survey 2010/2011*. Islamabad: Ministry of Finance.

Social protection and safety nets

Redistribution can be possible through social transfers, including social assistance benefits and social insurance programs. Social protection and safety nets consist of policies and programs designed to reduce poverty and vulnerability by promoting efficient labor markets and enhancing their capacity to manage economic and social risks. Pakistan has a network of direct and indirect social protection mechanisms. Indirect provisions include the Employees' Old Age Benefit Institution (EOBI) and Workers Welfare Fund (WWF), while direct transfers include Zakat, Pakistan Bait-ul-Mal (PBM), Benazir Income Support Programme (BISP), Punjab Sasti Roti (cheap bread) Programme, and market-based interventions (microfinance).

Total transfers through all programs showed a net increase of 69% in terms of grants and 39% in terms of beneficiaries in 2009/2010. Of the total grants, 78% or PRs42.3 billion were in the budgetary mode whereas 22% or PRs11.7 billion were in the non-budgetary mode. A large proportion of about 59% of grants was disbursed through BISP. Disbursements in all programs were made to 6 million beneficiaries in 2009/2010, which was 39% more than the previous year. A total of PRs33 billion under the micro credit program was also disbursed, which was 15% higher than the previous year.

However, the budgetary allocations for social safety nets declined in 2011/2012 and now stand at 0.24% of GDP, which is low compared with other Asian developing countries. The poverty scorecard survey suggests that out of 6 million poor households that have been identified as eligible for obtaining a PRs1,000 per month installment under the BISP, 65% of children in the identified families were out of school. Thus, there is a need to ensure that children of those families who are beneficiaries of BISP through conditional cash transfers are enrolled in school. This will not only enhance human capabilities of the poor but also have a positive impact on poverty and income distribution.

Policy lessons

This chapter analyzed the trends and examined the drivers of inequality in Pakistan during the past five decades. The worsening of inequality during the 1960s may have been due to the pursuit of a growth strategy based on the rapid economic growth paradigm. Inequality remained high during the 1970s, despite nationalization of all major industries, which led to a decline in economic growth. Inequality declined during the 1980s when growth rates were high, suggesting a weak link between growth and inequality in Pakistan.

The worsening of inequality in the 1990s may, to some extent, have been due to globalization and liberalization that led to an increase in the premium for skilled labor and reduction in the wages for unskilled labor and an increased wage gap in Pakistan. The adverse effects on inequality may have been amplified by financial liberalization because inequality was found to be the highest in the finance sector.

Empirical evidence suggests that while trade and financial liberalization may have been important drivers of inequality in Pakistan over the past two decades, other important factors, including partial implementation of reform and its backtracking, may have compromised the positive effects of trade and financial liberalization. In addition, structural drivers of inequality, such as unequal access to education and health, along with highly unequal land ownership patterns, are also important determinants of inequality in Pakistan. Some policy lessons can be drawn from the analysis.

First, the widening wage gap due to a decline in the wages for unskilled labor is because minimum wage increases announced by the government were not sufficient to compensate for inflation. There is a need to revise wages consistent with inflation rise to address equity issues in an overall economic framework.

Second, access to finance is still limited and barely covers 5–10% of the poor population. Thus, expansion in equal access to credit for the poor, who do not have collateral and connections, is important to reduce inequality.

Third, rapid economic growth mainly benefited the rich and increased the level of inequality since the early 2000s. Because income tax as a share of GDP is still very low compared with other countries, taxation has an important role to play in reducing inequality in Pakistan.

Fourth, unequal access to human capital is an outcome of low public spending on education and health. Public expenditure on human capital needs to be increased and the share of the education and health sectors in total pro-poor expenditure should be increased to the pre-fiscal adjustment level.

Fifth, public sector enterprises eat up a big chunk of scarce resources. There is a need for the government to exit from production and privatize these units.

Sixth, a persistent rise in generalized and untargeted subsidies will increase inequality. These subsidies put pressure on the government to resort to borrowing, which results in higher inflationary tendencies that severely affect the poor and thus increases inequality.

Seventh, there is great potential to increase the tax-to-GDP ratio currently from 9.2% to 13% of GDP by reducing exemptions for agricultural income, remittances, and export income, and by increasing tax rates on urban immovable property. Higher tax revenue would enable the government to raise expenditure on pro-poor activities and will thus reduce inequality of opportunity as well as inequality of income.

Eighth, there is a need to improve the governance profile. This would enhance the impact of redistributive policies of taxes and expenditures that directly benefit low- and middle-income groups to provide equal access to opportunities. These policy lessons are important to achieve inclusive growth, made possible by reducing inequality of opportunities, creating economic opportunities, and ensuring equal access to the opportunities for all segments of the population.

Last, on the research side, the estimation of a consistent series of income distribution data is important to draw an unambiguous conclusion about the impact of policy reform on inequality and its comparison across Asian countries. By doing so, one can get a better understanding of past trends and the pattern of inequality.

References

Anwar, T. 1996. Structural Adjustment and Poverty: The Case of Pakistan. *Pakistan Development Review*. 35 (4). pp. 911–26.

——. 2002. The Impact of Globalization and Liberalization on Growth, Employment and Poverty: A Case Study of Pakistan. *WIDER Discussion Paper* No. 2002/17. Helsinki, Finland: United Nations University World Institute for Development Economics Research.

——. 2004. Recent Macroeconomic Developments and Implications for Poverty and Employment in Pakistan: The Cost of Foreign Exchange Reserves Holdings in South Asia. *Working Paper* No. 17. Canberra: Australia South Asia Research Centre, Australian National University.

——. 2005. Long-Term Changes in Income Distribution in Pakistan: Evidence Based on Consistent Series of Estimates. *Discussion Paper* No. 3 CRPRID. August. Islamabad.

——. 2006. Trends in Absolute Poverty and Governance in Pakistan: 1998–99 and 2004–05. *Pakistan Development Review.* 45 (4). pp. 777–93.

——. 2007. Growth and Sectoral Inequality in Pakistan: 2001–02 to 2004–05. *Pakistan Economic and Social Review*. 45 (2). pp. 141–54.

——. 2009. Measuring Inequality of Consumption and Opportunities in Pakistan, 2001–02 and 2004–05. *Pakistan Economic and Social Review.* 47 (2). pp. 157–81.

——. 2010. Role of Growth and Inequality in Explaining Changes in Poverty in Pakistan. *Pakistan Development Review.* 49 (1). pp. 1–17.

Anwar, T., S. K. Qureshi, and H. Ali. 2004. Landlessness and Rural Poverty in Pakistan. *Pakistan Development Review.* 43 (19). pp. 855–74.

Asian Development Bank (ADB). 2008. *Pakistan: Poverty Assessment Update*. Manila.

——. 2012. *Asian Development Outlook 2012: Confronting Rising Inequality in Asia.* Manila.

Azfar, J. 1973. The Distribution of Income in Pakistan: 1966–67. *Pakistan Economic and Social Review.* 11. pp. 40–66.
Banerjee, A. V., and A. F. Newman. 1993. Occupational Choice and the Process of Development. *Journal of Political Economy.* 101 (2). pp. 274–98.
Bergan, A. 1967. Personal Income Distribution and Personal Savings in Pakistan, 1963–64. *Pakistan Development Review.* 7 (2). pp. 160–212.
Beyer, H., P. Rojas, and R. Vergara. 1999. Trade Liberalization and Wage Inequality. *Journal of Development Economics.* 59. pp. 103–23.
de Kruijk, H., and M. Leeuwen. 1985. Changes in Poverty and Income Inequality in Pakistan during the 1970s. *Pakistan Development Review.* 24 (3–4). pp. 407–22.
Galiani, S., and P. Sanguinetti. 2003. The Impact of Trade Liberalization on Wage Inequality: Evidence from Argentina. *Journal of Development Economics.* 72. pp. 2–17.
Galor, O., and J. Zeira. 1993. Income Distribution and Macroeconomics. *Review of Economic Studies.* 60. pp. 35–52.
Government of Pakistan. 2006. Economic Survey 2006. Islamabad: Ministry of Finance.
——. 2008. Economic Survey 2008. Islamabad: Ministry of Finance.
——. 2011. Economic Survey 2010/2011. Islamabad: Ministry of Finance.
——. 2012. Economic Survey 2012. Islamabad: Ministry of Finance.
Government of Punjab. 2003. *Punjab-Poverty Reduction Strategy Paper (P-PRSP).* Lahore: Planning and Development Board.
Haq, K. 1964. A Measurement of Inequality in Urban Personal Income Distribution in Pakistan. *Pakistan Development Review.* 4 (4). pp. 623–64.
Idrees, M. 2006. Analysis of Income and Consumption Inequality in Pakistan. PhD thesis submitted at Quad-i-Azam University, Islamabad.
Khandkar, R. 1973. Distribution of Income and Wealth in Pakistan. *Pakistan Economic and Social Review.* 11 (1). pp. 1–39.
Kuznets, S. 1955. Economic Growth and Income Inequality. *American Economic Review* 45. pp. 1–28.
Mahmood, Z. 1984. Income Inequality in Pakistan: An Analysis of Existing Evidence. *Pakistan Development Review.* 23 (2–3). pp. 365–79.
Naseem, S. M. 1973. Mass Poverty in Pakistan: Some Preliminary Findings. *Pakistan Development Review.* 12 (4). pp. 312–60.
Pakistan Bureau of Statistics. 2001. *Poverty in the 1990s.* Islamabad: Statistics Division.
——. 2008. *Pakistan Social and Living Standard Measurement Survey (PSLM) 2007/08.* Islamabad.
——. 2011. *Pakistan Social and Living Standard Measurement Survey (PSLM) 2010/11.* Islamabad.
Planning Commission. 2006. *Pakistan Millennium Development Goals Report 2005.* Islamabad: Centre for Research on Poverty Reduction and Income Distribution.
Salman, Z., and M. Javed. 2011. The Impact of Trade Liberalization on Wage Inequality: Case of Pakistan. Paper presented at the 27th Annual General Meeting and Conference of Pakistan Society for Development Economics, Islamabad.
State Bank of Pakistan. 2002. *Financial Sector Assessment: 1990–2000.* Karachi: Research Department.
Wood, A. 1999. Openness and Wage Inequality in Developing Countries: The Latin American Challenge to East Asian Conventional Wisdom. In R. Baldwin *et al.* eds. *Market Integration, Regionalism and the Global Economy.* Cambridge, UK: Cambridge University Press.
World Bank. 2003. *Poverty in Pakistan: Vulnerabilities, Social Gaps, and Rural Dynamics.* Washington, DC: World Bank.
——. 2006. *Summary of Key Findings and Recommendation for Pakistan: Poverty, 2004–05.* Islamabad: World Bank.
——. 2010. *Country Partnership Strategy, FY 2010–13.* Report No. 53553-PK. Islamabad: World Bank.
——. 2012. *Worldwide Governance Indicators, 2012 Update.* http://info.worldbank.org/governance/wgi/index.asp (accessed December 2012).

17 Accounting for inequality in India

Evidence from household expenditures

J. Salcedo Cain, Rana Hasan, Rhoda Magsombol, and Ajay Tandon

Introduction

While poverty and inequality have long been central to discussions about the Indian economy, they have received special attention by policy makers and researchers in recent years. There are two related reasons for the heightened interest in poverty and inequality. First, the Indian economy has been among the faster growing economies in the developing world since the 1980s. The efficacy of economic growth on poverty reduction in a country with widespread poverty is quite naturally a subject of considerable interest. Second, while market-oriented economic reforms, initiated in the 1980s and accelerated in the 1990s, are widely believed to lie behind high growth, there is considerable concern that the main beneficiaries of these reforms have been those at the higher end of the income distribution. In other words, there is concern that while India's economy is growing faster than it used to, lower income groups – and especially the poor – have not significantly participated in or benefited from growth.

Recent analysis of National Sample Survey (NSS) quinquennial round data on consumer expenditures provides qualified support for such concerns. Chaudhuri and Ravallion (2007) used national accounts and NSS data up to 1999 to examine whether and how growth has been uneven in India (and the People's Republic of China [PRC]) and the implications of this unevenness for evolution of inequality and poverty.[1] They note that growth in agriculture has been slow and increasingly lagged that in industry and services. Further, rural incomes have grown more slowly than urban incomes. Because a regression of poverty rates on growth across either the different production sectors or rural and urban areas indicates that growth in agriculture and in rural areas, more generally, is a powerful driver of poverty reduction, the recent pattern of growth in India has not been particularly pro-poor. Turning specifically to the issue of inequality, Chaudhuri and

[1] The NSS data used or discussed in this chapter pertain to year-long surveys undertaken from January 1983 to December 1983 (NSS round 38), July 1993 to June 1994 (NSS round 50), July 1999 to June 2000 (NSS round 55), and July 2004 to June 2005 (NSS round 61). For expositional convenience, we refer to the surveys in terms of the starting year of a particular round rather than the number of the round. Thus, we refer to data for NSS round 50 as data from 1993, and so on.

Ravallion (2007) noted that the data from the NSS suggest increases in inequality during 1993–1999, with growth in per capita expenditures of the already well-off dominating those of other groups. However, it is difficult to arrive at a firm conclusion. The ambiguity stems from the comparability of the data on consumer expenditures across the two quinquennial round NSS surveys undertaken in 1993 and 1999 on account of different recall periods used for determining household consumption.[2] Chaudhuri and Ravallion's analysis was based on an adjustment to consumption expenditures due to Sundaram and Tendulkar (2003). As they pointed out, however, if they were not to make any adjustments to the original data, a much more pro-poor pattern of growth in consumption expenditures would emerge. Indeed, unadjusted data would reveal growth in per capita expenditures of the poorest percentile to be around double that of those at the upper end of the distribution. Given the controversy about the different adjustments proposed to make the 1993 and 1999 data comparable, it is not surprising that many analysts have keenly awaited the release of the 61st round of the NSS consumption expenditure survey undertaken over 2004–2005, given that this survey reverted to the recall periods used in 1993.

Based on this latest quinquennial round survey, Dev and Ravi (2007) found that poverty unambiguously declined during 1983–2004. Not only have poverty rates fallen, the absolute number of poor in 2004 is estimated to be lower than in either 1983 or 1993; however, they also found that the average annual percentage point reduction in poverty rates between 1993 and 2004 was lower than that during 1983–1993. Growth in per capita consumption has been higher during the more recent period and, according to their analysis, increases in inequality during 1993–2004 account for the slowdown in the extent of poverty reduction.

While the release of the 2004 consumption expenditure survey has pretty much settled the debate on whether inequality has increased since the early 1990s, the question of what explains this increase remains. Addressing this question is the central focus of this study and we utilize consumption expenditure data from the NSS surveys to shed light on why inequality increased during 1993–2004.

This study is related to two strands of the literature. One is the literature that analyzes changes in inequality using what Bourguignon *et al.* (2005) call the microeconomic approach. In contrast to the macroeconomic approach, which typically relies on aggregate measures of inequality and uses regression analysis

[2] Since the 1950s, NSS consumption expenditure surveys have used a 30-day recall period. The 55th round of the survey, undertaken in 1999–2000, adopted two recall periods for food, one based on a 7-day recall and the other on the standard 30-day recall. Because the question on the 7-day recall came before the 30-day recall (columns for the two recalls appear side by side against each consumption item in the questionnaire), most researchers agree that consumption expenditures recorded are driven by the 7-day recall (i.e., the 30-day recall is essentially a prorated version of the 7-day recall). Pilot surveys have strongly suggested that the shorter recall period yields, on average, higher consumption expenditures (on a prorated basis, of course), quite possibly due to a tendency for respondents to forget some items of consumption the longer the recall period. A comprehensive discussion of this and related issues in the context of the NSS consumption expenditure surveys is provided by the papers in Deaton and Kozel (2005).

to understand the determinants of inequality and its change, the microeconomic approach relies on the analysis of individual-level or household-level data from either labor force surveys or household surveys. These data are utilized to decompose inequality and changes in inequality into various observable factors. The idea is to get an understanding of the underlying processes that drive inequality and its change. Different methodologies have been used to carry out the decompositions. One of the most common is to decompose changes in inequality measures by population subgroups. Alternative and more powerful decompositions have been proposed by Bourguignon *et al.* (2005); Juhn *et al.* (1993); and Fields (2003), among others. However, insofar as the experience of developing countries is concerned, these decompositions have been applied primarily in the context of Latin American and East Asian countries (see, for example, the work of Alatas and Bourguignon (2005) and Ferreira and Paes de Barros (2005) who use the approach of Bourguignon *et al.* (2005) to investigate inequality in Indonesia and Brazil, respectively).

Of course, there is a literature on the factors accounting for inequality in India using the microeconomic approach, and this is the second strand of the literature to which this study is related. By and large, this work documents and tries to explain the rise in wage inequality observed during 1983–1999 (Chamarbagwala 2006; Kijima 2006). Focusing on full-time urban male workers, Kijima found that wage inequality (as measured by wage differentials between the 90th and 10th percentiles of the wage distribution) started increasing in the 1980s and was mainly attributable to the increases in the returns to skills (captured via educational attainment). She ascribed this increase in the "skills premium" to skill-biased technological change that raised the demand for skilled workers faster than the supply of skilled workers increased. Chamarbagwala included all wage and salaried workers in her analysis and came to a similar conclusion.

Our study is distinct from the work on wage inequality in India on several counts (in addition to incorporating more recent data). First, it focuses on consumption inequality using data on household per capita expenditures. Given the unavailability of data on the distribution of household income in India, a careful documentation of consumption inequality and the factors accounting for it and its change has its value, especially because a drawback of any analysis of wage inequality in India is that it must either miss out the self-employed, or use some procedure to impute their earnings.[3] This is because the NSS employment–unemployment surveys – the most comprehensive source of wage data in India – only record earnings from wage and salaried workers. As it turns out, self-employment is very important to the livelihoods of Indian households, and not just in rural areas. Based on the NSS consumption expenditure survey data that we use in our study, 43% of urban households in 2004 are categorized as

[3] Kijima predicted the earnings of the self-employed based on Mincerian wage equations. Not only does this assume that the relationship between observable characteristics and earnings are identical across wage/salary earners and the self-employed, it also assumes that this relationship fully explains earnings of the self-employed completely.

relying on self-employment income. The corresponding number in rural areas is 56%. Second, our analysis of inequality proceeds in a very different way from the work on wage inequality. We use a regression-based decomposition method developed by Fields (2003) to uncover the proximate factors associated with increases in inequality. We then extend this analysis in various ways, including examining whether economic liberalization may be linked to the pattern of results we get.

The empirical findings of this study are as follows. First, inequality in per capita expenditures increased during 1993–2004 in terms of a number of measures of inequality. Second, increases in inequality have not precluded reductions in poverty, however (a point also stressed by Dev and Ravi (2007)). In fact, per capita expenditures have increased for every statistical percentile group of individuals. As a result, the incidence of poverty has declined regardless of which poverty line one uses.[4] Third, insofar as the increases in inequality are concerned, they are much more of an urban phenomenon. Fourth, increases in "returns to education" account for a fairly large part of the increases in urban inequality.[5] Fifth, the increases in returns to education have been particularly pronounced in education-intensive services (such as communications, finance, insurance, real estate, and other business services) and education-intensive occupations (professional/technical, managerial/administrative, and clerical occupations). Finally, we find evidence that those industries that experienced greater liberalization in the 1990s experienced greater increases in returns to education.

Data

This study's analysis is based on household-level data from three large sample rounds of the NSS consumption expenditure surveys: round 38, carried out from January to December 1983; round 50, carried out from July 1993 to June 1994; and round 61, carried out from July 2004 to June 2005. To ensure comparability of expenditure data across rounds, we use information on expenditures based on a 30-day recall.[6] We restrict our attention to the rural and urban sectors of 16 major states.[7] However, because of its prominence (as well as its size), we also include data from urban Delhi in our analysis. Our estimates of poverty (headcount ratios)

---

[4] This result holds for not only the poverty rate, but also the poverty gap and squared poverty gap.

[5] We use the term "returns to education" as shorthand for the difference in log per capita expenditures that arise from differences in educational attainment across households controlling for various observables. Educational attainment may be captured in terms of either levels of education or years of education of the household head.

[6] Estimates of consumption expenditure in round 38 are based on a uniform recall period of 30 days while those from rounds 50 and 61 can be based on a mixed recall period (i.e., 365 days for five subgroups of goods and services purchased with low frequency and 30 days for the remaining items) as well as a uniform recall of 30 days for all goods and services.

[7] After 2000, three new states were formed: Chattisgarh, formerly part of Madhya Pradesh; Jharkhand, formerly part of Bihar; and Uttaranchal, formerly part of Uttar Pradesh. Some of our analysis draws upon state-level information. In order to maintain consistency across years, we do not consider these new states separately and instead consider the earlier state boundaries.

are based on state-wide official poverty lines. We also use these poverty lines to work out implicit price indexes that vary spatially as well as temporally (with urban Delhi 2004 as the base). These price indexes are then applied to current household expenditures in order to adjust them not only for price changes over time, but also for price differentials across states and between rural and urban areas within states. Both poverty and inequality measures are computed on a per capita basis by dividing household expenditures by household size. We also experiment with estimating inequality on a per adult equivalent basis.

In principle, inequality estimates (and decompositions) based on expenditures adjusted for spatial price differentials are superior to those based on current expenditures, where the implicit assumption is of common prices everywhere in the country. In practice, however, the situation is not as clear because any deficiencies of the official poverty line will carry over to the implicit price indexes we use. One particular problem is that price differences across rural and urban areas may get exaggerated due to the fact that part of the difference in monetary values between the rural and urban official poverty lines stems from different calorie norms that are implicit in the rural and urban poverty lines: 2,400 calories per person per day in rural areas and 2,100 calories per person per day in urban areas. This problem can be alleviated by keeping the analysis of poverty and inequality of urban and rural areas separate. A second problem with using the official poverty lines for deriving price indexes is that the specific weights used for aggregating price indexes of individual consumption goods and services implicit in the official poverty lines may not be the most appropriate to use for analysis of inequality issues.[8] We leave this question as an issue for future research to address.

Poverty and inequality in India: 1983 to 2004

Table 17.1 presents estimates of poverty, as captured by headcount ratios, based on official poverty lines for rural and urban areas (based on data for 16 states plus urban Delhi).[9] The table also presents the rates of change in poverty during 1983–1993 and during 1993–2004. How fast have poverty rates fallen? The rate of poverty reduction in the rural sector as a whole was similar across both periods. If anything, the rate during 1993–2004 was slightly better. As can be seen from Table 17.1, the compounded average annual reduction in poverty in the more recent period is 2.7% per annum versus 2.0% for the earlier period. The situation

[8] The underlying price indexes are based on the same prices used for the CPI-AL (i.e., consumer price index for agricultural labor) and CPI-IW (i.e., consumer price index for industrial workers) series, but re-weighted on the basis of consumption patterns of people around the poverty line during 1973–1974.

[9] The figures using the official poverty lines differ from the India-wide numbers published by the Planning Commission, Government of India, for the corresponding years on two counts. First, our state coverage is different. As noted above, we are working with the rural and urban areas of 16 states plus urban Delhi. Second, our poverty estimates are calculated using unit-level records, while those from the Planning Commission are extrapolated from published tables on per capita expenditures across various expenditure classes.

Table 17.1 Poverty, growth, and inequality decompositions

Headcount ratios	*1983*	*1993*	*2004*
Rural	46.2	37.2	27.7
Urban	42.3	33.2	26.3

Growth and inequality decompositions	*1983–1993*	*1993–2004*
Rural		
Annual percentage change in poverty (%)	−2.04	−2.65
Absolute change in poverty (%)	−8.98	−9.51
Growth component (%)	−6.65	−11.56
Redistribution component (%)	−2.34	2.05
Urban		
Annual percentage change in poverty (%)	−2.30	−2.08
Absolute change in poverty (%)	−9.19	−6.83
Growth component (%)	−9.67	−12.39
Redistribution component (%)	0.47	5.56

Source: Authors' estimates based on consumption expenditure surveys by National Sample Survey Office, Ministry of Statistics and Programme Implementation, Government of India, New Delhi, India.

in the urban sector is a little different, with the rate of poverty reduction having fallen during 1993–2004.[10]

The finding that the rate of poverty reduction during 1993–2004 was roughly similar (slightly higher in the rural sector and slightly lower in the urban sector) to that achieved during 1983–1993 is surprising in view of the fact that India's economy grew faster in the later period. While per capita GDP grew by 3.1% per annum during 1983–1993, it grew by 4.6% during 1993–2004 (World Bank various years). Why did the rate of poverty reduction not increase (significantly)? Does the answer have to do with slow growth of average per capita expenditures as captured by the NSS data? As is by now well known, there can be wide discrepancies between national account statistics and household survey data on consumption expenditure of households. Has the pattern of growth in consumer expenditures tended to favor the nonpoor over the poor?

Table 17.1 also sheds light on this. The lower part of the table presents decompositions of poverty reduction over 1983–1993 and 1993–2004 into growth and distribution components using the method of Datt and Ravallion (1992).[11] The growth component of poverty reduction is computed as the reduction of poverty that would result if the actual growth experienced had taken place in the context of unchanged distribution. The distribution component of poverty reduction

[10] This result is not due to the inclusion of the data from Delhi. For example, excluding Delhi, the reduction in urban poverty during 1983–1993 is 2.24%, while the reduction during 1993–2004 remains at 2.08%.

[11] Growth is of survey-based mean per capita consumption expenditure.

Table 17.2 Inequality estimates

	Per capita expenditure			*Expenditure per adult equivalent*		
	1983 *(1)*	*1993* *(2)*	*2004* *(3)*	*1983* *(4)*	*1993* *(5)*	*2004* *(6)*
Rural						
Gini	31.2	28.5	29.8	30.3	27.2	28.2
GE(0)	16.3	13.6	14.9	15.3	12.5	13.5
GE(1)	19.2	17.0	19.6	17.9	15.7	17.7
GE(2)	52.5	42.8	50.2	45.9	41.0	43.0
Urban						
Gini	33.9	34.2	37.8	32.0	32.4	35.9
GE(0)	18.9	19.3	23.6	16.9	17.4	21.2
GE(1)	21.5	23.3	28.9	19.1	21.3	26.1
GE(2)	34.4	72.6	82.8	29.7	72.2	70.9

Source: Authors' estimates based on consumption expenditure surveys by National Sample Survey Office, Ministry of Statistics and Programme Implementation, Government of India, New Delhi, India.

is the reduction of poverty that would result if the distributional change actually registered had taken place in the context of zero growth. There are several interesting features of the results. First, the main driver for poverty reduction in both periods has been the growth component. This is consistent with many previous studies (see Fields (2001) for a detailed overview of findings from around the developing world). Second, the growth component was much larger in the second period. However, changes in the distribution of per capita expenditures during 1993–2004 worked against the poor so that the positive impact of growth on poverty reduction was reduced, especially in the urban sector.

This suggests that inequality increased during 1993–2004, especially in urban areas. We thus turn to a direct examination of inequality estimates. Table 17.2 presents various estimates of inequality. In addition to the Gini coefficient, inequality indexes belonging to the generalized entropy (GE) class of inequality measures are also provided: GE(0) or the mean log deviation; GE(1) or the Theil index; and GE(2) or half the square of the coefficient of variation. The GE(0) is especially sensitive to expenditures at the bottom of the distribution, GE(2) is more sensitive to expenditures at the top of the distribution, and GE(1) exhibits a constant responsiveness across all ranges of expenditures. The Gini coefficient is more sensitive to expenditures around the middle of the distribution.

Table 17.2 also distinguishes between inequality estimates based on per capita expenditures and estimates that take into account the effects of household composition and scale effects due to size. Thus, instead of working only with household expenditures expressed in per capita terms (columns 1–3), we also consider household expenditures in per adult equivalent terms (columns 4–6). The adult equivalence scale that we use for this is the Organisation for Economic Co-operation and Development (OECD) equivalence scale, which assigns a value of

1 to the first household member, 0.7 to each additional adult, and 0.5 to each child (household members below 15 years of age) (OECD 2005).

Comparing either columns 1 and 2 or 4 and 5, we see that during 1983–1993 all inequality estimates for the rural sector declined, while in the urban sector all estimates increased, albeit marginally in most cases (the GE(2) measure is the exception). Next, comparing either columns 2 and 3 or 5 and 6, we see that with only one exception, all inequality estimates during 1993–2004 increase in both the rural and urban sectors. The inequality increases in rural areas are generally quite marginal, however. Those in urban areas have been larger. The exception is a slight decline in GE(2) for the urban sector when inequality is estimated in per adult equivalent terms. Given the possibility that GE(2) is more susceptible to outliers, especially compared with inequality measures such as the Gini and GE(1), it seems prudent not to make too much of the trends in GE(2). Once we do this, the overall flavor of the results is clearly one of very similar qualitative results across the per capita and per adult equivalent estimates of inequality. We therefore focus the remainder of our discussion in terms of the more familiar inequality estimates based on per capita terms.[12] The increase in inequality during 1993–2004, especially in urban areas, suggests that richer individuals have experienced faster growth in terms of their consumption expenditures than poorer individuals. This can be confirmed visually by using an increasingly popular graphical tool for inequality analysis, the growth incidence curve (GIC). The GIC shows growth in per capita expenditures at different statistical percentiles of the expenditure distribution over the time period between two surveys.

The GICs for various time periods and sectors are presented in Figure 17.1. The shape of the GIC provides information on how growth in expenditure is distributed. As can be seen from the GIC for rural India during 1983–1993 (Panel A), growth was broadly downward sloping, i.e., those at the lower (higher) end of the distribution saw their per capita expenditure levels grow more quickly (more slowly) than mean growth. This pattern of the distribution of growth in per capita expenditures changed during 1993–2004 (Panel B). The extremely well off – those in the top 5 percentile – experienced faster growth in their expenditures than most of the rest of the population. Expenditures of most others – from around the 5th percentile to the 95th percentile – increased by between 1.0% and less than 1.4%. Only the extremely poor experienced more than average growth in their expenditures.

In contrast, the GIC for the urban sector goes from having no clear pattern during 1983–1993 (Panel C) to having a clear upward slope during 1993–2004 (Panel D). Thus, the better-off (statistically) have seen faster growth in their expenditures.[13] It is important to note that while the GICs reveal the pattern of

---

[12] It may be noted that the main qualitative results of the analysis in the following section, i.e., regression-based decomposition of inequality and changes in it, remained unchanged whether we measure inequality in per capita terms or per adult equivalent terms.

[13] It may be noted that the behavior of the GE(2) estimates during 1983–1993 for the urban sector (i.e., an increase in the GE(2)) appears to be at variance with the behavior of the GIC in Panel C (i.e.,

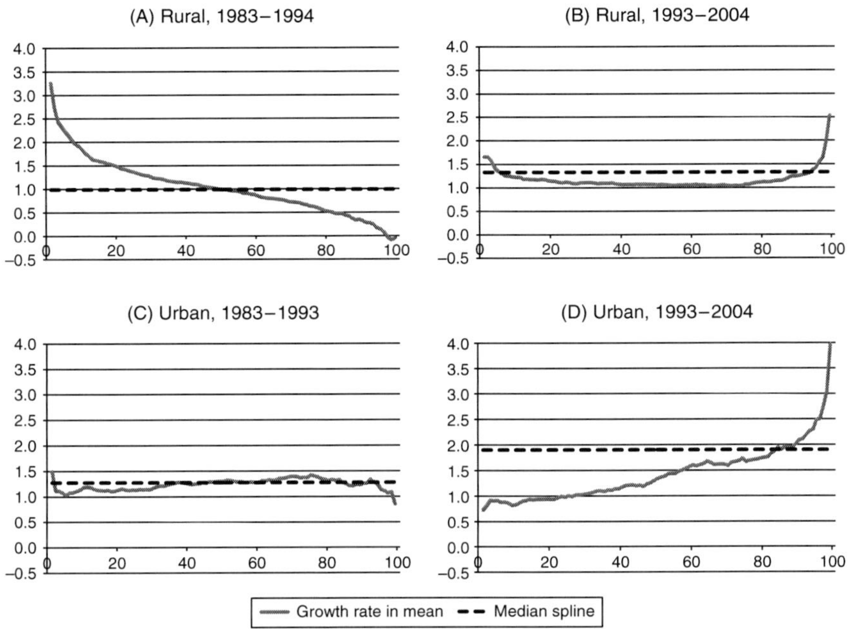

Figure 17.1 Annualized growth in real per capita expenditures by percentile (%).

expenditure growth to favor the better-off during 1993–2004, especially in urban areas, they also reveal that growth rates of expenditures have been positive at all percentiles.

Thus, all measures of absolute poverty would show a decline in poverty regardless of the monetary value of the poverty line. More generally, the fact that per capita expenditure levels have increased at each percentile of the distribution means that, despite increasing inequality over time, social welfare has improved during 1993–2004 from the standpoint of social welfare functions that are anonymous and increasing in expenditure. In other words, the 2004 distribution "first order dominates" the 1993 distribution.

Accounting for inequality between 1993 and 2004

As we have seen, inequality increased during 1993–2004, marginally in the rural sector and more substantially in the urban sector. What factors account for inequality and its changes during 1993–2004? In this section, we use

relatively low growth in per capita expenditures at the top of the distribution). A closer examination of the micro data revealed that per capita expenditures shot up within the top half of the top percentile. This reinforced the point made earlier in the text regarding the susceptibility of the GE(2) measure to outliers and extreme values.

a regression-based decomposition technique developed by Fields (2003) to determine what proportion of total inequality and its change can be accounted for by various observable household characteristics. It is crucial to point out that decomposition techniques provide a description of how various household characteristics are related to inequality. Their results do not imply causation. Nevertheless, used with caution, the results can be suggestive of the deeper factors explaining or driving inequality and can be a useful tool in analyzing inequality.

Mean per capita expenditures by household characteristics

Over which household characteristics should inequality be decomposed? In answering this question, we are obviously limited to choosing from what is available in the NSS consumption expenditure survey data. Nevertheless, there is some information available. In addition to knowing the state and sector in which a household is located and whether or not a household belongs to a scheduled caste or tribe group, we also have information on the household head's gender and level of educational attainment, and the principal production sector and occupation that form the main source of household income.[14] We consider five categories for the principal production sector of the household: (i) agriculture, (ii) manufacturing industry, (iii) non-manufacturing industry (mining, utilities, and construction), (iv) modern services (finance, insurance, and real estate; and public administration, education, scientific, research, and health and medical subsectors), and (v) traditional services (remaining services such as wholesale and retail trade, restaurants and hotels, community and personal services, etc.); three occupation groups: (i) high-skilled occupations (professional/technical and managerial occupations), (ii) medium-skilled occupations (clerical and sales occupations), and (iii) low-skilled occupations (agricultural workers, production workers, and service workers); and four levels of educational attainment: (i) below primary, (ii) primary, (iii) secondary, and (iv) tertiary and above.[15,16]

---

[14] Scheduled castes are the bottom rung of the hierarchy in the Hindu caste system. Scheduled tribes are groups outside the caste system.

[15] As is explained later, the regression-based decomposition of education's contribution to inequality into various factors requires that education enter the analysis not in terms of categories but as a continuous variable (such as years of education). We convert the various (more disaggregated) levels of educational attainment into equivalent years of education using the following assignment: (i) not literate: 0 years; (ii) nonformal education: 1 year; (iii) below primary: 2.5 years; (iv) primary level: 5 years; (v) middle school: 8 years; (vi) secondary level: 12 years; and (vii) tertiary and above: 15 years.

[16] Especially in rural areas, we would expect landholdings to be potentially important drivers of inequality and its change. Unfortunately, data considerations prevented us from including this variable in the analysis of rural inequality. In particular, we found the number of sample agricultural households in the rural sector with no landholdings to be less than 1% in both 1983 and 2004. In 1993, however, such households constituted as much as 8% of total sample agricultural households. It is very likely that a spike in such households in 1993 is due to data entry errors (e.g., miscoding missing data as 0 – there are similar issues with some other variables in the 1993 data).

These characteristics of households suggest natural groupings over which inequality and its changes may be decomposed. Before considering the results of these decompositions, however, it is instructive to consider how the distribution of the population and average per capita expenditures vary across these household characteristics. Table 17.3 provides information on this. Although our focus in this section is on explaining the increases in inequality during 1993–2004, Table 17.3 also provides numbers for 1983.

Table 17.3 confirms the importance of agricultural and low-skill livelihoods to the rural population (columns 1–3). In contrast, the urban population is more likely to depend on traditional services, although modern services and manufacturing are also important, with both accounting for around a fifth or more of the urban population's single most important source of livelihood during the three years considered (columns 4–6). Not surprisingly, household heads are, on average, much better educated in urban areas than rural areas. The population in both areas, however, has a very similar proportion of households that have a male as the household head – between 93% and 94% over the years. Turning to the information on average real per capita expenditures (columns 7–16), it is clear that higher education of the household head and household incomes based mainly on modern services and/or high-skill work are associated with the highest per capita expenditures on average in all years and for both rural and urban sectors.

The table also reveals that average per capita expenditures grew faster in urban areas during both 1983–1993 and 1993–2004. Additionally, per capita expenditures within both sectors grew faster in 1993–2004 when compared with 1983–1993. Especially during 1993–2004, those households whose heads were college-educated, engaged in the service sector (particularly its modern subcomponent), and had a high-skilled occupation (i.e., professional, technical, and managerial occupations) experienced the fastest growth in their per capita expenditures. Households belonging to scheduled caste and scheduled tribe groups, on the other hand, experienced slower growth in per capita expenditures than others. In view of the number of dimensions in which gender biases can exist, including possible discrimination in the labor market, an interesting finding from the table is that mean per capita expenditures are higher among female-headed households in the rural sector.[17]

While Table 17.3 suggests that the returns to higher education and certain production sectors and occupations may be driving the increases in inequality documented in the previous section, it does not demonstrate whether this actually has been the case. The regression decompositions, to which we now turn, inform us on this.

[17] Our result that mean per capita expenditures are higher among female-headed households is consistent with the findings of Dreze and Srinivasan (1997). Based on the data for rural households from round 42 of the NSS consumption expenditure survey (1986–1987), they note that, on average, per capita consumption expenditures for female-headed households are a little higher when compared with those of male-headed households. Furthermore, this result is robust to different assumptions about adult equivalence scales.

Regression-based decompositions

The regression-based decomposition technique developed by Fields (2003) enables us to answer two questions. First, how much inequality in per capita expenditures can be accounted for by various household characteristics? Second, to what extent do these characteristics account for the change in inequality over time? The answer to the first question – pertaining to the level of inequality – applies to a broad class of inequality measures, including the Gini coefficient and the generalized entropy measures. Answers to the second question – pertaining to changes in inequality – depend on the inequality measure being adopted, however.

Answering the first question entails taking two steps. In the first step, the log of per capita expenditures is regressed on various household characteristics:

$$\ln(Y_{it}) = \alpha_t + \beta_t X_{it} + \varepsilon_{it} \tag{17.1}$$

where the i refers to the household and t denotes year, Y refers to the per capita expenditures of the household, and X is a vector of explanatory variables composed of relevant household characteristics. These include the household head's age, age squared, a dummy variable for gender, and dummy variables for educational attainment; dummy variables for the industry and occupation comprising the main economic activity of the household; state dummies; and a dummy for whether or not the household belongs to a scheduled caste or tribe group. The various dummy categories for the production sector, occupations, and education are shown in Table 17.3.

In the second step, the estimated coefficients on the various explanatory terms are used to derive the share of the log variance of per capita expenditures attributable to each of the j household characteristics:

$$S_j(\ln Y) = \frac{\beta_j \times \sigma(X_j) \times cor(X_j, \ln Y)}{\sigma(\ln Y)} \tag{17.2}$$

where β_j is the estimated coefficient of the jth household characteristic, and X_j is the value taken on by the jth household characteristic. For example, a share of 0.1 for gender means that 10% of the log variance of per capita expenditures can be accounted for by gender. For household characteristics that are captured by more than one dummy variable, such as educational attainment of the household head (captured by dummy variables for primary, secondary, and tertiary education – those with less than a primary education being the excluded category), a consolidated share can be obtained by combining the shares pertaining to each of the individual educational categories. Thus, continuing with the example of educational attainment, a consolidated share for education can be computed as the sum of the individual shares for the three included educational categories, primary, secondary, and tertiary educations (i.e., $S_{\text{EDUC}} = S_{\text{EDUC-PRIMARY}} + S_{\text{EDUC-SECONDARY}} + S_{\text{EDUC-TERTIARY}}$).

Table 17.3 Distribution of population and average real monthly per capita expenditures

Groups	*Distribution of population (urban Delhi, %)*						*Average real monthly per capita expenditure (2004 rupees)*									
	Rural			*Urban*			*Rural levels*			*Rural annual change (%)*		*Urban levels*			*Urban annual change (%)*	
	1983	*1993*	*2004*	*1983*	*1993*	*2004*	*1983*	*1993*	*2004*	*1983–1993*	*1993–2004*	*1983*	*1993*	*2004*	*1983–1993*	*1993–2004*
	(1)	*(2)*	*(3)*	*(4)*	*(5)*	*(6)*	*(7)*	*(8)*	*(9)*	*(10)*	*(11)*	*(12)*	*(13)*	*(14)*	*(15)*	*(16)*
Production sector																
Agricultural	78.2	74.3	67.6	9.7	9.1	6.6	756	803	894	0.6	1.0	710	695	849	−0.2	1.8
Manufacturing industry	6.7	6.7	7.6	25.9	22.3	21.6	800	882	1,009	0.9	1.2	825	984	1,153	1.7	1.4
Nonmanufacturing industry	3.0	4.2	7.5	7.3	9.3	11.1	789	807	881	0.2	0.8	803	874	890	0.8	0.2
Traditional services	8.6	10.5	13.1	37.5	39.1	42.2	769	887	1,064	1.4	1.7	793	898	1,063	1.2	1.6
Modern services	3.6	4.3	4.2	19.6	20.3	18.5	1,118	1,257	1,544	1.1	1.9	1,113	1,274	1,633	1.3	2.3
Occupation																
High-skilled	2.5	3.4	4.3	12.6	15.2	18.4	1,182	1,270	1,589	0.7	2.1	1,283	1,503	1,800	1.5	1.7
Medium-skilled	5.8	7.2	8.0	30.3	30.0	29.4	844	997	1,156	1.6	1.4	909	1,034	1,228	1.2	1.6
Low-skilled	91.7	89.4	87.7	57.1	54.8	52.3	758	807	901	0.6	1.0	735	793	887	0.7	1.0
Level of education of household head																
Below primary	73.6	68.3	56.2	40.9	36.2	28.3	714	759	827	0.6	0.8	655	684	735	0.4	0.7
Primary	21.2	22.4	29.7	32.1	28.5	32.0	887	923	1,010	0.4	0.8	791	866	948	0.9	0.8
Secondary	4.3	7.5	11.3	18.2	22.2	24.7	1,134	1,143	1,224	0.1	0.6	1,104	1,165	1,318	0.5	1.1
Tertiary and above	0.9	1.9	2.8	8.8	13.0	15.1	1,259	1,416	1,714	1.1	1.8	1,522	1,683	2,108	1.0	2.1

Continued

Table 17.3 Continued

Groups	*Distribution of population (urban Delhi, %)*						*Average real monthly per capita expenditure (2004 rupees)*									
	Rural			*Urban*			*Rural levels*			*Rural annual change (%)*		*Urban levels*			*Urban annual change (%)*	
	1983	*1993*	*2004*	*1983*	*1993*	*2004*	*1983*	*1993*	*2004*	*1983–1993*	*1993–2004*	*1983*	*1993*	*2004*	*1983–1993*	*1993–2004*
	(1)	*(2)*	*(3)*	*(4)*	*(5)*	*(6)*	*(7)*	*(8)*	*(9)*	*(10)*	*(11)*	*(12)*	*(13)*	*(14)*	*(15)*	*(16)*
Gender of household head																
Male	94.5	94.5	93.8	94.5	93.8	93.1	772	834	948	0.7	1.2	860	978	1,163	1.2	1.6
Female	5.5	5.5	6.2	5.5	6.2	7.0	806	882	992	0.9	1.1	792	897	1,043	1.2	1.4
Social group																
Scheduled tribe/caste	28.5	31.8	30.7	15.0	17.0	18.5	626	703	779	1.1	0.9	676	735	847	0.8	1.3
Others	71.6	68.2	69.3	85.0	83.0	81.5	833	899	1,027	0.7	1.2	888	1,021	1,224	1.3	1.7
All	100	100	100	100	100	100	774	837	951	0.8	1.2	857	973	1,155	1.2	1.6

Source: Authors' estimates based on consumption expenditure surveys by National Sample Survey Office, Ministry of Statistics and Programme Implementation, Government of India, New Delhi, India.

The same applies to age of the household head, which enters on its own and in terms of its square, i.e., the shares for the age and age-squared term can be summed to arrive at a consolidated share for age.

Significantly, under certain conditions, which include the assumption that the log linear model for per capita expenditures is appropriate, the shares from equation (17.2) also apply to standard inequality measures such as the Gini coefficient (see Fields (2003) for details). Thus, the shares can also be described more generally as "factor inequality weights."

Answering the second question, i.e., the extent to which the household characteristics considered here account for the change in inequality over time, is therefore straightforward. Suppose we decompose changes in the Gini coefficient in urban India over 1993 and 2004. Let S_{j93} and S_{j04} represent the shares of the log variance of per capita expenditures for 1993 and 2004, respectively, for the jth household characteristic (or factor inequality weights for j). The change in the share of the Gini coefficient explained by factor j across the two years may be computed as $[S_{j04} \times Gini_{04} - S_{j93} \times Gini_{93}]/[Gini_{04} - Gini_{93}]$.

Columns 1, 2, 4, and 5 of Table 17.4 describe the contribution of various household characteristics to inequality in consumption expenditures in 1993 and 2004. The table also presents estimates of the Gini coefficient both for expositional convenience and also because they may differ slightly from those reported in Table 17.2. This can happen because the Ginis reported here are based on the data from sample households that have non-missing values for all the household characteristics being considered.[18] For those household characteristics that enter equation (17.1) with nonlinear terms (age) or as a string of dummy variables (e.g., education), the reported share is the consolidated share obtained by combining the pertinent individual shares.

Focusing on the upper half of Table 17.4 – which pertains to inequality decompositions based on a specification for equation (17.1) in which educational attainment is captured by dummies representing different levels of education – we can infer that the household characteristics included in our analysis are able to account for between 20% and 24% of inequality in rural areas (columns 1 and 2) and between 33% and 38% of inequality in urban areas (columns 4 and 5). For both rural and urban areas, these household characteristics are able to account for inequality to a greater degree in 2004 as compared with 1993. Although a lot of inequality is accounted for by the residual term even in 2004, the residual's contribution to changes in the Gini coefficient during 1993–2004 is much less, as we shall see.

---

[18] A careful check of the data also revealed there to be what are surely errors in data entry. In particular, some rural households engaged in agriculture were recorded as having an occupation code of "000," i.e., physicists. The profile of per capita expenditures of these households and education of household heads fitted those of other agricultural households. This problem was quite minor in the 1983 and 2004 data, but particularly severe in the 1993 data. We proceeded by dropping such observations from our analysis.

Table 17.4 Contribution to expenditure inequality and its change over 1993–2004

Variables	*Rural*			*Urban*		
	Contribution to inequality (%)		*Contribution to change in Gini (%)*	*Contribution to inequality (%)*		*Contribution to change in Gini (%)*
	1993 (1)	*2004 (2)*	*(3)*	*1993 (4)*	*2004 (5)*	*(6)*
Education measured in levels of education						
Age[a]	0.66	0.93	8.33	0.06	0.27	2.49
Gender	0.04	0.01	−0.81	−0.05	−0.09	−0.51
Social group	3.23	3.52	11.46	1.67	1.84	3.64
Production sector[a]	0.99	1.16	5.82	1.94	2.46	7.96
Occupation[a]	1.08	1.56	14.71	4.24	5.28	16.28
Level of education[a]	6.50	7.93	47.10	20.89	22.70	41.84
State[a]	7.82	8.81	35.93	4.95	6.01	17.22
Residual	79.66	76.08	−21.99	66.30	61.54	11.19
Gini[b]	28.46	29.50		33.95	37.16	
Education measured in years of schooling						
Age[a]	0.69	0.97	8.64	0.06	0.31	2.95
Gender	0.05	0.02	−0.80	−0.10	−0.14	−0.56
Social group	3.06	3.42	13.28	1.56	1.81	4.45
Production sector[a]	0.91	1.16	8.01	1.96	2.64	9.83
Occupation[a]	1.05	1.63	17.52	4.89	6.06	18.44
Years of education	7.39	8.28	32.66	19.87	21.33	36.77
State[a]	7.90	8.83	34.31	4.97	5.88	15.51
Residual	78.96	75.68	−14.17	66.78	62.13	12.95
Gini[b]	28.46	29.50		33.95	37.16	

Notes:

[a]The contribution of these variables is cumulative and is obtained by combining the contributions of constituent variables (for example, the total contribution of age is made up of two terms, age and age squared).

[b]The Gini coefficients reported here are not necessarily identical to those reported in Table 17.2 because sample observations with missing data on any of the included household characteristics were dropped.

Source: Authors' estimates based on consumption expenditure surveys by National Sample Survey Office, Ministry of Statistics and Programme Implementation, Government of India, New Delhi, India.

In rural areas in 2004, two factors each come close to accounting for nearly 10% of inequality: the state in which a household resides (9%) and the educational attainment of the household head (8%). Being a member of a scheduled caste or tribe has accounted for between 3% and 3.5% of inequality over both years. The remaining household characteristics account for even more negligible amounts of inequality. Interestingly, being a member of a scheduled caste or tribe accounts for even less inequality in urban areas – less than 2% in either 1993 or 2004.

By far the most important factor driving urban inequality is education, accounting for between 21% and 23% of inequality in 1993 and 2004, respectively. The sum of all other household characteristics does not match the amount of inequality accounted for by education.[19] Though not shown here, the importance of education of the household head is even higher if the inequality decompositions do not include the occupation and production sector that generate households' earnings.

This should not be surprising given that the choice of one's occupation and industry of employment is correlated with education. Thus, in rural areas, education accounts for between 8% and 9% of inequality in 1993 and 2004, while it accounts for 25% and 28% of inequality in urban areas. Of course, these estimates are probably overestimates given that education is not the only factor that determines occupation and production sector. Nevertheless, they may be seen as an indicator of the upper bound on the contribution of education to inequality, while the numbers based on the specification that includes occupation and production sector can be thought to represent a lower bound.

The impressive role of education notwithstanding, it needs to be noted that all the included household characteristics still leave a majority of inequality levels unaccounted for in both rural and urban sectors and in both 1993 and 2004. However, the included household characteristics do a much better job in accounting for changes in inequality. Data columns 3 and 6 of Table 17.4 describe how increases in the Gini coefficient during 1993–2004 were accounted for by each of the included household characteristics. Taken together, these household characteristics are able to explain the majority of the increases in the Gini – a large majority in the case of the urban sector. Educational attainment has the most dramatic impact on inequality changes, accounting for 47% of the total change in the Gini coefficient during 1993–2004 in the rural sector, and 42% in the urban sector. The second most important factor is state, accounting for 36% of the increase in the Gini coefficient in the rural sector and 17% in the urban sector. Interestingly, occupation, which is not an important factor in the levels of decomposition, is important in the change in decomposition, accounting for almost 15% of the increase in the Gini coefficient in the rural sector and 16% in the urban sector. Not surprisingly, the impact of educational attainment on changes in the Gini coefficient is even higher if the inequality decompositions are carried out without occupation (and production sector). In this case, education accounts for 53% of the increase in the Gini coefficient for the rural sector and 57% for the urban sector (not shown).

The role of education

Given the importance of education of the household head in accounting for the increases in inequality during 1993–2004, it is worthwhile to further analyze

[19] An unusual feature of the results in Table 17.4 is the negative values for gender in columns 4 and 5. Although the coefficient on the male dummy in equation (17.1) (β_{male}) is estimated to be negative, the raw correlation between the male dummy and ln Y is positive in urban areas. Thus, S_{male} in equation (17.2) is negative. Though this presents some awkwardness in interpretation, it is ultimately a feature of little consequence. Executing the analysis without the inclusion of the male dummy makes little difference to the results of this study.

its role in increasing inequality. In particular, we can follow Fields (2003) and ask to what extent education's contribution to increasing inequality has been due to (i) greater inequality in expenditures between households whose heads have different educational attainments (presumably reflecting increasing inequality in earnings between heads with different educational attainments), (ii) greater inequality in educational attainments, and/or (iii) an increase in the correlation between educational attainment and per capita expenditures.[20]

Answering this question is easier if we introduce education into equation (17.1) as a continuous variable rather than a string of dummy variables. This allows us to neatly decompose the change in the share of inequality in per capita expenditures attributable to years of education as

$$\Delta S_{\mathrm{EDUC\_YRS}}(\ln Y) \approx \Delta\beta_{\mathrm{EDUC\_YRS}} + \Delta\sigma(X_{\mathrm{EDUC\_YRS}}) + \Delta cor(X_{\mathrm{EDUC\_YRS}}, \ln Y) - \Delta\sigma(\ln Y) \qquad (17.3)$$

where the Δ operator denotes percentage change (see Fields (2003) for details).

With educational attainment included in terms of years of education, education still contributes to increases in inequality in both rural and urban areas.[21] This can be seen from the lower half of Table 17.4. The overall patterns are similar to using levels of education for measuring educational attainment. Most importantly, education continues to be the single most important factor accounting for increases in the Gini coefficient in urban areas, even when it is captured in terms of years of education (37%). Its relative importance in rural areas takes a bit of a hit. Nevertheless, it still accounts for a substantial share of increase in the Gini coefficient during 1993–2004 (33%).

Table 17.5 shows the results of the decomposition of equation (17.3) for rural and urban areas, with the first row describing the contribution of years of education to inequality levels, or in other words the factor inequality weight of years of education, as reported in the lower half of Table 17.4. The first two columns of Table 17.5 show the various terms of equation (17.3) in levels for 1993 and 2004. The last column shows the four left-hand side terms of equation (17.3), each divided by the change in the factor inequality weight of years of education.

---

[20] Admittedly, the use of the education of the household head may be problematic in this application; however, two things give us confidence that our analysis is meaningful. First, using an alternative variable such as the mean years of schooling among adult household members as a proxy for mean years of schooling among working household members (unfortunately, information on the labor force status of household members is not available in 2004) does not change our results dramatically. Second, analysis of the NSS employment–unemployment survey suggests that the household head plays a key role in generating household earnings. Among urban households whose working members were engaged in only wage or salaried work (in other words, households for which we can meaningfully compute total weekly earnings), the share of weekly earnings accounted for by the household head was as high as 87% on average in 2004. In the rural sector, the share was as high as 79% on average.

[21] As noted earlier, footnote 15 describes how we assign years of education to the various levels of educational attainment.

Table 17.5 Decomposing the contribution of years of education to changing inequality over 1993–2004

	Components of education's factor inequality weight		*Percent change in education's factor inequality weight explained by percent change*
	1993 *(1)*	*2004* *(2)*	*(3)*
Rural			
Education's factor inequality weight (%)	7.39	8.28	
Coefficient on years of education	0.030	0.029	−0.437
Standard deviation of years of education	4.070	4.544	0.966
Correlation between per capita expenditures and years of education	0.288	0.307	0.548
Standard deviation of per capita expenditure	0.482	0.485	0.055
Urban			
Education's factor inequality weight (%)	19.87	21.33	
Coefficient on years of education	0.043	0.049	1.825
Standard deviation of years of education	5.371	5.294	−0.197
Correlation between per capita expenditures and years of education	0.498	0.516	0.503
Standard deviation of per capita expenditure	0.575	0.621	1.086

Note: Numbers in the last column may not tally with those in the previous two columns on account of rounding.

Source: Authors' estimates based on consumption expenditure surveys by National Sample Survey Office, Ministry of Statistics and Programme Implementation, Government of India, New Delhi, India.

The coefficient on years of education – often referred to as the Mincerian return to education in the context of wage equations – decreases in rural areas and increases in urban areas. The standard deviation of years of education also behaves differently across rural and urban sectors, increasing in the former and decreasing in the latter. Put differently, inequality in years of schooling in the rural sector has been widening, while in the urban sector it has been declining. Since household heads have become more educated on average in both sectors (Table 17.3), the increase in the standard deviation of years of education in rural areas probably reflects the effects of increasing educational attainments in a population with generally low average educational attainments. For example, while the average years of schooling among household heads was only 3 years in rural areas in 1993, it was almost 7 years in urban areas. By 2004, these had increased to 4 years in rural areas and close to 8 years in urban areas. In contrast to the coefficient and standard deviation of years of education, the correlation between per capita expenditures and years of education is found to increase in both rural and urban areas.

All these suggest that the channels through which education has contributed to growing inequality are different across the rural and urban sectors. In the rural sector, increasing inequality in the years of education among household heads was a key factor putting upward pressure on inequality. Changes in the "returns" to education were, in fact, equalizing. In contrast, inequality in urban areas increased largely because the returns to education increased. Inequality in the years of schooling actually declined.

What explains these patterns? An examination of estimates of the marginal effects of education on per capita expenditures by occupation groups and by production sectors/industries can shed useful light. These are derived from a slightly modified version of the expenditure equation (17.1), whereby the dummies for occupations and production sectors do not appear isolated, but instead as interactions with years of education of the household head in two separate regressions (i.e., one which involves dummies for production sectors and the other which involves dummies for occupation groups).[22] In order to get more clarity regarding the relationship between education and labor market opportunities, we consider occupation and production sectors at a more disaggregated level than that considered so far (i.e., 7 occupations and 12 production sectors, as opposed to 3 occupations and 5 production sectors considered earlier).

Table 17.6 describes the resulting marginal effects of years of education on per capita expenditures in columns 1–4. Focusing on the first two data columns, which describe the marginal effects in 1993 and 2004 in rural areas, we see that 4 of 11 industries and 2 of 6 occupational groups experience declines in marginal effects. Marginal effects are unchanged in one industry and two occupation groups. While relatively large increases in marginal effects (i.e., 0.01 points or more) take place in the mining, utilities, and communications industries, data columns 5 and 6 show that these industries together cover only 1.2% of the rural population. Including trade, education, and other services – industries that see some increase in marginal effects – raises the coverage of the rural population to around 12%. On the other hand, the four industries that experience any decline in marginal effects cover almost 18% of the rural population. Turning to the changes in marginal effects across occupation groups, the two occupation groups that experience a decline in marginal effects cover almost 24% of the population while those experiencing an increase in marginal effects cover less than 4%.

[22] As noted in footnote 20, using an alternative variable, such as mean years of schooling among adult household members, in the analysis gave similar results. The results are available from the authors.

Table 17.6 Marginal effects of years of education, distribution of population, and average number of years of schooling by industry and occupation groups

	Marginal effects of years of education				*Distribution of population (%)*				*Average number of years of schooling*			
	Rural		*Urban*		*Rural*		*Urban*		*Rural*		*Urban*	
	1993 (1)	*2004 (2)*	*1993 (3)*	*2004 (4)*	*1993 (5)*	*2004 (6)*	*1993 (7)*	*2004 (8)*	*1993 (9)*	*2004 (10)*	*1993 (11)*	*2004 (12)*
By industry												
Agriculture[a]					74.3	67.6	9.1	6.6	2.4	3.5	3.7	4.9
Mining	0.038	0.059	0.059	0.073	0.8	0.7	1.5	1.1	2.3	3.1	5.8	6.6
Manufacturing	0.039	0.036	0.053	0.057	6.7	7.6	22.3	21.6	3.3	4.2	6.6	7.2
Utilities	0.049	0.06	0.067	0.061	0.3	0.3	1.4	1.1	6.3	7.4	8.7	10.0
Construction	0.021	0.017	0.045	0.043	3.1	6.6	6.3	8.9	2.4	3.1	3.7	4.6
Trade	0.035	0.036	0.046	0.052	5.4	7.1	20.3	24.8	4.2	5.3	6.5	7.5
Transportation	0.049	0.037	0.048	0.056	2.0	3.4	9.8	10.5	3.5	4.2	5.5	6.4
Communication	0.026	0.042	0.047	0.064	0.1	0.3	0.7	1.3	9.6	9.4	10.2	10.7
Finance, insurance, real estate, and business services	0.062	0.061	0.063	0.077	0.4	0.6	3.9	5.3	9.7	9.6	12.0	11.8
Public administration	0.048	0.048	0.054	0.066	1.9	1.4	11.0	7.6	8.4	8.9	10.2	10.4
Education, science, research, and health services	0.045	0.047	0.053	0.065	2.0	2.2	5.3	5.6	10.7	10.7	11.4	11.9
Other services	0.025	0.029	0.036	0.046	2.9	2.3	8.2	5.7	3.5	4.0	5.0	5.7

Continued

Table 17.6 Continued

	Marginal effects of years of education				*Distribution of population (%)*				*Average number of years of schooling*			
	Rural		*Urban*		*Rural*		*Urban*		*Rural*		*Urban*	
	1993 *(1)*	*2004* *(2)*	*1993* *(3)*	*2004* *(4)*	*1993* *(5)*	*2004* *(6)*	*1993* *(7)*	*2004* *(8)*	*1993* *(9)*	*2004* *(10)*	*1993* *(11)*	*2004* *(12)*
By occupation												
Professionals/technical	0.047	0.047	0.058	0.069	2.7	2.6	9.2	8.4	9.9	10.4	12.0	12.6
Manager/administrative	0.061	0.061	0.071	0.077	1.0	2.0	6.7	10.8	5.0	6.5	9.9	10.0
Clerical	0.045	0.048	0.049	0.061	1.9	1.7	11.5	9.6	9.2	9.4	10.8	11.1
Sales	0.036	0.035	0.045	0.051	5.0	5.9	17.7	19.0	4.3	5.4	6.8	7.8
Services	0.034	0.035	0.045	0.05	1.9	2.3	7.8	7.9	3.4	4.3	5.6	6.0
Production labor	0.031	0.026	0.04	0.042	13.3	18.0	38.1	37.7	3.0	3.6	4.8	5.5
Agricultural labor[a]					74.30	67.50	8.90	6.70	2.40	3.50	3.60	4.90

Note:
[a]The comparison group for industrial categories is agriculture and the comparison group for occupational categories is agricultural worker.

Source: Authors' estimates based on consumption expenditure surveys by National Sample Survey Office, Ministry of Statistics and Programme Implementation, Government of India, New Delhi, India.

Interestingly, the essentially stagnant returns to education in rural areas coexist with a fairly broad-based expansion in the average years of schooling across industries and especially occupation groups (data columns 9 and 10). Average years of education decline marginally for only two industries: (i) communication and (ii) finance, insurance, real estate, and other business services. Both are quite intensive in education in the first place.[23]

It appears that the structure and nature of production in the rural sector continues to remain essentially similar during 1993–2004 in that even though there has been some transition from agriculture to industry and services in the rural sector, the new jobs are not generally intensive in education.[24] Alternatively, where they have been more intensive in education, they have been only slightly more so, so that whatever increases in education have taken place have been more than enough to meet the increased demand for education. Put differently, slow structural transformation together with an expansion in the supply of education for virtually every occupation and production sector group represents a very plausible explanation for the fall in the overall coefficient on years of education reported in Table 17.5.

In contrast to the picture in rural areas, the marginal effects of years of education in urban areas increase in 9 out of 11 industries and for all occupation groups. The two industries that experience declines cover only around 10% of the urban population. Of the industries that experience relatively large increase in marginal effects (i.e., an increase of 0.01 points or more), five belong to the services sector (the sixth is mining). Significantly, four of the five service sectors are relatively intensive in education. As may also be seen from column 12 of Table 17.6, the average number of years of schooling among household heads in each of these industries is about 10 years or more in 2004 – considerably higher than the overall average of 7.6 years in urban areas. Similarly, the two occupations that experience relatively large increases in the marginal effects of education (professional/technical and clerical occupations) are the most intensive in education on average. Significantly, and in contrast to the picture in rural areas, increases in the marginal effects of years of education in the urban sector are accompanied by a broad-based expansion in the average years of schooling. This finding is very similar to that of Kijima (2006) insofar as wage inequality in the urban sector during 1993–1999 is concerned.

What is the quantitative impact of increasing marginal effects of education in production sectors and occupation groups relatively intensive in education

[23] Although the average years of education increases for all occupational groups and a large majority of production sectors, there is a stable pattern in terms of the ranking of the years of education across occupations and production sectors, which are likely to be linked with broad notions of productivity. Indeed, the Spearman rank correlation in years of education is 0.97 across production sectors and 1 across occupation groups.

[24] Thus, while there is a relatively large drop in agriculture and agricultural occupations (groups that display fairly low levels of educational achievement and could thus be characterized as low productivity), this decline is countered to a large degree by an expansion of the population covered by construction and production labor occupations (also groups that display fairly low levels of educational achievement).

on urban inequality (which cover 20% and 29% of the urban population – see columns 7 and 8 of Table 17.6)? We address this question based on a simple decomposition exercise in the spirit of Juhn *et al.* (1993). Using the estimates of the modified expenditure equation for 2004, whereby years of education enters both directly and through an interaction with industry dummies and occupation dummies separately, we construct a hypothetical earnings distribution and examine the resulting estimates of inequality. The hypothetical distribution holds constant all observable characteristics of households and household heads, the estimated coefficients on all observables except those relating to years of education, and the residuals. For the coefficients on the years of education variables (i.e., direct as well as interacted), we substitute the estimated 2004 coefficients with the 1993 coefficients for particular groups of industries or occupations. Thus, the contribution of years of education of some groups of industries or occupations to per capita expenditures is evaluated using estimated coefficients for 2004, while others are evaluated using the 1993 coefficients. Inequality estimates can then be generated using the hypothetical distribution of per capita expenditures and compared with the estimates generated from the actual distribution of per capita expenditures in 2004. Any resulting difference across the inequality estimates is then solely due to whether or not the effects of years of education are being evaluated using 1993 or 2004 coefficients for a particular group of industries or occupations. The bigger the difference, the bigger the contribution of changes in returns to years of education to inequality.

Table 17.7 provides inequality estimates for various hypothetical distributions. For convenience, the first row reproduces inequality estimates from the actual distribution of expenditures in 2004. The numbers in the second row are based on a scenario where the contribution of years of education to per capita expenditures (via both the direct and interaction terms) for the four education-intensive service industries is based on their estimated 1993 coefficients. For the remaining industries, the estimated 2004 coefficients are used. As may be seen, the Gini coefficient from this hypothetical distribution is almost 1.2 points lower than the actual 2004 Gini of 37.2. In contrast, a hypothetical distribution based on evaluating the effects of education on per capita expenditures of the other industries on the basis of their estimated 1993 coefficients and using the estimated 2004 coefficients for the four service industries, yields a Gini of 36.9 or only 0.3 points lower than the actual 2004 Gini. In other words, the changes (increases) in the marginal effects of education among the 20% of the urban population covered by the four education-intensive service industries reported in Table 17.6 is by far the more important driver of increasing inequality during 1993–2004 in comparison with changes in the marginal effects of education among the 80% of the urban proposition covered by the remaining industries. Something very similar occurs for the other measures of inequality.

Table 17.7 also shows inequality estimates associated with hypothetical distributions based on differential effects of education across various occupational groups. A comparison of these inequality estimates shows that increasing marginal effects of education on account of the 29% of the urban population covered by

Table 17.7 Urban inequality estimates for actual and hypothetical distributions, 2004

Distribution	*Gini* (1)	*GE(0)* (2)	*GE(1)* (3)	*GE(2)* (4)
Actual distribution	37.16	22.7	27.9	83.32
Hypothetical distributions				
Education-intensive services only	36.00	21.31	26.19	70.96
Other industries	36.85	22.30	27.59	86.03
Education-intensive occupations only	35.97	21.28	26.25	77.83
Other occupations	37.16	22.69	27.99	84.98
Professional/technical and managerial	36.27	21.63	26.53	77.17
Other occupations	36.88	22.35	27.76	85.92

Note: Education-intensive services include communications; finance, insurance, real estate, and business services; public administration; and education, science, research, and health services. Education-intensive occupations include professional/technical, managerial/administrative, and clerical occupations.

Source: Authors' estimates based on consumption expenditure surveys by National Sample Survey Office, Ministry of Statistics and Programme Implementation, Government of India, New Delhi, India.

education-intensive occupations is a much more important driver of inequality increases than increasing marginal effects of education of the remaining occupation groups. Interestingly, education-intensive occupations include not only professional/technical and managerial/administrative occupations, but also clerical occupations. Indeed, if we omit clerical occupations from our education-intensive occupations and estimate inequality for our hypothetical distributions, we find that increasing marginal effects of education among the revised education-intensive occupations account for less of the actual increase in inequality than took place. This may be seen by comparing, for example, the Gini coefficients for "Education-intensive occupations only" and "Professional/technical and managerial" (35.97 versus 36.27). The former is based on a hypothetical distribution that evaluates the effects of education on per capita expenditures for clerical workers using their 1993 coefficients on years of education; the latter is based on a hypothetical distribution that evaluates the effects of education using clerical workers' 2004 coefficients on years of education. Thus, increases in the returns to education among clerical workers during 1993–2004 are associated with almost a one-third point increase in the Gini coefficient.

Liberalization

The results of the previous subsections have shown that increasing inequality in India has essentially been an urban phenomenon. Additionally, an important driver of increasing inequality in urban areas has been increases in the returns to education, especially in relatively education-intensive service sectors. This leads to the question of what explains the increases in the returns to education. Some recent work focusing on wage inequality in the Indian context has tried to provide an answer. On the basis of a "demand–supply" analysis used by Autor *et al.*

(1998), Kijima (2006) argued that increasing returns to education (or skills, using her terminology) among full-time urban wage-earning males from 1993 to 1999 was driven by relative demand for college-educated workers increasing faster than their relative supply. She speculated that the liberalization of trade policies and industrial deregulation in the early 1990s may have had something to do with this. Chamarbagwala (2006) analyzed this issue further. Like Kijima, she found that wage inequality between college-educated and less educated groups increased over the 1980s and 1990s, and that the increases in relative demand for college-educated workers was the main driving force. She then proceeded to use the factor content approach and converted trade flow data (relating to both manufactured goods and services) into labor supply equivalents in order to measure the impact of trade on relative demand. She found evidence that trade has indeed increased demand for college-educated workers relative to other workers.

We pursue the links between liberalization and increased returns to education a little further in the context of increases in inequality in per capita expenditures in urban India during 1993–2004. Our approach is different from that of Chamarbagwala, however. We do not utilize the factor content approach to examine the effects of liberalization. Instead, we use a policy-based measure of liberalization because the effects of liberalization on economic outcomes work not so much through trade flows per se, but through changes in the prices of products, as different industries experience varying amounts of liberalization. Moreover, there is an endogeneity problem in working with trade flows given that trade flows are partly influenced by wages. We also do not make any attempt to distinguish between supply-side and demand-side factors in influencing inequality. Rather, we work within the framework of our expenditure equation to explore the direct effects of liberalization on the returns to education – the single most important observable characteristic associated with increasing inequality in urban India. In particular, we estimate expenditures' equations with interactions between our years of education variable and a measure of liberalization that categorizes industries, or subsectors, at the 2- or 2.5-digit level (as per the 1987 National Industrial Classification of India) as closed, moderately liberalized, or significantly liberalized.

An explanation regarding our measure of liberalization is required. Insofar as agriculture and manufacturing industries are concerned, we utilize information on tariff rates and nontariff barrier (NTB) coverage rates in 1992 and 2003 in order to categorize 45 industries in terms of how liberalized they were in 1993 and 2004. The implicit assumption here is that protection rates affect labor market outcomes with a 1-year lag.[25] We define an industry as closed if its NTB rate

[25] The information on industry-level tariff rates and NTB coverage rates is from Pandey (1999) and Das (2008). Pandey reported these for various years over the period 1988–1998. Das (2008) updated these for various years up to 2003 using the methodology of Pandey. The industrial classification used by Pandey and Das corresponds to that used in India's input–output tables. The input–output industries correspond to either industries at the 3-digit level as defined in India's National Industrial Classification (NIC) 1987 or groups of 3-digit NIC industries within a 2-digit NIC industry. We took simple averages of tariff rates and NTB coverage rates to arrive at the final protection data for the 45 agricultural and industry sector we work with.

is 80% or more or if its tariff rate is 100% or more. An industry is significantly liberalized if its NTB rate is less than 20% and the tariff rate is less than 50%. If it is neither, the industry is defined as moderately liberalized. We use such a classification scheme for two reasons. First, as is explained in the following text, our data on liberalization in services is in this form. Second, the specific cut-offs we employ are based on an examination of the pattern of tariff rates and NTB rates across industries. For example, while it may seem odd to classify an industry as liberalized on the basis of a tariff rate that is less than 50% (and for which the NTB rate is less than 20%) and not a much smaller number, the fact of the matter is that tariff rates in India in the early 1990s were routinely above 100%. Thus, a tariff rate of 50% or less arguably represents a high degree of liberalization.

Categorizing service sector industries is more challenging. Due to the nature of services, there is nothing corresponding to the protection data that exists for the agriculture and manufacturing sectors. Fortunately, a World Bank (2004) study on India's services sector provides useful information on the extent to which service industries were liberalized by the early 2000s. In particular, the study considered the following to construct an index of liberalization for industries or subsectors in services: (i) Is the subsector open to the domestic private sector? (ii) Is the subsector open to foreign investment? and (iii) Is there an independent regulatory body and/or is the level of regulation adequate for the subsector? If the answer to all three is "YES," the subsector is deemed to be significantly liberalized. If one or two of the answers are "NO," the subsector is moderately liberalized. Finally, if the answer to all three questions is "NO," the subsector is treated as closed.[26,27] While this information helps us to categorize the various service subsectors in

---

[26] We combined information provided on the degree of liberalization across subsectors provided in Figures 6 and 14 and Annex Table 1 of World Bank (2004). We also needed to augment this information in several ways before we could classify all services subsectors. For example, we treated subsectors such as public services, sanitation services, and recreational services as closed/nontraded given that provision by the private sector, domestic or foreign, is either prohibited or nonexistent. We also had to make a judgment for some other subsectors that were not considered by the World Bank study. For example, we coded commission agents in the same way that the World Bank study coded wholesale trade, given that the work of commission agents appears to be more in the line of wholesale trade and not retail trade activities. Similarly, we used information on policy on foreign direct investment (FDI) to categorize subsectors within utilities. While the utilities are not part of services, the principle of using information on whether or not FDI is permitted within the subsector is similar to that used by World Bank (2004) for the services subsectors. We thank Deepak Mishra for a useful discussion on the methodology used by World Bank (2004). A full breakdown of production sectors by degree of liberalization is available from the authors.

[27] While it would have been ideal to have information on the three variables separately, this is not available. Nevertheless, this is not too much of a drawback in the context of India's industrial and trade policy regime of the 1980s and 1990s. In particular, the trade liberalization of 1991 was accompanied by widespread domestic deregulation whereby industrial licensing requirements to which Indian manufacturing industries had previously been subject were removed. Since the widespread industrial delicensing, as it was called, did not necessarily apply to service sector industries, having a liberalization variable that captures not only a service subsector's openness to foreign investments but also whether it is open to domestic private sector or not is useful.

terms of whether or not they were liberalized in 2004, it does not provide specific information for 1993. We experiment with two possibilities for 1993: first, that all of the service subsectors were closed; and second, that each of the subsectors was liberalized one level lower than in 2004 (i.e., a subsector classified as significantly liberalized in 2004 was moderately liberalized in 1993, and so on).

Table 17.8 presents estimates of expenditure equations estimated by pooling data over 1993 and 2004 and augmented by our measure of liberalization. The liberalization variable can take three values: (i) if closed (or nontraded), (ii) if moderately liberalized, and (iii) if significantly liberalized. For expositional convenience, we only report the coefficients involving years of education and our liberalization measure. Column 1 describes the results for a specification that includes, in addition to our standard regressors, a year dummy for 2004 and an interaction term between years of education and liberalization.

The coefficient on the interaction term is positive and statistically significant at the 1% level. The size of the estimated coefficient implies that the marginal effect of years of education for a household relying on an industry that moved from being closed to significantly liberalized would increase by almost 17% (i.e., from 0.049 to 0.057). Column 2 adds the liberalization measure on its own as a regressor. Interestingly, while the interaction term involving liberalization and years of education remains statistically significant, the direct term on liberalization is insignificant. This suggests that liberalization does not have an across-the-board impact on household expenditure. Instead, its impact on household expenditures appears to be very much conditional on the education of a household. The more educated a household, the more liberalization seems to benefit it. Column 3 shows the coefficient on years of education varying across 1993 and 2004. As expected on the basis of results from the previous subsections, the direct effect of years of education on per capita expenditures are larger in 2004. As for the interaction term involving years of education and liberalization, this remains positive but is no longer significant. Column 4 is like column 3, except that it drops the consistently insignificant direct term on liberalization. Both interaction terms involving years of education, i.e., the terms relating to the dummy year for 2004 and liberalization, are now positive and statistically significant. However, the size of the coefficient on the interaction between years of education and liberalization is diminished. This is important because it suggests that at least a part of the "impact" of liberalization found in columns 1 or 2 may be a "time" effect given that there is a clear trend for industries to become more liberalized over time.

Columns 5 to 8 are similar to the first four except that they allow the effects of liberalization on returns to education to vary across the three broad production sectors, agriculture, industry, and services via the use of three-way interaction terms between years of education, liberalization, and dummies for the three broad production sectors. This is useful given the very different approaches we have used to categorize liberalization across production sectors (i.e., services and the remaining) and the nature of production across the sectors. Overall, the results are very similar to those in the first four columns. The most important feature is that it is liberalization within the industry, and especially in services sectors, that seems

Table 17.8 Expenditure equations and liberalization (education measured in years of education)

Variable	*(1)*	*(2)*	*(3)*	*(4)*	*(5)*	*(6)*	*(7)*	*(8)*
EDUCYRS	0.045***	0.044***	0.045***	0.044***	0.045***	0.044***	0.045***	0.044***
EDUCYRS × LIB	0.004***	0.005***	0.001	0.003***				
LIB		−0.008	0.018			−0.014	0.010	
EDUCYRS × YEAR2004			0.008***	0.006***			0.007**	0.006**
EDUCYRS × AGRICULTURE × LIB					−0.001	0.000	−0.003	−0.002
EDUCYRS × INDUSTRY × LIB					0.003***	0.004**	0.002	0.002***
EDUCYRS × SERVICES × LIB					0.006***	0.007***	0.003	0.004***
R^2	0.34	0.34	0.34	0.34	0.34	0.34	0.34	0.34

* $p < 0.1$; ** $p < 0.05$; and *** $p < 0.01$.

Note: Age, age-squared, and gender of the household head, social group of the household, and dummies for industries, states, and for the year 2004 are included in all regressions but not shown in the table.

Source: Authors' estimates based on consumption expenditure surveys by National Sample Survey Office, Ministry of Statistics and Programme Implementation, Government of India, New Delhi, India.

to drive the overall positive relationship between expenditures and liberalization among better educated households. It may be noted that all these results hold even when the coding of service subsectors' liberalization status in 1993 is based on the second alternative, whereby each subsector is treated as one level less liberalized than in 2004.

While our results on liberalization must necessarily be treated as tentative, they appear to be both interesting and novel. Although there is considerable literature that examines the impact of economic liberalization on inequality, it mainly focuses on effects of trade liberalization in agriculture and industry. Yet, it seems inappropriate to leave out services from the analysis. As is clear from World Bank (2004), there is a very real sense in which the service sector has experienced liberalization. In addition to liberalization on account of domestic deregulation, foreign providers have also been allowed entry to serve domestic markets (or international markets as in the business process outsourcing industry, etc.). Moreover, not just in India but also in other developing countries, the services sector employs many more than the industry sector. Given the potential for liberalization to have important distributional implications, the omission of analysis on the nexus between liberalization and inequality involving the services sector is a glaring one and the results presented here represent a first step in filling the gap.

Concluding remarks

It is useful to summarize the key findings of this study. First, prior to 1993, there was no clear pattern to changes in inequality. During 1993–2004, however, there has been an increase in inequality in both rural and urban sectors. Second, the increases in rural inequality are relatively marginal. They are more substantial in the urban sector. Third, of various household characteristics considered in this study, educational attainment of the household head turns out to be the single most important proximate factor driving inequality increases (as measured by the Gini coefficient). Fourth, in the urban sector, inequality increased to a large degree because the returns to education increased. Inequality in educational attainment in terms of years of schooling actually declined. Fifth, the increase in returns to education has been particularly pronounced among households relying on employment in the services sector, especially the subcomponent that has been a relatively intensive user of more educated workers. Though only covering around 20% of the urban population, increasing returns to education among this group have been quantitatively more important in driving inequality increases than that among the remaining population. Sixth, in a similar way, increases in the returns to education among occupations that are more intensive in education have been more important in driving increases in inequality. These occupations include not only professional/technical occupations and managers/administrators but also clerical occupations – a group not commonly discussed in the literature but one that experienced a large increase in the marginal effects of education during 1993–2004. Finally, we find that within the industry and services sectors, subsectors that experienced greater liberalization in the 1990s registered larger increases in returns to education in 2004. However, we cannot establish causality, nor can we identify channels through which liberalization may be raising returns to education. For example, while skill-biased technical change induced by liberalization may be at work – a possibility raised by Kijima (2006) in the context of Indian wage inequality – it is also possible that liberalization has created new opportunities for workers who can play a catalytic role during periods of transformation (Cragg and Epelbaum 1996). While professional/technical workers and managers/administrators would very much fit the description of such workers, workers in clerical occupations may also have played a role, given their key function of recording, organizing, storing, and retrieving information related to production processes. Disentangling the key channels that are operating is something we leave for future research.

An important question that arises in the context of our results is how the increases in inequality should be viewed, i.e., are they a largely benign feature of a growing economy, or do they merit a clear response? Additionally, to the extent that they merit a response, what form should it take? The following points can be brought up in favor of the more benign view on increasing inequality. First, notwithstanding the increases registered, levels of inequality based on NSS expenditure data are by no means particularly high when considered from an international perspective. For example, in comparison with 22 other Asian economies, the Gini coefficient for India turns out to be right in the middle (Asian Development Bank 2007).[28] Second, increases in inequality do not preclude reductions in poverty, or more generally, improvements in the standard of living of the population at large – something which the data support. Third, increases in inequality may well be part and parcel of the growth process of a developing economy. As Nobel laureate Arthur Lewis put it:

> Development must be inegalitarian because it does not start in every part of an economy at the same time. Somebody develops a mine, and employs a thousand people. Or farmers in one province start planting cocoa, which grows in only 10% of the country. Or the Green Revolution arrives to benefit those farmers who have plenty of rain or access to irrigation, while offering nothing to the other 50% in the drier regions.
>
> (Lewis 1954)

While Lewis' view that development is inherently inegalitarian may not be strictly correct in the aggregate – the experience of East Asia's newly industrialized economies is one that led many economists to believe that growth need not entail a worsening of inequality – there appears to be considerable force behind his point that the process of development is unlikely to start in every part of an economy

---

28 The comparison of Gini coefficients across 22 Asian economies does not control for spatial variation in prices within countries.

at the same time.[29] Indeed, our finding of households that relied on sectors within industry and services that were liberalized to a greater degree and that experienced larger increases in per capita expenditures, could be construed as supporting this notion.

However, there are some difficulties with the benign view. First, by focusing only on income or expenditure inequalities, we ignore the sharp inequalities in education and health that characterize the Indian landscape (ADB 2006; Bardhan 2007). Arguably, these inequalities represent the most pernicious of inequalities, i.e., those driven by circumstances beyond the control of individuals and which give rise to inequality of opportunities. Second, even if we were to focus on income or expenditure inequalities, it is difficult to argue that the recent increases in India are simply a by-product of a still nascent growth process that cannot start everywhere at the same time. The data presented in this study, combined with recent studies of economic growth in India, suggest that the nature of the growth process under way in India has been skewed toward generating new and better economic opportunities for a narrow minority of the Indian labor force: those employed in education-intensive services and occupations. Indeed, the positive association that we find between liberalization and per capita expenditures works through education in that it is the better educated who benefit more from liberalization in a given industry or services subsector. Of course, it is possible that the demand for workers of all types has increased (more or less equally), but that the small supply of college-educated professionals has meant rapid increases in earnings for them. However, the story of economic growth in India over the past decade or so suggests that this is not what is going on. As Bosworth *et al.* (2007) have argued, India's growth over the 1990s and early 2000s has not created enough jobs "for the bulk of the population that is not particularly well-educated." Unlike East Asia's fast-growing economies, India's growth has been driven by services and not manufacturing. Moreover, it is the growth of the modern component of services that stands on firmer ground statistically speaking (Bosworth *et al.* 2007). Given that modern services tend to have the highest intensity of college-educated workers, their ability to generate high productivity (and higher-paying) jobs for the typical member of India's labor force is, in all probability, quite limited, even if we can count on this sector to continue growing at a fast pace.[30]

A strategy of expanding the supply of higher educated individuals is unlikely to be effective in tackling the issue of inequality in a meaningful way – even if we were to assume that the extra college graduates could be obtained without a

[29] A comparison of inequality trends over the past 20 years would show that inequality in the People's Republic of China – a country whose rates of economic growth and track record in poverty reduction are something that most (if not all) developing countries want to emulate – has increased by far more than it has in India (Asian Development Bank 2007; Chaudhuri and Ravallion 2007). While not all of the increase in inequality can be ascribed to the sort of processes that Lewis described (see Dollar (2007); Knight (2008)), a nontrivial part probably is.

[30] Moreover, even the quantum of jobs that can be generated by this sector in the best of scenarios would not be sufficient for soaking up the large degree of underemployment characterizing the Indian labor force.

deterioration in the quality of the new college degrees. To the extent that increasing returns to education (the factor identified in this study as the single most important proximate cause of increasing urban inequality) are driven by the returns to particular occupations or industries – something which seems to be true not just for India but also in several other countries (see Mehta *et al.* (2007)) – increasing the share of college education in the population per se will not do much to raise incomes generally.

For growth to lead to a more rapid rise in standards of living for India's workforce at large, raising productivity in agriculture and expanding the manufacturing sector will be vital. Moreover, insofar as manufacturing is concerned, it is a more dynamic labor-intensive sector in the organized sector that is sorely needed for generating large numbers of jobs that match the skill/education profile of the average Indian worker. As Panagariya (2008) has put it, "the challenge of transformation facing India is that of creating an environment that allows unskilled-labor-intensive manufacturing to grow rapidly and rise as a proportion of the GDP." Efforts to create such an environment and also raise productivity in agriculture may well turn out to be the most effective way to fight inequality.

Acknowledgments

We would like to thank Gary Fields for useful discussions on regression-based methods for decomposing inequality and Poonam Gupta, Deepak Mishra, and anonymous referees of *World Development* for providing helpful comments and suggestions on various aspects of this study. This study is an output of an ADB technical assistance project (RETA 6364: Measurement and Policy Analysis for Poverty Reduction). The views presented here are those of the authors and not necessarily those of either the Asian Development Bank or the World Bank.

References

Alatas, V., and F. Bourguignon. 2005. The Evolution of Income Distribution during Indonesia's Fast Growth, 1980–96. In F. Bourguignon, F. H. G. Ferreira, and N. Lustig, eds. *The Microeconomics of Income Distribution Dynamics in East Asia and Latin America.* New York, NY: World Bank and Oxford University Press.

Asian Development Bank. 2006. *Key Indicators 2006: Measuring Policy Effectiveness in Health and Education.* Manila.

——. 2007. *Key Indicators 2007: Inequality in Asia.* Manila.

Autor, D., L. Katz, and A. Krueger. 1998. Computing Inequality: Have Computers Changed the Labor Market? *Quarterly Journal of Economics.* 113. pp. 1169–213.

Bardhan, P. 2007. Poverty and Inequality in [the People's Republic of] China and India: Elusive Link with Globalization. *Economic and Political Weekly.* September 22. pp. 3849–52.

Bosworth, B., S. M. Collins, and A. Virmani. 2007. Sources of Growth in the Indian Economy. *National Bureau of Economic Research Working Paper* No. 12901. Cambridge, MA: National Bureau of Economic Research.

Bourguignon, F., F. H. G. Ferreira, and N. Lustig. 2005. *The Microeconomics of Income Distribution Dynamics in East Asia and Latin America.* New York, NY: World Bank and Oxford University Press.

Chamarbagwala, R. 2006. Economic Liberalization and Wage Inequality in India. *World Development.* 34 (12). pp. 1997–2015.

Chaudhuri, S., and M. Ravallion. 2007. Partially Awakened Giants: Uneven Growth in [the People's Republic of] China and India. In L. A. Winters and S. Yusuf, eds. *Dancing with Giants: [People's Republic of] China, India and the Global Economy.* Washington, DC: World Bank.

Cragg, M. I., and M. Epelbaum. 1996. Why Has Wage Dispersion Grown in Mexico? Is It the Incidence of Reforms or the Growing Demand for Skills? *Journal of Development Economics.* 51 (1). pp. 99–116.

Das, D. 2008. Trade Barriers Measurement: A Methodological Overview. Processed. Economics and Research Department. Manila: Asian Development Bank.

Datt, G., and M. Ravallion. 1992. Growth and Redistribution Components of Changes in Poverty: A Decomposition with Applications to Brazil and India in the 1980s. *Journal of Development Economics.* 38. pp. 275–95.

Deaton, A., and V. Kozel. 2005. *The Great Indian Poverty Debate.* New Delhi: Macmillan India Ltd.

Dev, S. M., and C. Ravi. 2007. Poverty and Inequality: All-India and States, 1983–2005. *Economic and Political Weekly.* February 10. pp. 509–21.

Dollar, D. 2007. Poverty, Inequality, and Social Disparities during [the People's Republic of] China's Economic Reform. *World Bank Policy Research Working Paper* No. 4253. Washington, DC: World Bank.

Dreze, J., and P. V. Srinivasan. 1997. Widowhood and Poverty in Rural India: Some Inferences from Household Survey Data. *Journal of Development Economics.* 54 (2). pp. 217–34.

Ferreira, F. H. G., and R. Paes de Barros. 2005. The Slippery Slope: Explaining the Increase in Extreme Poverty in Urban Brazil, 1976–96. In F. Bourguignon, F. H. G. Ferreira, and N. Lustig, eds. *The Microeconomics of Income Distribution Dynamics in East Asia and Latin America.* New York, NY: World Bank and Oxford University Press.

Fields, G. 2001. *Distribution and Development: A New Look at the Developing World.* New York, NY: Russell Sage.

——. 2003. Accounting for Income Inequality and Its Changes: A New Method with Application to the Distribution of Earnings in the United States. *Research in Labor Economics.* 22. pp. 1–38.

Juhn, C., K. Murphy, and B. Pierce. 1993. Wage Inequality and the Rise in Returns to Skill. *Journal of Political Economy.* 101 (3). pp. 410–42.

Kijima, Y. 2006. Why Did Wage Inequality Increase? Evidence from Urban India 1983–99. *Journal of Development Economics.* 81. pp. 97–117.

Knight, J. B. 2008. Reform, Growth and Inequality in [the People's Republic of] China. *Asian Economic Policy Review.* 3 (1). pp. 140–58.

Lewis, W. A. 1954. Economic Development with Unlimited Supplies of Labour. *The Manchester School.* 22 (2). pp. 139–91.

Mehta, A., J. Felipe, P. Quising, and S. Camingue. 2007. Changing Patterns in Mincerian Returns to Education and Employment Structure in Three Asian Countries. *Center for Global Studies Paper* No. 06. Santa Barbara, CA: Institute for Social, Behavioral, and Economic Research, University of California.

Organisation for Economic Co-operation and Development. 2005. *What Are Equivalence Scales?* http://www.oecd.org/eco/growth/OECD-Note-EquivalenceScales.pdf (accessed June 2012).

Panagariya, A. 2008. *India: The Emerging Giant.* New York, NY: Oxford University Press.

Pandey, M. 1999. *NCAER Report on Trade Protection in India.* New Delhi, India: National Council of Applied Economic Research.

Sundaram, K., and S. D. Tendulkar. 2003. Poverty in India in the 1990s: Revised Results for All-India and 15 Major States for 1993–94. *Economic and Political Weekly.* 38 (November 15). pp. 4865–73.

World Bank. 2004. *Sustaining India's Services Revolution*. Washington, DC: World Bank.

——. World Development Indicators. http://devdata.worldbank.org/data-query/ (accessed June 2012).

Index